LEGISLATIVE SERIE

Congressional Deskbook

The Practical and Comprehensive Guide to Congress

SIXTH EDITION

Judy Schneider
Michael L. Koempel
Contributing Author: Robert Keith

TheCapitol.Net
Alexandria, VA 2012

For over thirty years, TheCapitol.Net and its predecessor, Congressional Quarterly Executive Conferences, have been training professionals from government, military, business, and NGOs on the dynamics and operations of the legislative and executive branches and how to work with them.

Our training and publications include congressional operations, legislative and budget process, communication and advocacy, media and public relations, testifying before Congress, research skills, legislative drafting, critical thinking and writing, and more.

Our publications and courses, written and taught by *current* Washington insiders who are all independent subject matter experts, show how Washington works.™ Our products and services can be found on our web site at *<www.TheCapitol.Net>*.

TheCapitol.Net is a nonpartisan firm.

The Training Edition of the *Congressional Deskbook* is included as part of the program materials in our public and custom Capitol Hill Workshop.

TheCapitol.Net has delivered custom, on-site training for hundreds of clients. For more information about bringing training to your organization, see our web site at *<TCNCustom.com>* or call us for details: 703-739-3790, ext. 112.

The Legislative Series from TheCapitol.Net also includes the *Legislative Drafter's Deskbook* and the *Congressional Directory*, which is updated annually. The spiral-bound *Directory* of the members of the U.S. Senate and the U.S. House of Representatives includes: member photos in full color; wire-spiral binding for easy, lay-flat use; member biographical data; office locations; phone and fax numbers; Twitter ID and email addresses where available; list of key congressional staff; district office information; a fold-out map of Capitol Hill; and much more. See *<TCNDir.com>* for more information.

Citation Form—URLs: We use a standard style for all web addresses, also known as Uniform Resource Locators (URLs). URLs appear in text next to the first mention of the resource being described, and are surrounded with open and close angle brackets.

For URLs that have the standard web addressing form at the beginning of the URL of "http://www." we show only the initial "www." For example, the URL "http://www.domainname.com" will appear in text and tables as *"<www.domainname.com>."*

For URLs that begin with anything other than "www.," such as "http://thomas.loc.gov," the URL will appear in text and tables as *"<http://thomas.loc.gov>."* For example, the URL "http://www3.domain.gov" will appear in text and tables as *"<http://www3.domain.gov>."*

Design and production by Zaccarine Design, Inc., Chicago, IL; zacdesign@mac.com.
Ebook conversion by Paula Reichwald *<igossi.com>*.

PO Box 25706
Alexandria, VA 22313-5706
703-739-3790 Toll free: 1-877-228-5086
<www.TheCapitol.Net>

v 6.0
LCCN: 00213909

Softcover (2081)
ISBN 13: 978-1-58733-208-1

Hardcover (1800)
ISBN 13: 978-1-58733-180-0

Ebook (2395) (color where available)
ISBN 13: 9781587332395
Amazon Kindle: 978-1-58733-250-0
B&N nook: 978-1-58733-251-7
Google Editions: 978-1-58733-252-4

Summary Table of Contents

Table of Contents

Back of the Book

Acknowledgments

As we worked on the sixth edition of the *Congressional Deskbook*, we again reflected on our debt to family, friends, and colleagues who assisted us in numerous ways in writing the first edition of this book, and who have continued to support us in the work of revising for subsequent editions. We once again must thank especially Dianne Hunt, Mike's wife, and Jean Yavis Jones, a dear friend, who assisted us in every phase of the writing. They helped get us back on track whenever we began to lose sight of our goal. We are also especially thankful to Bob Keith, a colleague at the Congressional Research Service, who contributed generously with his lucid writing to the chapter on the federal budget process in the first, second, fifth, and current editions. Mike also thanks Gabriel Koempel for his patience in sharing his dad with the evening, weekend, and holiday demands of writing and updating a book.

We are fortunate to have worked at the Congressional Research Service with exceptional people whose daily concern is service to Congress. We also are fortunate to have friends and colleagues in the media, government affairs, executive agencies, congressional offices, policy organizations, and universities. The experiences and knowledge of these people are certainly reflected in our perspective in writing this book. Some friends and colleagues whom we would like to thank specifically for their roles in this book over the years are Mildred Amer, Eugene Boyd, Joe Cantor, Bob Cuthriell, Paul Dwyer, Eric Fischer, Peggy Garvin, Sharon Gressle, Bill Heniff Jr., Henry Hogue, Bob Keith, Nancy Kervin, Jennifer Manning, Jack Maskell, Lynne McCay, Mary Mulvihill, Ilona Nickels, Walter Oleszek, Charlotte Preece, Harold Relyea, Mort Rosenberg, Steve Rutkus, Jim Saturno, Steve Stathis, Jeffrey Weinberg, Clay Wellborn, Leneice Wu, and Linda Zappasodi. Each has helped make this book better.

We could not have written or revised this book without the experiences we shared with members of Congress and congressional staff for more than forty years. We began our professional careers working on Capitol Hill as congressional staffers. From the beginning, we learned important lessons from members and staff. Those lessons became the focus of this book, and continue to inform this book as Congress evolves and members and staff conduct their work differently as each new Congress unfolds. Our affection and respect for the men and women who serve the nation in Congress and the staff who work in committees, personal offices, and administrative offices is constant. We are grateful to members and staff for information used in this book. For their assistance on several editions of the book, we must specifically thank former Representative Karen Thurman and Representative Jan Schakowsky and congressional staffers Cathy Hurwit, Nora Matus, and Ellen McCarthy.

Finally, and most importantly, this book would probably not have been written without the encouragement of Chug Roberts of TheCapitol.Net. Chug is serious about serving people inside and outside Washington who wish to understand Congress at a very practical level. The challenges of all editions of this graphically complex book were ably handled by production editor Catherine Zaccarine. We are very grateful to TheCapitol.Net for its encouragement, support, and vision, and for the opportunity to continue this book to its sixth edition.

Judy Schneider
Michael L. Koempel
June 2011

About the Authors

Michael L. Koempel is a senior specialist in American national government at the Congressional Research Service, a department of the Library of Congress. He worked previously for Congressional Quarterly Inc., and on the staffs of a U.S. representative and a state governor. Mr. Koempel holds a bachelor's degree from Georgetown University's School of Foreign Service and a law degree from The Catholic University of America, and is admitted to practice law in the District of Columbia.

Judy Schneider is a specialist on Congress at the Congressional Research Service, a department of the Library of Congress, and an adjunct scholar at The Brookings Institution. She worked previously for Senate and House committees, including the Senate Select Committee to Study the Senate Committee System. Ms. Schneider was selected as a Stennis Fellow for the 108th Congress, and received the Women in Government Relations (WGR) Distinguished Member Award in 2004. Ms. Schneider is a frequent speaker and lecturer on Congress and legislative procedures. She holds bachelor's and master's degrees from The American University.

Chapter 7

Robert Keith, who worked at the Congressional Research Service from 1974–2010, was a specialist in American national government. He specialized in legislative procedure and the federal budget process, focusing particularly on the development and consideration of budget resolutions, reconciliation bills, authorization and appropriations acts, revenue and debt-limit legislation, and proposals to change the budget process. He now consults on the budget process and other issues of federal governance.

The views expressed in this book are those of the individual authors. They do not represent the views of their employers or of TheCapitol.Net.

About the Authors

Preface

In its physical presence, the Capitol symbolizes our national political life. In this magnificent building, one senses the history of the nation. Paintings depict historical events. Visitors listen to whispers at the location of John Quincy Adams' desk in the Old House Chamber, now National Statuary Hall. Busts of the vice presidents, who served as presidents of the Senate, line the Senate chamber and corridors. Presidents are inaugurated at the Capitol, and they deliver their State of the Union addresses in the House chamber. When one walks the Capitol corridors, one feels the presence of presidents, of renowned and nearly forgotten members of Congress, and of millions of visitors. It is in the Capitol Rotunda that a few Americans have lain in state, most recently President Ford. This is the place where national and foreign dignitaries have come to witness history or to be a part of it, from the Marquis de Lafayette to Julia Ward Howe to Frederick Douglass to Winston Churchill to the Apollo astronauts to Nelson Mandela.

Most importantly, the Capitol houses Congress. The Congress that the founding fathers designed over 200 years ago has been a strong and vibrant institution throughout its history. More than 11,900 members have served in the House and Senate. They have come from all walks of life, from privileged backgrounds and from lives of hardship, and at different ages and times in their careers and lives. Each member comes to Congress with parochial concerns, but, as a legislature, Congress acts for the entire nation.

While many Americans might think first of the president when they think of the federal government, the founding fathers placed Congress first in the Constitution, in Article I. They gave it authority "To make all Laws which shall be necessary and proper for carrying into Execution the foregoing Powers [enumerated in Article I], and all other Powers vested by this Constitution in the Government of the United States, or in any Department or Officer thereof." *(Art. I, sec. 8, cl. 18.)* Our democratic system of representative government is centered on a strong, independent legislative branch. Our government is not a parliamentary democracy with a party's or coalition's control of both the executive and legislature and the prime minister and cabinet drawn from the parliamentary majority.

The founding fathers created an open institution, and the men and women who have served in Congress have fostered that openness. The Capitol and congressional office buildings are physically open to visitors every day. Even with the increased security concerns following the tragic events in the fall of 2001, Congress has tried to accommodate its own and the citizenry's desire to meet and visit and observe in the Capitol and the congressional office buildings.

All but a few committee meetings are open to anyone who wishes to attend, and the rules of the House and Senate essentially require meetings to be open. One can sit in the House and Senate visitors' galleries and watch floor proceedings, or stay at home or at the office and watch the proceedings live on television. Journalists have ready access to members, committee meetings, and floor proceedings, and report news in every medium. Votes cast by individual members in committee and on the House floor are readily available to the public in both congressional documents and web sites and in private print and electronic publications. Anyone can request a meeting with his or her representative or senator, and will be accommodated if at all possible. With its openness, Congress mediates between the federal government and the American people.

The founding fathers and the men and women who have served in Congress have also created a system of parliamentary procedures that values political consensus and, thus, makes legislation difficult to enact into law. The Constitution requires majority support on a measure in each chamber before the measure is sent to the president, who can then veto it. Unless a two-thirds majority in each chamber votes to override a president's veto, the measure dies. House rules generally enable a majority to work its will, but the rules still protect the minority party or minority viewpoint in many ways. Senate rules protect individual senators' prerogatives in nearly all instances, making it difficult for Senate leaders to process legislation.

Because of this openness, difficulty in enacting legislation, and Congress' political nature, it is easy to criticize Congress. In the best American tradition, we satirize politicians for their human and political foibles. Mark Twain long ago commented, "It could probably be shown by facts and figures that there is no distinctly native American criminal class except Congress." Will Rogers also satirized Congress, yet his statue stands today in the Capitol. It faces the center doors to the House of Representatives where he could "keep an eye on Congress" for the country.

But, for its foibles, it is in Congress that slavery was debated, the West was opened to homesteaders, a national economy was fostered, war was declared on five occasions, the rights of labor were secured, GIs returning from World War II were given new opportunities, the vote was extended step-by-step to every adult American, and federal financial support for education at all levels, health care, retirement security, and other programs of national welfare were enacted. Demagogues and bad public policy have held sway at times, but other forces in Congress arose ultimately to defeat them. The ability of Congress to correct course, usually because it has heard the voice of the people, is a unique and valuable part of our political heritage.

Is it possible for members of Congress, congressional staff, Capitol Hill visitors, and congressional critics to understand all that Congress has been and can be? It is easy to lose that perspective when mired in daily toil and daily headlines. Who fully appreciates the continuity of the Constitution and of Congress as its enduring embodiment? Few probably reflect regularly or at all on the Constitution. One has a sense that many think of the Constitution as a document from long ago rather than as the beacon that guides government day after day. Who outside Congress learns more than a few facts about the legislative process or tries to understand its impact on lawmaking? Even the number of scholars who study the legislative process is small. How do members, staff, visitors, and critics think about the complexities of the relationship among the three branches of government? Do they know the many options and opportunities available? It is tempting to focus, as the media often do, on who is "up" and who is "down" on a given day or political topic, as though each day of policymaking in Congress is part of a baseball season rather than an ongoing constitutional activity.

In this book we share our observations and experiences with readers who study Congress, who work there as members or staffers, who cover the institution as journalists, or who try to influence it as advocates, lobbyists, or citizens. Scores of books and studies about Congress are published each year. Some address legislative or budget procedures. Others detail documents that are generated on Capitol Hill or catalogue available Internet resources. Some explore an aspect of congressional history, or tell the story of Congress through a biography, voting patterns, leadership styles, or individual legislation. This book owes much to earlier books and studies. In some ways, it is a synthesis of these publications; in other ways, it is a complementary volume.

We decided that another book on Congress was not superfluous, but should provide as much practical information on the operations of this institution as possible in one volume. In this book, we cover legislative, budget, and special procedures; how various procedures relate to each other; the forms and impact of political competition on Capitol Hill; overviews of the election, lobbying, and ethics laws and rules that regulate congressional behavior; the work of congressional, committee, and administrative offices; and the variety of congressional documents.

Young and idealistic, we came to the Congress as staffers forty years ago. We wanted to make a difference and take part in the next evolution of a 200-year tradition. Between us, we worked for individual members and committees and for different parties. Both of us now work for a nonpartisan legislative support agency. All these years later, we are still excited to be working in the Capitol and congressional office buildings and assisting members and staff in their work.

Experience has not tempered our idealism or awe. It has added realism. We appreciate Congress' greatness, in part because we understand its weaknesses. One must see Congress as a whole and in its parts, and recognize that understanding comes in knowing the relationship between them. One must look not only at a member's committee assignments, but at what those assignments may mean for policy outcomes. One must consider not only rules and procedures, but what strategic and tactical choices members face each day. Dozens of documents are generated daily, and one must know their significance. As this book explains, beginning on the first page, when Congress acts, it is a complex process that has four indivisible aspects—people, politics, policy, and procedure.

Judy Schneider
Michael L. Koempel
June 2011

Introduction

As the name *Congressional Deskbook* implies, this book is meant to be kept close at hand for answering the variety of questions that arise daily in monitoring, interacting with, and studying Congress. The book is organized for daily use in answering questions, but it may be read in sections, by chapters, or in its entirety, as the reader chooses.

The sixth edition was extensively revised to reflect significant changes on Capitol Hill since the fifth edition and also to reflect changes in *Deskbook* readers' needs and their suggestions. We revised and reorganized chapters. For example, Chapter Three was completely rewritten to present the extensive changes in lobbying and ethics laws in the last several Congresses, providing the government relations professional with the necessary information to interact with counsel in planning and implementing government relations activities, and providing government relations professionals and members of Congress and congressional staff alike with essential information on the ethics regime in which representatives and senators work.

Regarding changes in *Deskbook* readers' needs and their suggestions, when we wrote the first edition of this book in 1999, the World Wide Web was still new and print was still the dominant source of congressional information. Government relations tools online and software were still taking shape, and congressional offices still dealt largely with paper letters, documents, and records. Webcasting was unknown on Capitol Hill. That was then. Today, the congressional information world and online government relations management is technologically much more sophisticated, and congressional offices work largely in an electronic environment, with few items still existing exclusively in print. Most importantly, *Deskbook* readers are savvy and sophisticated workers in this electronic environment. We no longer perceived a need for the chapter on private and government information providers and electronic research tips found in previous editions of the *Deskbook*, and dropped it from the sixth edition We reorganized monitoring information in the *Deskbook*, so that, for example, key components of former chapters on the Capitol complex and on monitoring and researching Congress were combined in a new, targeted Chapter Eleven on Viewing and Visiting Congress.

Chapter One attempts to create an image of what it is like to be a member of Congress. It describes the competition that imbues every aspect of the institution and the fragmented life of a member.

Chapters Two and Three guide the reader through some of the major pressures affecting members of Congress. These pressures come from campaigns and elections, lobbyists, and the ethics environment. The chapters provide an overview of the laws and congressional rules that affect members, staff, and the individuals who interact with them.

Chapter Four explains the support structure of Congress. It identifies components of the expense allowance system, staff positions and responsibilities, and the work of support offices. This chapter orients the reader to congressional staff roles.

Chapter Five describes the organization of Congress. It addresses not only the structures of the committee system and of the leadership hierarchy, but also how committee assignments are made and leaders are selected. It describes the early organization activities of the House and Senate following a general election.

Chapter Six describes the legislative process in detail. It explains hearings and committee markup strategies and methods of obtaining floor consideration of legislative initiatives. Amendments between the chambers and conference procedures are explained. The chapter describes options available to leaders and members throughout the legislative process.

Chapter Seven demystifies the federal budget process. It includes discussion of the president's role in budgeting, the congressional budget process, authorizations, and appropriations. It explains the terminology, concepts, and procedures of the budget process, such as reconciliation.

Chapter Eight discusses procedures and powers in Congress' relations with the executive, the judiciary, and the states and localities. It also explains some of the ways in which Congress deals procedurally with defense and foreign policy. Topics in this chapter include confirmation of presidential appointees to executive and judicial posts, the role of legislative history, fast-track procedures, the War Powers Act, alternative procedures for selection of a president and vice president, constitutional amendments, and unfunded mandates.

Chapters Nine and Ten identify and explain the use of congressional documents. Subjects include the forms and versions of legislation, laws and implementing executive documents, official rules and procedure manuals, and party and administrative publications.

Chapter Eleven guides the reader in viewing the House and Senate in session on C-SPAN, and also guides the reader around Capitol Hill so that the visitor might orient herself before a trip to the Capitol or one of the congressional office buildings. This chapter also includes a checklist for tracking legislative action and tips on communicating with members and committees and their staffs.

A case study in Chapter Twelve ties the legislative process, legislative documents, and other topics in the book together as it takes a measure enacted into law in the 106th Congress through the legislative steps from inception to public law. Document excerpts are displayed, and explanatory texts and annotations accompany each excerpt.

A cumulative, expanded glossary complements the individual glossaries and definitions that appear in individual chapters. All of the web sites listed throughout the book are cumulated in a table. This list is followed by an index to the book.

Chapter One

Being a Member of Congress

1

Analysis

§ 1.00 Introduction

The purpose of this book is to provide government affairs professionals, government officials, journalists, students of Congress, librarians, and other interested people, including members of Congress and congressional staff, particularly those new to Congress or seeking or taking on more senior roles, with a practical guide to Congress. The book offers an orientation to Congress, assisting the reader in understanding how Congress works and why it works the way it does.

The authors each have over thirty-five years' experience in American government. First as congressional staff, and then as analysts, writers, and educators, we have worked to understand and explain Congress to members and to congressional staff and to people whose profession requires a solid understanding of Congress. Based on our experiences, we designed this book to answer the variety of questions about Congress that arise daily in the work of individuals with a professional interest in Congress.

This chapter seeks to paint a picture of the congressional environment, especially from the perspective of a member of Congress.

§ 1.10 Who . . . Gets . . . What!

Walter Kravitz, our late colleague at the Congressional Research Service (CRS), began his lectures and speeches by asserting the immediately and comfortably obvious: "Congress is a political institution." Then he would pause a long time, and silently watch discomfort gradually but relentlessly take hold of his listeners. Their faces showed they were becoming very uncertain about the meaning of the word *political*.

Kravitz would finally ask, "What do I mean by that?" Answering his own question, he would practically shout, "WHO . . . GETS . . . WHAT!" He would pause again briefly and then begin a litany: "Who gets what in terms of benefits, preferences, advantages? Who gets what in terms of North versus South? City versus rural areas? Rich versus poor? Business versus labor? Republican versus Democrat? Who gets dams or highways or research? That's what I mean by political—who gets what!" And on he would continue with more examples until it was painfully obvious to all listening that *political* means *who gets what.*

§ 1.20 Congress, the Political Institution

A member of Congress takes to Washington all the aspirations, desires, and conflicted sentiments of his constituency, and serves as one of 435 representatives, five delegates, one resident commissioner, and one hundred senators, all of whom have their own constituencies, each with its own aspirations, desires, and conflicted sentiments. It is worth noting the number of Democratic candidates in 2006 who had experience as servicemen in Iraq—a war still underway as of 2011—who ran in opposition to the war. Yet other Democratic and Republican freshmen ran on positions in support of the war or in support of a change in mission without necessarily endorsing an immediate withdrawal. Candidates with each of these views won. Somehow, these 541 men and women make national policy.

The policymaking process in Congress—the means for determining who gets what—is not easy.

It can be partisan, fractious, slow, cumbersome, and frustrating. It can even seem craven as each member seeks advantages for her constituency. If we find it difficult to settle differences in our daily lives, how much more difficult must it be for members of Congress to make policy as they represent all 300-plus million of us?

The framers of the Constitution well understood competition between groups of people and regions, and created Congress to provide an outlet for debating and deciding the common good, balancing one interest against others in the process.

The rules of procedure and organization that each chamber has developed exist equally for the use of proponents and opponents of any proposition. At each step of the legislative process, proponents must build a new majority to get to the next step. Or, opponents may try to build a new majority to stop a proposition that they have not yet been able to stop. Outside groups—constituents, lobbyists, the president and his administration, and the media—are never far from the fray, and they pressure, pressure, pressure to influence the outcome. Finally, it is important always to recognize that not just one proposition at a time is moving in Congress, but many propositions, offering individual members and groups of members numerous opportunities to trade for support or opposition on more than one of these. These multiple propositions also restrain members—the colleague one alienates on one vote may be the colleague one needs on another vote.

At each step of the legislative process, proponents and opponents must build their majorities within larger groups. A committee is larger than a subcommittee, a chamber is larger than a committee, and the two houses voting on a conference report are larger still.

Winning a majority in Congress is not usually based on denying members—and thereby their constituents—a stake in the outcome of a piece of legislation. Winning a majority is more likely based on giving as many members as needed for a majority a stake in the outcome—by compromising, old-fashioned logrolling, papering over differences, trading for legislative support elsewhere, or exchanging favors within or outside Congress. To become a law, a measure must pass the House and Senate in identical form.

A piece of legislation must also pass the test of having sufficient political support to gain the president's signature to become law. The president, however, might veto a measure for any number of reasons, including a different sense of what the nation wants or needs. For Congress then to override a presidential veto requires a two-thirds supermajority in each chamber. On those infrequent occasions when a veto is overridden, political consensus in Congress must be very high.

It is in the power of the presidential veto that one can clearly see what the phrase "co-equal branches of government" means. Unless there are two-thirds of the members of each chamber willing to vote to override a veto, almost the equivalent of Congress speaking with one voice, the power of the sole executive—the president—is equal to the votes of more than 280 representatives and more than 60 senators, assuming all members are present and vote overwhelmingly for a measure. But few controversial measures pass Congress by majorities within striking distance of the two-thirds required for a veto override. The president's exercise of the veto should be seen as a constitutional action first and a political action second.

Two examples illustrate the power of the president in lawmaking. The Republican-controlled Congress was frustrated by President Bill Clinton's vetoes of appropriations bills in late 1995 as Congress tried to dictate the terms of achieving a balanced budget. Two shutdowns of the federal government ensued, for a total of twenty-seven days, and the public by wide margins blamed Congress. Congress ultimately responded with appropriations measures that the president was willing to sign. In 2007, Democrats in Congress and their supporters believed voters put Democrats back in the majority in Congress to stop funding for the war in Iraq, and Congress in May sent President George W. Bush an appropriations bill with a troop withdrawal or redeployment time frame. The president vetoed the measure, and a majority of the House, but only 222 of 425 representatives present, cast their votes for an override. Congress responded with an appropriations measure that nearly all Republicans voted for and a large majority of Democratic representatives voted against.

At every stage of the legislative process, and in every alliance made during the legislative process, Congress is a political institution, deciding who, including the president, gets what.

§ 1.30 A Member of Congress as Politician, Policymaker, and Parliamentarian

To be a successful member of Congress, a person must be a politician, policymaker, and parliamentarian. In the role of politician, a member must have the self-confidence to represent a large, diverse constituency. A constituency, in turn, expects its member of Congress, in the role of policymaker, to advance its interests and vote on the major issues of the day. Less visible to a constituency is the member of Congress in the role of parliamentarian, acting within the rules, precedents, and practices of the House or Senate to represent the constituency's interests and sentiments, and make policy for the entire nation. All three roles are constantly in play, thereby shaping the work of a member of Congress.

Politician

As a politician, a prospective or elected member of Congress can look in the mirror and see a person with a gift that most of us do not have—the capacity to campaign for and win a congressional election. He knows how to raise money; how to manage a campaign operation; how to rally a crowd; how to debate; how to listen; how to learn what issues matter to an individual, a constituency group, or a constituency generally; and how to advocate for himself or herself and for key issues. (*See Chapter Two: Pressures on Congress: Campaigns and Elections.*)

Once elected, the member of Congress can put the same skills to work in committee and on the House or Senate floor representing a congressional district or a state. The goal is to make policy—who gets what. The member's interests might be parochial or national or both; they might be simple or complex; they might be quite focused or fairly broad. The member has to be the same self-confident advocate with congressional colleagues as with constituents, able to speak persuasively one-on-one to a committee chair or ranking minority member and equally able to speak persuasively to the House or Senate in session.

Each member of Congress looks out for his own political interests in party and leadership meetings. A member wants to follow party leaders, unless they lead in a direction that would create political problems back home. The member must balance personal political needs against any stance taken by party leaders. A member might even want to have a role in the leadership, perhaps within the party's whip structure, but still maintain some flexibility in the relationship so she can speak for a different point of view or vote against the party leadership when necessary politically.

A principal challenge for any member is to be successful in a group. A *group* in Congress is not a *team*, as we might think of a sports team with everyone working together in various support roles to accomplish the clear goals of offense, defense, and winning. A group in Congress also lacks the formal system of direction or command that exists in business, the military, or even executive agencies, where a superior can give an order to subordinates with some degree of assurance that it will be carried out.

A member of Congress, in contrast, constantly functions within groups of different sizes, composition, like-mindedness, partisanship, purpose, role, structure, and so on. While some members of a group might have positions of power or discretion, such as the chair of a committee or a leader of a chamber, members are largely equal in many circumstances. No one is, or will be allowed to be, fully in charge since each state or district and set of supporters and other conditions are different for each member. A member must be skillful and adaptive in a variety of group structures to be a successful politician and policymaker.

Policymaker

As a policymaker, a member must be in command of facts, arguments, perspectives on a problem, and the advantages of particular policy or legislative solutions and the disadvantages of others. A member of Congress must also be able to manage her relationships with party and committee leaders. A member will need her leaders' assistance and even indulgence on matters critical to the member's constituency or political well-being.

Members of Congress might say that their views are rarely swayed by a colleague's speech. That may be true. However, it is equally true that their views are never positively swayed by a colleague who is unprepared or uninformed. More experienced members might be tolerant of a junior member learning a new policy issue. They are not accepting of another member who is not in command of facts and arguments for a point of view, who speaks loudly in ignorance, or who makes implausible arguments.

As policymakers, members introduce bills, ask questions in hearings, offer amendments in committee markup and in the chamber, debate and vote in committee and in the chamber, and maneuver inside and outside of conferences to protect or kill provisions in measures submitted to conference. All their actions are intended to advance to the degree possible their constituents' interests and their own policy and legislative positions.

In leading a chamber of policymakers, party leaders have the tough job of putting together majorities (or even supermajorities in the instance of veto override attempts or, in the Senate, motions to invoke cloture). They need to put together these majorities without compromising core party positions. Leaders must also stop opposing viewpoints from gathering momentum. To build a majority on some matter within a chamber, leaders first seek a majority within their parties. Leaders try to enforce party discipline through favors, threats, or even a member's isolation. (*See Chapter Five, Organizing Congress: Members, Leaders, and Committees.*)

Parliamentarian

As a parliamentarian, a member of Congress must understand chamber structure and the procedures through which members try to advance or impede policy in the form of legislation. Does the member introduce a bill or offer an amendment? If an amendment, should it be offered in a committee or on the floor? When? Is one committee more receptive to a policy solution than another? What opportunities or limitations will exist in committee because of the markup vehicle chosen? How does a member get time to speak on the floor? What can he do during that time? What is the optimal time? All these questions, options, and choices come into play as a member works within a chamber's procedures to realize a policy goal through the legislative process.

Congress has a formal structure. Each house of Congress follows laws, rules, precedents, and practices that apply in its chamber. Each chamber is very different. The strategies that work in the House, a majoritarian institution, are different from those that work in the Senate, an institution where the individual senator reigns supreme. Representatives who are elected to the Senate often find the first year or so to be a frustrating experience. It seems so difficult to get anything done in the Senate, compared with the practices of the House. (*See Chapter Six, Legislating in Congress: Legislative Process; Chapter Seven, Legislating in Congress: Federal Budget Process; and Chapter Eight, Legislating in Congress: Special Procedures and Considerations.*)

To be effective and realize policy goals, a member of Congress must use all his skills and abilities as a politician, policymaker, and parliamentarian—both inside and outside committees and chambers, and at all stages of the legislative process.

Congress and Its 541 Members

In contrast to the roles of politician, policymaker, and parliamentarian, what images do Americans carry of members of Congress? Most citizens have images of a teacher in a classroom, a businessman or woman in an office, a programmer at a computer, a carpenter building a house, a therapist helping a patient, or an entertainer on stage. They have strong, largely accurate images of people at work. They generally think well of people in various professions, even if they have had a bad experience with an individual in any profession.

With members of Congress, Americans might very well have somewhat or largely positive images of their own representatives and senators, yet dismiss Congress as a whole because it is made up of "politicians." Even worse, they might dismiss it because it represents America too well—a lack of consensus in Congress usually reflects a lack of consensus in the country.

To avoid the cynical view of Congress held by many Americans, how might someone interacting regularly with Congress try to imagine it as a whole, as a working institution? One possible way is to imagine Congress as a living organism, with a skeleton, nervous system, and muscular system. The skeleton is legislative procedure and the organization of Congress for processing legislation, which gives each chamber an enduring structure. The nervous system is complex, and involves all the avenues for information to reach members, committees, and leaders, such as the stimuli of elections, constituents, the president, lobbyists, the media, perceptions of problems, dissatisfaction with the status quo, events at home, events abroad, and the individual interests of members. The muscular system of Congress, which gives it the capacity to act, results in policymaking. Competing legislation is drafted, hearings are held, information is gathered, arguments are devised, and advocacy takes place inside and outside Congress. This image offers a way one might view Congress as a whole, in its capacity to act and to change.

The framers did not create Congress to achieve specific legislative results. They created it to process (or stop) legislation and to make law, whatever the outcome might be. A Congress that was largely controlled by Democrats for forty years until the 1994 elections worked just as well as a policymaking institution for Republicans who controlled it for twelve years until the 2006 elections. The policy results for Congress under Democratic control were different from the policy results under Republican control, and the policy results developing after the 2010 election seem to be different from those of earlier Democratic and Republican majorities. The framers, in fact, could not have anticipated modern political parties, but created a legislature where a majority, however composed, could win—in passing or stopping legislation. The stimulus of issues, the making of policy, and the procedural structure are just as important and evident today as they were in 1994, 1894, or 1794.

A member of Congress works as a politician, policymaker, and parliamentarian within a complex structure. He is one of 541 members motivated by different constituencies and personal and professional interests. To be successful, a member must combine roles skillfully within this complex structure.

§ 1.40 Obligations and Perquisites

With election come obligations to constituents, one's chamber, and the public and interests affected by one's role, and to the next election campaign.

If a member intends to seek reelection, she must be attentive to a constituency—through case work, visits home, prompt response to mail, and so on. Sometimes, proposed legislation could have a direct, adverse impact on a district or state. Constituents expect their members of Congress to defeat the legislation—not just do everything possible to defeat it, but defeat it. Think of how hard and how long the Nevada delegation, no matter what party or chamber, has fought the storage of civilian nuclear reactor waste in its state.

The obligations to a representative's constituency nowadays also require the member's presence in the home district every weekend. The demand of this kind of obligation is felt more keenly by representatives than senators, but no member who will seek reelection can afford to spend many weekends in Washington, or in places other than her home district.

A member might also serve on as many as three or four committees and many more subcommittees. However, meetings often conflict so that a member might spend a morning running from one important markup to another as well as fitting in other commitments. Floor votes occur regularly on Tuesday, Wednesday, and Thursday afternoons and often well into those nights. Floor votes may occur on other days as well. Meetings on specific legislation with chamber leaders, other party members, or allied members might take place at any time to try to work out problems, get commitments, or strategize. Formal party meetings are regularly scheduled, but informal party meetings can occur at any time. To participate in the politics of Congress, a member must be present and working.

The members' appearances and participation in events contribute significantly to their workloads. A member must choose which events to attend (and for how long), which to respond to with more than regrets (and how to respond), and which to decline. Home state and Washington lobbyists, interest group representatives, important constituents such as business or labor leaders, and constituent delegations or deputations want meetings. A member's staff needs to schedule time to discuss legislative initiatives. A member's family would like to be remembered somewhere in the schedule.

Another important consideration in daily, weekly, and monthly schedules is the need to focus on reelection. A reelection campaign starts as soon as an election is won, and neither party now waits for an election year or the selection of an opposition candidate to begin targeting members whom they perceive to be vulnerable or whom they wish to test for vulnerability. Negative attacks on freshmen members might start with their swearing-in. Representatives and delegates must face the electorate again in just two years. (The Puerto Rican resident commissioner has a four-year term.) Senators have six years between elections, but they cannot rest on their laurels for long. Each member must raise money for each campaign. Nearly every representative must set aside some time each week just to keep in touch with principals in his campaign organization, campaign contributors, and politicians back home. Members might go as often as once or twice a week to the Democratic or Republican headquarters in Washington to telephone their political advisors back home and their campaign contributors.

Senators' reelection campaigning is much less visible than that of representatives during the first three or four years of their terms. Yet, senators also must keep in touch with principals in their campaign organizations, raise money, and speak with home-state politicians. Senators seek to build large campaign funds by the fourth year of their terms, to ward off challengers or to ensure that a challenger knows a race will be hard-fought.

Members who wish to become leaders—in committee or in their chamber—must today prove themselves to be prodigious fund-raisers, and contribute to their party and to their colleagues.

Many activities are important, and all must be accommodated somehow. Private time or "think time" is rare once a day starts. A plane or train ride home to the state or district becomes catch-up time for reading—so long as another member, an administration official, a lobbyist, or an important constituent is not also on the plane or train and desiring a conversation.

It is all too common for a member's workday in Washington to begin before 8:00 a.m. and continue well into the night. A day in the district or state might be just as long or even longer. A member of Congress almost always has one eye on a watch, frequently rechecks her daily schedule, cannot be separated from a cell phone or BlackBerry®, and is often accompanied by a staffer who seems to be urging the member to leave wherever they are only moments after their arrival. On foot or by car, staffers are always picking up or dropping off a member and assisting with some aspect of the member's personal life as well as attending to the official one. (*See Chapter Four, Supporting Congress: Allowances and Staff.*)

One must imagine holding the job of a member of Congress to appreciate the attributes required. To be effective—to ensure that one's constituency is well served—requires exceptional skills and endurance.

The Honorable. . .

Election and congressional service also bring recognition and perhaps even adulation. Congratulatory mail and phone calls flow in after an election. Past and potential contributors want to associate with a successful candidate. People want to work in a congressional office; hundreds of résumés arrive in the temporary congressional mailboxes of members-elect. Party leaders are eager to get relations off to a good start. In less than two months after the election, the member's swearing-in ceremony is carried on C-SPAN, and dozens of well-wishers join the member in swearing-in festivities in Washington.

Subsequent speeches in floor and committee proceedings are carried on C-SPAN, and excerpts might be broadcast elsewhere. National newspapers and news services seek comments from senators on everything; state and local newspapers want the views of representatives as well; and members are now expected to have a presence online. Congressional leaders, administration officials, and the president seek the support of members of Congress on important votes. Lobbyists also want members' support, and all sorts of home-state and national organizations want members to give speeches, meet their boards of directors, and shake hands with their employees. Invitations to events, including perhaps a state dinner at the White House, arrive by the bagful. Constituents visiting Washington cannot leave town without taking the opportunity to say hello. These activities, largely flattering, are part and parcel of the politics of Congress.

For members, there are a number of smaller perquisites that accompany election and further indicate a change in status. Members of Congress and their spouses receive pins when the members are sworn in. The pins have the practical effect of facilitating the members' and their spouses' movement throughout the Capitol complex. But they are also the mark of an elite fraternity. There are also VIP parking lots for members of Congress and other dignitaries set aside at the Washington, DC, airports, Reagan Washington National and Dulles International. Again, it is a practical and cost-effective arrangement to deal with VIPs' cars, but, out of the millions of passengers who pass through those two airports each year, members are some of the few who are treated specially.

There are many flattering aspects and emotional rewards to being a member of Congress. Whether in Washington or traveling, a member of Congress is generally extended every courtesy. Most simply stated, being a member of Congress makes others pay attention.

§ 1.50 Ever-Changing and Unpredictable Schedules

Daily and weekly schedules in Washington, as well as district or state schedules, are major preoccupations of every congressional office. Scheduling a member's time is a job that often involves a scheduling assistant, a chief of staff, and a district or state director, in addition to the member. The watchword is *contingency*.

The first item to consider is whether the chamber in which the member serves is in session, when it is in session, and when there will be votes. The next item involves when the committees, subcommittees, and groups on which the member serves will meet and what their business will be. The legislative assistants and committee staff provide the scheduling team with information to assist them in setting priorities and ensuring the member's legislative interests are accommodated. The

1

§ 1.51

Example of a Senior House Member's Daily Schedule

November 9 (Tuesday)

8:00a–9:30a	Democratic Women Candidates Networking Breakfast to promote Democratic agenda regarding education and children Location: Capital Hilton, Congressional Meeting Room, 1001 16th St., NW
9:00a	Democratic Caucus to discuss the budget and appropriations Notes: special guest—White House Chief of Staff John Podesta Location: B-339 Rayburn
9:00a	Morning Hour
10:00a	Ways and Means Committee (W&M)—full committee hearing on President Clinton's new Social Security plan Location: 1100 Longworth
10:00a	House convenes—measures under suspension
11:00a	Prescription drug press conference with Hillary Clinton, Leader Gephardt, Whip Bonior, others Notes: staff—Helen Location: Rayburn Gold Room (2168)
11:30a	Democratic Women Candidates' Networking Lunch Notes: keynote speaker—Hillary Clinton Location: Capital Hilton, Congressional Meeting Room, 1001 16th St., NW
12:30p	Joint Health/Medicare task force meeting on Medicare prescription drug benefits Notes: staff—Jeff; pizza and drinks to be served Location: HC-9, Capitol
1:30p–2:00p	W&M Democrats to discuss minimum-wage bill Location: 1129 Longworth
2:00p	Sue Esserman to brief W&M Democrats and Democratic advisory group on World Trade Organization (WTO) Ministerial Notes: staff—Nora Location: H-137, Capitol
2:30p	Bob Quaine of the Kidnapped & Hostage program in Spring Hill to discuss silent survival signals Notes: staff—Bob
2:30p	White House ceremony giving the Congressional Gold Medal to the Little Rock Nine, the nine black students to integrate Little Rock's Central High School Notes: Members asked to arrive at 2:30; ceremony in the East Room from 2:45–3:45; reception in State Dining Room from 3:45-4:45
3:00p	W&M markup on minimum-wage bill Notes: staff—Bob Location: 1100 Longworth
3:30p	W&M Democrats and WTO labor advisory group Democrats' briefing on WTO Ministerial Notes: staff—Nora Location: H-137, Capitol
4:00p	Major Walker and various representatives from the Marine Corps Liaison to follow up on last week's meeting, answer Member's previous questions Notes: staff—Nora
4:30p	New Democratic Coalition "top of the week" meeting Notes: featuring John Podesta Location: HC-8, Capitol
5:00p	Members only briefing on WTO Ministerial Location: H-137, Capitol
6:30p–8:30p	Congressional Black Caucus reception to honor the Little Rock Nine Location: Great Hall, Jefferson Building, Library of Congress

§ 1.52

Example of a Freshman House Member's Daily Schedule

Thursday, March 18

7:59a–9:14a	Breakfast for another Member—National Democratic Club
8:00a–9:00a	Breakfast reception for another Member—National Democratic Club
9:00a–9:45a	Copanelist with another Member opening the 1999 Consumer Assembly; two staffers to accompany—Washington Plaza Hotel, 10 Thomas Circle, NW
9:00a–9:45a	WHIP Meeting—HC-9
9:01a–10:01a	GOVERNMENT REFORM SUBCOMMITTEE HEARING (preventing and treating drug abuse, government witnesses)—2247 Rayburn
9:30a–10:00a	SPEAKER'S CLOSED MEETING OF THE HOUSE to discuss highly classified material relating to emerging ballistic missile threats, followed later today by House action on HR 4—House Chamber
10:00a–10:30a	SMALL BUSINESS COMMITTEE MARKUP: HR 536 (SBA district offices)—2360 Rayburn
11:00a–11:30a	Meet with representative of American Immigration Lawyers' Association from Member's district to discuss immigration matters; staffer present—Member's office
12:00 noon	HOUSE convenes: HR 4 scheduled (missile defense policy), votes expected
12:00p–1:15p	Luncheon with National Newspaper Association editors and publishers; staffer to accompany—Montpelier Room, 6th floor, Madison Building, Library of Congress
2:00p–2:15p	Meet with parent of a campaign volunteer; staffer present—Member's office
2:30p–3:00p	Meet with a representative of State Podiatric Medical Association—Member's office
3:00p–3:45p	Meet with representative of Indo-American Democratic Organization; two staffers present—Member's office
4:00p–4:15p	Meet with representative of State Press Association—Member's office
4:30p–5:00p	Staff meeting on upcoming recess activities—Member's office
5:00p–9:00p	Reception at 5:00 followed by dinner and awards presentation 6:00p–9:00p for Center for Women Policy Studies; Member to speak and make presentation (business attire)—Hyatt Regency Washington on Capitol Hill, 400 New Jersey Ave., NW

member's personal staff might want to reserve time, and there might be personal events or family needs and plans to be protected in a schedule.

Most staff know the flight and train options for going to the district or state and returning. Possible events in the home district or state over a weekend are factored in. There are town hall meetings, breakfasts, lunches, receptions, dinners, events, and requests for meetings for which RSVPs are waiting, and quasi-official activities such as party conference or caucus meetings, briefings by legislative branch or administration staff, various meetings of like-minded members, and legislative

§ 1.53

1

Excerpt from House's Daily Schedule (GOP Source)

One of the principal jobs of the party whips in both parties in both chambers is to keep party members apprised of the floor schedule. The parties' whips' web sites in both chambers are listed in § 9.30, Sites for Committee, Scheduling, and Member Information. On any day, a reader will find different and useful supporting information available through the two parties' leaders' web sites.

ERIC CANTOR LEADER'S WEEKLY SCHEDULE
MAJORITY LEADER MAJORITYLEADER.GOV (202)225-4000

Week of May 23, 2011

Monday, May 23rd
On Monday, the House will meet at 2:00 p.m. for legislative business. Votes will be postponed until 6:30 p.m.

Legislation Considered Under Suspension of the Rules:

1) **H.R. 1407** - Veterans' Compensation Cost-of-Living Adjustment Act of 2011
(Sponsored by Rep. Jon Runyan / Veterans' Affairs Committee)
2) **H.R. 1627** - To amend title 38, United States Code, to provide for certain requirements for the placement of monuments in Arlington National Cemetery, and for other purposes
(Sponsored by Rep. Jeff Miller / Veterans' Affairs Committee)
3) **H.R. 1383** - Restoring GI Bill Fairness Act of 2011, as amended
(Sponsored by Rep. Jeff Miller / Veterans' Affairs Committee)
4) **H.R. 1657** - To amend title 38, United States Code, to revise the enforcement penalties for misrepresentation of a business concern as a small business concern owned and controlled by veterans or as a small business concern owned and controlled by service-disabled veterans
(Sponsored by Rep. Marlin Stutzman / Veterans' Affairs Committee)
5) **H.R. 1893** - To amend the Internal Revenue Code of 1986 to extend the funding and expenditure authority of the Airport and Airway Trust Fund, to amend title 49, United States Code, to extend the airport improvement program, and for other purposes
(Sponsored by Rep. John Mica / Transportation and Infrastructure Committee)

Tuesday, May 24th, and the Balance of the Week
On Tuesday, the House will meet at 10:00 a.m. for legislative business and recess immediately. The House will reconvene at approximately 11:00 a.m. for the purpose of receiving, in a joint meeting with the Senate, the Honorable Binyamin Netanyahu, Prime Minister of Israel.

On Wednesday, the House will meet at 10:00 a.m. for morning hour and 12:00 p.m. for legislative business.

On Thursday, the House will meet at 9:00 a.m. for legislative business. Last votes for the week are expected no later than 3:00 p.m.

On Friday, the House will meet in Pro Forma session.

S. 990 - A bill to provide for an additional temporary extension of programs under the Small Business Act and the Small Business Investment Act of 1958, and for other purposes, as amended (Suspension, 40 Minutes of Debate)
(Sponsored by Sen. Mary Landrieu / Small Business Committee)

H.R. 1216 - To amend the Public Health Service Act to convert funding for graduate medical education in qualified teaching health centers from direct appropriations to an authorization of appropriations (Subject to a Rule)
(Sponsored by Rep. Brett Guthrie / Energy and Commerce Committee)

H.R. 1540 - National Defense Authorization Act for Fiscal Year 2012 (Subject to a Rule)
(Sponsored by Rep. Buck McKeon / Armed Services Committee)

Possible consideration of legislation relating to expiring provisions of the USA PATRIOT Improvement and Reauthorization Act of 2005 and Intelligence Reform and Terrorism Prevention Act of 2004 (Subject to a Rule)
(Judiciary Committee / Permanent Select Intelligence Committee)

Committee Activity of the Week
Education and the Workforce Subcommittee on Health, Employment, Labor and Pensions Hearing on "Corporate Campaigns and the NLRB: The Impact of Union Pressure on Job Creation" (Thursday, May 26th at 10:00 a.m.)

§ 1.54

Excerpt from House's Daily Schedule (Democratic Source)

Party entities in the House and Senate provide various forms of information on their respective chamber's daily, weekly, and long-term schedules. The parties' scheduling web sites in both chambers appear in § 9.30, Sites for Committee, Scheduling, and Member Information. The starting point with party-provided information on floor action begins with so-called whip information, shown here.

OFFICE OF DEMOCRATIC WHIP STENY H. HOYER

THE WEEKLY WHIP

democraticwhip.gov • (202) 225-3130

FRIDAY, APRIL 29, 2011

FIRST VOTE OF THE WEEK:	LAST VOTE PREDICTED:
Monday 6:30 p.m.	**Thursday 3:00 p.m.**

Legislative Program - 51600 | Floor Information - 57400 | Whip Information - 53130

*****MEMBERS ARE ADVISED THAT ANY EXPECTED ABSENCES SHOULD BE REPORTED TO THE WHIP'S OFFICE AT X5-3130.**

MONDAY, MAY 2, 2011
On Monday, the House will meet at 2:00 p.m. for legislative business with votes postponed until 6:30 p.m.

Suspensions (2 Bills)

1) H.R. 1423 - To designate the facility of the United States Postal Service located at 115 4th Avenue Southwest in Ardmore, Oklahoma, as the "Specialist Micheal E. Phillips Post Office" (Rep. Cole – Oversight and Government Reform)
2) H.R. 362 - To redesignate the Federal building and United States Courthouse located at 200 East Wall Street in Midland, Texas, as the "George H. W. Bush and George W. Bush United States Courthouse and George Mahon Federal Building" (Rep. Conaway – Transportation and Infrastructure)

TUESDAY, MAY 3, 2011
On Tuesday, the House will meet at 10:00 a.m. for Morning Hour debate and 12:00 p.m. for legislative business.

H.R. 1213 – Repeal mandatory funding provided to States in the Patient Protection and Affordable Care Act to establish American Health Benefit Exchanges (Rep. Upton – Energy and Commerce) (Subject to a Rule)

H.R. 1214 – Repeal mandatory funding for school-based health center construction (Rep. Upton – Energy and Commerce) (Subject to a Rule)

WEDNESDAY, MAY 4, 2011 AND THE BALANCE OF THE WEEK
On Wednesday, the House will meet at 10:00 a.m. for Morning Hour debate and 12:00 p.m. for legislative business. On Thursday, the House will meet at 9:00 a.m. for legislative business with last votes no later than 3:00 p.m. On Friday, no votes are expected in the House.

H.R. 3 – No Taxpayer Funding for Abortion Act (Rep. Smith (NJ) – Judiciary/Energy and Commerce/Ways and Means) (Subject to a Rule)

H.R. 1230 – Restarting American Offshore Leasing Now Act (Rep. Hastings (WA) – Natural Resources) (Subject to a Rule)

Possible Consideration of H.R. 1229 – Putting the Gulf of Mexico Back to Work Act (Rep. Hastings (WA) – Natural Resources) (Subject to a Rule)

Continued on page 15

§ 1.54 (continued)

OFFICE OF DEMOCRATIC WHIP STENY H. HOYER

THE WEEKLY WHIP

democraticwhip.gov • (202) 225-3130

Additional Floor Information

The Rules Committee is scheduled to meet on the following days:

- Monday, May 2, 2011 at 5:00 p.m. to report a Rule for **H.R. 1213** – To Repeal the Mandatory Funding Provided to States in the Patient Protection and Affordable Care Act to Establish American Health Benefit Exchanges. We expect a Structured Rule and Amendments must be submitted to the Rules Committee by **10:00 a.m. on Monday, May 2, 2011.**
- Monday, May 2, 2011 at 5:00 p.m. to report a Rule for **H.R. 1214 –** To Repeal Mandatory Funding for School-Based Health Center Construction. We expect a Modified Structured Rule which may require that amendments be pre-printed in the Congressional Record prior to their consideration. Amendments should be submitted for printing in the Congressional Record on the legislative day of **Monday, May 2, 2011.**
- Monday, May 2, 2011 at 5:00 p.m. to report a Rule for **H.R. 3 –** No Taxpayer Funding for Abortion Act. We expect a Closed Rule.
- Wednesday, May 4, 2011 at 3:00 p.m. to report a Rule for **H.R. 1229** – Putting the Gulf of Mexico Back to Work Act and **H.R. 1230** – To require the Secretary of the Interior to conduct certain offshore oil and gas lease sales. We expect a Structured Rule for both bills. Amendments for H.R.1229 must be submitted to the Rules Committee by **10:00 a.m. on Tuesday, May 3, 2011** and Amendments for H.R. 1230 must be submitted to the Rules Committee by **10:00 a.m. on Wednesday, May 4, 2011.**

Announcements on the amendment processes can be found on the Rules committee website at: http://democrats.rules.house.gov/

strategy meetings that compete for a specific place on the schedule. No matter how senior or junior they may be, all members are very, very busy. (*See § 1.51, Example of a Senior House Member's Daily Schedule; and § 1.52, Example of a Freshman House Member's Daily Schedule.*)

A scheduling assistant's work does not end when he puts a schedule for the next day in a member's hands. The schedule rarely works as planned, and much of the day might be spent rearranging meetings and other commitments to accommodate changes.

Changes can result from additions to or deletions from agendas in committees or on the floor. Party leaders might also require a member's presence on short notice—a member does not say "I'm unavailable" to the Speaker or to party leaders. An event inside Congress or outside anywhere in the world—such as party leaders announcing an agreement with the White House on an important matter, a foreign crisis that leaves American citizens in harm's way, the sudden death of a member of Congress, or similar events—can have an immediate effect on every member's activities and schedule. A chamber might adjourn or recess early for the week or stay in session longer than announced. Many occurrences can scramble plans. (*See § 1.53, Excerpt from House's Daily Schedule (GOP Source); and § 1.54, Excerpt from House's Daily Schedule (Democratic Source).*)

§ 1.55

Floor Discussion of Schedule Changes

The negotiation of schedules is a time-consuming but important activity on Capitol Hill. Everyone desires predictability, but it is difficult for congressional leaders to deliver it.

The excerpt below is representative of congressional concerns over unpredictability in scheduling. The excerpt was taken from a House floor colloquy between House Majority Leader Dick Armey, R-TX, and House Appropriations Committee Ranking Member David Obey, D-WI, on Thursday, June 15, 2000. The House was considering amendments to the fiscal year 2001 Interior appropriations bill. The Republican leadership expressed its hope on Wednesday, June 14, to complete all floor votes by 6:00 p.m. Thursday. As Thursday afternoon wore on, representatives became anxious about making evening airline flights to their home districts. Finally, Obey raised the scheduling question with Armey in formal debate, and ultimately offered a preferential motion for the Committee of the Whole to rise. (*See § 6.120, Committee of the Whole: Amendment Process*.)

The motion was defeated on a recorded vote, 183 to 218. The Obey-Armey colloquy began about 5:20 p.m. The colloquy and vote on the motion consumed about thirty minutes. The House worked late and finally adjourned for the week on Friday morning, June 16, at 1:25 a.m.

> Mr. Obey: . . . I would simply like to ask if the leadership intends to keep the commitment which was announced to the House (to take no votes after 6:00 p.m. today) or whether the rumors are true that we hear that they now intend to be in until 9:00.
>
> Mr. Armey: . . . We worked out an agreement last night that we thought would give us good progress. We had high hopes of continuing this work and completing it by 6:00 today. But as we can see, we are approaching that hour; and we are not near completion.
>
> Mr. Obey: . . . Let me simply say that the problem, as has been brought to my attention by a number of members, is that the schedule published by the leadership indicates legislative business, no votes after 6:00 p.m. . . . But I regret that the leadership has seen fit to upset the ability of each individual member to get back to their district. . . .
>
> Mr. Armey: . . . [O]ur agreement that we made last night was in full understanding of the need and the commitment to complete this, where the floor manager said, and I think in good faith and with all good intention, that they would do everything they could to finish by 6:00. Unfortunately, given their best efforts, they have not been able to achieve that. . . .
>
> Mr. Obey: . . . We were told that the intention of the leadership was that we were leaving at 6, that the committee should do its best to be done by 6, but there was a clear understanding that the members would be allowed to leave as scheduled at 6:00.

Planning weekend and weeklong visits to the home district or state can also be fraught with anxiety when chamber leaders are unable to give commitments on an adjournment or recess or when members are required to return earlier than anticipated. (*See § 1.55, Floor Discussion of Schedule Changes.*) Weather can also upset travel plans for leaving or returning to Washington, and for maintaining a schedule at home. Compared with Washington schedules, however, members at home are better able to make and stick to schedules. Principal scheduling problems at home tend to result from overcommitment, insufficient travel time between event locations, and weather conditions affecting travel.

Mindful of the problems of alienation and exhaustion caused by congressional schedules, leaders and members have discussed a variety of scheduling options since the 1990s, but none of the alternatives has taken hold. Both chambers looked at options such as three weeks in session and one week not in session each month. The House looked at the possibility of eliminating evening votes, and went so far as to build a "family room" for members' children near the House floor, just off Statuary Hall.

Nothing has happened to make congressional committee and floor schedules more predictable, although the Republican-controlled House in the 112th Congress (2011–2013) sought to introduce more predictability to the days and weeks in session. Members have also not changed their behavior in traveling routinely to their districts or states, and constituents have not changed their expectations for members to be physically present in their districts or states as often as possible.

Within this demanding and shifting framework, a member's time and attention are resources that must be strategically and tactically deployed. Effectiveness in Congress is often based on a member taking the right step at the right time and being in the right place at the right time. Committee markups, floor debate and votes, constituent visits, calls to campaign contributors, purposeful chats with party leaders, and other important activities must be accommodated in the swirl of ever-changing and unpredictable schedules.

§ 1.60 Family Life

In addition to public and institutional pressures and demands, a member faces the challenge of balancing public and private lives. The demands of congressional service take a toll on a member's family and family life.

Just a little over a generation ago, most members' families lived in the Washington area. Today, most members' families live in the home district or state. It is a key difference in congressional life. Washington is a very expensive city compared with many of the places that members call home. To relocate a family and provide comparable housing, schools, and lifestyle is beyond many members' means. In Washington, spouses and children are cut off from the network of family and friends in their hometowns. Members, therefore, end up maintaining two residences, even if one is a tiny or shared apartment on Capitol Hill. Some members with families back home even stay in their Washington office rather than rent another place to live, although the House and Senate discourage that.

Whether a member's family lives in Washington or elsewhere, the toll on family and personal life is high. A spouse can become a stranger when one is a member of Congress. The time it takes to be a member of Congress can be a factor in a marriage's breakup. Even when a family is in Washington and a member goes to his district or state a bit less frequently or for a shorter period of time, the schedule of the House or Senate in session seems to preclude a regular home life. As mentioned in § 1.50, there has been discussion of "family friendly scheduling" in the last several Congresses, but no identifiable changes have endured.

Moreover, congressional families reflect changes in American life. Many spouses work. Delayed childbearing has affected members, too, with many of them, including an increasing number of women members, having young children at the same time they are building their congressional careers. For these and other reasons, Congress in session has become the temporary location for many members. A family and the constituents back home make the district or state the member's principal residence and workplace. Members are in Washington three or four days a week and not at all when there is a week-long recess.

A generation ago, members of Congress got to know each other fairly well. Members, spouses, and families socialized together. Members themselves would also socialize at activities such as weekly poker games. That is much less common among junior members today. Some representatives, in reaction, have attempted to create some common ground. Two bipartisan family "retreats" were organized at Hershey Park, PA, just after the convening of the 105th and 106th Congresses, to enable House members and their families to socialize together. The 107th and 108th Congresses' retreats were held at the Greenbrier resort in White Sulphur Springs, WV, but no subsequent bipartisan or family retreats have been held. Congressional spouse organizations also attempt to provide a common ground. (*See § 4.201, Congressional Spouse Organizations.*)

Senators' lives seem to have been affected somewhat less dramatically than those of representatives. A senator is somewhat more likely to have grown children rather than be a parent of young children during her Senate service, and the relentless travel to the home state is principally a feature of the last two years of a term. It is also somewhat less common for a senator's spouse and family to reside in the home state rather than in the Washington area.

Like the trade-offs between obligations and perquisites, the honor and rewards of serving in Congress come at a price. A member's family might be unprepared for its new status and regular separation from one parent. A member might be unprepared for the loneliness of having family far away.

§ 1.70 Staying in Congress

Another change in congressional service involves members' departures from Congress after a few terms.

The median number of terms or years that a member might be expected to serve in Congress has declined for some time. A generation ago, a newly elected member could reasonably expect to be reelected. Members frequently served twenty years or more before retirement. Reelection rates for the House—members choosing to run for reelection—are historically over 90 percent. At the beginning of the 112th Congress, the median number of terms served by representatives was four (eight years). Reelection rates for the Senate are historically below those for the House, but are still high. At the beginning of the 112th Congress, the median number of years served in the Senate was eight.

However, members whose seats are safe, who have no problem raising campaign funds, who hold positions of influence within Congress, and who contribute substantially to legislation regularly decide not to run for reelection. Why is this commitment to a career in Congress eroding?

Members of Congress cite many dissatisfactions with the congressional way of life as it has evolved over a generation. Some of these are as follows:

- high toll on personal and family life
- living with guilt over trying and being unable to be all things to all people, especially loved ones

- life in a fishbowl
- backbreaking schedule
- loss of time to think and be expert
- partisanship of Congress
- anonymity among colleagues that goes with a three-and-one-half-day-a-week presence in Washington
- endless fund-raising and the cost of campaigns
- influence of special interests
- negative campaigning, which has become year-round and includes groups affiliated with one's own party as well as the opposition party
- perceived irrelevance and intransigence of Congress in solutions to national problems
- vacuous, symbolic, and partisan legislation and votes on the congressional agenda
- perception of parties' lack of interest in governing
- relatively low salary for the work and high cost of being a member of Congress
- need for a higher salary to provide family needs, such as college costs
- decline of interest in public service
- term limits as a political issue and as a reality in committee and subcommittee chairmanships
- stronger interest in other careers

The hardship of congressional life is undeniable. Even the most self-confident and politically gifted member might choose to make a change after a few terms.

However, turnover might also reflect generational changes in how Americans view their jobs. Many workers in modern America hold several jobs in the course of a lifetime, in contrast to the norm in their grandparents' generation, when a successful career might have meant working for just one or two employers. In part, the shorter tenure of members of Congress could simply reflect larger national trends.

Whatever the reason for a member departing after a few terms, the departure means a loss of expertise and of political experience in Congress. National problems are complex and not easily mastered in a short time. Even with knowledge or expertise, members need political experience to identify and engineer legislative solutions. For the professional interacting with Congress, the shorter tenure presents both opportunities and challenges in developing working relationships, understanding congressional dynamics, and advocating and facilitating legislative solutions. (*See Chapter Three, Pressures on Congress: Lobbying and Congressional Ethics.*)

§ 1.80 Chapter Summary and Discussion Questions

What does it mean to be a member of Congress? A member is more than a legislator. He must be a representative of a district or state, a policy expert, a parliamentarian, a persuasive speaker and good listener, a constant candidate for reelection and fund-raiser, and a small businessman or -woman in charge of a congressional staff and, perhaps, a congressional committee or leadership office. Travel to and from one's district or state must be considered part of the job. All members also have a personal side, as a spouse or parent or child with aging parents.

Many members serve many years in Congress, but more members now serve a limited number of terms or years before leaving Congress to exercise other career options.

Discussion Questions

- Many congressional observers speak of the "three Ps." What are they and what is important about each of them to a member's success as a legislator?
- Thinking about the many roles and jobs of a member of Congress, make a list of the kinds of activities that are likely to be a possibility every day.
- Local, regional, national, and international events can redirect the attention of some members of Congress, or all members of Congress, and change its schedule. Identify one of these events, and check the *Congressional Record* or other sources to see how the congressional schedule was affected in the immediate aftermath of the event.
- If you were a newly elected member of Congress, what factors would you consider in deciding whether or not to relocate your family to the Washington, DC, area?
- What aspects of service in Congress—and getting elected and reelected to it—would you find distasteful or discouraging? Why? How do you think a member might overcome or accept a similar aversion?

Chapter Two

Pressures on Congress: Campaigns and Elections

2

Analysis

§ 2.00 Introduction

From the moment of his first election to Congress until the last day of service, a member is subjected to pressures from numerous sources, including constituents, media, executive officials, and lobbyists. A major pressure present is that the next election is always right around the corner. No one serves in Congress unless elected to it, although some senators are appointed temporarily to fill a vacancy until an election is held. (*See § 5.10, Members of Congress: Service, Qualifications, Characteristics, and Filling Vacant Seats.*)

Candidates must be organizers and managers able to put together a campaign organization, raise money, and develop a campaign strategy. Incumbents may have advantages in an election with an established campaign organization, additional sources of campaign funds, relationships with media that cover a campaign, and a tendency of voters to stick with a known politician. Party support is integral in a general election campaign, and the parties have many ways of supporting their candidates.

A candidate's future constituents, or an incumbent's current constituents, are the most important political component of any campaign, because they are the voters. An incumbent must have conducted his tenure with them foremost in her considerations, and a candidate must try to convince them that she better understands and will better represent their political desires and aspirations.

In the last two or three decades, fund-raising has become a huge responsibility and consumer of time for candidates for Congress. Campaigns are very expensive, and contributors are limited in what they may give to an individual for each election in which the individual is a candidate. Raising and spending campaign funds is highly regulated by federal law, Federal Election Commission and other federal agencies' regulations, and House and Senate rules. (*See also § 3.50, Congressional Ethics; § 3.60 Regulated Activities; and § 4.50, Franking Privilege.*) This chapter examines key aspects and concepts of law, regulations, and rules that apply to candidates for Congress.

An election does not always result in a clear determination of which candidate won and which other candidates lost. In many instances, courts in the state where there was a contested election are able to resolve the question in applying state law to issues of election administration. The House and Senate, however, have authority under the Constitution to make a determination of a winner in a contested election, and have developed mechanisms to do so.

The Constitution calls for a census to be conducted at the beginning of each decade for the purpose of apportioning seats in the House to the states. Congress by law limited the size of the House to 435 seats, and the Constitution guarantees each state one seat in the House, however small its population might be. All other seats are apportioned on the basis of a formula. Following apportionment after the most recent decennial census, the states with more than one seat redistrict so that the districts have approximately equal population, minorities have opportunities to win seats, and other redistricting goals are honored. New districts will be in effect in most if not all states for the 2012 elections.

Amendments to the Constitution and federal laws made pursuant to constitutional provisions ensure that all adult citizens may vote. Constitutional amendments have guaranteed voting rights to women, minorities, and citizens over eighteen years of age. Constitutional amendments and laws have prohibited state and local laws and behaviors that interfere with the right to vote.

§ 2.10 Campaigns and Elections

A member of Congress is an independent entrepreneur whose business is advancing her political career. An individual might have many motives for seeking a seat in Congress. These motives may include looking after the public good or tackling a tough policy problem in the public interest; a desire for public service; a wish to bring the perspective of the candidate's occupation to elective office; a positive or negative personal response to the issues of the day; a concern for the country being left to a candidate's descendants; and myriad other reasons. An individual must have political skills to act on those motivations, get elected to Congress, achieve her goals as a member of Congress, and communicate achievements to the public and the media.

The Democratic and Republican Parties (and sometimes other parties or entities) try to recruit candidates to run for open seats and seats occupied by incumbent members of Congress running for reelection. But the parties must rely on people motivated to run and politically skillful in doing so. The parties offer many forms of help, but a candidate for Congress is largely in charge of building his own volunteer and paid campaign organization, raising money, and developing a campaign strategy. This is true the first time a candidate runs for office and every time thereafter. The political tenor of the times can also bring many people new to politics into political activity and a run for public office. This phenomenon has occurred numerous times during the country's history, including the 2010 elections. To attract volunteers, media attention, and financial support, a candidate must project confidence that he can win. To remain attractive, a candidate must back up that confidence with evidence that he is running a campaign that can succeed. The goal is to get elected in the first place and to get reelected until the member resigns or retires voluntarily.

The advantages of incumbency—better fund-raising ability, more-automatic media attention, an existing corps of campaign volunteers, and so on—sometimes make it hard for the parties to attract candidates willing to take on incumbents, but high motivation, innate skill, and other factors can yield surprisingly strong contenders who are not party officials' choice. And, especially for some open House seats, the key fight is for the Democratic or Republican nomination: the party tilt of some districts typically makes one party's nominee a favorite in the general election. (*See § 2.11, 2012 and 2014 Congressional Election Information.*)

Still, in any election, many House seats and most Senate seats are considered competitive to some degree, whether in a convention, primary, or general election, and incumbent members of Congress running for reelection have learned not to take anything for granted. In the 2010 election, four representatives and two senators were defeated in primaries or conventions, and fifty-two representatives and two senators were defeated in the general election. (In addition, nineteen representatives and eight senators retired. Eleven representatives ran for another office but were defeated. Six representatives and one senator ran for another office and succeeded in the quest.) An incumbent member tries to act preemptively to reduce the chances of a tough reelection campaign. By raising as much money as possible as early as possible, responding quickly to any criticism, and not allowing a primary or general election opponent to characterize her record without response, an incumbent attempts to control public perceptions of her popularity and political strength. Further, by putting a "spin" on her own record and an opponent's, and not being reluctant to use "negative advertising" if it is expected to work, an incumbent attempts to influence public and media perceptions. An incumbent must also be conscious of what is being posted on web sites, or blogs, and social media as another avenue of attack, pressure, or support. The use of social media and other electronic tools by candidates, supporters, and opponents are additional tools in election campaigns. Members have campaign and official web sites, and most have begun their own blogs and social media sites to have a stronger, more active presence on the Internet. As an entrepreneur in the business of advancing a political career, a member is always vigilant to an opponent trying to "take market share."

These preemptive moves serve other purposes as well. They motivate campaign volunteers and likely supportive voters. They also send a message of confidence to home-district or home-state elected officials of the same party, both warding off potential primary challengers and motivating these other political professionals to affiliate with and support a successful member of the party team. They counteract advertising by interest groups intended to arouse constituents against a member or against his stand on a particular issue. A member needs to prevent openings for opponents within his party as well as from the other parties.

One of the biggest concerns for congressional candidates is fund-raising. Campaign finance data from the 2010 elections reveals why. In that election, 109 incumbent representatives raised more than $2 million each and twelve incumbent senators raised more than $10 million each. The Center for Responsive Politics (*<www.opensecrets.org>*), analyzing campaign-finance reporting to the Federal Election Commission (*<www.fec.gov>*), found that the average winning candidate for the House spent over $1.4 million, and the average winning candidate for the Senate spent nearly $9.8 million. So-called self-funders who have the wealth to fund their own campaigns can also have an enormous impact on an election campaign, although the self-funded candidate who spent the most in 2010—more than $50 million—lost a race in a Senate open seat. In total, candidates for the House and Senate in the 2010 election spent over $1.8 billion. Some members and candidates relish fund-raising, and raise large sums of money for their parties as well as for themselves. Many others resent the time it takes and the distraction it presents. The political parties and interest groups raise and spend hundreds of millions more in support of or opposition to specific candidates and specific election issues. Defenders of private money in campaigns argue that it is part of free speech and the marketplace of ideas, while critics argue the system of fund-raising contributes to conflicts of interest, favoritism to moneyed interests, and legislative stalemate. (*See § 2.70, Federal Campaign Finance Laws.*)

A member of Congress likely spends part of a week in Washington using telephones at Democratic or Republican party offices on Capitol Hill to call financial supporters. For any candidate, fund-raising via the Internet is also rapidly growing to compete with direct mail and other fund-raising methods a candidate might use. A member will likely also attend several of the hundreds of fund-raisers each month for her party, its leadership, various colleagues, or several like-minded political committees, as well as for himself or herself, or sponsor such events. Townhouses, apartments, and buildings on Capitol Hill, owned by consultants, law firms, and associations, are available for those events, as are other offices and restaurants dotting Capitol Hill and bordering neighborhoods. A member needs to make appearances in her own behalf, and to make personal appearances both in Washington and in the home districts or states of at least some party colleagues.

§ 2.11

2012 and 2014 Congressional Election Information

See <*TCNCE.com*>

Election Day 2012 is November 6, and Election Day 2014 is November 4. Federal law (2 U.S.C. 7) designates the first Tuesday after the first Monday in November, in even-numbered years, as election day for federal offices. Before election day, in each biennial cycle, the major political parties (and perhaps smaller parties) in each state will have held various kinds of conventions, and many states will have held major-party primaries and perhaps runoffs. Nearly all aspects of election administration are the responsibility of the individual states; Congress has not extensively exercised its constitutional authority to regulate federal election administration.

In addition to candidacies and candidate fund-raising that commences as soon as the previous general election is over, the earliest filing deadline is in December of the odd-numbered year in Illinois, unless states change their law.

Announcements of incumbent members' and challengers' plans can occur early, although, by the time all primary runoffs are completed, it may be just a month until the general election. As of August 2011, in anticipation of the 2012 general election, seventeen representatives and eight senators had announced their retirement at the end of the 112th Congress (2011–2013), although some were retiring because they were pursuing other offices. Members who had not announced their retirement are assumed to be running for reelection, but retirement announcements continue well into the general election year.

In the 2011–2012 election cycle, many members postponed announcements of their plans pending the completion of their state's redistricting. They had to decide not only whether to run for reelection but also, if running, what district to run in. Five representatives and one senator also resigned by August 2011, although one representative resigned so that he could accept appointment to the vacant Senate seat. A resignation so early in a Congress triggers a special election for a House seat, to be held soon after the early resignation and not usually postponed to a distant date for a previously planned election. In most states, the governor makes an appointment to a vacant Senate seat. (*For information on filling vacant House and Senate seats, see § 5.10, Members of Congress: Service, Qualifications, Characteristics, and Filling Vacant Seats.*)

The methods by which major-party and independent- or third-party candidates get their names on the general-election ballot are different in each state. Registration dates differ from state-to-state, and congressional primary dates in some states may be different in years in which the state holds a presidential primary (for example, 2012, 2016, 2020) than in the non-presidential election years.

Some states have "sore loser" laws to prevent an individual who lost his party's nomination from getting on the general election ballot. Some states allow an individual to pursue two offices at once, such as the presidency and a House or Senate seat. In addition, between each general election some number of states amend various elements of their election laws.

The web sites of the secretaries of state's election divisions or the independent state election boards provide a variety of information: important dates for registration and primaries, links to state and federal laws, early voting and absentee ballot information, past election statistics, and candidate lists, among other election-related information. Information that has become critical in recent elections are liberalization of early voting and absentee ballot laws. Election divisions or election boards are also sources of information on these state laws. Some comparisons of states' election laws can be found on the web sites of the National Association of State Election Directors, <*www.nased.org*>; the National Association of Secretaries of State, <*www.nass.org*>; and the National Conference of State Legislatures, <*www.ncsl.org*>, under the category of Legislatures and Elections.

For the reader's convenience, a telephone number for each state's election authority is provided below, in addition to each state's election authority's web site. Information is also provided for the District of Columbia and the five territories' election authorities. For current information and live links, see <*TCNCE.com*>.

Continued on page 27

§ 2.11 (continued)

- **Alabama** 800-274-8683
  www.sos.alabama.gov/elections/
- **Alaska** 866-952-8683
  www.elections.alaska.gov
- **American Samoa**
  684-633-4116
  www.americansamoa electionoffice.org
- **Arizona** 602-542-8683
  www.azsos.gov/election
- **Arkansas** 800-482-1127
  www.sos.arkansas.gov/ elections/
- **California** 916-657-2166
  www.sos.ca.gov/elections/
- **Colorado** 303-894-2200
  www.sos.state.co.us/ pubs/elections/
- **Connecticut** 860-504-6100
  www.ct.gov/sots/cwp/ view.asp?a=3&q=415810
- **Delaware** 302-739-4277
  http://elections.delaware.gov
- **District of Columbia**
  202-727- 6511
  www.dcboee.org
- **Florida** 850-245-6200
  http://election.dos.state.fl.us
- **Georgia** 404-656-2871
  www.sos.ga.gov/elections/
- **Guam** 671-477-9791
  http://gec.guam.gov
- **Hawaii** 800-442-8683
  www.hawaii.gov/elections
- **Idaho** 208-334-2852
  www.sos.idaho.gov/ elect/eleindex.htm
- **Illinois** 217-782-4141
  www.elections.il.gov
- **Indiana** 317-232-3939
  www.in.gov/sos/elections/
- **Iowa** 888-767-8683
  www.sos.state.ia.us/elections/
- **Kansas** 785-296-4561
  www.kssos.org/ elections/elections.html
- **Kentucky** 800-246-1379
  http://sos.ky.gov/elections
- **Louisiana** 800-883-2805
  www.geauxvote.com
- **Maine** 207-624-7736
  www.maine.gov/sos/cec/elec
- **Maryland** 800-222-8683
  www.elections.state.md.us
- **Massachusetts** 800-462-8683
  www.sec.state.ma.us/ele/
- **Michigan** 888-767-6424
  www.michigan.gov/sos/ 0,1607,7-127-1633- - -,00.html
- **Minnesota** 877-600-8683
  www.sos.state.mn.us/ index.asp?page=4
- **Mississippi** 800-829-6786
  www.sos.ms.gov/elections.aspx
- **Missouri** 800-669-8683
  www.sos.mo.gov/elections
- **Montana** 888-884-8683
  http://sos.mt.gov/elections/
- **Nebraska** 402-471-2555
  www.sos.ne.gov/elec/
- **Nevada** 775-684-5705
  http://nvsos.gov/elections/
- **New Hampshire** 603-271-3242
  www.sos.nh.gov/electionsnew.html
- **New Jersey** 877-658-6837
  www.njelections.org
- **New Mexico** 505-827-3600
  www.sos.state.nm.us/ sos-elections.html
- **New York** 800-367-8683
  www.elections.state.ny.us
- **North Carolina** 919-733-7173
  www.sboe.state.nc.us
- **North Dakota** 800-352-0867
  www.state.nd.us/sos/electvote
- **Northern Marianas Islands**
  670-664-8683
  www.votecnmi.gov.mp
- **Ohio** 877-767-6446
  www.sos.state.oh.us/ elections.aspx
- **Oklahoma** 405-521-2391
  www.ok.gov/elections/
- **Oregon** 866-673-8683
  www.sos.state.or.us/elections
- **Pennsylvania** 717-787-5280
  www.electionreturns. state.pa.us/
- **Puerto Rico** 787-777-8675
  www.ceepur.org
- **Rhode Island** 401-222-2345
  www.elections.ri.gov/
- **South Carolina** 803-734-9060
  www.scvotes.org/
- **South Dakota** 605-773-3537
  www.sdsos.gov
- **Tennessee** 877-850-4959
  www.tn.gov/sos/election/
- **Texas** 800-252-8683
  www.sos.state.tx.us/elections/
- **Utah** 801-538-1041
  www.elections.utah.gov
- **Vermont** 802-828-2464
  www.vermont-elections.org
- **Virginia** 800-552-9745
  www.sbe.virginia.gov
- **Virgin Islands** 877-773-1021
  www.vivote.gov
- **Washington** 800-448-4881
  www.sos.wa.gov/elections/
- **West Virginia** 304-558-6000
  www.sos.wv.gov/elections/
- **Wisconsin** 866-868-3947
  http://gab.wi.gov
- **Wyoming** 307-777-5860
  http://soswy.state.wy.us/ Elections/Elections.aspx

For current information and live links, see <*TCNCE.com*>.

§ 2.12

Members' Support for Candidates

Democratic Leader Nancy Pelosi
Democratic Whip Steny H. Hoyer
Assistant Democratic Leader James E. Clyburn
Democratic Caucus Chair John B. Larson
DCCC Chairman Steve Israel
Congressman Xavier Becerra
DCCC Chair of Recruitment Allyson Schwartz
& The DCCC Recruitment Committee

Invite you to

MEET OUR 2012 CANDIDATES

Wednesday, May 11, 2011
5:00 PM – 6:00 PM

International Brotherhood of Teamsters Headquarters
25 Louisiana Ave NW
Washington, DC

For more information, please contact Amy Strathdee at (202) 485-3420 or
to RSVP contact Ashley McNeil at McNeil@dccc.org

Contributions or gifts to the Democratic Congressional Campaign Committee are not tax deductible. Federal law requires us to use our best efforts to collect and to report the name, mailing address, occupation and name of employer of individuals whose contributions exceed $200 in an election cycle. Corporate contributions are impermissible by federal law.

Paid for and Authorized by the Democratic Congressional Campaign Committee

A member is expected to raise money and make appearances for the party's other candidates for Congress if the member has leadership ambitions within her chamber. These activities put a member into circumstances where she is appearing in opposition to incumbent members of the other party—its leaders, who are perhaps peers; its chairs or ranking minority members and other committee members, who may overlap in committee assignments; and fellow members of the same state delegation. The ubiquity of campaign demands on party members contributes to difficulty in Congress in policymaking between the parties. (*See § 2.12, Members' Support for Candidates.*)

One of the first chores of a freshman member is raising money to retire any campaign debt and get a start on the first reelection campaign, especially where there was a narrow or unexpected win. Members' chiefs of staff are also used as fund-raisers for their boss' party, with fund-raising events featuring their presence for contributors.

Congressional leaders, aspiring leaders, and many individual members also maintain political action committees (PACs), so-called leadership PACs, which they use to support their party's candidates for Congress. (*See § 2.70, Federal Campaign Finance Laws.*) This support can even extend to advertising not specifically related to a campaign, such as a testimonial for a member on a vote he has cast. Party leaders, such as each chamber's majority and minority leaders and the House Speaker, may have political responsibilities broader even than their leadership PAC, including not only fund-raising for their party and its members but also messaging and communications, political operations, coordination with the incumbent president (or the presidential candidate) of their party, and coordination of their PACS and campaign organization.

Members are expected to support their party's congressional campaign committees—the National Republican Congressional Campaign Committee, the Democratic Congressional Campaign Committee, the National Republican Senatorial Committee, and the Democratic Senatorial Campaign Committee. These committees are headed by members, and many other members participate not just as contributors but as chairs of special fund-raising, recruitment, and outreach efforts. The congressional campaign committees may levy assessments on their party's members, expecting higher payments from chamber and committee leaders, prospective chamber and committee leaders, and members with wealthy districts or proven fund-raising records than from rank-and-file members. Party committees run media and public relations campaigns to create a political environment conducive to their party winning seats in the House or Senate; develop messages, conduct polling and opposition research, and undertake other essential campaign-related work; fund-raise for both contributions to candidates and independent expenditures; and engage in the gamut of potential campaign activities. They set goals for potential candidates of their party before committing financial support, and make decisions on how to deploy their financial resources in support of their party's candidates: whom to support, how and for how long to support them, and when to end support or to make a late commitment to a campaign with surprise momentum. They also decide what role to play in special elections.

Members are also occasionally called on to assume the chairmanships of the Democratic or Republican National Committee.

As part of her fund-raising effort, a member of Congress must interact with Washington, DC-based lobbyists and PAC representatives, and with home-district or home-state interests. Those back-home interests are every bit as critical to successful fund-raising and reelection as donations from Washington-based organizations. In addition, the back-home interests more often represent voters. Because of the need for campaign cash, however, candidates also often turn to out-of-state areas of wealth, participating in fund-raisers in places such as Los Angeles, New York, and Silicon Valley. Retired members with substantial campaign cash on hand have also become an important source of campaign funds. In some races, the amount of money a candidate raises in his home state versus the amount raised outside the state can become an issue.

As described below (*§ 2.20, Constituency Pressure*), constituents seem to have ever greater expectations of a member of Congress. They expect his regular presence in the district or state, and they expect a member to play an ombudsman role in dealing with their local and personal matters at the federal level. A member must be vigilant in service to constituents and case work, and must set standards for congressional office staff in ensuring quick and responsive attention to mail, phone calls, visits, and other contacts. A member is expected to "bring home the bacon," helping local entities with their federal grantsmanship and assisting their home states and communities in other ways.

To deliver for constituents and enhance her political profile, a member of Congress seeks committee assignments that support career ambitions. An assignment to a key committee can also open larger fund-raising opportunities. A member might also seek to cast a wider net of interests and influence by obtaining appointments to task forces and party committees dealing with specialized subjects. A member might also join one or more congressional special-interest caucuses, or even organize a caucus, to demonstrate commitment to an interest or to the solution to a policy problem.

A member must be conscious of the public record she builds—what bills and amendments to sponsor or cosponsor, what to say in debate, and how to cast votes in committee and on the floor. In recent Congresses, members cast politically difficult votes on economic stimulus, extension of the Bush-era tax cuts, health care, financial services, climate change, and public debt reduction. On some votes, Democrats risked alienating liberal support by a vote one way and centrist and independent voters with a vote another way. Republicans, on the other hand, risked alienating their small-government supporters by a vote one way and many centrist and independent voters with a vote another way. All members, however they voted, opened themselves to a range of criticism in the media and in online outlets ranging from web sites and blogs to social media—for failing to push liberals' favored options, for failing to check government's role and spending, or for failing demonstrate moderation and compromise. Votes on so-called omnibus bills can be particularly troublesome, because an opponent might try to tie a member's vote to just one item out of the several hundred that appear in an omnibus measure. How will constituents receive each bill introduced or cosponsored or each vote cast? How will interests at home or in Washington react? How might an opponent attack an initiative or a vote? Is the record being built consistent with the past, and can that consistency be sustained in the future?

Come election day, running with sufficient funds in campaign coffers and with records anticipated to please constituents, the national mood nonetheless matters. The electorate was genuinely angry when it went to the polls in 1994 and ended forty years of Democratic control of the House. Members who seemed to be in tune with their constituents were tossed out of office along with those who had "bounced" checks at the "House bank" or had other political problems. In 2006, the congressional elections seemed to be as much a referendum on the war in Iraq and the perceived failures of the Bush administration as a decision on individual Republican and Democratic candidates. By 2010, the pendulum swung back, and fifty Democratic House incumbents and two Democratic Senate incumbents lost in the general election, losing control of the House to Republicans and cutting Democratic control of the Senate to four seats.

Presidents also know how to apply pressure and how to reward allies. President Bush, for example, showed his attractiveness as a fund-raiser throughout every election cycle. He also began his presidency by taking his campaign for congressional enactment of his tax-cut proposal to the home states of then-Senate Democratic leader Tom Daschle, wavering Democrats, and senators representing states where Bush had done well. He ended the 2001–2002 cycle making numerous appearances on behalf of Republican candidates for both chambers. By the 2006 election, the president continued to be a strong fund-raiser, but he was asked to make few appearances on behalf of his party's congressional candidates. President Obama similarly proved to be a strong fund-raiser and exceptional at motivating young and minority voters. But, during the 2010 election many incumbent Democrats distanced themselves from the national Democrats and from President Obama. His legislative program, passed with great fanfare by a unified Democratic majority, proved to be an albatross around the necks of members from districts and states that had elected split party tickets over the course of previous elections. President Obama remained a strong fund-raiser but operated with Republicans resurgent in Congress.

It is difficult for members to make commitments on a measure or a future vote early in the legislative process. Who knows what might end up in legislation on the floor? Who knows before the moment of a vote what the alternatives might be, if any? For this and other reasons, "absolutely," "never," "definitely," and similar words are not often part of the vocabulary of an experienced member of Congress regarding legislation and floor votes. Members of Congress expect their party leaders to protect their interests in the votes that arise. Can a divisive or difficult vote be prevented from occurring, diluted in its difficulty, or handled indirectly through a procedure that avoids a direct vote? May a member take a pass on a vote important to party but anathema to her district or state? Might a member choose party unity over home interests in some instances?

Like most people, a member of Congress wishes to be successful in his job—to be thought well of, to have influence, to win reelection, and so on. A member wants a successful legislative track record to run on. A member might also have ambitions beyond the current office. A representative might want to become a senator or governor at some future point, or a member might want to be president, a Cabinet secretary, an ambassador, or a Supreme Court justice. These career ambitions must also be weighed in a member's political conduct.

§ 2.20 Constituency Pressure

Congress was designed by the founding fathers as a representative body—two equal chambers whose job is to make laws in the national interest that reflect the interests of members' states and constituents. Members might feel pulled in different directions by the views of their parties or by their own perceptions of national interest, and these views might sometimes conflict with sentiment in their home districts or states. However they have conducted themselves and whatever legislative record they have built, representatives every two years and senators every six years answer to the specific group that decides their fate: their constituents.

Some issues resonate more in one district or state than in another. Some members know that they will be reelected by a comfortable margin while others know every election campaign will be a close race. A member with a secure seat may be able to take the lead on an issue, even at the risk of alienating some voters, or might be able to spend more time on national concerns. A member in a competitive district or state may need to put his representational role ahead of a legislative role. Attention to constituent concerns often accelerates as elections approach, a phenomenon especially

§ 2.21

Examples of Constituent Outreach

How Congressman Altmire Can Serve You.

Veterans' Affairs and Military Families

Veterans of the U.S. Armed Services are encouraged to contact the office with questions regarding filed claims, medical coverage policies, or eligibility for coverage. Members of the Armed Forces and National Guard and Reserve, and their families, can also call on me for assistance with a broad range of problems and challenges.

Medicare and Social Security

Questions regarding the Medicare prescription drug benefit and problems with the Social Security Administration such as lost or delayed checks, disability application status, Social Security application procedures, survivor benefits, or Supplemental Security Income (SSI) should be directed to my office.

Loans and Grants for Students and Organizations

Helping constituents obtain federal funding is an important part of serving in Congress. Students seeking a guide to the federal aid process and organizations seeking federal grants should visit my website, www.altmire.house.gov.

Academy Nominations

Each year, Members of Congress nominate qualified students for admission into our nation's renowned military service academies. Please contact my office for eligibility and application information.

U.S. Representative Allyson Y. Schwartz
Representing the 13th Congressional District of Pennsylvania

FOR IMMEDIATE RELEASE
March 21, 2011

CONTACT: Tali Israeli 202-225-6111

Thursday, March 31st at 10:30 a.m.

SCHWARTZ TO HOST CENSUS INFORMATION SESSION TO HELP BUSINESS AND COMMUNITY LEADERS TAP INTO DEMOGRAPHIC DATA

On Thursday, March 31st, the office of U.S. Rep. Allyson Schwartz will host a hands-on presentation with representatives from the U.S. Census Bureau to better inform Philadelphia-area businesses, non-profits, and civic associations on how to identify and access valuable economic, demographic and social data available from the census enumeration. The workshop is free and open to the general public, and is geared toward helping businesses and non-profits better understand how Census data can inform strategic planning decisions and how to best utilize online Census data.

The event, *The Census and You: Accessing 2010 Data*, is an overview of key highlights and features of the 2010 Census and American Community Survey. Presenters from the Census will work through detailed information on how to access publicly available Census data, including being able to export and download information.

Civic associations and individuals can view a statistical portrait of their community, as well as the numerical basis for distribution of federal funds for infrastructure and services.

For more information, or to RSVP, contact Schwartz's Philadelphia office at 215-335-3355.

WHO: Representatives from the Office of U.S. Rep. Allyson Schwartz
Representatives from the U.S. Census Bureau
Local businesses, non-profits and civic organizations

WHEN: Thursday, March 31, 2011
10:30 am to 12:00 pm

WHERE: CORA Services
8640 Verree Road
Philadelphia, PA 19111

####

8th District Constituent Services Contact Information:

Each location has staff specifically trained to help assist you.

Washington, DC
516 Cannon HOB
Washington, DC 20515
Phone: 202.225.6531, Fax: 202.225.3013
Hours: Mon-Fri 8:30AM-5:30PM

Tifton
127-B N. Central Ave.
Tifton, GA 31794
Hours: Mon-Fri 8:30AM-5:30PM

Dublin
Laurens County Courthouse
101 N. Jefferson St, 2nd Floor
Dublin, GA 31021
Please contact the Warner Robins office to make an appointment

Warner Robins
230 Margie Dr. Suite 500
Warner Robins, GA 31088
Phone: 478.971.1776, Fax: 478.971.1778
Hours: Mon-Fri 8:30AM-5:30PM

I'm honored to serve as your representative in Washington and want to make you aware of the many services available to you through our offices. —Austin

Assistance with Federal Agencies:
Do you have questions or concerns about Social Security, IRS, Passports, Veterans Issues, Medicare, HUD, USDA, or other federal agencies? If so, please contact one of our Constituent Services Representatives in our Dublin, Tifton, or Warner Robins offices, and they'll be pleased to assist you.

U.S. Capitol Tours and House Gallery Passes:
Interested in viewing the House or Senate in session? You may obtain gallery passes from our Washington office. If you'd like a tour of the Capitol, please contact the Washington office with your travel dates.

Our offices may also assist you with:
- Capitol Flag requests and Washington D.C. Tourist Attractions
- Military Service Academy Nominations
- Washington D.C. and District Congressional Internships

Find Congressman Scott on Twitter, Facebook and YouTube.
AustinScott.House.Gov

---

noticeable in the Senate, where it is six years between elections. The tendency to emphasize local concerns also often increases with the competitiveness of a race. Members must know their constituency to survive.

Members of the House represent districts that, after the 2010 census, includes an average of 710,767 people. District sizes ranged from Rhode Island's two districts with just over 527,000 people,

§2.22

Example of Member's Newsletter or Report

Members prepare periodic newsletters for their constituents, and they also prepare specialized reports on major state or district issues and policies. Below, Senator Dianne Feinstein (D-CA), explains the need to reauthorize the Lake Tahoe Restoration Act.

Dear Californian:

Lake Tahoe is a national treasure. Her alpine beauty has drawn and inspired people for centuries, from poets and artists like John Muir and Mark Twain to countless millions of people the world over.

But the "Jewel of the Sierra" is in trouble, threatened by invasive species – such as the quagga mussel, which could devastate the lake's biology and the regional economy – as well as pollution and drought. If we don't take robust action, we could lose Lake Tahoe and the Tahoe Basin to any number of serious threats. Fourteen years ago, former President Bill Clinton and Vice President Al Gore held a Presidential Forum at Lake Tahoe. The Forum signaled a renewed federal commitment to the restoration of the Lake Tahoe Basin, in partnership with the States of California and Nevada, as well as the Tahoe community.

In 2000, I cosponsored the Lake Tahoe Restoration Act, which began a 10-year, $900 million clean-up effort. The bill authorized $300 million in federal funds to be spent on efforts to restore Lake Tahoe. This partnership launched more than 269 environmental projects and restoration activities all around the lake.

But this funding expires this year, so that's why in January 2011 I introduced legislation to extend the Lake Tahoe Restoration Act by another 10 years. This legislation will authorize $415 million to combat invasive species, improve water clarity, reduce the threat of catastrophic wildfire, and restore the environment.

We must continue the job begun a decade ago. But we cannot do this alone. We need your help and support. Together we can preserve this precious natural resource.

Sincerely,

Dianne Feinstein

U.S. Senator

to Montana's single district with 989,415 people. Senators represented states ranging in population from 563,626 (Wyoming) to just under 37.3 million (California). Large and diverse constituencies make it difficult for members to gauge constituent opinion on every issue. Few districts or states are solely rural, suburban, or urban. Most areas now contain a cross-section of these kinds of interests. Most districts and states are heterogeneous—they include citizens, immigrants, schoolchildren, parents, and retirees, and people with diverse ethnic backgrounds, occupations, educational levels, and socioeconomic status.

No member of Congress seeking reelection can afford to take her constituency for granted. The levels of expectations for service, for reflecting a constituency's views, for being home often, and for

§ 2.23

Example of Privacy Act Release Form

In order to facilitate the exchange of information with federal agencies on case work and to protect the privacy of an individual's records held by the federal government, congressional offices use Privacy Act release forms.

PRIVACY RELEASE AND CONSTITUENT INFORMATION FORM

The Honorable James M. Inhofe:

I hereby authorize you and/or your staff to request information from the appropriate Federal Agency or Department in reference to my inquiry. This authorization includes written correspondence, telephonic or any other means of communication. The Federal Agency or Department is authorized to furnish copies of any documents, correspondence or information relative to my inquiry.

Name ____________________ Email ____________________

Address ____________________ City/St/Zip ____________________

Home phone __________ Cell __________ Work __________ Fax __________

Complete only the sections applicable to your case:

Social Security # ____________________ VA Claim # ____________________

Military ID/Branch ____________________ OPM # ____________________

OWCP Claim# ____________________ Alien # INS ____________________

Other ____________________ Receipt# INS ____________________

Briefly explain the problem below. Attach copies of any relevant documents.

____

____

____

____

____

____

____

____

____

____

____ use back of page, if necessary.

Have you contacted another office regarding this issue? If so, who and when? __________

Do you authorize release of information to another party or your attorney? If so, who?

Name ____________________ Phone ____________________

Signature ____________________ Date: ____________________

Please return to:

U. S. Senator James M. Inhofe
1924 S. Utica #530
Tulsa OK 74104
918-748-5111
Fax: 918-748-5119

U. S. Senator James M. Inhofe
1900 NW Expy #1210
Oklahoma City OK 73118
405-608-4381
Fax: 405-608-4120

being responsive are very high. (*See § 2.21, Examples of Constituent Outreach.*) Members try their best to meet those expectations. Failure to do so may provide an opening for a challenge within a member's own party in a primary, from the other major party, or even from a third party in a general election. (*See § 2.22, Example of Member's Newsletter or Report.*)

§ 2.24

Constituent Service Reflected in Member's Newsletter

The excerpt from Rep. Chris Van Hollen's newsletter shows two good examples of case work, one on behalf of individuals and one to assist a local organization. In the former instance, Van Hollen cites his intervention with the president.

Getting Things Done for the 8th District

Securing Local Investments

Working with state and local officials, we have brought important funding to our community for transportation projects, education programs and public safety efforts. In July I had the privilege of presenting a $1.3 million Head Start grant to the Lourie Center for Infants and Children in Rockville.

Chris speaks with a family about Head Start at the Lourie Center in Rockville.

Helping the Disabled

This fall I visited the Bethesda Naval Hospital, which has developed an innovative and successful program hiring disabled individuals from our local community to work in its kitchen and cafeteria. Many of these individuals have worked there for more than twenty years. They are hard-working, reliable and beloved by the naval officers and staff. The Administration had selected these positions to be bid out to private contractors, leaving these disabled employees on the verge of losing their jobs. I wrote to the President about this injustice and am pleased that as a result of our timely intervention, these disabled individuals have been able to keep their jobs and the sense of dignity that comes with them.

Case Work and Grants

Case work refers to helping individuals or small groups of constituents, including local governments, in their dealings with federal government agencies. How well a member conducts case work can be key to reelection. A congressional office may perform advocacy or referral functions for as many as several thousand cases a year, ranging from tracking down missing Social Security checks to expediting a passport application to clearing up immigration cases to facilitating consideration of a community's grant application for some public project. (*See § 2.23, Example of Privacy Act Release Form.*) Constituents have been known to forgive a member for a controversial vote. However, they can be less forgiving when case work is ignored or mishandled. (*See § 2.24, Constituent Service Reflected in Member's Newsletter; and § 2.25, Case Work Outreach.*)

Members also have duties and favors to perform for constituents. A very important duty is to nominate appointees to the U.S. service academies. In states and districts where there are many applicants for these appointments, members use interview boards and other mechanisms to make choices.

Favors for constituents include arranging tours for visitors to Washington, flying flags over the Capitol to commemorate special occasions, obtaining congratulatory messages from the White House, and making congratulatory speeches on the House or Senate floor. (*See § 2.26, Assistance to Constituents.*)

Pork-barrel politics is often used to describe what members do to try to obtain federal funds for public-works projects, federal installations, grants, and other benefits for their districts or states.

§ 2.25

Case Work Outreach

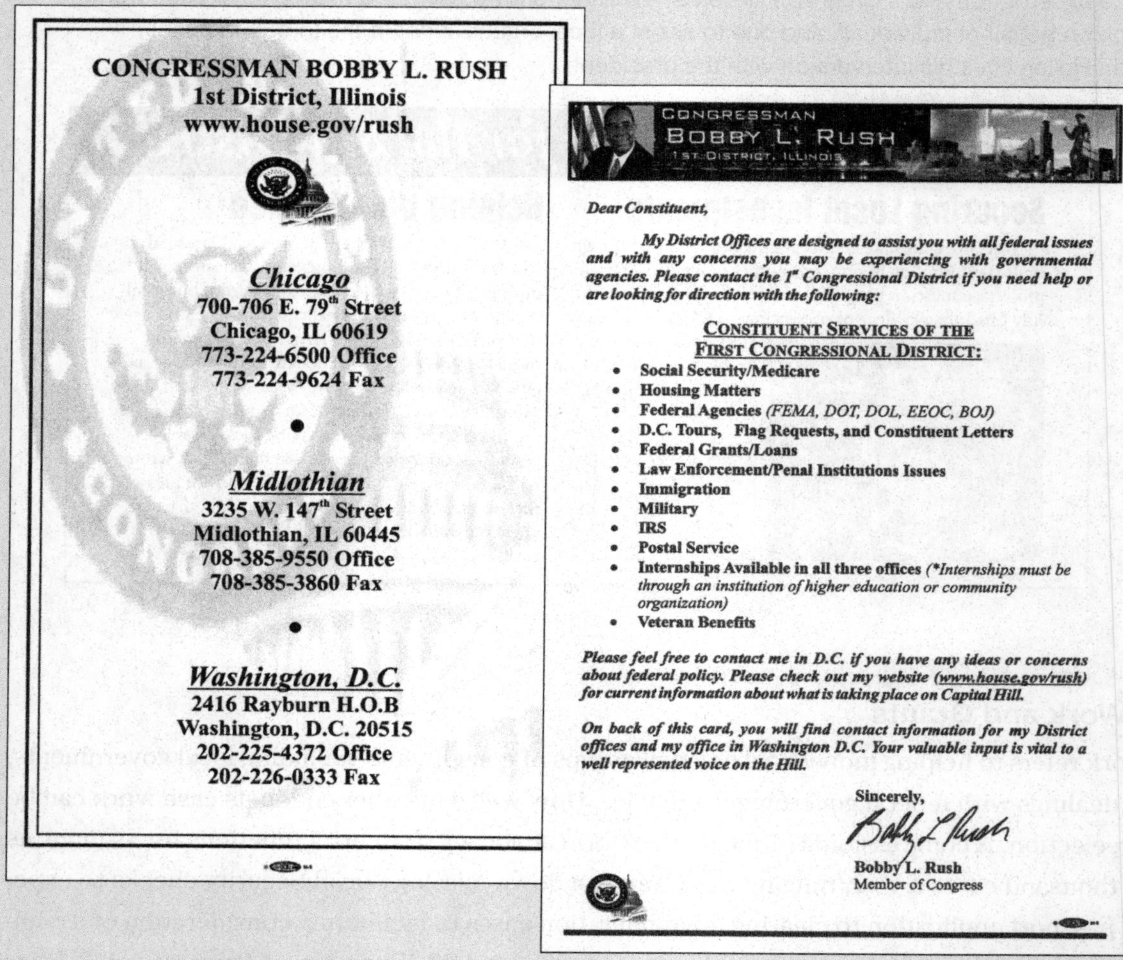

CONGRESSMAN BOBBY L. RUSH
1st District, Illinois
www.house.gov/rush

Chicago
700-706 E. 79th Street
Chicago, IL 60619
773-224-6500 Office
773-224-9624 Fax

•

Midlothian
3235 W. 147th Street
Midlothian, IL 60445
708-385-9550 Office
708-385-3860 Fax

•

Washington, D.C.
2416 Rayburn H.O.B
Washington, D.C. 20515
202-225-4372 Office
202-226-0333 Fax

CONGRESSMAN
BOBBY L. RUSH
1ST DISTRICT, ILLINOIS

Dear Constituent,

My District Offices are designed to assist you with all federal issues and with any concerns you may be experiencing with governmental agencies. Please contact the 1st Congressional District if you need help or are looking for direction with the following:

CONSTITUENT SERVICES OF THE FIRST CONGRESSIONAL DISTRICT:

- **Social Security/Medicare**
- **Housing Matters**
- **Federal Agencies** *(FEMA, DOT, DOL, EEOC, BOJ)*
- **D.C. Tours, Flag Requests, and Constituent Letters**
- **Federal Grants/Loans**
- **Law Enforcement/Penal Institutions Issues**
- **Immigration**
- **Military**
- **IRS**
- **Postal Service**
- **Internships Available in all three offices** *(*Internships must be through an institution of higher education or community organization)*
- **Veteran Benefits**

Please feel free to contact me in D.C. if you have any ideas or concerns about federal policy. Please check out my website (www.house.gov/rush) for current information about what is taking place on Capitol Hill.

On back of this card, you will find contact information for my District offices and my office in Washington D.C. Your valuable input is vital to a well represented voice on the Hill.

Sincerely,

Bobby L. Rush
Member of Congress

The federal government also buys goods and services from private suppliers, and government contracts are let to companies around the country. Federal research and development programs disburse billions of dollars to universities, federal laboratories, and private companies. Members try to obtain allocations of these kinds of funds for their districts or states in both the legislative process and the grant-making process, but the public reaction to widespread use of earmarks to obtain such funds resulted in a broad curtailment of many forms of pork-barrel spending. (*See § 7.80, Authorizations and Appropriations Processes.*)

Members of Congress attempt to assist their constituents with information and links on their web sites to federal, private, and other grant resources. For example, many link to the Catalog of Federal Domestic Assistance, <*www.cfda.gov*>, and to other sources to identify and apply for federal grants.

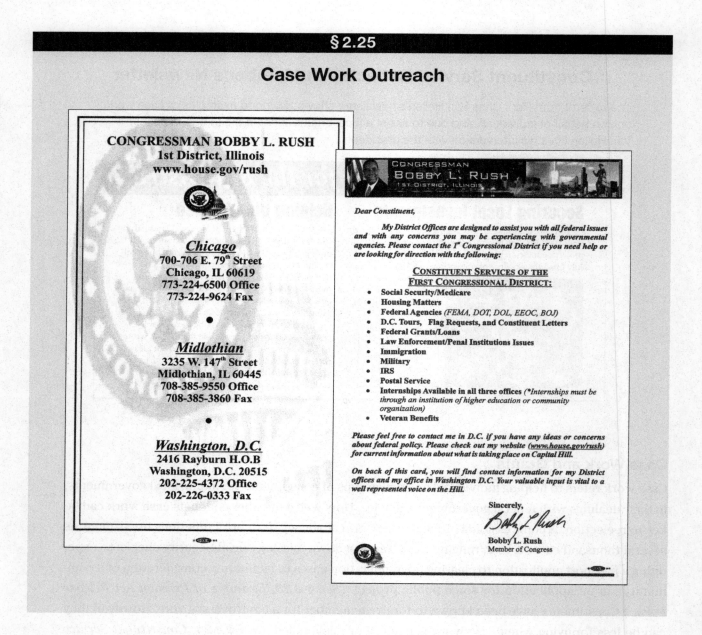

§ 2.26

Assistance to Constituents

TABLE OF CONTENTS

2

HOW TO CONTACT OUR LOCAL COMMUNITY COLLEGES

Caldwell Community College and Technical Institute
2294 Community College Drive
Boone, NC 28607
828-297-3811
www.cccti.com

Catawba Valley Community College
2550 Highway 70 SE
Hickory, NC 28602
828-327-7000
www.cvcc.edu

Davidson Community College Davie County Campus
1205 Salisbury Road
Mocksville, NC 27028
336-751-2885
www.davidson.cc.nc.us.

Forsyth Technical C.C.
2100 Silas Creek Parkway
Winston-Salem, NC 27103-5197
336-723-0371 ext. 7253
www.forsyth.tec.nc.us.

Mitchell Community College
500 West Broad Street
Statesville, NC 28677
704-878-3200
www.mitchell.cc.nc.us.

Rockingham C.C.
P.O. Box 38
Wentworth, NC 27375-0038
336-342-4261 ext. 333
www.rcc.cc.nc.us.

Surry Community College
Box 304
Dobson, NC 27017
336-386-8121 ext. 204
www.surry.cc.nc.us.

Wilkes Community College
1328 Collegiate Drive
Wilkesboro, NC 28697
336-838-6100
www.wilkes.cc.nc.us.

Be sure all mail is addressed to the attention of the Admissions Office.

The North Carolina Community College System (NCCCS) is composed of 59 community colleges statewide. Information about community colleges, student services, financial aid and different fields of study can be found on the NCCCS website at:

http://www.ncccs.cc.nc.us.

5

Joe Manchin
United States Senator for West Virginia

Information for the Greatest Generation

It is my great pleasure to serve West Virginia. This brochure will provide information about the services available to seniors. However, if you need assistance, or have an issue or concern, do not hesitate to write, fax, e-mail, call, or stop by my office.

SOCIAL SECURITY BENEFITS

Depending on age and work history, you may be eligible for Social Security retirement benefits as early as age 62. You may also be eligible for benefits based on your spouse's work history, even if you are divorced. If you choose to draw benefits at age 62 be aware that your monthly payments will be less than if you wait until full retirement age. Most seniors are not eligible for Medicare until age 65 even if they draw their retirement at age 62.

To make an appointment at your local Social Security office, call 1-800-772-1213, or visit www.ssa.gov. If you are hard of hearing, call toll-free: 1-800-325-0778 weekdays between 7 a.m. and 7 p.m.

CONTACT ME

Charleston • 300 Virginia Street East • Suite 2630 • Charleston, WV • 25301 • 304-342-5855

Martinsburg • 217 West King Street • Room 238 • Martinsburg, WV • 25401 • 304-264-4626

Washington, DC • 311 Hart Senate Office Building • Washington, DC • 20510 • 202-224-3954

WWW.MANCHIN.SENATE.GOV
Follow me on Twitter @ **SEN_JOEMANCHIN**

§ 2.27

Tips for Contacting Members of Congress

Common sense probably tells us that hateful, insulting, or threatening communications do not work. In the current sensitive environment, such communications are also likely to be referred to federal investigators.Vague, unfocused, or nebulous requests for action or assistance are also ineffective.

Types of Communication

1. Letters, Faxes, and Email
   - Be brief and to the point
   - Write at the proper time in the legislative process
   - Use your own language
   - Stick to one issue for each communication
   - Personalize the issue
   - Write to your own representative or senator
   - Clearly identify the legislation, using bill numbers if possible
   - Know your facts
   - Be polite and positive
   - Speak for yourself
   - Ask for a reply and include your phone number and postal address, even on email
   - Write on personal stationery, if a letter

2. Telephone Calls
   - Be brief, to the point, and considerate of the member's time constraints
   - Identify yourself as a concerned constituent
   - Indicate the issue
   - Be specific about the action you want
   - Be courteous and polite
   - Compose your thoughts before the call
   - Follow up with a thank-you note

3. Personal Visits
   - Be brief, to the point, and considerate of the member's time constraints
   - Thank the staffer or member by name
   - Put a human face on your issue
   - Begin the meeting by thanking the office for any prior help
   - Respect member's or staffer's opinion
   - "Connect the dots" for the member or staff: explain why the member's help is needed and what specifically the member can do to help

Mail from Home

Constituent pressure manifests itself in the form of millions of letters, postcards, faxes, emails, phone calls, and personal visits to members each year, asking assistance or urging support or opposition on issues before Congress. Although many contacts are the result of advocacy-group activity, many are in the form of individual letters, calls, and other communications sent by individual constituents on particular matters important to them.

Most offices have policies on responding to constituent mail. Mail from the district or state is always answered, usually on a one-week or two-week turnaround. (However, following the delivery of anthrax spores to Capitol Hill via the U.S. mail in fall 2001, letters to members and committees of Congress are delayed by irradiation and inspection procedures.) Mail from outside the district or state may be answered if a member aspires to statewide or national office or has become associated with an issue. Or, mail from outside a member's district or state might be referred to a member representing that other district or state. (*See § 4.50, Franking Privilege.*)

Mail from constituents, lobbyists, and other members serves as a barometer of opinion on a par-

§ 2.28

Addressing Correspondence to Members of Congress

Written communications with members and committees of Congress can be very effective. They are not as easily forgotten as a conversation, they exist as a record for both the sender and the recipient, and they allow a perspective or argument or request to be laid out in a full and thoughtful manner.

Both email and printed correspondence have advantages and disadvantages. Email is rapidly delivered and, to be effective, is short and to the point. Correspondence management systems in congressional offices can handle email efficiently. One disadvantage is that email is treated on Capitol Hill as a commodity—so many for a proposition and so many against. Another disadvantage is that a single email is easily overlooked in the volume of correspondence received by congressional offices.

Printed correspondence lends seriousness to a communication, is not easily overlooked, and is not typically treated as a commodity. It suffers a severe disadvantage, however, in that letters to congressional offices go to an off-site inspection facility before being delivered, resulting in a significant delivery delay.

The information in this exhibit applies principally to printed correspondence, although the salutations are applicable to both email and printed correspondence.

Addressing Letters to an Individual Member

Honorable [name of representative]
[room number, building]
e.g., 1111 Longworth House Office Building
U.S. House of Representatives
Washington, DC 20515

Dear Representative [last name]:

Honorable [name of senator]
[room number, building]
e.g., 123 Russell Senate Office Building
U.S. Senate
Washington, DC 20510

Dear Senator [last name]:

Addressing Letters to a Committee Chair

Committee on [name]
[room number, building]
e.g., 2222 Rayburn House Office Building
U.S. House of Representatives
Washington, DC 20515

Dear Chairman [last name]:

Committee on [name]
[room number, building]
e.g., 123 Dirksen Senate Office Building
U.S. Senate
Washington, DC 20510

Dear Chairman [last name]:

ticular issue. Most offices pay particular attention when incoming mail is heavy on an issue, especially when that mail comes from the home district or state. (*See § 2.27, Tips for Contacting Members of Congress; and § 2.28, Addressing Correspondence to Members of Congress.*)

Members' Travel to the District and State

Representatives' districts are statewide in only seven states. Most representatives, therefore, are better known to their constituents than the senators representing a state. Representatives are often more involved in local affairs, or in local affairs with a federal dimension. They also run for reelection every two years, and are almost always campaigning. Representatives usually do not receive

§ 2.29

Constituent Outreach Meetings

Senator Lamar Alexander & Senator Bob Corker

cordially invite you to attend their constituent breakfast

Tennessee Tuesday

Coffee and doughnuts with your Tennessee Senators
Tuesdays at 9:00 a.m.
When the Senate is in session

Please call ahead to confirm room location
(202) 224-3344 or (202) 224-4944 (Alexander)

Congressman James Lankford Invites You to a Community Forum

We are looking forward to seeing you at one of our upcoming community forums.

Monday, August 15
6:00-7:30 PM
EOC Tech
4601 N Choctaw Road, Choctaw, OK 73020

Tuesday, August 16
6:00-7:30 PM
Francis Tuttle Technology Center – Portland Campus
3500 NW 150th Street, Oklahoma City, OK 73134

Thursday, August 18
6:00-7:30 PM
CPN Cultural Heritage Center
North Reunion Hall
1702 S Gordon Cooper Drive, Shawnee, OK 74801

Contact: Mona Taylor 405.234.9900

Contact Senator Feinstein

Washington, DC Office
331 Hart Senate Office Building
Washington, DC 20510
(202) 224-3841
http://feinstein.senate.gov

San Francisco Office
One Post Street
Suite 2450
San Francisco, CA 94104
(415) 393-0707

Los Angeles Office
11111 Santa Monica Blvd.
Suite 915
Los Angeles, CA 90025
(310) 914-7300

Fresno Office
2500 Tulare Street
Suite 4290
Fresno, CA 93721
(559) 485-7430

San Diego Office
750 B Street
Suite 1030
San Diego, CA 92101
(619) 231-9712

the same level of media coverage as their counterparts in the Senate. Moreover, because they usually share a media market with other representatives, they must work harder to make themselves known and stay in the public eye. Add these and other factors together and one understands why members of the House return home much more frequently than senators.

On average, representatives make about forty trips to their home districts each year. Some may fly across the continent nearly every weekend, and House schedules try to accommodate the flight schedules to the West Coast. For example, votes are not generally held before 6:30 p.m. on Mondays

§ 2.30

Advertising Constituents' Access to a Member

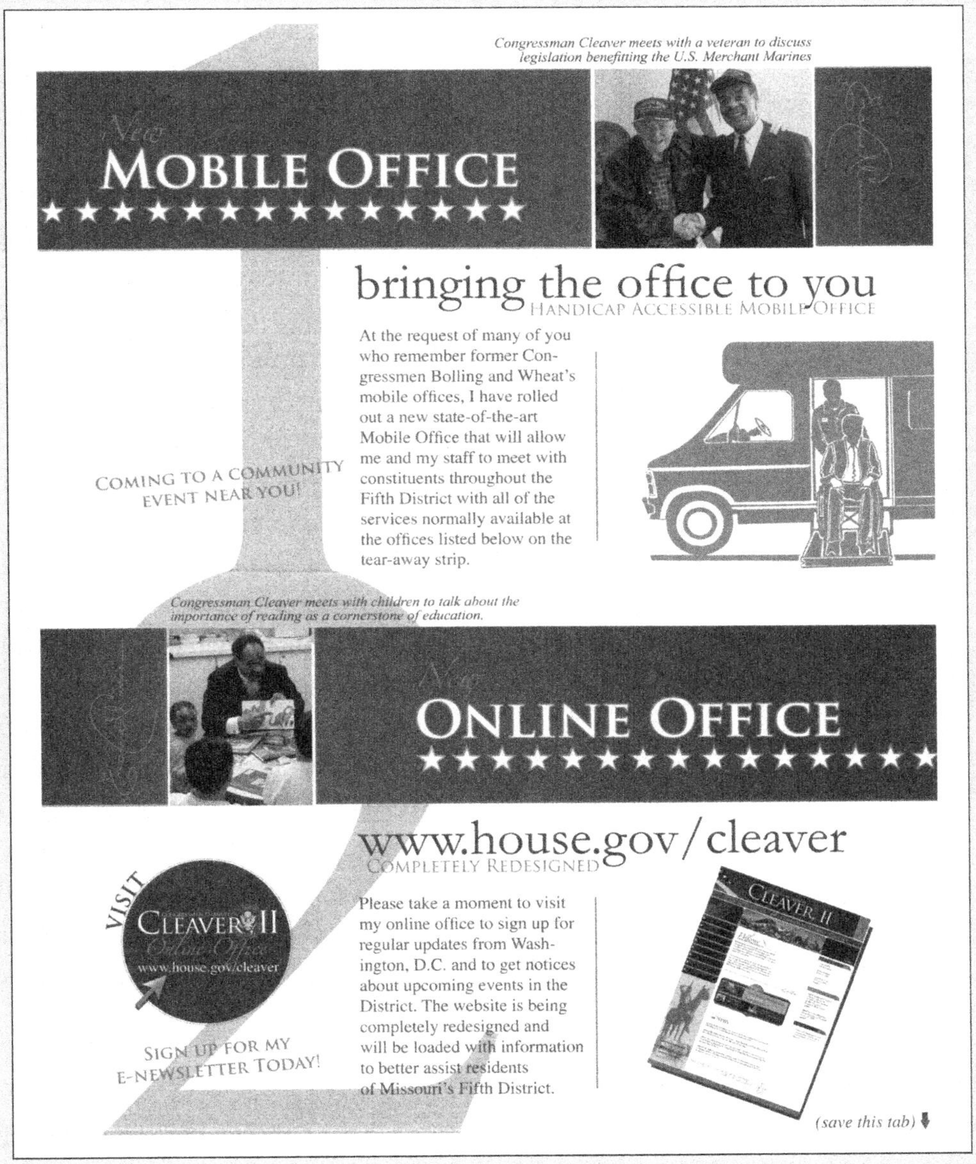

or Tuesdays, because one flight popular with members from California arrives at Washington, DC's Dulles International Airport at 5:00 p.m.

Senators generally do not return home as often as representatives, although that usually depends on the distance of a state from Washington, DC, the convenience of airline flight schedules, the Senate's schedule, and the balance of time until the next election. There are always exceptions, however—Delaware's senators return home by train nearly every night.

As an acknowledgment of the importance of going home, the House schedules district work peri-

§ 2.31

Example of Community Holiday Event

Congressman Xavier Becerra
and his family

invite you to attend
The 31st Congressional District's 17th Annual

HOLIDAY PARTY

Saturday, December 12, 2009
4:00–6:00 PM

featuring
Live Music • Festive Food
Door Prizes • Crafts for Kids

Center for the Arts, Eagle Rock
2225 Colorado Boulevard, Eagle Rock, California 90041

Bring the kids!
Please bring a new unwrapped toy to brighten the holidays for a local child in need.

Call (213) 484-8961 to RSVP

Parking on nearby streets and in Bank of America's parking lot (2263 Colorado Boulevard)

ods, and the Senate schedules nonlegislative periods, to allow "long weekends" or full weeks to be spent in home districts and states.

Members in Their Home Offices. At home, members usually maintain several district or state offices. The staff in those offices have responsibility for much of an office's case work and day-to-day contact with constituents. Although all offices do outreach to constituents, some offices hire a designated staffer to do outreach for the member. When in the district or state, a member usually works at one or more of his offices at least part of the time. (*See § 2.29, Constituent Outreach Meetings.*)

A member may also convene town meetings to obtain the views of voters and generate goodwill publicity. It is important to demonstrate interest in and awareness of local sentiment. Some members have instituted regular practices to achieve this goal. For instance, for supermarket Saturdays, a member goes to a different supermarket in her district each Saturday at an announced time. Between a lot of visiting and a little grocery shopping, a member of Congress is seen by constituents to be engaged in a normal activity, down-to-earth, and in touch—not having "gone Washington." (*See § 2.30, Advertising Constituents' Access to a Member; and § 2.31, Example of Community Holiday Event.*)

Constituents Come to Washington

From Memorial Day to Labor Day, Washington, DC, is one of the most-visited cities in the world. Families come to see the sights, and often wish to see their representatives and senators in Congress. They might come to discuss legislative issues of national importance, to discuss parochial concerns about their communities, or just to get visitors' gallery passes to the House and Senate chambers and information about Washington's museums. Washington, DC, is also the destination of choice of school groups across the country, particularly in the spring of each year. In addition to class trips, many students participate in programs run by the Close-Up Foundation, American Youth Scholarship Foundation, and other organizations promoting civic education or public service. Members regularly make presentations to student groups, and hire students as interns. (*See § 2.32, Internship Opportunities in a Congressional Office.*)

§ 2.32

Internship Opportunities in a Congressional Office

Congressional Internship Program for Individuals with Intellectual Disabilities

HOUSE INTERNSHIP PROGRAM REP. GREGG HARPER

2011 Spring Internship Program

FEBRUARY 14 – MAY 6, 2011

ABOUT THE PROGRAM

Established by Rep. Gregg Harper, R-Miss., the Congressional Internship Program for Individuals with Intellectual Disabilities is a unique program designed to give students with varying intellectual disabilities an opportunity to gain congressional work experience.

Last year, working in conjunction with George Mason University's Mason LIFE Program – a postsecondary education program for young adults with intellectual disabilities – and the Committee on House Administration, Harper launched the internship program with four Mason LIFE students and six House offices. After only one semester, the program tripled in size with nearly twenty Congressional offices participating.

Today, Harper continues to expand the program to accommodate additional students so that they are afforded the same exciting educational and enrichment opportunities typically afforded to congressional interns working here in the nation's capital.

HOW THE PROGRAM WORKS

The 2011 Spring Program will be a 12-week internship that runs from Monday, February 14, 2011, through Friday, May 6, 2011. **Each participating office will host a Mason LIFE student and his or her work coach for one two-hour session each week.** During the two-hour sessions, which are held Monday and Friday mornings and afternoons, the interns will work with their congressional office and their work coach to complete various office tasks as assigned.

In addition to fulfilling their weekly office responsibilities, the interns will have an opportunity to enjoy various enrichment activities coordinated by the program administrators. Some of the prior enrichment activities have included Capitol tours and trips to one of the many Smithsonian museums nearby.

HOW TO GET INVOLVED

If your office is interested in participating in the 2011 Spring Program, please contact Salley Wood with the Committee on House Administration at 5-7043, or via email at Salley.Wood@mail.house.gov.

Whatever the reason and whatever the time of day or time of year, members and their staff are expected to meet with visiting constituents and respond to their concerns and needs. Ideally, of course, a constituent should leave the office feeling that he was treated specially. Part of that special treatment comes from home-state offerings of snacks and beverages stocked by members' offices, from peanuts to candy to juice to soft drinks.

Congressional offices provide passes to the chambers' visitors' galleries and brochures on museums and other tourist attractions. When possible, special tours to Washington sights (such as the Capitol or the White House) are arranged. Generally, constituents are met by staff. Walking through the Capitol complex, one regularly sees a staffer showing around a family or group of students. A staffer might also take visitors to a committee meeting to see a member, or may accompany them to the chamber's gallery. This enables visitors not only to see the member but also to see the legislative process in action. For visitors, meeting with a staffer is always nice, but they generally want to meet the member. Whenever possible, a visit with the member is arranged. (*See also § 2.29, Constituent Outreach Meetings.*)

§ 2.40 Reapportionment and Redistricting

Every ten years, an additional election pressure is added for incumbent candidates for House seats. As required by the Constitution, a census is taken, and seats in the House are then reapportioned by law among the states, based on each state's population relative to all other states. After the House seats are reapportioned, state legislatures, commissions created by state law, or state or federal courts take over and redraw congressional district boundaries. Subject to federal and state laws and court decisions, including Supreme Court decisions, the body doing the redistricting tries to obtain an equal population in each district in a state. Redistricting goals might include favoring a political party in some of the districts, or trying to accomplish other purposes, such as the creation of districts with a majority of minority population or with geographical compactness. Court cases are used to challenge districting decisions, and several states have redistricted or considered redistricting during a decade.

Reapportionment following the 2010 census was completed without challenges. For the 113th though 116th Congresses, six states gained one seat each in the House of Representatives—Arizona, Georgia, Nevada, South Carolina, Utah, and Washington. One state gained two seats—Florida, and one state gained four seats—Texas. Eight states lost one seat—Iowa, Louisiana, Massachusetts, Michigan, Missouri, New Jersey, and Pennsylvania. Two states—New York and Ohio—each lost two seats. The seats apportioned to all of the other states remained the same.

Under the Constitution, seats in the House of Representatives are apportioned among the states. They are reapportioned every ten years following the decennial census. Every state is entitled to one seat under the Constitution, and seven states, because of their relatively small population in the 2010 census, have just one seat. These states are Alaska, Delaware, Montana, North Dakota, South Dakota, Vermont, and Wyoming. (These same seven states also were apportioned one seat each following the 2000 census.) California, the largest state, was apportioned fifty-three seats, the same number apportioned after the 2000 census.

State representation in the U.S. Senate is not affected by reapportionment. Under the Constitution, each state has two senators, no matter how large or small a population it has. Nonvoting representation of American Samoa, the District of Columbia, Guam, the Northern Marianas Islands, Puerto Rico, and the Virgin Islands in the House is also not affected by reapportionment. Puerto Rico has one resident commissioner, and the other five jurisdictions have one delegate each. (*See § 5.21, Delegates in the House of Representatives.*)

The usual explanation for a shift of seats is the more rapid growth of some states in relation to other states. A state might lose population from one decennial census to the next, but only Michigan did in the 2010 census. The table in § 2.41 shows the apportionment population of each state in the 2000 and 2010 censuses, the numeric and percent change from 2000, and the total seats and change in seats following reapportionment. The map that follows the table illustrates the relative growth of the fifty states.

Apportionment is based on the total resident population of each of the fifty states, but also includes federal employees (principally military personnel) stationed abroad. The combined total is called the apportionment population. Excluded from the calculation are foreign officials such as other nations' ambassadors, nonresident citizens of other nations, and residents of the District of Columbia, commonwealths, and territories.

Congress in 1911 first set the number of seats in the House at 435; this size was made permanent in 1929. When seats in the House are reapportioned following a census, each state is first allocated one seat (to meet constitutional requirements), and the remaining 385 seats (with fifty states) are apportioned according to each state's population in the latest census. Several formulas have been used over the past 200 years, but, since the 1940 census, the method of equal proportions has been used. *(See an explanation of the method of equal proportions and other useful information on reapportionment at <www.census.gov/population/apportionment/index.html>.)*

The 2010 census date, following the practice for most twentieth-century censuses, was April 1. Federal law required the Census Bureau within nine months (no later than December 31, 2010) to deliver to the president the population totals and allocation of U.S. House seats for each state. The Census Bureau released this information to the public December 21, 2010. Within a week of the convening of the 112th Congress, the president was required to transmit this information to the clerk of the House, who then, within fifteen days, was required to notify each state governor of the number of representatives to which the state was entitled.

Redistricting

Using census data within the guidelines established by federal and state laws and federal and state court decisions, the states followed their own procedures to draw new congressional districts for the 2012 elections. That is the second step, following reapportionment, in determining representation in the U.S. House of Representatives. ("Redistricting" also refers to procedures employed at the state and local level to obtain population equality in state legislative districts and local representational units. Those procedures are not covered here.)

Federal law requires single-member districts. The federal Voting Rights Act, among its provisions, requires some states to obtain "preclearance" of redistricting plans from the U.S. Justice Department. (States covered in whole or in part by the preclearance provisions of the Voting Rights Act are Alabama, Alaska, Arizona, California, Florida, Georgia, Louisiana, Michigan, Mississippi, New Hampshire, New York, North Carolina, South Carolina, South Dakota, Texas, and Virginia.) Congress has not chosen to exercise its constitutional authority (*art. I, sec. 4, cl. 1*) to prescribe other criteria for state legislatures to use in redistricting. (See *§ 2.90, Laws Protecting and Extending the Franchise.*)

Federal court decisions applicable to state redistricting include "one person, one vote," the

§ 2.41

Change in States' Population and Seats in the House of Representatives

State	2000 Census Apportionment population	2010 Census Apportionment population	Change from 2000 Total	Change from 2000 Percent	Seats	Seat change from 2000
Alabama	4,779,736	4,447,100	332,636	7.5	7	
Alaska	710,231	626,932	83,299	13.3	1	
Arizona	6,392,017	5,130,632	1,261,385	24.6	9	+1
Arkansas	2,915,918	2,673,400	242,518	9.1	4	
California	37,253,956	33,871,648	3,382,308	10.0	53	
Colorado	5,029,196	4,301,261	727,935	16.9	7	
Connecticut	3,574,097	3,405,565	168,532	4.9	5	
Delaware	897,934	783,600	114,334	14.6	1	
Florida	18,801,310	15,982,378	2,818,932	17.6	27	+2
Georgia	9,687,653	8,186,453	1,501,200	18.3	14	+1
Hawaii	1,360,301	1,211,537	148,764	12.3	2	
Idaho	1,567,582	1,293,953	273,629	21.1	2	
Illinois	12,830,632	12,419,293	411,339	3.3	18	-1
Indiana	6,483,802	6,080,485	403,317	6.6	9	
Iowa	3,046,355	2,926,324	120,031	4.1	4	-1
Kansas	2,853,118	2,688,418	164,700	6.1	4	
Kentucky	4,339,367	4,041,769	297,598	7.4	6	
Louisiana	4,533,372	4,468,976	64,396	1.4	6	-1
Maine	1,328,361	1,274,923	53,438	4.2	2	
Maryland	5,773,552	5,296,486	477,066	9.0	8	
Massachusetts	6,547,629	6,349,097	198,532	3.1	9	-1
Michigan	9,883,640	9,938,444	-54,804	-0.6	14	-1
Minnesota	5,303,925	4,919,479	384,446	7.8	8	
Mississippi	2,967,297	2,844,658	122,639	4.3	4	
Missouri	5,988,927	5,595,211	393,716	7.0	8	-1
Montana	989,415	902,195	87,220	9.7	1	
Nebraska	1,826,341	1,711,263	115,078	6.7	3	
Nevada	2,700,551	1,998,257	702,294	35.1	4	+1
New Hampshire	1,316,470	1,235,786	80,684	6.5	2	

Continued on page 47

§ 2.41 (continued)

State	2000 Census Apportionment population	2010 Census Apportionment population	Change from 2000 Total	Change from 2000 Percent	Seats	Seat change from 2000
New Jersey	8,791,894	8,414,350	377,544	4.5	12	-1
New Mexico	2,059,179	1,819,046	240,133	13.2	3	
New York	19,378,102	18,976,457	401,645	2.1	27	-2
North Carolina	9,535,483	8,049,313	1,486,170	18.5	13	
North Dakota	672,591	642,200	30,391	4.7	1	
Ohio	11,536,504	11,353,140	183,364	1.6	16	-2
Oklahoma	3,751,351	3,450,654	300,697	8.7	5	
Oregon	3,831,074	3,421,399	409,675	12.0	5	
Pennsylvania	12,702,379	12,281,054	421,325	3.4	18	-1
Rhode Island	1,052,567	1,048,319	4,248	0.4	2	
South Carolina	4,625,364	4,012,012	613,352	15.3	7	+1
South Dakota	814,180	754,844	59,336	7.9	1	
Tennessee	6,346,105	5,689,283	656,822	11.5	9	
Texas	25,145,561	20,851,820	4,293,741	20.6	36	+4
Utah	2,763,885	2,233,169	530,716	23.8	4	+1
Vermont	625,741	608,827	16,914	2.8	1	
Virginia	8,001,024	7,078,515	922,509	13.0	11	
Washington	6,724,540	5,894,121	830,419	14.1	10	+1
West Virginia	1,852,994	1,808,344	44,650	2.5	3	
Wisconsin	5,686,986	5,363,675	323,311	6.0	8	
Wyoming	563,626	493,782	69,844	14.1	1	
Total*	308,745,538	281,421,906	27,323,632	9.7	435	

* Includes the population of the 50 states and the District of Columbia.

requirement of equal district populations (not voting populations) within a state. Other court decisions have interpreted the Constitution—particularly the Fourteenth Amendment's Equal Protection Clause—and the Voting Rights Act to offer guidance to the states on creating "majority-minority districts," the use of race as a factor in redistricting to remedy past discrimination, the "compactness" of districts, and other factors. (See *§ 2.90, Laws Protecting and Extending the Franchise.*) Once a state has adopted a redistricting plan, it is subject to court challenge and possibly to legislative or court revision.

Many states also have laws that govern redistricting. These laws discourage splitting political units, favor compact districts, and set forth other goals.

In most states, the legislatures enact redistricting plans, which are then submitted to the governor for approval or veto. Other states use commissions to create redistricting plans. In some states, failure by the legislature to act can send responsibility for redistricting to a commission.

Under federal law, the Census Bureau, by April 1, 2011, was to provide the governors and state legislatures with the population data that their states needed to redistrict. States have some discretion in what data they may request, and they receive data by political jurisdiction, such as county; by census geographical units, such as census tracts; and by other geographical units, such as voting precincts.

Although laws and court decisions govern redistricting decisions, redistricting is a political process. It is particularly painful to congressional incumbents in states that have lost seats. Unless one or more incumbents retire, two incumbents are likely to face each other in a primary if they are of the same party, or in a general election if they are of opposing parties.

However, redistricting is also viewed as an opportunity by Democrats and Republicans to strengthen their respective party's representation in Congress. A party might attempt to add its party's voters to a marginal district to shore up its strength in that district, or it might add its party's voters to a district that has favored the other party's candidates in an attempt to destabilize the district's voting pattern. The parties might make a deal to create districts favorable to each party or to favor each party's incumbents. Influential state legislators facing term limits and having political ambitions of their own might try to create districts favorable to their own future campaigns for Congress. Some congressional incumbents are very popular or very unpopular with state legislators, and might reap the rewards or agonies of their standing.

Even in states that gain seats, redistricting can be a problem for incumbents. Where a party controls both houses of the legislature and the governorship, it often uses this power to increase the likelihood of winning additional districts, both existing, albeit revised, and new. In states with commission redistricting, there can be a sense of unpredictability and lack of influence by politicians over the outcome. And, the addition of districts due to reapportionment offers additional opportunities for drafting district lines to favor a party, a racial or ethnic group, a socioeconomic group, or another set of voters.

It is no wonder that U.S. representatives are actively involved in redistricting. Some hire lobbyists to represent them in their state's capital while they are working in Washington, DC, and their districts. Others spend time and effort keeping up contacts from their time in their state's legislature. Some support their party's state legislators and legislative candidates politically.

Still, incumbent representatives must be circumspect in another way. U.S. House rules proscribe the use of official funds for redistricting activities.

A legislative reopening of a state's congressional district is also possible where party control of a state's elective offices shifts. In a challenge to Texas' 2003 mid-decade redistricting, the U.S. Supreme Court did not find anything "inherently suspect" in the action. (*League of Latin American Citizens (LULAC) v. Perry*, No. 05-204, slip op. (548 U.S. 399, 2006).) Texas successfully redistricted for the 2004 election, but the court challenge resulted in an additional change for the 2006 election, based on a Voting Rights Act violation. Where a court-ordered map has been imposed, legislatures also sometimes make subsequent adjustments. (*To view district maps, see the Census Bureau's web site at <www.census.gov> and search for "2010 Census Redistricting," and the U.S. Geological Survey's web site at <www.nationalatlas.gov/printable/congress.html>. Some secretaries of state's election divisions or independent state election boards also have district maps on their web sites. See the URLs for these web sites at § 2.11. Local media web sites and state legislature and redistricting commission web sites are also sources.*)

§ 2.50 Term Limits

In recent years, Congress was under pressure to enact term limits applicable to members of Congress. A number of states have enacted limits on the number of terms a person may serve or serve consecutively in the state legislature. The attempt by some states to extend term limits to members of Congress, however, was stopped by a Supreme Court decision, *U.S. Term Limits Inc. v. Thornton*, 514 U.S. 779 (1995), which found an Arkansas congressional term-limits statute unconstitutional. Nevertheless, some members of Congress have voluntarily pledged to their constituents not to run for reelection after serving a certain number of terms. As time has gone on, fewer members or candidates for Congress seem to have made a pledge, and some members seem to be repudiating it and doing so without losing significant votes in reelection.

§ 2.60 Election Challenges

The House and Senate are empowered by the Constitution to be ". . . the Judge of the Elections, Returns and Qualifications of [their] own Members. . . ." (*Art. I, sec. 5, cl. 1.*) Following each election, the House Administration Committee on behalf of the House, and the Rules and Administration Committee on behalf of the Senate, consider election challenges. Most of these are disposed of expeditiously by the committees. However, investigations into challenges can go on for a long time, and even result in a seat being declared vacant and a new election ordered.

House

In the contemporary Congress, the House is likely to choose to employ the procedures established for resolving contested House elections established in the Federal Contested Elections Act (*P.L. 91-138; 83 Stat. 284*), whereby a candidate for a House seat may challenge the election for that seat. (A member or member-elect or another person could also challenge the seating of a member-elect, although not under the provisions of the contested elections act, and the House could refer the matter to the House Administration Committee for its consideration and recommendations.)

After a winner has been declared by the appropriate state authority, the candidate challenging the election initiates House action by filing a notice with the clerk of the House and by serving the notice on the member-elect. The notice is to state "with particularity the grounds" on which the election is contested. The member-elect must respond, and may do so with defenses; with a motion to dismiss, based on various assertions, which will be decided by the House Administration Committee; or with a motion for a more definite statement of notice, which the House Administration Committee would rule on.

While these proceedings are unfolding, the new Congress might convene. Normally, the member-elect, possessing "credentials" from the state election authority—an election certificate considered to be prima facie evidence of the outcome of an election—is seated. The member-elect may be sworn in with other members-elect, or asked to stand aside and be sworn in separately. In either case, the House retains the authority to decide the contested election at a future date. In addition, further proceedings, either administrative or judicial, may take place in the state where the contested election occurred. The House Administration Committee, which has jurisdiction over contested elections, might be inclined to wait for these proceedings to conclude before undertaking its own consideration of the contested election.

The Federal Contested Elections Act, in addition to governing the notice, response, and motions, contains provisions dealing with time limits or deadlines, depositions, affidavits, subpoenas, default, penalties, and dismissal, and requires that all documents developed in the course of state and Federal Contested Elections Act proceedings be filed with the clerk of the House. This documentation provides the basis under the act for the committee's consideration of a contested election.

The House Administration Committee might discharge its consideration in a number of ways, with the result of a simple resolution (H. Res.) reported from the committee for the consideration of the House. The committee might form a task force to do the committee's preliminary work, hold hearings, or conduct its own field work, in addition to or as a supplement to considering the documentary record. Although it has normally been reluctant to do so, the committee might undertake a full or partial recount.

Upon the completion of its work, the House Administration Committee makes its recommendation to the House. The committee might recommend dismissal of the challenge, the seating of a specific candidate, an investigation of fraud and other problems with the election, a declaration that the seat is vacant and a new election is to be held, or a variation on these choices. The resolution is privileged in the House, and the House might decide it with or without debate, with or without amendment, and by voice or recorded vote.

Following the 1996 general election, for example, a challenge in the House was not settled until early 1998. In the House, the incumbent, Republican Bob Dornan, was defeated for reelection by just under 1,000 votes, and challenged the election under the provisions of the Federal Contested Elections Act. Dornan alleged that noncitizens had voted illegally in the election in favor of Democrat Loretta Sanchez. The House Oversight Committee (now House Administration) appointed a task force to investigate. The challenge continued until the House voted, 378 to 33, on February 12, 1998, to end the investigation.

As a later example, when the 110th Congress convened January 4, 2007, an election challenge had been noticed for Florida's Thirteenth Congressional District. Vern Buchanan, a Republican, had been certified as the winner of the election by the Florida election authority, the secretary of state, and, following normal House practice even for a contested seat, Buchanan was sworn in with the other members-elect.

Prior to the swearing-in of the members-elect, Rep. Rush Holt, D-NJ, posed a parliamentary inquiry to the Speaker, asking whether the losing candidate, Democrat Christine Jennings, had filed a notice of contest with the clerk and what effect Buchanan's seating had on the contested election.

The Speaker responded that the notice had been filed with the clerk, that the "House remains the judge of the elections of its Members," and that the seating was "without prejudice to the contest over the final right to that seat that is pending under the statute. . . ."

A further parliamentary inquiry was then posed by Rep. Adam Putnam, R-FL, asking whether Buchanan "has been certified by the Secretary of State as duly elected from the 13th District of Florida." The Speaker stated that Putnam was correct.

The central argument in the contested election involved an apparent undervote by 18,000 voters in Sarasota County (in this instance, in relation to all county voters who voted), which Jennings claimed was caused by a malfunction of the electronic voting machines. The undervote was very high compared to neighboring counties.

The difference between the winner, Buchanan, and the loser, Jennings, was only 368 votes of more than 338,000 votes cast. The Florida Elections Canvassing Commission ordered a recount, with the difference then showing 369 votes, and certified the election. Jennings filed a contested election suit in state court, alleging that perhaps thousands of votes had been lost due to malfunctioning voting machines. The trial judge denied Jennings' request for access to the voting machines manufacturer's proprietary hardware, software, and source code. An appellate court on June 18, 2007, upheld the trial judge's decision, stating that the judge had followed the law and that Jennings had failed to show "irreparable, material injury" to the trial proceedings. Jennings eventually abandoned her court challenge.

On December 20, 2006, Jennings filed with the House a notice of contest under the Federal Contested Elections Act, and, after his swearing in, Buchanan filed a motion to dismiss, arguing that Jennings' evidence was speculative. The chair of the House Administration Committee established a three-member task force to oversee the election contest, with two Democrats, who were in the majority in the House, and one Republican. The task force found sufficient credibility in Jennings' claims to approve an investigation of her challenge, and immediately obtained the Government Accountability Office's services to investigate the voting machines. The task force subsequently approved GAO's work plan and assured the contestants' access to information about GAO's protocols and work.

GAO's effort was the second review of the voting machines' functionality and reliability. Immediately after the election, the Florida secretary of state ordered an audit of the machines, and released the results in February 2007, stating there was no evidence of a discrepancy between the certified election results and the votes actually cast.

In October 2007, GAO sought authority from the task force for further testing, and, in February 2008, reported to the task force its finding that its testing statistically eliminated the possibility that the voting machines contributed to the undervote and, therefore, its conclusion that further testing was unwarranted. The task force voted unanimously to dismiss the election contest. The House Administration Committee then unanimously approved a resolution to dismiss the election contest, stating in its report on the resolution that "only clear and convincing evidence can provide the basis to overcome the presumption of regularity accorded a State's certified results." The resolution was adopted on a voice vote by the House on February 25, 2008.

Senate

In contrast to the House, the Senate does not act on contested elections pursuant to a statute. The Senate tends to consider each election contest uniquely, although precedents, such as having the Senate Rules and Administration Committee conduct an investigation and make a recommendation to the Senate, may play an important role. Two modern cases of contested elections illustrate the structure and flexibility of the Senate's consideration of election challenges.

In a Senate race in Louisiana in 1996, Mary Landrieu, a Democrat, and Woody Jenkins, a Republican, fought for an open seat, which Landrieu won by fewer than 6,000 votes out of more than 1.7 million cast. Jenkins charged voter fraud, and asked that the seat be declared vacant and a new election ordered. The Senate seated Landrieu "without prejudice" to the Senate's constitutional right to make a later decision on dismissing Jenkins' petition, seating Jenkins, setting aside the election, or taking another action. The Rules and Administration Committee's investigation, which began with a bipartisan adoption of supplementary committee rules to govern the investigation, became a partisan investigation, from which the Democratic committee members withdrew. The investigation lasted until the committee voted unanimously on October 1, 1997, to end it.

In an earlier instance, following a New Hampshire Senate race in 1974, the Senate voted to declare the seat vacant and seek a new election. Although several ballot counts emerged in New Hampshire following the election, the final count, which was used to certify the winner, provided only a two-vote win to the Republican candidate, former Rep. Louis Wyman. The Democratic candidate, former state insurance commissioner John Durkin, filed a petition to contest the election with the Senate, and sought to have the Senate seat him based on one of the earlier ballot counts. When the Senate convened, it voted against a proposal to seat Wyman and another proposal to declare the seat vacant, and voted instead to refer the matter to the Senate Rules and Administration Committee.

The Rules and Administration Committee agreed on a procedure to review about 3,500 ballots from the more than 32,000 that were questioned by one or both candidates. The committee ultimately agreed on how voters had cast all but twenty-seven of these ballots, and reported to the Senate a resolution that allowed the full Senate to vote on each of the twenty-seven ballots and on eight questions of procedure related to recounts of certain precincts, voting machines that allegedly malfunctioned, and other matters. For each item, the Senate would be choosing between Wyman and Durkin, and presumably by its votes deciding the winner, or at least pointing the way for the Rules and Administration Committee to determine a winner.

Deadlock ensued on the Senate floor for six weeks as the parties largely voted as blocs, with just enough Democrats voting with Republicans to defeat motions to invoke cloture. This situation continued until Durkin reversed his position of opposition to a new election, on which Senate Democrats had supported him. The Senate voted July 30, 1975, to declare the seat vacant. A new election was held September 16, which Durkin won with just over 53 percent of the vote. He was sworn in September 18.

Two other contested Senate elections, in contrast, were resolved by action in state courts following the 2008 and 2010 elections.

In the 2008 case of challenger Democrat Al Franken and incumbent Republican Norm Coleman in the 2008 Minnesota Senate contest, Franken ultimately prevailed, but Minnesota was without a senator for six months.

On election day, November 4, 2008, more than 2.9 million voters cast ballots in the Minnesota Senate race. In mid-November, the state canvassing board adopted a report showing that Coleman received 206 more votes than Franken. Since a difference of less than one-half of one percent separated the votes cast for Coleman and Franken, the board directed the secretary of state to oversee a manual recount. This process lasted more than six weeks, identified 933 absentee ballots that had been erroneously excluded from counting, and resulted in a new tally that gave Franken a lead of 225 votes.

Coleman contested the election results and sought the certificate of election by filing suit in state court. Following a trial, the judge ordered another 351 absentee ballots counted, which increased Franken's lead over Coleman to 312 votes. Coleman appealed the decision to the Minnesota Supreme Court.

In its decision on June 30, 2007, the Minnesota Supreme Court.held that the state canvassing board's certification constituted prima facie evidence that Franken had been elected, and, therefore, Coleman bore the burden of proof to show that the board's certification had been erroneously given. The supreme court indicated it would not set aside a finding of fact unless Coleman demonstrated that a finding was clearly erroneous, but that it would review conclusions of law de novo. Coleman challenged procedures for counting absentee ballots and the inclusion in the tally of votes in one precinct where some of the ballots were lost before the recount.

The court ruled, essentially, that voters must follow fully the provisions of the state statute for voting absentee, and rejected Coleman's contention that voters need only substantially comply. During the trial, the court had identified ten categories of ballots that could not be considered to be legally cast for failure to comply with one or more statutory requirements. The court also rejected Coleman's argument that local election officials applied the absentee ballot law differently in different locales. The court upheld the trial court's finding that local officials acted consistently and that individual local procedures could be attacked only if they were applied with the intent to discriminate among absentee voters, which Coleman failed to do. In its discussion of these issues, the court rejected Coleman's due process and equal protection claims. The court also rejected two challenges Coleman made to trial procedures concerning evidence.

On the matter of the missing ballots, the Minnesota Supreme Court upheld the lower court's finding that the precinct's votes were properly counted in the absence of a showing of fraud or misconduct that called the voting machine returns into question.

The court concluded by saying that Franken was "entitled [under Minnesota law] to receive the certificate election. . . ." Coleman conceded the election the same day the court handed down its decision, and Franken was sworn in as Minnesota's junior senator on July 7, 2007.

A 2010 Senate election challenge dealt with the application of principles and provisions of election law to the rare issue of counting write-in votes that could change the outcome of an election. In the Alaska Senate race, challenger Joe Miller won the Republican primary over incumbent Lisa Murkowski. Murkowski subsequently decided to mount an independent write-in campaign for the Senate seat; Alaska did not have a "sore-loser" law preventing her from subsequently running in the general election, having lost the Republican nomination. Once the Alaska division of elections on

November 17, 2010, completed tallying write-in votes for the general election, Murkowski led Miller by 10,420 votes, with Miller having challenged 8,553 of write-in votes that had been counted.

On November 9, 2010, Miller sued in federal district court, seeking to stop election officials from counting write-in votes where Murkowski's name was not written or spelled precisely. When the vote counting was completed, the federal judge issued a temporary injunction to prevent certification of the election, but redirected Miller to state court for a ruling on challenges under Alaska election law. Miller filed his suit in state court, and lost at the trial level. He took an appeal to the Alaska Supreme Court, which ruled on December 22, 2010.

The Alaska Supreme Court stated that it had always interpreted election statutes to prevent the disenfranchisement of voters and to allow a voter's intent to prevail. The court rejected Miller's argument that Murkowski's name needed to be written or spelled perfectly. The court held that the Alaska statute and the court's precedents required election officials to disregard misspellings and other variations in writing a candidate's name to effectuate a voter's intent. The court nonetheless approved of action of election officials of not counting ballots where the oval had not been filled in next to the name of a write-in candidate. Alaska law required a mark in the oval, and allowed any mark in the oval to indicate the choice of a write-in candidate.

The court also rejected Miller's contention that election officials applied standards in the hand counting of write-in votes that disadvantaged him. The court said it had examined the record and found that consistent standards had been followed and that Miller's counting observers had been afforded the opportunity to challenge every write-in ballot. In its discussion of these issues, the court rejected Miller's due process and equal protection claims. The court also ruled against Miller's challenges to more technical aspects of Alaska election administration. The court concluded by saying "there are no remaining issues raised by Miller that would prevent this election from being certified."

After the ruling, Miller announced that he would not pursue further legal proceedings to prevent certification. On December 28, 2010, the federal district judge lifted the injunction and dismissed Miller's case. Murkowski took office on January 5, 2011, with other senators elected to a new term.

Seating a Member Meeting Constitutional Qualifications

While these examples deal with House and Senate judging elections of their members, either house might need to determine the constitutional qualifications of a member-elect to serve. In a landmark decision, the U.S. Supreme Court enunciated a limitation on congressional judgments on seating a member-elect related to these qualifications. The case stemmed from the House's refusal to seat a member-elect, but the court's opinion presumably applies to the Senate as well. Rep. Adam Clayton Powell, D-NY, was reelected to his House seat in the 1966 election. Rather than seat Powell, the Speaker directed him to step aside while the other members-elect were sworn. The House did not seat Powell but agreed to a resolution to establish a select committee to consider Powell's qualifications, his involvement in a civil case in New York in which he had been held in contempt, and his alleged misconduct involving a misappropriation of funds that was the subject of an investigation at the end of the preceding 89th Congress. The resolution also disallowed Powell from being seated pending House action on the select committee's report. The select committee subsequently recommended seating Powell, but censuring and fining him and depriving him of his seniority.

When the House considered the resolution embodying the select committee's recommendations, it approved an amendment to the resolution, and then agreed to the resolution as amended. The resolution as amended excluded Powell from the House and declared his seat vacant. Powell sued Speaker John McCormack and other House officers. Powell argued that he must be seated if he met the constitutional qualifications for a representative—twenty-five years of age, a citizen for seven years, and a resident of the state from which elected. Following lower-court decisions, the Supreme Court granted certiorari, settled arguments against the federal courts' jurisdiction and the matter's justiciability, and supported Powell's claim to his seat. The Court held that "in judging the qualifications of its members Congress is limited to the standing qualifications prescribed in the Constitution." (*Powell v. McCormack*, 395 U.S. 486 (1969).)

§ 2.70 Federal Campaign Finance Laws

Election campaigns for the House and Senate are subject to numerous laws and regulations, and no one may pursue a candidacy for a House or Senate seat outside of this legal framework. These laws and regulations include federal election, tax, communications, and criminal laws; Federal Election Commission (FEC), Internal Revenue Service (IRS), and Federal Communications Commission (FCC) regulations and rulings; chamber rules and their interpretations by the House and Senate ethics committees; and state laws and regulations. The general intent of the proscriptions in these laws and regulations is to prevent or minimize conflicts of interest by candidates for Congress, protect the integrity of citizens' exercise of the franchise, and prevent diversion of public funds to political purposes.

The federal campaign laws applicable to congressional campaigns (principally 2 U.S.C. 431 et seq.) reflect several principles:

- private financing, not public financing
- no ceilings on candidates' expenditures from their campaign or their personal funds
- periodic disclosure of receipts and expenditures as the principal means of enabling the public to assess candidates' campaign-finance activities
- ceilings on contributions made by individuals, parties, and political action committees (PACs) to House and Senate candidates (PACs are entities that receive contributions and make expenditures under campaign finance laws.)
- prohibitions on entities that may contribute to House and Senate candidates

Campaign funding fully covered by federal laws and regulations, such as an individual's donation to a congressional candidate's campaign, is called *hard money*. Campaign funding that is legal but only partially or immaterially regulated is called *soft money*. Candidates may only raise hard money for new campaigns.

While there have been numerous proposals for public financing of congressional campaigns, Congress has not enacted such a proposal. The system of private financing and unlimited expenditures remains intact, although the costs of congressional campaigns, the time consumed by fundraising, and the role of wealthy contributors (and candidates) invite frequent criticism. The current system seems to prevail because of concerns about the advantages of incumbency that a challenger's fund-raising must overcome, potential electoral distortions in a public-funding system, limitations on spending as a direct or indirect limitation on constitutionally protected speech, and other issues.

A frequent complaint of congressional candidates is the significant amount of time they must spend on fund-raising because of both the high costs of campaigns and the ceilings that exist on individual and other contributions, as explained below. Squeezed between high campaign costs and low campaign contribution ceilings, House candidates conduct fund-raising year-round; for Senate candidates, fund-raising cannot be confined to the last one or two years of a six-year term.

This explanation of federal campaign finance law applicable to congressional candidates is not intended as legal advice but rather as an overview of some of the principles and provisions of the law. The campaign finance laws are very complex and expert legal advice is needed to understand the applicability of the law to a particular action or circumstance. This overview is intended to assist a government affairs professional in discussing political action with counsel.

Contributions

A candidate for the House or Senate *must* establish and register with the FEC a principal campaign committee. A candidate may in addition establish or authorize and register other committees as a part of his campaign, known as affiliated committees. The candidate's principal campaign committee and any affiliated committees are considered to be one committee for purposes of contribution limits. Once a campaign committee is registered, periodic reporting of contributions to it and spending by it begins, as explained below. References in this section to a candidate's campaign committee include both the principal campaign committee and affiliated committees.

A potential candidate is allowed a grace period to explore a run for a seat in the House or Senate, without registration or reporting, but must follow many campaign finance laws and rules in that period. Once she crosses a threshold of announcing a candidacy or taking actions that a candidate would take, for example, ballot qualification, the time for registration has arrived. Raising or spending $5,000 or more is also an indication of candidacy, although the actions the potential candidate undertakes during the exploratory period will decide whether that level of funding is determinative of a candidacy that must establish and register a principal campaign committee.

A candidate for Congress may not solicit campaign contributions on federal property, although member-to-member solicitations are exempt. A congressional candidate may not designate a federal facility as the location for receiving contributions. Should a donor send a contribution to a congressional office, the contribution must be forwarded promptly, not using the frank, to the member's campaign committee.

A candidate's campaign committee receives contributions in support of the candidate's campaign. Contributions may not be made directly to the individual who is running for office, and benefits that accrue to a candidate may be considered by the FEC to be reportable campaign contributions. A contribution is anything of value that is given, loaned, or advanced to support a candidate's campaign. A contribution may be accepted only if it is allowed under the law and FEC regulations.

A contribution may be money, although a campaign committee may not accept a cash donation of more than $100 from any contributor or of more than $50 from an anonymous donor. A contribution may be earmarked for a specific candidate and received by the candidate's campaign committee through an intermediary, such as an entity like EMILY's List or the Susan B. Anthony List. A contribution may be in-kind, that is, an item or service given without charge or at a discount specific to the campaign committee. A campaign worker picking up the cost of an item or service for the campaign committee might under some circumstances be considered to be making an in-kind contribution. A contribution may be the cost of a ticket to a campaign event or of an item sold there, but the ticket or sales price is the contribution, not the net proceeds after deducting costs. A loan is also a contribution, unless it is made by a usual lender under usual terms. An extension of credit is also a contribution, unless it is made by a usual seller under usual terms.

Each contributor is limited in what the contributor may give to a candidate's campaign committee, including, as mentioned above, both a candidate's principal campaign committee and any affiliated committees. The limit starts anew for *each* campaign in which a candidate participates, so that a contributor may designate a contribution for, and give up to the maximum amount for, a primary election, a general election, each runoff election, and any special election primary, primary runoff, special election, or special election runoff. A candidate may also set up another, separate fund if his election is subject to a recount.

A party caucus or convention may qualify as a primary if it selects a party's House or Senate candidate. A third-party candidate is entitled to separate primary election as well as general election fund-raising, even when there is no primary for her candidacy. FEC regulations allow such candidates to determine a date separating the primary and general election periods.

Campaign finance law and regulations require separation in a campaign committee's accounting system of contributions collected for different elections, determine the circumstances under which funds given for one election may be used to finance another election or pay off its debts, and govern the retirement of debts after an election and the continuation, evolution, or termination of a campaign committee. The principles and provisions of these regulations are not examined here.

Contribution limits apply during a two-year election cycle, and the amounts described below apply in the 2011–2012 election cycle. The limits for individuals, for "other" political committees (such as the political committee of a state or local candidate), and for the combined donations of a national party committee and a Senate campaign committee, are indexed for inflation in odd-numbered years. The limits for PACs and parties are not indexed.

First, an individual may give up to $2,500 for each election in which a candidate runs. (Individuals are also limited to donating $46,200 to all candidates in a two-year election cycle.)

Second, a PAC that supports multiple candidates and meets other organizational criteria under campaign finance law and regulations may give up to $5,000 for each election. (Two or more PACs controlled by the same entity, such as a corporation or labor union, are considered to be affiliated committees, subject to one contribution limit.) The Center for Responsive Politics (<*www.opensecrets.org*>), analyzing campaign-finance reporting to the Federal Election Commission (<*www.fec.gov*>), reported that campaigns in total for the 2010 election raised 62 percent of their funds from individuals and 28 percent from PACs.

Third, a state, district, or local party committee may donate up to $5,000 for each election. (A district or local committee is presumed to be affiliated with its state committee, with all donations considered to be from one donor, unless the committees can meet FEC criteria to demonstrate independence from one another.)

Fourth, a national party committee may donate up to $5,000 for each election, although a special limit of $43,100 for *each period of a primary and general election* applies to the combined donations of a national party committee and a Senate campaign committee to a Senate candidate's campaign committee.

Fifth, an "other" political committee may donate up to $2,500 for each election, although a contribution of more than $1,000 might trigger registration as a federal political committee.

Sixth, a House or Senate candidate's campaign committee may contribute up to $2,000 to another House or Senate candidate's campaign committee for each election.

Contributions in other forms are also allowed by law and regulation. Party committees may make coordinated expenditures and independent expenditures. National committee parties and state party committees may make expenditures coordinated with a campaign in connection with the *general election* of a candidate, spending from their own resources. The national party committees have a limit on their spending for each House and Senate candidate; the state party committees have the same limit on their spending for each House and Senate candidate within their state. The national party committees and the state party committees may authorize other party committees, such as the national congressional and senatorial committees and local party committees, to spend against these limits.

The limits are determined by a formula, which for 2011 allowed coordinated party expenditures for House nominees in states with one representative of $88,400; for House nominees in other states of $44,200; and for Senate nominees a range from $88,400–$2.46 million.

State and local party committees may, however, engage in the preparation and distribution of campaign materials, such as bumper stickers and yard signs, and of candidate lists, such as sample ballots. Subject to certain criteria, these activities are not defined as contributions under campaign finance law and regulations.

Party committees (and other entities recognized under campaign finance and federal tax laws) may make unlimited independent expenditures advocating the election or defeat of a specific candidate. "Independent" means that these expenditures do not occur in concert with a candidate or a candidate's campaign committee. These entities spend tens of millions of dollars in election cycles.

A candidate's campaign committee may also join with one or more other political committees, normally other candidate and party committees, for joint fund-raising. This activity is regulated under campaign finance law and regulations, and may not be used to evade contribution limits applicable to the participants in the activity.

Any entity, even ones prohibited from making a contribution, as explained below, may donate legal or accounting services to assist a campaign committee in complying with the federal campaign finance law. Restrictions exist on how these services may be provided, such as disallowing the entity providing the service from hiring additional staff to provide the service or back up employees providing the service.

An individual may donate his services without making an in-kind contribution so long as the donor is not compensated by anyone for the services. A volunteer who is a corporation or labor union employee or member may also use the entity's facilities for other "incidental" campaign work (up to an hour a week). The entity will not then be considered to have made a contribution to a campaign, although the volunteer must reimburse the entity for more than incidental use, resulting in an in-kind contribution to the campaign committee. Volunteer activities on the Internet also do not necessarily result in a contribution to a campaign committee, even if performed at a volunteer's place of employment.

Volunteers may use their homes, community rooms, and church halls without making a contribution to a campaign committee, although a community room or church hall must be regularly used for noncommercial purposes, without regard to political affiliation. Volunteers may also spend up to $1,000 for events in these locations (for each candidate for each election) without being considered to have made a contribution. An individual may incur unreimbursed transportation expenses of $1,000 and unlimited associated meals and lodging for a campaign committee for each election without making a contribution.

A vendor of food and beverages may offer a campaign committee a discount of up to $1,000 for each election, so long as the discount is not below the cost of the items, without making a contribution. Two or more campaigns may share expenses without a contribution having been made, so long as costs are appropriately apportioned. In addition, one candidate may positively mention another candidate in her campaign materials and that mention does not constitute a donation to the second candidate's campaign. A candidate's endorsement also does not alone constitute a contribution to another candidate.

Just as there are limits on amounts that may be contributed to a candidate's campaign committee, there are limits and prohibitions on who may make a contribution. A candidate's campaign committee may not accept a contribution from the treasury funds of corporations, labor unions, or national banks. Rather, such entities may establish PACs, more specifically, separate segregated funds, also called connected PACs, which solicit PAC donations from individuals, such as members, employees, or shareholders, associated with the sponsoring entity. A candidate's campaign committee, a party committee, or a PAC may rent at a normal rate, or use in the same manner as community or civic groups, a corporation's or labor union's facility for a purpose such as a fund-raiser.

If a candidate is employed, her compensation is considered to be personal funds exempt from reporting. If, however, the candidate is paid an amount in excess of hours worked or for work not performed, the additional compensation is considered a contribution. If the employer is a corporation, labor union, or national bank, a contribution in the form of such compensation would be prohibited.

A candidate's campaign committee may not accept contributions from federal government contractors. While contributions are banned from corporations that are also contractors, this prohibition applies as well to partnerships, sole proprietorships, and individuals.

Contributions are not allowed from foreign nationals, that is, an individual who is not a U.S. citizen or a noncitizen without permanent residency status. The U.S. subsidiaries of foreign parent corporations may establish connected PACs if specific criteria ensuring the independence of the PAC from foreign support and administration are met.

Certain prohibitions apply to individuals, as well. One individual may not contribute in the name of another, and individuals may not be reimbursed for their contributions. A minor may be a contributor, but the contribution must be made voluntarily and knowingly with the minor's own money.

It is illegal for a candidate to solicit a contribution from an individual on public assistance or from a federal employee. A member of Congress may not solicit or accept a contribution from employees in his congressional office.

A candidate may donate or lend to her campaign not subject to any contribution limit, but contributions or loans from family members are subject to the same limits applicable to all individuals. A candidate's donations or lending to her campaign must be reported, and law and regulations determine whether and how candidate loans may be repaid.

Spending

A candidate's campaign committee may pay for expenses such as salaries, rent, travel, office supplies, and other operating expenses. It may make loan repayments, and, subject to various criteria, make donations to state and local candidates, transfers to party committees, and contributions to committees supporting or opposing ballot questions. Restrictions apply to air travel, with restrictions applicable to House candidates different from those applicable to Senate candidates.

A candidate for the House or Senate who is not an incumbent member of Congress may receive a salary from her principal campaign committee. The salary is limited to the lesser of a member of Congress' salary or what the candidate received as earned income the previous year. A family member might be a paid campaign worker if he provides a bona fide service to the campaign and the salary reflects a fair market value for his services.

In general, however, campaign funds may not be converted to personal use, such as for mortgage payments, food consumed at home, clothing, or tuition payments. There are narrow exceptions to these presumptively personal expenditures when a campaign nexus can be established, for example, payment for a candidate to learn Spanish in order to communicate with constituents. The FEC applies a test of asking whether the expense would exist in the absence of the candidacy to determine whether an expense is campaign-related or personal or should be an exception to what would otherwise be personal.

Solicitations and other communications from a candidate's campaign committee must carry a disclaimer stating that they were paid for by the authorized committee. A candidate's radio and television communications also require compliance with the "stand by your ad" provision of campaign finance law, with the candidate stating she approved of the advertisement and, on television, showing the candidate or an image of the candidate.

Broadcasters, including cable systems, must provide "reasonable access" to their broadcasting schedule for candidate advertisers and must make advertising time available to candidates for what is known as the "lowest unit broadcast rate." The purpose of this privilege is to make available to candidates the same rates available to a broadcaster's most-favored advertisers. The rate requirement is in effect forty-five days before a primary election and sixty days before a general election.

Reporting

Campaign finance law requires campaign committees to keep records of contributions and to report contributions aggregating over $200 from each individual donor and contributions of any amount from a political committee. For an individual donor, the information to be recorded is the amount, date of receipt, full name, address, occupation, and employer. For a political committee, the information to be recorded is the amount, date of receipt, and name and address.

Additional reporting is required for so-called bundled contributions received from lobbyists or lobbyist PACs. A bundled contribution is one forwarded by or credited to a lobbyist or lobbyist PAC. If a campaign committee receives two or more such bundled contributions exceeding a threshold of $16,200 (in 2011) within a semiannual or quarterly period, it must report them. The campaign committee must report the name and address of a lobbyist or lobbyist PAC that provides bundled contributions exceeding the reporting threshold, the employers of the lobbyist, and the aggregate amount of bundled contributions forwarded by or credited to the lobbyist or lobbyist PAC during the reporting period.

Campaign committees must also keep records of all disbursements and have supporting documentation for any disbursement exceeding $200.

A candidate's principal campaign committee must file periodic reports on financial activity until all debts have been paid and a termination report has been filed with and accepted by the FEC. Quarterly reports are due on April 15, July 15, October 15, and, for the year-end report, January 31. In an election year, additional reports are required. A pre-election report is required twelve days before each election, such as a primary, general election, or runoff. A post-general election report is due thirty days after the general election. A campaign committee must also file so-called 48-hour notices of contributions of $1,000 or more received in the last twenty days before an election. A notice must be filed within forty-eight hours of receipt of such a contribution. (Therefore, such contributions received in the last forty-eight hours before election day are exempted from this reporting.)

House candidates must file with the FEC; filings must be made electronically if contributions or expenditures are expected to exceed $50,000. Senate candidates file on paper with the secretary of the Senate. House reports are available at the House Legislative Resource Center (B-106 Cannon House Office Building; 202-226-5200), and Senate reports are available at the Senate Public Records Office (SH-232 Hart Senate Office Building; 202-224-0758). All reports are available for public inspection at the FEC's public records office and on its web site (<*www.fec.gov*>). The FEC levies administrative fines on late filers and nonfilers.

Leadership PACs

A candidate for a House or Senate seat may also establish her own PAC, popularly called a leadership PAC, which is a political committee directly or indirectly established and controlled by the candidate. Strictly, it is a nonconnected PAC, that is, not a PAC affiliated with a corporation, labor union, or membership organization such as a trade association or professional society. It is not the principal campaign committee or an affiliated committee of the candidate and does not influence an election on the candidate's behalf.

A leadership PAC is subject to the same receipt limit of $5,000 applicable to other PACs. It may receive contributions from individuals, party committees, other PACs, other political committees, and from candidate campaign committees. It may donate as a PAC, which limits contributions to $5,000 for each candidate for each election. A candidate's leadership PAC may donate up to $5,000 for each election to the candidate's own campaign committee.

Candidates' campaign committees and leadership PACs may only receive hard money as contributions, that is, money that is fully covered by federal laws and regulations. The kinds of contributions just described are hard money. Campaign funding that is legal but only partially or immaterially regulated is called soft money. Candidate campaign committees and leadership PACs may not receive soft money contributions. Candidates for Congress are also limited in their participation in events for raising permitted soft-money contributions, such as for state or local parties.

Leadership PACs must also report contributions, including contributions bundled by lobbyists, and their spending.

§ 2.80 Federal Campaign Finance-Related Laws and Rules

A theme of both federal law and the rules of the House and Senate is to segregate official and political activity. (Political activity is used here in a popular, not legal, sense to describe an array of activities, political or campaign-related, that are described in federal law, regulation, and chamber rules and their interpretations.) In general, a member of Congress may not use his office, its staff, its equipment, or official funds for political activity. He may not use campaign funds to support official activities, such as operating a congressional office, or convert campaign funds to personal use.

While congressional staff may not, in general, engage in political work in congressional offices or in the course of performing their congressional office duties, they might "volunteer" their time to congressional campaigns at other locations and at other times. Nonetheless, an office scheduler may coordinate a member's schedule with a campaign office. On some occasions, a congressional staffer might go off the congressional payroll while performing extensive campaign work or might reduce her official hours and salary commensurate with reduced official duties and increased campaign duties. A congressional staffer may also concurrently draw a congressional salary and, for campaign work, a campaign salary. A senator may, in addition, designate up to three of her congressional staff, at least one of whom is in the senator's Washington, DC, office, to handle campaign funds for the senator's or a group of senators' campaign committee.

Laws and rules also attempt to reduce some of the advantages of incumbency. As mentioned in § 4.50 (*Franking Privilege*), mass mailings—500 pieces or more, largely identical in content—must be postmarked not fewer than ninety days before an election in which a representative is a candidate for any public office and not fewer than sixty days before an election in which a senator is a candidate for any public office. The House prohibition pertains to all mass communications, for example, announcements of "town hall" meetings. In addition, both the House and Senate regulate and monitor the use of the frank in recognition of its purposes in the conduct of congressional business rather than for campaign activities.

Also, for a representative, official travel must be paid from official funds. Travel cannot be designated as official if it originates or ends at a campaign event, and official travel may not be combined with or related to travel paid with campaign funds. For a senator's travel, reimbursement is allowed for actual transportation and disallowed for other travel-related expenses during the sixty days before a primary or general election in which the senator is a candidate, unless the candidacy is uncontested. Allocation of travel expenses between campaign funds and official funds is permitted when a trip has a "mixed purpose" of both official and campaign-related activities.

Campaign-related restrictions also exist, among others, for using House and Senate recording studios, video and audio from the House and Senate floors, mobile offices, and House and Senate office equipment, as well as for making campaign advertisements in congressional offices. In addition, the House considers redistricting to be a political activity, and, for the most part, disallows use of official funds related to a member's redistricting expenses. The Ethics in Government Act (*5 U.S.C. App. 101*) requires candidates for Congress to file financial disclosure forms. Candidates for the House file their reports with the clerk of the House and candidates for the Senate file with the secretary of the Senate. (*See also § 3.50, Congressional Ethics; § 3.60, Regulated Activities; § 4.30, House Allowances for Staff, Office, and Other Expenses; and § 4.40, Senate Allowances for Staff, Office, and Other Expenses.*)

§ 2.90 Laws Protecting and Extending the Franchise

A major theme in Congress' involvement with elections is extending and enhancing the exercise of the franchise. The Constitution gave Congress certain powers over elections (*art. I, sec. 4, cl. 1*), and congressional enforcement powers were included in amendments subsequently ratified that enhanced the right to vote.

Many extensions in the exercise of the franchise have taken place through constitutional amendments, which were submitted to the states and ratified. In the Fifteenth Amendment (1870) to the Constitution, the right to vote was guaranteed without reference to "race, color, or previous condition of servitude." The Seventeenth Amendment (1913) provided for the direct popular election of senators, who to that point were elected by state legislatures. In the Nineteenth Amendment (1920), the right to vote was guaranteed without reference to sex. In the Twenty-Third Amendment (1961), the District of Columbia was provided presidential electors. The Twenty-Fourth Amendment (1964) barred the poll or other tax in denying or abridging the right to vote. And the Twenty-Sixth Amendment (1971) extended the right to vote to citizens who had reached the age of eighteen.

In addition, Congress has used its legislative powers to enhance the exercise of the franchise. Four statutes of broad impact representative of congressional concerns include the Voting Rights Act (*42 U.S.C. § 1971 et seq.*), as amended; the National Voter Registration Act (*42 U.S.C. § 1973gg–gg-10*); the Uniformed and Overseas Absentee Voting Act (*42 U.S.C. § 1973 ff–ff-6*), as amended; and the Help America Vote Act (*P.L. 107-252; 116 Stat. 1666*).

Originally enacted in 1965, the Voting Rights Act has been renewed by Congress on four occasions. While Congress initially wished to address the disenfranchisement of African-American citizens in Southern states, the original act and its extensions have also covered other parts of the citizenry subject or potentially subject to disenfranchisement. Over the course of its history, the act and amendments to it have ended literacy tests and curtailed English-language literacy requirements, required bilingual election materials and assistance in certain circumstances, enabled challenges to election laws that denied or abridged voting rights, required Justice Department or U.S. district court "preclearance" of changes in election and related laws in counties and states with previous discriminatory voting practices, allowed federal workers to register voters and watch polls, and prevented disenfranchisement in presidential elections through registration requirements that exceeded thirty days. The Voting Rights Act authorized citizens and the federal government to sue to address discriminatory voting practices and procedures, and proscribed any jurisdiction in the United States from enacting an election law to "deny or abridge" voting rights on the basis of race, color, or language-group membership.

Some provisions of the Voting Rights Act are temporarily authorized, and Congress must pass legislation to continue these provisions in force. Congress extended the 2007 expiration to 2032 with a bill signed into law by President George W. Bush (*P.L. 109-246*). The new law reinvigorated preclearance requirements, which Congress found had been limited contrary to congressional intent by Supreme Court decisions.

Congress also began to address issues of accessibility for disabled persons through an amendment to the Voting Rights Act in 1982 (*P.L. 97-205*). A provision in this law allowed a disabled person to have assistance from another person chosen by the voter. Congress followed up in 1984 with the Voting Accessibility for the Elderly and Handicapped Act (*P.L. 98-435*), requiring accessibility in polling places and registration facilities and availability of registration and voting aids for handicapped and elderly individuals. Additional requirements were included in the Help America Vote Act, which is described below.

The National Voter Registration Act of 1993, also called the "motor voter law," addressed the issue of states' voter registration practices, which Congress perceived as an impediment to voting participation. The principal national standards that Congress set in the law included the following: (1) allowing an application for a driver's license or renewal also to serve as a voter registration application; (2) allowing mail-in voter registration; (3) mandating other public offices (including public-assistance offices) to serve as voter registration sites; and (4) circumscribing procedures for dropping a voter from a voter registry.

The Uniformed and Overseas Citizens Absentee Voting Act allows military personnel, their dependents, and overseas voters who no longer maintain a residence in the United States to register and vote absentee in federal elections. Overseas voters register in the jurisdiction of their last residence, and registrations must be honored for applications received at least thirty days before an election. States must also establish systems to allow military and overseas voters to request voter registration and absentee ballot applications online and by mail. Under the law, the U.S. Postal Service carries voting materials free of charge.

In response to the breakdowns in election administration in the 2000 general election, Congress responded with the Help America Vote Act. It authorized several grant programs to states, establishing, requirements and standards for voting systems and election administration. It created the Election Assistance Administration to implement the grant programs and other provisions of the law and to test and certify voting systems. This entity was also authorized to issue voluntary guidelines for voting systems, replacing authority previously vested in the Federal Election Commission. Grants could be used to eliminate punch-card and lever voting machines, improve election administration, and make polling places accessible. The largest grant program at least partially funded state plans for activities such as procuring statewide voter registration systems. The law required the use of provisional ballots, and mandated disability access and other changes at polling places. The law also amended the military and overseas voting law to overcome problems that were identified in the 2000 election.

Other powers of Congress also bear on its legislating in the area of elections. For example, Congress has established the Tuesday after the first Monday in November as the day for electing federal officials. The Constitution provides for a decennial census, which is to be used, among other purposes, to apportion seats in the House of Representatives. Through law and appropriations, Congress has implemented these constitutional provisions. (*See § 2.40, Reapportionment and Redistricting.*) As described earlier in this section, Congress has submitted constitutional amendments to the states, which have been ratified, and enacted laws dealing with the election of the president and vice president of the United States. These laws include implementation of the constitutional provisions dealing with presidential electors. (*See § 8.90, Congress and the Executive: Presidential Election and Succession; and § 8.91, Electoral College.*)

On five occasions in the 1970s, Congress enacted campaign-finance laws applicable to the election of federal officials. It has regularly debated changes to those laws since then, and in 2002 passed the Bipartisan Campaign Reform Act. Highlights of these laws applicable to congressional candidates are discussed in § 2.70 (*Federal Campaign Finance Laws*).

§ 2.100 Chapter Summary and Discussion Questions

No one serves in Congress unless elected to it, although some senators are appointed temporarily to fill a vacancy until an election is held. Many different motivations exist for an individual to run for Congress and, if elected, to run for reelection. The national political parties also play a part in selecting candidates by recruiting individuals to run. Independent parties or third parties also play an important electoral role in some states or districts.

Candidates must be good organizers and managers when putting together a campaign organization, raising money, and developing a campaign strategy. Incumbents may have advantages in an election with an established campaign organization, additional sources of campaign funds, relationships with media that cover a campaign, and a tendency of voters to stick with a known politician.

Candidates, especially if they are incumbents, must be active in promoting their candidacy and in warding off potential competitors in both their own party and the opposition party. Media coverage, constituent service, and early, successful campaign fund-raising all contribute to a sense of a candidate's electability and invincibility. A strategy for the Internet and social media must also now be a part of any tenure in office and campaign.

A candidate's future constituents, or an incumbent's current constituents, are the most important political component of any campaign, since they are the voters. Constituents are also a source of campaign funds and campaign volunteers. An incumbent must have conducted her tenure with them foremost in the incumbent's considerations, and a candidate must try to convince them that she better understands and will better represent their political desires and aspirations than the incumbent. A candidate must be thoughtful in the policy positions she takes, and an incumbent must be thoughtful in the legislative and representational record he builds. While most incumbents running for reelection are successful, a number of incumbents are vulnerable to primary or general election challenges in every election and lose renomination or reelection.

Since most incumbents are successful in their reelection campaigns, retirement from Congress is normally voluntary, occurring at the incumbent's initiative. Term limits, such as apply to some state legislators, do not apply to members of Congress, although some members voluntarily place a term limit on their service in Congress.

In the last two or three decades, fund-raising has become a huge responsibility and very time-consuming for candidates for Congress. Campaigns are expensive, and contributors are limited in what they may give to an individual for each election in which the individual is a candidate. Incumbent members of Congress spend a portion of each week they are in Washington fund-raising for themselves and for their party and fellow party candidates. The average winning House campaign in 2010 spent over $1.4 million, and the average winning Senate campaign spent nearly $9.8 million.

The four national congressional party organizations—the Democratic Congressional Campaign Committee, the National Republican Congressional Committee, the Democratic Senatorial Campaign Committee, and the National Republican Senatorial Committee—are critical sources of campaign funds for individual candidates and for spending on behalf of the party and on behalf of individual candidates. On the other hand, incumbents are expected to raise money for their party and for other party candidates, and members of Congress spend part of each week in Washington sponsoring or attending fund-raisers for purposes other than their own reelection. Many members of Congress also maintain so-called leadership political action committees (PACs) to raise money to donate to other candidates' campaigns.

Raising and spending campaign funds is highly regulated by federal law, Federal Election Commission (FEC) and other federal agencies' regulations, and House and Senate rules. No one may pursue a candidacy for a House or Senate seat outside of this legal framework, and congressional candidates must register their campaign with the FEC. Federal elections are privately financed, not publicly financed. This chapter examined key aspects and concepts of law, regulations, and rules that apply to candidates for Congress.

The principles that underlie campaign finance laws are that ceilings do not exist on candidates' spending from their campaign or personal funds, but that they do exist on contributions to candidates made by individuals, parties, and political action committees (PACs). Candidate campaigns may not accept contributions from corporations, labor unions, or national banks, but these entities may establish PACs, which are separate entities that receive contributions and make expenditures under campaign finance laws. Members of Congress also establish PACs, called leadership PACs. Periodic disclosure of receipts and expenditures is required of every campaign, but only some types of donors to campaigns must reveal contributions or sources of their funding.

Campaign funding fully covered by federal laws and regulations is referred to as hard money, and campaign funding that is legal but only partially or immaterially regulated is called soft money. Congressional candidates may raise only hard money for their campaigns.

A campaign may accept a contribution for each election in which the candidate is involved, for example, both a primary and a general election. The campaign may accept the maximum amount from each type of donor for each election; an individual donor may contribute $2,500 to a campaign for a primary and another $2,500 to the same candidate for the general election. The individual donor is nonetheless subject to an overall contribution ceiling of $46,200 to all federal candidates in all campaigns in a two-year election cycle. A PAC could give up to $5,000 for each election. Political parties are allowed to make contributions to campaigns, expenditures coordinated with campaigns (subject to a limit established by a formula), and independent expenditures not coordinated with campaigns.

Solicitations of funds must carry a disclaimer stating they were paid for by a candidate's campaign, and campaign advertisements are subject to "stand by your ad" requirements that a candidate or her image appear in an ad to say the candidate approved it. In-kind contributions, discounts, and volunteer services are allowable under campaign finance laws, but the circumstances of a donation may determine whether it is allowable, is a reportable contribution, and is subject to a limit.

A candidate who is not a member of Congress may receive a salary from his campaign, but it is limited to the lesser amount of a congressional salary or the candidate's last year's income. Campaign funds may not be converted to personal use.

Detailed reporting of receipts (from any individual source totaling $200 or more) and of expenditures is required quarterly. Special reporting is required for certain contributions received through the efforts of lobbyists. Additional reports are required in an election year.

An election does not always result in a clear determination of which candidate won and which candidates lost. In many of these instances, election authorities and courts in the state where there was a contested election are able to resolve the question by applying state law to issues of election administration. The House and Senate, however, have authority under the Constitution to make a determination of a winner in a contested election, and have developed mechanisms to do so. The House has delegated initial authority to investigate election challenges to the House Administration Committee, acting under the Federal Contested Elections Act. The Senate tends to act ad hoc in deciding how to resolve a contested Senate election.

The Constitution calls for a census to be conducted at the beginning of each decade for the purposes of apportioning seats in the House by population of the states. Congress by law limited the size of the House to 435 seats, and the Constitution guarantees each state one seat in the House, however small its population might be. All other seats are apportioned on the basis of a formula. The 2010 census resulted in ten states losing one or two seats, and eight states gaining between one and four seats. Reapportionment may result from a state growing faster or slower than the national average.

Each state has two seats in the Senate no matter how large or small its population.

Following apportionment, states with more than one seat redistrict so that the districts have equal population, minorities have opportunities to win seats or affect election outcomes, and other redistricting goals are honored. New districts are expected to be in effect in most if not all states in time for the 2012 elections. States have authorized different entities to redistrict: its state legislature, a commission, or a combination. State and federal courts are also frequently drawn into redistricting contests to choose a final plan.

Amendments to the Constitution and federal laws made pursuant to constitutional provisions ensure that all adult citizens may vote. Constitutional amendments have guaranteed voting rights to women, minorities, and citizens over eighteen years of age. Constitutional amendments and laws have prohibited state and local laws and behaviors that interfere with the right to vote.

Discussion Questions

- Both incumbent members of Congress and nonincumbent challengers have advantages and disadvantages in contemplating the next election. List five important advantages and five important disadvantages for each and discuss these. Select one disadvantage for each and discuss how an incumbent or challenger might deal with her disadvantage.
- Pick a congressional campaign in your area to follow or analyze, and evaluate one or more candidates' campaign web sites and social media uses for qualities such as information (answers to questions, such as issue positions, that you might have), currency, positive or negative campaign messages, treatment of opponents, and solicitation of contributions and volunteers. Explain your conclusions from your observations.
- Read the section in this chapter about the ways in which members of Congress interact with their constituents. Check with your member of Congress on when he will next make a public appearance at home, and plan to attend. Select an issue that interests you, learn more about it, and prepare some questions to ask your member of Congress about the issue. Try also to anticipate what he might say by checking the member's congressional web site and news web sites covering your area. How does what you have learned change the way you have formulated your questions?
- In your state, redistricting occurred following the 2010 census. Using news sites for your state and, perhaps, the legislature's web site and other web sites, learn what process was used for redistricting congressional seats. If you live in a state with a single congressional seat, learn what process was used for redistricting state legislative seats. Was a commission used, and what authority did it have? Was your state's redistricting plan subject to review by the Department of Justice? Was the redistricting authority able to agree to a plan, or was a suit filed in a state or federal court? If so, what was the court's decision?
- Read the section of this chapter dealing with the election challenges in the Senate races in Minnesota and Alaska. What did the state courts decide that was intended to prevent the disenfranchisement of voters? What did the state courts decide that resulted in the disenfranchisement of voters? How did the courts justify their decisions?
- Much has been written and said about whether congressional campaigns should be publicly financed or continue to be privately financed. You could conduct a research project on this debate. Or, to gain an introductory understanding of the debate, pick one organization on each side of this issue, read the information on each organization's web site, and compare the arguments favoring each side of the debate. What was your original point of view on the debate? How was it influenced or changed by what you learned?
- The section of this chapter on campaign finance lists many prohibitions on contributions to members of Congress. For example, an incumbent member of Congress may not solicit a contribution on federal property, may not use her office, staff, or office equipment for campaign purposes, and may not use campaign funds to operate her congressional office. How might these specific prohibitions further ethical standards and behavior in Congress?
- The average winning House campaign in 2010 spent over $1.4 million, and the average winning

Senate campaign spent nearly $9.8 million. Individual donors are limited to contributions of $2,500 to a candidate for an election, and PACs are limited to $5,000 to a candidate for an election. Assuming private funding of campaigns will continue, would you leave these limits in place, lower them, or raise them? What arguments might you make for each of these decisions? What decision do you favor, and why?

- Although Congress arguably has the constitutional authority to make a law prohibiting or requiring voters to present identification in order to vote, it has not chosen to do so. This requirement, however, is now under debate in many states, or has recently been under debate. Learn about current law and this debate in your state. What are the arguments for requiring the presentation of identification? What are the arguments against it? What is your view on this issue? Why?

Chapter Three

Pressures on Congress: Lobbying and Congressional Ethics

3

Analysis

§ 3.00 Introduction

Along with the campaign-finance laws discussed in Chapter Two, lobbying laws and congressional ethics laws and rules form a regulatory triad circumscribing the behavior of members of Congress. Whether they apply to members of Congress or congressional staff on the one hand or to individuals outside Congress on the other hand, these laws and rules are intended to regulate relationships between the two groups. While criminal or civil liability or other consequences can attach to the violation of a law or rule, the laws and rules set limits that protect all parties to these political relationships. Therefore, it is just as important for a government affairs professional to be aware of these laws and rules as it is for a member of Congress and congressional staffer.

This chapter addresses lobbying interactions with Congress, not between lobbyists and their clients or organizational membership. It highlights regulated aspects of the relationship between lobbyists and Congress. The chapter also addresses additional ethics laws and rules applicable to service in Congress and the consequences of violations.

This chapter provides examples of instances where lobbyists and members or staff nonetheless ignored the red lights and barriers and proceeded with illegal activity that resulted in jail terms and fines.

It is important to keep in mind that constituents "lobby" their members of Congress, and many registered lobbyists represent membership organizations whose members live in communities throughout the United States. In other words, many lobbyists represent us as individual citizens and voters. For the individual for whom lobbying is a profession, however, numerous laws and rules apply to the individual's pursuit of her profession and to her relationships with members of Congress and staff. With their thresholds of what constitutes lobbying activity, these laws and rules seek to exempt citizens from lobbying their members of Congress.

It has become commonplace for members of Congress and congressional staff to pursue careers in lobbying after their service in Congress. Their political understanding, network of contacts, knowledge of congressional procedures and operations, and experience in the congressional policymaking environment make them invaluable assets to a lobbying entity. Lobbyists working on Capitol Hill are always on the lookout for potential recruits for their organizations.

Members of Congress and staff are also subject to numerous constraints in their service in Congress, irrespective of any relationship with a lobbyist. These constraints affect their office operations, and they are discussed here as well as in Chapter Four, Supporting Congress: Allowances and Staff. They also affect members' non-congressional income, financial disclosure, post-congressional employment, and legislative work. The House and Senate Ethics Committees act on potential ethics violations, deferring, however, to the Justice Department when DOJ is pursuing a criminal investigation of a member or staff member.

§ 3.10 Lobbying Pressures

After the federal government, a feature of Washington that most Americans would probably call to mind is special interests or, simply, lobbyists. Self-representation or representation of an interest predates the Constitution, was anticipated by James Madison in *Federalist No. 10*, and was enshrined in the Bill of Rights as part of the First Amendment set of freedoms.

A lobbyist's role is straightforward—to contact and persuade one or more members of Congress to take a legal action. A lobbyist might seek to obtain or prevent a member's sponsorship of a bill or amendment. A lobbyist might seek a member's support on a vote in committee or on the floor in composing a majority for or against a measure or amendment, or might request the member to phone a committee chair or subcommittee chair to alert the chair regarding a matter before the panel that affects a segment of the population or the economy. A lobbyist might suggest that a member contact a department or agency to request that fair consideration be given to a problem, or might request any other number of actions. The first issue for a lobbyist is access.

Citizens and even members of Congress themselves can lose track of the value of lobbying. People may deplore the means often associated with lobbying, such as high-priced meals, entertainment, travel that appears more involved with pleasure than work, and campaign contributions.

The saga of lobbyist Jack Abramoff confirmed many people's darkest beliefs about the world of lobbying as grand jury indictments, trials, and guilty pleas exposed corruption in Washington, DC, Florida, and Guam. Abramoff was found guilty or pleaded guilty to multiple fraud counts, tax evasion, conspiracy to bribe public officials, and other acts. Many other individuals whom he brought into his schemes were also convicted or pleaded guilty.

All are also appalled when greed overtakes the judgment of a member of Congress, such as the criminal conduct that led to convictions during recent Congresses of Representatives Bob Ney, Randy "Duke" Cunningham, and William Jefferson, and the alleged behavior of other Democratic and Republican representatives that has led to ongoing investigations and interim House actions, such as depriving members under an ethical cloud of certain committee positions or assignments.

Yet, for lobbyists and the interests they represent, critical matters are at stake. The means of influence that some lobbyists use should not be confused with the purposes for which lobbyists work. For a corporation, the business' ability to make a profit, conduct its operations, control costs, or compete may be a major issue. For a labor union, governmental and business decisions might have eroded previously enjoyed worker rights. For a group of individuals sharing similar physical traits, having equal opportunities in all phases of life might still be a goal rather than a reality. For a group of citizens united by an idea, such as a cleaner environment or access to health care or a federal government less pervasive in economic affairs, these citizens might see their highest calling as having that idea validated in law. For a small business, nonprofit organization, or local government, a federal grant or loan may be perceived as the difference between failure and success. For a government contractor, Congress' or the administration's choice of what to buy and how to buy it can affect the company's profitability and competitiveness for years. Indeed, it is interesting to note that specific industrial and individual corporations have been criticized as ineffective in policy debates because their Washington lobbying presence was too low-key. If lobbyists do not inform members of Congress of the stakes of a decision, and help them make that decision, the opportunities for members to be well-informed may be limited.

Congress in its constitutional role is a mediating institution, the place in the national government where those competing interests foreseen by Madison could battle without bloodshed over the public interest. A special-interest organization's Washington presence probably includes at least the monitoring of the executive departments, regulatory agencies, and the courts, and, nationally, might include state and even local representation. Some organizations might focus on regulatory policy or court challenges as their principal means of influencing the direction of public policy. But most special-interest organizations concerned with public policy lobby Congress. Access to Congress is open to all individuals and groups.

On nearly any issue, however, the work of the lobbyist today involves more members with more diverse backgrounds. The old concept of the "iron triangle" between committees or subcommittees, executive agencies, and interest groups does not adequately explain lobbying relationships today. More players participate inside and outside of Congress.

Inside, Congress is decentralized, and members look out for their own political needs. Members are well-educated. They are diverse, not only in the numbers of women and minority-group members now serving in Congress but also in their backgrounds, accomplishments, and pre-Congress careers. Among the membership, there is a broad array of knowledge and experience to draw on. Senators represent states that seem to be growing more heterogeneous in their populations each year, providing senators with even more perspectives to be accommodated. Many House districts seem less heterogeneous than whole states as "majority-minority" districts are created, suburban areas are populous enough to comprise their own districts distinct from cities, and districts are created that have a strong partisan tilt.

No two members of Congress are alike. Two members may often or even routinely vote alike and may have campaigned for each other. They will nonetheless have differences. A lobbyist should know as much as possible about a member before meeting with the member or one of her staffers. Each member probably has an economic base in her district or state, the interests of which she will defend to the point of offending other members. The interest might be sugar beets or cars or coal or pristine beaches or food stamps or public employees. A member might also represent a district or state with a strong profile on one or more or a cluster of issues, such as gun rights or gun control, abortion rights or pro-life, inner-city needs or rural needs, or liberal causes or conservative causes. It is now easier than ever to find such information in a member's official web site, political web site, and social network pages, blogs, and other postings, and in other traditional and newer places such as home-state media web sites, Washington, DC-based media web sites and publications, and the congressional political parties' web sites.

It is incumbent on the lobbyist to know the member, her record of bills introduced and votes, and who and what the member represents in Congress. A lobbyist should not ask a member to vote against a core interest, might explore in some instances whether there is a middle ground, and should not vilify a member for a position on one issue when she might be an ally on the next issue to come along.

Outside Congress, many groups participate in policymaking. They do direct lobbying, share information with like-minded group members, stimulate grassroots actions, engage in media strategies, manage political action, and undertake other activities, such as conducting or supporting research and conducting public opinion surveys. At any one time, many groups and lobbying coalitions are at work on the many legislative issues active, or possibly to become active, on Capitol Hill. No one group seems to have a clear shot at attaining any policy goal. Attaining a goal or a compromise, or even trying and falling short, involves multifaceted lobbying, grassroots, political action, public relations, and media activities orchestrated by very smart, organizationally skilled people, some of whom never go to Capitol Hill and some of whom are not even located in Washington. The media, likewise, comprise well-educated, aggressive reporters, editors, bloggers, radio and television personalities, and other commentators, who can define issues in ways critical to the success or failure of a lobbying campaign and who quickly publicize upcoming votes, congressional favors to special interests, positions taken by members of Congress, proponents' and opponents' views, and other information.

The political parties also have realigned so that the Democratic Party in Congress is more consistently the party of "liberal" members and the Republican Party is more consistently the party of "conservative" members. There still are members from along the political spectrum in each party in Congress, but the parties as a whole are more partisan than they have been in much of the last sixty years. Their backers are also more partisan and more vocal on an array of issues, and either become engaged or are invited by party leadership to become engaged in rallying support for or opposition to legislative issues.

Regarding access in its most literal sense, lobbyists, just like everyone, have been affected by security measures on Capitol Hill. (*For a description of Capitol Hill security changes, see § 4.114, Capitol Security.*)

§ 3.20 Congress as an Open Institution

Congress is open through its individual members and their Washington and district or state staffs. A constituent, a lobbyist, or an administration representative will be received; virtually no caller is turned away. A staff member will meet with a visitor. Most lobbying contacts with a congressional office are initially and often principally with staff members. A lobbyist can build relationships with members through staff over the course of time, becoming known for the information and other services he can provide. Lobbying requires patience and persistence.

With the high turnover of congressional staff, a lobbyist might even find an advantage in the effort that this change in contacts entails. If a staff member simply changes offices, the lobbyist might end up with a contact in another congressional office, probably a contact who received or promoted the change. In the office that lost the staff member, the lobbyist might have an advantage in providing continuity for a new staff member. A lobbyist quickly learns that it is important to be gracious to all members of a congressional staff—the lobbyist will want the scheduler as well as the chief of staff and the legislative aides to know him. (*See Chapter Four, Supporting Congress: Allowances and Staff.*)

Lobbyists have another longer-range purpose in getting to know members and staff—identifying potential future lobbyists. Lobbying is an alternative career to working on Capitol Hill, in the executive branch, or elsewhere, and many members and staff decide at some point to parlay their contacts, issue knowledge, and political acumen into lobbying. (*See § 3.60, Regulated Activities.*)

Every member of Congress, except one retiring from elective office, needs campaign funds. A portion of nearly every member's campaign fund-raising for reelection is based on contributions from political action committees (PACs). Another substantial percentage is based on contributions from people of means inside and outside a district or state, including individual lobbyists in Washington,

DC, all of whom have a political interest in supporting a member financially. For Washington, DC, fund-raising events, it is common for one or more members of Congress to sponsor an event for another member or a challenger and make available to that person their own lobbying and other sources of campaign funds. A lobbyist might have a role in an organization's PAC, engage in other political activities, some of which may directly support one member's or several members' political campaigns, and be a contributor himself or herself. Lobbyists are valued campaign advisors and workers, and every two years they hit the campaign trail when Congress adjourns for the next election. Members also desire endorsements and recognition, which lobbyists can play a role in causing to happen. (*See § 2.10, Campaigns and Elections.*)

A lobbyist's contribution to a member's campaign fund, or a contribution by the lobbyist's employer's or client's PAC, is not a claim to the member's allegiance. The breadth of individuals and PACs that contribute to a winning campaign reduces the influence of any one contributor. It can nonetheless be a means of obtaining access and a hearing from the member on a matter of concern to a lobbyist. Contributions may be closely related to a member's position in Congress. The committees on which the member serves will generate additional contributions from certain PACs and individual contributors with interests before those committees. Members generally in accord with a PAC's or individual contributor's positions might receive relatively more contributions.

Congress is also open to lobbyists through individual member's constituents. Members are attuned to contacts from their constituents, even if those contacts have been orchestrated as part of a lobbying campaign. Members take seriously the letters, postcards, faxes, emails, phone calls, visits, remarks at town meetings, and other contacts they have with constituents. While several individual letters or individual office visits might make a compelling case on some issue, members also take cognizance of the volume of constituent calls and letters as part of their decision-making on an issue, even when a lobbyist's grassroots campaign stimulated an outpouring of constituent mail. The quality of the message, however, matters in communications notable for their volume.

The multiplication in the variety of forms by which constituents can contact members, the inexpensiveness and ease of these communications, and their ubiquitousness make it easy for a constituent to initiate contact with a member of Congress. Computer databases coupled with the different communication forms also make it easy for a lobbyist to conduct a grassroots campaign and to get the right messages to the right members at the right time in the right volume. As members also know, an organization's resources can be put to work for the member or a challenger in a future election. Members, too, use computer databases to target particular constituents. (*See § 3.21, Grassroots Training; and § 3.22, Example of Grassroots Campaign.*)

The increasing population of districts and states and the expectations of constituents for members' presence have also meant that members have turned to additional methods for keeping in touch with constituents, such as *town meetings* and *supermarket Saturdays*. In addition to traditional events such as plant visits, speeches to local organizations, and appearances at events such as fairs and parades, these forums provide another avenue for grassroots activity by lobbyists. A lobbyist can organize citizens to turn out at a member's public events. The lobbyist, or the constituent sharing the lobbyist's perspective, can express views in a diverse public forum, question a member of Congress, and inform fellow constituents at the same time. Similarly, a lobbyist can make and main-

§ 3.21

Grassroots Training

Nearly all associations engage in some type of rallying or training of an association's members to ensure that members of Congress have heard firsthand about the association's legislative concerns and priorities from one or more constituents—the *grassroots*. Members are attentive to constituents. While they cannot possibly satisfy all the competing legislative desires of each constituent or group of constituents, they will usually do everything they can to appear interested and not alienate anyone. Associations, whether located in Washington, DC, a state capital, or another major city, understand this, and attempt to get the "grassroots" to articulate the association's positions to their own members of Congress.

The American Dietetic Association held a "legislative symposium" in 1997, which included training on grassroots action. It is representative of many associations' efforts. The following is an excerpt from one of the training materials handed out at the symposium:

How to Play the Grassroots Game

Do you think of yourself as a political leader? You should! To understand why, first we'll take a look at what political people say about politics.

All Politics Is . . .

All Politics Is Local

The favorite saying of the late House Speaker Thomas P. "Tip" O'Neill (D-MA) was "all politics is local." Because "all politics is local," the voice of the American Dietetic Association will not be heard without **Grassroots Communication**.

Here are some applications of the "all politics is local" principle. **All politics is local** means:

- It isn't an issue in Washington until it's an issue back home.
- Constituents can have more influence over elected officials than party leaders do. Even if there is a Republican or Democratic position on an issue, individual elected officials frequently tell their party leaders, "I have to vote my district."
- A local example of how something works will have more influence than a national statistic.
- Elected officials tend to believe that what is best for their district is in the national interest.
- Elected officials measure communications by how many people the communicator knows locally.
- Elected officials measure communications by how much effort is involved locally.
- The oldest rule in politics is flatter the king; in a democracy the voter is king.

All Politics Is Personal

All politics is personal means that in **Grassroots Communication**:

- The credibility of the messenger determines the credibility of the message.
- A story involving people is more memorable than an argument based on logic.
- Put your personal endorsement behind your message.
- Different people can tell different stories.
- Elected officials sometimes take a position simply because they have been asked.
- Elected officials see every person as a potential voter, contributor, and campaign volunteer.

Continued on page 79

§ 3.21 (continued)

All Politics Is Competitive

Finally, "all politics is competitive." To govern is to choose, and each governmental choice affects some people better than others.

During the health-care reform debate, dozens of organizations involving millions of citizens attempted to make their voices heard.

All politics is competitive means:

- The political process is dominated by people who make an effort to make their voices heard.
- People and groups who have the most to gain or lose by legislation usually make the most effort to influence the process.
- Even a compromise is usually the result of competition.

TheCapitol.Net offers Capitol Hill Day/Washington Fly-In/Legislative Day training (*see <CapitolHillDay.com>*), and the *Pocket Guide to Advocacy on Capitol Hill* (*see <PocketGuideToAdvocacy.com>*).

tain contact with district and state staff, and make general requests for meetings with constituents when a member is home.

In this same vein, a lobbyist can encourage a committee or specific members to conduct field hearings. The lobbyist can provide local witnesses to bolster the members' understanding of a specific perspective on an issue, and turn out an audience for the hearing. A lobbyist may also suggest to her principals the idea of invitations to members for local site visits.

Congress is open to lobbyists in that it is decentralized. Party leaders rely mostly on persuasion to work their will, and they must accommodate the sentiments of individual or small groups of members to put together majorities. In addition to the formal committee structure, there are congressional member organizations (CMOs are groups of members organized around a specific legislative interest), party task forces, leadership task forces, and other entities concerned with policy.

These entities often sponsor events on Capitol Hill, including seminars and unofficial hearings. (*See § 5.120, Informal Groups and Congressional Member Organizations (CMOs).*) There are thus many access points and opportunities where a lobbyist's concerns might be shared and where the lobbyist's information is welcome. In this decentralized environment, where voting majorities can be difficult to assemble, lobbying coalitions can be effective, or even essential, to reaching members, where a coalition works on its own or as an ally of the majority leadership, the minority leadership, or a group of sympathetic members.

Lobbyists should not overlook other opportunities to build relationships, such as the annual charity fund-raisers where a team of lobbyists faces off against a team of members in ice hockey or basketball, or where women members play softball against women journalists.

This decentralization can also mean hard work for lobbyists because committee leaders or party leaders are limited in what they can do to bring or keep their members in line. On key votes, for example, negotiations might proceed with little advance knowledge of what the winning political

§ 3.22

Example of Grassroots Campaign

In the past decade, the Juvenile Diabetes Foundation organized and gave a name to its "grassroots advocacy movement run by the volunteers" of the foundation. It was called the "Promise to Remember Me Campaign." To simplify as much as possible for the grassroots advocates what they were supposed to do in meetings with members of Congress, which included having their photos taken with their members, the foundation provided the following guidance:

JDF Promise to Remember Me Campaign
TALKING POINTS for Congressional Meetings

- Thank the Member for the meeting and for posing for the photograph with you
- Tell your PERSONAL STORY about diabetes and that you are a JDF advocate
- Ask for increased funding for diabetes research
- Ask for a doubling of the National Institutes of Health (NIH) budget

and policy combination might be, or how and when it might be implemented procedurally. In such instances, many members' votes might remain in play until the last moment. A lobbyist has an opportunity to play a role at all stages of the legislative process, whether or not the lobbyist's position accords with majority sentiment.

Congress is open to lobbyists in the equality of its members. Freshman representatives are courted by their leadership for their votes just as much as other members are courted. A representative in the majority party might chair a subcommittee by his second term (or sooner); in the minority party, he might be the ranking member on a subcommittee in that same short time. Multiple committee assignments provide members with additional opportunities to diversify their expertise and influence. Representatives interested in serving in the Senate might attempt Senate election after just a short time in the House. The Senate, because of its rules, has always been a more egalitarian chamber than the House. Today it is even more so, with some freshman senators of the majority party chairing subcommittees in their first year. Members also often have ambitions rising up the leadership ladder in their party in their chamber. A lobbyist, therefore, has the opportunity to build relationships at the beginning of a member's career that can prove useful over time.

Congress is open to lobbyists in that its members and staff are voracious consumers of information. Even if a member begins with a firm opinion on an issue, she is always looking for additional, plausible justifications for that position and new persuasive arguments to raise with colleagues. If a justification is based on a positive or negative impact on the member's constituents, it is a justification the member must acquire. A principal job for any lobbyist is purveying informa-

3

§ 3.23

Meeting Tips for a Lobbyist

The following tips for a lobbyist conducting a meeting with a member of Congress or congressional staffer first appeared in the August 1989 issue of *Association Management*, the monthly periodical of the American Society of Association Executives. The tips remain as timely today as they were when published.

Thou Shalt Lobby

It's an association commandment—so learn how to do it right

By Steve Charton

As simple as they seem, the following 10 guidelines are the keys to successful lobbying. They have served me well for more than 20 years.

1. Never tell a lie.
Your reputation is everything. If you don't know the answer to a question, pledge to get one as soon as possible. You lose your credibility permanently if you lie.

2. Be patient.
Public officials, whether elected or appointed, have many parties vying for their attention. Use your time constructively to work on your presentation while you wait your turn.

3. Be courteous.
Public officials and their employees and representatives are human and expect common courtesy. Plus, they may be more helpful if you treat them with respect.

4. Be brief.
Get in and out of an official's office quickly. Show that you know how valuable his or her time is.

5. Get to the point.
Don't beat around the bush. Keep embellishments to a minimum.

6. K.I.S.S.
Keep it simple, stupid. Don't be too technical, too detailed, too complex, or too oblique. Get to the point, cover the basics, and make sure the official understands your main point. Don't be condescending either.

7. Keep your group small.
An unwieldy group can make everyone uncomfortable, distract from your message, and waste valuable time getting set up.

8. Plan your pitch.
Make sure that a great deal of consideration goes into your positions. Develop, rework, and refine your stance in advance—not in front of the official you want to impress.

9. Practice, practice, practice.
Repeat your presentation over and over until it is a work of art. Nothing is more impressive to a public official than a smooth and professional presentation. Nothing is less impressive than to go in unprepared and stumble through your case. Involve all participants in practice sessions to avoid dissension and duplication among your delegation.

10. Don't forget to close.
Always ask for the official's vote or support.

Steve Charton is executive vice president, Arkansas Telephone Association, Little Rock.

tion—preferably reliable and authoritative information. It may, of course, be biased to support the lobbyist's position, but it must be credible. The right information must also be delivered at the right time in the legislative process—not too early but never too late. (*See Chapter Six, Legislating in Congress: Legislative Process; and Chapter Seven, Legislating in Congress: Budget Process.*) A lobbyist or knowledgeable officials in her client organization might also convey information formally as witnesses at committee hearings. (*See § 3.23, Meeting Tips for a Lobbyist.*)

This voracious need for information includes national and local media and public relations. Along with a grassroots strategy, a full lobbying effort today must include media and public relations strategies and polling. What happens to sway public opinion and convey that opinion to Congress can make a difference. For example, advertising against President Clinton's early health-care initiative (the widely seen "Harry and Louise" ads) was credited for its part in stopping the initiative in Congress. Since public concern over health care was a major issue, opponents of the president's initiative needed to convince constituents that his initiative was not the answer. From the lobbyist's perspective, members and constituents must read and hear about the lobbyist's concerns or perspectives both in Washington and in the home districts or states.

In the last two decades, the intensity and approaches of national lobbying campaigns for and against legislation and nominations has increased. Lobbying campaigns outside of Washington using public relations; media relations; ingenious symbols, ideograms, events, and other devices; rallies; social media and other online campaigns; and grassroots organization have been directed at broad matters of national significance and narrow matters of regional or local interest. More specifically, they have been directed at specific members of Congress who are viewed as persuadable, or at variance with their constituents in their apparent position, or politically vulnerable, or soon facing reelection. These lobbying campaigns, occurring year-round as different issues come to the fore, have been financed by national and state political parties, interest and advocacy groups, and individuals or groups of individuals of all political stripes.

An administration can also do a full-court press on its highest priorities. With complementary media buys and public relations activities by the national political party and well-funded, supportive private groups, an administration can deploy the president, vice president, Cabinet officers, and other officials across the country to speak directly to regional and local media, interested groups such as business or labor organizations, and citizens.

These kinds of campaigns aimed at Congress were used in the last decade:

- 2001 Bush tax cuts.
- Iraq war resolution and subsequent votes on funding for it.
- Two Bush and two Obama appointments to the Supreme Court.
- Bush Social Security proposal.
- Obama proposals on health care, financial institution regulation, and climate change.
- Organized labor's proposed "card check" legislation.
- "Net neutrality."
- Other administration, congressional, and interest-group initiatives.

In each instance, millions of dollars were spent on advertising in states and districts of members who were viewed as persuadable to support or oppose, or as able to be pressured, if enough constituents were persuaded by the media campaign and made their views known to the member. Advertising also opposed alternatives to the majority party's proposal, if a member of Congress or an interest group was promoting an alternative. If votes occurred, hundreds of thousands more dollars were spent to thank or attack members for their votes when interest groups perceived members needed support for a tough vote or could be weakened politically for a tough vote the other way. Other techniques, including rallies, appearances at town hall meetings, social media exchanges, and email communications, also played major roles. Traditional lobbying—like buttonholing members—was part of much larger influence enterprises.

In recent Congresses, another lobbying trend seems to be coming into maturity. Existing groups and new groups that support Democrats politically are focusing on the positions and votes of Democratic members of Congress. These groups seem to be seeking to ensure a political orthodoxy among Democratic members and in legislative outcomes in Congress. For example, CODEPINK, a women's peace organization, established a permanent presence on Capitol Hill and targeted Democratic members and Obama administration officials appearing at congressional hearings. Republican members were pressured by groups on the right to adhere to certain positions, where threats of electoral retribution resonated in policymaking. Groups operating under the Tea Party banner, for example, sought to hold members whose election they supported accountable for specific policy positions, votes, and points of view. Members of both parties straying from a group's perception of the right position or vote on a matter may find themselves the subject of radio and television advertising, harsh questioning at local constituent meetings, insistent visitors in their Washington and home offices, email and letter-writing campaigns, blog attacks, threats of primary challenges, and other forms of pressure. These actions are current and immediate; they are not being saved solely for a member's reelection campaign.

A lobbying organization and the individual lobbyist might step back and assess how it has been conducting its lobbying effort. Has it been win at all costs? Has it been "leave nothing on the table," depriving the loser of any face-saving retreat? Was it "I'm losing so I'm going to take my marbles and go home?" Has there been a long-term strategic gain or a short-term tactical win that will ultimately be viewed as a Pyrrhic victory? Conversely, has there been only a short-term setback in a long-term, strategically sound project? Has impatience overcome judgment? Long-term victories are won by long-term majorities with broad support for a policy in American society.

§ 3.30 Lobbying Laws

With recognition of First Amendment freedoms, Congress has chosen to regulate lobbying in an attempt to reduce and minimize possible corruption. While lobbying laws are regulatory and criminal statutes, they are not intended to interfere with advocacy, but to regulate potentially corrupt or corrupting aspects of lobbying interactions and require disclosures so that the electorate may assess its members' representation in Congress. The following description characterizes aspects of this regulation; it does not offer specific legal or professional advice on compliance with federal law.

Lobbying is regulated principally by the Lobbying Disclosure Act of 1995 (*109 Stat. 691; 2 U.S.C. § 1601 et seq.*), as amended by the Lobbying Disclosure Technical Amendments Act of 1997 (*112 Stat. 38*) and the Honest Leadership and Open Government Act of 2007 (*121 Stat. 735*). Lobbying is also subject to tax, appropriations, labor, and criminal laws, House and Senate rules, and other laws and rules. Potential criminal law violations and punishments increased with passage of the Lobbying Disclosure Act (LDA) and Honest Leadership and Open Government Act (HLOGA), requiring any entity that plans to engage in lobbying activities to be cautious. Individual members, individual House and Senate committees, and the congressional party caucuses might also issue additional guidelines for the staff of that member, committee, or caucus, such as staff's relationship to a family member who is a lobbyist. The LDA requires registration with the clerk of the House and the secretary of the Senate. The LDA requires quarterly and semiannual filings. Some restrictions apply to members of Congress and congressional staff, some to lobbyists, and some to members, staff, and lobbyists.

The text of the LDA, guidance issued pursuant to the act, registration and reporting forms, and other information is available on the web sites of the clerk of the House (*<http://lobbyingdisclosure.house.gov>*) and the secretary of the Senate (*<http://senate.gov>*, then select "Legislation & Records" then "Lobbying Disclosure"). The clerk of the House's Legislative Resource Center (B-106 Cannon HOB; 202-225-5200) maintains the registration and reporting forms. The secretary of the Senate's Office of Public Records (SH-232 Hart Building; 202-224-0758) performs the same function for the Senate.

Campaign finance laws, a small portion of which are examined in Chapter Two, are separate from lobbying laws. However, a provision of the Honest Leadership and Open Government Act imposed a new campaign finance disclosure requirement on lobbyists, which is explained below. Recall also that lobbying laws do not reach many activities such as media relations meant to influence Congress or constituents if they are conducted independently of what lobbying laws define as lobbying contacts, although some entities such as charities or federal contractors may be subject to limits or disclosures under tax or other laws.

Certain representation of foreign entities not covered by the Lobbying Disclosure Act is covered by the Foreign Agents Registration Act (FARA) (*22 U.S.C. § 611 et seq.*). FARA, which requires registration with the Department of Justice, specifies that registrants must file "informational material" generated by the foreign interest and to keep records for inspection (*<http://fara.gov>*). Restrictions applicable to registrants under FARA or to members of Congress and congressional staff in their dealings with registrants under FARA are not discussed here.

Recall that lobbying laws apply to lobbying the executive branch of the federal government as well as the legislative branch, and that the president has also issued guidance on lobbying and the role of lobbyists applicable to the executive branch. Only lobbying of Congress is discussed in this chapter.

§ 3.40 Factors Affecting Application of Laws and Rules

Criteria and Thresholds. The Lobbying Disclosure Act (LDA) establishes criteria and thresholds for registration, reporting, and, tacitly, termination of a registration. Registration, reporting, and termination must be done electronically.

In general, the thresholds require registration for a "lobbying firm" *for each client* from whom the lobbying firm expects *income from lobbying activities* to exceed $3,000 during a quarter. For an entity employing in-house lobbyists, registration generally must occur if *expenses for lobbying activ-*

ities are expected to exceed $11,500 during any three-month period. Information to be disclosed in a registration includes the identification of individual lobbyists and general policy issue areas.

The thresholds are adjusted every four years. The amounts here reflect the January 2009 adjustments.

In addition, for purposes of registration, a lobbyist is defined as an individual who is employed or retained by a client entity for compensation. The services provided include more than one "lobbying contact," and "lobbying activities" constitute 20 percent or more of the individual's services during a three-month period. In general, a lobbying contact is an electronic, written, or oral communication with a member of Congress, a congressional officer, or a congressional staff member. Lobbying activities include lobbying contacts and activities in support of those contacts.

If a lobbyist makes more than one lobbying contact and spends more than 20 percent of his time on lobbying activities, the lobbying firm or the entity employing in-house lobbyists must register if lobbying activities exceed the applicable monetary threshold. A lobbying firm or an entity employing in-house lobbyists must register within forty-five days, as provided in the Lobbying Disclosure Act, with the clerk of the House and the secretary of the Senate. (*See § 3.41, Lobbying Registration Form.*)

Registrants must report quarterly their lobbying, including lobbyist identification, specific issues on which lobbying occurred (not general issues or solely bill numbers), lobbying contacts, and income (for lobbying firms) or spending (for entities with in-house lobbyists) over $5,000. Entities employing in-house lobbyists must also disclose payments to lobbying firms, if any, and portions of dues paid that were used for lobbying, if any. Quarters end on the last day of March, June, September, and December, and reports are due within twenty days of the end of a quarter. Quarterly reporting continues until a registration is terminated, whether or not there is lobbying to report.

If a lobbyist was a "covered official" under the Lobbying Disclosure Act in the previous twenty years (but since enactment), that must be disclosed in a lobby registration or, if the lobbyist is employed subsequent to a registration, in the appropriate quarterly report.

Registrants *and* individual lobbyists must also file a semiannual report (in July and January) on contributions, discussed further below. This form must also be filed until a registration is terminated.

Foreign interests generally must register under FARA, except for foreign commercial or other private interests that meet the registration criteria of the Lobbying Disclosure Act. Those interests do not register under FARA, but must register with the clerk and the secretary under the Lobbying Disclosure Act. The official activities of foreign diplomats are exempt from either registration.

Context. The application of the Lobbying Disclosure Act and other laws regulating lobbying often depends on context in addition to criteria and thresholds. For example, in providing guidance on the Lobbying Disclosure Act, the clerk of the House and the secretary of the Senate use an example of a former congressional chief of staff who leaves congressional employment and enters private law practice. The former chief of staff waits more than a year before contacting her former office (thus honoring post-employment restrictions), and then calls that office to speak to a staff member about the status of legislation affecting the interests of one of her clients. Although the law would normally exempt this kind of communication as an "administrative request," the guidance comments that the identity of the person asking questions and that person's relationship to the office

§ 3.41

Lobbying Registration Form

There are three forms, one for registration (shown below), one for reporting, and one for contributions. All forms must be filed electronically (*see § 3.30*). The Lobbying Registration (LD-1DS) Sample Form can be seen at <*lobbyingdisclosure.house.gov*>.

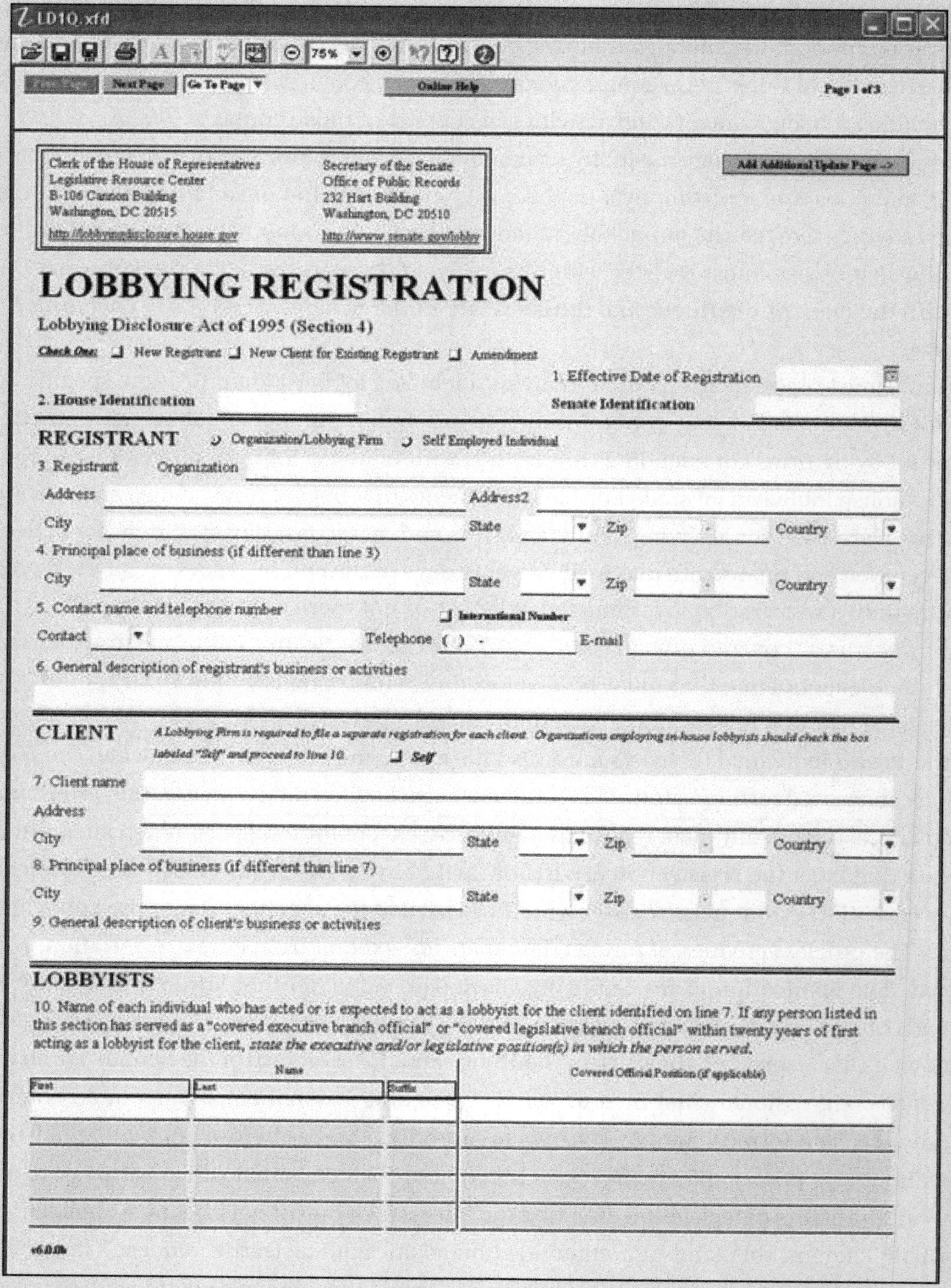

LD10.xfd

First Page | Next Page | Go To Page | Online Help | Page 1 of 3

Clerk of the House of Representatives
Legislative Resource Center
B-106 Cannon Building
Washington, DC 20515
http://lobbyingdisclosure.house.gov

Secretary of the Senate
Office of Public Records
232 Hart Building
Washington, DC 20510
http://www.senate.gov/lobby

Add Additional Update Page ->

LOBBYING REGISTRATION

Lobbying Disclosure Act of 1995 (Section 4)

Check One: ☐ New Registrant ☐ New Client for Existing Registrant ☐ Amendment

1. Effective Date of Registration

2. House Identification Senate Identification

REGISTRANT ○ Organization/Lobbying Firm ○ Self Employed Individual

3. Registrant Organization

Address Address2

City State Zip Country

4. Principal place of business (if different than line 3)

City State Zip Country

5. Contact name and telephone number ☐ International Number

Contact Telephone ( ) - E-mail

6. General description of registrant's business or activities

CLIENT *A Lobbying Firm is required to file a separate registration for each client. Organizations employing in-house lobbyists should check the box labeled "Self" and proceed to line 10.* ☐ *Self*

7. Client name

Address

City State Zip Country

8. Principal place of business (if different than line 7)

City State Zip Country

9. General description of client's business or activities

LOBBYISTS

10. Name of each individual who has acted or is expected to act as a lobbyist for the client identified on line 7. If any person listed in this section has served as a "covered executive branch official" or "covered legislative branch official" within twenty years of first acting as a lobbyist for the client, *state the executive and/or legislative position(s) in which the person served.*

Name			Covered Official Position (if applicable)
First	Last	Suffix	

v6.0.0b

Continued on page 87

§ 3.41 (continued)

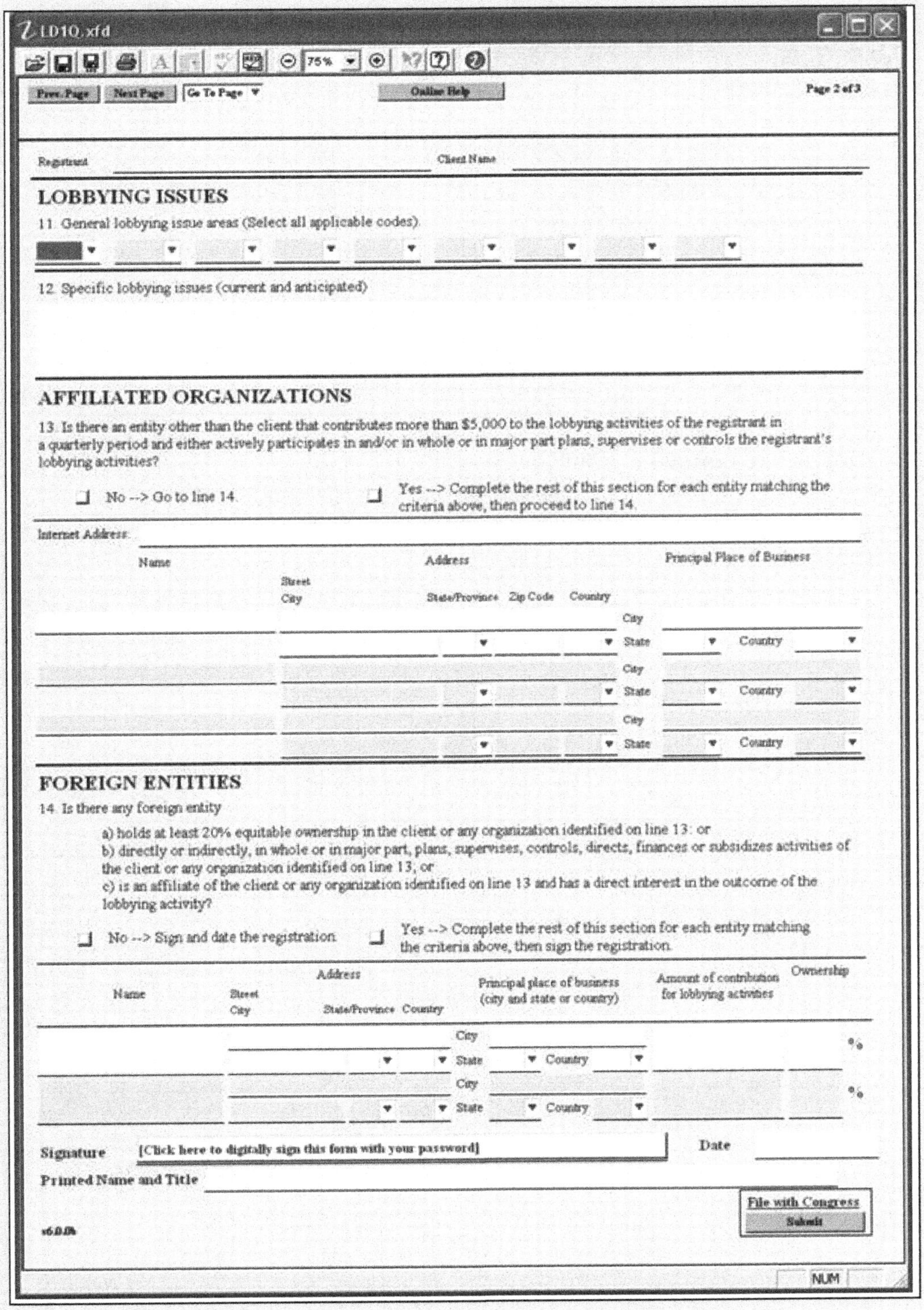

LD10.xfd

75%

Prev. Page | Next Page | Go To Page | Online Help | Page 2 of 3

Registrant ______ Client Name ______

LOBBYING ISSUES

11. General lobbying issue areas (Select all applicable codes).

12. Specific lobbying issues (current and anticipated)

AFFILIATED ORGANIZATIONS

13. Is there an entity other than the client that contributes more than $5,000 to the lobbying activities of the registrant in a quarterly period and either actively participates in and/or in whole or in major part plans, supervises or controls the registrant's lobbying activities?

☐ No --> Go to line 14. ☐ Yes --> Complete the rest of this section for each entity matching the criteria above, then proceed to line 14.

Internet Address:

Name	Address: Street, City, State/Province, Zip Code, Country	Principal Place of Business
		City / State / Country
		City / State / Country
		City / State / Country

FOREIGN ENTITIES

14. Is there any foreign entity

a) holds at least 20% equitable ownership in the client or any organization identified on line 13: or

b) directly or indirectly, in whole or in major part, plans, supervises, controls, directs, finances or subsidizes activities of the client or any organization identified on line 13, or

c) is an affiliate of the client or any organization identified on line 13 and has a direct interest in the outcome of the lobbying activity?

☐ No --> Sign and date the registration. ☐ Yes --> Complete the rest of this section for each entity matching the criteria above, then sign the registration.

Name	Address: Street, City, State/Province, Country	Principal place of business (city and state or country)	Amount of contribution for lobbying activities	Ownership
		City / State / Country		%
		City / State / Country		%

Signature [Click here to digitally sign this form with your password] **Date**

Printed Name and Title

File with Congress | Submit

v6.0.0h

NUM

Continued on page 88

§ 3.41 (continued)

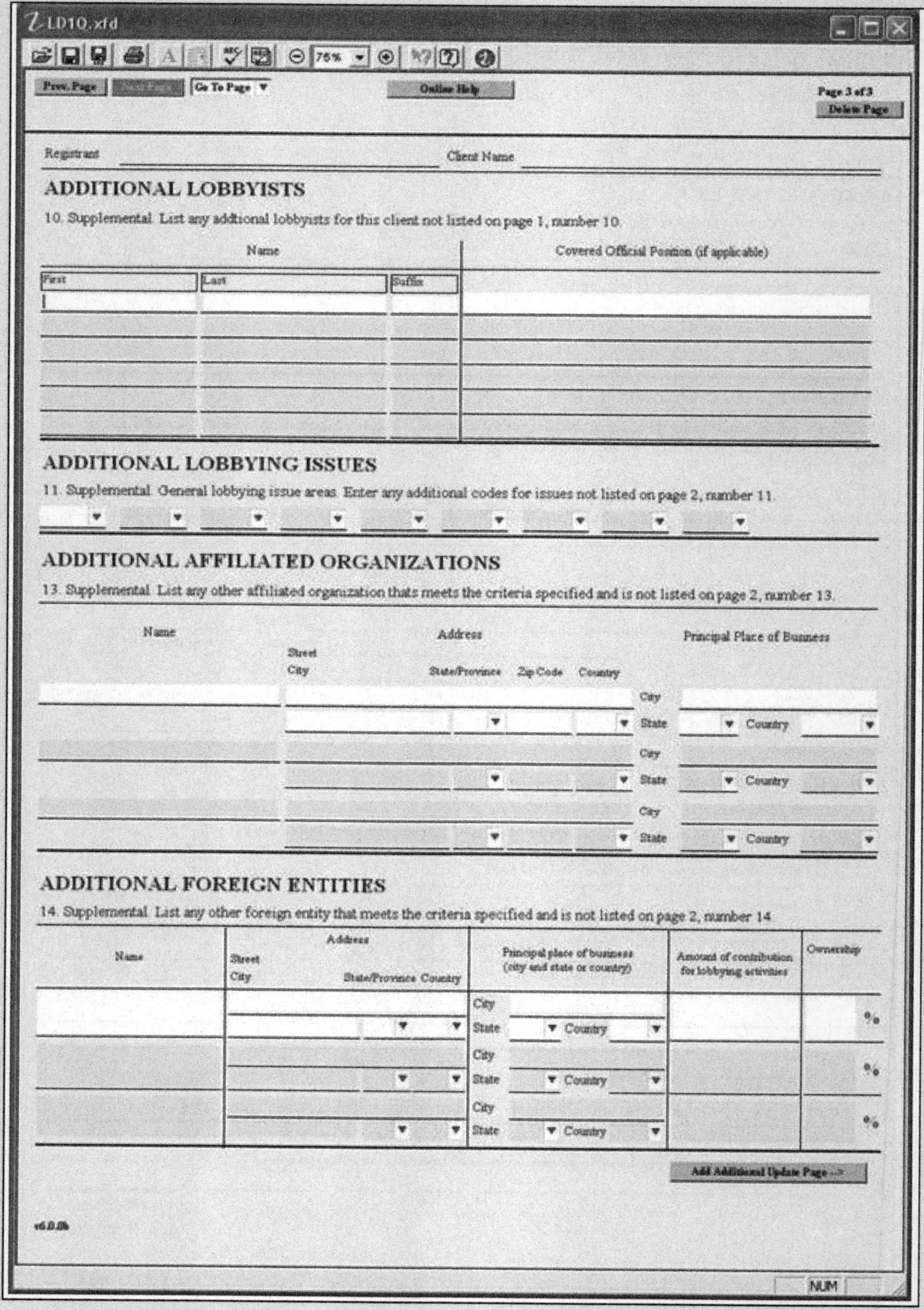

LD1Q.xfd

Prev. Page | Next Page | Go To Page | Online Help | Page 3 of 3 | Delete Page

Registrant ____________ Client Name ____________

ADDITIONAL LOBBYISTS

10. Supplemental. List any additional lobbyists for this client not listed on page 1, number 10.

Name			Covered Official Position (if applicable)
First	Last	Suffix	

ADDITIONAL LOBBYING ISSUES

11. Supplemental. General lobbying issue areas. Enter any additional codes for issues not listed on page 2, number 11.

ADDITIONAL AFFILIATED ORGANIZATIONS

13. Supplemental. List any other affiliated organization thats meets the criteria specified and is not listed on page 2, number 13.

Name	Address: Street, City, State/Province, Zip Code, Country	Principal Place of Business
		City; State; Country
		City; State; Country
		City; State; Country

ADDITIONAL FOREIGN ENTITIES

14. Supplemental. List any other foreign entity that meets the criteria specified and is not listed on page 2, number 14.

Name	Address: Street, City, State/Province, Country	Principal place of business (city and state or country)	Amount of contribution for lobbying activities	Ownership
		City; State; Country		%
		City; State; Country		%
		City; State; Country		%

Add Additional Update Page -->

v6.0.0b

NUM

are important factors. In the example, the guidance states, "Presumably [the law firm's client] will expect the call to have been part of an effort to influence the member, even though only routine matters were raised at that particular time."

Kind of Organization. The kind of organization engaged in lobbying or wishing to engage in lobbying affects the application of various lobbying laws. Organizations exempt from taxation under the Internal Revenue Code may be restricted in their lobbying activities. Different criteria apply to different kinds of tax-exempt organizations. Special rules apply to religious organizations under the Lobbying Disclosure Act, and certain tax-exempt organizations have the option of using IRC definitions of lobbying or definitions under the Lobbying Disclosure Act.

Parent and subsidiary entities or chapters might be considered one entity or separate filing entities. The criteria of the Lobbying Disclosure Act are meant to apply to lobbying that is compensated so that the law reaches professional lobbyists and their activities. Lobbying firms and organizations with in-house lobbyists that meet the criteria and thresholds of the Lobbying Disclosure Act must register and report. Because of the criteria for registering and reporting, a group of homegrown volunteers should still be aware of the law.

Coalitions and Associations. The Lobbying Disclosure Act attempts to identify principals behind coalitions and associations that conduct lobbying activities. While the law generally provides that a coalition or association should be identified as the client of a lobbying firm, it also requires that additional disclosures be made of entities that contribute more than $5,000 toward the coalition's lobbying activities *and* that actively participate in planning and controlling its lobbying activities.

Federal Funds. If an organization receives federal funds, lobbying laws might apply if the organization lobbies or desires to lobby. For the most part, congressionally appropriated funds may not be used for lobbying so that federal officers and employees may not conduct lobbying campaigns. Federal contractors, grantees, borrowers, and parties to cooperative agreements may not use federal funds for lobbying, and certain tax-exempt organizations ("§ 501(c)(4)" organizations) may not lobby if they wish to receive federal grants, loans, or other awards.

Individual Lobbyist. Officials in both Congress and the executive branch are covered by post-employment restrictions once they leave federal service. A former member of the House may not lobby either house of Congress for one year after leaving office; a two-year restriction applies to senators. (Moreover, a former member who is a registered lobbyist or foreign agent is disallowed certain perquisites available to former members, such as access to the Hall of the House.) In general, a highly paid staffer of a House member's office may not lobby his former office for one year after leaving the member's office. Similarly, a highly paid House committee staffer may not lobby his former committee or its members and their staff for one year after leaving the committee staff. A Senate staffer is disqualified from lobbying the Senate for one year after leaving Senate employment. Additional restrictions may apply based on an individual's access during government service to certain information or negotiations. Various restrictions in law and executive orders apply to former executive-branch employees. A lawyer who is engaged in lobbying would also be covered by rules of professional conduct.

Under House and Senate rules, the relationship of an individual to a member of Congress may also affect that related person if she is registered as a lobbyist or is employed by a registered lobbyist. In the House, a member's staff, including, if applicable, the member's committee or leadership staff, may not have a lobbying contact, as defined in the Lobbying Disclosure Act, with the member's spouse.

In the Senate, the same prohibition on a senator's personal, committee, and leadership staff applies not only to a senator's spouse but also to a senator's other immediate family members. In addition, all other senators and their staffs, whether personal, committee, or leadership, may not have a lobbying contact with any senator's spouse. There is an exception to this latter prohibition, however. If a senator's spouse was a registered lobbyist at least one year before the senator's most recent election or at least one year before the senator's marriage to the individual, the latter prohibition does not apply. The prohibition remains in effect against the senator's staff being lobbied by the senator's spouse.

Kind of Activity. Some activities undertaken by certain kinds of people are not covered as lobbying activities, for example, public officials acting in an official capacity and journalists gathering news. Hearings testimony is also exempted, as is a response to a specific request for information from a member of Congress. The Lobbying Registration Act clearly covers "lobbying contacts," but an organization's efforts to get others to contact members of Congress, such as through public relations or the kind of activity that is often called grassroots lobbying, is not alone generally considered a lobbying contact for an organization—unless it is in support of lobbying contacts. As was seen in the example above involving the former congressional chief of staff, an activity not legally characterized as a lobbying activity might be converted to one, based on the attributes of the activity.

Disclosures in Communications. When making an oral communication, a lobbyist, if asked, must disclose her registration and client and, if the client is a foreign entity, identify that fact. If a lobbyist makes a written communication in behalf of a foreign client, the lobbyist must identify the foreign client and her registration.

Similarly, if an individual makes a lobbying contact, that individual may request that the official or employee contacted disclose if she is an official covered by the Lobbying Disclosure Act.

Gifts. Aspects of Congress' *gift rules* are summarized in § 3.60 (*Regulated Activities*), but some aspects of these rules apply in specific ways to lobbyists. Unlike the Lobbying Disclosure Act, the gift rules are not laws but House and Senate rules that are applicable to members and staff. They are also complex. Nonetheless, lobbyists should be knowledgeable of the chambers' gift rules so that they may certify their understanding of these rules and their adherence to them, as explained under Contributions Reporting, below. Some applications of the gift rules affecting lobbyists include the following:

- In general, a gift to a representative or senator or a congressional staff member is not allowed unless it fits into one of the exceptions in the House or Senate gift rule.
- Gifts include items, services, a discount from market value, travel, hospitality, and gestures of friendship, and may even include gifts between family members when one individual is a member of Congress or congressional staff member and the other individual is a lobbyist.
- A registered lobbyist, an individual listed as a lobbyist on a registration or report, or an organization registered and employing a lobbyist may not make a gift to a member of Congress or congressional staff member if the donor "has knowledge that the gift or travel may not be accepted" under House or Senate rules, as applicable.

- Prohibitions are enforceable by civil and criminal penalties.
- In general, a member or congressional staff member (including part-time and temporary staff and consultants) may not accept a gift from a registered lobbyist or an entity employing lobbyists. However, if the gift fits into one of twenty-three specific categories of acceptable gifts in the House, or twenty-four categories in the Senate, meeting each of the criteria for a specific category of gift, a member or congressional staff member may accept the gift, even if the gift is made by a lobbyist. For example, members and staff may accept food or refreshments of a "nominal value" and not part of a meal, or items of "nominal" or "little intrinsic" value such as baseball caps, even if the source of the gift is a lobbyist.
- Hospitality from a lobbyist cannot be considered an exception to the ban on gifts from lobbyists when the lobbyist gives a member of Congress a campaign contribution in the course of the hospitality. The exception applies to events sponsored by political organizations.
- Donations to the legal defense fund of a member of Congress or congressional staff member may not be accepted from a lobbyist.
- A member of Congress or congressional staff member may accept gifts of friendship from a lobbyist, if that person qualifies under criteria defining that relationship, such as the lobbyist paying personally for the gift and the existence of a history of gift exchange. A gift exceeding $250 in value, however, must be approved by the House Ethics Committee or Senate Select Ethics Committee for members and staff of the respective chambers.
- A gift to a family member may be considered a gift to a member or congressional staff member in certain circumstances and thereby subject to the gift rule limitations and exceptions.
- A member of Congress or congressional staff member may not accept a gift of personal hospitality in a lobbyist's home unless all criteria of the exceptions for relatives or personal friendship are met. If the gift of hospitality exceeds $250 in value, it must be approved by the respective ethics committee.
- An entity "maintained or controlled" by a member of Congress or congressional staff member may not receive "anything" from a lobbyist.
- While a charitable donation may be made in lieu of an honorarium, a charitable donation may not be made by a lobbyist upon the designation or recommendation of a member of Congress or congressional staff member.
- An event for members of Congress or congressional staff members, sponsored by or affiliated with an "official congressional organization," may not receive a contribution from a lobbyist.
- Representatives and senators may not participate at an event at a national political convention held in the member's honor if the event is sponsored by a lobbyist or an entity employing lobbyists.

A member or congressional staff member may not solicit a gift and may not accept gifts for personal gain. Reporting requirements might also apply to gifts, such as those applicable to gifts to members and some highly paid congressional staff when filing their annual financial disclosure forms.

A lobbyist must also beware of gifts or campaign contributions that might be construed as having an intent or connection related to an official act by a member or congressional staff member. That could trigger the application of the federal bribery or illegal-gratuities statute. In addition, each lobbying organization, other entities employing lobbyists, and each lobbyist must file a Form LD-203 certifying that the filer has read and understands the House and Senate gift rules and has not knowingly violated them, as explained below under Contributions Reporting.

Gifts of Travel. A gift of travel involving a lobbyist or an agent registered under the Foreign Agents Registration Act—including sponsoring, planning, or organizing travel, or traveling with a member of Congress or congressional staff member—is disallowed in many, if not most, instances.

Travel for official business, such as a subcommittee field hearing, may not be paid for by a private entity. Travel for a member's or congressional staff member's outside business or employment or for certain personal activities unrelated to official duties, and travel based on personal friendship, might be paid for by a private entity. Travel for fund-raising or campaign activities may be paid for by a political organization or by a member's campaign committee. These kinds of travel are examined further in § 3.60, Regulated Activities. In addition, members and congressional staff members may not normally accept local travel, generally defined as travel within thirty-five miles of the Capitol building or within thirty-five miles of a district office.

Travel connected to a member's or staff member's duties as officeholder might be paid for by a private entity, and the principal themes of this allowance related to lobbyists are discussed here. Additional discussion appears in § 3.60, Regulated Activities.

Travel connected to duties may include a "meeting, speaking engagement, fact-finding trip, or similar event," in the words of the House and Senate gift rules. If the events scheduled during travel are "substantially recreational," the travel is not considered to be connected with a member's or staff member's duties. Travel connected to duties is allowed as a reimbursement to the House or Senate under the gift rule.

An entity retaining or employing registered lobbyists, however, may make a gift of travel solely for a one-day event connected to a member's or congressional staff member's duties, including one night's lodging and related meal expenses. (Under very limited circumstances, and determined on a case-by-case basis, a second night's stay may be allowed by the relevant chamber's Ethics Committee.) The sponsoring entity must have a direct relationship with the event and location occasioning the travel; multiple sponsors of travel for an event must each meet the criteria of the gift rule. A lobbyist may not sponsor or pay travel expenses and may not accompany a member or congressional staff member on a trip. A lobbyist may not initiate the proposal for travel or a guest list, but may have de minimis involvement in planning or organizing a trip.

Although it might employ lobbyists, an institution of higher education may sponsor travel connected to a House member's or congressional staff member's duties, and the institution's lobbyists may participate in planning and organizing a trip and may accompany members and staff members on the trip. A comparable exception applies in the Senate to charitable entities, which hold a tax status under section 501(c)(3) of the Internal Revenue Code. A lobbyist's participation in planning such travel, however, must be de minimis, and the lobbyist may not accompany the senator or Senate staff member.

Travel expenses allowed for privately sponsored travel include "reasonable" expenses for transportation, food, and lodging. Entertainment or recreation could be disallowed. A family member may also accompany a member or congressional staff member, and that individual's expenses may also be covered by the private entity sponsoring the travel.

Privately sponsored travel must be approved by the Committee on Ethics for each congressional participant in advance of the travel. The sponsor must provide a "private sponsor travel certification form" to each member and congressional staff member to whom it has offered travel. The form discloses information about the trip and sponsor and certifies various statements, such as that neither a registered lobbyist nor a registered foreign agent is financing any part of the trip.

Each member and congressional staff member must then complete a traveler form and submit it and the sponsor travel certification form, respectively, to the House Ethics Committee or Senate Select Committee on Ethics. On the traveler form, the member or staff member must justify the connection of the trip to his duties. A member must certify for a staff member that the travel is authorized and is conducted in connection with the staff member's official duties. A member or staff member wishing to conduct privately sponsored travel must obtain the committee's permission before the travel commences.

Within fifteen days of completion of a trip (House), or thirty days (Senate), each member and congressional staff member must file with the clerk of the House or the secretary of the Senate, respectively, a post-travel form, disclosing actual expenses and other information about the trip, and attaching the pre-travel documentation. Privately sponsored travel is also likely to meet the threshold for inclusion on the financial disclosure forms that members and many congressional staff must file.

Travel sponsored by the federal government or a state or local government is excepted from the operation of the gift rule. Travel sponsored by foreign governments and international organizations may be excepted under the terms of the Foreign Gifts and Decorations Act or the Mutual Educational and Cultural Exchange Act. Lobbyist and foreign agent involvement in planning or organizing travel by domestic or foreign governments or in accompanying members and congressional staff on such travel is not prohibited.

As already noted, a gift or campaign contribution might be construed as having an intent or connection related to an official act by a member or congressional staff member that could trigger the application of the federal bribery or illegal-gratuities statute. In addition, each lobbying organization, other entities employing lobbyists, and each lobbyist must file a Form LD-203 certifying that the filer has read and understands the House and Senate gift rules and has not knowingly violated them, as explained below under Contributions Reporting.

Contributions Reporting. Whether or not a registered entity or individual lobbyist has made a "contribution," each lobbying organization, each entity employing lobbyists, and each lobbyist must file a contributions report semiannually, by July 30 covering January through June and by January 30 covering July through December. (This report may become a quarterly report during the 112th Congress (2011–2013); a change would be announced on the web sites of the clerk of the House, *<http://clerk.house.gov>* and the secretary of the Senate, among other sources.) This report has a two-fold purpose: to disclose certain contributions and, as indicated in the discussions of gifts, to certify that the filer has read and understood the House and Senate gift rules (House Rule XXV and Senate Rule XXXV) and has not knowingly violated them. Even if a filer has no contributions to disclose, the filer must still complete the contributions report to make the certification concerning the House and Senate gift rules.

The information and contributions to be disclosed are several and varied. Also note that the required reporting by a member of Congress under the federal campaign finance law (*2 U.S.C. § 434*) may preclude the necessity of reporting contributions described here to honor or recognize the member.

- The name of any political action committee (PAC) established or controlled by the filer (an example in the clerk and secretary's guidance on the Lobbying Disclosure Act indicates that service on a PAC's board is a position of "control");
- A contribution of more than $200 in the aggregate during the reporting period to a federal candidate or officeholder, leadership PAC, or political party committee;
- A contribution to an event to honor or recognize a member of Congress or congressional staff member and other information about the event;
- A contribution to an entity named for a member of Congress or congressional staff member or to an entity in recognition of that official and other information about the contribution;
- A contribution to an entity established or controlled by a member of Congress or congressional staff member or to an entity designated by that official, which includes a contribution to an entity designated by an official in lieu of an honorarium; and
- A contribution to a meeting or similar event held by or in the name of a member of Congress or congressional staff member.

A contributions report must also disclose contributions over $200 to presidential library foundations and presidential inaugural committees. A contribution to a presidential transition organization is reportable under the Presidential Transition Act (*3 U.S.C. § 102 note*).

§ 3.50 Congressional Ethics

A member of Congress works in an environment with numerous ethical rules, and with constraints on official, political, and personal activities. These limits exist in laws, regulations, chamber rules, interpretations, and practices. The expectations of members' constituents also contribute to ever-tightening acceptable norms of behavior.

There are a number of places where one can begin research on congressional ethics, including the following:

House

- House Committee on Ethics (until the 112th Congress, the Committee on Standards of Official Conduct), which has a web site of current and historical information, some of which is highlighted in this list, *<http://ethics.house.gov>*.
- *House Ethics Manual*, last published in 2008; individual chapters are accessible from the left navigation bar on the committee web site, *<http://ethics.house.gov>*.
- Committee advisory memoranda, known as "pink sheets."
- House Code of Official Conduct/House Rule XXIII.

- House Rule X, clause 1(q) (Ethics Committee's jurisdiction); Rule X, clause 11(g)(4) (committee's duty to investigate an unauthorized release of intelligence information in the possession of the Permanent Select Committee on Intelligence); Rule XI, clause 3 (functions of the committee); and Rule XXV, clause 5(h) and (i) (committee's duties pertinent to the House "gift rule")—available on the web site of the House Committee on Rules, *<http://rules.house.gov>*.
- Rules of the Ethics Committee.
- Office of Congressional Ethics, established in 2009 to receive from the public allegations of House members', officers', or staff's ethics violations, and, where a review finds merit to an allegation, to refer the matter to the Ethics Committee for disposition, *<http://oce.house.gov>*.
- *Members' Congressional Handbook*, available on the web site of the Committee on House Administration, *<http://cha.house.gov>*.
- *Committee Handbook*, available on the web site of the Committee on House Administration, *<http://cha.house.gov>*.
- *Franking Manual* and related franking information, available on the web site of the Committee on House Administration, *<http://cha.house.gov>*.

Senate

- Senate Select Committee on Ethics, which has a web site of current and historical information, *<http://ethics.senate.gov>*.
- *Senate Ethics Manual* (S.Pub. 108-1), last published in 2003, available on the web site of the Senate Ethics Committee.
- Committee interpretative rulings and other guidance are either listed on the committee's home page or appear in appendices to the *Senate Ethics Manual*.
- Senate Code of Official Conduct, Senate Rules XXXIV–XLIV.
- Senate standing orders creating and assigning duties to the Ethics Committee (*Senate Manual*, §§ 77–80), available from the GPO's Federal Digital System (*<http://fdsys.gov>*, select "Browse Collections" then "Senate Manual").
- The Senate Ethics Committee's rules of procedure.
- *United States Senate Handbook*, updated in October 2010 and available only on the Senate internal web site.
- *Regulations Governing the Use of the Mailing Frank*, available on the Senate Ethics Committee's web site.

House and Senate

- Code of Ethics for U.S. Government Service (H.Con.Res. 175, 85th Cong.; 72 Stat., Part II, B12 (1958)), which appears in an appendix to the *House Ethics Manual*, *<http://ethics.house.gov>*.
- Honest Leadership and Open Government Act of 2007 (P.L. 110-81; 121 Stat. 735 (2007)).
- Ethics in Government Act of 1978 (P.L. 95-521; 92 Stat. 1824 (1978)) and other ethics laws, in *Compilation of Federal Ethics Laws*, prepared by the U.S. Office of Government Ethics, *<www.usoge.gov>*.

- Congressional Management Foundation, *Setting Course: A Congressional Management Guide* (Washington, DC: Congressional Management Foundation, 2010), Chapter 16, Managing Ethics.

The House Ethics Committee attempts to to respond to ethics questions from organizations and individuals outside of the House after serving House members and staff. The committee only accepts a complaint from the public if it is "certified in writing" by a member of the House. The committee may be contacted by telephone, 202-225-7103, or in writing, Committee on Ethics, 1015 Longworth HOB, U.S. House of Representatives, Washington, DC 20515. (*For explanation of the availability of committee advice to the public, see the committee's web site, <http://ethics.house.gov>.*)

The Office of Congressional Ethics (OCE) was created in March 2009 to *receive* complaints from the public about the ethical conduct of members of the House, House officers, and House staff members. It is not a House committee, but an independent, nonpartisan office governed by a board of directors comprising private citizens. Upon the written request of two board members (one of whom is appointed by the Speaker and one by the minority leader), OCE reviews allegations of misconduct by a member, officer, or staff member of the House. If two members make a request for an investigation and the investigation continues through two required phases of review, then four members of the board may refer the matter to the House Ethics Committee with a recommendation for further review or dismissal. If four members fail to support referral for either further review or dismissal, the matter is referred as unresolved to the Ethics Committee. OCE may be contacted though its web site, *<http://oce.house.gov>*, by phone: 202-225-9739, or by mail: PO Box 895, Washington, DC 20515. OCE is located at 425 Third Street SW, Washington, DC.

The Senate Ethics Committee also attempts to respond to ethics questions from organizations and individuals outside of the Senate after serving senators and staff. The committee may accept a complaint from an individual who is not a senator, Senate officer, or Senate staff member. The telephone number is 202-224-2981. The committee is located at SH-220 Hart Building, Washington, DC 20510.

There are many aspects and considerations involved in the application of ethics laws and rules in a particular situation. There are laws that apply to both representatives and senators, yet different chamber rules, interpretations, and practices apply in the House and Senate. Differing rules may apply to members' spouses, children, and staff. Therefore, it is prudent to get a professional opinion on a specific activity before it is undertaken. A government affairs professional might have every good intention in offering a service or courtesy to a member of Congress. However, she may inadvertently be running afoul of a well-established ethics norm.

Members are not exempt from civil or criminal liability. They are subject to prosecution for violations of federal, state, and local criminal law. A severe sentence was handed down to Representative William Jefferson following his federal conviction in 2009 on eleven counts involving conspiracy to solicit bribes, solicitation of bribes, depriving citizens of honest services, money laundering, and racketeering. (Jefferson was found not guilty on five other counts, including additional honest services violations and violation of the Foreign Corrupt Practices Act.) Jefferson was sentenced to thirteen years in prison and ordered to forfeit over $470,000 in proceeds from his illegal activities involving business ventures in Africa. (Jefferson remained free pending appeal; his appeal was based in part on a dispute by defense counsel over what constituted an official act as opposed to private business activities by a member of Congress.) The Democratic Caucus removed Jefferson from his seat on the Ways and Means Committee in the course of the Justice Department's investigation, a year in advance of his indictment, and Jefferson resigned from the Small Business Committee after his indictment. Jefferson was defeated for reelection prior to his trial and conviction.

Representative Randy "Duke" Cunningham pleaded guilty in U.S. district court in 2005 to bribery, mail fraud, wire fraud, and tax evasion. He resigned his seat and was subsequently sentenced to eight years and four months in jail and ordered to pay over $1.5 million in taxes, penalties, and interest to the U.S. Treasury.

Representative Bob Ney pleaded guilty to making false statements and conspiracy related to gifts from lobbyist Jack Abramoff, and was sentenced to thirty months in prison.

Representative Vito Fossella of New York was sentenced by a Virginia court to five days in jail and fined for driving while intoxicated in Virginia. Fossella was not a candidate for reelection.

Representative Patrick Kennedy was sentenced by a District of Columbia court after pleading guilty to driving under the influence of drugs. Kennedy was placed on twelve months of probation, and required to complete fifty hours of community service, submit to random urine screenings, and to pay fines of $350. A ten-day jail sentence and additional fines were suspended pending successful completion of the plea agreement.

Members who become the subject of a federal investigation can lose privileges in Congress, such as Representative Jefferson did, but also be punished at the polls. In 2008, Jefferson managed to win the Democratic primary runoff, but was defeated in his overwhelmingly Democratic district by Republican Anh "Joseph" Cao, as presidential candidate Barack Obama took 72 percent of the vote in the district.

Another member who lost privileges in Congress and was subsequently punished at the polls was Representative Alan Mollohan. Initially, Mollohan was accused of extensive improper reporting on his financial disclosure forms. He amended the forms, and stepped down as the ranking Democrat on the House Standards of Official Conduct Committee. About the same time, Mollohan was accused as an Appropriations Committee member of steering earmarks to nonprofits with which he had relationships. When Mollohan was later named chair of the appropriations subcommittee that oversaw the Justice Department, he recused himself from deliberations involving funding for the Federal Bureau of Investigation (FBI) and other units of the Justice Department.

Mollohan was the subject of a four-year Justice Department inquiry into his relationships with the nonprofits and private entities. Nonprofit officials, some of whom were also co-investors with Mollohan in profitable private endeavors, included friends, former staff, and family, and were also major contributors to Mollohan's campaigns. While the U.S. attorney for the District of Columbia ultimately announced that the investigation was terminated without filing charges, the allegations became an issue in the Democratic primary in 2010, and Mollohan lost the primary due in part to the resonance of the ethics allegations.

Representative John Doolittle was caught up in the scandal surrounding former lobbyist Jack Abramoff, who faced multiple prosecutions related to his influence-peddling and other schemes. Doolittle's wife's home-based business benefited from its relationship with Abramoff, but apparently performed no work for payments received from Abramoff. After an FBI search of the Doolittles' home, Doolittle stepped down from his seat on the Appropriations Committee and from his position in the Republican leadership. After protestations against the federal investigation, he chose not to run for reelection.

A member's legal troubles might first come to light in another investigation, in spending for legal representation, or in the receipt of subpoena from a grand jury. All three were present in what became the downfall of Representative Bob Ney. The Senate Select Committee on Indian Affairs conducted an investigation into tribal lobbying, with one of its hearings exposing Ney's congressional activities in support of an Indian tribe client of Jack Abramoff. Ney began accumulating large legal fees, which he paid from his campaign fund, which were reported to the Federal Election Commission. He later set up a legal defense fund, with the approval of the House Standards of Official Conduct Committee. Around the same time, Ney received a subpoena from the grand jury investigating Abramoff's activities. Under House Rule XVIII, a member, officer, or staff member must promptly notify the Speaker in writing upon the receipt of a subpoena, and the Speaker must promptly inform the House.

Ney was implicated in plea agreements in the Abramoff scandal, and was forced to relinquish the chairmanship of the House Administration Committee after Abramoff's plea agreement. While separate incidents involving an exchange of favors for gambling trips to London led to a plea agreement, the case against Ney based on those trips allowed prosecutors to press for an agreement covering the Abramoff relationship.

Ney pleaded guilty to a conspiracy charge covering a number of offenses and a charge of making false statements to the House, which included his failure to disclose gifts on his financial disclosure forms and falsifying his travel reports. Ney admitted to soliciting and accepting gifts in exchange for the performance of official congressional acts. He was sentenced to thirty months in prison and directed to receive treatment for alcohol abuse, fined $6,000, placed under supervised release for two years for each count, required to perform one hundred hours of community service during each two years of parole, and required to participate in alcohol treatment and submit to alcohol and drug tests during parole. After his plea, at the time of the 2006 election, Ney resigned from Congress; he would have been barred from his subcommittee chairmanship on the Financial Services Committee and from participation in any committee deliberations had he chosen to serve the balance of his term.

Congressional staff can also be caught in criminal investigations. A staff member for former Representative Curt Weldon, for example, failed to report his wife's income on his financial disclosure form. She was employed by a nonprofit entity on whose board Weldon served. The staff member pleaded guilty to conspiracy to commit wire fraud in attempting to obtain federal funds for the entity.

A number of congressional staff members were caught up in the Abramoff scandal. For example, a staff member of the House Transportation and Infrastructure Committee pleaded guilty to conspiracy to commit honest services wire fraud, and was sentenced to prison, probation, community service, and a fine. In exchange for gifts, he had used his position to aid Abramoff. A chief of staff to former Representative Ernest Istook pleaded guilty to the same charge, based on similar allegations, and was sentenced to four months in a halfway house and five years' probation.

An aide to former Senator Christopher Bond pleaded guilty to making false statements on his tax return related to illegal gifts he received. Staff members have also been prosecuted for defrauding the House or Senate in obtaining various forms of payments.

Congressional corruption cases and ethics violations do not often go to trial in federal court or to formal hearing in the congressional ethics committees. Among the reasons for this infrequent occurrence are that bribery (the issue if not the allegation underlying many public corruption cases) is difficult to demonstrate, evidentiary support for a trial is weak, plea bargaining might conclude an investigation, the member resigns or does not seek reelection, or the member is defeated in a primary or general election. The corruption case against Senator Ted Stevens added a new reason why a trial might not occur: prosecutorial misconduct led a federal judge to throw out Stevens' conviction.

Stevens was indicted on seven counts for an eight-year period of accepting gifts from an oil pipeline services and construction firm and its chief executive, for not disclosing the gifts, and for taking actions as a member of Congress requested by the firm's chief executive. The first count stated that Stevens concealed the receipt of hundreds of thousands of dollars of things of value, which were listed in the indictment, by failing to report these as gifts on his financial disclosure forms. The first count also listed the actions Stevens took as requested by the firm's chief executive. The other six counts pertained to each year's financial disclosure forms, 2001–2006. He was not charged with performing official congressional acts for the firm or its chief executive. After his indictment, Stevens stepped down as ranking minority member of the Senate Commerce, Science, and Transportation Committee and of the Defense Subcommittee of the Appropriations Committee. He also requested a jury trial be rapidly scheduled so that the case might conclude before the 2008 general election, in which he would be a candidate for reelection.

Stevens pleaded not guilty, indicating before the trial and in his testimony at trial that he believed his financial disclosure forms were accurate. Stevens' wife also testified, explaining the renovation of the Stevens' Alaska home and her payment for renovation services. Whether renovation projects were gifts from the oil pipeline services firm was a principal issue in the trial. Stevens was convicted of making false statements just a week before the election, and lost the election to Democrat Mark Begich by little more than one percentage point.

Before, during, and after the trial, Stevens' attorneys sought dismissal of the case based on prosecutorial misconduct related to evidence. The U.S. district judge throughout the trial was forced to deal with the prosecution's failure to provide the defense with exculpatory evidence and with the prosecution's handling of evidence. After the trial, an FBI agent who participated in the Stevens investigation alleged misconduct by others involved in the case. In addition, in preparation for post-trial motions, a new team of Justice Department lawyers uncovered additional evidence that should have been provided to the defense. Attorney General Eric Holder then asked the judge to dismiss the case with prejudice (meaning a new trial could not be sought), "in consideration of the totality of the circumstances." The judge overturned the conviction and, in addition, ordered a criminal investigation of the prosecutors' conduct.

Conviction of a crime could result in an additional penalty for a member of Congress, in addition to jail time, fines, and other forms of punishment. If a member of Congress is convicted of certain crimes, he is deprived of creditable service under federal retirement systems, the consequence being that the member loses his federal pension benefits. The member could, however, receive back his own retirement plan contributions. The crimes include but are not limited to bribery, illegal gratuities, honest services fraud, obstruction of justice, and perjury. Members of Congress, like most federal officials, lose their pension benefits if convicted of the crimes of treason, espionage, and related national security criminal laws.

In addition, members are subject to disciplinary procedures in their respective chambers. The Constitution states (*art. I, sec. 5, cl. 2*): "Each House may . . . punish its Members for disorderly Behaviour, and, with the Concurrence of two thirds, expel a Member." Each chamber has disciplined members for violations of law and congressional rules, including ethics rules. Each has also disciplined members for actions that are not explicitly disallowed in law or rules, but that bring discredit or disrepute on the House or Senate. However, the jurisdiction of the House and Senate is over sitting members, not former members. The most serious disciplinary action that a chamber may take is expulsion, which, as the Constitution provides, requires a two-thirds vote. Each chamber has a variety of other responses to "disorderly Behaviour," including censure, reprimand, and lesser disciplinary actions, which the chambers and their ethics committees tend to shape and name to suit the offense and the response that is desired to be made to it.

In the 107th Congress (2001–2003), the House expelled Rep. James Traficant, D-OH, following his criminal conviction for conspiracy to violate the federal bribery statute, receiving an illegal gratuity in violation of the federal bribery statute, violating the federal obstruction of justice statute, conspiracy to defraud the United States, and filing a false tax return. He was sentenced to seven years in prison. (*See <http:ethics.house.gov> and search for Traficant.*) The House Standards of Official Conduct Committee, as it was then named, conducted an investigation and reported a resolution to expel Traficant, which the House agreed to.

House

Since the Traficant expulsion in 2002, a number of House members have been the subject of allegations or investigations. Allegations sometimes received no official House attention, but served as an embarrassment to one or more members. The allegations may have not been a violation of a rule or law, or may have lacked probative value or have been untrue.

Some allegations might have been considered by the Ethics Committee, the Office of Congressional Ethics, or both. They may have been dismissed, or they may have resulted in the lightest of rebukes. The Ethics Committee might also have offered guidance to all members as a consequence of an allegation against one or more members. Allegations against some members resulted in their punishment by the Ethics Committee or the House.

Examples of various outcomes from recent Congresses are listed here, with the Standards of Official Conduct Committee referred to consistently as the Ethics Committee:

- The most severe punishment since the Traficant case was meted out to Representative Charles Rangel. In the 111th Congress (2009–2011), the House approved a resolution of censure of Rangel, reported by the Ethics Committee. A censure resolution requires the member to go to the well of the House, where the presiding officer, normally the Speaker, reads aloud the resolution of censure. Rangel submitted to this process, and was also required to pay unpaid taxes to appropriate tax authorities. Following Rangel's initial referral of his own case to the Ethics Committee after adverse publicity about his conduct, the committee conducted a more than two-year investigation, but its subsequent trial was short-circuited when Rangel asked for more time after the investigation to prepare for trial, having recently severed his relationship with his counsel. The committee denied his request, convicted him of eleven counts of ethics and House rules violations, and recommended the House censure him for his violations. Six counts involved Rangel's fund-raising for a center at the City College of New York named in his honor: principally, he used congressional resources for this private activity, and solicited and received donations from entities with business before Congress. The other transgressions involved inaccurate financial disclosure forms, violations of the Code of Ethics for U.S. Government Service for failing to observe various federal, state, and local laws, and violation of the House Code of Conduct in his conduct. Rangel's argument that committee counsel did not find evidence of corruption or personal gain was unpersuasive in committee or on the floor. During the course of the investigation, Republicans on several occasions brought resolutions to the floor to establish immediate consequences for Rangel's ethical problems, but the Democratic majority deflected these challenges procedurally. Rangel, however, eventually lost his chairmanship over an unrelated ethics violation, and the Democratic Caucus in the 112th Congress reelected Rangel to the committee but denied him the ranking minority member position under the Republican majority.

- While the House in the 109th Congress (2005–2007) lost jurisdiction over Representative Mark Foley when he resigned after his sexually explicit emails with congressional pages came to light, the House nonetheless referred to the Ethics Committee a resolution for an investigation of the scandal. The committee chose to investigate the conduct of members, officers, and staff for potential violations of the Code of Conduct and other applicable rules and standards. The committee did not find violations by the individuals with some knowledge of the Foley matter, but stated in its report: "[A] pattern of conduct was exhibited among many individuals to remain willfully ignorant of the potential consequences of former Representative Foley's conduct with respect to House pages." The committee also stated that its report was a reminder to members, officers, and staff that "they are obligated to pursue specific and non-specific allegations of improper interactions between a Member or House employee and a participant in the House Page Program. . . ." The committee seemed to have established a standard to be followed in the future.
- Following its review, the Office of Congressional Ethics forwarded to the Ethics Committee findings that Representative Sam Graves' 2004 invitation to a Small Business Committee hearing on renewable fuels issued to a businessman created the appearance of a conflict of interest. Representative Graves' wife and the individual were both investors in two renewable fuels companies. The Ethics Committee found no House rule prohibited the appearance of a conflict of interest in an invitation to a hearing.
- The Ethics Committee concluded an investigation into travel to business conferences during 2007 and 2008 by six members, with the committee finding in 2010 that the travel was provided in violation of the House gift rule. The travel was paid for by private entities

employing lobbyists and lasted more than one day. Five members had received committee clearance for the travel, as required by the gift rule, but obtained their clearance based on false information provided to them by travel organizers. These members were exonerated of wrongdoing since they did not knowingly accept the travel in violation of the gift rule, but they were still required by the committee to pay the U.S. Treasury for the costs of their travel. A sixth member, Representative Charles Rangel, however, was required to pay the costs of his travel and, in addition, was publicly admonished by the committee since his staff knew that the travel was being paid for in violation of the gift rule. Rangel also lost his chairmanship of the Ways and Means Committee. The committee also referred to the Department of Justice its findings that the conference organizers supplied false information, and the department has charged one individual with making false statements to the federal government.

- Representative Curt Weldon was directed by the Ethics Committee to repay $23,000 to sponsors of a trip taken in 2003 by the representative and a number of his family members. The committee found the trip to be officially connected and therefore subject to the House gift rule, disallowing payment for expenses for most family members.
- Representative Tom Feeney was ordered by the Ethics Committee to pay over $5,600 to the U.S. Treasury to cover the costs of a 2003 trip that was primarily recreational in nature and possibly paid for by an entity other than that reported, in violation of the House gift rule.
- In 2006 the Ethics Committee published conditions for the management of Representative John Conyers' office following an investigation of news accounts of demands made on his staff for campaign-related work and personal services, potentially in violation of several standards of behavior. Conyers agreed to conditions of office management not required of members, including written policy statements on staff duties and a prohibition on the voluntary performance of campaign-related work.
- Representative Laura Richardson was cleared by the Ethics Committee in 2010 of violations of the House gift rule and of requirements related to her financial disclosure form related to a home she owned in Sacramento, California. The committee found that she had not received favored treatment from a mortgage lender and that, without Richardson's knowledge, a mortgage broker had created false documents to include in a mortgage application.
- Eight representatives—members of both parties—were the subject of a June 2010 investigation by the Office of Congressional Ethics. The probe resulted from campaign fund-raisers held around the time the House was considering financial services reform legislation, and examined an appearance of impropriety, because of the proximity in time, that there was special access or influence or a linkage between campaign donations and official activity. The OCE recommended no further action in five of the cases, but referred three cases to the Ethics Committee for further action. While the Ethics Committee may be sensitive to fund-raising that occurs around the same time as legislative action, it chose in these cases to endorse the recommendations of its staff that there was no appearance of impropriety and that no rules or laws were broken. The staff recommendations observed

that fund-raising was conducted by professional fund-raisers who did not have contact with the members or their legislative staffs; the timing of the fund-raisers and House action were coincidental; the members had well- and long-established positions on the legislation; the members' official acts were based on the members' legislative concerns and not requests of donors; and legislation was not discussed during members' brief appearances at the fund-raisers.

3

Senate

In the 107th Congress (2001–2003), the Senate Ethics Committee issued a "letter of admonition" (*<http://ethics.senate.gov/downloads/pdffiles/torricelli.pdf>*) to Sen. Robert Torricelli, D-NJ, for "poor judgment," violation of the Senate gift rule, and, consequently, violation of financial disclosure requirements, based on a relationship between the senator and an individual, David Chang, whom the committee stated "was attempting to ingratiate himself, in part through a pattern of attempts to provide you (Sen. Torricelli) and those around you with gifts over a period of several years when you and your Senate office were taking official action of benefit to Mr. Chang. . . ." Torricelli, at the time the committee released the letter, was in the midst of a reelection campaign. He subsequently ended his campaign, and was replaced on the ballot.

In the 111th Congress (2009–2011), the six members of the Ethics Committee signed a "public letter of qualified admonition" to Senator Roland Burris, D-IL, severely criticizing his conduct in seeking an appointment to the Senate and in his conduct in investigations and public statements involving his appointment after his seating in the Senate. Burris was appointed to fill the vacancy resulting from Senator Barack Obama's resignation. The committee noted that, while some of Burris' actions occurred before his seating, they were "inextricably linked" to his appointment and were therefore within the committee's jurisdiction. It specifically condemned Burris' omissions from his affidavit and testimony to the gubernatorial impeachment committee of the Illinois House of Representatives; contradictory statements lacking in candor, including to the Ethics Committee, regarding contacts with the Illinois governor's associates on an appointment to the Senate; and a strong and inappropriate implication to the brother of Illinois Governor Rod Blagojevich, not specifically a quid pro quo, to raise campaign funds for the governor in exchange for appointment to the Senate. The committee found that Burris "should have known" that he provided "incorrect, inconsistent, misleading, and incomplete information" to the Senate, the public, and to investigatory authorities. While his conduct was not criminally actionable, the committee stated that its legal authority extended to improper conduct reflecting on the Senate.

In addition to the Torricelli and Burris admonitions, the Senate Select Committee on Ethics in recent years took other actions on other alleged ethical transgressions. These actions have included:

- While both the Justice Department and the Federal Election Commission ended their investigations without further action their investigations into ethics allegations against Senator John Ensign, the Senate Ethics Committee appointed a special counsel in early 2011 to conduct its own inquiry into possible violations of Senate ethics rules and federal law. Ensign had admitted to an affair with a campaign worker who was also the wife of one of his top congressional aides. Ensign was alleged to in remorse have sought post-employment lobbying work for his aide and to have provided assistance to the aide's clients in governmental matters, a possible violation of the post-employment restrictions on former members and highly paid congressional staff. Ensign's parents also apparently made a $96,000 gift to the campaign worker with whom Ensign had the affair, her husband, and their two children, a possible violation of campaign finance laws. The Ethics Committee investigation could pursue its own course based not only on these laws but also on other laws and Senate ethics rules. Ensign stepped down from his leadership position as chair of the Senate Republican Policy Committee after acknowledging the affair and, in early 2011, announced that he would not be a candidate for reelection in 2012. A few months later, he resigned from the Senate. While the Ethics Committee then lost jurisdiction over Ensign, it still issued a damning report of its investigation into his conduct. The findings included that Ensign conspired to violate and abetted the violation of his aide's post-employment contact ban, that Ensign and his parents made false and misleading statements to the Federal Election Commission, that a portion of his parents' gift to the Ensigns constituted an illegal campaign contribution, and that he despoiled relevant documents and engaged in potential obstruction of justice, among other findings. The Ethics Committee voted unanimously to release the report and to refer findings related to violations of federal law to the Justice Department and Federal Election Commission. The chair and vice chair claimed time on the Senate floor to explain the committee's decision-making and its acceptance of the special counsel's investigation. Ensign then remained in legal jeopardy. Ensign's former Senate aide had already been indicted for lobbying Ensign in violation of the post-employment restrictions in federal lobbying law.

- A different legal matter ensnared Senator Larry Craig. In 2007, he was arrested in a Minneapolis-St. Paul International Airport men's restroom, accused of soliciting sex in a police sting operation. Craig pleaded guilty to a misdemeanor charge of disorderly conduct, but, once the guilty plea and incident that occasioned it became known, Craig unsuccessfully sought to withdraw his plea. His sentence called for payment of $575 and suspension of a jail term of 10 days and another $500 fine conditioned on his not committing a similar offense in the next year. Craig stepped down from his ranking minority member position on the Veterans' Affairs Committee and on two subcommittees, one on the Appropriations Committee and one on the Energy and Natural Resources Committee. He announced that he would not run for reelection. The Ethics Committee conducted its own investigation, ultimately issuing a public letter of admonition in 2008. The committee's letter admonished Craig for attempting to withdraw his plea when guilty, in violation of the Code of Ethics for Government Service, and for using campaign funds for legal expenses without the committee's approval.
- Senator David Vitter avoided both criminal prosecution and an ethics investigation related to allegations that he solicited for prostitution. The Ethics Committee in a letter to Vitter in 2008 dismissed a complaint that it received concerning Vitter's potential violation of Senate rules. The complaint was dismissed without prejudice, meaning the committee could open an investigation at a later time. The committee noted that the alleged conduct occurred

before Vitter's Senate candidacy and service; that he had not been criminally charged; and that his conduct had not involved improper use of his office or status. The committee did not directly rebuke Vitter, but stated that, were the alleged conduct of solicitation for prostitution proven to be true, committee members would find the conduct "reprehensible." While Vitter was subsequently reelected, the episode was embarrassing, leading him to publicly confess to "sin," and jeopardized what political observers considered a likely safe reelection bid.

- Senators Christopher Dodd and Kent Conrad received mortgages through a mortgage company's V.I.P. program, which a public interest group alleged might constitute a violation of the gift rule. The Ethics Committee dismissed the complaint in 2009, finding the senators did not "knowingly" accept a gift as required by the prohibition in the gift rule, but it criticized the senators' judgment. The committee commented in its letters to the senators that they should have been vigilant in determining whether they were being extended preferential treatment, based on warning signs such as notice to them that their loans were being considered through the lender's V.I.P. program. Dodd's circumstances were of particular public interest since he served as chair of the Senate's Banking, Housing, and Urban Affairs Committee.

3

§ 3.60 Regulated Activities

Ethics training has increased in recent years, and is now required for new staff. In the House and the Senate, any new staff member must receive ethics training within sixty days of an individual's hiring. Ethics training has also been given to new representatives and senators and to staff who were already employed when House and Senate rules were changed in 2007.

What follows is a description of some of the types of activities regulated by congressional ethics laws, rules, interpretations, and practices. Each activity is accompanied by a characterization of the norm regulating the activity, but these characterizations are neither exhaustive nor statements or interpretations of specific laws or rules. (*See also §§ 4.10–4.50 in Chapter Four, Supporting Congress: Allowances and Staff.*)

This list also does not necessarily describe the norms applicable to party conferences and caucuses, congressional staff, family members, the vice president in his role as president of the Senate, or others whose activities might be covered by congressional ethics norms. In general, however, laws and rules applicable to members are often applicable to their staffs as well.

Office Expenses. Members may not use their official allowances or federal property for political purposes, and campaign contributions may not be used to support official activities or to defray official expenses. In general, neither money nor in-kind contributions may be accepted to support official activities, but there are exceptions to this principle, such as the loan or display of a home-state product or artifact.

Campaign Activities. A congressional staffer might engage in limited forms of political work on her own time, but a staffer engaging only nominally in official duties and performing political work might trigger the operation of various antifraud statutes against a member. Members are also proscribed under law from a number of campaign-related activities, such as promising assistance in obtaining federal employment in exchange for a political contribution and, in general, soliciting or receiving political contributions in a federal building.

Gifts. A gift may not be accepted unless it falls into one of twenty-three exceptions in the House or twenty-four exceptions in the Senate. A member or staff member may not accept a gift from a lobbyist, except as explained above (*§ 3.30, Lobbying Laws*). The principal exceptions allowing a gift to be accepted are as follows:

- The gift must have a de minimis value, so that a gift of under $50 value from one source may be accepted, and a total of not more than $100 in gifts may be accepted from a single source in a year. Items with a value of under $10 do not count toward the $100 limit. A lobbyist may not take advantage of this rule unless she qualifies under another exception, such as being a family member.
- Family gifts are allowed.
- Gifts from friends are also allowed, but subject to conditions and criteria to prevent circumvention of the gift rule. A gift may be accepted when it is given on the basis of friendship and not because of the position of the recipient as a member of Congress, officer of the House or Senate, or congressional employee. In addition, there must be a history of gift exchange, the gift must be paid for by the individual giving the gift, and gifts were not given to other members of Congress, officers, or employees. Acceptance of a gift with a value of more than $250 must be approved by the respective chamber's Ethics Committee.
- A gift of a meal must fall under one of the exceptions, such as de minimis value or provision by a family member.
- A gift of personal hospitality is allowed where the hospitality is not provided by a lobbyist or foreign agent or is paid for by the host.
- A member, officer, or staff member may attend a so-called widely attended event such as a convention or exhibition as a guest when he will participate in the event or the event is appropriate to the performance of his duties, regardless of a lobbying connection to the sponsor of the event.
- Similarly, food and refreshments offered other than as part of meal may be considered to be of nominal value, allowing an exception to the gift rule for receptions, even if the sponsor is a lobbyist or employs lobbyists.

Other exceptions include, but are not limited to, inheritances, political contributions, and home-state products for display or, if of little individual value, for distribution.

Solicitation or acceptance of a gift related to an official act can trigger the federal bribery or illegal-gratuity statute, and solicitation of a gift is not allowed under any circumstances.

Travel. As a general rule, travel purposes cannot be mixed and sources of payment for travel may not be mixed. For example, travel for an official purpose, such as a field hearing, may not be combined with travel for a political fund-raiser. Travel paid for by the House or Senate may not include travel expenses paid for by a private entity, although it is possible that an event, such as a widely attended event, might coincide with official travel and that members could therefore attend the event where the sponsor waived the admission fee.

A gift of travel must be related to a member's or staff member's official duties. If a gift of such travel has been proposed, then a representative or House employee may accept travel lasting for up to four days in the continental United States or for up to seven days for travel to Alaska, Hawaii, the territories, or international travel. A senator or Senate employee may accept travel for up to three days for domestic travel and for up to seven days for international travel. Since the travel is linked to a member's or staff member's official duties, it has been interpreted to be a reimbursement to the House or Senate.

As explained above (*§ 3.30, Lobbying Laws*), a lobbyist or organization employing lobbyists may neither pay for nor participate in a gift of travel, unless the organization is an institution of higher education (House) or a section 503(c)(3) tax-exempt organization under the Internal Revenue Code (Senate). As also explained, there is an exception for one-day travel for an organization that employs lobbyists.

3

Expenses allowed are those reasonable to the accomplishment of the purpose of the travel. Recreational expenses are not allowed, although it is possible that such an expense might qualify under the de minimis rule. Entertainment expenses are not allowed if the entertainment is not available to all attendees as an integral part of the event that occasioned the travel, although, again, such an expense might qualify under the de minimis rule. One relative may accompany the member or staff member on official travel, with expenses paid by the sponsor.

Privately funded travel of any type must be approved in advance by the respective chamber's Ethics Committee. The member or staff member must submit, thirty days in advance, a set of documents: a copy of the invitation (in the Senate), a form completed by the sponsor of the travel certifying adherence to specified aspects of the gift rule, and, for staff, an authorization form. The respective committee must give its approval before travel begins. Once the travel is completed, the member or staff member must file within fifteen days with the clerk of the House, or thirty days with the secretary of the Senate, a disclosure form of expenses and of the meetings and events attended.

There are other kinds of exceptions to the operation of the gift rule as it pertains to travel. For example, it does not apply to a member's or staff member's outside business activities or to political activities.

Representatives in most circumstances are also prohibited from flying on private, corporate aircraft, although members who own a plane may continue to use it for congressionally related purposes.

Charitable Events. Specific House and Senate rules apply to member attendance at charitable events. Members of Congress may accept an invitation to a charitable event when the sponsor waives any fees for participating in aspects of the event open to all participants. The House requires, however, that net proceeds of the event are for the benefit of a section 501(c)(3) organization exempt from taxation under the Internal Revenue Code; transportation and lodging are paid by the organization; and the free attendance is provided by the organization. The Senate requirements are different. The charitable event may not be "substantially recreational," and the expenses to be paid must meet the same requirements as those for officially connected travel.

Honoraria. Honoraria are prohibited, but an event sponsor may pay up to $2,000 to a charity in lieu of an honorarium. Payment of such an honorarium must be made directly to the charity by the provider of the honorarium. Neither the member nor a relative of the member may receive a finan-

§ 3.61

House and Senate Financial Disclosure Form

UNITED STATES HOUSE OF REPRESENTATIVES CALENDAR YEAR 2010 FINANCIAL DISCLOSURE STATEMENT	Form A For use by Members, officers, and employees	Page 1 of ___
Name:	Daytime Telephone:	

Filer Status	☐ Member of the U.S. House of Representatives	State: ______ District: ______	☐ Officer or Employee	Employing Office:	(Office Use Only)
Report Type	☐ Annual (May 16, 2011)	☐ Amendment	☐ Termination	Termination Date:	***A $200 penalty shall be assessed against anyone who files more than 30 days late.***

PRELIMINARY INFORMATION — ANSWER EACH OF THESE QUESTIONS

I. Did you or your spouse have "earned" income (e.g., salaries or fees) of $200 or more from any source in the reporting period? **If yes, complete and attach Schedule I.**	Yes ☐	No ☐	VI. Did you, your spouse, or a dependent child receive any reportable gift in the reporting period (i.e., aggregating more than $335 and not otherwise exempt)? **If yes, complete and attach Schedule VI.**	Yes ☐	No ☐
II. Did any individual or organization make a donation to charity in lieu of paying you for a speech, appearance, or article in the reporting period? **If yes, complete and attach Schedule II.**	Yes ☐	No ☐	VII. Did you, your spouse, or a dependent child receive any reportable travel or reimbursements for travel in the reporting period (worth more than $335 from one source)? **If yes, complete and attach Schedule VII.**	Yes ☐	No ☐
III. Did you, your spouse, or a dependent child receive "unearned" income of more than $200 in the reporting period or hold any reportable asset worth more than $1,000 at the end of the period? **If yes, complete and attach Schedule III.**	Yes ☐	No ☐	VIII. Did you hold any reportable positions on or before the date of filing in the current calendar year? **If yes, complete and attach Schedule VIII.**	Yes ☐	No ☐
IV. Did you, your spouse, or a dependent child purchase, sell, or exchange any reportable asset in a transaction exceeding $1,000 during the reporting period? **If yes, complete and attach Schedule IV.**	Yes ☐	No ☐	IX. Did you have any reportable agreement or arrangement with an outside entity? **If yes, complete and attach Schedule IX.**	Yes ☐	No ☐
V. Did you, your spouse, or a dependent child have any reportable liability (more than $10,000) during the reporting period? **If yes, complete and attach Schedule V.**	Yes ☐	No ☐	**Each question in this part must be answered and the appropriate schedule attached for each "Yes" response.**		

EXCLUSION OF SPOUSE, DEPENDENT, OR TRUST INFORMATION — ANSWER EACH OF THESE QUESTIONS

TRUSTS—Details regarding "Qualified Blind Trusts" approved by the Committee on Ethics and certain other "excepted trusts" need not be disclosed. Have you excluded from this report details of such a trust benefiting you, your spouse, or dependent child?	Yes ☐	No ☐
EXEMPTION—Have you excluded from this report any other assets, "unearned" income, transactions, or liabilities of a spouse or dependent child because they meet all three tests for exemption? Do not answer "yes" unless you have first consulted with the Committee on Ethics.	Yes ☐	No ☐

The complete House Financial Disclosure Form can be found on the House Committee on Ethics web site: *<http://ethics.house.gov>*.

Continued on page 109

cial or tax benefit from the donation. Neither an employee of the member nor a relative of an employee may receive a financial or tax benefit from the donation. In addition, if a charitable contribution in lieu of an honorarium is made for a representative by a registered lobbyist or registered foreign agent, then the representative must file a report with the clerk of the House. Travel expenses, however, may be covered or reimbursed.

Outside Earned Income. Certain categories of outside earned income are proscribed; for example, paid professional services such as law, real estate sales, and insurance sales, and compensation for services as an officer or board member of an organization. A member may not represent a person or entity in a private capacity before a federal agency or a federal court, whether compensated or not, and, in general, may not contract or benefit from a contract with the federal government. Outside earned income is limited to 15 percent of Executive (Branch) Level II pay (15 percent of $179,700 in 2011, or $26,955. The current Executive Level II rate of pay can be found on the U.S. Office of Personnel Management's web site, *<http://opm.gov>*, select "Salaries & Wages" then "Executive Schedule.").

§ 3.61 (continued)

House and Senate Financial Disclosure Form

UNITED STATES SENATE FINANCIAL DISCLOSURE REPORT
FOR ANNUAL AND TERMINATION REPORTS

Last Name	First Name and Middle Initial	Annual Report **Calendar Year Covered by Report:**	Senate Office / Agency in Which Employed
Senate Office Address (Number, Street, City, State, and ZIP Code)	Senate Office Telephone Number *(Include Area Code)*	Termination Report **Termination Date (mm/dd/yy):**	Prior Office / Agency in Which Employed

AFTER READING THE INSTRUCTIONS - ANSWER EACH OF THESE QUESTIONS AND ATTACH THE RELEVANT PART

	YES	NO		YES	NO
Did any individual or organization make a donation to charity in lieu of paying you for a speech, appearance, or article in the reporting period? If Yes, Complete and Attach PART I.			Did you, your spouse, or dependent child receive any reportable travel or reimbursements for travel in the reporting period (i.e., worth more than $335 from one source)? If Yes, Complete and Attach PART VI.		
Did you or your spouse have earned income (e.g., salaries or fees) or non-investment income of more than $200 from any reportable source in the reporting period? If Yes, Complete and Attach PART II.			Did you, your spouse, or dependent child have any reportable liability (more than $10,000) during the reporting period? If Yes, Complete and Attach PART VII.		
Did you, your spouse, or dependent child hold any reportable asset worth more than $1,000 at the end of the period, or receive unearned or investment income of more than $200 in the reporting period? If Yes, Complete & Attach PART IIIA and/or IIIB.			Did you hold any reportable positions on or before the date of filing in the current calendar year? If Yes, Complete and Attach PART VIII.		
Did you, your spouse, or dependent child purchase, sell, or exchange any reportable asset worth more than $1,000 in the reporting period? If Yes, Complete and Attach PART IV.			Do you have any reportable agreement or arrangement with an outside entity? If Yes, Complete and Attach PART IX.		
Did you, your spouse, or dependent child receive any reportable gift in the reporting period (i.e., aggregating more than $335 and not otherwise exempt)? If Yes, Complete and Attach PART V.			If this is your FIRST Report: Did you receive compensation of more than $5,000 from a single source in the two prior years? If Yes, Complete and Attach PART X.		

Each question must be answered and the appropriate PART attached for each "YES" response.

File this report and any amendments with the Secretary of the Senate, Office of Public Records, Room 232, Hart Senate Office Building, U.S. Senate, Washington, DC 20510. $200 Penalty for filing more than 30 days after due date.

This Financial Disclosure Statement is required by the Ethics in Government Act of 1978, as amended. The statement will be made available by the Office of the Secretary of the Senate to any requesting person upon written application and will be reviewed by the Select Committee on Ethics. Any individual who knowingly and willfully falsifies, or who knowingly and willfully fails to file this report may be subject to civil and criminal sanctions. (See 5 U.S.C. app. 4, § 104, and 18 U.S.C. § 1001.)

FOR OFFICIAL USE ONLY
Do Not Write Below this Line

Certification	Signature of Reporting Individual	Date (Month, Day, Year)
I CERTIFY that the statements I have made on this form and all attached schedules are true, complete and correct to the best of my knowledge and belief.		

For Official Use Only - Do Not Write Below This Line

	Signature of Reviewing Official	Date (Month, Day, Year)
It is the Opinion of the reviewer that the statements made in this form are in compliance with Title I of the Ethics in Government Act.		

The complete House Financial Disclosure Form can be found on the House Committee on Ethics web site: <*http://ethics.house.gov*>.

Financial Disclosure. Members and some highly paid congressional staff must file financial disclosure forms each year, by May 15 if it falls on a weekday or on the next business day, providing extensive information on earned and unearned income, assets, liabilities, and other financial and quasi-financial interests. The disclosure form is not a net-worth financial statement. (*See § 3.61, House and Senate Financial Disclosure Form.*)

Interns, Fellows, and Volunteers. In general, private interns, fellows, and volunteers may work in congressional offices, with consideration in their hiring being given to their affiliation with organizations having an interest in matters before Congress, the educational benefit such individuals will receive, the potential displacement of paid employees, and other factors. (*See § 4.100, Congressional Fellowships and Internships.*)

Case Work. Members are to avoid ex parte communications in departments' and agencies' adjudicatory proceedings. There are other situations involving departments and agencies, however, where a member might express judgment, such as when a proceeding is not adjudicatory.

Members also sometimes attempt to promote a business or nonprofit entity that they believe has an important product, technology, idea, or service. They might promote the entity to a federal agency as a good procurement opportunity or in legislation, such as through an earmark. If members fail to keep an arms-length relationship, or become overly zealous in assisting the entity, the relationship can become a basis for investigation by the respective chamber's ethics committee and a political problem for the affected members.

Members could also run into ethical trouble if they attempt to bestow official action, such as case-work assistance or access to a member, on political supporters, party members, or campaign contributors, while discriminating in extending or withholding the same official action from others, or even in taking punitive action. Both the House Committee on Standards of Official Conduct and the Senate Committee on Ethics sent communications to all members of their respective chambers reminding them of rules and guidance disallowing preferential treatment for a member's supporters and contributors.

Earmarks. Both chambers adopted new rules in 2007 to add transparency to member requests for earmarks. Transparency is not necessarily an attribute of ethical behavior, but members in each chamber believed that the volume of earmark requests and the background to the inclusion of some of them suggested potential ethical violations or increased potential for ethical violations. The response was not to ban earmarks but to require their disclosure and the public availability of certain information. An earmark might be for spending, providing a specific sum to a specific entity. It might be a limited tariff benefit, a favorable tariff provision benefiting ten or fewer entities. It might also be a limited tax benefit, a tax preference available to ten or fewer taxpayers (in the House rule) or a small group of taxpayers (in the Senate rule).

The House rule prohibits the House from considering legislation unless a list of earmarks in the legislation is available or there is a statement that no earmarks are included in the legislation. In the Senate, a motion to proceed to the consideration of legislation is not in order unless the chair or majority leader certifies that a list of earmarks and their requestors is available.

In disclosing an earmark in writing to the committee of jurisdiction, a member must provide her name, the name of the intended beneficiary or beneficiaries, and the purpose of the earmark. A representative must certify that neither she nor her spouse has a financial interest in the earmark requested. A senator must certify that neither she nor a family member has a financial interest. House committees must make earmark requests available for public viewing. Senate committees need make available only the certifications concerning financial interest. (*See also § 7.80, Authorizations and Appropriations Processes; and § 7.81, Limitations, Earmarks, and General Provisions.*)

House and Senate Republicans adopted an earmark moratorium for the 112th Congress.

Support of Noncongressional Entities. Members may not support outside organizations by lending or giving them franked envelopes, letterhead, or valuable items purchased with official funds. Post-employment restrictions on lobbying and advising foreign government interests apply for one year after a member leaves office. Similar one-year bans apply to highly paid personal staff, who may not lobby their former employer's office, and highly paid committee staff, who may not lobby their former committee.

Influencing Employment Decisions. Members may express their opinions on hiring in executive departments and agencies in limited circumstances. A member may make a recommendation for federal employment based only on personal knowledge. He, however, may express a judgment about a prospective appointee to a political position.

Under the Honest Leadership and Open Government Act (HLOGA), members and congressional staff who seek to influence an employment decision or practice of a private entity on the basis of political affiliation could be subject to criminal prosecution. The law prohibits an attempt to influence through taking or withholding, or offering or threatening to withhold, an official act, and also prohibits influencing, or offering or threatening to influence, the official act of another.

Post-Congressional Service Employment. Congress has in recent years strengthened ethics laws related to negotiating employment while still serving in Congress and to the cooling-off period following congressional service.

Representatives and senators must refrain from negotiating employment following the end of their congressional service until their successor is elected. If, however, they wish to begin negotiations, they may do so if they disclose the negotiations within three days of their commencement to the Ethics Committee (House) or secretary of the Senate. In addition, a senator may not begin negotiating employment that involves lobbying activities until after her successor has been elected. Highly paid House and Senate staff must also disclose to their respective Ethics Committee post-congressional employment negotiations within three days of the commencement of those negotiations.

Members and staff engaged in post-congressional service negotiations must recuse themselves from work that involves a conflict of interest or that creates an appearance of a conflict of interest.

Members and staff are also restricted in the immediate post-congressional service period from lobbying all or some portions of Congress. Representatives may not lobby the legislative branch for one year after the end of their congressional service, and senators may not lobby the legislative branch for two years. Highly paid House staff may not lobby the member or committee for whom they worked for one year, and highly paid Senate staff may not lobby anyone in the Senate for one year. In addition, all other former Senate staff are proscribed from lobbying the Senate office for which they worked for one year. No member or staff member may advise or represent a foreign entity for one year after the end of their congressional service or employment.

There are narrow exceptions to this post-congressional service restriction on lobbying, for example, if the former member or congressional staff member becomes a federal, state, or local executive in the applicable cooling-off period.

The federal statute intended to prevent former federal officials from "switching sides" also applies. A former member or congressional staff member with knowledge of trade or treaty negotiations who had access to non-public information may not seek to influence anyone in the legislative branch on that subject for one year after the end of their congressional service or employment.

Other Norms of Ethical Behavior. Both chambers have broad, unspecific standards of behavior to which members are expected to adhere. In the House, for example, the Code of Official Conduct, available on the Ethics Committee web site (<*http://ethics.house.gov*>) begins: "A Member . . . shall conduct himself at all times in a manner that shall reflect creditably on the House." In the Senate, the Senate Ethics Committee Rules of Procedure, available on the Ethics Committee web site

(<*http://ethics.senate.gov*>), implies there is a body of precedent that establishes what constitutes "improper conduct reflecting on the Senate." The Code of Ethics for Government Service, adopted by the 85th Congress on July 11, 1958, and which both chambers still employ as a norm of behavior, states: "Uphold the Constitution, laws, and legal regulations of the United States and of all governments therein and never be a party to their evasion."

§ 3.70 Chapter Summary and Discussion Questions

Lobbying is a highly regulated activity where laws, rules, and regulations seek to balance First Amendment rights with the mitigation of potential for corruption. This regulatory environment is intended to protect all parties engaged in influencing the legislative process and in legislative decision-making.

Lobbying is understood to be protected by the First Amendment as freedom to speak, assemble, and seek a redress of grievances. A lobbyist's job is to contact and persuade one or more members of Congress to take a legal action. While the citizenry is usually presented with the idea of insiders and special pleaders, the citizenry is what is represented by lobbyists. Businesses, labor unions, minority groups, citizens motivated by an ideal, local governments, government contractors, and others are all affected by decisions of the federal government, and they must let their legislators know how they are affected, lest their purpose is lost because members of Congress lacked information.

Congress is a very open institution, with citizens and lobbyists able to talk directly to members and congressional staff without many barriers. For lobbyists, members and staff are great consumers of information. Members are also interested in potential votes in elections and potential campaign contributions. Members and congressional leaders also look for allies among lobbyists who can help round up votes for a policy position. Congress is also a decentralized institution, with individual members willing to listen to many perspectives.

In balancing First Amendment rights with mitigating the potential for corruption, Congress has distinguished in law between the individual citizen or ad hoc citizens' group and the professional lobbyist. Only those individuals, or entities employing those individuals, who spend a certain amount of time and a certain amount of money on lobbying activities must register with the House and Senate and then report quarterly on their activities. The Lobbying Disclosure Act, as amended, has a number of tests to determine whether an individual is a lobbyist, or whether an organization employs lobbyists, and must register and report.

Existing laws, such as those prohibiting bribery, and new laws, such as the Honest Leadership and Open Government Act, make illegal many possible actions that a lobbyist could perform. While the prohibition on bribery has long existed, newer laws and rules prohibit gifts of meals, tickets, travel, and other things of value to a member of Congress or congressional staff member from a lobbyist. Members have not only been prohibited from accepting gifts from lobbyists but also must disclose additional information about their travel and other activities as members of Congress.

Members have been prosecuted in federal and state courts for violations of law, and they have been investigated by the Ethics Committee of their respective chamber and punished according to the severity of their ethical lapse. Members are not exempt from criminal prosecutions, and may be jailed or fined or otherwise punished on conviction. At the beginning of the twenty-first century, a representative was also expelled as allowed by the Constitution following his criminal conviction.

Members are also subject to numerous ethical laws and rules governing their service in Congress. Many rules govern their use of money and staff made available to them to do their work. Many rules require the strict separation of legislative work from campaign activity. Many rules prevent members' self-dealing and conflicts of interest. Other rules separate members' official work from their personal interests, and require financial disclosure statements and other disclosures to help ensure this separation as well as ethical behavior.

Discussion Questions

- What are some of the benefits to the nation from allowing lobbyists to seek to persuade members of Congress to understand or even adopt a certain perspective on an issue before Congress?
- Think about public policy issues that concern you and your perspective on them. What would you like to say to your members of Congress, and how might you go about persuading them, recognizing that they are probably hearing two, three, or more other perspectives on the same issues?
- Members of Congress come from specific places, with specific economies, population profiles, resources, and other features. Did you consider this in thinking about how to persuade your members of Congress? Read about your members, and think about how this knowledge might change your approach in trying to persuade them.
- What kind of grassroots campaign might you design to support your effort to persuade your members of Congress?
- In the sidebars in this chapter, there are several examples of how organizations conduct meetings with members of Congress. What do you think are the concerns about these meetings that the advice is meant to address?
- This chapter describes a number of ways in which Congress is open to lobbyists and to citizens. Would you describe this openness as a strength or weakness of Congress? Why?
- What changes might you make to laws or rules about lobbyists' access if you think Congress should be more open or less open to them? Would these changes be compatible with the First Amendment?
- Have you seen a television or online commercial about a public policy issue or member of Congress during times when there is no election? What has this commercial sought to tell you? What did you think about it? What effect do you think it might have had on the targeted member or on his constituents?
- If you were asked to summarize in one paragraph the key components of federal lobbying laws, what aspects or themes would you include? Try to write that paragraph.
- What effect on mitigating corruption do you think results from prohibiting lobbyists from making gifts of meals, tickets, travel, or other items of value? How persuasive with members of Congress do you think these gifts might have been before they were outlawed? Why?
- There are a number of examples of ethical lapses by members that are cited in this chapter.

There were obviously laws that made their actions illegal, and they nonetheless chose to engage in criminal activity. What effect do you think more laws or stricter laws added in recent years will have in preventing illegal activities by members of Congress?

- What are some of the roles and responsibilities of the House and Senate Ethics Committees that this chapter identified? If you were a member of Congress, would you like to be a member of the Ethics Committee? Why or why not?

Chapter Four

Supporting Congress: Allowances and Staff

4

Analysis

§ 4.00 Introduction

The work of Congress depends on thousands of people in addition to the members. Congressional staffers work in members' personal offices and in their district or state offices. Staffers are employed by committees, subcommittees, and leadership offices in a variety of professional and clerical positions. Members and committees are provided with salary allowances to hire staff. Additional employees work for limited periods as a result of numerous internships and fellowships sponsored by both government and private groups.

Members and committee are also provided with allowances for expenses, such as mail, subscriptions, training, security, and travel. Some of the principal rules and regulations governing spending by members are described in Chapter Three, Pressures on Congress: Lobbying and Congressional Ethics. Members and committees are also provided with office space, which is described in § 11.30, Guide to Public Buildings on Capitol Hill.

Each chamber has officials, such as the clerk of the House and sergeant at arms of the House and the secretary of the Senate and sergeant at arms for the Senate, with large staffs who support the legislative operations, financial management, and security of the chambers and their members and committees. Smaller units in each chamber have specialized duties. The architect of the Capitol, Capitol police, Office of Compliance, and attending physician support both chambers with a wide array of services throughout the Capitol complex.

Congress has also ensured that it has independent sources of information from the executive branch to support it in its legislative and oversight responsibilities. These legislative branch agencies are the Congressional Budget Office (CBO), Congressional Research Service (CRS), Government Accountability Office (GAO), Government Printing Office (GPO), and Library of Congress. Executive agencies, such as the Office of Management and Budget and the General Services Agency, also have important relationships in support of Congress.

§ 4.10 Pay and Allowances of Members

Like executives hired in many other positions, members, including the resident commissioner for Puerto Rico and the five delegates in the House, receive salaries, employee benefits, office space, supplies, and expense accounts to perform their jobs. They hire staff to assist them in discharging their responsibilities in office. Members operate fairly independently in managing their offices, but their management is subject to many laws, rules and regulations, and practices. (*See also § 3.50, Congressional Ethics.*) A chair or ranking minority member on a committee or subcommittee also wears a second hat as manager of resources for that entity. Congressional leaders also receive allowances to have staff and pay expenses, separate from their allowance as individual members of Congress. A vast bureaucracy, answerable to House and Senate officers, congressional leaders, and oversight committees, services members' offices and the committees on which members serve. Part of this bureaucracy keeps up the nation's premier public building, the U.S. Capitol, and the grounds and other buildings that surround it, in which members, their staff, the Supreme Court, and others work.

§ 4.20 Salary, Earned Income, and Benefits

The Constitution empowers Congress to set its own compensation, and the Twenty-Seventh Amendment provides that a variance in compensation voted by one Congress will not take effect until after the next intervening election. Congress last specifically voted to increase its pay in 1989 and 1991. It first adopted the Ethics Reform Act of 1989 (*P.L. 101-194; 103 Stat. 1716*), which raised representatives' and senators' salaries. (Representatives' salaries were raised by a greater amount than senators' in this legislation.) In 1991, Congress approved a Senate amendment to the fiscal 1992 legislative appropriations bill raising senators' salaries to equal those of representatives (*P.L. 102-90; 105 Stat. 447*).

As enacted, these two laws were also important in linking a pay increase to two changes affecting members' income. Receipt of honoraria was barred and other, outside earned income was limited to 15 percent of Executive (Branch) Level II (15 percent of $179,700 in 2011, or $26,955). The changes for representatives were included in the Ethics Reform Act, and the changes for senators were begun in the Ethics Reform Act and completed in the fiscal 1992 legislative branch appropriations bill.

House and Senate rules implement the honoraria ban and outside earned-income limit. Ethics laws and chamber rules allow a payment of up to $2,000 to be made to a charity in lieu of an honorarium. Payment of such an honorarium must be made directly to the charity by the provider of the honorarium. Neither the member nor a relative of the member may receive a financial or tax benefit from the donation. Neither an employee of the member nor a relative of an employee may receive a financial or tax benefit from the donation. These donations must also be reported on a member's financial disclosure statement.

Ethics laws and chamber rules proscribe certain categories of outside earned income, for example, compensation for professional services such as real estate and insurance sales, the practice of law, and service as an officer or board member of an organization. Any outside income and service as an officer or board member must be reported on a member's financial disclosure statement.

The Ethics Reform Act also created a revised means of automatic, annual salary increases for members of Congress and other highly paid federal officials, which has become the basis for congressional pay increases. (Another means of salary increases exists in law, which requires a congressional vote.) Under the Ethics Reform Act, the pay-increase formula is based in part on components of the Bureau of Labor Statistics' employment cost index. It is limited both by a 5 percent ceiling and by the size and effective date of adjustments to general schedule federal employees' base pay. Unless Congress votes to prohibit an increase, it automatically takes effect. (Congress under law might also modify the increase, but a question exists about whether that would trigger the operation of the Twenty-Seventh Amendment, thus postponing the increase to after the next election.)

Within the formula and limitations, members' pay increased on January 1, 2009, by 2.8 percent, to $174,000. The changes appear in the table on the next page. Congressional salaries were frozen at this level through December 31, 2012, as a consequence of legislation subsequently enacted. Over the years, a very few members have availed themselves of a law that allows them to return a portion of their salary to the Treasury for the purpose of federal debt reduction. To the extent members have returned salary, it has often been the portion of their salary attributable to a recent pay increase. *(For a table listing congressional pay, see <CongressPay.com>.)*

Like other federal employees, members of Congress may participate in the Federal Employees Health Benefits program, the Federal Employees Group Life Insurance program, and the federal retirement system. Members' pension contributions, benefit formulas, and years of service and retirement age for receiving an unreduced pension are different from other federal employees. In general, based on the presumption that the duration of congressional service is unpredictable, members and congressional staff contribute more in exchange for more generous retirement income. Social Security participation is mandatory.

Free outpatient care is available to members at the Naval Medical Center in Bethesda, MD, and Walter Reed Army Hospital in Washington, DC, a long-standing privilege also available to the president, vice president, and other government officials. In-patient care, however, must be paid at the rates set for these institutions by the Department of Defense. Members of Congress may also receive care at military clinics and hospitals, and that care must be paid for. *(See also 4.122, Office of the Attending Physician.)* Members must also pay the tax on wages for Medicare Hospital Insurance (Part A).

Office Held	**Salary on Jan. 1, 2012***
Vice President (President of the Senate)	$230,700
Speaker of the House	$223,500*
President Pro Tempore of the Senate, Senate Majority and Minority Leaders, and House Majority and Minority Leaders	$193,400*
Senators, Representatives, and, in House, Delegates and Resident Commissioner	$174,000*

** Frozen by law from January 1, 2009, until December 31, 2012. For a table listing congressional pay, see <CongressPay.com>.*

Upon retirement, resignation, or defeat for reelection, a member of Congress continues to enjoy certain perquisites. For example, floor privileges are allowed with certain limitations; access to reports of the Congressional Research Service continues; access to congressional fitness centers and dining rooms is permitted, with certain limitations; and a limited franking privilege exists for ninety days.

Finally, a member is entitled to an annual income tax deduction of up to $3,000 for living expenses while away from his home district or state.

§ 4.30 House Allowances for Staff, Office, and Other Expenses

In the House, a "member's representational allowance" (MRA) for representatives in 2011 averaged $1,447,065. (MRAs for the delegates and resident commissioners vary slightly.) The maximum amount in an MRA was $1,671,596, and the minimum amount was $1,356,975. The MRA is used by representatives, delegates, and the resident commissioner for staff salaries in Washington and district offices, office expenses in both locales, rent of district offices, and use of the *frank* for mail.

Each member receives the same amount in her MRA for staff salaries—$897,437 in 2011. An MRA does not include salary overhead. A member may not employ more than eighteen permanent staff in her Washington, DC, office and any district offices. Up to four other staffers may be employed if their positions are in classifications such as temporary or paid intern. The top salary that a member may pay a staffer in 2011 was $168,411.

Congressional staff pay, in general, is low, with full-time junior staff assistants earning as little as $25,000 on an annual basis in the high-cost Washington, DC, area. Staff are also expected to work long days, with unpredictable schedules, and to work at least some time on weekends and even holidays. Staff also regularly go off the congressional payroll as election day approaches so that they can work on their boss' or another candidate's campaign. Nonetheless, many young people are attracted to a position on Capitol Hill early in their career.

Capitol Hill is an exciting place to work and a unique learning environment. Congressional staff positions allow individuals to build résumés that are impressive to lobbying organizations, think tanks, foundations, nonprofit organizations, law firms, businesses, and other entities. Experienced individuals employed in the executive branch or in the private sector who worked previously on Capitol Hill also return to senior congressional staff positions, even if that means a salary cut. They are attracted by the excitement of Capitol Hill and the opportunity for further public service, the political arena, the public policy issues ascendant at a particular time, and the chance for further résumé building. Some individuals need a few more years of federal service in anticipation of their retirement, and find Capitol Hill a satisfying way to cap their careers.

A negative side of a congressional job is that it can end precipitously through a member's death, resignation, or election defeat. A change in a chairmanship or committee ranking member position can have the same effect for committee staff. There is no special help available for a congressional staffer who finds herself in this situation. Her network, skills, luck, and good fortune to be in the right place at the right time are a staffer's outplacement service.

The amount included in an MRA for office expenses varies because the allocation includes money for travel and for district office rent. In 2011, each member received in this account a base of $243,745. In addition, each member received money for travel based on a formula that included the distance from Washington, DC, to the point in his district farthest from Washington; a minimum amount of $6,200 was provided. Finally, using a formula based on the applicable per-square-foot rental charge the General Services Administration might incur in a district, money is provided for a total of 2,500 square feet in one or more district offices.

In addition to travel and district office rental, office expenses include office equipment, furnishings for district offices, computer equipment, office supplies, and telephone services, and perhaps lease charges for a car, "mobile district office" expenses, mailing-list purchases (as long as addresses are in the member's district, result from an arm's length transaction, and do not contain campaign-related or political party information), and subscriptions. There are a number of prohibitions on use of this allowance as well; for example, expenses for professional association and membership dues, holiday greeting cards, and relocation costs are not allowed.

Funds are included in an MRA to cover the costs of all franked mail from a member's Washington and district offices, including mass mailings, which are defined as 500 pieces or more, largely identical in content. This allocation is calculated individually for each member, based on the number of nonbusiness addresses in a district, and, in 2011, averaged $169,833. (*Some of the procedures and prohibitions applicable to use of the franking privilege are discussed in § 4.50, Franking Privilege.*)

Money is largely—but not completely—fungible among these three funds.

A separate allocation, not part of an MRA, provides *public document envelopes* to each representative.

A travel expense allowance is available for reelected and newly elected members and, for each, one staff member to travel to Washington to attend early organization meetings following a general election. For newly elected members, this allowance includes a per diem.

A number of ethics laws, rules, and guidelines surround the MRA and office operations. (*See § 3.50, Congressional Ethics.*) Some of these are as follows:

- A member is personally responsible for expenses that exceed her MRA.
- Funds in the MRA cannot be reallocated or transferred between years. (A year runs from January 3 of one year through January 2 of the next year.)
- A member may not use campaign or private funds to support his office, and a member may not pay for personal, social, or political expenses from an MRA.
- A member may not use committee resources for her office, or use an MRA for committee expenses.
- Neither the member nor a relative may benefit from spending from an MRA.
- Employees must perform duties commensurate with their compensation.
- With some exceptions that deal with changes of status after a person is employed, a member may not employ a relative.

Separate from the MRAs, all representatives, the resident commissioner, and delegates are provided with furnished office suites in one of the House office buildings. Parking for members and a portion of their staffs is provided in garages and other locations on Capitol Hill. In addition, other services are available:

- Numerous service providers operate in the "small city" on the House side of the Capitol and in the House office buildings: post offices; a credit union; a stationery shop and a gift shop; restaurants and cafeterias; private meeting rooms; a members' gymnasium; a staff fitness center; a travel reservation and ticketing service; beauty and barber shops; a dry cleaner; housekeeping, maintenance, and repair services; parking garages and parking areas for representatives and staff; a shuttle-bus service; in-house television and radio feeds; and the Capitol police. Many services charge normal retail rates or, in the case of the gymnasium, levy an annual fee. Services such as the post offices, dining halls, and beauty and barber shops are open to the public.
- The Chief Administrative Officer (CAO) staff supports the telecommunications, automation, finance, and personnel needs of a modern-day office environment. The General Services Administration assists members in obtaining and furnishing district office space. The House recording studio provides radio and television services for a fee and the photographic studio also provides services for a fee. Numerous government documents flow into a representative's office for office use or redistribution to constituents.

- Department and agency congressional liaison offices, and department and agency regional or state office contacts, facilitate the handling of congressional case work in the executive branch. Intern, volunteer, and fellowship programs support students and professionals in Washington and district offices. The Legislative Resource Center provides legislative documents, public disclosure of member and lobbyist records, and other services.
- The House general counsel may assist individual representatives on official matters. The House employment counsel provides assistance on employment law, and the House administrative counsel assists with questions on administrative issues. The House legislative counsel provides legislative drafting services, and the House parliamentarian provides procedural advice.
- Legislative and administrative staffs work under the management of the clerk of the House. Administrative staffs under the management of the House sergeant at arms, the CAO, and the architect of the Capitol assist with or facilitate the needs, concerns, or questions of any representative's office.
- The attending physician's office, health units in the office buildings, and the House chaplain serve the needs of representatives and staff. An annual fee is charged to members for regular use of the attending physician's services.
- The Congressional Budget Office and Government Accountability Office principally serve congressional committees with a variety of reports. The Congressional Research Service assists both committees and members with research and policy analyses. The Government Printing Office serves Congress' extensive document needs.
- Reporters from all media are present in the Capitol, providing ready access if a representative wishes to distribute press information or hold a press conference.

§ 4.40 Senate Allowances for Staff, Office, and Other Expenses

In the Senate, the total allocation for personnel, office, and other expenses varies with the population of the state that a senator represents and its distance from Washington. Thus, senators from populous states like California, the largest state with a population of over 37 million, have more financial resources available to them than senators from small-population states like Wyoming, the smallest state with a population of just over 563,000.

A senator has three funds available for the operation of his Washington and state offices. Two accounts support personnel: the administrative and clerical assistance allowance, which is based on population, and the legislative assistance allowance, which is the same for all senators. (Salary overhead is not included in these funds.) The third fund, with components based on population and distance of the home state from Washington, is the official office expense allowance, which covers travel, stationery, and other expenses. Money is largely—but not completely—fungible among these three funds.

A senator's administrative and clerical assistance allowance ranged in 2011 from $2,512,574 for a senator from a state with a population of less than 5 million to $3,993,206 for a senator from a state with a population of 28 million or more. The allowance covers staff in Washington and state offices.

The top salary that could be paid in 2010, the latest year for which a figure was officially available, was $169,459.

The second personnel fund, the legislative assistance allowance, in 2011 provided each senator with $508,377 to hire up to three legislative assistants. The primary purpose of this fund is to ensure that senators have sufficient legislative staff to support their committee work. The top salary that could be paid in 2011 was $169,459.

The third fund is the official office expense allowance, which has several components that are determined by formula. Compared with the House's equivalent allocation, this Senate fund covers fewer items. The Senate does not charge an individual senator's offices for some of the office expenses that are covered by a representative's allowance. For example, most of the costs of a representative's district office are charged against the individual member's representational allowance, while most costs of a senator's state office are not charged against the senator's official office expense allowance. In 2011, the official office expense allowance for a senator ranged from $128,585 to $465,922. (*See § 4.41, Senators' Official Personnel and Office Expense Account.*)

Some items covered by this allowance illustrate its components and, in some cases, the complexity of its administration:

- Telecommunications equipment and services, including both charges for standard equipment and services supplied or paid for by the Senate and additional costs and charges incurred by an individual senator.
- Stationery and office supplies purchased from the Senate stationery room as well as supplies purchased from commercial outlets or General Services Administration (GSA) stores, mailing lists, regular postage, and subscriptions.
- Expenses for state offices not otherwise covered, for example, cable television service charges, and additional office equipment for the Washington or a state office not included in the standard equipment supplied by the Senate.
- Travel expenses for senators and their staff, and, if a senator chooses, for individuals who are not Senate employees but who serve a limited time on an advisory group assisting a senator with nomination recommendations for federal judgeships, U.S. attorneys, U.S. marshals, or the U.S. service academies. Travel costs for a senator and her staff are also limited to "actual transportation expenses" in the sixty days preceding any election in which the senator's name appears on a ballot, unless the candidacy is uncontested and that fact is attested to by an appropriate state official.
- Recording and photographic services performed by the Senate recording and photographic studios or by commercial services.
- The "official mail account," which is totaled with the official office expense allowance and is based on the number of addresses in a senator's state. A senator may supplement official mail costs that exceed his allotment from other funds in the senator's official office expense allowance. In addition, $50,000 is available within a senator's official office expense allowance for "mass mailings"—that is, mailings of 500 or more pieces, largely identical in content. A senator may not increase the amount of money allotted for mass mailings.

§ 4.41

Senators' Official Personnel and Office Expense Account

In its report on the legislative branch appropriations bill for fiscal year 2007 (S. Rept. 109–267), the Senate Appropriations Committee included a table showing the proposed state-by-state allowances for senators' administrative and clerical assistance allowances, legislative assistance allowances, and official office expense allowances. That table is reproduced here.

State	A	B	C	D
Alabama	$2,512,574	$508,377	$184,991	$3,205,942
Alaska	2,512,574	508,377	253,277	3,274,228
Arizona	2,660,358	508,377	206,464	3,375,199
Arkansas	2,512,574	508,377	170,305	3,191,256
California	3,993,206	508,377	465,922	4,967,505
Colorado	2,586,463	508,377	192,466	3,287,306
Connecticut	2,512,574	508,377	160,486	3,181,437
Delaware	2,512,574	508,377	128,585	3,149,536
Florida	3,520,453	508,377	316,073	4,344,903
Georgia	2,882,034	508,377	221,720	3,612,131
Hawaii	2,512,574	508,377	280,364	3,301,315
Idaho	2,512,574	508,377	166,072	3,187,023
Illinois	3,103,716	508,377	265,292	3,877,385
Indiana	2,660,358	508,377	195,554	3,364,289
Iowa	2,512,574	508,377	170,934	3,191,885
Kansas	2,512,574	508,377	169,077	3,190,028
Kentucky	2,512,574	508,377	178,630	3,199,581
Louisiana	2,512,574	508,377	185,739	3,206,690
Maine	2,512,574	508,377	149,000	3,169,951
Maryland	2,586,463	508,377	171,883	3,266,723
Massachusetts	2,660,358	508,377	194,935	3,363,670
Michigan	2,955,932	508,377	233,327	3,697,636
Minnesota	2,586,463	508,377	189,010	3,283,850
Mississippi	2,512,574	508,377	169,968	3,190,919
Missouri	2,586,463	508,377	197,825	3,292,665
Montana	2,512,574	508,377	162,926	3,183,877
Nebraska	2,512,574	508,377	161,288	3,182,239
Nevada	2,512,574	508,377	176,913	3,197,864
New Hampshire	2,512,574	508,377	143,688	3,164,639
New Jersey	2,808,144	508,377	204,844	3,521,365
New Mexico	2,512,574	508,377	168,021	3,188,972
New York	3,567,727	508,377	318,250	4,394,354
North Carolina	2,882,034	508,377	220,482	3,610,893
North Dakota	2,512,574	508,377	150,646	3,171,597
Ohio	3,029,825	508,377	254,146	3,792,348

Continued on page 125

§ 4.41 (continued)

State	A	B	C	D
Oklahoma	2,512,574	508,377	181,706	3,202,657
Oregon	2,512,574	508,377	190,990	3,211,941
Pennsylvania	3,103,716	508,377	260,775	3,872,868
Rhode Island	2,512,574	508,377	139,066	3,160,017
South Carolina	2,512,574	508,377	176,473	3,197,424
South Dakota	2,512,574	508,377	152,539	3,173,490
Tennessee	2,660,358	508,377	196,101	3,364,836
Texas	3,804,103	508,377	370,394	4,682,874
Utah	2,512,574	508,377	171,812	3,192,763
Vermont	2,512,574	508,377	137,073	3,158,024
Virginia	2,734,250	508,377	197,171	3,439,798
Washington	2,660,358	508,377	216,441	3,385,176
West Virginia	2,512,574	508,377	148,773	3,169,724
Wisconsin	2,586,463	508,377	192,233	3,287,073
Wyoming	2,512,574	508,377	153,825	3,174,776

4

Senators-elect are provided with allowances for travel for themselves and two staff persons for attending early organization meetings, for telecommunications expenses, and for stationery expenses.

In addition to a furnished and equipped office in one of the Senate office buildings, separate allowances and perquisites cover many other office needs of a senator:

- Space for state offices in federal buildings or privately owned buildings, with the total amount of space allowed increasing with a state's population, to a maximum of 8,200 square feet for a state with a population of 17 million or more. GSA furnishes state offices, and the expense allocation available for that also increases with a state's population, from a minimum amount of $48,000. The Senate sergeant at arms provides standard office equipment for each state office.
- One mobile state office, including lease and operating costs (but not personnel).
- Blank stationery, letterhead, white envelopes, and public-document envelopes, allocated on the basis of state population, with a minimum of 180,000 pieces of letterhead and 180,000 white envelopes.
- An allocation from a computer services fund for lease or purchase of computer hardware and software and related training and support.
- With a senator's election or reelection, an allowance of $5,000 for furnishing the senator's personal office, reception area, and conference room. A senator entitled to a Capitol office is allowed $2,500 each term to purchase nonstandard furnishings for that office.
- Parking is provided to senators and a portion of their staffs in garages and other Capitol Hill locations.

- A limited number of plants available on loan from the Botanic Garden for a senator's office, two framed reproductions from a limited selection available on loan from the National Gallery of Art, and unmounted maps available on loan (or possibly free) from the U.S. Geological Survey.
- Numerous service providers operate in the "small city" on the Senate side of the Capitol and in the Senate office buildings: post offices; a credit union; a packaging service; a stationery shop and gift shop; restaurants and cafeterias; private meeting rooms; a travel reservation and ticketing service; beauty and barber shops; a members' gymnasium; storage lockers; housekeeping, maintenance, and repair services; parking garages and parking areas for senators and staff; a shuttle-bus service; in-house television and radio feeds; and the Capitol police. Many services charge normal retail rates or, in the case of the gymnasium, levy an annual fee. Services such as the post offices, dining halls, and beauty and barber shops are open to the public.
- The Senate sergeant at arms supports the telecommunications needs of a modern-day office environment. The Senate computer center provides an array of services. The Senate recording studio offers radio and television services for a fee, and the photographic studio also provides services for a fee. The General Services Administration assists senators in obtaining and furnishing state offices. Numerous government documents flow into a senator's office for office use or for redistribution to constituents.
- Department and agency congressional liaison offices, and department and agency regional or state office contacts, facilitate the handling of congressional case work in the executive branch. Intern, volunteer, and fellowship programs support students and professionals in Washington and home-state offices. The Senate historian's office and Senate library provide research and other services.
- The Senate legal counsel may assist individual senators, and the Senate chief counsel for employment provides assistance on employment law. The Senate legislative counsel provides legislative drafting services, and the Senate parliamentarian provides procedural advice.
- Legislative, administrative, and executive staffs work under the management of the secretary of the Senate. Administrative staff under the management of the Senate sergeant at arms and architect of the Capitol assist with or facilitate the needs, concerns, or questions of any senator's office.
- The attending physician's office, health units, and the Senate chaplain serve the needs of senators and their staffs. An annual fee is charged to senators for regular use of the attending physician's services.
- The Congressional Budget Office and Government Accountability Office principally serve congressional committees with a variety of reports. The Congressional Research Service assists both committees and members with research and policy analyses. The Government Printing Office serves Congress' extensive document needs.
- Reporters from all media are present in the Capitol, providing ready access if a senator wishes to distribute a press release or hold a press conference.

As with their House counterparts, senators spend from their allowances pursuant to a number of laws, Senate rules and regulations, and interpretations. Funds provided by the Senate must be used for official—not personal or political—purposes. Additional restrictions begin within sixty days of an election in which a senator's name appears on a ballot. The federal antinepotism law applies to hiring for a senator's office.

Both houses generally allow the use of only appropriated or personal funds for official expenses. Both houses also generally allow a third party to reimburse for expenses for services a member provided to the outside entity, such as travel expenses in conjunction with a speech at a conference or a fact-finding trip. *(See § 3.50, Congressional Ethics.)*

§ 4.50 Franking Privilege

Members of Congress by law are given the privilege of sending official mail under their signatures; members-elect and specified officers of each chamber, such as the clerk of the House and the secretary of the Senate, are also extended the franking privilege. "It is the policy of the Congress that the privilege of sending mail as franked mail shall be established under this section in order to assist and expedite the conduct of the official business, activities, and duties of the Congress of the United States." *(39 U.S.C. § 3210(a)(1).)* In its annual legislative-branch appropriations bill, Congress defrays postal charges for the costs of members exercising this privilege of office.

The use of the frank is regulated in the House and the Senate, respectively, by the House Commission on Congressional Mailing Standards (popularly called the "Franking Commission") and the Senate Select Committee on Ethics. Members are encouraged to consult the Franking Commission and the Select Ethics Committee with questions on use of the frank; representatives must seek clearance from the Franking Commission for mass mailings before they are mailed. Additional authority resides with the House Administration Committee and the Senate Rules and Administration Committee.

Numerous provisions of law, rules and regulations of the House and Senate, and advisory and interpretative opinions govern the use of the frank or affect its use. Following are some of these limits:

- Mail may not be personal, such as holiday greetings.
- Mail may not seek political support, mention candidacy, solicit funds, or electioneer (for example, advocate someone's election or defeat).
- The frank may not be lent to another person or organization or generally be used for the benefit of a third party.
- The frank may generally be used for newsletters, questionnaires, news releases, and the distribution of some types of publications (for example, the *Congressional Record*).
- Mass mailings—500 pieces or more, largely identical in content—must be postmarked not fewer than ninety days before an election in which a representative's name appears on any ballot and not fewer than sixty days before an election in which a senator's name appears on any ballot.
- Mass mailings must carry the disclaimer, "This mailing was prepared, published, and mailed at taxpayer expense."
- Representatives must get clearance for mass mailings (and other mass communications) from the Franking Commission. Mass mailings may not be mailed to addresses outside

representatives' districts, including, prior to an election based on new district lines, to addresses in newly redistricted areas.

- Senators must register their mass mailings with the secretary of the Senate. Senate mass mailings must be handled by the Senate service department, which certifies the cost of each mailing so that it can be charged against the $50,000 mass-mailing ceiling applicable to each senator's official office expense allowance.
- Overseas mail, express mail, and some other specific types of mail are not frankable.
- Former members may use the frank for limited purposes for up to ninety days following the end of their term.

A member whose mailing violates franking rules may be required to pay for the mailing. Recipients of mailings may complain to the House Franking Commission or the Senate Select Ethics Committee.

Both chambers have struggled to adapt their franking and other rules to members' ever-expanding use of electronic communications, including social media.

§ 4.60 Personal Staff

The first paid staff on Capitol Hill were hired by committees before the Civil War. By World War II, there were approximately 2,000 people in the personal offices of members of the House and Senate. Today, that number is approximately 14,000.

Being a staffer is not a nine-to-five job. Members can require staffers to work ten or more hours a day, often six days a week. Each member decides office policies on vacation and sick leave. Each staffer individually negotiates salary with the member, the member's chief of staff, or, possibly, an office manager. According to the Congressional Management Foundation, most personal staff are young and white, and a substantial portion are female. Senior positions are held predominantly by men. Many staff are recent college graduates with little previous full-time job experience.

As described in § 4.30 (*House Allowances for Staff, Office, and Other Expenses*), each House member has a member's representational allowance (MRA), which allows a member to hire up to eighteen permanent and four other staff, such as paid interns. Staff are divided between the Washington and district offices. The maximum House personal staff salary in 2011 was $168,411. Each employee must be paid at least minimum wage.

A senator's administrative and clerical assistance allowance varies with the size of a senator's state. For 2011, the allowance ranged from $2,512,574 for a senator representing a state with a population of less than 5 million people, to $3,993,206 for a senator representing a state with a population of 28 million people or more. The maximum staff salary in a senator's office in 2010, the latest year for which a figure was officially available, was $169,459. In addition, in 2011, the legislative assistance allowance authorized for each senator for the appointment of three legislative assistants was proposed at $508,377.

There is not a limit on the number of staff that a senator may hire with the administrative and clerical assistance allowance. Depending on a state's population, a senator might employ thirty to fifty staff, or even more for a larger state.

Staff from across Capitol Hill who serve in the National Guard or reserves are being called up for

§ 4.61

Staff Salary Data

2010 House and 2006 Senate Staff Salary Data

Position in Washington, DC, Office of Representative or Senator	Average Salary	Average Years in House Position	Years in Position in Senate
House Administrative Assistant/Chief of Staff	$136,588	6.7	
Senate Chief of Staff	$151,767		3–6
House Legislative Director	$87,674	4.5	
Senate Legislative Director	$116,952		1–3
House Press Secretary	$64,003	3.7	
Senate Press Secretary	$66,027		1–3
House Legislative Assistant	$48,762	3.1	
Senate Legislative Assistant	$66,789		1–3
House Systems Administrator	$33,675	6.6	
Senate Systems Administrator	$60,955		3–6
House Office Manager	$62,165	7.1	
Senate Office Manager	$78,266		3–6
House Scheduler	$51,869	5.5	
Senate Scheduler	$63,634		3–6

Source of data: U.S. House, Chief Administrative Office, *2010 House Compensation Study*, and U.S. Senate, Office of the Secretary of the Senate, *2006 U.S. Senate Employment, Compensation, Hiring and Benefits Study*. For congressional staff salaries, also see <*LegiStorm.com*>.

active duty. Pursuant to law, they are entitled to leave without loss in pay, time, or performance rating.

While individual member and committee offices determine how to fill positions, there are centralized résumé services in each chamber. Information on the Senate sergeant at arm's service is available on the Senate web site, <*http://senate.gov*>, select "Visitors," then select "Employment." Information in the House chief administrative officer's service is available on the House web site, <*http://house.gov*>, then select "Employment."

Personal Office Staff Functions

Personal staff work for a member in his representative and legislative capacities. They contact executive-branch agencies to assist constituents with bureaucratic tangles that affect the constituents' Social Security or veterans' benefits. Personal staff help private and governmental entities in their home states or districts secure grants or special-project funds, answer constituent mail, and, in many offices, initiate mail to constituents.

§ 4.62

Congressional Staff Organizations

Staff belong to numerous Capitol Hill-based membership organizations, such as teams in the congressional softball leagues (<*www.congsoftball.com*>, <*www.housesoftball.com*>, and <*www.senatesoftball.org*>). Some staff organizations are listed on the Commitee on House Administration web site, <*http://cha.house.gov*>. Here is a representative list of congressional staff organizations:

- Black Republican Congressional Staff Association
- Capitol Hill Chapter, Federal Bar Association
- Capitol Hill Toastmasters Club
- Congressional Asian Pacific American Staff Association
- Congressional Black Associates
- Congressional Chorus
- Congressional Hispanic Staff Association
- Congressional Hockey Caucus Staff Association
- Congressional Jewish Staff Association
- Congressional Legislative Staff Association
- Democratic Press Secretaries Association
- Democratic Women of Capitol Hill
- Equestrian Society
- Federalist Society–Capitol Hill
- House Chiefs of Staff Association
- Lesbian, Gay, Bisexual, and Transgender Congressional Staff Association
- Peace Corps Congressional Staff Association
- Professional Administrative Managers
- Rotary Club of Capitol Hill

Personal staff monitor legislation and issues to assist a member in her committee, floor, and constituency activities. They meet with constituents and representatives from interest groups on behalf of a member. Press staff work with the national and local media to keep them apprised of a member's activities. (*See also § 4.62, Congressional Staff Organizations.*)

Personal Staff Positions

Some of the principal positions and functions that appear in members' offices include the following:

- *Administrative Assistant* (*AA*) or *Chief of Staff* (*COS*)*:* The chief of staff coordinates and supervises the work of the entire staff and frequently serves as a political (not campaign) advisor to a member.
- *District/State Director:* The district/state director is the senior staffer in a state or district office, and supervises field representatives and other non-Washington staff.
- *Legislative Director* (*LD*)*:* The LD is usually the senior legislative assistant and supervisor of the legislative staff.
- *Legislative Assistant* (*LA*)*:* The LA drafts legislation and amendments (usually working with the Office of Legislative Counsel), monitors committee and floor action, and deals with constituents and lobbyists. In some offices, the LA also answers constituent correspondence. In most Senate offices, the LA works with a legislative correspondent.
- *Legislative Correspondent* (*LC*)*:* The LC drafts responses to letters and other communications sent to the member.

- *Case Worker:* A case worker is responsible for dealing with constituent problems with agencies, such as requesting compassionate leave for enlisted persons, or assisting homeowners and small businesses in obtaining aid after natural disasters. Case workers might also assist localities and nonprofits with grantsmanship and concerns arising in the course of participating in grant programs. In some offices, case workers do "outreach" to meet constituents on behalf of members.
- *Press Secretary or Press Assistant:* A press secretary is the member's chief spokesperson to the media. A press secretary composes press releases, writes newsletters, organizes press conferences, and undertakes other media-relations activities.
- *Systems Manager/Web Master:* The systems manager is responsible for computer hardware, software, and applications, and may also be responsible for maintaining a member's web site.
- *Office Manager:* Sometimes called executive assistant, the office manager deals with staff recruitment, pay, vouchers, use of space and equipment, and coordination between Washington and district or state offices.
- *Scheduler:* The scheduler manages competing demands for a member's time. (*See § 1.50, Ever-Changing and Unpredictable Schedules.*)

Although job titles usually connote a likely set of responsibilities, they do not necessarily indicate who is the most influential staffer in an office. For example, a member might rely on an AA to manage an office, but rely on a press secretary or district director for political advice that affects all aspects of the member's conduct and issue positions.

§ 4.70 Committee and Subcommittee Staff

Although the first full-time committee staff were hired in 1865 by the House Ways and Means Committee and the Senate Finance Committee, there were not many committee staff until relatively recently. The Legislative Reorganization Act of 1946 established a system of permanent professional staff for each standing committee; however, there were fewer than 400 committee staff in both chambers at that time. Since then, that number has risen sharply. Today there are approximately 1,300 House committee staff and nearly twice as many Senate committee staff.

There is great variation in the organization of committee staffs. Some committees are highly centralized, where all staff work for the full committee and help subcommittees as needed. Other committees are decentralized, with each subcommittee having its own staff.

A few committees employ a single nonpartisan staff. Most committees, however, divide their funds for hiring staff between the majority and minority parties, with the largest share accorded to the majority. Each party hires its own staff, although even the most partisan committees may share some administrative staff. The degree of bipartisanship between majority and minority staffs depends largely on the tone set by members: on some committees staff from both parties work closely with each other, while on other committees the relationship is more adversarial.

When there are separate majority and minority staffs, each party generally employs a top staff person called a staff director or minority staff director. A chief or general counsel may also be employed. (A staffer can wear more than one hat, so that, for instance, a chief counsel might also serve as staff director.) On behalf of the respective chair or ranking minority member, a staff director manages the party's staff and acts as liaison between the staff and the committee leader.

Staff are often classified into two groups—the professional staff and the administrative staff. Professional staff draft legislation, plan hearings, write committee reports, conduct investigations, prepare for floor action, and assist conference committees. Some professional staff titles include—in addition to staff director and chief counsel—counsel, specialist, investigator, professional staff assistant, press coordinator, and associate staff.

Administrative staff perform tasks such as keeping the schedule of hearings and meetings, controlling committee meeting rooms, getting committee documents published, maintaining files, and providing general support services. Some common administrative staff titles include chief clerk, staff assistant, clerk, and receptionist.

Job titles on committees can be misleading. For example, clerks on the Appropriations Committees are the top staff. Also, the staff director probably manages a committee staff but might not be the closest advisor to the committee chair or ranking member. Members might also rely on committee staff for some committee matters and personal staff for other committee matters.

§ 4.80 House of Representatives Committee Funding

Each standing and select committee of the House, except the Appropriations Committee, is required to submit an operating budget request for expenses over the two years of a Congress to the Committee on House Administration. The budget includes estimated staff salary needs and the cost of consulting services, detailees, printing, office equipment and supplies, travel for committee members and staff, and other administrative expenses. The House Administration Committee may hold hearings on each request and ask committee leaders to testify on behalf of their committees. The House Administration Committee marks up each request and packages the individual requests into an omnibus primary expense resolution.

The minority party is required to be "treated fairly in the appointment" of committee staff. Both parties as majority parties have often interpreted "fairly" to mean one-third of a committee's staff and resources for the minority.

The maximum committee staff salaries in 2011 were $172,500 a year for up to three staff (two majority and one minority), $170,696 a year for up to nine staff (six majority and three minority), and $168,411 a year for other committee staff.

§ 4.90 Senate Committee Funding

By January 31 of the first session of a Congress, each Senate committee, except the Appropriations and Ethics Committees, reports a resolution requesting funding for staff and expenses for a Congress. The Appropriations and Ethics Committees have permanent authorizations for staff salaries and expenses.

Each committee funding resolution is referred to the Committee on Rules and Administration. The committee may hold hearings on each request and ask other committees' leaders to testify on behalf of their committees. The Rules and Administration Committee marks up each request and packages all the requests into an omnibus funding resolution. The resolution recommends funding levels for the entire Congress, but allocates funding in two portions. In recent years, funding has been allocated for nineteen months in the first portion and twelve months in the second portion. The seven-month overlap allows committees to carry over to the second period any unexpended funds from the first period.

Each committee establishes a maximum level of staff that its budget can accommodate. By resolution, however, a majority of the minority party members of a committee may request at least one-third of the funds for hiring minority staff. Committees may also hire consultants or request that staff be detailed from federal agencies if they receive approval to do so from the Committee on Rules and Administration. Each senator also receives a legislative assistance allowance, separate from a committee's budget, to hire personal staff who handle committee work for the senator.

The maximum committee staff salary in 2010, the latest year for which a figure was officially available, was $171,315 a year.

§ 4.100 Congressional Fellowships and Internships

College students, graduate students, and professionals on sabbatical have opportunities to work on Capitol Hill. Executive agencies and private organizations sponsor fellowships and internships (the terms are often used interchangeably) in congressional offices. The following inventory lists some entities sponsoring major fellowship programs and highlights key information on each fellowship. The applications for many of these programs can be obtained on the appropriate web site. Interested individuals should also check on possible fellowships with other professional societies, educational institutions, foundations, and think tanks.

Internship opportunities, generally unpaid, can also be explored through individual congressional offices.

This section is on the web at <*TCNCF.com*>.

Fellowship Name and Sponsor	**Duration**	**Qualifications**	**Comments**
Asian Pacific American Institute for Congressional Studies <*http://apaics.org*>	Nine months (September–May)	Undergraduate or graduate degree	$20,000 stipend
Charles G. Koch Summer Fellow Program, Institute for Humane Studies at George Mason University <*http://theihs.org*>	Ten weeks during summer	Undergraduates, recent graduates, and graduate students, from all countries and studying in all majors are eligible	$1,500 stipend plus housing assistance
Congressional Black Caucus Congressional Fellows Program and Louis Stokes Urban Health Public Policy Fellows Program (and also internships) <*www.cbcfinc.org*>	Nine months	Full-time graduate or law students, recent college graduates, professionals with five or more years of experience pursuing part-time graduate studies, and faculty members interested in legislative process	$40,000 stipend and benefits for one-year Congressional Fellows

Fellowship Name and Sponsor	Duration	Qualifications	Comments
Congressional Fellows, American Political Science Association <*www.apsanet.org*>	Nine months, November–August	Political scientists, journalists, federal executives, health policy executives, and international scholars	$38,000 stipend and travel allowance (political scientists)
Congressional Hispanic Caucus Institute Fellowship Program (and also internships) <*www.chci.org*>	Eight weeks during summer, or nine months	College undergraduates, graduate students, and recent graduates	Stipend: $2,200 per month, $2,700 with graduate degree; plus travel
Congressional Science and Technology Policy Fellowships, coordinated by American Association for the Advancement of Science <*http://fellowships.aaas.org*>	One year, September–August	Ph.D. or equivalent doctoral-level degree, or master's degree in engineering and three years of post-degree professional experience	$74,000 stipend and benefits
The Heritage Foundation Internship Program <*http://heritage.org*>	Summer (nine to ten weeks), Spring and Fall (semester)	Rising college juniors or older, including recent college graduates, master's students, and law students	$7.25 per hour, Johnson Building Intern Housing Program available
LEGIS Fellows Program, Brookings Institution and Congressional Fellowship for Corporate Executives <*www.brookings.edu*>	Twelve months beginning in January, or seven-month winter or spring assignment (beginning in January or April)	GS-13 or uniformed service equivalent, two years of federal service in executive branch, and corporate executives with seven years management experience, respectively	Cost is $4,525 to $6,135
Native American Congressional Summer Internship Program, Morris K. Udall Foundation <*www.udall.gov*>	Ten weeks	Native American college students	$1,200 educational stipend plus expenses
Public Leadership Education Network <*www.plen.org*>	Summer session (two months)	Women undergraduate or graduate students	Course credit granted; internship fee charged
Robert Wood Johnson Health Policy Fellowships, sponsored by National Academy of Sciences, Institute of Medicine <*www.healthpolicyfellows.org*>	One year, September–August, with possible extension to December	Midcareer health professionals	Grants up to $165,000

Fellowship Name and Sponsor	Duration	Qualifications	Comments
Truman Scholars <*www.truman.gov*>	Ten-week summer institute in Washington	Undergraduate students pursuing careers in public service	Up to $30,000 merit-based grant toward graduate school
Washington Semester Fellows, American Politics Semester, sponsored by American University <*www.american.edu*>	One semester	College juniors or seniors	
Women's Research and Education Institute—Fellowship on Women and Public Policy <*www.wrei.org*>	January–September	Principally women graduate and post-graduate students, men may also apply	$1,450 per month stipend; $500 for health insurance, and up to $1,500 for tuition reimbursement

For internship and fellowship opportunities in the federal government for students, see <http://students.gov>, then select "Career development."

<TCNCF.com>

§ 4.110 Administrative Offices of the House

An administrative structure of legislative and nonlegislative staff supports the House in its legislative and representational roles and as a large, operating governmental entity. All House officers also have continuity of operations duties. (*See also § 4.121, Architect of the Capitol; and § 4.122, Office of the Attending Physician.*)

Chaplain

<http://chaplain.house.gov>

The chaplain is elected by the House, and serves the pastoral needs of members, their families, and congressional staff. The chaplain offers a prayer at the opening of each day's session. (*See § 4.111, Chaplains and Guest Chaplains.*)

Chief Administrative Officer

<http://cao.house.gov>

The chief administrative officer (CAO) is elected by the House to supervise its nonlegislative support services. The CAO may be removed by the Speaker or by the House. The CAO's staff, largely administrative and technical, is organized into several units in addition to the CAO's "immediate office," which oversees the media galleries in the Capitol, and issues the quarterly *Statement of Disbursements*, *<http://disbursements.house.gov>*, including:

- Administrative and Financial Services provides financial management and financial services to the House, such as administering House payroll and benefits processing expenses, offering advice on expenses, preparing the monthly financial statements procurement, and contract management. (*See § 4.112, Selling Products and Services to Congress.*)

§ 4.111

Chaplains and Guest Chaplains

Rev. Patrick Conroy, a Roman Catholic priest, was sworn in as the House chaplain on May 25, 2011. The Senate chaplain, Rear Admiral Dr. Barry C. Black (Ret.), a Seventh-day Adventist minister, was elected June 27, 2003. The chaplains are elected by their respective chamber to open the daily session with a prayer; serve as spiritual counselor to members, families, and staff; conduct Bible studies and discussion sessions; and officiate at weddings and funerals of members and on other special occasions.

Guest chaplains often deliver the daily invocation. Members contact their respective chamber chaplain to request approval to invite a guest chaplain. Guest chaplains are usually clergy from a member's home state or district. The guest chaplain may meet with the chamber chaplain before his appearance, to discuss the length—and often the tenor—of the daily prayer.

All 122 chaplains (sixty in the House and sixty-two in the Senate) have been Protestant, except three: a Catholic priest who served in the Senate for one year, and now Father Conroy and his immediate predecessor, Rev. Daniel Coughlin. Guest chaplains have represented many faiths.

- House Information Resources coordinates technology and communications products and services, including offering advice on technology purchases and integration, troubleshooting, contacting vendors, and managing computer security.
- Human Resources provides a variety of human resource management services, such as maintaining an employee assistance office, organizing training for congressional staff, and assisting offices with Americans with Disabilities Act services. Training sponsored by the House is supplemented by institutes and workshops offered by the Congressional Research Service and programs offered by other entities.
- Customer Solutions Center offers a number of services, including furnishing House offices, providing office equipment (including equipment and furnishings purchases for district offices), providing office supplies, managing the House office supply service and gift shop, managing the House postal operations and other specific services contracts, and maintaining video, audio, and photography services.

The administrative counsel within the CAO's immediate office reviews district office leases and car leases for compliance with House rules, and provides legal advice on administrative matters. The CAO also provides checklists and forms for closing a congressional office.

Clerk of the House

<http://clerk.house.gov>

At the convening of a new Congress, the clerk is elected by the House as its chief legislative officer. The clerk may be removed by the Speaker or the House. On the first day of a new Congress, the clerk presides over the House until the Speaker is elected. Throughout a Congress, the clerk has numerous powers and responsibilities. The clerk does the following, among other duties:

- receives and authenticates certificates of election
- maintains the *Journal of the House of Representatives of the United States*, and publishes the *Calendars of the United States House of Representatives and History of Legislation*

§ 4.112

Selling Products and Services to Congress

The House and Senate operate separately in vendor and procurement operations.

The House chief administrative officer (CAO) through the Office of Procurement Management is responsible for House procurement activities. Information on procurement policy and current procurement opportunities are listed on the CAO's web site, *<http://cao.house.gov>.*

The House has "privatized" some of its support services, increasing the number of procurement opportunities available in particular to services vendors. Some of the privatized services include restaurants, internal mail operations, and the beauty and barber shops.

The Senate sergeant at arms manages procurement activities through the Financial Operations Office, Procurement. Information on procurement policy is available at *<http://senate.gov>*, select "Visitors," then select "Procurement."

The architect of the Capitol (AOC) is also a purchaser of goods and services, with information available online at the AOC's web site, *<www.aoc.gov>.*

Some congressional procurement opportunities are advertised on the Federal Business Opportunities (Fed.Biz.Opps.Gov) web site, *<www.fbo.gov>.*

Other congressional officers also procure goods and services, and may be contacted directly.

- certifies the passage of bills and joint resolutions, and presents enrolled House bills and joint resolutions to the president
- prints and distributes the calendars of the House
- lists reports due to Congress from executive departments and agencies
- receives messages from the president and Senate when the House is not in session
- attests to and affixes the House seal to documents issued by an order of the House
- manages the House's institutional records, and assists members and departing members with their records through information such as the *Members Records Management Manual* and advice
- supervises the staff and manages the office of a member, delegate, or resident commissioner who dies, resigns, or is expelled, or in the event the House declares a vacancy in a congressional district
- maintains a web site of legislative information; extensive information about members, the House, Senate, and Capitol; and public disclosure information, including legislative disclosures such as signatories of discharge petitions (*see description of Legislative Resource Center below*)

Following are some of the principal units of the clerk's office:

- Legislative Operations comprises the various clerks who support the House's legislative activities. They are present working on the Speaker's dais when the House is in session. They also work behind the scenes processing the legislation introduced in and considered by the House, and preparing other documents.
- Official Reporters record the proceedings of the House for the *Congressional Record*, and also record the proceedings of House committees.

§ 4.113

Congressional Pages

Until August 2011, both the House and Senate were served by pages, high-school juniors of at least 16 years age who serve as messengers and assistants in the House or in the Senate. The House page program was discontinued in August 2011. Senate pages may be boys or girls; must be appointed to the Senate page program by a senator; and serve for a semester or for a summer session, although pages are sometimes reappointed for two semesters, two summer sessions, or both a school year and a summer.

Through its end in August 2011, the House authorized seventy-two pages, with up to forty-eight positions allocated to the majority and up to twenty-four to the minority. In the Senate, thirty pages are authorized, with up to eighteen positions allocated to the majority and up to twelve to the minority.

In addition to carrying messages and documents to or from member and committee offices from or to other locations in the Capitol complex, pages work in the Senate chamber. They assist Senate officers in setting up the Senate chamber for each day's activities, such as placing documents relevant to the day's agenda on each senator's desk. They also respond to senators on the floor by carrying documents to the dais, or carrying messages outside of the chamber.

The Senate has a page board that acts as the governing body for its page program. The sergeant of arms of the Senate supervises Senate pages. The pages live in a dormitory supervised by the page program staff. They take grade-level courses in a page school operated by the page program. The Senate page school is located at the Senate pages' residence hall. Pages receive a salary, and pay a housing and meals fee.

For historical information about the House page program, see <*http://pageprogram.house.gov*>. For information about the Senate page program, see <*http://senate.gov*> then select "Reference," "Virtual Reference Desk," "Pages."

- Publication Services provides liaison with the Government Printing Office, among other services.
- Legislative Computer Systems manages the functioning of the electronic voting system, among other responsibilities.
- Capitol Service Groups support the Democratic and Republican cloakrooms and other rooms set aside for special purposes for members, such as the Prayer Room.
- The House page program was previously managed by the clerk, who was also a member of the Page Board. (*See § 4.113, Congressional Pages.*)
- The Legislative Resource Center (LRC) distributes documents to the House and the public, providing the services of the former House Document Room. It also provides some library and research services to House offices. In its public-disclosure function, the LRC makes available for public review financial disclosure statements, foreign travel reports, gift and travel filings, mass mailings under members' franks, members' legal expense funds, member post-employment notices, and lobbying registrations and reports. (For campaign finance reports, the clerk's web site links to the Federal Election Commission's web site.) The LRC also distributes in print and on the clerk's web site official lists, for example, of members and committee assignments.

- Office of History and Preservation curates the House collection of art and artifacts, and is responsible for archiving and maintaining the official records of the House and its committees, and for giving advice to members on the archiving of their papers.
- The Employment Counsel offers legal advice to members and represents House offices in employment matters, including those arising under the Congressional Accountability Act.

General Counsel

Appointed by the Speaker, the general counsel provides legal advice to members, committees, officers, and employees on matters pertaining to their official duties, and represents them in litigation related to their official duties. The general counsel offers support to committees in their oversight and investigatory roles. Under the House rules establishing the Office of General Counsel, the Speaker consults on the office's direction with other members of the Bipartisan Legal Advisory Group, who are the majority leader, majority whip, minority leader, and minority whip.

The general counsel may also be assigned responsibility for filing an amicus brief in a case of importance to the House or even directed to represent the House as a litigant in lieu of representation by the Department of Justice. (The House general counsel is authorized by 2 U.S.C. 130f to appear in any court.) For example, under federal law (28 U.S.C. 530D), the attorney general must notify Congress when the Department of Justice will not defend the constitutionality of a law, will take the side against a law's constitutionality, or will not enforce a law. On February 23, 2011, the attorney general notified Congress that the executive would no longer defend the constitutionality of a provision of the Defense of Marriage Act (DOMA) (1 U.S.C. 7). (*See "Letter from the Attorney General to Congress on Litigation Involving the Defense of Marriage Act," February 23, 2011, at <www.justice.gov/opa/pr/2011/February/11-ag-223.html>.*) On March 9, 2011, by majority vote, the Bipartisan Legal Advisory Group directed the House general counsel to defend DOMA, where cases were on appeal in the courts of appeals for the First and Second Circuits.

Inspector General

<www.house.gov/IG>

Appointed jointly by the Speaker and the House majority and minority leaders, the inspector general conducts periodic audits of the financial and administrative activities of the House and of joint entities, and oversees the annual audit of the House. (Joint entities are legislative-branch agencies and offices shared by the House and the Senate, such as the architect of the Capitol.)

Office of the Law Revision Counsel

<http://uscode.house.gov>

The Office of the Law Revision Counsel, an office within the House, prepares and publishes the United States Code, which is a "consolidation and codification by subject matter of the general and permanent laws of the United States." This office maintains the U.S. Code, including classification tables for recently enacted laws, online. GPO Access also carries the Code online at *<www.gpoaccess.gov/uscode/index.html>*, and GPO sells the Code in printed, bound volumes.

§ 4.114

Capitol Security

To Capitol visitors, perhaps the five most noticeable components of increased Capitol security the last few years are the construction of the Capitol Visitor Center, inability to enter the Capitol without a guide, metal detectors and other security measures at building entrances, implementation of timed, ticketed tours of the Capitol, and street closures. These changes are part of a larger array of security-related activities, including:

- off-site irradiation and inspection of mail and other packages before delivery to congressional offices
- evacuation planning and training for office emergency coordinators, and allocation of emergency supplies and equipment
- security planning for state and district offices
- increased perimeter security with both police presence and barriers around the Capitol grounds and congressional office buildings, in addition to street closures
- restrictions on truck and bus traffic around the Capitol and congressional office buildings
- construction of permanent perimeter security structures aesthetically compatible with the Capitol and Olmsted landscape architecture
- increased police hiring and special training, and policies on use of lethal force
- increased personnel devoted to intelligence and threat assessment
- conduct of evacuation drills and security sweeps
- installation of notification systems
- installation of chemical and biological agents detection systems
- access of members to the federal government's emergency telephone system
- military transport for the Speaker
- implementation of security plans as threat levels change
- identification of alternate meeting sites for House and Senate
- continuity of operations planning
- changes in House rules, adopted at the beginning of the 108th and 109th Congresses, to provide the Speaker with additional authority in the event of an emergency

On a daily basis, the Capitol police, members and staff, and visitors must respond to the sudden implementation of security plans in response to real or potential emergencies and to changes resulting from other developments. Spontaneous events have included suspicious packages, suspicious substances, violations of airspace, computer attacks, discovery of weapons, weapons-wielding individuals, practical jokes, unauthorized demonstrations, power outages, and loss of water pressure, while planned events have included presidential visits to Capitol Hill, authorized demonstrations, addition of construction sites, and sidewalk closures. At times of heightened security, increased numbers of police, patrols, and K-9 units are visible to the public.

The severe wounding of Representative Gabrielle Giffords, death of six individuals, and injuries to thirteen more people in an assassination attempt on Giffords on January 8, 2011, in Tucson, Arizona, led to additional precautions. Members have sought security assessments of their state or district offices, and upgraded security measures in those offices. They have also sought security assessments of their homes, and have been permitted by the Federal Election Commission to use campaign funds

Continued on page 141

§ 4.114 (continued)

for home security measures. At the urging of the House and Senate sergeants at arms, members have appointed staff as law enforcement or security coordinators to provide liaison with local police, notify local police of member events, and undertake other security activities. U.S attorneys have successfully prosecuted some individuals who threatened violence against members and their families or staff.

In addition, each congressional office is also required under the Occupational Health and Safety Act, made applicable to Congress by the Congressional Accountability Act, *<http://compliance.gov>*, to have an emergency action plan, and each staff member must be trained in the plan. Assistance to offices in the development of a plan is available from the Office of Accountability and the Capitol police.

While the Law Revision Counsel is the official source of the Code, commercial publishers offer print and online versions with annotations and other features that make it easier to use and a much more powerful legal research tool.

(*For a more complete explanation of the U.S. Code, see § 9.70, Laws and Their Codification.*)

Legislative Counsel

<http://house.gov/legcoun>

Appointed by the Speaker, the legislative counsel and counsel's staff provide legislative drafting services and advice to leaders, committees, and members of the House.

Parliamentarian

Appointed by the Speaker, the parliamentarian and parliamentarian's staff advise the House's presiding officer on parliamentary procedure when the House is in session. On a nonpartisan and confidential basis, the parliamentarian also advises House leaders and members on parliamentary procedure at all other times. A very important function is to advise the Speaker on referral of measures, rulings on points of order, and responses to parliamentary inquiries. The parliamentarian compiles the precedents of the House, prepares the parliamentarian's notes for the *Constitution, Jefferson's Manual, and Rules of the House of Representatives of the United States*, and authors documents such as *How Our Laws Are Made*. *(See also § 10.40, Official Rules Publications of the House; and § 10.60, Other Congressional Sources of Information on Rules and Procedures.)*

Sergeant at Arms

<http://house.gov>, then select "The House Explained," "Officers and Organizations," then "Sergeant at Arms"

Elected by the House as chief protocol and law enforcement officer, the sergeant at arms maintains order in the House at the direction of the Speaker; executes orders of the Speaker; ensures that only individuals privileged to be on the House floor enter when the House is in session; and regulates the House galleries. The sergeant at arms also leads ceremonial processions at events such as joint sessions or meetings of Congress and presidential inaugurations. The mace, the symbol of the authority of the House and of the office of the sergeant at arms, is in the custody of the sergeant at arms.

The sergeant at arms has extensive responsibility for security for the House side of the Capitol, the House office buildings, and House garages and parking areas. This House officer provides various forms of support for major events in the Capitol and House office buildings. The sergeant at arms may investigate threats to members and crimes, and provide protective details. The sergeant at arms also bears security and other responsibilities for traveling congressional delegations. (*See § 4.114, Capitol Security.*) The sergeant at arms issues IDs to congressional staff, and manages the appointment desks for visitors with business in the Capitol. With the Senate sergeant at arms and the architect of the Capitol, the House sergeant at arms serves on the Capitol Police Board and the Capitol Guide Board. (*See § 4.123, Capitol Police.*)

The sergeant at arms may make funeral arrangements for representatives who die in office.

§ 4.120 Administrative Offices of the Senate

An administrative structure of legislative and nonlegislative staff supports the Senate in its legislative and representational roles and as a large, operating governmental entity. All Senate officers today have continuity of operations duties. (*See also § 4.121, Architect of the Capitol; and § 4.122, Office of the Attending Physician.*)

Chaplain

<www.senate.gov/reference/office/chaplain.htm>

The chaplain is elected by the Senate, and serves the pastoral needs of members, their families, and congressional staff. The chaplain offers a prayer at the opening of each day's session. (*See § 4.111, Chaplains and Guest Chaplains.*)

Legal Counsel

Appointed by the president pro tempore on the recommendation of the majority and minority leaders and elected by adoption of a Senate resolution, the legal counsel provides legal advice to members, committees, officers, and employees on matters pertaining to their official duties, and represents them in litigation related to their official duties. The legal counsel offers support to committees in their oversight and investigatory roles. Under the law establishing the Office of Legal Counsel, the legal counsel is responsible to the bipartisan joint leadership group consisting of the majority and minority leaders, president pro tempore, and the chairs and ranking minority members of the Judiciary and Rules and Administration Committees. When authorized by a two-thirds vote of the joint leadership group or by Senate resolution, the legal counsel defends the Senate, a committee or subcommittee, or member, officer or employee. Other procedures authorizing action apply in other circumstances (*2 U.S.C. 288 et seq.*).

Legislative Counsel

<http://slc.senate.gov>

Appointed by the president pro tempore, the legislative counsel and counsel's staff provide legislative drafting services and advice to leaders, committees, and members of the Senate.

§ 4.121

Architect of the Capitol

<www.aoc.gov>

The architect of the Capitol operates in a broad, complex web of responsibilities, is involved in numerous entities, and is accountable to several officers and committees of the House and Senate.

The buildings and grounds under the architect's authority include the Capitol and its grounds, which include the Taft Memorial, fountains, and other structures; the House and Senate office buildings, including the subways to the Capitol; the Library of Congress buildings and grounds, including two satellite buildings and, in Fort Meade, Maryland, and Culpeper, Virginia, two archival buildings; the Supreme Court building and grounds; the Thurgood Marshall Federal Judiciary Building and grounds; the Capitol police headquarters; the Botanical Garden and the adjoining outdoor National Garden; the Capitol power plant; and other buildings. The architect's duties in relation to these buildings include planning, operations, structural improvements and upkeep, construction and renovation, systems upgrades and maintenance, historic preservation, preservation of art and artifacts, landscaping and groundskeeping, and installation of physical security and life safety systems. "Green projects" have included installation of a vegetative roof on the Dirksen Senate Office Building. The architect also operates the Senate restaurants and furnishes Senate offices, and serves as civil defense coordinator for the Capitol complex.

Major projects include the rehabilitation of the Capitol dome, improvements to security within the Capitol complex, and life and fire safety improvement to the utility tunnels providing heating and cooling to Capitol Hill buildings, rehabilitation of the Cannon House Office Building, renovation of the indoor House parking garages, energy savings and efficiency of the Senate office buildings, and the Supreme Court roof replacement. The architect also bears partial responsibility for the arrangement of presidential inaugurations and other ceremonies held in the Capitol or on its grounds. The architect also moves member and committee offices after an election.

With the Capitol arguably the most important structure in Washington, DC, and with the extent of the federal presence on Capitol Hill, the architect plays an important role in District of Columbia planning. The architect is responsible for the master plan for the Capitol complex, and serves on the District of Columbia Zoning Commission, the Advisory Council on Historic Preservation, the National Capital Memorial Commission, and the Art Advisory Committee to the Washington Metropolitan Area Transit Authority, among various regional entities. Within the confines of the Capitol complex, the architect is an ex officio member of the U.S. Capitol Preservation Commission, and a member of the Capitol Police Board and the Capitol Guide Board, among various congressional entities. The architect's duties intertwine with those of the House's chief administrative officer, the Senate sergeant at arms, and other officers of the House and Senate.

In connection with his duties for the House, the architect is subject to the oversight of the House Administration Committee and the House Appropriations Committee. In connection with duties for the Senate, the architect is subject to the oversight of the Senate Rules and Administration Committee and the Senate Appropriations Committee. The Speaker, House Office Building Commission, Joint Committee on the Library, and other entities also play key policy and oversight roles.

A 1989 law established an appointment process for the architect and a ten-year term, with eligibility for reappointment (*2 U.S.C. 1801*). The law provides that a congressional commission recommend three names to the president, who then chooses an appointee. The appointment is subject to Senate confirmation. Upon confirmation, the architect is an officer of the legislative branch. On May 12, 2010, Stephen Ayers was confirmed as the second architect of the Capitol appointed under the law.

§ 4.122

Office of the Attending Physician

During normal weekday working hours and whenever the House or Senate is in session, emergency and nonemergency medical care is available from the Office of the Attending Physician and health units located in the Capitol and several of the congressional office buildings. The attending physician maintains an emergency response team to provide emergency care until a patient can be taken to an appropriate medical facility. The health units are staffed by registered nurses, who provide first aid and emergency nursing services.

The health units also provide services such as flu shots, injections of allergy medications, blood pressure screening and monitoring, some occupational-health nursing services, and other nonemergency services.

These services are available to members, congressional staff, Capitol police, and Senate pages. Emergency responses are made for Capitol visitors as well. An annual fee is charged to members for regular use of the office's services ($549 in 2011). Staffing and funding for the office have traditionally been shared by Congress and the Department of the Navy.

When mail containing anthrax spores was delivered to the office of then-Majority Leader Tom Daschle, the Office of the Attending Physician coordinated response for both the eradication of the contaminants and the testing and care of members and staff.

Parliamentarian

Appointed by the secretary of the Senate with the approval of the majority leader, the parliamentarian and parliamentarian's staff advise the Senate's presiding officer on parliamentary procedure when the Senate is in session. During a session, the parliamentarian or a member of his staff sits on the dais directly below the presiding officer. A very important function of the parliamentarian is to advise the presiding officer on referral of measures, rulings on points of order, and responses to parliamentary inquiries. On a nonpartisan and confidential basis, the parliamentarian also advises Senate leaders and senators on parliamentary procedure at all other times. The parliamentarian compiles the precedents of the Senate and prepares other documents such as *Enactment of a Law*. *(See § 10.50, Official Rules Publications of the Senate; and § 10.60, Other Congressional Sources of Information on Rules and Procedures.)*

Secretary for the Majority

<http://senate.gov>, then select "Reference," "Senate Organization," "Secretary for the Majority"

The secretary for the majority, selected by the majority leader, is an elected officer of the Senate. The secretary supervises the majority party's cloakroom, assigns chamber seats for majority-party senators, and works on and off the Senate floor to keep majority-party senators apprised of pending business. The secretary polls senators if requested by the leadership, monitors nominations on the *Executive Calendar*, performs other duties for the leadership as directed, and obtains *pairs* on votes for senators. The secretary for the majority is the repository of official minutes of majority-party conference meetings and of meetings of its policy and other committees. The secretary staffs the com-

§ 4.123

Capitol Police

<www.uscapitolpolice.gov>

Created in the early 1800s, the U.S. Capitol Police today exercises jurisdiction throughout the complex of congressional buildings and surrounding streets and parks. It protects life and property; prevents, detects, and investigates crimes; and enforces traffic regulations. It is called on to protect members and officers of Congress and their families throughout the United States in addition to its principal work on Capitol Hill. Assignments include protective services, investigations, drug enforcement, emergency response, hazardous devices, patrol, communications, K-9, and other activities. The police are overseen by the Capitol Police Board, which comprises the sergeants at arms of the House and Senate and the architect of the Capitol.

Congress has authorized an increase in the size of the police force in light of the increased security challenges and workload the force has confronted, particularly since the terrorist and anthrax attacks of 2001. Police personnel needs are also affected by the numbers of members of Congress who run for president, which can trigger the addition of security details beyond those normally accorded special protection, such as the Speaker. Like other Capitol Hill workers, the police force has had to confront personnel reductions caused by call-ups of National Guard and reserve units. (*See also § 4.114, Capitol Security*.)

mittee that arranges majority-party committee assignments, and maintains a file of senators' requests for committee assignments. The secretary also recommends to the leadership majority-party appointees to boards, commissions, and international conferences, and keeps records of those appointments.

Secretary for the Minority

<http://senate.gov>, then select "Reference,"
"Senate Organization," "Secretary for the Minority"

The secretary for the minority, selected by the minority leader, is an elected officer of the Senate. The secretary performs similar duties for the minority-party leadership and senators as the secretary for the majority performs for the majority party in the Senate.

Secretary of the Senate

<www.senate.gov/reference/office/secretary_of_senate.htm>
<www.senate.gov/artandhistory/history/common/briefing/secretary_senate.htm>

Elected by the Senate to provide legislative, financial, and administrative support to the Senate, the secretary of the Senate plays a key role in the Senate's operations. In addition, the secretary presides over the Senate in the absence of the vice president of the United States and pending election of a president pro tempore, and has custody of the Senate seal. The secretary is aided by an assistant secretary.

In a legislative role, the secretary's office comprises the various clerks, including the official reporters of debate, who support the Senate's legislative activities. They are present working on the dais when the Senate is in session. They also work behind the scenes processing the legislation introduced in and considered by the Senate and preparing other documents. One clerk position that exists in the Senate but not the House is the executive clerk, who prepares the *Executive Journal* and the *Executive Calendar*, recording activity on nominations, treaties, and resolutions pertaining to the Senate's executive business.

The secretary is the Senate's chief financial officer, responsible for accounting for all funds appropriated to the Senate and managing the disbursing office, headed by a financial clerk, which handles the Senate payroll, employee benefits, and all Senate-appropriated funds. The secretary also audits Senate financial activities, and issues the semiannual *Report of the Secretary of the Senate*, showing all disbursements over a six-month period.

The administrative offices under the secretary of the Senate, which include the following, serve the Senate or the public or both:

- Conservation and Preservation coordinates programs for the preservation of Senate records and materials.
- Security protects classified information.
- The Historical Office assists senators and committees with archives (including publishing the *Records Management Handbook*), performs research for use by senators and the public, assists researchers in access to Senate records, maintains senators' profiles in the online *Biographical Directory of the United States Congress*, and offers other services.
- The Library offers legislative, legal, and reference services to Senate offices, and makes its enormous collection of congressional and government documents available to senators and other authorized users.
- Public Records provides public access to financial disclosure forms, travel reports, Federal Election Commission reports, registrations of mass mailings, lobbying registration and reports, and other records.
- Printing and Document Services serves as liaison with the Government Printing Office.
- The Senate Curator administers museum programs of the Senate for the Capitol and Senate office buildings.
- Interparliamentary Services assists interparliamentary conferences and Senate delegations traveling overseas.
- The Stationery Room provides stationery and other office supplies, and the Gift Shop offers a variety of items.
- The Senate Page School is managed by the secretary, who serves as a member of the Page Board. (*See § 4.113, Congressional Pages.*)
- The Chief Counsel for Employment offers legal advice to members and represents Senate offices in employment matters, including those arising under the Congressional Accountability Act. The secretary of the Senate also administers other human resources programs.

In the event of a senator's death, the secretary manages the senator's staff until a successor is chosen. With the sergeant at arms, the secretary publishes *Closing a Senate Office Handbook.*

Sergeant at Arms

<www.senate.gov/reference/office/sergeant_at_arms.htm>

<www.senate.gov/artandhistory/history/common/briefing/sergeant_at_arms.htm>

Elected by the Senate as chief protocol and law enforcement officer and administrative manager, the sergeant at arms supervises the Senate floor and galleries. *Doorkeepers* ensure that only individuals privileged to be on the Senate floor enter when the Senate is in session. The sergeant at arms also regulates the Senate galleries and supervises Senate pages and other workers who serve the Senate. (*See § 4.113, Congressional Pages.*) The Senate gavel is entrusted to the care of the sergeant at arms.

In a protocol role, the sergeant at arms escorts official guests to the Senate, may make funeral arrangements for senators who die in office, and provides various forms of support for major events in the Capitol and Senate office buildings. The sergeant at arms leads the Senate wherever it goes as a body, such as to the House for a joint session or meeting or to the presidential inaugural platform.

The sergeant at arms has responsibility for security for the Senate side of the Capitol and its grounds, the Senate office buildings and grounds, and the senators themselves. The sergeant at arms enforces all rules governing the Senate side of the Capitol and the Senate office buildings, and may arrest violators. The sergeant at arms also bears security and other responsibilities for traveling congressional delegations. The sergeant at arms issues IDs to Senate staff, and employs the staff of the media galleries. With the House sergeant at arms and the architect of the Capitol, the Senate sergeant at arms serves on the Capitol Police Board and the Capitol Guide Board. (*See § 4.123, Capitol Police.*) The sergeant at arms is also custodian of property of the Senate. (*See also § 4.112, Selling Products and Services to Congress.*)

As an administrative manager, the sergeant at arms has the largest staff and budget in the Senate and supports the Senate in numerous ways. Following are some of the services provided by the sergeant at arms office:

- Security and emergency preparedness, including continuity of operations.
- Production of mass mailings and operation of the Senate mail system and post office.
- Administration of parking and of automobile fleet maintenance.
- Management of the Senate's furnishings, including their repair and moving, and equipment repair.
- Provision of services such as housekeeping and barber and beauty shops.
- Leasing of autos for Senate offices.
- Recording and photographic services, including operation of television cameras that record the Senate in session.
- Technology services ranging from network engineering to information security to Internet services to software acquisition to user support.
- Financial management.
- Human resources, which administers various employment programs, such as employee assistance, workers' compensation, and training; training sponsored by the Senate is supplemented by institutes and workshops offered by the Congressional Research Service and programs offered by other entities, including TheCapitol.Net, publisher of this book.

The sergeant at arms assists senators in establishing and maintaining their state offices. Senate pages are supervised by the sergeant at arms.

§ 4.130 Legislative-Branch Support Agencies

A handful of agencies within the legislative branch assist Congress in both its lawmaking and representational or informational roles. Some, like the Congressional Research Service, work exclusively for Congress, and their work products traditionally must be obtained through congressional offices. Others, such as the Government Accountability Office, make many of their work products available directly to the public in both print and electronic form, although the public release of some work might be delayed to give the requesting committee or member a first chance to read or release it.

Congressional Budget Office

<http://cbo.gov>

The Congressional Budget Office (CBO) explains its nonpartisan role in congressional policymaking as "helping the Congress formulate a budget plan, helping it stay within that plan, helping it assess the impact of federal mandates, and helping it consider issues related to the budget and to economic policy." CBO's mandate originated in the Congressional Budget and Impoundment Control Act of 1974. Its director is appointed jointly by the Speaker of the House and the president pro tempore of the Senate to a four-year term.

In fulfilling its role, CBO works first and foremost for the House and Senate Budget Committees. Its next priority is service to the four "money" committees—the House and Senate Appropriations Committees, which have jurisdiction over the discretionary portion of the federal budget, and the House Ways and Means and Senate Finance Committees, which have jurisdiction over taxation and full or partial jurisdiction over programs that are tax-based, such as Social Security and Medicare. It then serves Congress' authorizing committees, such as the House Agriculture Committee and the Senate Agriculture, Nutrition, and Forestry Committee. CBO handles individual member requests to the extent it can. (In its work with the tax committees, CBO uses revenue projections prepared by the congressional Joint Committee on Taxation, a bicameral study committee without legislative authority.)

In assisting the Budget Committees in preparing the annual congressional budget resolution, CBO prepares economic forecasts and projections, baseline budget projections, an analysis of the president's budget, and policy options. For most bills reported from committee, CBO prepares a cost estimate. It then tracks those bills and performs scorekeeping, a tabulation of the cumulative impact of congressional spending and revenue decisions. It also performs other economic and budget analyses and prepares policy options, often at the request of a specific committee. (*See Chapter Seven for an explanation of the federal budget process and CBO's role in it.*)

Finally, under the Unfunded Mandates Reform Act of 1995 (*109 Stat. 48*), CBO is required to provide committees with a determination of whether a reported measure contains a federal mandate, make an estimate of the direct costs of the mandate if specific criteria are met, and assess funding provided or needed to cover the mandate's costs. (*See § 8.201, Unfunded Mandates and Congressional Procedures.*) A document notification service is available at *<http://cbo.gov/listserver>*.

Congressional Research Service

<www.loc.gov/crsinfo/>

The nonpartisan Congressional Research Service (CRS) provides information services in many forms to all congressional offices—reports, confidential memoranda and briefings, seminars, a web site, audio and video programs, and research in a variety of formats. It also supports the Legislative Information System (LIS) used in congressional offices. CRS performs legislative research and analysis and policy analysis within a legislative context; provides research and analytical services related to legislative, budget, and other processes; and offers legal and constitutional research and analyses on legal issues. (Unlike the Government Accountability Office, CRS does not evaluate federal programs.) Through its research centers in the congressional office buildings and the Library of Congress' Madison Building and its staff of librarians, CRS also provides library research, reference, bibliographic, and other services. CRS responds to more than 500,000 congressional inquiries annually, exclusive of web site inquiries.

None of these services is available directly to the public. CRS reports may be obtained in print form through a member or committee office or, selectively, online through a member or committee web site. (A CRS product online through a member or committee web site may not be the latest version.) Members and committees also often release CRS confidential analyses in the course of hearings, floor debate, or press conferences, and CRS staff often testify at congressional hearings. A number of web sites, such as Open CRS, *<http://opencrs.com>*, also provide access to CRS reports, but the version might not be current. CRS bill digests, however, are available for legislation listed on THOMAS, *<http://thomas.gov>*.

Organizationally, CRS is a department of the Library of Congress, and CRS is headed by a director appointed by the librarian of Congress.

Government Accountability Office

<http://gao.gov>

In response to requests from committees or members or in fulfilling its legal and legislative responsibilities, the nonpartisan Government Accountability Office (GAO) provides reports, testimony, and briefings based on its audits and evaluations of government agencies, programs, and activities. Its work is often used by congressional committees in their oversight and investigatory roles, and GAO's work might well be the source of legislative provisions in reauthorization and other legislation. GAO also provides Congress with legal analyses and advice related to legislative proposals, legislative drafting, and potential policy changes to specific government agencies, programs, and activities. (*For an explanation of the criteria and procedures used by GAO to undertake work for Congress, see GAO's Congressional Protocols, available on the GAO web site: <http://gao.gov>, then search for "Congressional Protocols." See also § 4.131, Requesting GAO Assistance.*)

Testimony and completed reports (unless classified) are quickly made available to the public in print and through GAO's web site, although GAO may delay release of a report for up to thirty days if a congressional requestor asks for a delay. Lists and finding aids on the web site assist the users in identifying useful reports and other GAO documents. GAO also provides notices of newly released reports and testimony via email and other means.

§ 4.131

Requesting GAO Assistance

Committees and individual members regularly turn to the Government Accountability Office to request a variety of assistance. Here is a letter written in the 112th Congress by a bicameral, bipartisan group of members representing Ohio, who were seeking a GAO investigation of the disposition of NASA Space Shuttles.

In accepting work from Congress, GAO gives precedence to congressional mandates and to requests from committees. In considering accepting the request from the Ohio delegation, it would likely consider the relevance of the members' committee assignments to the subject of the request, the specificity of the request, GAO's ability to perform the request, the resources required for performance, and other factors.

Congress of the United States
Washington, DC 20515

April 12, 2011

The Honorable Gene Dodaro
U.S. Government Accountability Office
441 G Street, NW
Washington, D.C. 20548

Dear Mr. Dodaro:

We are writing to request that the Government Accountability Office (GAO) undertake a review of the policies and practices of the National Aeronautics and Space Administration's (NASA) and the Smithsonian's disposition of the shuttle program related property.

The National Aeronautics and Space Authorization Act of 2010 (Public Law No: 111-267) reiterated Congressional support for the existing NASA disposal plan. Section 603 of the Act states, "The orbiter vehicles shall be made available and located for display and maintenance through a competitive procedure established pursuant to the disposition plan developed under section 613(a) of the National Aeronautics and Space Administration Authorization Act of 2008."

The law regarding disposal of excess government property is clear, and NASA's disposition plan for the shuttle clearly affirms that NASA will follow it. NASA is bound to follow existing federal property disposal laws, including the Federal Property and Administrative Services Act. That law indicates that if the Space Shuttle Orbiters are declared surplus to NASA's needs, they need to be offered to other Federal agencies (including the Defense Department) before they can be offered to any organization outside the federal government.

While answering questions before the Senate and House Appropriations Commerce, Science, and Justice and Related Agencies Subcommittees, NASA Administrator Bolden stated that the decision on shuttle disposition was his alone based on the process he and his predecessors laid out – including a ten point selection criteria analyzed by a "team" within the organization. Any such GAO review should disclose the 10 criteria, the members of the team, and how the final decision was determined.

Continued on page 151

§ 4.131 (continued)

Specifically, we ask that GAO review how the disposition of the shuttle program related property carried out, and if NASA and the Smithsonian did so in accordance with all statutory and regulatory guidelines.

Thank you for your attention to this request.

Sincerely,

Sherrod Brown
United States Senator

Michael R. Turner
Member of Congress

Steve Austria
Member of Congress

Marcy Kaptur
Member of Congress

Steven C. LaTourette
Member of Congress

The laws under which GAO operates provide it with broad investigatory powers and broad access to agencies' information. Its authority and the interdisciplinary expertise that its audit and evaluation teams bring together enable GAO to measure the achievement of goals and objectives in federal programs, determine whether federal funds are being spent efficiently, and ensure compliance with federal law. Because of its work, GAO has developed a number of manuals that are available to the public.

In addition to responsibilities for special investigations, accounting standards, and other work affecting the executive branch, GAO reports to Congress pursuant to specific laws. For example, under the Congressional Review Act, the comptroller general reports to the committees of jurisdiction of both houses of Congress on major rules proposed by federal agencies. Under the Government Performance and Results Act, GAO plays a lead role in monitoring executive departments and agencies in their implementation of the law and reports its findings to Congress. And, in assisting Congress under the Congressional Budget and Impoundment Control Act of 1974, GAO reviews rescissions and deferrals of spending proposed by the president. (*See § 8.41, Congressional Review of Agency Rule Making; and Chapter Seven, Legislating in Congress: Federal Budget Process.*)

GAO is regularly assigned new duties or projects in new laws. For example, in the Patient Protection and Affordable Care Act (*P.L. 111-148*), GAO was directed, among other duties, to appoint members of the methodology committee of the Patient Centered Outcomes Research Institute and commissioners to the National Health Care Workforce Commission.

GAO is headed by the comptroller general. After receiving a list of candidates from a special bicameral, bipartisan commission, the president nominates the comptroller general to a fifteen-year term; the presidential appointment is subject to the Senate's confirmation. Gene Dodaro was confirmed by the Senate as comptroller general on December 22, 2010. Until July 2004, the agency's name was the General Accounting Office.

Library of Congress and Law Library of Congress

<http://loc.gov> and <http://loc.gov/law>

The Library of Congress is the most publicly oriented of the legislative-branch support agencies. Indeed, the number of domestic and foreign visitors, researchers, librarians with business at the Library of Congress, copyright registrants, guests for public events, visitors to its ever-expanding web resources, and so on, vastly exceeds the number of congressional requests the library receives. Yet, the Library of Congress is also a vital resource for members and committees of Congress.

In terms of subject matter, the library's collections are vast and comprehensive. It is only in the fields of technical agriculture and clinical medicine "where it yields precedence to the National Agricultural Library and the National Library of Medicine, respectively." Books and other items from the library's collections are available for lending to congressional offices, and research assistance related to special collections can be obtained. The Library of Congress makes its public rooms available to members for official events, and maintains a members' reading room in the Jefferson Building. And, the library serves members' constituents with *THOMAS*, the web-based legislative information system, *<http://thomas.loc.gov>*, online catalogs, an extensive web site including online research collections, social media accounts, and other services.

Finally, the Library of Congress maintains the world's largest law library, the collection of which includes both domestic and foreign legal materials available for use by the public. The law library seeks to obtain all primary legal and legislative sources and important secondary sources concerning the laws of all nations and legal systems. It also collects sources on the history of law, the philosophy of law, comparative law, and international law. The electronic version of this collection activity is reflected in the Global Legal Information Network, *<http://glin.gov>*. The law library staff serves Congress primarily with foreign-law research. Domestic legal research and analysis is performed by the Congressional Research Service's American Law Division, another part of the Library of Congress.

The Library of Congress is headed by the librarian of Congress, who is nominated by the president; the appointment is subject to Senate confirmation. The law librarian is appointed by the librarian of Congress.

§ 4.140 Government Printing Office

<www.fdsys.gov>

As the principal producer and disseminator of congressional documents, the Government Printing Office (GPO) is a key source of information—in both print and electronic (online and CD-ROM) formats—about Congress and its activities. As a legislative body, Congress needs fast, accurate printing services to assist it in the processing of legislation. GPO was established in 1860 to do just that.

Today, pursuant to the provisions of Title 44 of the U.S. Code, GPO is charged with printing, binding, and electronic information dissemination for Congress, the president, and federal agencies. GPO prints the *Congressional Record* and the *Federal Register* and makes both publications available online: <*http://fdsys.gov*>. GPO describes itself as the "digital platform for the federal government," amid congressional efforts to reduce the volume of printing and binding of legislative documents.

The congressional documents that GPO prints are distributed to the House Legislative Resource Center, the Senate Document Room, congressional committees, and elsewhere within Congress. Most documents are redistributed by those offices to members and congressional staff and to the public, but some are printed for the specific use of a committee or other congressional entity. In addition, most congressional documents are also available free online, for examination in depository libraries, or for purchase from GPO's superintendent of documents.

In addition to the printing of bills and resolutions and other legislative documents, GPO provides each congressional office with specific printed documents, as authorized by law, resolution, or regulation. These include the following:

- *Congressional Record*
- *Statutes at Large*
- *Congressional Directory* and *Congressional Pictorial Directory*
- *Federal Register* and *Presidential Papers*
- *U.S. Treaties* and *Other International Agreements*

Senators each receive a permanent edition of the *Congressional Record*, the *Senate Manual*, and other documents. Representatives each receive the *Constitution, Jefferson's Manual, and Rules of the House of Representatives of the United States*, a set of the U.S. Code, and other documents.

GPO provides members with franked, public-document envelopes, reprints from the *Congressional Record* (for a nominal fee), estimates of the cost of insertions exceeding two pages into the Extensions of Remarks section of the *Congressional Record*, and other services.

GPO also serves Congress and the public through its web site of frequently used documents, GPO's Federal Digital System: <*http://fdsys.gov*>. Many congressional web sites, the Library of Congress' THOMAS service, and other government and private web sites link to FDsys. It provides online access to congressional bills and resolutions, committee reports (including conference committee reports), public laws, the *Congressional Record*, the *Congressional Directory*, and a variety of other congressional documents. It also provides online access to the *Federal Register, Code of Federal Regulations*, and other executive-branch publications essential to the work of a government-relations professional. Many publishers and commercial online services buy content from GPO to index and reformat for their systems. Because GPO is the source, it will often have the information online first; however, other services often have more powerful search tools and more convenient features than GPO. (*See also Chapter Nine, Congressional Documents: Overview, Legislation and Laws.*)

As the administrator of the federal depository libraries program for nearly 1,300 libraries, GPO also makes these and other congressional, executive, and judicial documents available to federal depository libraries, <*http://gpo.gov/libraries*>. Located within public, university, and other libraries, federal depository libraries allow local, public access to current and historical documents that may not be available online. The depository libraries are staffed with librarians experienced in using those resources. GPO also maintains an online bookstore for congressional and other government documents: <*http://bookstore.gpo.gov*>.

§ 4.150 Congressional Accountability Act

Office of Compliance

<*www.compliance.gov*>

A key provision of the House Republican's 1995 "Contract with America" and the first new law of the Republican-controlled Congress, the Congressional Accountability Act (*P.L. 104-1; 109 Stat. 3*) extended application of eleven federal labor and nondiscrimination laws to Congress and the legislative branch. It superseded existing practices and regulations, and afforded legislative-branch staff with rights and redress provided to other government and private workers.

The laws made applicable by the Congressional Accountability Act were the following:

- Age Discrimination in Employment Act of 1967
- Americans with Disabilities Act of 1990
- Civil Rights Act of 1964
- Employee Polygraph Protection Act of 1988
- Fair Labor Standards Act of 1938
- Family and Medical Leave Act of 1993
- Labor-Management Dispute Procedures (part of Title 5 of the U.S. Code)
- Occupational Safety and Health Act of 1970
- Rehabilitation Act of 1973
- Veterans Reemployment Act of 1993
- Worker Adjustment and Retraining Notification Act of 1988

The law established the Office of Compliance, with authority over the legislative branch, to enforce the statutes and handle complaints of employees. It is headed by an executive director, hired by a board of directors that is appointed jointly by the Speaker, House minority leader, and Senate majority and minority leaders. Oversight is exercised by the House Administration Committee, Senate Rules and Administration Committee, and Senate Homeland Security and Governmental Affairs Committee. Congress created the office to avoid a potential separation-of-powers problem caused by executive administration of the act in the legislative branch.

For resolution of a grievance, an employee must bring his grievance to the Office of Compliance and follow a formal process of counseling, mediation, and hearing. After the mediation process, an employee can file a formal complaint and request an administrative hearing with the office or file a civil suit in U.S. district court. The act also provides for an appeals process from a decision made by a hearing officer. Members of Congress may not be held personally liable for any damage awards, and punitive damages are disallowed.

The Office of Compliance is also given authority to determine unionization rights of employees. However, unionization is not allowed for staffs of member, committee, and leadership offices, or for staff in other specified legislative-branch agencies and offices. The general counsel investigates OSHA, disability access, and other matters under the Congressional Accountability Act. The general counsel is also directed in the Congressional Accountability Act (*see <www.compliance.gov>*) to conduct occupational safety and health compliance inspections of all legislative branch facilities once in every Congress and to report findings to the Speaker, president pro tempore, and others.

The House and Senate Ethics Committees retained authority to discipline members, officers, and employees for violations of rules on nondiscrimination in employment. However, members of Congress were allowed to continue to consider party affiliation, residence, and "political compatibility" in making employment decisions.

§ 4.160 General Services Administration

<http://gsa.gov>

The General Services Administration (GSA) has congressional services representatives in each GSA region who serve over 1,400 House district and Senate state offices. The congressional services representatives coordinate requests for space, furnishings and equipment, and other office services (such as moving, custodial, and security services).

The congressional services representatives work under the policies and guidance provided by GSA's Office of Congressional and Intergovernmental Affairs, which works to ensure that GSA services for district and state offices are carried out in accordance with House and Senate rules and policies. GSA, in turn, works through the House's Office of the Chief Administrative Officer (under the policy guidance of the House Administration Committee) and the Senate Office of the Sergeant at Arms (under the policy guidance of the Senate Rules and Administration Committee). The House chief administrative officer and the Senate sergeant at arms provide the points of contact for congressional offices in obtaining GSA services. They also review leases for offices not in federal buildings.

In another service useful to both members of Congress and their constituents, GSA maintains online a searchable *Catalog of Federal Domestic Assistance*, facilitating research on grants and other federal funding available to governments, nonprofits, individuals, and other entities (*<www.cfda.gov>*). GSA also compiles the print version of the *Catalog*. (*See also <http://grants.gov>, managed by the Department of Health and Human Services.*) GSA maintains both online and other services to the American public, services for business, and services for government agencies that are useful to members of Congress and their constituents. These services include the consumer information center and the Federal Citizen Information Center. (*See <http://pueblo.gsa.gov>.*)

§ 4.170 Congressional Liaison Offices

Congressional liaison offices in executive departments and agencies are vital to congressional-executive relations. They might also be called congressional affairs offices, legislative relations offices, or some other appropriate name. A congressional liaison office responds to congressional requests for information and coordinates case work for congressional offices with an agency. It might coordinate an agency's legislative program and some or many aspects of appropriations requests. It also works with the Office of Management and Budget on legislative clearance. (*See § 4.180, Office of Management and Budget.*) Several agencies that handle congressional requests numbered in the thousands each year maintain offices in the House and Senate office buildings. (*See § 4.171, Liaison Offices on Capitol Hill.*)

§ 4.171

Liaison Offices on Capitol Hill

All departments and many agencies maintain congressional affairs offices, a point of contact for congressional offices with a specific department or agency. In addition, some of the departments and agencies that handle among the highest volume of congressional inquiries maintain offices within the House and Senate office buildings. These Capitol Hill offices are listed below. All area codes are 202.

Department or Agency	House		Senate	
	Room	Phone	Room	Phone
Air Force	B322 Rayburn	225-6656	SR-182 Russell	224-2481
Army	B325 Rayburn	225-3853	SR-183 Russell	224-2881
Coast Guard	B320 Rayburn	225-4775	SR-183 Russell	224-2913
Marine Corps	B324 Rayburn	225-7124	SR-182 Russell	224-4681
Navy	B324 Rayburn	225-7126	SR-182 Russell	224-4682
Office of Personnel Management	B332 Rayburn	225-4955	B332 Rayburn	225-4955
Social Security Administration	G3-L1, Rayburn	225-3133	G3-L1, Rayburn	225-3133
Department of State	B330 Rayburn	226-4640	B330 Rayburn	226-4640
Department of Veterans' Affairs	B328 Rayburn	225-2280	SH-321 Hart	224-5351

The General Services Administration Office of Congressional and Intergovernmental Affairs and Department of Health and Human Services Assistant Secretary for Legislation provide a good description of a liaison office's work. (*Excerpts appear in § 4.172, Duties of a Congressional Liaison Office.*)

The general counsel's office in departments and agencies is also involved in legislative relations, working closely with both the congressional liaison office and the head of the department or agency. (*Excerpts describing the responsibilities of two general counsel offices appear in § 4.173, General Counsel Offices.*)

Heads of departments and agencies and their personal staffs, budget offices, and program offices might all become involved at one time or another in liaison with Congress. Cabinet secretaries and other departmental officials and agency officials might testify at legislative, appropriations, oversight, and investigatory hearings. Responses to congressional case work might include policy decisions that require review by a senior departmental or agency official. Requests for information might involve regional, state, or field offices assisting in a response. When a congressional office is the client, departments and agencies tend to be responsive.

§ 4.172

Duties of a Congressional Liaison Office

General Services Administration's Office of Congressional and Intergovernmental Affairs

<http://gsa.gov/portal/category/21405>

The following excerpt from the General Services Administration web site offers a good summary of the work and responsibilities of a congressional liaison office.

General Information

The Office of Congressional and Intergovernmental Affairs serves as advisor to the Administrator and supervises and maintains agency liaison with all Members of Congress and Congressional committees.

The Office of Congressional and Intergovernmental Affairs: prepares and coordinates GSA's annual legislative program; communicates GSA's legislative program to the Office of Management and Budget (OMB), Congress, and other interested parties; works closely with OMB in the coordination and clearance of all proposed legislation impacting GSA and its programs; prepares comments and makes recommendations on all bills submitted by GSA to the President for final action; and initiates, coordinates, and presents briefings to Members of Congress and their staff on GSA programs and initiatives.

The Office also prepares, circulates, and finalizes agency reports/recommendations on GSA's position concerning bills (including drafts) which affect GSA's mission and responsibilities; coordinates and clears with OMB and other agencies GSA reports, positions on legislative initiatives, testimony, follow-up questions, and answers submitted to congressional committees; coordinates all activities associated with GSA's appearances before congressional committees including the development of strategy, designation of witnesses, and preparation of testimony; and represents GSA in meetings and discussions with other agencies on all legislative matters.

The Office also: coordinates preparation of reports mandated by statute to be forwarded to the Congress as required; serves as liaison with state and local government officials and their official national organizations on items concerning GSA; and prepares weekly GSA intergovernmental affairs report for the White House Director of Intergovernmental Affairs.

General Services Administration's Office of Congressional and Intergovernmental Affairs

The GSA web site previously listed procedures applicable to agency work with congressional offices, which remain of interest in understanding an agency's congressional liaison procedures:

5. Procedures. The following procedures will be followed in dealings with the Congress:

a. Hearing statements to be presented by GSA witnesses must first be submitted to the Office of Congressional Affairs for review. The congressional statements also require approval from the Office of Management and Budget before submission to the Congress; therefore, enough time must be allowed for both GSA and OMB to review the statements.

b. Congressional hearings dealing with matters of direct interest to GSA, whether or not GSA witnesses are involved, must be monitored by a member of the office of Congressional Affairs, and a brief memorandum listing the major issues covered at the hearing and the commitments made on behalf of the agency will be forwarded to the program office involved. The Office of Congressional Affairs will track and follow up on these commitments.

Continued on page 158

4

§ 4.172 (continued)

c. Associate Administrators and Heads of Services and Staff Offices are expected to take initiative and work diligently with the committee staffs on issues. Their dealings should be coordinated through the Office of Congressional Affairs, which will take the lead in contacting the Congress and will maintain the agency record. If legislative issues arise or requests are received for technical assistance in contacts between GSA's Office of Budget and the Congress, the Office of Congressional Affairs must be notified regarding the nature of the issues and of any further action needed.

d. Any GSA employee dealing directly with a Member of Congress and staff on policy issues or a subject involving an agency commitment must inform the Office of Congressional Affairs and the next higher level of management within the affected Service or Staff Office. When regional GSA congressional support representatives contact a Member or staff in providing and outfitting State and district offices, the Office of Congressional Affairs does not need to be contacted. Regional congressional support representatives must report to the Office of Administrative Services any situations that are not routine. The Office of Administrative Services will, when necessary, inform the Office of Congressional Affairs. Direct contacts that result in a meeting being scheduled that involves policy issues and agency commitments must be reported to the Office of Congressional Affairs before the meeting takes place.

e. All congressional correspondence, background material, and factsheets, whether initiated by GSA or in reply to an inquiry, whether for signature by the Administrator or a Service Head (excluding Regional Administrators), must be routed through the Office of Congressional Affairs for concurrence. Congressional correspondence signed by Regional Administrators must include a copy to the Office of Congressional Affairs.

f. Deadlines on requests for comment on legislation sent out by the Office of Congressional Affairs are to be honored by the Services and Staff Offices, which are expected to give the deadlines top priority. Normally, extensions to deadlines will not be granted by the Office of Congressional Affairs. The Office of Congressional Affairs will keep the Administrator informed of each service's compliance with deadlines.

g. When meetings are held to discuss legislation, projects, inquiries, or matters of congressional interest, a representative from the Office of Congressional Affairs must be invited to attend.

U.S. Department of Health and Human Services Assistant Secretary for Legislation

<www.hhs.gov/asl>

Cabinet departments have an assistant secretary charged with congressional liaison and often other responsibilities, as shown in this example:

Mission

The Office of the Assistant Secretary for Legislation (ASL) is responsible for the development and implementation of the Department's legislative agenda.

It provides advice on legislation and facilitates communication between the Department and Congress. The office also informs the Congress of the Department's views, priorities, actions, grants and contracts. ASL is the Department liaison with Members of Congress, staff, Committees, and with the Government Accountability Office (GAO).

The office provides support to the Secretary of Health and Human Services by:

- developing, transmitting, providing information about, and working to enact the Department's legislative and administrative agenda;

Continued on page 159

§ 4.172 (continued)

- supporting implementation of legislation passed by Congress;
- working closely with the White House to advance Presidential initiatives relating to health and human services;
- responding to Congressional inquiries and notifying Congressional offices of grant awards (GrantsNet, TAGGS) made by the Department;
- providing technical assistance regarding grants and legislation to Members of Congress and their staff and facilitating informational briefings relating to Department programs and priorities;
- managing the Senate confirmation process for the Secretary and the fourteen other Presidential appointees (HHS) who must be confirmed by the Senate;
- preparing witnesses and testimony for Congressional hearings;
- coordinating meetings and communications of the Secretary and other Department officials with Members of Congress;
- notifying and coordinating with Congress regarding the Secretary's travel and event schedule;
- coordinating Department response to Congressional oversight and investigations;
- acting as Departmental liaison with the Government Accountability Office (GAO) and coordinating responses to GAO inquiries; and
- serves as liaison to external organizations, including public and private interest groups, with respect to the legislative agenda.

§ 4.180 Office of Management and Budget

<www.whitehouse.gov/omb>

The Office of Management and Budget plays many roles of interest to Congress and important to the operation of the executive branch, but two roles in particular stand out as of interest to Congress: coordinating preparation and defense of the annual budget, and legislative coordination and clearance.

OMB organizes the preparation of the annual budget in the executive branch, and works to implement the president's guidance and decisions during that process. The OMB director and his staff bring all decisions together in the budget documents that the president submits to Congress. The OMB director is also one of the leadoff executive witnesses each year before several committees to explain the president's budget recommendations to Congress and to defend them, and continues to play a key role throughout the year as congressional committees draft appropriations, tax, and other budgetary legislation. (*For more information on OMB's budget role, see § 7.40, Presidential Budget Process.*)

OMB also seeks to ensure that the administration speaks with one voice through the system of legislative coordination and clearance. OMB Circular A-19 describes policies and procedures (*see <http://omb.gov>, then search for "A-19"*); it is supplemented occasionally by memoranda to department and agency heads from the OMB director (*see <http://omb.gov>, under "Information for Agencies" select "Memoranda"*). Legislative clearance and coordination covers legislation that agencies

§ 4.173

General Counsel Offices

The following two examples show the support that a general counsel's office gives an executive department in its relations with Congress.

U.S. Department of Transportation Office of the General Counsel

<www.dot.gov/ost/ogc/org/legislation/index.html>

The Office of Legislation, U.S. Department of Transportation, serves as legislative counsel to the Office of the Secretary in all modes of Transportation.

Its areas of responsibility include:

- Departmental legislation to be transmitted to Congress
- Departmental analysis of legislation pending before Congress
- Departmental analysis of legislation under consideration in the Administration
- Confirmation hearings of the Secretary, Deputy Secretary, and General Counsel
- Departmental testimony to be given by departmental witnesses before Congressional Committees
- Departmental analysis of testimony to be given by Administration witnesses before Congressional Committees
- Executive Orders
- Presidential Memoranda
- Proclamations

U.S. Department of Commerce Office of General Counsel

<http://commerce.gov/os/ogc>, under "Assistant General Counsels" select "Legislation and Regulations"

Office of the Assistant General Counsel for Legislation and Regulations

The Legislative Division works with various bureaus to develop and support the Department's legislative initiatives and is the focal point within the Department for coordinating the analysis of legislation, and developing and articulating the views of the Department on pending legislation. This office is the principal legal liaison with the Office of Management and Budget, working to obtain required clearances and interagency consensus on Departmental letters, reports, testimonies, and legislative proposals for delivery to the Congress. The office also represents the Department's views in interagency deliberations on legislative proposals and expressions of legislative views advanced by other agencies.

wish to transmit to Congress. The process allows other interested agencies to have input and for OMB to consider the draft legislation's compatibility with the president's legislative program. If the legislation is cleared, there will be "no objection" to the legislation, or it will be "in accord with the president's program," that is, it implements a portion of the president's legislative program. The agency makes this information known to Congress with its transmittal.

Legislative coordination and clearance similarly covers agency testimony and reports, critical to the committee stage of the legislative process.

As legislation moves to the floor of the House or Senate, OMB regularly prepares "statements of administration policy," or SAPS, on major legislation. Interested agencies, White House offices, and OMB each contribute to these documents, which are then made available to Congress. (*See examples of SAPs at §§ 12.08 and 12.13.*)

Finally, the president needs advice once legislation is submitted to him for his signature or veto. Agencies usually have forty-eight hours to submit their views, in the form of a letter signed by a presidential appointee in the agency, to OMB, which then prepares a memorandum for the president on the views submitted and its own analysis of the legislation. Agencies are also tasked with first drafts of signing or veto statements. (*For more information on these processes and OMB's role, see § 8.20, Congress and the Executive: Legislation.*)

§ 4.190 National Archives and Record Administration

<http://archives.gov/legislative>

The National Archives houses the Center for Legislative Archives, located in its downtown building at Pennsylvania Avenue and Seventh St., NW. The center preserves and makes available to researchers historic congressional documents, particularly those of House and Senate committees. The center's collection includes the *Journals* of the House and Senate; the *Congressional Record* and its predecessor publications, the *Globe* and *Annals of Congress;* the Guide to the U.S. Serial Set; the CIS congressional documents references; and historical works on Congress.

4

Two principal finding aids for congressional documents at the National Archives are:

- National Archives and Records Administration, *Guide to the Records of the United States Senate at the National Archives, 1789-1989 Bicentennial Edition*, S.Doc. 100-42, prepared under the direction of Walter J. Stewart, Secretary of the Senate, 1989 (*<http://archives.gov/legislative/guide/senate>*)
- National Archives and Records Administration, *Guide to the Records of the United States House of Representatives at the National Archives, 1789-1989 Bicentennial Edition*, prepared under the direction of Donnald K. Anderson, Clerk of the House of Representatives, 1989 (*<http://archives.gov/legislative/guide/house>*)

Committee records remain the legal property of the House and Senate, governed by House Rule VII and S.Res. 474 (96th Congress), respectively. In general, House records are closed for thirty years, and Senate records for twenty years. Sensitive records might be closed for fifty years. Policies for joint committee records are governed by House or Senate rules, depending on which chamber responsibility for a specific joint committee was assigned.

An Advisory Committee on the Records of Congress advises the archivist of the United States on the management and preservation of congressional records. The committee comprises the archivist, the clerk of the House, the secretary of the Senate, the historians of the House and Senate, and public members appointed by the House and Senate leadership. Committee decision-making in 2011, as an example of its duties, concerned the creation of a digital catalog of the congressional records at the Archives.

The documents and records of individual members of Congress are located in many places since many members donated their archives to local universities and historical societies. Two useful reference works for finding these collections are:

- Karen Dawley Paul, *Guide to Research Collections of Former United States Senators, 1789-1995: A Listing of Archival Repositories Housing the Papers of Former Senators, Related Collections, and Oral History Interviews* (Washington, D.C.: GPO, 1995)

- Cynthia Pease Miller, ed, *A Guide to Research Collections of Former Members of the United States House of Representatives, 1789–1987* (Washington, D.C.: The Office for the Bicentennial of the House of Representatives, 1988)

In addition, the information in these volumes and later information on the same subject appears with members' biographies in the *Biographical Directory of the United States Congress* (*<http://bioguide.congress.gov>*).

§ 4.200 Outside Groups

Several outside groups maintain close relationships with members and staff because of services these groups provide. Congressional spouses also organize for social and other purposes. (*See § 4.201, Congressional Spouse Organizations.*)

Bipartisan Policy Center

<http://bipartisanpolicy.org>

Founded in 2007 by four former Senate majority leaders—Democrats Tom Daschle and George Mitchell and Republicans Howard Baker and Robert Dole—the Bipartisan Policy Center tackles the major public policy issues of the day in "the tradition of . . . great moments in compromise by encouraging civil, respectable political discourse between the political parties." The great moments cited by the center range from the Connecticut Compromise at the Constitutional Convention that provided for a House of Representatives with representation based on population and a Senate with representation of two senators for each state to the Civil Rights Act of 1964 to President Obama's retention of Robert Gates as secretary of defense, the position to which he was appointed by President George W. Bush.

The center has proposed its own health care reform plan, under the leadership of Tom Daschle, and its own debt reduction plan, under the leadership of former Senator Pete Domenici and former CBO director, OMB director, and Federal Reserve Board member Alice Rivlin. It has ongoing projects in a number of policy areas led by former members of Congress and government officials, and seeks to channel partisan debate as "civil discourse" to recommend policy solutions.

Congressional Institute

<http://conginst.org>

The Congressional Institute was established in 1987 to provide information about Congress to the general public, and to encourage dialogue between Congress and the public on issues of national importance.

The institute conducts conferences, briefings, and seminars for members of Congress, congressional staff, and private-sector leaders. The institute has also assisted in the bipartisan House retreats.

Congressional Management Foundation

<http://cmfweb.org>

The Congressional Management Foundation (CMF) was founded in 1977 to assist members and staff in improving office management.

CMF provides management training programs for senior staff and consulting services for individual offices. CMF also conducts training for new senior staff during the early organization meetings. It publishes management books and reports, and provides advisory research services for staff.

§ 4.201

Congressional Spouse Organizations

- Congressional Club (Democratic and Republican spouses)
- Democratic Spouses Club
- Meager Means Investment Club (bipartisan)
- Spouses Club (Republican spouses)

National Academy of Public Administration

<http://napawash.org>

The National Academy of Public Administration undertakes studies for Congress and the executive "upon any subject of government." The academy comprises 680 fellows, both scholars and government practitioners, who serve on project panels and undertake other activities to aid government in improving its quality, performance, and accountability.

National Academy of Sciences

<www.nationalacademies.org>

The National Academy of Sciences has a "mandate that requires it to advise the federal government on scientific and technical matters." The academy comprises over 2,000 members and over 400 foreign associates who are engaged in scientific and engineering research. Members volunteer their time to work on committees created by Congress and the executive to conduct studies on science, technology, and medicine.

Stennis Center for Public Service

<www.stennis.gov>

Created by Congress as a legislative branch agency in honor of the late Senator John Stennis, D-MS, the Stennis Center's mandate is to "attract young people to careers in public service, to provide training for leaders in or likely to be in public service, and to offer development opportunities for senior congressional staff." Programs for congressional staff include the Congressional Staff Fellows Program and the Emerging Congressional Staff Leadership Program.

U.S. Association of Former Members of Congress

<http://usafmc.org>

The Former Members of Congress Association was founded in 1970 as a bipartisan and nonprofit educational, research, and social organization.

The association promotes public understanding of Congress, both domestically and internationally. The former members group, through its "Congress to campus" program, conducts education programs in high schools and colleges. Through its foreign policy seminars, the association travels throughout the world to meet with legislators from other countries to address common concerns.

The former members also routinely return to Washington for special events, such as a day on

Capitol Hill honoring their service. A biennial seminar on "life after Congress" is conducted for new former members to assist them in adjusting to life outside Congress. A number of former members also contributed to a book, *Inside the House: Former Members Reveal How Congress Really Works*, edited by Lou Frey Jr. and Michael T. Hayes (Lanham, MD: University Press of America, 2001).

Former members of Congress are extended certain privileges and courtesies by the House and Senate, with some restrictions if they are now lobbyists. They continue to have floor privileges, including to joint sessions or meetings. They have access to the Congressional Research Service and Library of Congress, priority after sitting members in testifying at hearings, seating in the members' dining rooms, access to congressional fitness facilities, and other courtesies. Departing members are allowed to make some purchases of office furnishings and equipment, may use the frank for certain purposes for ninety days, and are provided guidance on archiving correspondence and other print and nonprint items.

U.S. Capitol Historical Society

<http://uschs.org>

The Capitol Historical Society was founded in 1962 as a nonprofit, nonpartisan educational organization chartered to "enhance and perpetuate the history and heritage of the Capitol, its institutions and the individuals who have served in Congress and the Capitol."

The society holds programs on Congress for elementary and secondary schools and scholarly symposia. It works for the enhancement of the Capitol's collection of art and artifacts, and supports research on the art and architectural history of the Capitol and the careers of members of Congress. The society is publisher of *We the People: The Story of the U.S. Capitol.*

Woodrow Wilson International Center for Scholars

<http://wilsoncenter.org>

Congress Project: <http://wilsoncenter.org>, under "Programs" select "Congress Project."

The Wilson Center is a think tank created by Congress that sponsors scholars for extended periods of time in Washington, DC, so that policymakers might interact with them and benefit from diverse views presented in written work, seminars, and other formats. The Wilson Center sponsors the Congress Project, which "fosters a dialogue between scholars who study Congress and policymakers who have experience with how Congress works."

§ 4.210 Chapter Summary and Discussion Questions

Each member and each committee chair and ranking minority member is responsible for a large sum of money that enables the members and committees of Congress to perform their work. Each member draws a salary and benefits, and contributes to federal programs such as health insurance, life insurance, Social Security, and Medicare. Each member, committee chair, and ranking minority member is allocated funds for staff salaries, expenses ranging from stationery to travel, and franked mail. Numerous laws and chamber rules and regulations govern every aspect of spending these funds.

Members and committees are supported in each chamber by large bureaucracies under the supervision of officers of the House and Senate. Each chamber operates separately, with its own officers. The clerk of the House and the secretary of the Senate support their chambers' legislative activities. The House chief administrative officer and the secretary of the Senate manage their chambers' finances. The House chief administrative officer and the Senate sergeant at arms provide many administrative services, ranging from furnishings to technology, to their chambers. The sergeants at arms of each chamber are responsible for security. Other officers and staff provide specific services, such as each chamber's parliamentarian advising his respective presiding officer on the chamber's parliamentary proceedings.

The chambers also share the architect of the Capitol, who provides different services to each chamber; the Capitol police; the attending physician; and the Office of Compliance. The architect has jurisdiction over the buildings and grounds on Capitol Hill, including the Library of Congress and the Supreme Court. The Capitol police provide security throughout Capitol Hill. The attending physician provides routine and emergency care. The Office of Compliance implements the Congressional Accountability Act, making federal laws applicable to Congress, but avoiding constitutional separation of powers issues that could arise were enforcement of congressional compliance the responsibility of the executive branch.

Congress has also created separate entities in the legislative branch to provide it with information independent of the executive branch and free of the bias or partisanship of advocacy groups. The Library of Congress serves the public as well as Congress. The Congressional Research Service (CRS) provides research and analysis for Congress in its legislative and oversight roles. The Government Accountability Office (GAO) investigates and evaluates federal programs and agencies in aid of congressional lawmaking and oversight. The Congressional Budget Office (CBO) assists Congress in understanding the economic and fiscal environment in which it makes laws and in understanding the economic and fiscal consequences of its legislative actions. The Government Printing Office (GPO) provides congressional documents in print and digital forms.

The Office of Management and Budget, and the congressional liaison offices and general counsels of federal departments and agencies, play important informational roles in supporting congressional lawmaking and oversight. Some private groups have support of Congress as their principal purpose.

Discussion Questions

- What are the policies contained in the Ethics Reform Act affecting members' income that were identified in this chapter?
- Describe the health-care benefits available to members of Congress and determine how members pay for these benefits. Is it your impression that members are treated more generously than, less generously than, or the same as other Americans who work in organizations that provide employee health insurance?
- Prepare a table showing congressional salaries listed in this chapter and the top staff salaries that may be paid in member and committee offices in each chamber. What might explain the uniformity of some salaries and the variations in others?

- What office funds are available to representatives? To senators? What member expenses are covered by other entities in each chamber?
- Describe the restrictions on franked mail applicable in the House or Senate or both chambers. What might be some explanations for these restrictions?
- Compare the staff positions that exist in members' personal offices and in committees. What conclusions might you draw about the work of a personal office compared to the work of a committee based on the differences?
- Attempt to watch on C-SPAN the opening of the House and the Senate on three or four different days, and listen to the chaplains' prayers. What observations can you make about the content of these prayers? Can you find any connections between the prayers and the news of the day or the legislative activities that followed on that day?
- If you had to differentiate the work of the House chief administrative officer, clerk of the House, and House sergeant at arms by writing two sentences about each one, what would you write? If you had the same assignment for the secretary of the Senate and the Senate sergeant at arms, what would you write?
- How is the work of the House general counsel and the Senate legal counsel different from the work of the House and Senate legislative counsels? How is the work of the House and Senate parliamentarians different from these other officials?
- How are the responsibilities of the secretary for the majority and the secretary for the minority different from those of the secretary of the Senate?
- What might be the benefits to young people of the experience of serving as a page in the Senate?
- Read over the changes in Capitol security in recent years. Pick one specific action and research why that action is important to the security of a workplace.
- The architect of the Capitol has undertaken a multiyear renovation of the Cannon House Office Building. Do some research to learn about this building and the person for whom it was named, and find out about the renovation project and how the architect plans to accommodate the many offices in this building while the renovation is going on. You might want to start with the architect's web site.
- The legislative branch agencies that support Congress can be very interesting and professionally rewarding places to work. Check out the career information for each of these agencies on their web sites: for CBO, see "What We Do"; for GAO, see "Careers"; for the Library of Congress, see "Jobs & Fellowships"; for CRS, see *<http://loc.gov/crsinfo>*; and for GPO, see "Careers." What interests you? Why? What educational and other experiences are you likely to need to compete for a position that interests you?
- On the Office of Compliance web site, you will see a report, *Recommendations for Improvements to the Congressional Accountability Act.* Pick one of the sections of this report—safety and health, public access, or workplace rights—and read it. What is the board of directors recommending? Why? Why might Congress have exempted itself from complying with these provisions of law applicable to federal executive branch and private workplaces? What might make Congress change its policy to adopt the board's recommendations?

- Use THOMAS to pick a bill that has been introduced but on which there has not yet been any action, other than referral to a committee. If you worked in a congressional liaison office, what might you do to let the committee or committees with jurisdiction over the bill know that your agency favors or opposes the bill? If the bill was scheduled for floor action in the House or Senate, what might you do to let some or all representatives or some or all senators know your agency's position? Which of these actions (at the committee level and the chamber level) would you need to coordinate with OMB? In what way?
- Look at the web site of the U.S. Capitol Historical Society. What idea or ideas do you have for helping this organization "interpret the history of the Capitol" so that this history would be interesting and engaging to you?

Chapter Five

Organizing Congress: Members, Leaders, and Committees

5

Analysis

§ 5.00 Introduction

The structure and organization of Congress can have a tremendous impact on how policy decisions are reached. The selection of party leaders influences the legislative agenda. The selection of committee and subcommittee chairs and committee and subcommittee members can determine committees' policy outcomes. The choice of individuals in charge of the administrative organs of Congress can affect the services that a chamber provides its members.

The Constitution outlines the structure of Congress and places some constraints on membership qualifications and administration. Largely, however, the House of Representatives and the Senate are free to establish their own rules, create their own structures, and form their own systems of administration. In addition, the federal courts have generally found cases involving the internal affairs

§ 5.01

Constitutional Provisions Related to the Composition and Organization of Congress

TheCapitol.Net has a Pocket Constitution available: see *<http://TCNConst.com>*.

Guide	**Article I**
Bicameral legislature	**Section 1.** All legislative Powers herein granted shall be vested in a Congress of the United States, which shall consist of a Senate and House of Representatives.
Two-year term in House	**Section 2.**[1] The House of Representatives shall be composed of Members chosen every second Year by the People of the several States, and the Electors in each State shall have the Qualifications requisite for Electors of the most numerous Branch of the State Legislature.
Age, citizenship, and residency requirements for House	[2] No person shall be a Representative who shall not have attained to the Age of twenty five Years, and been seven Years a Citizen of the United States, and who shall not, when elected, be an Inhabitant of that State in which he shall be chosen.
Decennial census	[3] [*Part of original Constitution on counting for the census changed by section 2 of the Fourteenth Amendment.*] . . . The actual Enumeration shall be made within three Years after the first Meeting of the Congress of the United States, and within every subsequent Term of ten Years, in such Manner as they shall by Law direct. The Number of Representatives shall not exceed one for every thirty Thousand, but each State shall have at Least one Representative. . . . [*Specifies original number of representatives for each state.*]

Continued on page 172

§ 5.01 (continued)

Guide	Article I
Vacancies in House	[4] When vacancies happen in the Representation from any State, the Executive Authority thereof shall issue Writs of Election to fill such Vacancies.
House officers	[5] The House of Representatives shall chuse their Speaker and other Officers. . . .
Two senators for each state, and a six-year term for senators	**Section 3.**[1] The Senate of the United States shall be composed of two Senators from each State . . . for six Years; and each Senator shall have one Vote. [*Ellipses represent original text changed by first clause of the Seventeenth Amendment, which provided for direct popular election of senators.*]
Senate classes	[2] Immediately after they shall be assembled in Consequence of the first Election, they shall be divided as equally as may be into three Classes. The Seats of the Senators of the first Class shall be vacated at the Expiration of the second Year, of the second Class at the Expiration of the fourth Year, and of the third Class at the Expiration of the sixth Year, so that one third may be chosen every second Year. . . . [*Part of original Constitution on filling vacancies changed by second clause of the Seventeenth Amendment.*]
Age, citizenship, and residency requirements for senators	[3] No Person shall be a Senator who shall not have attained to the Age of thirty Years, and been nine Years a Citizen of the United States, and who shall not, when elected, be an Inhabitant of that State for which he shall be chosen.
Vice president is Senate president	[4] The Vice President of the United States shall be President of the Senate, but shall have no Vote, unless they be equally divided.
Senate officers	[5] The Senate shall chuse their other Officers, and also a President pro tempore, in the Absence of the Vice President, or when he shall exercise the Office of President of the United States.
Congress to assemble annually	**Section 4.**[2] The Congress shall assemble at least once in every Year, and such Meeting shall [be on the first Monday in December,] unless they shall by Law appoint a different Day. [*Original text in brackets was changed by Section 2 of the Twentieth Amendment.*]

Continued on page 173

§ 5.01 (continued)

Guide	Article I
Each house judges its own elections, returns, and qualifications	**Section 5.**[1] Each House shall be the Judge of the Elections, Returns and Qualifications of its own Members, and a Majority of each shall constitute a Quorum to do Business; but a smaller Number may adjourn from day to day, and may be authorized to compel the Attendance of absent Members, in such Manner, and under such Penalties as each House may provide.
Each house creates its own rules	[2] Each House may determine the Rules of its Proceedings, punish its Members for disorderly Behaviour, and, with the Concurrence of two thirds, expel a Member.
Journal of each house, and provision for vote requested by one-fifth of those present	[3] Each House shall keep a Journal of its Proceedings, and from time to time publish the same, excepting such Parts as may in their Judgment require Secrecy; and the Yeas and Nays of the Members of either House on any question shall, at the Desire of one fifth of those Present, be entered on the Journal.
Consent of both houses to adjourn	[4] Neither House, during the Session of Congress, shall, without the Consent of the other, adjourn for more than three days, nor to any other Place than that in which the two Houses shall be sitting.
Compensation, privilege from arrest, Speech and Debate clause	**Section 6.**[1] The Senators and Representatives shall receive a Compensation for their Services, to be ascertained by Law, and paid out of the Treasury of the United States. They shall in all Cases, except Treason, Felony and Breach of the Peace, be privileged from Arrest during their Attendance at the Session of their respective Houses, and in going to and returning from the same; and for any Speech or Debate in either House, they shall not be questioned in any other Place.
Limitation on holding an executive office	[2] No Senator or Representative shall, during the Time for which he was elected, be appointed to any civil Office under the Authority of the United States, which shall have been created, or the Emoluments whereof shall have been encreased during such time; and no Person holding any Office under the United States, shall be a Member of either House during his Continuance in Office.

Continued on page 174

5

§ 5.01 (continued)

Guide	
	Article II
President may convene Congress	**Section 3.** . . . he [*the president*] may, on extraordinary Occasions, convene both Houses, or either of them, and in Case of Disagreement between them, with Respect to the Time of Adjournment, he may adjourn them to such Time as he shall think proper. . . .
	Article VI
Oath of office	[3] The Senators and Representatives before mentioned . . . shall be bound by Oath or Affirmation, to support this Constitution; but no religious Test shall ever be required as Qualification to any Office or public Trust under the United States. [*Text represented by ellipses refers to executive and judicial officers of the United States and the states.*]
	Fourteenth Amendment
Apportionment	**Section 2.** Representatives shall be apportioned among the several States according to their respective numbers, counting the whole number of persons in each State, excluding Indians not taxed. But when the right to vote at any election for the choice of electors for President and Vice President of the United States, Representatives in Congress, the Executive and Judicial officers of a State, or members of the Legislature thereof, is denied to any of the male inhabitants of such State, being twenty-one years of age, [*provision affected by Twenty-Sixth Amendment*] and citizens of the United States, or in any way abridged, except for participation in rebellion, or other crime, the basis of representation therein shall be reduced in the proportion which the number of such male citizens shall bear to the whole number of male citizens twenty-one years of age in such State.
Disqualification from service in Congress for certain acts	**Section 3.** No person shall be a Senator or Representative in Congress . . . who, having previously taken an oath, as a member of Congress, or as an officer of the United States, or as a member of any State legislature, or as an executive or judicial officer of any State, to support the Constitution of the United States, shall have engaged in insurrection or rebellion against the same, or given aid or comfort to the enemies thereof. But Congress may by a vote of two-thirds of each House, remove such disability. [*Text represented by ellipses deals with other office holders.*]

Continued on page 175

§ 5.01 (continued)

Guide	
	Seventeenth Amendment
Popular election of senators	The Senate of the United States shall be composed of two Senators from each State, elected by the people thereof, for six years; and each Senator shall have one vote. The electors in each State shall have the qualifications requisite for electors of the most numerous branch of the State legislatures.
Vacancies in the Senate	When vacancies happen in the representation of any State in the Senate, the executive authority of such State shall issue writs of election to fill such vacancies: *Provided*, That the legislature of any State may empower the executive thereof to make temporary appointments until the people fill the vacancies by election as the legislature may direct.
	This amendment shall not be so construed as to affect the election or term of any Senator chosen before it becomes valid as part of the Constitution.
	Twentieth Amendment
New congressional term begins at noon on January 3 in odd-numbered years	**Section 1.** The terms of the President and Vice President shall end at noon on the 20th day of January, and the terms of Senators and Representatives at noon on the 3d day of January, of the years in which such terms would have ended if this article had not been ratified; and the terms of their successors shall then begin.
Annual congressional session	**Section 2.** The Congress shall assemble at least once in every year, and such meeting shall begin at noon on the 3d day of January, unless they shall by law appoint a different day.
	Twenty-Seventh Amendment
Congressional compensation	No law varying the compensation for the services of the Senators and Representatives shall take effect until an election of Representatives shall have intervened.

TheCapitol.Net has a Pocket Constitution available: see <*TCNConst.com*>.

5

of the House and Senate to be nonjusticiable. (*See § 5.01, Constitutional Provisions Related to the Composition and Organization of Congress.*)

This chapter describes both the constitutional characteristics of Congress, such as Senate classes and the qualifications of representatives and senators, and the membership characteristics of the individuals who compose the House and Senate. It also describes concepts such as sessions of Congress, including lame-duck sessions, shows the partisan control of the modern Congress, and describes some of the organizational prerogatives of the party majority.

This chapter addresses the organization of Congress. It describes the decisions reached before the swearing-in of a new Congress, leadership structures, and the committee and subcommittee systems. It also describes the affinity groups in Congress, informally called caucuses, and the boards and commissions on which members of Congress serve.

§ 5.10 Members of Congress: Service, Qualifications, Characteristics, and Filling Vacant Seats

The Constitution in Article I established a bicameral (two-house) legislature comprising the House of Representatives and the Senate. Article I tells us that there must be at least one representative from each state in the House and exactly two senators from each state in the Senate. With fifty states, there are one hundred senators. (*See § 5.01, Constitutional Provisions Related to the Composition and Organization of Congress.*)

Seven states have just one representative, but, as a result of the decennial 2010 census, the most

§ 5.11

Senate Classes

See <*TCNSC.com*>

The Constitution provides that senators are elected to six-year terms. The Constitution also provides that one-third of the senators are to be elected every two years, and that after the first election of the Senate "they shall be divided as equally as may be into three Classes." (*Art. I, sec. 3, cl. 2.*) As states joined the union, a state's two new senators were assigned to two classes in keeping with the constitutional requirement of near equal numbers of senators in each class.

Senators Whose Terms End in 2013 (Class 1)

Class I terms run from the beginning of the 110th Congress on January 3, 2007, to the end of the 112th Congress on January 3, 2013. Senators in Class I were elected to office in the November 2006 general election, unless they took their seat through appointment or special election.

Democrats

Akaka, Daniel K. (D-HI)
Bingaman, Jeff (D-NM)
Brown, Sherrod (D-OH)
Cantwell, Maria (D-WA)
Cardin, Benjamin L. (D-MD)
Carper, Thomas R. (D-DE)
Casey, Robert P., Jr. (D-PA)
Conrad, Kent (D-ND)
Feinstein, Dianne (D-CA)
Gillibrand, Kirsten E. (D-NY)
Klobuchar, Amy (D-MN)
Kohl, Herb (D-WI)
Manchin, Joe, III (D-WV)
McCaskill, Claire (D-MO)
Menendez, Robert (D-NJ)
Nelson, Ben (D-NE)
Nelson, Bill (D-FL)
Stabenow, Debbie (D-MI)
Tester, Jon (D-MT)
Webb, Jim (D-VA)
Whitehouse, Sheldon (D-RI)

Continued on page 177

§ 5.11 (continued)

Republicans

Barrasso, John (R-WY)
Brown, Scott P. (R-MA)
Corker, Bob (R-TN)
Hatch, Orrin G. (R-UT)
Heller, Dean (R-NV)
Hutchison, Kay Bailey (R-TX)
Kyl, Jon (R-AZ)
Lugar, Richard G. (R-IN)
Snowe, Olympia J. (R-ME)
Wicker, Roger F. (R-MS)

Independents

Lieberman, Joseph I. (I-CT)
Sanders, Bernard (I-VT)

Senators Whose Terms End in 2015 (Class 2)

Class II terms run from the beginning of the 111th Congress on January 3, 2009, to the end of the 113th Congress on January 3, 2015. Senators in Class II were elected to office in the November 2008 general election, unless they took their seat through appointment or special election.

Democrats

Baucus, Max (D-MT)
Begich, Mark (D-AK)
Coons, Christopher (D-DE)
Durbin, Richard J. (D-IL)
Franken, Al (D-MN)
Hagan, Kay R. (D-NC)
Harkin, Tom (D-IA)
Johnson, Tim (D-SD)
Kerry, John F. (D-MA)
Landrieu, Mary L. (D-LA)
Lautenberg, Frank R. (D-NJ)
Levin, Carl (D-MI)
Merkley, Jeff (D-OR)
Pryor, Mark L. (D-AR)
Reed, Jack (D-RI)
Rockefeller, John D., IV (D-WV)
Shaheen, Jeanne (D-NH)
Udall, Mark (D-CO)
Udall, Tom (D-NM)
Warner, Mark R. (D-VA)

Republicans

Alexander, Lamar (R-TN)
Chambliss, Saxby (R-GA)
Cochran, Thad (R-MS)
Collins, Susan M. (R-ME)
Cornyn, John (R-TX)
Enzi, Michael B. (R-WY)
Graham, Lindsey (R-SC)
Inhofe, James M. (R-OK)
Johanns, Mike (R-NE)
McConnell, Mitch (R-KY)
Risch, James E. (R-ID)
Roberts, Pat (R-KS)
Sessions, Jeff (R-AL)

Senators Whose Terms End in 2017 (Class 3)

Class III terms run from the beginning of the 112th Congress on January 3, 2011, to the end of the 114th Congress on January 3, 2017. Senators in Class III were elected to office in the November 2010 general election, unless they took their seat through appointment or special election.

Democrats

Bennet, Michael F. (D-CO)
Blumenthal, Richard (D-CT)
Boxer, Barbara (D-CA)
Inouye, Daniel K. (D-HI)
Leahy, Patrick J. (D-VT)
Mikulski, Barbara A. (D-MD)
Murray, Patty (D-WA)
Reid, Harry (D-NV)
Schumer, Charles E. (D-NY)
Wyden, Ron (D-OR)

Republicans

Ayotte, Kelly (R-NH)
Blunt, Roy (R-MO)
Boozman, John (R-AR)
Burr, Richard (R-NC)
Coats, Daniel (R-IN)
Coburn, Tom (R-OK)
Crapo, Mike (R-ID)
DeMint, Jim (R-SC)
Grassley, Chuck (R-IA)
Hoeven, John (R-ND)
Isakson, Johnny (R-GA)
Johnson, Ronald H. (R-WI)
Kirk, Mark (R-IL)
Lee, Mike (R-UT)
McCain, John (R-AZ)
Moran, Jerry (R-KS)
Murkowski, Lisa (R-AK)
Paul, Rand (R-KY)
Portman, Rob (R-OH)
Rubio, Marco (R-FL)
Shelby, Richard C. (R-AL)
Thune, John (R-SD)
Toomey, Patrick J. (R-PA)
Vitter, David (R-LA)

The current Senate Classes can be seen online at <*TCNSC.com*>.

§ 5.12

Membership Changes, 112th Congress, First Session

Changes after July, 2011, and subsequent Congresses are available online at: <*CongressProfile.com*>.

House

State and District	Former Member and Party	Date of Death or Resignation	New Member and Party	Date of Swearing-in
New York, 26th District	Christopher Lee, R	Resigned February 9, 2011	Kathy Hochul, D	June 1, 2011
California, 36th District	Jane Harman, D	Resigned February 28, 2011	(special election on July 12, 2011)	
Nevada, 2nd District	Dean Heller, R	Resigned May 9, 2011	(special election on September 13, 2011)	
New York, 9th District	Anthony Weiner, D	Resigned June 21, 2011		

Senate

State	Former Member and Party	Date of Death or Resignation	New Member and Party	Date of Swearing-in
Nevada	John Ensign, R	Resigned May 3, 2011	Dean Heller, R	Appointed to fill vacancy; sworn in May 9, 2011

populous state, California, has fifty-three representatives in the 113th–116th Congresses, one for each of its fifty-three congressional districts. Seats in the House of Representatives are apportioned according to population, and Congress by law has provided that the total number of representatives is 435. In addition there are five delegates—one each from American Samoa, the District of Columbia, Guam, the Northern Mariana Islands, and the Virgin Islands—and a resident commissioner from Puerto Rico, as explained later in this section. (*See § 2.40, Reapportionment and Redistricting.*)

Different rules for proceedings evolved in the House and Senate—in part because of their difference in size, in part because senators were appointed by their state legislatures until ratification of the Seventeenth Amendment in 1913, in part because of an earlier perspective of senators as "ambassadors" from their states, and for other reasons. The House is a *majoritarian institution* where majority sentiment on an issue is usually able to work its will and, at least on the floor, to do so in a relatively short time. Senate rules, on the other hand, provide numerous protections to the individual senator and to minority points of view; hence, the *filibuster*—the use of extended debate and dilatory motions—is a feature of the Senate.

Members and, by interpretation, their aides, have a limited protection in what they say because of the Speech and Debate Clause of the Constitution, but both chambers have rules and practices of decorum to which their members must adhere. The Constitution also protects members from arrest under certain circumstances, but the provision is obsolete because the circumstances to which it applied no longer exist. However, each house may punish its members and, on a two-thirds vote, even expel a member.

Finally, a member may not hold another federal office while serving in Congress.

For a further explanation of clauses of the Constitution applicable to Congress and its members, see *Constitution of the United States of America: Analysis and Interpretation*, available in print from the Government Printing Office and online through GPO's Federal Digital System, <*www.fdsys.gov*>, select "Browse Collections," then select "Constitution of the United States of America: Analysis and Interpretation."

In addition to the differences in size and constituency between the House and the Senate, representatives face elections every two years while senators serve six-year terms. The Constitution provided that there would be three "classes" of senators so that one-third of seats in the Senate (a class) would be up for election every two years. *(See § 5.11, Senate Classes.)*

§ 5.13

Party Switchers

House

Rodney Alexander, LA—became Republican, Aug. 6, 2004

Ralph Hall, TX—became Republican Jan. 2, 2004

Senate

Richard Shelby, AL—became Republican, Nov. 9, 1994

Joseph Lieberman, CT—became Independent Democrat, January 12, 2007

Changes after July 2011, and subsequent Congresses are available online at: <*CongressProfile.com*>.

Qualifications for Office and Vacancies in Office

The Constitution also provides that representatives and senators must be residents of the states from which they are elected, and that representatives must be twenty-five years of age or older and senators thirty years of age or older to take office. Foreign-born individuals can serve in Congress. However, a representative must have been a citizen for seven years; a senator, for nine years. *(See § 5.14, Selected Characteristics of the 112th Congress; additional characteristics appear in §§ 5.15–5.23.)*

In the event of a House seat vacancy, a special election is held unless the date of the general election is so close that the state's governor decides to hold the special election concurrent with the general election. *(See below for additional information on House vacancies.)*

In the event of a Senate seat vacancy, nearly every state allows a governor to make a temporary appointment to the seat. The majority of states allow the appointee to serve until the next general election, although some states allow the appointee to serve until the general election after the next general election if the vacancy occurred within a few weeks of an upcoming general election. The minority of states require there to be a special election (depending on when the next general election occurs), and it is in some of these states that the governor is also disallowed from making a temporary appointment to a vacant seat.

There are other variations in the appointment to a vacant Senate seat. In some states, for example, the appointee must be of the same political party as the individual who had occupied the seat. Some states even require that the political party provide the governor with a list of potential appointees. In some states, an individual is allowed to run for the Senate while also running as his party's candidate for president or vice president, which could result in a vacancy in the Senate seat. *(See § 5.12, Membership Changes, 112th Congress, First Session.)*

While it is clear that a vacancy due to a death occurs after an election has taken place, there was

§ 5.14

Selected Characteristics of the 112th Congress

Information current as of July 2011.
The authors keep this information updated online at <*CongressProfile.com*>.

Party Alignment[1]

	Democrats	Republicans	Independents
House[2]	192	240	0
Senate	51	47	2[3]

1. *For history of party control from the 80th Congress through the 112th Congress, see § 5.51.*
For current party alignment see TheCapitol.Net web page <*PartyNumbers.com*>.
2. *Includes two vacancies, two Democratic and one Republican (see § 5.12, Membership Changes, 112th Congress).*
3. *The two independent senators caucus with the Democrats.*

Median Age, and Oldest and Youngest Members

	Median Age	Oldest Democratic and Republican Members	Youngest Democratic and Republican Members
House	57	**John D. Dingell,** D-MI, b. July 8, 1926	**Jared Polis,** D-CO, b. May 12, 1975
		Ralph M. Hall, R-TX, b. May 3, 1923	**Aaron Schock,** R-IL, b. May 28, 1981
Senate	62	**Frank Lautenberg,** D-NJ, b. Jan. 23, 1924	**Kirsten Gillibrand,** D-NY, b. Dec. 9, 1966
		Richard G. Lugar, R-IN, b. April 4, 1932	**Mike Lee,** R-UT, b. June 4, 1971

Median Service, and Most Senior Members

	Median Service	Most Senior Democratic and Republican Members, and Date Current Service Began
House	Service beginning 2003	**John D. Dingell**, D-MI, Dec.13, 1955 (twenty-nine consecutive terms)
		C.W. Bill Young, R-FL, Jan. 3, 1971 (twenty consecutive terms)
Senate	Service beginning 2003	**Daniel K. Inouye,** D-HI, Jan. 3, 1963
		Richard G. Lugar, R-IN, Jan. 4, 1977
		Orrin Hatch, R-UT, Jan. 4, 1977

Members Serving from States with One Representative

Don Young, R-AK
John Carney, D-DE
Denny Rehberg, R-MT
Rick Berg, R-ND
Kristi Noem, R-SD
Peter Welch, D-VT
Cynthia Lummis, R-WY

Continued on page 181

§ 5.14 (continued)

Other Information

Professions: More members of Congress have backgrounds in business than in any other occupation. Business is the most common occupation for representatives, followed by public service. Law, however, is the dominant profession for senators, followed by public service.

Education: All but a handful of representatives have attended at least some post-high school college, community college, or technical school. All senators have at least some post-high school education. All but 27 representatives and one senator have at least an associate's degree. All other representatives and senators have at least a bachelor's degree, and over 260 representatives and senators have advanced degrees—doctorates, or degrees in law or medicine. Over 70 members of Congress hold at least one degree from an Ivy League university, and many others have degrees from other selective private and public American and British universities and the U.S. Military and Naval Academies.

Religion: The majority of members of Congress claim affiliation with Protestant denominations, but the largest representation of a religious denomination is Roman Catholic. There have long been many members of the Jewish faith, and there are now representatives who are adherents to the Muslim and Buddhist faiths.

Women Members: Seventy-five women (51 Democrats and 24 Republicans) serve in the House; three of the Democratic women are delegates. Seventeen women (12 Democrats and 5 Republicans) serve in the Senate.

Minority Members: There are 44 African-American members in the House (42 Democrats and 2 Republicans). Fifteen of the Democratic members are women, two of whom are delegates. There are 26 Hispanic members of the House (19 Democrats and 7 Republicans). Two Democratic members are a delegate and the resident commissioner. Five Democratic women and two Republican women are Hispanic. There are two Hispanics, one of each party, serving in the Senate. There are 11 members of Asian and Pacific Islander heritage, all but one of whom are Democrats. Two Democrats are delegates. Two senators are of Asian heritage, one of whom is also of Native Hawaiian heritage. One Republican representative is Native American.

Sexual Orientation: There are several openly gay men and women members of the House.

Military Service: There are 90 representatives and 25 senators who have served in the military, including the reserves and the National Guard. Three senators and two representatives are veterans of World War II, and there are veterans in Congress of each conflict since then. There are 18 representatives and 4 senators who completed their service after 9/11 or who continue to serve.

Turnover in Membership: A hallmark of the last three elections has been the turnover in the House and Senate. As a consequence, approximately one-third of House Democrats and one-half of House Republicans began service since the 2006 elections, and 60 senators (three-fifths of the Senate) began their service in the past decade. In the 2010 elections, five former representatives and one former senator who had not served in the 111th Congress (2009-2011) were elected; some had not served for a longer period than just the previous Congress. Fourteen senators elected since 2006 had previous House service. The numbers of House and Senate freshman members in the last three elections, including members elected in a special election on the same day as the general election, are shown in this table:

House				Senate			
Year	All Freshmen	Democrats	Republicans	Year	All Freshmen	Democrats	Republicans
2006	55	42	13	2006	10	8*	1
2008	55	33	22	2008	10	8	2
2010	96	9	87	2010	16	3	13

*In addition, an independent senator was elected who caucuses with the Democrats.

§ 5.15

Senators in the 112th Congress Who Previously Served in the House of Representatives

Information current as of July 2011.
The authors keep this information updated online at <*CongressProfile.com*>.

Service in the House is often a political stepping-stone to the Senate. Nearly half the Senate in the 112th Congress had previous House service. Because of its small size relative to the House, the Senate's political dynamics can be affected by small changes in its membership. Some observers, for example, think that the influx of former House members—twenty-five just since 2001 serving in the 112th Congress—has made the Senate more partisan and more oriented toward constituent service, attributes more often associated with the House than the Senate. The last member to serve in the House after serving in the Senate was Claude Pepper, D-FL (House, 1963–1989; Senate, 1936–1951).

Senator	Service in House	Year Entered Senate
Daniel Akaka	1977–1990	1990
Max Baucus	1975–1978	1978
Roy Blunt	1997–2011	2011
John Boozman	2001–2011	2011
Barbara Boxer	1983–1993	1993
Sherrod Brown	1993–2007	2007
Richard Burr	1995–2005	2005
Maria Cantwell	1993–1995	2001
Benjamin L. Cardin	1987–2007	2007
Thomas Carper	1983–1993	2001
Saxby Chambliss	1995–2003	2003
Dan Coats	1981–1989	1989*
Tom Coburn	1995–2001	2005
Thad Cochran	1973–1978	1978
Mike Crapo	1993–1999	1999
Jim DeMint	1999–2005	2005
Richard Durbin	1983–1997	1997
John Ensign	1995–1999	2001
Lindsey Graham	1995–2003	2003
Charles Grassley	1975–1981	1981
Tom Harkin	1975–1985	1985
Dean Heller	2007–2011	2011
James Inhofe	1987–1994	1994
Daniel Inouye	1959–1963	1963

* Coats served in the Senate 1989-1999. He was not a candidate for reelection in 1989. In 2010, Coats ran again for the Senate and won, beginning his new service in 2011.

Senator	Service in House	Year Entered Senate
Johnny Isakson	1999–2005	2005
Tim Johnson	1987–1997	1997
Mark Kirk	2001–2010	2010
Jon Kyl	1987–1995	1995
John McCain	1983–1987	1987
Robert Menendez	1993–2006	2006
Barbara Mikulski	1977–1987	1987
Jerry Moran	1997–2011	2011
Bill Nelson	1979–1991	2001
Rob Portman	1993–2005	2011
Jack Reed	1991–1997	1997
Harry Reid	1983–1987	1987
Pat Roberts	1981–1997	1997
Bernard Sanders	1991–2007	2007
Charles Schumer	1981–1999	1999
Richard Shelby	1979–1987	1987
Olympia Snowe	1979–1995	1995
Debbie Stabenow	1997–2001	2001
John Thune	1997–2003	2005
Pat Toomey	1995–2005	2011
Mark Udall	1999–2009	2009
Tom Udall	1999–2009	2009
David Vitter	1999–2005	2005
Roger Wicker	1995–2007	2007
Ron Wyden	1981–1996	1996

§ 5.16

Former Governors Serving in the 112th Congress

Information current as of July 2011.
The authors keep this information updated online at <*CongressProfile.com*>.

Governors often seek election to the Senate. Having won a statewide office already, they are able to mount another statewide campaign. A former governor is likely to be conversant with the range of policy issues confronting Congress.

Member	Party and State	Service as Governor
Sen. Lamar Alexander	R-TN	1979–1987
Sen. Thomas Carper	D-DE	1993–2001
Sen. John Hoeven	R-ND	2000–2010
Sen. Mike Johanns	R-NE	1999–2005
Sen. Joe Manchin	D-WV	2005–2010
Sen. Ben Nelson	D-NE	1991–1999
Sen. James Risch	R-ID	2006
Sen. John Rockefeller	D-WV	1977–1985
Sen. Jeanne Shaheen	D-NH	1997-2003
Sen. Mark Warner	D-VA	2002-2006

concern over what was state law and, despite that, what should be done in the 2000 and 2002 elections following deaths *before* the election. Senate candidate Mel Carnahan (Missouri in 2000), Senate candidate, Sen. Paul Wellstone, D-MN, and House candidate, Rep. Patsy Mink, D-HI (both in 2002), died before the respective elections but after ballots had been printed. The practice in nearly all states in the interest of orderly election administration has been to set a cutoff date for replacing candidates (whether a candidate resigns her candidacy or dies), and to proceed after that date even if a candidate should die. The practice in Congress, in judging elections, has been to consider a seat vacant if the deceased candidate obtains the greatest number of votes in the election. Laws for filling the vacancy are then followed, and that is what happened in filling the vacancies caused by Carnahan's and Mink's deaths. In Minnesota, a replacement candidate was named for the general election.

Continuity of the House

Following the terrorist attacks of September 11, 2001, members of Congress and others have become concerned over continuity of government for the legislative branch should many members be killed or disabled in a terrorist attack. Plans for continuity of government and continuity of operations exist or are being further developed, but attention to succession for representatives continues. Governors are able to act quickly in most states to name replacement senators. However, the Constitution requires House vacancies to be filled by special election. A number of proposals have been made,

§ 5.17

Numbers of Former State and Local Elected Officials Serving in the 112th Congress

Information current as of July 2011.
The authors keep this information updated online at <CongressProfile.com>.

State legislatures and state, regional, county, city, and other local offices are the political training grounds of many members of Congress, including delegates. Because of the number of federal aid and regulatory programs affecting states and localities, former state and local officials elected to Congress are often able to take part quickly in many policy debates in Congress. Many members with experience in state legislatures held leadership positions in their chamber or key legislative committees. In addition to these officials, the 112th Congress includes former Cabinet secretaries and ambassadors, executive and administrative officials from all levels of government, White House staff, presidential and congressional campaign staff, nonprofit and think-tank officials, and national, state, and local party officials. Sen. John Kerry, D-MA, was his party's 2004 presidential nominee, and Sen. John McCain, R-AZ, was his party's 2008 presidential nominee. Other members have run active campaigns for their party's presidential nomination. Many members, before or since being elected to Congress, have served as delegates to their parties' national political conventions.

Former Local and Regional Elected Officials	Former State Legislators	Former State Officials Elected Statewide
House: 139	House: 227	House: 16
Senate: 26	Senate: 43	Senate: 29

§ 5.18

Members of Congress Who Subsequently Served on the Supreme Court

Congressional service has been a route to appointment to the Supreme Court.

Served in House of Representatives and on Supreme Court

John Marshall
Joseph Story
Gabriel Duvall
John McLean
Henry Baldwin
James Wayne
Philip Barbour
Nathan Clifford
Mahlon Pitney
William Strong
Joseph McKenna
William Moody
Fred M. Vinson

Served in Senate and on Supreme Court

William Paterson
Oliver Ellsworth
Levi Woodbury
Salmon P. Chase
Stanley Matthews
Howell Jackson
Edward D. White
Hugo L. Black
Harold Burton
Sherman Minton
David Davis (resigned from Supreme Court to serve in Senate)

Served in Both House of Representatives and Senate, and on Supreme Court

John McKinley
Lucius Q.C. Lamar
George Sutherland
James F. Byrnes

§5.19

Former Judges Serving in the 112th Congress

Information current as of July 2011.
The authors keep this information updated online at <*CongressProfile.com*>.

Because state and local judgeships are often elective, members of the judiciary are sometimes attracted to congressional service.

Member	Party and State	Type of Judge
Sen. John Cornyn	R-TX	Justice, Texas Supreme Court
Sen. Roger F. Wicker	R-MS	Municipal judge
Rep. Robert B. Aderholt	R-AL	Municipal judge
Rep. G. K. Butterfield	D-NC	Superior court judge; justice, North Carolina Supreme Court
Rep. John Carter	R-TX	Municipal judge; district court judge
Rep. Lloyd Doggett	D-TX	Justice, Texas Supreme Court
Rep. John J. Duncan Jr.	R-TN	County criminal court judge
Rep. Louie Gohmert	R-TX	District court judge; Texas Court of Appeals, chief justice
Rep. Charles A. Gonzalez	D-TX	Municipal judge; judge, county court at law; district court judge
Rep. Al Green	D-TX	Justice of the peace
Rep. Ralph M. Hall	R-TX	County judge
Rep. Alcee L. Hastings	D-FL	U.S. district court judge
Rep. Sheila Jackson-Lee	D-TX	Municipal judge
Rep. Hank Johnson	D-GA	Magistrate court judge
Rep. Gregory W. Meeks	D-NY	State workers' compensation judge
Rep. Ted Poe	R-TX	District court judge
Rep. Steven R. Rothman	D-NJ	Surrogate court judge

5

including a constitutional amendment to allow governors to appoint representatives under certain circumstances. As an interim step, the House amended its rules at the beginning of the 108th Congress to deal with some contingencies: enabling the Speaker to secretly designate his successors should his office become vacant, allowing the Speaker to declare an emergency recess, and codifying the practice of adjusting the whole number of the House in the case of vacancies. The House amended its rules again at the beginning of the 109th Congress, providing a method for establishing a "provisional quorum" in the case of a catastrophic event. Under the rule, if the House is without a quorum due to a catastrophic circumstance, a quorum would be a majority of the "provisional number" of the House.

§ 5.20

Members of the 112th Congress Who Were Congressional Pages

Information current as of July 2011.
The authors keep this information updated online at <*CongressProfile.com*>.

Pages are high-school juniors, at least sixteen years old, both male and female, who serve members of the House and Senate by delivering packages and messages throughout the Capitol complex. They also serve on the floor of each house. (*See § 4.113, Congressional Pages*.)

House

Dan Boren, D-OK
Jim Cooper, D-TN
Ander Crenshaw, R-FL
John D. Dingell, D-MI
Rush D. Holt, D-NJ
Ben Quayle, R-AZ

Senate

Michael Bennet, D-CO
Mike Lee, R-UT
Mark Pryor, D-AR
Roger F. Wicker, R-MS

During the 109th Congress, Congress passed legislation that was signed by the president to provide an expedited time table in "extraordinary circumstances" for filling House vacancies through special elections (*P.L. 109-55, Title III*). These extraordinary circumstances were defined as existing when the Speaker of the House announced that there were over one hundred vacancies in the House. If the Speaker makes such an announcement, the governor of any state with a vacancy must schedule a special election within forty-nine days, unless a general election or a special election for that vacancy has already been scheduled to occur within seventy-five days of the Speaker's announcement. Candidates are to be chosen by political parties within ten days of the Speaker's announcement, or states may prescribe another method of choosing candidates, including a primary. Additional provisions of the law dealt with expedited judicial review of a challenge to the Speaker's announcement; accommodation of military and overseas voters voting absentee; and the continuing applicability of various federal statutes protecting the franchise.

Post-Election Events

More routinely, members can also change their party affiliations after election to Congress. One party might well seek to attract potential defectors from the other party. In states without a "sore loser" law, a candidate may switch party affiliation before an election to appear on the general election ballot. (*See § 5.13, Party Switchers.*)

From time to time, the outcome of an election might be challenged because two candidates obtained nearly the same number of votes or because some irregularity is alleged. In any case, the Constitution provides that the House and Senate "shall be the Judge of the Elections, Returns and Qualifications of its own Members." (*Art. I, sec. 5, cl. 1.*) Investigatory work is usually conducted in the House by the House Administration Committee and in the Senate by its Rules and Administration Committee if state administrative or judicial processes are unable to settle candidate challenges. (*See § 2.10, Campaigns and Elections.*)

§ 5.22

Members of the 112th Congress Who Have Served as Congressional Staff

Information current as of July 2011.
The authors keep this information updated online at <*CongressProfile.com*>.

Numerous members of the 112th Congress served in congressional staff positions before their election. Some senators served on Senate staffs; others served on House staffs. One senator served on the Capitol police force. Some House members served on Senate staffs; others served on House staffs.

This list was compiled from information in the *Congressional Directory,* the *Biographical Directory of the United States Congress* (*online version*), official and campaign web sites, and press sources. Included are members who served as either permanent staff or fellows. If the source provided the name of the office for whom a member worked, it is included; if the office was not provided, the term "congressional staff" is noted. Some members listed here and others not listed also served as interns and campaign workers; this list does not show those relationships.

Many congressional staff who seek election to Congress fail in the attempt. However, service on Capitol Hill offers great political training and unparalleled exposure to national issues and politics. As is evident from the list below, many former congressional staff have been successful in seeking election to Congress.

Current Member	Staff on Which Member Served
Sen. Lamar Alexander	Sen. Howard Baker
Sen. Barbara Boxer	Rep. John Burton
Sen. Dan Coats	Rep. Dan Quayle
Sen. Susan Collins	Sen. William Cohen; Senate Committee on Governmental Affairs
Sen. Tom Harkin	Rep. Neal Smith
Sen. Mark Kirk	Rep. John Edward Porter; House Committee on International Relations
Sen. Joseph Lieberman	Sen. Abraham Ribicoff
Sen. Mitch McConnell	Sen. Marlow Cook
Sen. Harry Reid	Capitol Police
Sen. Pat Roberts	Sen. Frank Carlson; Rep. Keith Sebelius
Sen. Olympia Snowe	Rep. William Cohen
Sen. John Thune	Sen. James Abdnor
Sen. Roger F. Wicker	Rep. Trent Lott; House Committee on Rules
Rep. Jason Altmire	Rep. Pete Peterson
Rep. Charles Bass	Rep. William Cohen; Rep. David Emery
Rep. Gus Bilirakis	Rep. Don Sundquist
Rep. Jo Bonner	Rep. Sonny Callahan
Rep. Dan Boren	Rep. Wes Watkins
Rep. Ken Calvert	Rep. Victor Veysey

Continued on page 188

5

§ 5.22 (continued)

Current Member	Staff on Which Member Served
Rep. Dave Camp	Rep. Bill Shuette
Rep. Dennis Cardoza	Rep. Gary Condit
Rep. Hansen Clark	Rep. John Conyers
Rep. William Lacy Clay, Jr.	House Doorkeeper
Rep. Tom Cole	National Republican Congressional Committee
Rep. Jerry Connolly	Senate Foreign Relations Committee
Rep. John Conyers, Jr.	Rep. John D. Dingell
Rep. Jim Costa	Rep. John Krebs
Rep. Mark Critz	Rep. John Murtha
Rep. Peter A. DeFazio	Rep. James Weaver
Rep. Rosa L. DeLauro	Sen. Christopher Dodd
Rep. Charlie Dent	Rep. Don Ritter
Rep. Norman D. Dicks	Sen. Warren Magnuson
Rep. Robert Dodd	House Government Reform Committee
Rep. JoAnn Emerson	National Republican Congressional Committee
Del. Eni F.H. Faleomavaega	House Committee on Interior and Insular Affairs
Rep. Bob Filner	Sen. Hubert Humphrey; Rep. Don Fraser
Rep. Jeff Fortenberry	Senate Subcommittee on Intergovernmental Relations
Rep. Barney Frank	Rep. Michael Harrington
Rep. Marcia Fudge	Rep. Stephanie Tubbs-Jones
Rep. Cory Gardner	Sen. Wayne Allard
Rep. Chris Gibson	Rep. Jerry Lewis; House Defense Appropriations Committee
Rep. Bob Goodlatte	Rep. M. Caldwell Butler
Rep. Tim Griffin	House Government Reform Committee
Rep. Frank Guinta	Rep. Jeb Bradley
Rep. Jeb Hensarling	National Republican Senatorial Committee; Sen. Phil Gramm
Rep. Jaime Herrera Beutler	Rep. Cathy McMorris Rodgers
Rep. Mazie Hirono	Sen. Spark Matsunaga
Rep. Kathy Hochul	Rep. John LaFalce; Sen. Daniel Patrick Moynihan
Rep. Rush D. Holt	Rep. Bob Edgar
Rep. Bill Huizenga	Rep. Peter Hoekstra
Rep. Randy Hultgren	Rep. Dennis Hastert
Rep. Steve Israel	Rep. Richard Ottinger
Rep. Sheila Jackson-Lee	House Select Committee on Assassinations
Rep. Barbara Lee	Rep. Ron Dellums
Rep. Jerry Lewis	Rep. Jerry Pettis

Continued on page 189

§ 5.22 (continued)

Current Member	Staff on Which Member Served
Rep. Daniel Lipinski	Rep. Rod Blagojevich; Rep. Richard Gephardt
Rep. Zoe Lofgren	Rep. Don Edwards
Rep. Dan Lungren	Rep. Bill Colmer; Sen. Bill Brock
Rep. Kevin McCarthy	Rep. Bill Thomas
Rep. James P. McGovern	Rep. John Moakley; Sen. George McGovern
Rep. Patrick Meehan	Sen. Arlen Specter
Rep. John L. Mica	Sen. Paula Hawkins
Rep. James P. Moran	Senate Committee on Appropriations
Rep. Pete Olson	Sen. Phil Gramm; Sen. John Conyer
Rep. Nick Rahall	Sen. Robert Byrd
Rep. Denny Rehberg	Rep. Ron Marlenee; Sen. Conrad Burns
Rep. Laura Richardson	Rep. Juanita Millender-McDonald
Rep. David Rivera	Sen. Connie Mack
Rep. Tom Rooney	Sen. Connie Mack
Rep. Peter Roskam	Rep. Tom DeLay; Rep. Henry Hyde
Rep. Paul Ryan	Sen. Robert Kasten; Senate Committee on Small Business; Rep. and Sen. Sam Brownback
Rep. Tim Ryan	Rep. James Traficant
Del. Gregorio Kilili Camacho Sablan	Sen. Daniel Inouye
Rep. James Sensenbrenner	Rep. J. Arthur Younger
Rep. Jackie Speier	Rep. Leo Ryan
Rep. Mac Thornberry	Rep. Tom Loeffler; Rep. Larry Combest
Rep. Pat Tiberi	Rep. John Kasich
Rep. Fred Upton	Rep. David Stockman
Rep. Chris Van Hollen	Senate Committee on Foreign Relations; Sen. Charles Mathias
Rep. Nydia M. Velázquez	Rep. Edolphus Towns
Rep. Peter J. Visclosky	Rep. Adam Benjamin; House Committee on Appropriations
Rep. Greg Walden	Rep. Denny Smith
Rep. Anthony D. Weiner	Rep. Charles Schumer
Rep. Frank R. Wolf	Rep. Ed Biester
Rep. Rob Woodall	Rep. John Linder
Rep. John Yarmuth	Sen. Marlow Cook
Rep. C.W. Bill Young	Rep. William Cramer
Rep. Todd Young	Sen. Richard Lugar

5

§ 5.23

Vice Presidents Elected to the Senate

Five individuals have been elected to the Senate after serving as vice president. One, Andrew Johnson, was vice president to Abraham Lincoln and became president upon Lincoln's assassination.

John Calhoun, SC
Hannibal Hamlin, ME
Andrew Johnson, TN
Alben Barkley, KY
Hubert Humphrey, MN

§ 5.21 Delegates in the House of Representatives

In addition to 435 representatives, the House's membership includes five delegates—one each from American Samoa, the District of Columbia, Guam, the Northern Mariana Islands, and the Virgin Islands—and one resident commissioner from Puerto Rico. There are no practical differences between the positions of delegate and resident commissioner.

In a 1902 law, Puerto Rico was granted representation in the House; the position of resident commissioner was created. In a 1970 law, the District of Columbia was authorized to elect a delegate to the House. This same privilege was extended by law to Guam and the Virgin Islands in 1972, to American Samoa in 1978, and to the Northern Mariana Islands in 2008. Delegates and the resident commissioner are treated equally with representatives in the allocation of members' representational allowances, salary, and other perquisites available to representatives.

Delegates and the resident commissioner may do any of the following:

- introduce bills and resolutions
- speak on the House floor
- serve on committees and accrue seniority in the same manner as other members of their party on those committees
- fully participate in committee activities, including offering amendments and motions, and voting during markups
- chair subcommittees

§ 5.30 Terms and Sessions of Congress

A term of Congress lasts for two years, beginning at 12:00 noon on January 3 of odd-numbered years, about two months after the latest general election. Congress might decide to convene a new term and swear in members on another day, but members of the previous Congress cease collecting their pay at noon on January 3, and members of the new Congress begin collecting theirs at that time. The 112th Congress convened on January 5, 2011. (*See § 5.31, Terms of Congress.*)

A term of Congress in contemporary practice comprises first and second sessions. The first session occurs within the first calendar year covered by the term—2011 for the first session of the 112th Congress. The second session occurs in the second calendar year—2012 for the second session of the 112th Congress. When the 112th Congress convened on January 5, it convened its first session. There is not usually any legislative significance attached to the sessions, but they fulfill the Twentieth Amendment requirement that Congress assemble "at least once in every year."

A session of Congress continues until Congress adjourns the session *sine die*, that is, without (*sine*) any day (*die*) to return or reconvene. When the second session of a Congress convenes, legislative work picks up where it left off in the first session; for example, a bill on which there were sub-

§ 5.31

Terms of Congress

To see a table listing all terms of Congress, see <*TermsofCongress.com*>.

Congress	Years	Congress	Years	Congress	Years
80th	1947–1949	94th	1975–1977	108th	2003–2005
81st	1949–1951	95th	1977–1979	109th	2005–2007
82nd	1951–1953	96th	1979–1981	110th	2007–2009
83rd	1953–1955	97th	1981–1983	111th	2009–2011
84th	1955–1957	98th	1983–1985	112th	2011–2013
85th	1957–1959	99th	1985–1987	113th	2013–2015
86th	1959–1961	100th	1987–1989	114th	2015–2017
87th	1961–1963	101st	1989–1991	115th	2017–2019
88th	1963–1965	102nd	1991–1993	116th	2019–2021
89th	1965–1967	103rd	1993–1995	117th	2021–2023
90th	1967–1969	104th	1995–1997	118th	2023–2025
91st	1969–1971	105th	1997–1999	119th	2025–2027
92nd	1971–1973	106th	1999–2001	120th	2027–2029
93rd	1973–1975	107th	2001–2003	121st	2029–2031

committee hearings and markup could be considered in full committee markup and be reported to the committee's parent chamber.

When Congress adjourns *sine die* at the end of a second session, the uncompleted work of that Congress remains uncompleted. Legislation at any stage of the legislative process dies. Work must begin again with the introduction of legislation after the new Congress convenes. (*See § 5.33, Résumé of Congressional Activity, 111th Congress (2009–2011).*)

It is possible for Congress to convene other sessions within its two-year term. It is also possible under the Constitution for the president to reconvene Congress within or between sessions. The threat of the president calling Congress back is sometimes used tactically to extract an extra effort from Congress toward completing a specific legislative action. With the first session of a Congress comprising nearly a full calendar year and the second session often concluding just a few weeks before the next general election, it is somewhat unlikely that there would be another session within a two-year term.

If Congress considers the need to reconvene following a general election possible or probable, it does not adjourn *sine die* before the election. If it reconvenes following an election, the ensuing work period is referred to colloquially as a lame-duck session. (*See § 5.32, Lame-Duck Sessions of Congress, 1935–2010.*)

During a session, the House and Senate might adjourn or recess during a day or at the end of a

§ 5.32

Lame-Duck Sessions of Congress, 1935–2010

Congress	Date Pre-Election Session Ended	Date Post-Election Session Began	Date Post-Election Session Adjourned Sine Die
76th Congress, 3rd Session (1940–1941)	Congress stayed in session		Jan. 3, 1941
77th Congress, 2nd Session (1942)	Congress stayed in session		Dec. 16, 1942
78th Congress, 2nd Session (1944)	Sept. 21, 1944	Nov. 14, 1944	Dec. 19, 1944
80th Congress, 2nd Session (1948)	Aug. 7, 1948	Dec. 31, 1948	Dec. 31, 1948
81st Congress, 2nd Session (1950–1951)	Sept. 23, 1950	Nov. 27, 1950	Jan. 2, 1951
83rd Congress, 2nd Session (1954)	Aug. 20, 1954	Senate: Nov. 8, 1954	Senate: Dec. 2, 1954
91st Congress, 2nd Session (1970–1971)	Oct. 14, 1970	Nov. 16, 1970	Jan. 2, 1971
93rd Congress, 2nd Session (1974)	Oct. 17, 1974	Nov. 18, 1974	Dec. 20, 1974
96th Congress, 2nd Session (1980)	Senate: Oct. 1 House: Oct. 2, 1980	Nov. 12, 1980	Dec. 16, 1980
97th Congress, 2nd Session (1982)	Oct. 1, 1982	Senate: Nov. 29 House: Nov. 21, 1982	Senate: Dec. 23 House: Dec. 21, 1982
103rd Congress, 2nd Session (1994)	Oct. 8, 1994	Nov. 28, 1994	Senate: Dec. 1 House: Nov. 29, 1994
105th Congress, 2nd Session (1998)	Oct. 21, 1998	House: Dec. 17, 1998	House: Dec. 19, 1998
106th Congress, 2nd Session (2000)	Senate: Nov. 2 House: Nov. 3, 2000	House: Nov. 13 Senate: Nov. 14, 2000	House: Dec. 15 Senate: Dec. 15, 2000
107th Congress, 2nd Session (2002)	House: Nov. 4 Senate: Nov. 4, 2002	House: Nov. 7 Senate: Nov. 7, 2002	Senate: Nov. 20 House: Nov. 22, 2002
108th Congress, 2nd Session (2004)	House: Oct. 9 Senate: Oct. 11, 2004	House: Nov. 16, Dec. 6 Senate: Nov. 16, Dec. 7, 2004	House: Nov. 24, Dec. 7 Senate: Nov. 24, Dec. 8, 2004
109th Congress, 2nd Session (2006)	House: Sept. 29 Senate: Sept. 29, 2006	House: Nov. 13, Dec. 5 Senate: Nov. 13, Dec. 4, 2006	House: Nov. 15, Dec. 8 Senate: Nov. 16, Dec. 8, 2006
110th Congress, 2nd Session (2008)	House: Oct. 3 Senate: Oct. 2*, Nov. 3, 2008	House: Nov. 19, Dec. 9 Senate: Nov. 6*, Nov. 17, Dec. 8	House: Nov. 20, Dec. 10, Jan. 3 (2009) Senate: Nov. 20, Dec. 11, Jan. 2* (2009)
111th Congress, 2nd Session (2010)	House: Sept. 30 Senate: Sept. 29*, Nov. 1, 2010	House: Nov. 15, Nov. 29 Senate: Nov. 4*, Nov. 15, Nov. 29, 2010	House: Nov. 18, Dec. 22 Senate: Nov. 19, Dec. 22, 2010

* Senate continued meeting in pro forma session on approximately every third day.

§ 5.33

Résumé of Congressional Activity, 111th Congress (2009–2011)

Every measure introduced in Congress has a two-year life cycle. Legislation to be enacted into law must pass in identical form both the House and Senate and be signed by the president. Some measures must be introduced in several Congresses before sufficient political support is generated for them to be enacted into law. Other measures authorize programs for several years, and Congress does not need to consider another authorization bill until the end of that period. Although it is difficult to assess the workload of a given Congress, scholars generally base a Congress' success on certain factors, including workload, time in session, and legislation enacted.

This table identifies some common measures of legislative activity in the 111th Congress.

Activity	House	Senate
Days in session	286	349
Public bills enacted into law	265	118
Measures passed	1,888	1,047
Bills introduced	6,562	4,059
Joint resolutions introduced	107	42
Roll-call votes	1,647	696
Congressional Record pages of proceedings	24,497	25,216

* For current information, see <*CongressByTheNumbers.com*>.

day, setting the next day and time of their meeting. The House might recess during a day to take a break from its proceedings for some reason, and it then will adjourn at the end of a day. The Senate, however, sometimes prefers to recess at the end of a day so as not to trigger a new legislative day the next day. (*The reasons for this Senate practice are explained in § 6.160, Senate Scheduling. See also § 5.34, Joint Meetings and Joint Sessions.*)

Secret Sessions

Secret sessions, also called closed or executive sessions, are held in the House and Senate chambers, with the galleries closed to the press and the public. (*An executive session of the Senate should not be confused with executive business, as explained in § 6.180, Senate Calendars and Legislative and Executive Business before the Senate.*) Secret sessions are held at the request of any member, and are convened to discuss issues of national security, confidential information, and sensitive executive communications. Senate deliberations during impeachment trials may be held in secret session.

To convene in secret session, a member makes a nondebatable motion to resolve into secret session. Proceedings in secret session are not published in the *Congressional Record* unless the chamber votes to release them.

§ 5.34

Joint Meetings and Joint Sessions

In 1789 and 1790, meetings of the two chambers were held in the Senate chamber in Federal Hall in New York. From 1790 to 1793, such meetings were held in the Senate chamber in Congress Hall in Philadelphia. From 1794 to 1799, meetings of the two chambers were held in the hall of the House chamber. When the Congress moved to Washington in 1800, the Senate chamber hosted the two houses. Since 1809, with few exceptions, these meetings have been held in the House chamber.

There are four terms that are used to describe times when the House and Senate meet together. The distinction among the four is not always clear or consistent.

A **joint session** is a formal meeting that occurs when both houses adopt a concurrent resolution. A joint session, for example, is usually what the sessions are called to count electoral votes and receive the State of the Union message.

A **joint meeting** occurs when each chamber agrees by unanimous consent to meet with the other chamber. Addresses by foreign dignitaries or special guests, as well as commemorative gatherings, occur in joint meetings.

- Joint meetings for foreign dignitaries have included Winston Churchill, Clement Atlee, Haile Selassie, Charles de Gaulle, Anwar Sadat, Yitzhak Rabin, Margaret Thatcher, Lech Walesa, Vaclav Havel, Nelson Mandela, Hamid Karzai, Ayad Allawi, Ellen Johnson Sirleaf, and King Abdullah.
- Joint meetings for special guests have included General Douglas MacArthur, the Apollo astronauts, and General William Westmoreland.
- Joint meetings for commemorative gatherings have included the fiftieth anniversary of World War II, Friendship 7, the first orbital space flight, the first lunar landing, the centennial of Harry Truman's birth, and the bicentennial of the 1st Congress.
- Joint meeting in New York City to honor the city on its recovery from the September 11, 2001, terrorist attack.

A **joint reception** occurs when a concurrent resolution calls for the Senate to recess to meet with the House, but the Senate adjourns instead. For example, a joint reception was held for the 1939 visit of King George VI of England.

The inauguration of the president is referred to as a **joint gathering**, although in recent years it has been held pursuant to concurrent resolution and thus would be a joint session.

The Speaker of the House presides over both joint sessions and joint meetings, with one exception: the vice president as the president of the Senate or the president pro tempore of the Senate presides over the counting of electoral votes. The two chambers normally convene on the day of the joint meeting or joint session, and then recess to conduct the joint meeting or joint session in the House chamber after the Senate as a body proceeds across the Capitol to the House chamber.

Secret sessions are rare. Since 1929, when the Senate ended its practice of considering treaties and nominations behind closed doors, it has held fewer than sixty secret sessions, including six in 1999 to discuss impeachment proceedings against President Clinton. The last secret Senate session occurred in 2005 to discuss the war in Iraq. Since 1830, the House has met in secret session only a handful of times, the most recent in 2008 during debate on the Foreign Intelligence Surveillance Act.

§ 5.40 Early Organization Meetings

Since the mid-1970s, both chambers have convened early organization meetings in November or December of even-numbered years to prepare for the start of the new Congress in January. These meetings serve educational, organizational, and social purposes.

The educational sessions range from meetings on legislative procedures and staff hiring to seminars on current policy issues. These sessions are taught by current members of Congress, former members, government practitioners, and academic experts. Issue sessions generally focus on the substance of issues, previous attempts at legislative changes, administration policy, and the outlook for action in the new Congress.

The organizational sessions serve new members as their first introduction to Congress and to each other. Some meetings are conducted for all freshmen and some for all members of the incoming Congress. Some meetings are organized by party affiliation. At these early organization meetings, class officers are elected, party leaders selected, and chamber officers chosen. Regional representatives to steering committees are named. Candidates for chair of selected committees are interviewed or elected, and members of those committees might be chosen. Each of these actions involving committees is then subject to official ratification by the House or Senate at the start of the Congress.

Room selection drawings and room assignments are also accomplished during the early organization meetings. (*See § 11.30, Guide to Public Buildings on Capitol Hill.*)

The House Administration Committee and the Senate majority and minority leaders organize the chamber-specific official orientation programs for members-elect and their families. Orientation handbooks are provided, which describe the official rules of the chamber relating to staff hiring, ethics regulations, office equipment (including computer hardware and software), roles of the chamber officers, services of the legislative support agencies, and the like. Several sessions are devoted to these topics.

Separate, simultaneous programs are held for spouses and designated staff of members-elect. Spouse organizations are responsible for the spouse sessions. The spouse sessions, in addition to being social in nature, help spouses understand the congressional schedule and pressures on family life.

The Congressional Management Foundation, in conjunction with the House Chiefs of Staff Association, has conducted the sessions for House staff of newly elected members for the last several Congresses. These sessions are designed to assist the new chiefs of staff, or individuals designated by the newly elected members to lead the set-up of their offices, in planning, budgeting, and setting up an office. The Congressional Management Foundation often conducts similar programs for Senate staff of newly elected senators.

Following orientation sessions for members-elect, the returning members join the members-elect for party organization meetings. At these sessions, the parties generally meet separately, although dinners are often hosted by the respective leadership for all members. Other evening events are held for members of only one party. (*See § 5.41, A Representative Early Organization Schedule: 108th Congress.*)

§ 5.41

A Representative Early Organization Schedule: 108th Congress

Overview: Schedule of Events

Monday, November 11

All day	Registration
6:00pm	Welcome Reception hosted by Representative Steny H. Hoyer
6:00pm	Majority Whip's Dinner
8:00pm	Welcome Reception hosted by House Administration Chairman Robert W. Ney

Tuesday, November 12

8:00–8:45am	Members and Family Room Continental Breakfast for Members-Elect and Spouses
8:45–9:00am	Class Picture at Capitol Steps
9:15am–1:00pm	Committee on House Administration Program for Members-Elect
12:00–2:00pm	Luncheon hosted by Rep. Steny Hoyer, Ranking Minority Member, Committee on House Administration
1:00–2:00pm	Republican Member Lunch and Discussion
2:30–4:30pm	Members-Elect Meeting with Speaker, Majority Leader, Majority Whip, House Republican Conference and Deputy Majority Whip
2:30–5:00pm	Democratic Leadership Orientation Program
6:30–10:00pm	Dinner Hosted by Rep. Nancy Pelosi, Minority Whip Dinner Hosted by Rep. Martin Frost, Chairman, Democratic Caucus
6:00–10:00pm	Speaker's Dinner at Statuary Hall–Capitol
6:00–7:00pm	Reception and Candlelight Tour of Capitol
7:00–10:00pm	Dinner

Wednesday, November 13

7:00–8:00am	Breakfast for Republican New Members with Conference Vice Chair, Congresswoman Deborah Pryce
7:00–8:00am	Breakfast hosted by Rep. Nancy Pelosi, Minority Whip
7:30–10:00am	Breakfast hosted by Rep. Robert Menendez, Vice Chairman, Democratic Caucus
7:30–8:30am	Democratic Members-Elect Breakfast at Hyatt Regency on Capitol Hill
8:15am–12:00pm	Committee on House Administration Members-Elect Program
8:15am–4:15pm	Spouses Program
12:00–12:30pm	Members-Elect Meeting with Speaker and Minority Leader
12:30–1:30pm	Lunch Sponsored by Congressman Tom Reynolds
12:30–1:45pm	Lunch Hosted by Rep. Steny Hoyer, Ranking Minority Member, Committee on House Administration
2:00–5:00pm	Democratic Leadership Orientation Program
2:00–4:00pm	Conference Activities Begin
6:00–9:00pm	Minority Leader's Dinner, Statuary Hall, The Capitol
6:30–9:00pm	Representative Roy Blunt Reception and Dinner
Time TBD	Tour of West Wing of White House
8:30–10:30pm	Dessert Reception hosted by Representative Nancy Pelosi, Minority Whip

Thursday, November 14

9:00am	Democratic Caucus
7:00–8:30am	Republican Policy Committee Breakfast sponsored by Congressman Chris Cox
8:30–9:00am	Rain Date for Class Picture
10:00am–2:00pm	Conference Activities
8:00am–4:15pm	Designated-Aide Program Sponsored by Congressional Management Foundation (CMF)
3:00–6:00pm	NRCC Activities
7:00–9:00pm	Committee on House Administration Reception
Time TBD	Reception Hosted by Congressman Rogers

Friday, November 15

Time/Place TBD	Begin NRCC Activities
9:00am	Democratic Caucus

Committee on House Administration • 2002 New Member Orientation

In addition to the formal House and Senate programs, other orientation sessions are available to new members. Several organizations hold policy seminars. Harvard University's Institute of Politics presents a several-days-long policy program for newly elected House members soon after the official organization concludes. The Heritage Foundation holds a several-days-long seminar on policy issues for both Senate and House members-elect. In January, soon after the swearing-in, the Congressional Research Service conducts a several-days series of policy and procedural briefings for newly elected House members and their families.

§ 5.50 Party Leadership

The party leadership is responsible for bringing order and efficiency in a body comprising individualistic legislators. Former Speaker of the House Dennis Hastert said his job was to "keep the trains moving on time." A former Senate leader once described his job as "janitor," and another said it was like "herding cats."

Party leaders serve both institutional and partisan functions. The majority leadership sets the agenda, determines legislative priorities and political strategies, schedules measures for floor action, assesses support for legislation, and rounds up votes for passage. The minority leadership devises strategies for upsetting the plans of the majority, unless, of course, there is agreement on the legislation.

The basic function of the party leaders is to bring coherence and efficiency to a decentralized institution. As institutional leaders, they are responsible for knowing rules and procedures, and for organizing the committee system and chamber administrative machinery. The majority leadership has the added responsibility of scheduling measures for floor consideration. As leaders of their political parties in their chambers, the leaders meet with committee chairs and ranking minority members to discuss political strategies and legislative priorities, assess support and opposition to the leadership's initiatives, round up votes, and serve as congressional spokesmen for their parties' positions. *(See § 5.51, Party Control of Congress, 80th through 112th Congresses.)*

§ 5.60 House Leadership

This section briefly describes the majority and minority party leadership in the House. The reader should keep in mind that House rules favor the majority.

Speaker of the House. The position of Speaker is established by the Constitution. The Speaker is the most senior officer of the House and third most senior official in the federal government. Institutionally, the Speaker presides over the House, refers measures to committee, makes rulings on points of order, has priority right of recognition on the floor, and sets the agenda. The Speaker appoints members to task forces, commissions, conference committees, some legislative committees, and select and special committees. The Speaker oversees the management of support functions. By tradition, the Speaker only occasionally participates in floor debate and seldom votes.

The Speaker is elected by majority vote of the House. Candidates are nominated by their respective party caucus or conference. On rare occasions, such as at the beginning of the 109th Congress, other candidates, in addition to those nominated by the party caucus or conference, have had their names put in nomination. The Speaker does not have to be a member of Congress, but all Speakers have been representatives..

§ 5.51

Party Control of Congress, 80th through 112th Congresses

Party control in Congress indicates a party has the majority of members in a chamber.

Membership may change throughout a Congress, due to deaths, resignations, or party switching by members. Twice in history, in the 65th Congress (1917–1919) and in the 72nd Congress (1931–1933), party control in the House changed from that based on the election results. In the 65th Congress, there were 210 Democrats, 216 Republicans, and 7 members of other parties. These 7 members affiliated with the Democrats, thereby making the Democrats the majority party in the 65th Congress. In the 72nd Congress, the election yielded 216 Democrats, 218 Republicans, and 1 member of a third party. By the time the 72nd Congress met on December 7, 1931, 14 representatives-elect had died (including Speaker Nicholas Longworth). Special elections to fill the vacancies resulted in a net gain of 4 seats for the Democrats, giving them control of the House.

When the 107th Congress convened, the Senate was split at 50 members each for the Democrats and Republicans. Because Vice President Cheney was a Republican and could vote in the event of a tie vote, Republicans organized the chamber, but only after a "power-sharing agreement" was negotiated between the parties. Then, on June 6, 2001, Republican Sen. James Jeffords, VT, declared himself to be an independent who would caucus with the Democrats to organize the Senate. The power-sharing agreement remained partially in effect.

In January 1959, Alaska was declared a state, and, in August 1959, Hawaii was declared a state. In the House, the admission of Alaska and Hawaii to the Union was accommodated by a temporary increase in the number of House members, to 436 in the 86th Congress for the 1 seat allocated for Alaska, and 437 in the 87th Congress for the 1 seat allocated for Hawaii. The number was returned to 435 in the 88th Congress following the 1960 census and apportionment. In the 86th Congress, there were 98 senators to accommodate 2 Alaskan senators. In the 87th Congress, the Senate reached its current level of 100 senators, reflecting the addition of the 2 Hawaiian senators.

The following table depicts party control at the start of a Congress. In Congresses where the numbers do not total 100 in the Senate or 435 in the House, there were vacancies at the start of the Congress. The numbers above 435 for the House in the 86th and 87th Congresses provided the seats for Alaska and Hawaii.

	Senate			House		
Congress	Democrat	Republican	Other	Democrat	Republican	Other
80th Congress (1947–1949)	45	51		188	246	1
81st Congress (1949–1951)	54	42		263	171	1
82nd Congress (1951–1953)	48	47	1	234	199	2
83rd Congress (1953–1955)	46	48	2	213	221	1
84th Congress (1955–1957)	48	47	1	232	203	
85th Congress (1957–1959)	49	47		234	201	
86th Congress (1959–1961)	64	34		283	153	
87th Congress (1961–1963)	64	36		262	175	
88th Congress (1963–1965)	67	33		258	176	

Continued on page 199

§ 5.51 (continued)

	Senate			House		
Congress	**Democrat**	**Republican**	**Other**	**Democrat**	**Republican**	**Other**
89th Congress (1965–1967)	68	32		295	140	
90th Congress (1967–1969)	64	36		248	187	
91st Congress (1969–1971)	58	42		243	192	
92nd Congress (1971–1973)	54	44	2	255	180	
93rd Congress (1973–1975)	56	42	2	242	192	1
94th Congress (1975–1977)	60	37	2	291	144	1
95th Congress (1977–1979)	61	38	1	292	143	
96th Congress (1979–1981)	58	41	1	277	158	
97th Congress (1981–1983)	46	53	1	242	192	1
98th Congress (1983–1985)	46	54		269	166	
99th Congress (1985–1987)	47	53		253	182	
100th Congress (1987–1989)	55	45		258	177	
101st Congress (1989–1991)	55	45		260	175	
102nd Congress (1991–1993)	56	44		267	167	1
103rd Congress (1993–1995)	57	43		258	176	1
104th Congress (1995–1997)	48	52		204	230	1
105th Congress (1997–1999)	45	55		207	226	2
106th Congress (1999–2001)	45	55		211	223	1
107th Congress (2001–2003)	50	50		211	221	2
108th Congress (2003–2005)	48	51	1	205	229	1
109th Congress (2005–2007)	44	55	1	201	232	1
110th Congress (2007–2009)	49	49	2	233	202	
111th Congress (2009-2011)	56	41	2	256	178	
112th Congress (2011-2013)	51	47	2	193	242	

For the current party control of Congress, see TheCapitol.Net web page <*PartyNumbers.com*>.

Majority Leader. The majority leader is the second most senior official in the House and the day-to-day manager of business on the floor. In concert with the other majority-party leadership, the majority leader builds and manages her party's consensus on legislation. The majority leader is elected by the party caucus or conference.

§ 5.61

The Parties' Whip Structures

The parties in the House and Senate have an extensive array of whips assisting the elected majority and minority whips. The majority and minority whips appoint a number of deputy, assistant, or regional whips. Each party also elects zone whips, sometimes referred to as regional whips. Additional whips represent classes of members, such as freshmen members.

The titles associated with the various whip positions are not consistent between Congresses, between parties, or even within a party. Some members identify themselves as regional whips, when they might more accurately be called at-large whips, or vice versa. Party lists that identify whips elected or appointed by the party leadership may not consistently include whips selected by other groups. Different sources may identify different whip structures.

Because the whip organization is not made public, the table depicts only the breadth of the whip structure.

Whip	House Democrats	House Republicans	Senate Democrats	Senate Republicans
Senior Chief Deputy Whip	1			
Chief Deputy Whip	9	1	1	1
Deputy Whip	12	17	2	7
Assistant Whip		49*		
Regional Whip	24*			
At-Large Whip	70*			

* Estimate

Majority Whip. The majority whip persuades members to support her party's position on votes, and also measures and rounds up support for party positions. Assisted by a network of assistant whips—including chief deputy whips, regional whips, and class whips—the majority whip is elected by her party caucus or conference. The term "whip" comes from British parliamentary practice, which adapted it from fox hunting. The "whipper in" is the term for the person responsible for keeping the fox hounds from leaving the pack. (*See § 5.61, The Parties' Whip Structures.*)

Minority Leader. The minority leader is the senior official for his party, who works within the party to set an agenda, message, and strategy. He can appoint minority party members to task forces and commissions. The minority leader is elected by the party caucus or conference.

Assistant. A position unique within the House Democratic Caucus, the assistant works with other Democratic leaders on communication, message, and research. The assistant is selected by the Democratic leader.

Minority Whip. The minority whip persuades members to support her party's position on votes, and counts votes. To do the whip's job, she is assisted by a network of assistant whips, including regional whips and class whips. The minority whip is elected by her party caucus or conference.

Democratic Caucus. The caucus serves as the organizational vehicle for all House Democrats and is led by two officers elected by the caucus: chair and vice chair. The caucus hosts meetings and serves as the primary vehicle for communicating the party message to members.

Democratic Congressional Campaign Committee. Appointed by the Democratic leader, the chair and co-chairs oversee the political unit of House Democrats.

Republican Conference. The conference serves as the organizational vehicle for all House Republicans. It is led by three officers elected by the conference: chair, vice chair, and secretary. The conference hosts meetings and serves as the primary vehicle for communicating the party message to members.

Republican Policy Committee. Elected by the Republican Conference, the chair assists party leaders in designing, developing, and executing policy ideas. The chair appoints a vice chair.

Republican Congressional Campaign Committee. Elected by the Republican Conference, the chair and executive committee oversee the political unit of House Republicans.

§ 5.70 Senate Leadership

This section briefly identifies the majority and minority leadership in the Senate. The reader should keep in mind that the Senate is not hierarchical and that policy ideas are often worked out in social settings such as each party's Tuesday policy lunches.

President Pro Tempore. By tradition the longest serving member of the majority party, the president pro tempore is elected by the Senate to this constitutional but largely ceremonial position.

Majority Leader. The majority leader is the most senior Senate official, who manages the day-to-day business of the Senate floor. The majority leader is responsible for working with each committee on legislation and scheduling the sequence and manner of debate on legislation. The majority leader has priority recognition on the floor under Senate precedents. The majority leader is elected by his party caucus or conference.

Assistant Majority Leader (Majority Whip). The majority whip persuades members to support party positions on votes, and measures and rounds up support for party positions. The majority whip is elected by the party caucus or conference, and is assisted by an appointed chief deputy whip.

Minority Leader. The minority leader is the senior official for his party. The minority leader is elected by his party caucus or conference.

Assistant Floor Leader (Minority Whip). Elected by party members, the minority whip serves as the second-ranking leader for the minority. Assisted by a chief deputy whip, the minority whip counts votes and works to persuade members to support party positions.

Democratic Conference. The conference serves as the organization vehicle for Senate Democrats and is led by a chair, vice chair, and secretary elected by the conference. The chair is called majority leader or minority leader depending on which party controls the Senate.

Democratic Conference Vice Chair. The conference vice chair works with the conference chair to advance the party agenda.

Democratic Conference Secretary. The conference secretary works with the conference chair to advance the party agenda.

Democratic Policy Committee. The policy development arm of the Senate Democrats, the Policy Committee works with the Democratic leader to develop policy proposals. The chair and vice chair are appointed by the Democratic leader. The committee includes three regional chairs.

Democratic Senatorial Campaign Committee. Appointed by the Democratic leader, the chair oversees the political unit of Senate Democrats. A vice chair for outreach and policy is appointed by the chair.

Democratic Steering and Outreach Committee. Appointed by the Democratic leader, the chair of the committee is responsible for building coalitions.

Democratic Committee on Committee Outreach. Appointed by the Democratic leader, the chair and vice chair are responsible for maintaining communication among committee leaders.

Senate Republican Conference. The conference serves as the organizational vehicle for Senate Republicans and is led by a chair and vice chair elected by the conference. The conference hosts periodic meetings and is the primary vehicle for communicating party message. The conference chair is called majority leader or minority leader depending on which party controls the Senate.

Republican Policy Committee. The Policy Committee, and its elected chair, assists other Senate leaders in designing, developing, and executing policy ideas.

Republican Steering Committee. The steering committee, led by an appointed chair and vice chair, is responsible for making committee assignments.

National Republican Senatorial Committee. The campaign committee serves as the political unit of Senate Republicans. It is led by a chair who is appointed by the Republican Conference, and a vice chair appointed by the chair.

§ 5.80 Committees and Subcommittees

Types of Committees

There are three types of committees. "Standing committees" are permanent entities with legislative authority identified in chamber rules, that is, authority to report legislation to their parent chamber. House Rule X and Senate Rule XXV list the jurisdiction of each committee. Referral is determined primarily by committee jurisdiction. (*See § 6.30, Referral of Legislation to Committee.*)

"Select committees" or "special committees" (the terms are interchangeable) are temporary panels created for a specified period of time and with a specific mandate. Most select committees do not have legislative authority. Select or special committees are created by simple resolution.

"Joint committees" are made up of members of both chambers. Joint committees are generally permanent panels with study or administrative authority, established in law or by concurrent resolution.

Committee Sizes and Ratios

In both the House and Senate, the respective party leaders begin interparty and intraparty negotiations over individual committee sizes and ratios before the early organization meetings. They continue the discussions during the organization meetings. Occasionally, the negotiations continue until the beginning of the new Congress. Committee sizes are modified each Congress, but generally not by more than a few seats. Committee sizes are included in Senate rules, but not followed. They are not in House rules.

§ 5.81

House and Joint Committee Ratios in the 112th Congress

Information current as of July 2011.
The authors keep this information updated online at <*CongressByTheNumbers.com*>.

Committee	Republicans	Democrats
Agriculture	26	20
Appropriations	29	21
Armed Services	35	27
Budget	22	16
Education and the Workforce	23	17
Energy and Commerce	31	23
Ethics	5	5
Financial Services	34	27
Foreign Affairs	26	20
Homeland Security	19	14
House Administration	6	3
Intelligence, Permanent Select	12	8
Judiciary	23	16
Natural Resources	27	21
Oversight and Government Reform	23	17
Rules	9	4
Science, Space, and Technology	23	17
Small Business	15	11
Transportation and Infrastructure	33	26
Veterans' Affairs	15	11
Ways and Means	22	15

Joint Committees

Committee	House		Senate	
	Republicans	Democrats	Democrats	Republicans
Economic	6	4	6	4
Library	3	2	3	2
Printing	3	2	3	2
Taxation	3	2	3	2

§ 5.82

Senate Committee Ratios in the 112th Congress

Information current as of July 2011.
The authors keep this information updated online at <CongressByTheNumbers.com>.

Committee	Democrats	Republicans
Agriculture, Nutrition, and Forestry	11	10
Appropriations	16	14
Armed Services[1]	14	12
Banking, Housing, and Urban Affairs	12	10
Budget[2]	12	11
Commerce, Science, and Transportation	13	12
Energy and Natural Resources[2]	12	10
Environment and Public Works[2]	10	8
Finance	13	11
Foreign Relations	10	9
Health, Education, Labor, and Pensions[2]	12	10
Homeland Security and Governmental Affairs[1]	9	8
Judiciary	10	8
Rules and Administration	10	8
Small Business and Entrepreneurship[1]	10	9
Veterans' Affairs[2]	8	7
Indian Affairs	8	6
Select Ethics	3	3
Select Intelligence	8	7
Special Aging	11	10

1. Sen. Joseph Lieberman, an Independent Democrat, receives his committee assignments from the Democrats and is counted as a Democrat for determining committee ratios. He serves on this committee.
2. Sen. Bernard Sanders, an independent, receives his committee assignments from the Democrats and is counted as a Democrat for determining committee ratios. He serves on this committee.

Ratios on House and Senate committees generally reflect party strength in the chamber. However, it is commonly acknowledged that House ratios are done in the aggregate (allocation of total number of committee seats), rather than on a committee-by-committee basis. This is done in part to attain a "working majority" on the more sought-after committees. Senate ratios also allow for a "working majority." However, ratios more closely approximate party strength in the chamber as a whole. (*See § 5.81, House and Joint Committee Ratios in the 112th Congress; and § 5.82, Senate Committee Ratios in the 112th Congress.*)

Committee sizes or ratios might change during a Congress if, in the leaders' political views, there is a change in the party makeup of a chamber.

Subcommittees

Most committees form subcommittees to share specific tasks with the full committees. Subcommittees are responsible to—and work within the guidelines established by—their parent committees. House rules impose a limit of five subcommittees for most committees. Senate committees are not limited by Senate rule in the number of subcommittees they may create. The House Appropriations Committee has twelve subcommittees, and the Senate Appropriations Committee has twelve subcommittees. (*See § 7.82, New Appropriations Subcommittee Organization.*)

Some subcommittees have independent, autonomous staff; others do not, using instead full committee staff as needed. Some subcommittees have the authority to mark up legislation; others do not. Some subcommittees conduct only hearings.

§ 5.90 Committee Leadership

A committee chair calls meetings and establishes the committee agenda. The chair arranges hearings, presides over hearings and markups, controls the selection of staff and expenditures from the committee budget, manages some or all of a measure reported from the committee on the floor for the majority party, and recommends conferees. The ranking minority member performs these functions for the minority-party members on a committee.

In the House, selection of committees' party leaders is determined by party rules. For the Democrats, nominations are drawn up by the Democratic Steering Committee and then elected by secret ballot by the entire Democratic Caucus. Republicans also rely on their Steering Committee to select committee leaders. The Republican Steering Committee is controlled by the party leader.

In the Senate, the Democratic Steering and Coordination Committee selects committee leaders generally based on seniority. The full Democratic Conference votes on the selection. For the Republicans, each committee selects its leader, subject to approval by the full Republican Conference.

In both the House and Senate, no member may chair more than one standing committee. In addition, Republican members in both chambers have imposed term limits on their committee and subcommittee leaders. Under the restrictions, committee or subcommittee leaders may not serve more than six years as leader. The House rule became effective in 1995. The Senate rule was agreed to in 1995 to become effective in 1997, but it was not fully implemented until 2005. Republicans also included term limits in House rules in 1995, which Democrats retained for the 110th Congress when they took majority control but repealed in the 111th Congress. When Republicans regained the majority in the 112th Congress, they reinstated the House committee chair term limits rule. (*See § 5.91, House Committee Chairs and Ranking Minority Members and Their Tenure; and § 5.92, Senate Committee Chairs and Ranking Minority Members and Their Tenure.*)

House and Senate rules also allow a full committee chair and ranking minority member to serve ex officio as a member of any of a committee's subcommittees. Some House committees allow ex officio members to vote; others do not. Senate rules prohibit ex officio members from voting. Most committees allow ex officio members to be counted toward establishing a quorum.

§ 5.91

House Committee Chairs and Ranking Minority Members and Their Tenure

House Rule X, cl. 5(c)(2) addresses term limits for committee and subcommittee chairs. The rule does not address term limits for ranking minority members or term limits for members who accrue time as both chairs and ranking minority members. With the exception of the Committee on Rules, no member may serve as a chair of the same standing committee, or of one subcommittee of a standing committee, for more than three consecutive Congresses. Service for less than a full session of Congress does not count against a chair's term limit. Republican Conference rules go further than House rules. Conference rules limit Republican members to three consecutive terms as chair or ranking minority member of a standing, select, joint, or ad hoc committee or subcommittee beginning with the 104th Congress.

Committee	Chair	Year Became Chair	Year to Relinquish Chair	Ranking Minority Member	Comments
Agriculture	Frank Lucas	2011	2015	Collin Peterson	Rep. Lucas spent two years as ranking member (2009–2011)
Appropriations	Harold Rogers	2011	2017	Norm Dicks	
Armed Services	Howard "Buck" McKeon	2011	2017	Adam Smith	Rep. McKeon served part of one year as chair of Education and the Workforce (2006)
Budget	Paul Ryan	2011	2015	Chris Van Hollen	Rep. Ryan spent two years as ranking member (2009–2011)
Education and the Workforce	John Kline	2011	2017	George Miller	
Energy and Commerce	Fred Upton	2011	2017	Henry Waxman	
Ethics	Jo Bonner	2011	n/a	Linda Sanchez	
Financial Services	Spencer Bachus	2011	2013	Barney Frank	Rep. Bachus spent four years as ranking member (2007–2011)
Foreign Affairs	Ileana Ros-Lehtinen	2011	2015	Howard Berman	Rep. Ros-Lehtinen spent two years as ranking member (2009–2011)
Homeland Security	Peter King	2011	2013	Bennie Thompson	Rep. King served part of two years as chair (2005-2007) and four years as ranking member (2007–2011)
House Administration	Dan Lungren	2011	2013	Robert Brady	Rep. Lungren spent two years as ranking member (2009–2011)
Judiciary	Lamar Smith	2011	2015	John Conyers	Rep. Smith spent two years as ranking member (2009–2011)
Natural Resources	Doc Hastings	2011	2015	Edward Markey	Rep. Hastings spent two years as ranking member (2009–2011)
Oversight and Government Reform	Darrell Issa	2011	2015	Elijah Cummings	Rep. Issa spent two years as ranking member (2009–2011)
Rules	David Drier	2011	n/a	Louise Slaughter	
Science, Space, and Technology	Ralph Hall	2011	2017	Eddie Bernice Johnson	
Small Business	Sam Graves	2011	2017	Nydia Velazquez	
Transportation and Infrastructure	John Mica	2011	2013	Nick Rahall	Rep. Mica spent four years as ranking member (2007–2011)
Veterans' Affairs	Jeff Miller	2011	2017	Bob Filner	
Ways and Means	Dave Camp	2011	2013	Sander Levin	

Also see TheCapitol.Net's Congressional Directory: <*CongressDirectory.com*>.

§ 5.92

Senate Committee Chairs and Ranking Minority Members and Their Tenure

Republican Conference rules address the issue of term limits for committee chairs and ranking minority members. Although the rule was agreed to in 1995, it was not made effective until 1997. A clarification to the rule was needed to say that senators could serve no more than six years as chair and six years as a ranking minority member of a single committee. If a senator has already served six years as chair of a committee, she could not become the ranking member. Time served as ranking member must come before, or interrupt, the six years of service as chair. With the change of party control of the Senate in 2001 as a result of the party switch to independent from Republican of former Sen. James Jeffords, the interpretation of the rule was addressed once again. In general, the 107th Congress was viewed by the Republican Conference as not counting against a senator's term limits. Because of the complexity of the Republican Conference rule, and its effect on all Republican senators, the exact language of the rule is provided here:

> "B. Standing Committee Chair/Ranking Member Term Limits: (1) A Senator shall serve no more than six years, cumulatively, as Chairman of the same standing Committee. This limitation shall not preclude a Senator from serving for six years, cumulatively, as Chairman of other Committees, in series, if the Senator's seniority and election by Committee members provides the opportunity for such additional service. (2) Service as Ranking Member shall also be limited to six years, cumulatively, in the same pattern as described in (1) above. Time served as Ranking Member shall not be counted as time served as Chairman. Once a Senator has completed six years as Chairman of a committee, there will be no further opportunity for that Senator to serve as Ranking Member of that same committee if control of the Senate shifts and Republicans go into the minority. The opportunity for service as Ranking Member, outlined in (2) above, takes place either before or in interruption of the Senator's six year term as Chairman, not after."

Because the term limit is a Republican Conference rule, rather than a Senate rule, it does not apply to Democratic senators.

Committee	Chair	Ranking	Comments
Agriculture, Nutrition, and Forestry	Debbie Stabenow	Pat Roberts	
Appropriations	Daniel Inouye	Thad Cochran	Sen. Cochran served two years as chair (2005–2007)
Armed Services	Carl Levin	John McCain	
Banking, Housing, and Urban Affairs	Tim Johnson	Richard C. Shelby	Sen. Shelby served four years as chair (2003–2007)
Budget	Kent Conrad	Jeff Sessions	
Commerce, Science, and Transportation	John D. Rockefeller	Kay Bailey Hutchison	
Energy and Natural Resources	Jeff Bingaman	Lisa Murkowski	
Environment and Public Works	Barbara Boxer	James M. Inhofe	Sen. Inhofe served four years as chair (2003–2007)

Also see TheCapitol.Net's Congressional Directory: <*CongressDirectory.com*>.

Continued on page 208

§ 5.92 (continued)

Committee	Chair	Ranking	Comments
Finance	Max Baucus	Orrin Hatch	
Foreign Relations	John Kerry	Richard G. Lugar	Sen. Lugar served four years as chair (2003–2007)
Health, Education, Labor, and Pensions	Tom Harkin	Mike Enzi	Sen. Enzi served two years as chair (2005–2007)
Homeland Security and Governmental Affairs	Joseph I. Lieberman*	Susan M. Collins	Sen. Collins served four years as chair (2003–2007)
Judiciary	Patrick J. Leahy	Charles Grassley	
Rules and Administration	Charles Schumer	Lamar Alexander	
Small Business and Entrepreneurship	Mary Landrieu	Olympia J. Snowe	Sen. Snowe served four years as chair (2003–2007)
Veterans' Affairs	Patty Murray	Richard Burr	
Indian Affairs	Daniel Akaka	John Barrasso	
Select Committee on Intelligence	Dianne Feinstein	Saxby Chambliss	Republican Conference rules on term limits affect only standing committees
Special Committee on Aging	Herb Kohl	Bob Corker	Republican Conference rules on term limits affect only standing committees

* Independent Democrat

Also see TheCapitol.Net's Congressional Directory: <*CongressDirectory.com*>.

§ 5.100 House Committee and Subcommittee Assignment Process

Committee assignments often determine the character and course of a member's career. New members generally seek assignment to committees that address issues with which they are familiar, as well as issues important to their districts and states and key to their political ambitions. (*See § 5.101, Member Press Release; and § 5.102, Example of a Senior Committee Member's Activities.*) Committee assignments are also important to the party leaders who organize the chamber. Committee assignments shape the composition of the committees. In making assignments to committees, party leaders balance the wishes of the members against the sometimes differing political needs of the party. Both House rules and party rules (Democratic Caucus and Republican Conference) address the assignment process. (*See § 5.103, House Committee Assignment Request Form.*)

Numbers and Limitations on Committee Assignments. In general, no member may serve on more than two standing committees and four subcommittees of those committees, a total of six slots. As noted in § 5.104 (*Categories of Committees in the House of Representatives*), both parties designate categories of committees and generally limit service to one exclusive committee, although

§ 5.101

Member Press Release

Home » Media Center » Press Releases

Congresswoman Terri A. Sewell Selected to Serve on House Committee on Agriculture and the House Committee on Science and Technology

SHARE

Jan 19, 2011 | Issues: Jobs and Economy, Education

WASHINGTON, DC – Today, Congresswoman Terri A. Sewell (AL-7) was selected by House leadership to serve on the House Committee on Agriculture and the House Committee on Science and Technology.

The House Committee on Agriculture creates farm policy and drafts legislation to protect the interests of rural America. The committee's jurisdiction includes rural development, agricultural colleges, farming, nutrition, renewable energy, conservation, bioterrorism, forestry and many others.

"I am excited and honored to have the opportunity to serve on the House Committee on Agriculture," said Rep. Sewell. "By serving on this committee, I have the opportunity to advocate for the critical needs of the 7th Congressional District of Alabama. I will promote innovative legislation that will strengthen our small businesses, our land grant institutions, support both urban and rural economic development and work to improve the nutritional challenges facing our children, seniors and families. This committee assignment will help to ensure that America remains a dominant exporter of agricultural goods, which will create and protect good-paying, cutting-edge jobs in the district and across the country."

The House Committee on Science and Technology is responsible for overseeing research and development programs at many different federal agencies, including the National Aeronautics and Space Administration (NASA), the Department of Defense (DOD), the Environmental Protection Agency (EPA), the Department of Homeland Security (DHS), the Federal Aviation Administration (FAA) and many others.

"I look forward to serving on the House Committee on Science and Technology," said Rep. Sewell. "As a member of this committee, I have the ability to promotelegislation that will improve economic development in the 7th Congressional District and throughout the State of Alabama. This includes introducing legislation in emerging scientific industries, encouraging the creation of public-private partnerships and investing in education and workforce development. Scientific advancement is one of the keys to U.S. competitiveness in a global marketplace, and this committee assignment will produce innovative opportunities for the advancement of science, technology and education as we move in to the future."

"I am pleased to have Congresswoman Sewell join the House Committee on Science, Space and Technology," said Rep. Eddie Bernice Johnson (D-TX), Ranking Member on the Committee on Science and Technology. "As Ranking Member of the Committee, I look forward to working with Congresswoman Sewell as we further explore opportunities to positively affect science and technology."

###

Contact: Allison Abney
(202) 225-2665
allison.abney@mail.house.gov

5

§ 5.102

Example of a Senior Committee Member's Activities

The Home Grown Economy: Foods from Local Farms as an Economic Development Tool

Conference sponsored by Congressman Collin Peterson

Monday, April 2, 2007
University of Minnesota, Morris

In conjunction with University of Minnesota including:
Minnesota Institute of Sustainable Agriculture (MISA)
Northwest Regional Sustainable Development Partnership
University of Minnesota, Morris
University of Minnesota Extension Service
West Central Regional Sustainable Development Partnership
West Central Research & Outreach Center

UNIVERSITY OF MINNESOTA

Program Schedule

8:00—9:00 a.m. **Registration**

9:00—9:30 a.m.
Welcome & Introductions—Michael Sparby, Project Development Director, AURI; Chancellor Jacqueline Johnson, University of Minnesota, Morris and Congressman Collin Peterson, Chair U.S. House Agriculture Committee

9:30—10:15 a.m.
Economic Realities of the Region—Ken Meter, MPA, Crossroads Resource Center

10:15—10:30 a.m. **Break**

10:30—11:15 a.m.
Woodbury County Experience—Organic Agriculture as Economic Development—Robert Marqusee, Director, Rural Economic Development for Woodbury County, Iowa

11:15—11:45 a.m.
Community Supported Agriculture—Farm to Consumer Business Model
- *Carol Ford, Owner, Garden Goddess Produce*
- *Ruth Ann Karty, Counsel, Southwest Small Business Development Center*
- *Dorothy Rosemeier, Executive Director, West Central Regional Sustainable Development Partnership (Moderator)*

11:45—12:45 p.m. **Locally Grown Foods Lunch and Exhibits Open**

12:45—1:15 p.m.
New Value Chain Panel—Keeping Value Added Dollars Local
- *Don Struxness, Co-owner, Double D Natural Meats*
- *Todd Churchill, Owner, Thousand Hills Cattle Company*
- *Jessi Gurr, Manager, Pomme de Terre Foods Coop*
- *Terry VanDerPol, Program Oganizer, Land Stewardship Project (Moderator)*

1:15—1:45 p.m.
Consumer Attitudes towards Local Foods—Robert P. King, Professor and Department Head of Applied Economics, University of Minnesota

1:45—2:00 p.m. **Break**

2:00—2:45 p.m.
Institutional and Retail Demand Creates Rural Opportunities
- *Jim Ennis, Midwest Food Alliance*
- *Don Kulick, District Manager, Sodexho Campus Services*
- *Jim VanDerPol, Pastures A Plenty Farm & Company*
- *Sandy Olson-Loy, Vice Chancellor for Student Affairs, University of Minnesota, Morris (Moderator)*

2:45—3:30 p.m.
Market Opportunities for Agriculture of the Middle—Frederick L. Kirschenmann, Leopold Center for Sustainable Agriculture

About the Keynote Speakers' Presentations

Ken Meter, MPA, President of Crossroads Resource Center
Growing homegrown economies in rural Minnesota requires a solid grasp of current economic realities. It's impossible to successfully develop a locale without knowing how its economy currently works, and it is difficult for a community to attract investors without solid data. West Central and Northwest Minnesota have been national pioneers in adopting local economic analysis as a tool for homegrown development. The finding from these studies, performed by Ken Meter of Crossroads Resource Center, shows the region has more assets than is commonly believed, but also highlight some of the key challenges ahead.

Robert Marqusee, Director of Rural Economic Development for Woodbury County, Iowa
Woodbury County, Iowa, has taken significant; precedent-setting steps to make local, organic food produced on family farms a key component of its rural economic development program. In June 2005, the Board of Supervisors passed a first-in-the-nation policy that provides a property tax break to landowners who convert farmland to certified organic production. In January 2006 the Board followed up by passing another breakthrough policy – when the county buys food it must be organically produced and processed within a 100-mile radius of the courthouse in Sioux City. Marqusee will talk about his enthusiasm for these programs and why they provide an opportunity to revitalize his region's rural economy.

Robert P. King, Professor and Department Head of Applied Economics, University of Minnesota
When asked if they prefer to buy local foods, food shoppers almost always answer, "Yes." But what are their reasons for preferring local foods and how do they define "local"? This presentation will summarize findings on attitudes toward local foods from a survey of 500 food shoppers in Twin-Cities metro area supermarkets, natural food stores, and farmers' markets. These findings can help producers and food retailers more effectively market locally produced foods.

Fred Kirschenmann, Philosopher, Leopold Center for Sustainable Agriculture, Iowa State University
Markets in the food industry have been changing dramatically in recent years. Direct markets in the form of Farmers Markets, CSA's, internet sales and other arrangements have grown dramatically. Organic sales have continued to grow at the rate of 20% a year for over ten years. And supermarkets have featured "store within a store" sections that feature highly differentiated food products. But perhaps the biggest demand for highly differentiated food products has emerged in the food service sector---restaurants, health care institutions and school systems. This growing market presents an opportunity for the farmers who fall between these direct markets and the mass production commodity markets. These new markets provide unique opportunities for mid-sized, independent family farms since they have all of the qualities that these markets desire. We will explore what we need to do to help farmers transition to these new markets and how to insure that they receive a fair share of the value obtained through these new markets.

Beginning List of Exhibitors

- AURI (Agriculture Utilization Research Institute)
- Sustainable Farming Association of Minnesota
- SBDCs (Small Business Development Centers)
- Land Stewardship Project
- Minnesota Grown
- Minnesota Department of Agriculture
- Renewing the Countryside
- U.S. Small Business Administration
- Minnesota Department of Employment and Economic Development (DEED)
- West Central Initiative Fund
- Southwest Minnesota Initiative Foundation
- Northwest Minnesota Initiative Foundation
- Upper Minnesota Valley Regional Development Commission
- Mid-Minnesota Regional Development Commission
- University of Minnesota
- And more!

Welcome!

As your Representative in Congress, one of my top priorities is to help develop economic opportunities for citizens in our rural agricultural economy. One of the most promising current developments is the growing interest in local food supply chains.

Businesses and consumers throughout the nation are showing increasing interest in locally grown, fresh, healthy food and that is creating new opportunities for farmers and rural communities. Localized supply chains, or new value chains can provide opportunities for profit for farmers and other rural entrepreneurs and main street businesses who want to participate in processing and distribution of food from the farm field to the local dinner plate. These value chains can be short, consisting only of a direct relationship between the farmer and the end user or they can be longer chains that include local processing and distribution functions to meet the needs of larger retail and institutional customers.

My goal in sponsoring this conference is to provide my constituents with an opportunity to learn about and explore how these new value chains can become an economic development engine for farmers, rural communities and development organizations and how we can all work together to satisfy market demands.

I hope you will join us and I know you'll have a pleasant, educational and productive day!

Sincerely,

Collin C. Peterson, Member of Congress

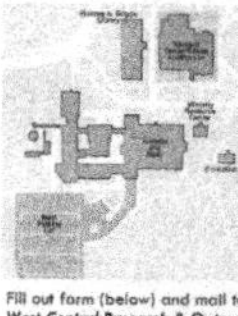

Conference Location: University of Minnesota, Morris Campus Student Center

Parking: Park in West Parking Lot on campus, 2nd Street

For directions to Morris and campus, go to: **www.morris.umn.edu/visitor**

Hotel Reservations—Conference rate at Prairie Inn in Morris, $51.30 for one, $56.70 for two, call 800-535-3035 and indicate Congressman Peterson's conference.

Conference registration fee payable to:
University of Minnesota
- By March 26, 2007: **$35**
- Student Rate: **$10**

Fill out form (below) and mail to:
West Central Research & Outreach Center
46352 State Hwy 329
Morris, MN 56267 *Att: Julie Larson*

OR register and pay online by 3/26/07 at:
www.regionalpartnerships.umn.edu

For weather concerns on day of conference, call 218-847-5056

Name ____________________

Organization or Business ____________________

Mailing Address ____________________ City ____________________

State __________ Zip __________ Phone __________ E-mail __________

____ I have special needs. Please contact me.

§ 5.103

House Committee Assignment Request Form

COMMITTEE ASSIGNMENT REQUEST FORM FOR INCOMING REPUBLICAN MEMBERS

108th Congress

(MUST BE RETURNED BY 12 NOON ON DECEMBER 2, 2002)

____
Member's Name

____
State & District

<u>108th Congress Committee Request</u>

1st Choice: ______________________________

2nd Choice: ______________________________

3rd Choice: ______________________________

4th Choice: ______________________________

5th Choice: ______________________________

Comments: ______________________________

____

____

Staff Contact & Phone Number: ______________________________

RETURN TO: Republican Steering Committee
Speaker's Office, H-209, the Capitol
Washington, DC 20515

*****PLEASE RETURN BY 12 NOON ON DECEMBER 2, 2002*****

§ 5.104

Categories of Committees in the House of Representatives

Category	Democrats	Republicans
Exclusive	Appropriations	Appropriations
	Energy and Commerce (for service on the panel in the 104th and subsequent Congresses)	Energy and Commerce
	Financial Services (for service on the panel beginning in the 109th)	Financial Services
	Rules	Rules
	Ways and Means	Ways and Means
Nonexclusive	Agriculture	Agriculture
	Armed Services	Armed Services
	Budget	Budget
	Education and the Workforce	Education and the Workforce
	Energy and Commerce (for service on the panel occurring in the 104th and earlier Congresses)	
	Financial Services (for service on the panel prior to the 109th Congress)	
	Foreign Affairs	Foreign Affairs
	Homeland Security	Homeland Security
	House Administration	
	Judiciary	Judiciary
	Natural Resources	Natural Resources
	Oversight and Government Reform	Oversight and Government Reform
	Science, Space, and Technology	Science, Space, and Technology
	Small Business	Small Business
	Transportation and Infrastructure	Transportation and Infrastructure
	Veterans' Affairs	Veterans' Affairs
Exempt	Ethics	Ethics
	Select Intelligence	Select Intelligence

a member can serve on the Budget or House Administration panels while on an exclusive committee. A Republican member of the Rules Committee can take a leave of absence from a standing committee to serve on Rules without losing seniority on the standing committee. Both parties allow service on two nonexclusive committees.

For Democrats and Republicans, service on the Standards of Official Conduct Committee is exempt from assignment limitations. Under House rules, service on this committee is limited to three Congresses during any five successive Congresses.

Service on the Budget Committee is limited to no more than four Congresses in any six successive Congresses for both Democrats and Republicans.

Party Organization Role. Both the Democrats and Republicans give their assignment function to steering committees, comprising the elected leadership, members elected from regions, and members appointed by the leadership. Representatives from specific classes are often also represented.

The steering committees vote by secret ballot to arrive at individual recommendations for assignments, and forward these recommendations to the respective party caucus or conference. Although procedures exist to appeal steering committee recommendations, it is rare for the party to overturn a slate. Once ratified by the party, the House votes on each resolution comprising the committee lists for each party.

Subcommittee Assignment Process. Under House rules, members are generally limited to service on four subcommittees. Party rules and practice, however, govern the subcommittee assignment process. In Democratic Caucus rules, Democrats formally provide for a bidding process based on full committee seniority, whereby each member selects one choice before any member receives a second subcommittee assignment. Republicans leave the decision on subcommittee assignments to each individual committee leader. Many Republican committee leaders employ a bidding process similar to the one used by the Democrats.

§ 5.110 Senate Committee and Subcommittee Assignment Process

Numbers and Limitations on Committee Assignments. Senate rules establish three categories of committees, popularly called "A," "B," and "C." (*See § 5.111, Categories of Committees in the Senate, for a list of the committees within each category.*) Each party also designates so-called "super A" committees. Senators are restricted to service on two "A" committees and one "B" committee. They are also restricted to service on one "Super A" committee. There are no restrictions on service on "C" committees. The limitations are often waived, and senators who serve on additional panels may be referred to as having "grandfather" rights on the additional committees.

Subcommittee Assignment Process. Neither Senate rules nor party rules discuss how subcommittee assignments are made. However, there are two prevalent practices. Under one practice, the full committee chair exercises discretion in selecting subcommittee members. Under the other common practice, senators choose assignments in a bidding process in order of seniority on the full committee, similar to the way the House members select subcommittee assignments.

There are limitations on subcommittee assignments. A senator may not serve on more than three subcommittees of each "A" committee (except Appropriations), and two subcommittees of a "B" committee. Because the full committee limitations are often waived, the subcommittee limitations are also often waived. There are no restrictions for service on "C" committees. The "C" committees, however, rarely create subcommittees.

§ 5.111

Categories of Committees in the Senate

"A" Committees	"B" Committees
Agriculture, Nutrition, and Forestry	Budget
Appropriations*	Rules and Administration
Armed Services*	Small Business and Entrepreneurship
Banking, Housing, and Urban Affairs	Veterans' Affairs
Commerce, Science, and Transportation	Special Aging
Energy and Natural Resources	Joint Economic
Environment and Public Works	
Finance*	**"C" Committees**
Foreign Relations*	Select Ethics
Health, Education, Labor, and Pensions	Indian Affairs
Homeland Security and Governmental Affairs	Joint Library**
Judiciary	Joint Printing**
Select Intelligence	Joint Taxation

* Categories are listed in Senate Rule XXV; however, Democratic and Republican party rules each designate four "A" committees as so-called "Super A" committees.

** The committee is not listed in Senate Rule XXV; it is treated as a "C" committee for assignment purposes.

§ 5.120 Informal Groups and Congressional Member Organizations (CMOs)

Informal groups, caucuses, congressional member organizations (CMOs)—the terms all relate to the same thing: they refer to ad hoc social or policy groups comprising a limited number of members of Congress from one or both houses. The groups are not recognized in chamber rules and are voluntary associations. Some have long lineages; others appear for just a few Congresses. They operate outside the formal committee structure and apart from the official party organizations. However, caucuses are an important link in the policy chain. Members joining these entities initiate policy actions, and their work touches on all aspects of the legislative arena.

Caucuses vary in membership, range of interest, issue focus, activity, and strategy. Some are formed to influence policy; some serve as information clearinghouses. Some represent constituency interests; others are aimed primarily at the orientation of new members. Some groups exist to develop member expertise on an issue; others exist to serve as liaison with outside organizations. Some groups are partisan; others are bipartisan. Some represent members of one chamber only; others are bicameral. Some meet frequently; some meet occasionally; some never meet. These groups represent the many policy and other concerns of the members of Congress.

Most groups have chairs, and many also have co-chairs. Groups that are made up mostly of House members often have steering or executive committees. Larger caucuses often organize their members into subgroups representing regional or ideological perspectives. Almost all groups rely on staff from their members' personal offices to do the work of the caucus.

§ 5.121

Selected Caucuses and Informal Groups

A list of Congressional Member Organizations (CMOs) is available on the web site of the Committee on House Administration: *<http://cha.house.gov>*, or by searching the web for "Congressional Member Organizations."

Type of Caucus or Member Organization	Example	Comments
Industry issues	Congressional Bicameral High-Speed and Intercity Passenger Rail Caucus	Bipartisan and bicameral
	Congressional Steel Caucus	Bipartisan House members
	Congressional Travel and Tourism Caucus	Bipartisan House members
	Congressional Wireless Caucus	Bipartisan House members
	Congressional Bourbon Caucus	Bipartisan and bicameral
National constituency	Congressional Caucus on Foster Care	Bipartisan Senate members
	Congressional Black Caucus	Bipartisan and bicameral
	Congressional Caucus for Women's Issues	Bipartisan and bicameral
	Congressional Hispanic Caucus	Bipartisan and bicameral
	Congressional Public Service Caucus	Bipartisan and bicameral
	Vietnam-Era Veterans in Congress	Bipartisan and bicameral
Regional	Congressional Western Caucus	Bipartisan House members
	Western States Senate Coalition	Bipartisan Senate members
	Northeast-Midwest Congressional Coalition	Bipartisan and bicameral
	Northern Border Caucus	Bipartisan House Members
State/district	Rural Health Care Coalition	Bipartisan House members
	Congressional Urban Caucus	Bipartisan House members
	Congressional Long Island Sound Caucus	Bipartisan and bicameral
	Rural Education Caucus	Bipartisan Senate members
Personal interest	Congressional Arts Caucus	Bipartisan House members
	Congressional Caucus on CPAs and Accountants	Bipartisan and bicameral
	Congressional Caucus on Missing and Exploited Children	Bipartisan House members
	Congressional Sportsmen's Caucus	Bipartisan and bicameral
Party issues	Blue Dog Coalition	"Conservative" House Democrats
	New Democrat Coalition	"Moderate" House Democrats
	Progressive Caucus	"Progressive" House Democrats
	Republican Study Committee	Social and economic conservative House Republicans
	Tuesday Group	"Moderate" House Republicans

5

Caucuses, CMOs, and informal groups can be categorized by type. They represent industry issues, national constituencies, regional concerns, state or district issues, personal interests, and party or political agendas. (*See § 5.121, Selected Caucuses and Informal Groups.*)

CMOs are registered with the House Administration Committee as informal groups of members who "share official resources to carry out activities," according to regulations promulgated by the Committee on House Administration. These CMOs do not receive office space and cannot use the congressional frank. They are, however, officially recognized informal groups. CMOs are the successors to what were called *legislative service organizations* before the 104th Congress. A number of legislative service organizations restructured into CMOs. In the 112th Congress, over 300 CMOs were registered with the Committee on House Administration. A list of Congressional Member Organizations is available on the committee's web site: *<http://cha.house.gov>*. Congressional staff organizations are also listed on the committee's web site. The Senate does not have a counterpart registration system for such informal groups.

Members of CMOs in the House and informal groups in the Senate are subject to rules and ethics codes of their respective chambers. The CMOs and informal groups may not hire staff or use official funds for such expenses as stationery. Members may list their membership in a CMO or informal group on their own stationery, and may use a portion of their own web sites for information on a CMO or informal group.

§ 5.130 Commissions and Boards

In addition to their other responsibilities, many members serve on commissions, boards, and other entities that Congress has created to oversee or study various governmental or quasi-governmental organizations, commemorations, or public policy issues. These organizations might also be used as decisionmaking bodies within or outside Congress. Appointment power might lie within Congress.

Members of Congress appoint individuals from their states and districts to the U.S. service academies. In addition, members serve on the boards of visitors to the academies. For example, the board of visitors of the U.S. Air Force Academy includes four senators and five representatives. Statute provides for the board and its composition. The senators include the chair of the Armed Services Committee or her designee and three senators appointed by the president pro tempore of the Senate or the vice president; two of these appointees must be members of the Appropriations Committee. Members also serve on entities such as the board of trustees of the John F. Kennedy Center for the Performing Arts and the board of regents of the Smithsonian Institution. The president pro tempore of the Senate and the Speaker of the House also name private citizens to serve on the Social Security Advisory Board.

Certain events are well worth commemorating in explaining to the American citizenry and the world what is the meaning of the United States of America. For example, Congress established the Abraham Lincoln Bicentennial Commission. Its membership comprised two senators, one appointed by the majority leader and one by the minority leader; two representatives, one appointed by the Speaker and one by the minority leader; and six citizens, two each appointed by the Senate majority leader and Speaker and one each appointed by the Senate and House minority leaders.

Congress regularly uses a commission or similar form to provide itself with input on public policy issues outside of the normal process of committee hearings and other information channels or to monitor developments in policy areas where it has acted or has delegated authority to the executive. For example, because of grave concerns in the Senate over negotiations leading up to the Kyoto accords on global warming, the Senate passed a resolution giving expression to those concerns and creating an observer group of twelve senators appointed by the majority and minority leaders. In paving the way in law for China's membership in the World Trade Organization, Congress created the Congressional-Executive Commission on China, comprising nine senators appointed by the president pro tempore of the Senate, nine representatives appointed by the Speaker, and five executive officials appointed by the president (<*www.cecc.gov*>). Congress had similarly established a monitoring entity in agreeing to the treaty on Security and Cooperation in Europe, the U.S. Helsinki Commission (<*www.csce.gov*>).

The House also promotes the building of democratic institutions in selected foreign nations though the House Democracy Partnership, under the auspices of a board comprising twenty representatives: <*http://hdac.house.gov*>.

Within Congress, decision-making has been entrusted to entities such as the House Page Board (two members appointed by the Speaker and two by the minority leader), the House Office Building Commission (the Speaker and two representatives appointed by the Speaker), and the Senate Office Building Commission (nine senators appointed by the president pro tempore). Congressional influence on decision-making extends beyond Capitol Hill with membership on entities such as the National Capital Planning Commission, which provides overall planning guidance for federal land and buildings in the national capital region; the chairs of the Senate Committee on Homeland Security and Governmental Affairs and the House Committee on Oversight and Government Reform, or their designees, serve as ex officio members.

§ 5.140 Chapter Summary and Discussion Questions

Summary

- Article I of the Constitution vests all legislative power in Congress, and establishes a bicameral national legislature comprising the House of Representatives and the Senate.
- Article I and other provisions of the Constitution address the composition of the House and Senate, meetings and votes, enumerated powers, and many other aspects of congressional conduct and authority.
- Representatives are elected to two-year terms, and senators are elected to six-year terms, with one-third of the senators standing for election in a general election. House vacancies are filled by special elections, but most Senate vacancies are filled temporarily by gubernatorial appointments.
- House membership includes not only representatives but also five delegates and one resident commissioner.
- The House is more diverse than the Senate, and both comprise members from numerous occupations, religions, and ethnicities. Neither chamber fully reflects the composition of

American society. Many members have extensive political backgrounds in elective, appointive, and other public service positions.

- Congress meets early in each calendar year, and meets throughout the year until adjourning its first session (in an odd-numbered year) and its second session (in an even-numbered year). If Congress meets after a general election in the even-numbered year, that session is called a lame-duck session.
- Congress typically holds several joint meetings or joint sessions each year, one to receive the president's State of the Union address and others to allow noted Americans and foreign leaders to address members of the House and Senate meeting together.
- The party that wins the majority of seats in the House or the Senate organizes that chamber. Its leaders set the chamber's legislative agenda, and its members chair and have the majority of seats on the chamber's committees.
- The Speaker of the House is a position identified in the Constitution. The Speaker or his designee presides over the House. The Speaker is the House's leader and also the majority party's leader. The majority leader manages floor business for the majority party.
- By precedent, the majority leader of the Senate leads the Senate. He determines the Senate floor schedule and has certain rights, such as the right of recognition before other senators if he is seeking recognition when another senator is not already speaking.
- Each party in each chamber has a caucus comprising all party members: the House Democratic Caucus, the House Republican Conference, the Senate Democratic Conference, and the Senate Republican Conference.
- In addition, members in one or both chambers organize hundreds of social and policy-oriented caucuses to draw attention to specific issues.
- All members seek to serve on one or more committees in their chamber. Committees hold hearings, conduct oversight, and develop legislation, and their members gain expertise in issues dealt with by their committees. Each party caucus has a mechanism for making committee assignments.
- Each committee is headed by a chair, who sets her committee's agenda.
- Each committee is subdivided into several subcommittees. The committee chair can largely determine what role a committee's subcommittees play in the development of legislation.
- Members of Congress also serve on boards and commissions that Congress has created. Some of these boards have policy duties, such as the boards of visitors of the service academies. Others monitor executive or even international developments in certain policy areas in behalf of Congress.

Discussion Questions

- What are the qualifications for an individual to serve in the House of Representatives? In the Senate?
- States are the political units to which seats in the House and Senate are assigned. How large is the House, and how are seats there allocated among the states? How large is the Senate, and how are seats there allocated among the states?

- The Constitution provides different procedures for filling vacant seats in the House from those in the Senate. What are these differences?
- What are some of the other constitutional differences between the House and Senate? What are some of the ways that the House and Senate have developed that reflect these constitutional differences?
- In looking at the characteristics of the members of the 112th Congress, what characteristics reflect American society as a whole? What characteristics does the whole of American society have that are not reflected in the makeup of Congress?
- Do you think that the differences between the composition of Congress and broader American society affect policymaking? Or, do you think that members reflect the points of view of American society, and that the differences between the composition of Congress and broader American society is inconsequential or irrelevant?
- Some politicians argue that more female members would change the policy agenda in Congress, while other argue that the agenda would not change but the policymaking environment would be different with a greater emphasis on cooperation and problem solving. What do you think about these perspectives?
- With so many politicians with extensive résumés serving in the House and Senate, do you think service in Congress is considered a promotion for a politician? Why might that be the case?
- What legislative authority do delegates and the resident commissioner exercise?
- What happens to legislation that is pending when Congress adjourns *sine die* at the end of two years?
- Since World War II, the president has only once called Congress into special session. Conduct research to identify that occasion, the reasons cited by the president, and the response of Congress to the president's request.
- How are the roles of the Speaker of the House and the majority leader of the Senate comparable? How are they different?
- What do party whips do?
- What are some of the formal organizations or entities in Congress (aside from the floor of each chamber) where members might debate policy? What are some of the informal organizations?
- How are committee and subcommittee chairs in each chamber selected? What reasons might you come up with to explain why Republicans have sought to impose term limits on chairs?
- What limits exist in each chamber for the numbers of committees on which a member may serve?
- Compare the two systems—House and Senate—by which committees are categorized to ensure as many members as possible have assignments to important committees.
- Identify some of the important committees. Why might members want to serve on those committees? Look up these committees' legislative jurisdiction in House and Senate rules. Identify other factors after describing the committees' policymaking authority that might make these committees attractive to individual members.

- Identify two or three subcommittees in each chamber that sound interesting to you. Using the parent committees' web sites and other sources, such as the *Congressional Record*, learn what these subcommittees have done in the 112th Congress. What conclusions can you draw about the work of subcommittees?
- Review the list of congressional caucuses on the web site of the House Administration Committee. Select one to research. What role has the caucus played in congressional policymaking?

Chapter Six

Legislating in Congress: Legislative Process

Analysis

§ 6.00 Introduction

If an idea or problem attracts the attention of policymakers, opinion leaders, and the public, it might begin to build political momentum. That momentum may lead members of Congress to introduce legislation, committees to hold hearings and markups, chamber leaders to schedule floor time, and the president to approve the resulting legislation. The legislative process is activated by policy proponents attempting to see a policy enacted into law. (*See § 6.01, Legislative Process Flowchart.*)

But, many problems can occur along the way. The framers of the Constitution devised a system that makes legislation difficult to pass—two very different chambers comprising members from fifty states must agree to the identical proposition by majority votes, and the president must then agree with Congress. Each member is concerned with different local, regional, political, personal, and other interests. The rules of the House and the Senate that build on the bare-bones constitutional system further add to the difficulty of making law by ensuring adequate consideration of proposals, allowing the airing of alternative points of view, and establishing procedural stages through which proposals must pass. In addition, each member of Congress is accountable in elections for his performance in office. This democratic cornerstone of the Constitution requires that members constantly weigh the sentiments of their constituencies against their own positions on legislation to determine how to cast their votes. (*See § 6.02, House Rules Citations; and § 6.03, Senate Rules Citations.*)

What follows is an analysis of the legislative process in Congress—a distillation and description of both major, well-known stages of the process and more nuanced points that play a critical role in members' ability to advance or impede legislative proposals. The explanations that supplement the text—definitions of specific terminology, examples, and resources—assist in understanding, monitoring, and participating appropriately and effectively in the policymaking process.

Additional, special legislative procedures applicable to budget legislation, the Senate's executive business, and other kinds of legislation and oversight are described in Chapters Seven and Eight. Congressional documents are described in Chapters Nine and Ten. Tracking of legislative action is described in § 11.50. A working example of the legislative process is the subject of Chapter Twelve.

§ 6.01

Legislative Process Flowchart

<LegislativeProcessFlowchart.com>

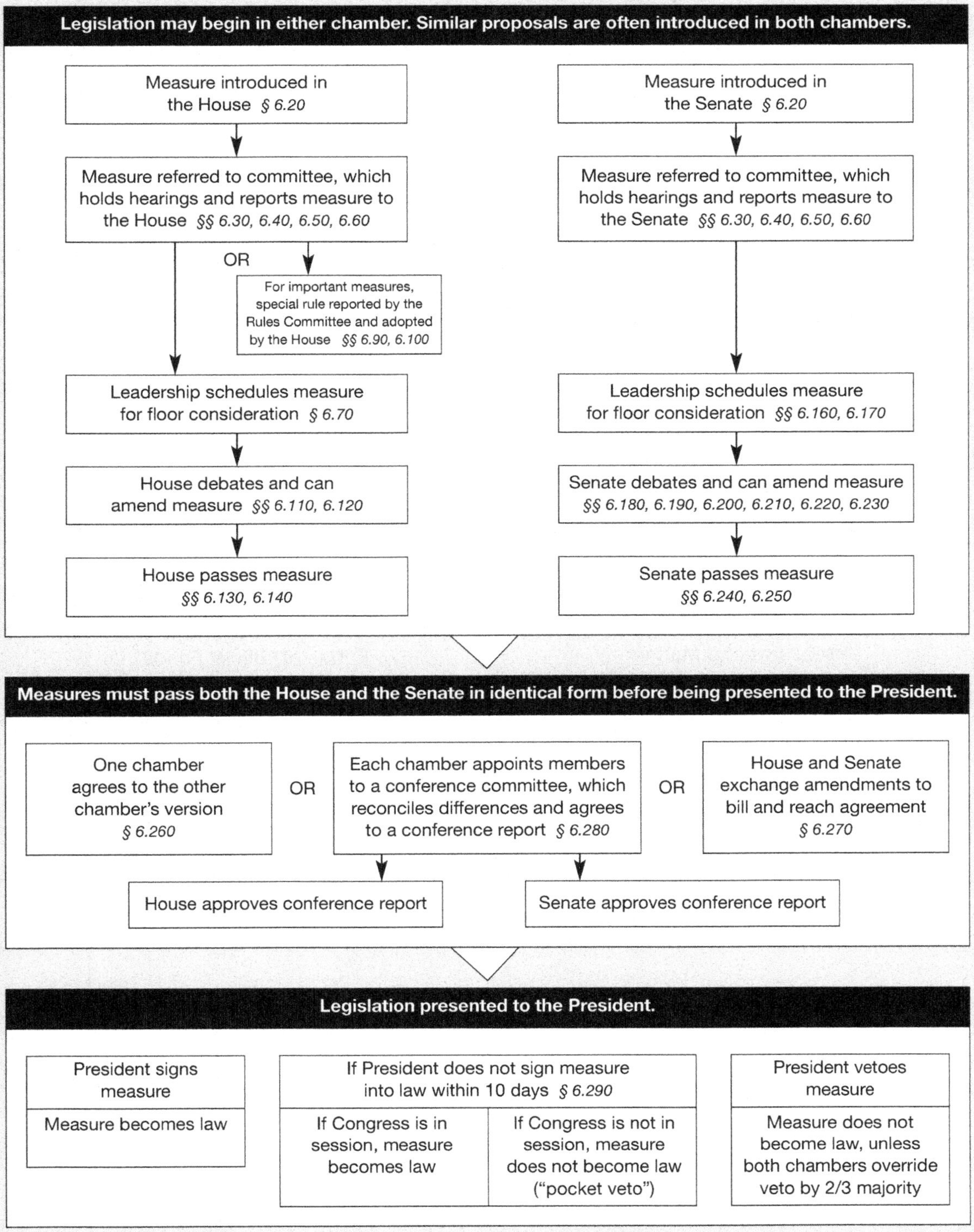

§ 6.02

House Rules Citations

House Rule Number	Subject Heading
I	The Speaker
II	Other Officers and Officials
III	The Members, Delegates, and the Resident Commissioner
IV	The Hall of the House
V	Broadcasting the House
VI	Official Reporters and News Media Galleries
VII	Records of the House
VIII	Response to Subpoenas
IX	Questions of Privilege
X	Organization of Committees
XI	Procedures of Committees and Unfinished Business
XII	Receipt and Referral of Measures and Matters
XIII	Calendars and Committee Reports
XIV	Order and Priority of Business

House Rule Number	Subject Heading
XV	Business in Order on Special Days
XVI	Motions and Amendments
XVII	Decorum and Debate
XVIII	The Committee of the Whole House on the State of the Union
XIX	Motions Following the Amendment Stage
XX	Voting and Quorum Calls
XXI	Restrictions on Certain Bills
XXII	House and Senate Relations
XXIII	Code of Official Conduct
XXIV	Limitations on the Use of Official Funds
XXV	Limitations on Outside Earned Income and Acceptance of Gifts
XXVI	Financial Disclosure
XXVII	Statutory Limit on the Public Debt
XXVIII	General Provisions

§ 6.03

Senate Rules Citations

Senate Rule Number	Subject Heading
I	Appointment of a Senator to the Chair
II	Presentation of Credentials and Questions of Privilege
III	Oaths
IV	Commencement of Daily Sessions
V	Suspension and Amendment of the Rules
VI	Quorum-Absent Senators May Be Sent For
VII	Morning Business
VIII	Order of Business
IX	Messages
X	Special Orders
XI	Papers-Withdrawal, Printing, Reading of, and Reference
XII	Voting Procedure
XIII	Reconsideration
XIV	Bills, Joint Resolutions, and Preambles Thereto
XV	Amendments and Motions
XVI	Appropriations and Amendments to General Appropriations Bills
XVII	Reference to Committees, Motions to Discharge, Reports of Committees, and Hearings Available
XVIII	Business Continued from Session to Session
XIX	Debate
XX	Questions of Order
XXI	Session with Closed Doors
XXII	Precedence of Motions
XXIII	Privilege of the Floor
XXIV	Appointment of Conferees
XXV	Standing Committees
XXVI	Committee Procedure
XXVII	Committee Staff
XXVIII	Conference Committees, Reports, Open Meetings
XXIX	Executive Sessions
XXX	Executive Session-Proceedings on Treaties
XXXI	Executive Session-Proceedings on Nominations
XXXII	The President Furnished with Copies of Records of Executive Sessions
XXXIII	Senate Chamber-Senate Wing of the Capitol
XXXIV	Public Financial Disclosure
XXXV	Gifts
XXXVI	Outside Earned Income
XXXVII	Conflict of Interest
XXXVIII	Prohibition of Unofficial Office Accounts
XXXIX	Foreign Travel
XL	Franking Privilege and Radio and Television Studios
XLI	Political Fund Activity, Definitions
XLII	Employment Practices
XLIII	Representation by Members

6

§ 6.04

Selected Procedures: House and Senate Rules

Procedure	House Rule Citation	Senate Rule Citation
Amendment Process	XVI	XV
Appropriations Process	XXI	XVI
Committee Jurisdiction	X	XXV
Committee Procedure	XI, XIII	XXVI
Committee Referral	XII	XVII
Conference Committees	XXII	XXIV, XXVIII
Debate	XVII	XIX
Motions	XVI	XV
Order of Business	XIV	VIII
Outside Earned Income	XXVI	XXXVI
Voting	XX	XII

§ 6.10 Types of Measures

Legislation is the form in which policy ideas are translated into a procedural vehicle for consideration by a chamber. There are four types of legislative measures Congress may consider, in addition to the Senate's consideration of treaties and nominations. (*See § 6.11, Legislation Glossary.*)

Bills

A bill is the most commonly used form for legislation. A bill is prefixed with an *H.R.* in the House and with an *S.* in the Senate. A number assigned at the time of introduction signifies the order in which a bill was introduced during a Congress. A bill becomes law only if it is passed with identical language by both houses and signed by the president or passed over his veto. Under certain circumstances, a bill can become law without the president's signature. (*See § 6.290, Presidential Action on Enacted Measures.*) The bill form is used for authorization or reauthorization of federal policies, programs, and activities, among its many lawmaking purposes. (*See § 9.40, Legislation for Lawmaking: Bills and Joint Resolutions; and § 7.80, Authorizations and Appropriations Processes.*)

Joint Resolution

A joint resolution is a legislative measure used for purposes other than general legislation. A joint resolution is designated *H. J. Res.* or *S. J. Res.* in the House and Senate, respectively. Like a bill, it has the force of law when passed by both houses and signed by the president or passed over his veto. Joint resolutions are also used for proposing amendments to the Constitution, in which case a joint

§ 6.11

Legislation Glossary

Act: Legislation that has passed both houses of Congress and been signed by the president or passed over his veto, thus becoming law. Also, parliamentary term for a measure that has been passed by one chamber and engrossed.

Bill: Measure that becomes law when passed in identical form by both houses and signed by the president or passed over his veto. Designated as *H.R.* or *S.* (*See also Joint Resolution*.)

Blue-Slip Resolution: House resolution ordering the return to the Senate of a Senate bill or amendment that the House believes violates the constitutional prerogative of the House to originate revenue measures.

By Request: A designation on a measure, which appears next to the sponsor's name, indicating that a member has introduced a measure on behalf of the president, an executive agency, or a private individual or organization.

Christmas-Tree Bill: Jargon for a bill containing many amendments unrelated to the bill's subjects; usually refers to Senate measures.

Clean Bill: A measure reported from a House committee that reflects the revised version of a measure considered in markup and repackaged into a new bill with a new number.

Commemorative Bill: Legislation designating a federal holiday or recognizing a particular issue, such as National Ice Cream Day or National Breast Cancer Awareness Month. Commemorative bills are currently disallowed in the House of Representatives.

Companion Bill: Identical or very similar bills introduced in both houses.

Concurrent Resolution: Used to express the sentiment of both houses on some matter without making law. Also used to carry out the administrative business of both houses. It does not require presidential approval or become law, but requires passage in identical form by both houses to take effect between them. Designated as *H. Con. Res.* or *S. Con. Res.*

Enacting Clause: Phrase at the beginning of a bill that gives it legal force when enacted: "Be it enacted by the Senate and House of Representatives of the United States of America in Congress assembled. . . ."

Engrossed Measure: Official copy of a measure as passed by one chamber, including the text as amended by floor action. Measure is certified by the clerk of the House or the secretary of the Senate.

Enrolled Measure: Final official copy of a measure as passed in identical form by both chambers and then printed on parchment. Measure is certified by the chamber of origin and signed by the Speaker of the House and the president pro tempore of the Senate before it is sent to the president.

Executive Document: A document, usually a treaty, sent by the president to the Senate for its consideration and approval.

Joint Resolution: Similar to a bill, though limited in scope (for example, to change a minor item in existing law). Becomes law when passed in identical form by both houses and signed by the president. It also is the form of legislation used to consider a constitutional amendment. A constitutional amendment requires a two-thirds vote in each house but does not require the president's signature. Designated as *H. J. Res.* or *S. J. Res.* (*See also Bill*.)

Continued on page 230

6

§ 6.11 (continued)

Law/Public Law/Private Law: Act of Congress signed by the president or passed over his veto.

Official Title: Statement of a measure's subject and purpose that appears above the enacting clause.

Omnibus Bill: A measure that combines the provisions of several disparate subjects into a single measure. Examples include *continuing resolutions* that might contain a number of the annual appropriations bills.

Original Bill: A measure drafted by a committee and introduced by its chair when the committee reports the measure back to its chamber. It is not referred back to the committee after introduction.

Popular Title: The informal, unofficial name or the short title by which a measure is known.

Preamble: Introductory language in a bill preceding the enacting clause. It describes the reasons for and intent of a measure. In a joint resolution, the language appears before the resolving clause. In a concurrent or simple resolution, it appears before the text.

Private Bill: A measure that generally deals with an individual matter, such as a claim against the government, an individual's immigration, or a land title. In the House, a private bill is considered via the Private Calendar on the first and third Tuesdays of each month.

Public Law: Act of Congress that has been signed by the president or passed over his veto. It is designated by the letters *P.L.* and numbers noting the Congress and the numerical sequence in which the measure was signed; for example, P.L. 112-7 was an act of Congress in the 112th Congress and was the seventh measure to become law during the 112th Congress.

Resolution/Simple Resolution: Sentiment of one chamber on an issue, or a measure to carry out the administrative or procedural business of one chamber. It does not become law. Designated as *H. Res.* or *S. Res.*

Resolution of Inquiry: A simple resolution calling on the president or the head of an executive agency to provide specific information or papers to one or both houses.

Resolving Clause: First section of a joint resolution that gives legal force to the measure when enacted: "Resolved by the Senate and House of Representatives of the United States of America in Congress assembled. . . ."

Rider: Term for an amendment unrelated to the subject matter of the measure to which it was attached. Usually associated with policy provisions attached to appropriations measures.

Slip Law: First official publication of a law, published in unbound single sheets or pamphlet form.

Star Print: A reprint of a measure, amendment, or committee report to correct errors in a previous printing. The first page carries a small black star. Rarely used today, with technology mitigating the need.

A larger glossary is located at the back of the book and online at <*TCNLG.com*>.

resolution passed in exactly the same form by a two-thirds vote in both chambers is submitted directly to the states rather than to the president. (*See § 9.40, Legislation for Lawmaking: Bills and Joint Resolutions.*)

Concurrent Resolution

A concurrent resolution deals with the internal affairs of both chambers and requires approval by both houses but is not sent to the president. Therefore, it does not have the force of law. A concurrent resolution is designated *H. Con. Res.* or *S. Con. Res.* in the House and Senate, respectively. Examples of concurrent resolutions are those providing for the adjournment of Congress or the congressional budget resolution. Nonbinding policy opinions of both chambers, such as "sense of the Congress," are traditionally in the form of concurrent resolutions. (*See § 9.50, Legislation Effective within Congress: Simple and Concurrent Resolutions.*)

Resolution (Simple Resolution)

A simple resolution deals with the internal workings of only one chamber or with nonbinding public-policy statements. Designated *H. Res.* or *S. Res.* in the House and Senate respectively, a simple resolution does not require the concurrence of the other chamber or approval by the president. Special rules from the House Rules Committee, the creation of a select and special committee, and funding resolutions for individual committees are in the form of simple resolutions. (*See § 9.50, Legislation Effective within Congress: Simple and Concurrent Resolutions.*)

6

§ 6.20 Drafting and Introducing Legislation

Sources of Legislation

Although legislation can be introduced only by members of Congress, ideas for legislation emanate from many sources. Members and their staffs may develop ideas based on promises made during election campaigns. The media also bring attention to issues that may need legislative solutions. Special-interest groups, and their lobbyists in Washington, often provide detailed ideas for legislation they want to see enacted. Constituents, either as individuals or groups, often suggest legislation to their own members of Congress. The executive branch is a key initiator of legislative proposals. The president in his State of the Union address to Congress outlines his priorities for the year, which may lead to legislation. Executive departments and agencies transmit drafts of legislation to Congress. Foreign governments often ask Congress to take up specific legislation, or seek ratification of certain treaties.

Drafting Legislation

Members and staff seek assistance in drafting legislation from the Office of Legislative Counsel in their respective chambers. The nonpartisan attorneys in these offices provide expert technical assistance in drafting bills, resolutions, and amendments. Legislative counsel are not only proficient in drafting but also knowledgeable about the substance of issues and the legislative process.

The Senate Committee on Rules and Administration has set drafting priorities for the Senate Office of Legislative Counsel. These priorities are measures in conference, measures pending on the floor, measures pending before a committee, and measures to be prepared for individual senators.

§ 6.21

House Cosponsorship Form

U.S. House of Representatives

Congress: ____________
Session: ____________
Date: ____________

Pursuant to clause 7 of Rule XII of the Rules of the House Representatives, the following sponsors are hereby added to:

H.R. ____________ H.Con. Res. ____________
H.J. Res. ____________ H.Res. ____________

1) ____________	21) ____________
2) ____________	22) ____________
3) ____________	23) ____________
4) ____________	24) ____________
5) ____________	25) ____________
6) ____________	26) ____________
7) ____________	27) ____________
8) ____________	28) ____________
9) ____________	29) ____________
10) ____________	30) ____________
11) ____________	31) ____________
12) ____________	32) ____________
13) ____________	33) ____________
14) ____________	34) ____________
15) ____________	35) ____________
16) ____________	36) ____________
17) ____________	37) ____________
18) ____________	38) ____________
19) ____________	39) ____________
20) ____________	40) ____________

Member Signature: ____________

§ 6.22

Sample "Dear Colleague" Letter

Congress of the United States
Washington, DC 20515

May 2, 2011

Cosponsor the Farm Dust Regulation Prevention Act

Dear Colleague:

The U.S. Environmental Protection Agency (EPA) is in the midst of a regular five- year review of the Clean Air Act's National Ambient Air Quality Standard (NAAQS) for Particulate Matter (PM). One form of regulated matter, coarse PM (i.e. dust), is kicked up by driving on unpaved roads or by farmers working in their fields, and is composed primarily of ground up dirt and naturally occurring organic materials. The EPA is considering a more stringent standard which a recent study shows many rural areas will not be able to meet.

For this reason, we have introduced **H.R. 1633, the Farm Dust Regulation Prevention Act,** which would restore common sense by removing these burdensome, job-threatening regulations and give certainty to rural America. H.R. 1633 would stop the EPA in its current review from imposing more stringent dust standards for one year. Additionally, it would afford states and localities the flexibility to address any rural dust issues before the federal government would have the authority to do so. If unregulated at the state or local level, the Administrator could not regulate this type of dust unless the EPA could put forth findings of substantial adverse health effects caused by the dust and a report that benefits of rural dust regulation outweigh economic costs in the local communities.

The EPA has long recognized that the health evidence from rural dust is inconclusive, yet the EPA has continued to regulate it in the same manner as other forms of PM, for which the health evidence is more certain. While the levels at which EPA regulates PM may generally be achievable in urban areas, they are difficult, if not impossible, to achieve in rural areas, without threatening the agriculture industry and other rural-based economic activity.

Further regulation of dust by EPA would unnecessarily and severely hamper the ability of farmers, ranchers, and other agribusinesses to continue to conduct business, and could result in lost jobs throughout the rural economy. That is why we have acted to restore common sense by introducing this legislation. If you are interested in cosponsoring H.R. 1633, please contact Renee Latterell in Rep. Noem's office (renee.latterell@mail.house.gov), Bryan Wood in Rep. Hurt's office (bryan.wood@mail.house.gov), Katy Siddall in Rep. Boswell's office (Katy.Siddall@mail.house.gov), or Dusty Holley in Rep. Kissell's office (Dusty.Holley@mail.house.gov).

Sincerely,

Robert Hurt
Member of Congress

Kristi Noem
Member of Congress

Leonard Boswell
Member of Congress

Larry Kissell
Member of Congress

6

The House legislative counsel, as the senior attorney in the office, is appointed by the Speaker of the House. The Senate legislative counsel is appointed by the president pro tempore of the Senate. The staff attorneys are hired by the legislative counsel. Legislative counsel are typically assigned to work with specific committees or on specific subjects. Also see *Legislative Drafter's Deskbook*, by Tobias A. Dorsey.

Introducing Legislation

The legislative process formally begins when a measure is introduced. Approximately 10,000 measures are introduced in each two-year Congress. Only a member can introduce legislation. There is no limit on the number of measures a member can introduce or on the issues such measures may address (with a few exceptions such as the House bar on commemorative legislation).

The Constitution stipulates that all revenue measures must originate in the House. House origination is the custom for appropriations bills as well. (When the Senate initiates a measure that the House believes affects revenues and sends it to the House, the measure is returned to the Senate by a so-called *blue-slip resolution*. The Senate may act on revenue measures before the House does, but it must wait for a House revenue measure to be sent to it before it can complete its legislative actions.) All other measures can originate in either the House or the Senate. Many pieces of legislation are introduced in both chambers as *companion bills*.

In the House, a measure is introduced by placing it in the *hopper*, a mahogany box that sits on the rostrum in the House chamber. Measures can be introduced only whenever the House is in session and sitting as the House. (*See § 6.110, Committee of the Whole: Debate.*) In the Senate, measures can technically be introduced only during the *morning business* portion of the *morning hour*. However, in practice they are introduced throughout the day. A senator need only hand a measure to a clerk at the desk in the chamber. In the Senate, a statement is often made on the floor or inserted in the *Congressional Record* when a measure is introduced.

On introduction, a measure is assigned a number by a bill clerk. The numbers are assigned sequentially throughout a Congress. Occasionally, a member will ask to reserve a specific number. For example, H.R. 2020 might be reserved for a measure affecting eye care, or S. 23 might be reserved to honor basketball star Michael Jordan. At the beginning of a new Congress, the first few bill numbers are often reserved for the majority-party leadership to signal their legislative priorities for Congress; the next few bill numbers might be reserved for the minority. Senators, by tradition, rarely introduce legislation until after the president delivers his State of the Union address.

Measures remain active between the two sessions of a Congress. If they are not enacted into law, they die with the adjournment of the Congress in which they were introduced. Treaties, however, which are considered only by the Senate, remain pending from one Congress until they are approved or formally withdrawn by the president, since the Senate is a *continuing body*.

House and Senate rules permit a member to introduce a measure at the request of the president, an executive agency, or a private individual although that member may be opposed to the legislation. The courtesy to introduce legislation on behalf of someone is granted because neither the president nor any person other than a member can introduce legislation. In such a case, "by request" appears on the measure following the name of the sponsor.

Cosponsorship

House and Senate measures may have numerous sponsors in addition to the member who proposes the legislation. It is common in both chambers for the key proponent of a measure to send a *Dear Colleague* letter (in print or electronically) to other members requesting their support for the legislation by cosponsoring its introduction. An original cosponsor signs on and is listed on the legislation when it is introduced. Cosponsors can be added throughout the legislative process until a measure is reported from a committee, or, in the Senate, at any time by unanimous consent. Names of cosponsors added after introduction appear in the *Congressional Record*, and in subsequent printings of a measure. A member can be removed as a cosponsor only by unanimous consent on the House or Senate floor. (*See § 6.21, House Cosponsorship Form; and § 6.22, Sample "Dear Colleague" Letter.*)

§ 6.30 Referral of Legislation to Committee

Once introduced in the House or Senate, or passed by one chamber and sent to the other, the vast majority of measures is referred to committee. Referral to committee occurs so that a committee can scrutinize the legislation by holding hearings and gauging sentiment for its enactment, and, if the committee proceeds to markup, proposing amendments to the parent chamber or writing, introducing, and reporting a new measure.

To which committee(s) a measure is referred can have a significant impact on its fate. Referral of a measure is based on a committee's jurisdiction, which, in turn, is determined by a variety of factors. The principal factor in making a referral is Rule X in the House or Rule XXV in the Senate. Each rule lists the broad subject matter within the purview of each standing committee, although not all issues within a committee's jurisdiction are identified. In addition, these jurisdictional descriptions do not explicitly identify jurisdiction over particular measures, executive-branch departments and agencies, or programs operated within those departments. Accordingly, the formal provisions of the rules are supplemented by an intricate series of precedents and informal agreements.

A referral decision is formally the responsibility of the Speaker for the House and the presiding officer for the Senate. In practice, however, the parliamentarian in each chamber advises these officials on an appropriate referral.

House of Representatives

In addition to House Rule X, precedents and agreements affect referral decisions. In general, these precedents dictate that once a measure has been referred to a given committee, the measure's subject matter remains the responsibility of that committee. The precedents further presume that amendments to laws that originated in a committee are within the purview of that committee as well.

Formal agreements, drafted between committees to stipulate their understanding of jurisdictional boundaries, also influence referral decisions. These agreements are usually in the form of an exchange of letters between committee chairs or in the form of memoranda of understanding between chairs and are often entered in the *Congressional Record* during debate on a measure when it comes to the floor for consideration. The letters and memoranda are also often kept in committees' so-called *jurisdiction files* and with the parliamentarian. (*See § 6.31, Sample Jurisdictional Agreement.*)

§ 6.31

Sample Jurisdictional Agreement

January 4, 2007 CONGRESSIONAL RECORD—HOUSE **H15**

Ms. SLAUGHTER. Madam Speaker, I ask unanimous consent to insert in the RECORD a jurisdictional memorandum of understanding between the chairmen-designate from the Committee on Transportation and the Committee on Homeland Security.

The SPEAKER pro tempore. Is there objection to the request of the gentlewoman from New York?

There was no objection.

MEMORANDUM OF UNDERSTANDING BETWEEN THE COMMITTEE ON TRANSPORTATION AND INFRASTRUCTURE AND THE COMMITTEE ON HOMELAND SECURITY

January 4, 2007

On January 4, 2005, the U.S. House of Representatives adopted H. Res. 5, establishing the Rules of the House for the 109th Congress. Section 2(a) established the Committee on Homeland Security as a standing committee of the House of Representatives with specific legislative jurisdiction under House Rule X. A legislative history to accompany the changes to House Rule X was inserted in the Congressional Record on January 4, 2005.

The Committee on Transportation and Infrastructure and the Committee on Homeland Security (hereinafter "Committees") jointly agree to the January 4, 2005 legislative history as the authoritative source of legislative history of section 2(a) of H. Res. 5 with the following two clarifications.

First, with regard to the Federal Emergency Management Agency's, FEMA, emergency preparedness and response programs, the Committee on Homeland Security has jurisdiction over the Department of Homeland Security's responsibilities with regard to emergency preparedness and collective response only as they relate to terrorism. However, in light of the federal emergency management reforms that were enacted as title VI of Public Law 109-295, a bill amending FEMA's all-hazards emergency preparedness programs that necessarily addresses FEMA's terrorism preparedness programs would be referred to the Committee on Transportation and Infrastructure; in addition, the Committee on Homeland Security would have a jurisdictional interest in such bill. Nothing in this Memorandum of Understanding affects the jurisdiction of the Committee on Transportation and Infrastructure of the Robert T. Stafford Disaster Relief and Emergency Assistance Act and the Federal Fire Prevention and Control Act of 1974.

Second, with regard to port security, the Committee on Homeland Security has jurisdiction over port security, and some Coast Guard responsibilities in that area fall within the jurisdiction of both Committees. A bill addressing the activities, programs, assets, and personnel of the Coast Guard as they relate to port security and non-port security missions would be referred to the Committee on Transportation and Infrastructure; in addition, the Committee on Homeland Security would have a jurisdictional interest in such bill.

This Memorandum of Understanding between the Committee on Transportation and Infrastructure and the Committee on Homeland Security provides further clarification to the January 4, 2005 legislative history of the jurisdiction of the Committees only with regard to these two specific issues. The Memorandum does not address any other issues and does not affect the jurisdiction of other committees.

JAMES L. OBERSTAR,
Chairman-designate, Committee on Transportation & Infrastructure.
BENNIE G. THOMPSON,
Chairman-designate, Committee on Homeland Security.

Announcement by Rules Committee Chair Related to a Committee's Jurisdiction

January 4, 2007 CONGRESSIONAL RECORD—HOUSE **H6**

RULES OF THE HOUSE

Ms. SLAUGHTER. Mr. Speaker, I offer a privileged resolution (H. Res. 5) and ask for its immediate consideration.

The Clerk read the resolution, as follows:

H. RES. 5

Resolved, That upon the adoption of this resolution it shall be in order to consider in the House the resolution (H. Res. 6) adopting the Rules of the House of Representatives for the One Hundred Tenth Congress. The resolution shall be considered as read. The previous question shall be considered as ordered on the resolution to its adoption without intervening motion or demand for division of the question except as specified in sections 2 through 4 of this resolution.

****

Continued on page 237

§ 6.31 (continued)

January 4, 2007 CONGRESSIONAL RECORD—HOUSE

Renews the standing order approved during the 109th Congress that prohibits registered lobbyists from using the Members' exercise facilities.

Mr. Speaker, I consider it to be a great honor to have a chance to address our House on the first day of the 110th Congress. That is what serving as a Representative in this body is, an honor.

****

Today, the men and women of America have given us a very special gift. We have the ability to leave our mark on the future of our Nation. It is the only gift Members of Congress should ask for, and one we must cherish for the good of all. Let us begin.

Mr. Speaker, I would like to take this opportunity to reaffirm the jurisdiction of the Committee on Small Business as contained in House Rule X, clause 1(p). The Committee's jurisdiction includes the Small Business Administration and its programs, as well as small business matters related to the Regulatory Flexibility Act and the Paperwork Reduction Act. Its jurisdiction under House Rule X, clause 1(p) also includes other programs and initiatives that address small businesses outside of the confines of those Acts.

This reaffirmation of the jurisdiction of the Committee on Small Business will enable the House to ensure that it is properly considering the consequences of its actions related to small business.

Mr. Speaker, I reserve the balance of my time.

Several other factors may influence the referral of a measure. The committee assignment of the sponsor often serves as a signal that a bill should be referred to a committee on which the sponsor serves. The timing of a measure's introduction can also influence its referral; for example, introduction following a series of issue hearings held by a committee could signal that the panel wants to legislate on the issue it recently studied.

Under House Rule X, the Speaker usually designates a "primary" committee to receive a referral. If other panels have jurisdictional responsibilities over some of the issues in the measure, they may receive a *sequential* referral. The language of a referral affecting more than one committee would be "to the Committee on XXXX, and in addition, to the Committee on YYYY." The primary panel is always named first. A referral can also designate specific titles or sections of a measure within each committee's responsibility. More common, however, is a referral for "issues within the jurisdiction of the committee." Referral without designation of a primary committee can be made under "exceptional circumstances." A sequential referral may be made after a measure's introduction or after the primary committee reports the measure.

The Speaker has authority to impose a time limit on committees receiving a referral. Sometimes the time limit is determined at the time of referral; sometimes a time limit is imposed after a measure has been referred. (*See § 6.32, Sample of House Referral.*)

Senate

Under Senate Rule XVII, measures are referred to committee based on "the subject matter which predominates" in the legislation, commonly referred to as *predominant jurisdiction*. The Senate generally refers a measure to a single committee based on this rule and the jurisdictions enumerated in Senate Rule XXV.

§ 6.32

Sample of House Referral

I

110TH CONGRESS
1ST SESSION

H. R. 1064

To amend title 39, United States Code, to extend for 2 years the provisions under which the special postage stamp for breast cancer research is issued.

IN THE HOUSE OF REPRESENTATIVES

FEBRUARY 15, 2007

❶ Sponsor

❷ Original cosponsors

❸ Explanation of the referral

❶ Mr. BACA (for himself, Mr. MOORE of Kansas, Ms. MCCOLLUM of Minnesota, Mr. VAN HOLLEN, Mr. FARR, Mrs. MALONEY of New York, Mr. FORTUÑO, Mr. MORAN of Virginia, Mr. MCDERMOTT, Mr. CONYERS, Mr. CLEAVER, Mr. DINGELL, Mr. NEAL of Massachusetts, Mrs. MCCARTHY ❷ of New York, Mr. ELLISON, Mr. BURTON of Indiana, Mrs. JONES of Ohio, Mr. AL GREEN of Texas, Mr. NADLER, Mr. STARK, Mr. SCOTT of Georgia, Ms. HOOLEY, Mrs. BOYDA of Kansas, Mr. MICHAUD, Mr. KLEIN of Florida, Mr. MCINTYRE, Mr. KILDEE, Mr. GEORGE MILLER of California, Mr. SHAYS, Mr. GRIJALVA, Ms. ROYBAL-ALLARD, Mr. TERRY, Mr. BOSWELL, Mr. GENE GREEN of Texas, Mr. DENT, Mr. HINCHEY, Mr. HINOJOSA, Mr. CHANDLER, Mr. WEINER, Mr. SHIMKUS, Ms. WASSERMAN SCHULTZ, Mr. COOPER, Mr. HONDA, Mr. HOLT, Mr. ORTIZ, Mr. YOUNG of Alaska, Mr. HALL of Texas, Mrs. SCHMIDT, Mr. BERMAN, Mr. PRICE of North Carolina, Mr. DELAHUNT, Ms. KAPTUR, Ms. KILPATRICK, Mr. PATRICK J. MURPHY of Pennsylvania, Ms. HIRONO, Mr. ENGEL, Mr. ABERCROMBIE, Ms. BERKLEY, Mr. SHERMAN, Mr. KING of New York, and Mr. DOGGETT) introduced the following bill; which was ❸ referred to the Committee on Oversight and Government Reform, and in addition to the Committees on Energy and Commerce and Armed Services, for a period to be subsequently determined by the Speaker, in each case for consideration of such provisions as fall within the jurisdiction of the committee concerned

---

A BILL

To amend title 39, United States Code, to extend for 2 years the provisions under which the special postage stamp for breast cancer research is issued.

Predominant jurisdiction allows a measure to be guided to a specific committee, so that the referral predetermines its fate. Many senators, as well as lobbyists, understand that they can influence the legislative agenda by learning how creative drafting of a measure can possibly affect its referral. For example, is tobacco an agricultural issue within the purview of the Agriculture Committee, generally friendly to tobacco? Or, is tobacco a health risk, an issue within the predominant purview of a less friendly Health, Education, Labor, and Pensions Committee? Or, is the issue about tobacco advertising, and thus within the predominant purview of the Commerce, Science, and Transportation Committee? The drafting of a measure on tobacco is not simple if one wants a specific committee to obtain the referral.

The rule further allows a measure to be referred to more than one panel if an issue crosses jurisdictional boundaries or predominance is not clear-cut. Such *multiple referrals* are not common, in part because they are typically made by unanimous consent after negotiations among affected committee chairs. A joint motion made by the majority and minority leader for multiple referrals is also allowed under Senate Rule XVII, but it has never been used.

Finally, under Senate Rule XIV, the majority leader, his designee, or any senator may follow a set of procedures that allow a measure to be placed directly on the Senate's legislative calendar without referral to committee. Placement there, however, does not guarantee that floor action will ever be scheduled. *(See § 6.160, Senate Scheduling.)*

§ 6.40 Committee Hearings

Perhaps the most visible of all congressional actions is the committee hearing. As Woodrow Wilson wrote, "It is not far from the truth to say that Congress in session is Congress on public exhibition, whilst Congress in its committee rooms is Congress at work."

Types of Committee Hearings

Committees and their subcommittees hold hundreds of hearings each year. These hearings are nearly always one of four types.

Legislative Hearings. These hearings typically occur when there is a measure under consideration or when a committee is collecting information so it can draft legislation. Witnesses give their own or their organizations' views on a measure's provisions. They might also express views on competing proposals for legislation that a committee could develop with the input received in hearings and from other sources.

Investigative Hearings. These hearings are not directly connected with legislation, but are called to examine a subject in which a committee has an interest. These hearings are sometimes held when there is possible evidence of wrongdoing or criminal activity by specific individuals.

Oversight Hearings. These hearings are held to ensure that executive agencies are carrying out programs in the manner Congress intended.

Confirmation Hearings. These hearings are held to question presidential appointees when Senate confirmation is required and to investigate nominees' qualifications.

Rules That Govern Hearings

Each committee is required by its respective chamber's rules to adopt and publish rules of procedure. A committee's rules generally apply to its subcommittees, although some rules contain specific procedures for subcommittees. Many committee rules address hearings.

Notice and Scheduling. Under both House and Senate rules, the chair of a committee or subcommittee must publicly announce the date, place, and subject matter of a hearing at least one week in advance in the Daily Digest section of the *Congressional Record*, unless the chair and ranking member—or the committee by majority vote—determines that there is good cause to begin the hearing sooner. (*See § 6.41, Committee Hearings Schedule.*)

Senate committees may not hold a hearing after the Senate has been in session for two hours, or after 2:00 p.m. when the Senate is in session, whichever is earlier. This Senate rule is often waived by unanimous consent on the Senate floor or by agreement between the Senate majority and minority leaders. House hearings can be held at any time, except during a joint session or meeting of the House and Senate.

Open Hearings. Hearings must be open to the public and the media unless the committee, in open session, decides by record vote to close a hearing. Hearings may be closed if discussion of the subject matter might endanger national security, compromise sensitive law-enforcement information, or violate a rule of the parent chamber. If testimony would defame, degrade, or incriminate a person, the testimony must be taken in closed session if a majority of committee members determines that the testimony might be problematic. Testimony taken in closed session can be released only by majority vote of the committee.

Quorums. Individual committees set their own quorum requirements to conduct a hearing. However, House rules require that not fewer than two members be present. Senate committees usually allow a single senator to be present to conduct a hearing. Individual House committee rules also set a quorum requirement for waiving a hearing notice, but House rules disallow the quorum from being less than one-third. Senate committees have no comparable rule. Finally, for House committees, a majority of members of a committee constitutes a quorum for authorizing a subpoena or closing a committee session.

Subpoena Power. Both House and Senate committees are authorized to issue subpoenas to witnesses and for documents. The rules of each committee delineate the procedures for issuing a subpoena. When a committee adopts its rules at the beginning of a Congress, it must decide how to issue subpoenas. A committee might determine that a subpoena can be issued under the signature of the chair or that the concurrence of the ranking minority member is required. Alternatively, it might choose to authorize a subpoena only by a majority vote of the committee.

Witnesses. Witnesses must be invited to appear before a committee or subcommittee. A formal letter of invitation is usually sent under the name of the chair or, sometimes, the chair and ranking minority member. Occasionally, a committee will ask for written witness testimony in lieu of an appearance before the committee. An organization or individual may also request an invitation to appear or to submit testimony for a hearing record. (*See § 8.75, Committee Investigations and Witness Protections.*)

§ 6.41

Committee Hearings Schedule

SENATE COMMITTEE ON
HOMELAND SECURITY
&GOVERNMENTAL AFFAIRS

ABOUT THE COMMITTEE • SUBCOMMITTEES • HEARINGS • PRESS • ISSUES • LEGISLATION & NOMINATIONS • DOCUMENTS • RESOURCES

HEARINGS

SHARE / PRINT

All Hearings Select Congress

June 2011

09th [Border Corruption: Assessing Customs and Border Protection and the Department of Homeland Security Inspector General's Office Collaboration in the Fight to Prevent Corruption]
10:00 AM

May 2011

26th BUSINESS MEETING
Dirksen Senate Office Building, room SD-342
2:30 PM

25th Assessing Efforts to Eliminate Improper Payments
Dirksen Senate Office Building, room SD-342
2:30 PM

25th How to Save Taxpayer Dollars: Case Studies of Duplication in the Federal Government
Dirksen Senate Office Building, room SD-342
10:00 AM

24th Stimulus Contractors Who Cheat on Their Taxes: What Happened?
Dirksen Senate Office Building, room SD-342
2:30 PM

23rd Protecting Cyberspace: Assessing the White House Proposal
Dirksen Senate Office Building, room SD-342
10:30 AM

19th Ten Years After 9/11: Is Intelligence Reform Working? Part II
Dirksen Senate Office Building, room SD-342
1:30 PM

18th BUSINESS MEETING (Part II)
Dirksen Senate Office Building, room SD-342
9:45 AM

17th Addressing the U.S. Postal Service's Financial Crisis
Dirksen Senate Office Building, room SD-342
10:30 AM

12th Ten Years After 9/11: Is Intelligence Reform Working? Part I
Dirksen Senate Office Building, room SD-342
2:30 PM

11th BUSINESS MEETING (Part I)
Dirksen Senate Office Building, room SD-342
10:00 AM

10th JOINT HEARING: Roadmap for a More Efficient and Accountable Federal Government: Implementing the GPRA Modernization Act
Dirksen Senate Office Building, room SD-562
2:30 PM - 5:00 PM

05th Understanding the Power of Social Media as a Communications Tool in the Aftermath of Disasters
Dirksen Senate Office Building, room SD-342
10:00 AM

Hearings Calendar

May 2011

S	M	T	W	T	F	S
1	2	3	4	5	6	7
8	9	10	11	12	13	14
15	16	17	18	19	20	21
22	23	24	25	26	27	28
29	30	31				

Related Links

All Hearings

Hearing Archives

6

§ 6.42

Sample Truth in Testimony Form

Committee on the Budget

Witness Disclosure Requirement – "Truth in Testimony"
Required by House Rule XI, Clause 2(g)

	Yes	No
Your Name:		
1. Will you be representing a federal, State, or local government entity? (If the answer is yes please contact the committee).		
2. Please list any federal grants or contracts (including subgrants or subcontracts) which you have received since October 1, 2002:		
3. Will you be representing an entity other than a government entity?		
4. Other than yourself, please list what entity or entities you will be representing:		
5. Please list any offices or elected positions held and/or briefly describe your representational capacity with each of the entities you listed in response to question 4:		
6. Please list any federal grants or contracts (including subgrants or subcontracts) received by the entities you listed in response to question 4 since October 1, 2002, including the source and amount of each grant or contract:		
7. Are there parent organizations, subsidiaries, or partnerships to the entities you disclosed in response to question number 4 that you will not be representing? If so, please list:		

Signature: ______________________ Date: ______________

Please attach this sheet to your written testimony.

§ 6.43

Celebrity Witnesses

As a means of generating publicity and public support for public-policy issues, committees have turned increasingly in recent years to "celebrity witnesses." Celebrity witnesses who have testified at hearings before House and Senate committees in recent years, and the issues on which they testified, include the following:

Environmental and Agricultural Issues

- Ted Danson—American Oceans Campaign
- Jessica Lange—Farm bill

Health Issues

- Michael J. Fox—Parkinson's disease research
- Mary Tyler Moore—Diabetes disease research
- Ben Vereen—Deafness research
- Sally Field—Osteoporosis
- Jack Klugman—Cancer research
- Diane Keaton—Cancer research
- Olivia Newton John—Cancer research
- Jason Alexander—Scleroderma research
- Shawn Colvin—Drug addiction
- Robert Guillaume—Drug addiction
- Katie Couric—Colon cancer research
- David Hyde Pierce—Alzheimer's disease research
- Elton John—HIV/AIDS
- Julia Roberts—Rett syndrome
- Nick Jonas–Diabetes disease research

International Issues

- Richard Gere—Tibet
- Sam Waterston—Immigration

Labor Issues

- Charlton Heston—Unemployment benefits
- Muhammad Ali—Regulation of boxing

Treatment of Animals

- Alec Baldwin—End to animal testing
- Kim Basinger—End to animal testing

Other

- Denyce Graves—Arts funding
- Pearl Jam—TicketMaster dispute
- Martin Short—Foster parents
- Jack Nicklaus—Education
- Elmo—Music education
- Stephen Sondheim, Arthur Miller, Wendy Wasserstein—Playwrights' Licensing Antitrust Initiative Act
- Bobby McFerrin—Arts funding
- Edward James Olmos—Volunteer service programs
- Doris Roberts—Ageism in media
- Mickey Rooney–Elder abuse

House and Senate chamber rules, as well as individual committee rules, generally require a witness to file a specific number of copies of her prepared written statement in advance of an appearance. A nongovernmental witness appearing before a House committee is also required to comply with the so-called *truth in testimony* rule, which states that the witness should file a résumé and disclose the amount and source of any grant or contract money received from the federal government in the current or two preceding fiscal years. (*See § 6.42, Sample Truth in Testimony Form.*)

The minority party is entitled to one day of hearings to call its own witnesses if a majority of minority members of the committee so requests.

See also *Testifying Before Congress*, by William N. LaForge.

6

§ 6.44

Field Hearing Announcement

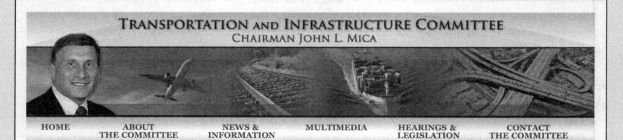

TRANSPORTATION AND INFRASTRUCTURE COMMITTEE
CHAIRMAN JOHN L. MICA

HOME | ABOUT THE COMMITTEE | NEWS & INFORMATION | MULTIMEDIA | HEARINGS & LEGISLATION | CONTACT THE COMMITTEE

HEARING

DEVELOPING TRUE HIGH-SPEED RAIL TO THE NORTHEAST CORRIDOR: STOP SITTING ON OUR FEDERAL ASSETS

Grand Central Terminal, Northeast Balcony -- New York, New York

January 27, 2011

Field hearing of the Committee on Transportation and Infrastructure:

Grand Central Terminal
Northeast Balcony
87 East 42nd Street
New York, NY 10017

Background Information

RELATED INFORMATION

Developing High-Speed Rail for Northeast Corridor Focus of Congressional Hearing

Statements of Chairman Mica & Chairman Shuster from Hearing on Northeast Corridor High-Speed Rail

Witness Testimonies

The Honorable Michael Bloomberg
The Honorable Ed Rendell
Mr. Thomas Hart
Ms. Petra Todorovich
Mr. Perry Offutt
Mr. Robert Scardelletti

Search this site
Search

IN THIS SECTION

Hearings
Markups
Legislation

SUBCOMMITTEES

Aviation
Coast Guard and Maritime Transportation
Economic Development, Public Buildings and Emergency Management
Highways and Transit
Railroads, Pipelines and Hazardous Materials
Water Resources and Environment

QUICK LINKS

Members
Jurisdiction
Speaker of the House
Majority Leader
Majority Whip
Republican Conference
Minority T&I Web Site

INTERACT

House Transportation and Infrastructure Committee
2165 Rayburn House Office Building

Conducting Hearings

Each committee determines if witnesses will appear individually or in a panel. In a panel format, committee members usually hold their questions until all panelists have made their presentations. A committee must also determine whether to swear in a witness.

Protocol and tradition dictate that members of Congress wishing to testify at hearings do so before other witnesses testify. Executive-branch officials and former members are also afforded consideration in the order in which they appear. A "celebrity witness" is likely to be placed to generate maximum media coverage. A witness generally summarizes his written testimony before a committee. *(See § 6.43, Celebrity Witnesses.)*

As a general practice, each House member is entitled to five minutes of questioning of each witness. However, the chair and ranking member can designate specific members or staff to pursue extended questioning of up to thirty minutes on behalf of their party's members. It is also possible for members to ask witnesses to respond to questions in writing after a hearing is concluded. Many Senate committees also have adopted committee rules limiting senators to five minutes for each witness.

An individual committee's rules spell out the order in which members are recognized to question witnesses. Many committees recognize members in order of their seniority on the committee. Several panels recognize members based on their "order of appearance" at a hearing, giving priority to those members who arrive early.

Most hearing rooms are equipped with small, color lights on the witness table. The green light is turned on when a member is recognized to speak or ask questions of a witness. The red light signifies a member's time has expired. An amber or orange light signifies that a member's time will soon expire. The committee chair or committee clerk controls the lights, but the lights are not always strictly monitored or even turned on. In many hearing rooms, digital clocks rather than lights have been installed on both the dais and the witness table.

Most committee hearings are held in Washington, DC. In recent years, however, committees have increased their use of *field hearings*. A field hearing is conducted the same way as a hearing in Washington, but is held in the home district or state of the member calling the hearing or in a locale relevant to the subject of the hearing. Field hearings allow local residents to attend or testify without coming to Washington. *(See § 6.44, Field Hearing Announcement.)*

(For information on hearings transcripts and printed hearings, see § 10.10, Committee Documents.)

§ 6.50 Committee Markup

When hearings are completed, a committee may meet to *mark up* a measure. The connotation of a markup session is that the language of the original measure is analyzed line-by-line or section-by-section, and then *marked up*, that is, changed or amended. *(See § 6.51, Committee Markup and Reporting Glossary.)*

The rules of each chamber provide only general guidance to committees for conducting markups. The rules of the House and the Senate are the rules of their committees "so far as applicable." Each

§ 6.51

Committee Markup and Reporting Glossary

Chairman's Mark/Staff Draft: Recommendation by chair of the measure to be considered in markup, usually drafted as a bill.

Clean Bill: New measure reported by a House committee, incorporating all changes made in markup. Measure, with new number, is introduced and referred to the committee, which then reports that measure.

Committee Report: Document accompanying measure reported from a committee, containing an explanation of the provisions of the measure, arguments for its approval, and certain other matters.

Cordon Rule: Senate rule that requires a committee report to show changes the reported measure would make in current law.

Mark: *See Vehicle.*

Minority, Supplemental, and Additional Views: Statements in a committee report, presenting individual or group opinions on the measure.

Ordered Reported: Committee's formal action of agreeing to report a measure to its chamber.

Original Bill: Bill drafted by a committee and introduced when the committee reports the measure to the chamber. Senate allows all committees to report original bills; House generally allows only the Appropriations Committee to do so.

Ramseyer Rule: House rule that requires a committee report to show changes the reported measure would make in current law.

Report/Reported: As a verb, formal submission of a measure to the chamber. As a noun, a committee document explaining the measure reported from committee. A report is designated *H. Rept.* in the House and *S. Rept.* in the Senate.

Vehicle/Legislative Vehicle: Term for legislative measure that is being considered.

A larger glossary is located at the back of the book and online at *<TCNLG.com>*.

committee must also adopt written rules governing its procedures. House and Senate committee rules cannot be inconsistent with their chambers' rules. Committee markups follow committee rules made pursuant to these two guidelines. Subcommittees generally are covered by full committee rules. In recent years, several committees have conducted all markups at the full committee level after hearings were held at the subcommittee level. Both chambers require that markup sessions be open to the public unless a committee decides in open session by majority vote to close the markup.

Vehicle for Consideration and Amendment

A markup begins with the chair calling up a particular measure for consideration by the committee. The text the chair intends for the committee to consider is referred to as the *markup vehicle*, and the chair has several alternatives from which to choose.

Introduced Measure. Using an introduced measure as the vehicle is the easiest way to conduct a markup. The chair notifies committee members that the vehicle for the markup will be the introduced bill, identifying the bill number and, often, the original sponsor. At House markups, the measure is usually read for amendment by section. By unanimous consent, the measure can be open for amendment at any point or title by title. At Senate markups, measures are usually open to amendment at any point. In either case, each section can be amended in *two degrees*. (*See First-Degree Amendment and Second-Degree Amendment in § 6.121, Amendment Process Glossary.*)

Subcommittee Reported Version/Committee Print. Many measures considered by a full committee have already received subcommittee action. If a subcommittee reports its version of a text to the full committee, the product is often printed and referred to as a *committee print*. The committee print can then be used as the markup vehicle. An alternative is for a committee or subcommittee chair to offer the subcommittee-reported version as an *amendment in the nature of a substitute* for the measure initially used as the markup vehicle. A third approach is for the subcommittee chair to introduce a new measure reflecting the subcommittee's changes to the earlier measure. This new measure could then be referred to the committee and used as the markup vehicle.

Staff Draft/Chairman's Mark. This option allows the committee to use as a vehicle a text that incorporates both changes made in subcommittee markup and additional changes negotiated afterward, yet before full committee markup. The product of these negotiations is incorporated into a *committee print*, often referred to as a *staff draft* or *chairman's mark*.

Amendment in the Nature of a Substitute. A chair sometimes prefers to offer an amendment in the nature of a substitute to the measure selected as the markup vehicle. This type of amendment, representing a full-text alternative, can be offered only at the outset of the amendment process, after the first section of the measure is read. (A full-text amendment can also be offered at the end of the markup process, but that practice is rare.)

Amendment Procedure

Committees do not actually amend measures during markup; instead, a committee votes on what amendments it wishes to recommend to its parent chamber. If a committee reports a measure with amendments, the parent chamber will ordinarily have to act on the amendments. How a panel conducts the amendment process in markup generally reflects procedures used in the chamber, possibly as modified by individual committee rules.

Reading the Measure. Bills must be *read* twice in committee. This second reading enables the amendment process to begin. Committees usually dispense with the first reading of a bill, either by unanimous consent or by a motion to dispense with the reading. A measure is not considered as read for a second time, for amendment, until a chair directs the clerk to read section one. A measure is usually read for amendment by section. By unanimous consent, a measure could be "considered as read and open for amendment at any point" or could be amended by title, or be open for amendment in another manner.

Recognition and Debate. In recognizing committee members to speak or offer amendments, the chair alternates between majority and minority members. The chair also often gives preference to more senior members. When a member offers an amendment, the clerk reads the amendment and

6

committee staff distribute copies of it. Reading of the amendment can be dispensed with by unanimous consent.

Before a sponsor speaks in support of an amendment, any committee member can either reserve or make a *point of order* against the amendment. A point of order must be reserved or made after the clerk reads the amendment, or it is distributed to all committee members, but before the sponsor begins to speak. A point of order is a parliamentary device for questioning whether an amendment, measure, or motion is within the rules of a chamber or of a committee. If a member makes a point of order, he must immediately explain the parliamentary violation. If a member reserves a point of order, the chair will probably indicate when the member must make or withdraw the point of order. Debate on a point of order occurs at the chair's discretion. Debate on an amendment may occur while a reservation of a point of order is pending.

If a point of order is sustained by a committee chair, the amendment cannot be offered. If the point of order is overruled, the amendment process can proceed. Although it is possible to appeal a chair's ruling—to question it—making a successful appeal is rare. (Although committee members and staff may seek advice from the parliamentarian before or during a markup, a parliamentarian is not present during a markup. Rather, a committee staff member is normally designated to be a committee's expert on chamber and committee rules.)

Amendments offered in House committee markups are considered under the five-minute rule; that is, any member may speak for up to five minutes. Additional time can be given by unanimous consent.

Amendments offered in Senate committee markups are generally not subject to debate limitations. Therefore, it is possible for opponents to filibuster an amendment. There is no Senate procedure for invoking cloture in a committee markup; however, several Senate committees have adopted committee rules to bring extended debate to an end.

An amendment may be agreed to or rejected by a voice, division, or roll-call vote. House committees may not use proxy voting; Senate committees may if a committee's rules authorize proxy voting. (*See § 6.131, House Voting Glossary.*)

Offering and Considering Amendments in House Markups. The most common method of conducting markups allows a member to offer an amendment to a section as it is read. When the last amendment to a section has been offered, the section is considered closed to further amendment, and the committee moves to the next section. By unanimous consent, amendments may be offered *en bloc*, that is, affecting more than one section of a measure.

Alternatively, the chair can open the bill to amendment at any point if unanimous consent is granted. This process enables members to offer amendments in an order convenient to the committee's members. Some committees use an amendment roster, a list agreed to in advance by all committee members, which provides the order in which amendments will be considered.

Another option is for the chair or another member, generally a senior majority member, to offer an amendment in the nature of a substitute. This is essentially a full-text alternative to the pending measure. This type of amendment can be offered only at the beginning or end of the markup process, and is itself open to amendment at any point (and may by unanimous consent be made original text for the purpose of further amendment). An advantage of an amendment in the nature of a substitute is that a motion can be made after any debate on the amendment to cut off further debate and amendments. This motion is called the *previous question.*

An amendment must be read in full unless reading is dispensed with by unanimous consent. An amendment can be withdrawn if no action has occurred on it. Amendments are permitted only in *two degrees*, and they must be *germane. (See definitions in § 6.121, Amendment Process Glossary.)*

Ending the Amendment Process in House Markups. After the last section of the measure has been read, any committee member can move the previous question. A member can also move to *close debate* or *end debate* on amendments or to *limit debate* to a specified time. Unlike the previous question, closing or limiting debate does not preclude offering additional amendments, but it does mean that all subsequent amendments are decided without debate.

Offering and Considering Amendments in Senate Markups. A measure is usually open to amendment at any point in Senate committees. However, a committee can decide by unanimous consent to structure the amendment process. Otherwise, amendments are considered in whatever order senators offer them.

An amendment must be read in full unless reading is dispensed with by unanimous consent. An amendment can be withdrawn if no action has occurred on it. Germaneness of amendments is generally not required during markup; however, Senate rules prohibit the floor consideration of substantive committee amendments containing significant matter outside the jurisdiction of the reporting committee. Amendments are permitted in two degrees. *(See First-Degree Amendment, Second-Degree Amendment, and Germaneness at § 6.121, Amendment Process Glossary.)*

Reporting

At the end of the amendment process, a chair normally entertains a motion to report a measure favorably to its parent chamber. The motion is not a request for unanimous consent. In each chamber, a majority of the committee must be physically present in the committee when a measure is reported. Although Senate committees generally allow the use of proxies, proxy votes may not affect the outcome of the vote to report a measure from committee.

Once the motion to report is agreed to, a bill is *ordered reported*; it is not actually *reported* until the committee report is filed in the chamber. While House committees are normally required to file a report, Senate committees have discretion whether to file one. When a committee orders a measure reported, it is incumbent upon the chair to report it "promptly" and to take all steps necessary to secure its consideration by the House. Staff are usually granted authority to make "technical and conforming" changes to the measure reported.

Options for Reporting. A committee can report a measure without amendment. This means that the committee has made no changes to the text of the measure as introduced.

Second, a committee can report a measure "as amended" with an amendment or multiple amendments—so-called *cut and bite amendments.* Multiple amendments could be considered individually or adopted *en bloc* on the floor.

Third, a House committee can report a *clean bill.* That is a new bill incorporating the text of amendments adopted in markup. A committee member, often the chair, introduces the new measure in the House; it receives a new number and is referred to committee. By unanimous consent, a clean bill can be "deemed reported," thereby voiding the need for another committee meeting.

A Senate committee may report an *original bill* that embodies a text agreed to in markup. This new bill is given its own number when it is reported or called up or at another time after committee action has been completed. Reporting an original bill avoids separate floor votes on the changes adopted in markup.

Fourth, a committee can report an introduced measure with an amendment in the nature of a substitute. This is similar to reporting a clean bill, but it retains the original measure's number.

Which option a committee chooses may influence how the measure is considered on the floor of the respective chamber.

Options on How to Report. A committee can report a measure "favorably." This means that a majority of a committee is recommending that the full House or Senate consider and pass a measure. Alternatively, a committee can report "unfavorably" or "adversely." This often implies that the majority-party leadership believes that a majority of House members support a measure even though a majority of the committee does not. Third, a committee can report "without recommendation." This means that a committee believes a measure should receive floor consideration even though it could not find a majority to agree on what to report.

§ 6.60 Committee Reports

When a committee sends a measure to the floor by reporting it from the committee, the committee usually files a written report to accompany the measure. The report describes the purpose and intent of the legislation, and explains the committee's action on the measure, including votes taken in markup. The report indicates changes proposed to existing law, provides information on the measure's cost, and contains other information. Individual member statements can also be included in the report. A committee report provides a useful substantive and political explanation of a committee's intent.

Description and Requirements

The cover page of a committee report, usually formatted by the Office of Legislative Counsel, provides the title of the bill, the date the report was ordered printed, the name of the chair submitting the report, and a notation to the legislation it accompanies. There is a reference to the inclusion of a Congressional Budget Office (CBO) estimate and to any minority, supplemental, or additional views that were filed. The cover page also identifies committee action on the legislation and the number of the report itself. (*See § 6.61, Reading the Cover Page of a House Committee Report.*)

A committee report's sections then begin, generally in the following sequence. The initial section provides a brief description of the purpose of the legislation, a brief summary of the bill itself (referred to as a "section-by-section"), and a legislative history of the legislation, including a detailed explanation of the actions taken by the committee in hearings and markup. A House report must contain details on all votes taken in committee on each amendment offered and on the motion to report, including how each member voted on each item. A hearing summary is often included as well. A committee report then addresses the need for the legislation and the intent of the measure; this portion of a report is often cited in court decisions and by future Congresses.

§ 6.61

Reading the Cover Page of a House Committee Report

❶ Committee reports, including those from conference committees, are numbered sequentially as the reports are filed by any committee with its parent chamber. "H. Rept." denotes a report from a House committee; "S. Rept." from a Senate committee. The numbers before the hyphen show the Congress; for example, "106" means 106th Congress. The numbers following the hyphen make up the unique, sequential number for the report.

❷ If a measure is referred to more than one committee, each committee reporting the measure uses the same report number. But, each committee's report is printed separately and designated a "part" of the report. In this example, all reports were H. Rept. 106-74, but the Banking Committee reported "Part 1" and a supplement, "Part 2." The report from the Commerce Committee was then "Part 3." (Part designations may appear in Roman numerals.)

❸ An identification of the measure, such as its "popular name" or "short title."

❹ The reporting date and the calendar designation; in this case, the "Union Calendar."

❺ The chair and committee reporting the measure.

❻ The notation of minority, supplemental, or additional views, if one or more committee members requested their inclusion.

❼ The measure that is being reported from the committee.

❽ A brief description of the measure and the committee's recommendation to the parent chamber.

❾ The report text begins, sometimes with a table of contents.

---

❶

106TH CONGRESS, *1st Session* } HOUSE OF REPRESENTATIVES { REPT. 106–74, Part 3

❷

❸ FINANCIAL SERVICES ACT OF 1999

---

❹ JUNE 15, 1999.—Committed to the Committee of the Whole House on the State of the Union and ordered to be printed

---

❺ Mr. BLILEY, from the Committee on Commerce, submitted the following

R E P O R T

together with

❻ ADDITIONAL VIEWS

❼ [To accompany H.R. 10]

❽ The Committee on Commerce, to whom was referred the bill (H.R. 10) to enhance competition in the financial services industry by providing a prudential framework for the affiliation of banks, securities firms, and other financial service providers, and for other purposes, having considered the same, report favorably thereon with an amendment and recommend that the bill as amended do pass.

CONTENTS

❾

57–325

§ 6.62

House Committee Reports: Required Contents

Requirement	Applies to
Statement of committee action on all record votes	Record vote to report measure of public character and on any amendment offered in committee
Statement of committee oversight findings and recommendations	Measure approved; all committees except Committees on Appropriations and Budget
Statement on new budget authority and related items	Measure (except continuing appropriations measure) providing new budget authority, new spending authority, new credit authority, or increase or decrease in revenues or tax expenditures
Statement of Congressional Budget Office (CBO) cost estimate and comparison, if submitted in timely fashion	Measure of public character; all committees except Committee on Appropriations
Statement of general performance goals and objectives, including outcome-related goals and objectives	Measure approved
Supplemental, minority, or additional views, if submitted in writing and signed, and filed within two calendar days	Measure approved; all committees except Committee on Rules
Recital on cover of report to show inclusion of certain material	Reports that include CBO cost estimate and comparison, oversight findings, and supplemental, minority, or additional views
Changes in existing law ("Ramseyer rule")	Measure that amends or repeals existing law
Statement of committee cost estimate	Measure of public character; Committees on Appropriations, House Administration, Rules, and Standards of Official Conduct are exempt; requirement does not apply if CBO cost estimate is in report
Determination regarding new advisory committee	Legislation establishing or authorizing establishment of advisory committee
Applicability to legislative branch, or statement explaining why not applicable	Measure relating to terms and conditions of employment or access to public services or accommodations
Statement of federal mandates	Measure of public character
Macroeconomic analysis	Ways and Means Committee; requirement does not apply if analysis is inserted in *Congressional Record*

A House report must include oversight findings and recommendations, CBO estimates, information on unfunded mandates (if appropriate), and a statement of authority. (*See § 6.62, House Committee Reports: Required Contents.*)

A Senate report must include cost estimates, a paperwork impact statement, a regulatory impact statement, and information on unfunded mandates (if appropriate). If a roll-call vote was ordered to report a measure, the report must also include the vote results. Finally, if appropriate, a statement explaining the extent to which the measure preempts any state, local, or tribal law must be provided. (*See § 6.63, Senate Committee Reports: Required Contents.*)

Ramseyer/Cordon. A comparative section in contrasting typefaces must be included in a committee report. It shows the text of a statute, or a part thereof, that is proposed to be amended or repealed. This section is usually prepared by each chamber's Office of Legislative Counsel. In House reports, this comparative section is eponymously called a "Ramseyer," and in Senate reports, a "Cordon." (These sections are named, respectively, for Representative Christian W. Ramseyer, R-IA, 1915–1933, and Senator Guy Cordon, R-OR, 1944–1955.)

§ 6.63

Senate Committee Reports: Required Contents

Committee reports must include:

- Record of roll-call votes
- Cost estimate prepared by Congressional Budget Office
- Regulatory impact statement
- Changes in existing law, a requirement called the "Cordon rule"
- Minority, supplemental, or additional views, if requested

Committee reports usually include:

- Text of committee's proposed amendments, if any
- Discussion of policy issue addressed
- Summary of committee's deliberations
- Discussion of committee's conclusions and recommendations
- Section-by-section analysis of measure's provisions and proposed amendments

Minority, Additional, and Supplemental Views. Views of individual committee members or groups of committee members are required to be included if a member or members request permission to include them. Minority views may be filed by committee members who are not minority-party members.

Individual Committee Requirements. Several House committees are required to include specific provisions in their committee reports. The Committee on Appropriations, for example, must provide a statement describing the effect of any provision of an appropriations bill that changes the application of a law, a list of appropriations for unauthorized expenditures, and a list of rescissions and transfers of unexpended balances.

In reports accompanying resolutions that change House rules, the Committee on Rules must include the text of the rule proposed to be changed and a comparative text showing the proposed change.

In reports on measures changing the Internal Revenue Code, the Committee on Ways and Means must include a tax complexity analysis prepared by the Joint Committee on Taxation. If the Ways and Means Committee reports legislation designated by the majority leader as major tax legislation, the report must include a *dynamic estimate* of the changes in federal revenues expected to result if the legislation is enacted.

(*For additional information on committee documents, see § 10.10, Committee Documents.*)

§ 6.71

House Calendars

When a measure is reported from committee, it is placed on a calendar. These calendars are lists of pending measures. The calendars are not agendas, because measures are not assigned a day for consideration until the leadership determines when a measure will come up for consideration.

Union Calendar: All legislation dealing with raising, authorizing, or spending money.

House Calendar: Non-money measures, and measures dealing with internal House matters.

Private Calendar: Bills dealing with relief of a private individual or group of individuals.

Discharge Calendar (Calendar of Motions to Discharge Committees): All motions to take (discharge) a measure from a committee through the discharge procedure.

§ 6.72

Daily Starting Times in the House

Starting times are usually announced early in each session by the majority-party leadership.

January 5, 2011, through February 1, 2011

- 2:00 p.m. on Monday (12:00 noon for morning hour)
- 12:00 noon on Tuesday (10:00 a.m. for morning hour)
- 10:00 a.m. on Wednesday and Thursday
- 9:00 a.m. on all other days

After February 1, 2011, until the end of the first session

- 2:00 p.m. on Monday (12:00 noon for morning hour)
- 12:00 noon on Tuesday (or 2:00 p.m. if no legislative business was conducted on preceding Monday) (2 hours prior for morning hour)
- 12:00 noon on Wednesday and Thursday
- 9:00 a.m. on all other days

For current information, see <*CongressSchedules.com*>.

§ 6.70 House Floor: Scheduling and Privilege

Once a measure has been reported from committee, it goes on a calendar. The majority-party leadership is responsible for determining whether a measure should come off its respective calendar and when it should receive floor consideration. Working with the Rules Committee, the leadership also influences how a measure is considered. (*See § 6.71, House Calendars; and § 10.20, Floor Documents.*)

Decisions on how a measure comes to the floor are made within strictures in House rules that limit the kinds of measures that can go to the floor. The concept of *privilege* is used to categorize such procedures. *Privileged business* consists of those measures and matters that members can bring up for consideration on the House floor and that are *privileged* to interrupt the regular order of business.

In the House, measures on certain calendars, or to be brought up for consideration subject to certain procedures, are privileged on certain days. These calendars and procedures are the Discharge and Private Calendars; District Day; Calendar Wednesday; and suspension of the rules. Business privileged on any day the House meets includes general appropriations bills; privileged reports from committees that have the right to report at any time, including special rules from the Rules Committee; and reported resolutions of inquiry. Amendments in disagreement and Senate amendments that do not require consideration in the Committee of the Whole are also privileged.

When the House is in session, it tends to follow meeting times announced by the majority-party leadership at the beginning of each session. (*See § 6.72, Daily Starting Times in the House.*)

(*For information on House floor documents, see § 10.20.*)

§ 6.80 House Floor: Methods of Consideration

There are numerous ways to bring a measure to the House floor for debate, possible amendment, and a vote on passage. A measure might come to the floor because of the calendar on which it was placed or because it is a certain day of the week or the month. Another measure might find its fate in the hands of the majority leadership, especially the Speaker of the House. One measure might come to the floor because it is noncontroversial, and another might make it there only after complex negotiations.

Unanimous Consent

Noncontroversial measures, which have been cleared by the respective party leaders, can come to the floor by unanimous consent. Once cleared, a member can ask permission to bring up the particular measure. A single objection by another member will stop the process. A member can, alternately, "reserve the right to object" in order to ask about the request, traditionally to check if the measure has been cleared by the minority party. Once the member seeking to bring up the measure responds, the member reserving the right to object withdraws the reservation, and the consent request is agreed to "without objection." This exchange, under the reservation, is all the discussion that occurs on a measure brought up by unanimous consent.

Suspension of the Rules

This procedure, for largely noncontroversial measures, accounts for more than half of all measures considered by the House. On Monday, Tuesday, and Wednesday of each week, and during the last six days of a session, the Speaker may recognize members to move to "suspend the rules and pass" a particular measure or conference report. Suspension measures can also be considered on other days by unanimous consent or pursuant to provisions of a special rule.

In the 112th Congress (2011–2013), the Republican majority adopted party guidelines to end the use of the suspension procedure to pass legislation honoring or commemorating people, events, and achievements, such as sports teams winning championships.

A measure traditionally will not be considered under the suspension procedure if it was controversial in committee. (The majority party's rules supplement House rules in guiding the leadership on legislative and other matters. However, party rules have no official status in House proceedings and cannot be a basis for a point of order.)

Debate on a motion to suspend the rules is limited to forty minutes, with twenty minutes controlled by a proponent and twenty minutes controlled by an opponent, regardless of party affiliation. In practice, a majority floor manager controls twenty minutes and a minority floor manager controls the other twenty minutes. Measures considered under this process are not subject to floor amendment, although the motion to suspend may incorporate an amendment. Because the motion would then be to "suspend the rules and pass the bill with an amendment," no separate vote is taken on the amendment. Points of order cannot be raised on a measure or conference report brought up under suspension of the rules.

To pass, a measure considered under the suspension procedure requires two-thirds of the members present and voting to vote for the motion. Unless a recorded vote is requested, however, a measure considered under this procedure can be passed by a voice vote.

Private Calendar

Bills on this calendar generally relate to individual immigration and claims matters and are placed there when reported by the Committee on the Judiciary or any committee considering a private bill. Measures on the Private Calendar can come to the floor on the first Tuesday of each month. At the discretion of the Speaker, private measures can also be considered on the third Tuesday of each month.

Each party often appoints *official objectors* to review bills on the Private Calendar. If an official objector has a concern about a bill, there can be an objection to its consideration. More often, however, the bill is "passed over, without prejudice." It gives sponsors a chance to address concerns before the bill comes up under the next call of the Private Calendar.

Each bill is called up automatically in the order in which it was reported from committee and placed on the Private Calendar. A bill is considered under a special procedure, called "in the House as in the Committee of the Whole." Under this process, there is no general debate, but members may speak for five minutes. There is usually little debate and measures pass by voice vote.

Discharge Calendar

Any member may file a motion with the clerk of the House to discharge a committee from consideration of any measure that has been pending before the committee for thirty legislative days. (*See § 6.81, Discharge Petition.*) A motion to discharge a special rule from the Committee on Rules can be filed if the special rule has been pending before that committee for seven legislative days. The Discharge Calendar is considered on the second and fourth Mondays of each month, although a measure eligible for discharge (by having 218 signatures on its discharge petition) must be on the Discharge Calendar for seven legislative days.

Discharge motions are considered in the House with twenty minutes of debate equally divided between a proponent and an opponent. The only intervening motion is a nondebatable motion to adjourn.

Special Rule

A measure not in order under the means discussed above generally comes to the floor under provisions of a *special rule*. A special rule sets the guidelines for a measure's consideration, including time for *general debate* and any limits on the *amendment process*. Most important and controversial legislation is considered under the terms of a special rule to enable the leadership to structure debate and amendments.

Rules are considered in the House under the *one-hour rule*, with time controlled by a majority floor manager. The majority floor manager customarily yields thirty minutes to the minority floor

§ 6.81

Discharge Petition

111th Congress
2nd Session

United States
House of Representatives

No. 0011

Motion to Discharge a Committee from the Consideration of a resolution

June 16, 2010

To the Clerk of the House of Representatives:

Pursuant to clause 2 of rule XV, I, Steve King of Iowa, move to discharge the Committees on Energy and Commerce, Ways and Means, Education and Labor, the Judiciary, Natural Resources, Rules, House Administration, and Appropriations from the consideration of the bill (H.R. 4972) to repeal the Patient Protection and Affordable Care Act; which was referred to said committees on March 25, 2010, in support of which motion the undersigned Members of the House of Representatives affix their signatures, to wit:

Wednesday, June 16, 2010		
1. Steve King	Iowa	05
2. Connie Mack	Florida	14
3. Michele Bachmann	Minnesota	06
Tuesday, June 22, 2010		
4. Todd Tiahrt	Kansas	04
Wednesday, June 23, 2010		
5. Marsha Blackburn	Tennessee	07
6. Tom Price	Georgia	06
7. Paul C. Broun	Georgia	10
8. Jerry Moran	Kansas	01
9. Tom Graves	Georgia	09
10. Rob Bishop	Utah	01
11. Joseph R. Pitts	Pennsylvania	16
12. Mike Pence	Indiana	06
Thursday, June 24, 2010		
13. Lynn A. Westmoreland	Georgia	03
14. Glenn Thompson	Pennsylvania	05
15. Jeb Hensarling	Texas	05
16. Louie Gohmert	Texas	01
17. Judy Biggert	Illinois	13
18. John Boozman	Arkansas	03
19. Kenny Marchant	Texas	24
20. Jim Jordan	Ohio	04

168. Ileana Ros-Lehtinen	Florida	18
169. Tim Murphy	Pennsylvania	18
170. Charles W. Dent	Pennsylvania	15
Tuesday, September 14, 2010		
171. Jim Gerlach	Pennsylvania	06
Wednesday, September 15, 2010		
172. Gene Taylor	Mississippi	04
Thursday, September 16, 2010		
173. Steve Buyer	Indiana	04

manager "for purposes of debate only." Accordingly, special rules can be amended only if the majority floor manager offers an amendment to the rule or yields time to another member to offer an amendment, or if the previous question on the rule is defeated. (The previous question is in the form of a motion ("I move the previous question"), which, if agreed to, cuts off further debate and the possibility of amendment.)

§ 6.90 Rules Committee and Special Rules

For most major legislation, it is the Rules Committee that determines if and how a measure will be considered on the floor. The Rules Committee is empowered to report *a special rule* in the form of a simple resolution (for example, H. Res. 123) to govern floor debate, the amendment process, and other procedures related to floor consideration of a measure. (*See § 6.91, Special Rules Glossary.*)

Requesting a Special Rule

When a committee reports a measure, the committee chair, usually by letter to the Rules Committee chair, requests that a Rules Committee hearing be scheduled on the measure. The letter often notes the type of rule requested, the amount of debate time needed, and whether any *waivers* of House rules are required. (*See § 6.92, Request for Special Rule.*) Individual members may also write to the Rules Committee requesting the opportunity to testify and make their cases for being allowed to offer amendments to the measure on the House floor. (*See § 6.93, Announcement on Amendments Prior to a Rules Committee Meeting.*)

Rules Committee Action

The Rules Committee hearing is typically scheduled after the majority leadership has decided to schedule floor time for a measure. The committee's hearing on this legislation resembles any other committee hearing, although only members of the House are witnesses. Following the hearing, the panel marks up a special rule, often drafted with the knowledge and input of the majority-party leadership.

Types of Special Rules

There are several types of rules the committee can craft. (*See § 6.94, Reading a Special Rule.*) Under each type, *general debate* is permitted for a specified period of time. Under an *open rule*, all *germane amendments* can be offered, provided they are offered in a timely manner, comply with all House rules, and fit on the *amendment tree*. Under a *closed rule*, no amendments can be offered to the bill. (*See § 6.120, Committee of the Whole: Amendment Process; and § 6.122, Basic House Amendment Tree.*)

Modified rules fall into several categories. A *modified open rule* generally requires that amendments be preprinted in the *Congressional Record*, and the special rule may place an overall time limit on the amendment process. A *modified closed rule*, often called a *structured rule*, permits only specified amendments, which are listed in the Rules Committee report. These amendments are normally debated for a specified period of time, with a proponent and an opponent, and usually the majority floor manager controlling the debate time.

§ 6.91

Special Rules Glossary

Closed Rule: Permits general debate for a specified period of time but permits no floor amendments. Amendments reported by the reporting committee are allowed.

Modified Closed Rule: Permits general debate for a specified period of time, but limits amendments to those designated in the special rule or the Rules Committee report accompanying the special rule. May preclude amendments to particular portions of a bill.

Modified Open Rule: Permits general debate for a specified period of time, and allows any member to offer amendments consistent with House rules subject only to an overall time limit on the amendment process or a requirement that amendments be preprinted in the *Congressional Record*.

Open Rule: Permits general debate for a specified period of time and allows any member to offer an amendment that complies with the standing rules of the House.

Queen-of-the-Hill Rule: A special rule that permits votes on a series of amendments, usually complete substitutes for a measure, but directs that the amendment receiving the greatest number of votes is the winning amendment.

Rise and Report: Refers to the end of proceedings in the Committee of the Whole, which sends the measure it has been considering back to the House for final disposition.

Self-Executing Rule: If specified, the House's adoption of a special rule may also have the effect of amending or passing the underlying measure. Also called a "hereby" rule.

Structured Rule: Another term for a modified closed rule.

Waiver Rule: A special rule that waives points of order against a measure or an amendment.

A larger glossary is located at the back of the book and online at <*TCNLG.com*>.

A *queen-of-the-hill rule* allows a specified number of full-text substitutes to a measure, with the amendment receiving the most votes being the only amendment deemed adopted. The *king-of-the-hill rule* has not been used in recent years. Under this procedure, the last amendment to receive a majority vote was the amendment adopted.

A *waiver rule* provides for consideration of amendments or measures that might otherwise be subject to points of order.

A *self-executing* or *hereby rule* stipulates that, upon adoption of the rule, the House is deemed to have passed a measure, adopted an amendment, or taken some other action. A self-executing rule precludes a separate vote on the measure, amendment, or action.

A special rule might include more than one of these features; for example, any of these types of rules might include waiver provisions.

Providing for Floor Consideration

A special rule designates which measure is to be considered on the floor; for example, a committee-reported bill or a so-called leadership alternative. (Leadership alternatives appear regularly.) After

6

§ 6.92

Request for Special Rule

Mike Rogers, Michigan, CHAIRMAN

Mac Thornberry, Texas
Sue Myrick, North Carolina
Jeff Miller, Florida
K. Michael Conaway, Texas
Peter T. King, New York
Frank A. LoBiondo, New Jersey
Devin Nunes, California
Lynn A. Westmoreland, Georgia
Michele Bachmann,, Minnesota
Thomas J. Rooney, Florida
Joseph J. Heck, Nevada

C.A. Dutch Ruppersberger, Maryland, RANKING MEMBER

Mike Thompson, California
Janice D. Schakowsky, Illinois
James R. Langevin, Rhode Island
Adam B. Schiff, California
Dan Boren, Oklahoma
Luis V. Gutierrez, Illinois
Ben Chandler, Kentucky

John A. Boehner, SPEAKER OF THE HOUSE
Nancy Pelosi, DEMOCRATIC LEADER

U.S. HOUSE OF REPRESENTATIVES
PERMANENT SELECT COMMITTEE
ON INTELLIGENCE

HVC-304, THE CAPITOL
WASHINGTON, DC 20515
(202) 225-4121

Michael Allen, STAFF DIRECTOR

May 6, 2011

The Honorable David Dreier
Chairman
Committee on Rules
U.S. House of Representatives
Washington, DC 20515

Dear Mr. Chairman:

I am writing to request that the Rules Committee grant a rule to provide for consideration of H.R. 754, the "Intelligence Authorization Act for Fiscal Year 2011." The Permanent Select Committee on Intelligence ordered H.R. 754 favorably reported to the House with an amendment in the nature of a substitute on March 10, 2011, and filed a report on the bill on May 3, 2011.

The bill covers only the remainder of Fiscal Year 2011 and enjoys bipartisan support. As such, the legislative provisions are intentionally limited in scope to focus our attention on providing necessary resources to the men and women of the Intelligence Community. Consistent with this intention, a structured rule may be appropriate for its consideration, at the discretion of the Committee. In addition, I request that the Committee waive all points of order against the bill as necessary, make the Intelligence Committee amendment in the nature of a substitute in order as original text for purposes of amendment, and make in order a manager's amendment to be offered by the Chairman of the Permanent Select Committee on Intelligence.

I appreciate that you have notified the Members of the House to provide copies of any amendments they wish to offer to the Committee on Rules no later than noon on Tuesday, May 10, 2011. Because the Intelligence Authorization Act deals with sensitive national security and intelligence programs, I hope that the Committee will also ensure that advance notice will be provided of any amendments to be offered to the bill.

Thank you for your consideration of these requests and your continued strong support of our nation's intelligence professionals.

Sincerely,

Mike Rogers
Chairman

§ 6.93

Announcement on Amendments Prior to a Rules Committee Meeting

Search

▸ Visit *the* Minority Page

House of Representatives
Committee on
RULES
David Dreier, Chairman

Home | About | Legislation | Amendments | News | Resources | Contact

Announcements

Print

Amendment Process Announcement for H.R. 1229

H.R. 1229 — To amend the Outer Continental Shelf Lands Act to facilitate the safe and timely production of American energy resources from the Gulf of Mexico.

April 26, 2011

Dear Colleague:

The Committee on Rules may meet the week of May 2nd to grant a rule that could limit the amendment process for floor consideration of H.R. 1229, to amend the Outer Continental Shelf Lands Act to facilitate the safe and timely production of American energy resources from the Gulf of Mexico. The bill was ordered reported on April 13th by the Committee on Natural Resources.

Any Member wishing to offer an amendment must submit an electronic copy of the amendment and description via the Committee's *website*. Members must also submit 30 hard copies of the amendment, one copy of a brief explanation of the amendment, and an *amendment log in form* to the Rules Committee in room H-312 of the Capitol by **10 a.m. on Tuesday, May 3, 2011**. Both electronic and hard copies must be received by the date and time specified. Members should draft their amendments to the *text of the bill as ordered reported* by the Committee on Natural Resources, which is available on the Rules Committee website.

Members should use the Office of Legislative Counsel to ensure that their amendments are drafted in the most appropriate format. Members should also check with the Office of the Parliamentarian, the Committee on the Budget, and the Congressional Budget Office to be certain their amendments comply with the rules of the House and the Congressional Budget Act. If you have any questions, please contact myself or Adam Jarvis of the Committee staff at extension 5-9191.

Sincerely,

DAVID DREIER

Related Links

- *Press Releases*
- *Announcements*
- *Blog*
- *Rules Resources*

6

§ 6.94

Reading a Special Rule

H. Res. 289

[Report No. 106–317]

Original Text of the Resolution

Providing for consideration of the bill (H.R. 1655) to authorize appropriations for fiscal years 2000 and 2001 for the civilian energy and scientific research, development, and demonstration and related commercial application of energy technology programs, projects, and activities of the Department of Energy, and for other purposes.

1. Authorizes the Speaker to transform ("resolve") the House into the Committee of the Whole House to consider the measure after adoption of the special rule.

1. *Resolved*, That at any time after the adoption of this resolution the Speaker may, pursuant to clause 2(b) of rule XVIII, declare the House resolved into the Committee of the Whole House on the state of the Union for consideration of the bill (H.R. 1655) to authorize appropriations for fiscal years 2000 and 2001 for the civilian energy and scientific research, development, and demonstration and related commercial application of energy technology programs, projects, and activities of the Department of Energy, and for other purposes.

2. Dispenses with the first reading of the bill. (Bills must be read three times before being passed.) Sets the amount of general debate time—one hour—and specifies which members control that time—in this instance, the chair and ranking minority member of the Committee on Science. Specifies that debate should be relevant to the bill.

2. The first reading of the bill shall be dispensed with. General debate shall be confined to the bill and shall not exceed one hour equally divided and controlled by the chairman and ranking minority member of the Committee on Science.

3. Sets reading for amendment one section at a time (or one paragraph at a time for appropriations bills), and provides that each member can speak for five minutes on each amendment. Because this special rule sets no limitations on amendments that can be offered, it is an open rule. Nonetheless, amendments still must comply with the House's standing rules, such as that on germaneness.

3. After general debate the bill shall be considered for amendment under the five-minute rule.

Continued on page 263

§ 6.94 (continued)

Explanation	Rule text
❹ Identifies text to be open to amendment in the Committee of the Whole. A special rule can provide that a committee-reported substitute be considered as an original bill for the purpose of amendment. Allowing a full-text substitute to be considered as an original bill is usually done to permit second-degree amendments to be offered.	❹ It shall be in order to consider as an original bill for purposes of amendment under the five-minute rule the amendment in the nature of a substitute recommended by the Committee on Science now printed in the bill. Each section of the committee amendment in the nature of a substitute shall be considered as read.
❺ Determines recognition order for offering amendments. Open rules customarily grant the chair of the Committee of the Whole discretion to give priority recognition to members who submitted their amendments for preprinting in the *Congressional Record*. Absent this provision, the chair would follow the custom of giving preferential recognition to members, based on seniority, who serve on the reporting committee, alternating between the parties.	❺ During consideration of the bill for amendment, the Chairman of the Committee of the Whole may accord priority in recognition on the basis of whether the Member offering an amendment has caused it to be printed in the portion of the Congressional Record designated for that purpose in clause 8 of rule XVIII. Amendments so printed shall be considered as read.
❻ A special rule that allows amendments to be offered might allow the chair of the Committee of the Whole to postpone votes on amendments, as shown here. The chair may reduce to five minutes the time for electronic voting on a postponed question, provided that the voting time on the first in any series of questions is not less than fifteen minutes.	❻ The Chairman of the Committee of the Whole may: (1) postpone until a time during further consideration in the Committee of the Whole a request for a recorded vote on any amendment; and (2) reduce to five minutes time for electronic voting on any postponed question that follows another electronic vote without intervening business, provided that the minimum time for electronic voting on the first in any series of questions shall be 15 minutes.
❼ Provides for transformation ("to rise") back to the House from the Committee of the Whole. This provision eliminates the need for a separate vote on a motion to rise and report.	❼ At the conclusion of consideration of the bill for amendment the Committee shall rise and report the bill to the House with such amendments as may have been adopted.
❽ Enables separate votes to occur in the House on each amendment approved by the Committee of the Whole. House rules require the House to vote on each amendment approved by the Committee of the Whole.	❽ Any Members may demand a separate vote in the House on any amendment adopted in the Committee of the Whole to the bill or to the committee amendment in the nature of a substitute.
❾ Expedites final passage. By automatically imposing the "previous question," intervening debate and the offering of motions is precluded. The only motion allowed is a motion to recommit.	❾ The previous question shall be considered as ordered on the bill and amendments thereto to final passage without intervening motion except one motion to recommit with or without instructions.

the House has voted to approve the rule, the rule normally then allows the Speaker to declare the House resolved into the *Committee of the Whole House on the State of the Union* (*Committee of the Whole*) for the consideration of the measure. (*See § 6.110, Committee of the Whole: Debate.*) The rule next generally waives the required *first reading* of a bill in full. Finally, the special rule states the amount of time available for discussion (called general debate), and further requires that debate be *germane.*

Structuring the Amendment Process

The special rule may address how the bill will be read for amendment; for example, by title, by section (which is the most common way), or open for amendment at any point. ("By section" is the default method for amending and would not typically be mentioned.) The rule also lays out the amendment process, although it does not state specifically that the rule is open, closed, or modified. The description of the amendment process in the rule enables one to classify and refer to the rule as open, closed, or modified. The chair of the Committee of the Whole may also postpone or cluster votes on amendments and reduce to not less than two minutes the time for clustered votes after a fifteen-minute vote on the first amendment in a series.

Facilitating Final Passage

The special rule makes the motion for the Committee of the Whole to *rise and report* automatic upon completion of the amendment process, and further allows for a *separate vote* in the House on any amendment agreed to in the Committee of the Whole. Finally, the rule allows a *motion to recommit* to be offered before a vote on *final passage*, which may be a *voice, division,* or *recorded vote.*

§ 6.100 Consideration of a Special Rule on the House Floor

When the House for parliamentary purposes is sitting as the House and has not resolved into the Committee of the Whole, House rules permit members, when recognized, to hold the floor for no more than one hour each. A special rule from the Rules Committee is privileged and is considered under this *hour rule.* (*See § 6.70, House Floor: Scheduling and Privilege.*) The *majority floor manager* for the Rules Committee, who calls up the simple resolution containing the special rule, customarily yields one half of this one hour to the control of a minority member of the committee, the *minority floor manager*, "for purposes of debate only."

When the House is meeting as the House, the Speaker or, more commonly, a Speaker pro tempore presides. The quorum in the House is a majority of the membership, or 218 representatives if there are no vacancies. (*See § 6.112, House versus Committee of the Whole.*)

Each floor manager then yields a portion of the time she controls to other members who wish to speak. The majority party has the right to close the debate—essentially to give the last speech. When all time has been consumed or yielded back, the majority floor manager "moves the previous question."

The *previous question* is a nondebatable motion that proposes to end debate on a measure, to preclude amendments, and to bring the House to a vote on a measure—in this case, the simple resolution containing the special rule. (A motion to adjourn, a motion to table, and a motion to recommit to committee are still in order.) The previous question requires a simple majority vote for adoption. After the previous question on a special rule is agreed to, there is a vote on adoption of the special rule.

There are three ways to offer amendments to a measure (such as a special rule) in the House sitting for parliamentary purposes as the House. First, a motion to recommit a measure can instruct a committee to report the measure back to the House with a specific amendment. The right to offer a motion to recommit is the prerogative of the minority party. Second, the majority floor manager can offer an amendment before the previous question is agreed to. In the case of a special rule, the majority party drafted the measure so that an amendment is rarely offered.

Third, an opponent of a measure can propose an amendment if she can gain control of the floor. To do this, the House would need to vote not to *order the previous question*, that is, to defeat it. Defeat of the previous question means that debate does not end, amendments are not precluded, and the resolution will not yet be voted on. If the previous question is defeated, a member, usually the minority floor manager, can proceed for one hour and offer an amendment to the special rule. At the end of the second hour, the minority floor manager would move the previous question on the measure and an amendment to it.

While neither the motion to recommit nor the defeat of the previous question routinely happen, the majority party occasionally mistakes majority sentiment. For example, when President Reagan's economic package was precluded from consideration in 1981 by the House by a special rule reported from the Rules Committee, the key vote was on ordering the previous question. A sufficient number of then-majority party Democrats joined Republicans to defeat the previous question and, subsequently, amend the special rule.

§ 6.110 Committee of the Whole: Debate

When the House is in session, it might be "sitting" in one of two ways for parliamentary purposes. For example, when the House considers and votes on a special rule, the House sits for parliamentary purposes as the House. The second way the House sits is as the *Committee of the Whole House on the State of the Union* (*Committee of the Whole*), a parliamentary device created to expedite consideration of a measure.

The House "resolves" into the Committee of the Whole either by unanimous consent or by adoption of a special rule. The Committee of the Whole is a committee consisting of all members of the House. The Committee of the Whole meets in the House chamber, is presided over by a chair appointed by the Speaker of the House, and has a quorum requirement of a hundred members. The mace, the symbol of the authority of the House, is removed from its pedestal when the Committee of the Whole is meeting and moved to a lower, less visible position near the Speaker's dais. (*See § 6.111, The Mace.*) Measures from the Union Calendar are considered in the Committee of the Whole. (*See § 6.112, House versus Committee of the Whole.*)

6

§ 6.111

The Mace

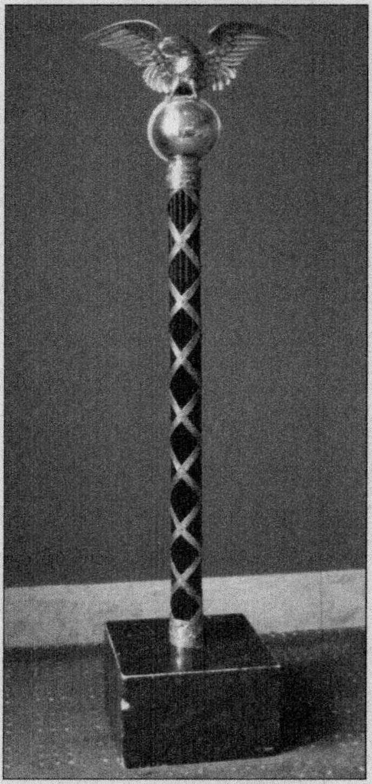

The mace is the symbol of authority of the House of Representatives. The following physical description of the mace appears with other information about the mace on the web site of the clerk of the House, at *<http://artandhistory.house.gov>*:

> The mace is 46 inches high and consists of 13 thin ebony rods representing the original 13 states of the union. The rods are bound together by four crossing ribbons of silver, pinned together and held at the bottom and at the top by silver bands. The bands are decorated with floral borders and a repoussé design. The name "Wm. Adams/Manufacturer/New York/1841." is engraved in the cartouche, located in the front center of the bottom band. This shaft is topped by a silver globe 4-1/2 inches in diameter and engraved with the seven continents, the names of the oceans, lines of longitude, and the major lines of latitude. The Western Hemisphere faces the front. The globe is encircled with a silver rim marked with the degrees of latitude, on which is perched an engraved solid silver eagle with a wingspan of 15 inches. The total weight of the mace is 10 pounds.

General Debate

General debate is a period of time set aside for discussing a bill as a whole. During this period, no amendments or motions are in order.

The special rule specifies the amount of time available for general debate and how the time is allocated. (For those measures that are brought up by unanimous consent, but considered in the Committee of the Whole, the consent request specifies the time set aside for general debate.) The special rule typically provides one hour of general debate on a measure, with time usually divided equally between the control of the chair and ranking minority member of the committee of jurisdiction. These two members are referred to as the *floor managers* of the measure. (Once a special rule is adopted, the Rules Committee members' role as floor managers ends.)

The chair of the Committee of the Whole recognizes the majority floor manager to open the general debate. The majority floor manager reserves the balance of time after concluding an opening statement. The minority floor manager then does the same. Thereafter, the two managers yield specific periods of time to individual members to speak on the measure.

Recognition by the chair of the Committee of the Whole usually alternates between the parties, although one party may yield to several members in a row to keep the remaining general debate time fairly equal between the parties. When a member who has been yielded time addresses issues that the manager does not want addressed, the manager reclaims the balance of time. Throughout the debate, it is common for the floor managers to inquire of the chair how much time remains. The floor

§ 6.112

House versus Committee of the Whole

House	Committee of the Whole
Established by Constitution	Established by House for consideration of a specific measure
Mace raised	Mace lowered
Speaker presides	Chair of Committee of the Whole presides, appointed by Speaker
One-hour rule	Five-minute rule for amendments; special rule from Rules Committee dictates procedure, after adoption of rule by House
Quorum of 218	Quorum of 100
One-fifth of members (44 with minimum quorum) to trigger a recorded vote	25 members to trigger a recorded vote
Motion for previous question in order	Motion for previous question not in order; motion to limit or end debate may be offered
Motion to recommit in order	Motion to recommit not in order
Motion to reconsider in order	Motion to reconsider not in order
Routine business of House in order	Routine business of House not in order

§ 6.113

Who Is Allowed on the House Floor?

In addition to the representatives and pages, a variety of staff have permanent or temporary privileges to be on the floor of the House.

Standing next to or near the presiding officer are the parliamentarian, sergeant at arms, clerk of the House, and Speaker's page. At the desk immediately in front of the Speaker are seated the journal clerk, tally clerk, and reading clerk. At the desk below the clerks are the bill clerk, enrolling clerk, and daily digest clerk. Reporters of debate sit at a table below the rostrum. Staff members of committees and individual representatives are allowed on the floor by unanimous consent.

(See § 11.11, House Floor Plan.)

§ 6.114

Committee of the Whole and the House: Stages of Action

- House resolves into Committee of the Whole
- General debate
- Measure read or considered for amendment
- Amendments debated under five-minute rule
- Committee of the Whole rises and reports
- House votes on Committee of the Whole-approved amendments
- Opportunity for motion to recommit
- House votes on final passage

managers are usually accompanied by committee staff, who can respond privately to questions from their party's members. (*See § 6.113, Who Is Allowed on the House Floor?*)

When all time for general debate has been consumed or yielded back, after the majority floor manager has concluded debate, general debate ends and the amendment process begins. (*See § 6.114, Committee of the Whole and the House: Stages of Action.*)

§ 6.120 Committee of the Whole: Amendment Process

Unless a special rule provides otherwise, a bill is usually read for amendment "by section." Bills can alternatively be read for amendment by title or be "open for amendment at any point." Reading a bill for amendment is referred to as the *second reading.*

When the first section of a measure is read, or *designated*, amendments recommended by the committee reporting the bill, called *committee amendments*, are first considered without being offered from the floor. A special rule often provides that committee amendments become part of the text of the measure for further amendment. (The text for purposes of debate or amendment is sometimes referred to as the *base text.*)

After committee amendments become part of the base text, individual members are then recognized to offer individual amendments. Priority recognition is given to members of the committee of jurisdiction, by seniority on the committee, with recognition usually alternating between the parties.

Amendments are debated under the *five-minute rule*, with the proponent and an opponent speaking first for up to five minutes each. Members may then make a motion to "strike the last word" or "strike the requisite number of words," that is, offer a pro forma amendment to gain five minutes to speak on an amendment. At the end of five minutes, the pro forma amendment is considered withdrawn. Time under the five-minute rule cannot be reserved, and a member may not speak more than once on an amendment. (*See § 6.121, Amendment Process Glossary.*)

If the special rule does not provide a cap on time for debating amendments, debate can be limited or ended by unanimous consent or by a motion to end or limit debate. (The previous question is not in order in the Committee of the Whole.) Such a motion may limit debate on a specific amendment, a section, or the entire measure. The motion can specify a specific time or a specific duration of minutes or hours for the consideration of amendments to continue. The motion may also designate how the remaining time is to be divided.

Legislation in recent Congresses has typically been considered pursuant to a structured rule. (*See § 6.90, Rules Committee and Special Rules.*)

Amendment Tree

An amendment to the base text is called a *first-degree amendment*. Such an amendment can be further amended by either a *substitute amendment* (which is also a first-degree amendment) or a *perfecting amendment*—a *second-degree amendment.* The substitute is also subject to a perfecting amendment. These four amendments constitute what is referred to as the *amendment tree.* Once an amendment to a measure is pending, either a perfecting amendment or a substitute amendment can be offered first. (*See § 6.122, Basic House Amendment Tree.*)

§ 6.121

Amendment Process Glossary

Amendment: Proposal of a member of Congress to alter the text of a measure.

Amendment in the Nature of a Substitute: Amendment that seeks to replace the entire text of the underlying measure. The adoption of such an amendment usually precludes any further amendment to that measure.

Amendment Tree: Diagram showing the number and types of amendments to a measure permitted by the chamber. It also shows the relationship among the amendments, their degree or type, the order in which they may be offered, and the order in which they are voted on.

"Bigger Bite" Amendment: Amendment that, although it amends previously amended language (not allowed under the rules), can be offered because it changes more of the measure than the original amendment.

Degrees of Amendment: Designation that indicates the relationship of an amendment to the text of a measure and of one amendment to another. Amendments are permitted only in two degrees.

En Bloc Amendment: Several amendments offered as a group, after obtaining unanimous consent.

First-Degree Amendment: Amendment offered to the text of a measure or a substitute offered to a first-degree amendment.

Five-Minute Rule: House rule that limits debate on an amendment offered in the Committee of the Whole to five minutes for its sponsor and five minutes for an opponent. In practice, the Committee of the Whole permits the offering of pro forma amendments, each debatable for five minutes.

Germaneness: Rule in the House requiring that debate and amendments pertain to the same subject as the bill or amendment under consideration. In the Senate, germaneness is not generally required.

Insert: Amendment to add new language to a measure or another amendment.

Perfecting Amendment: Amendment that alters—but does not substitute or replace—language in another amendment.

Point of Order: Objection to the current proceeding, measure, or amendment because the proposed action violates a rule of the chamber, written precedent, or rule-making statute.

Pro Forma Amendment: Motion whereby a House member secures five minutes to speak on an amendment under debate, without offering a substantive amendment. The member moves to "strike the last word" or "strike the requisite number of words." The motion requires no vote and is deemed automatically withdrawn at the expiration of the five minutes.

Second-Degree Amendment: Amendment to an amendment. It is also called a perfecting amendment.

Strike: Amendment to delete a portion of a measure or an amendment.

Strike and Insert: Amendment that replaces the text of a measure or an amendment.

Strike the Last Word/Strike the Requisite Number of Words: Also called a pro forma amendment. Means of obtaining time to speak on an amendment without offering a substantive change.

Substitute Amendment: Amendment that replaces the entire text of a pending amendment.

Unprinted Amendment: Senate amendment not printed in the *Congressional Record* before its offering. Unprinted amendments are numbered sequentially in the order of their submission during a Congress.

A larger glossary is located at the back of the book and online at <*TCNLG.com*>.

6

§ 6.122

Basic House Amendment Tree

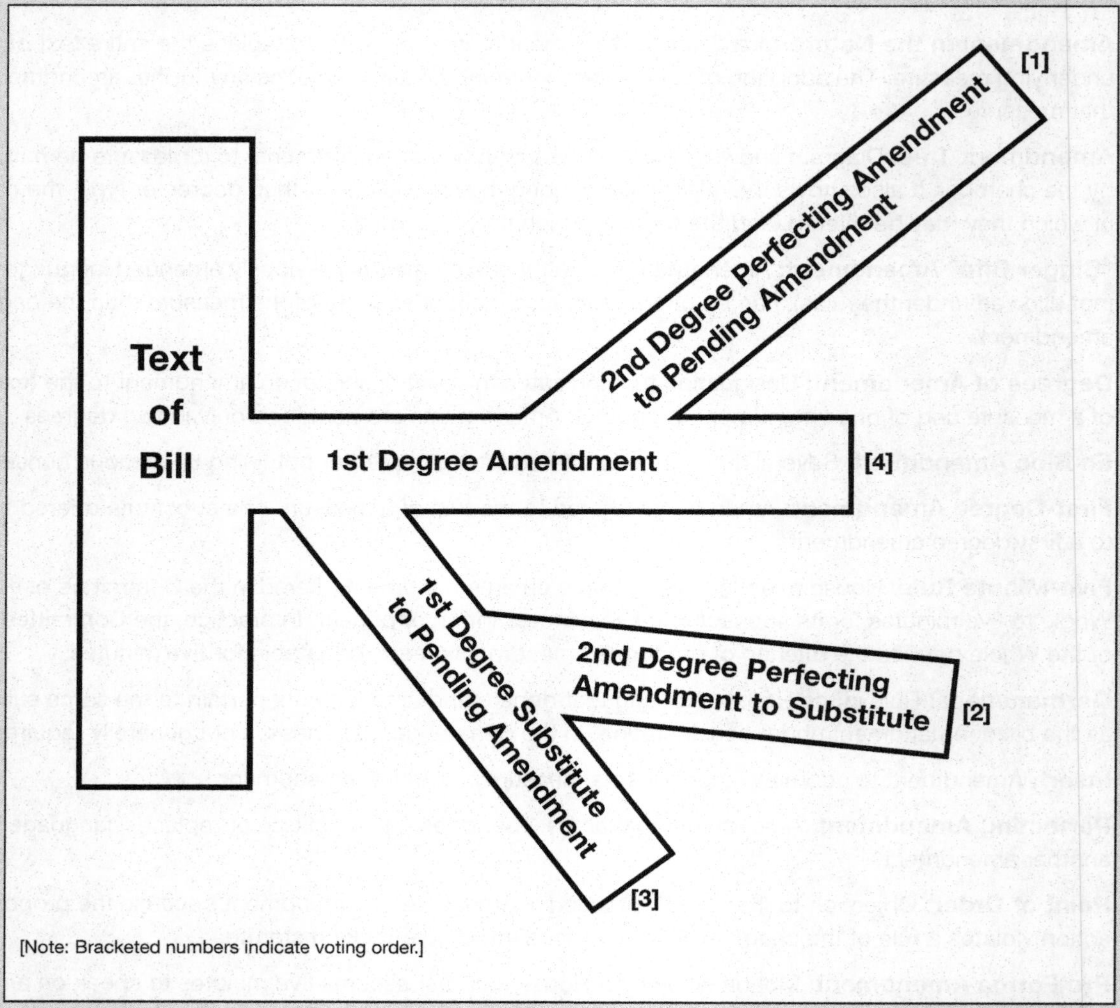

If all four of these amendments are pending, the order of voting is as follows:

1. the perfecting amendment to the amendment to the bill (a second-degree amendment)
2. the perfecting amendment to the substitute (a second-degree amendment)
3. the substitute (considered a first-degree amendment)
4. the base amendment to the text

When an amendment has been disposed of, a branch of the amendment tree is open. An additional amendment may then be offered, provided that the new amendment does not propose to change what has already been amended.

Restrictions on Amendments

In general, an amendment must be in writing at the time it is offered. The amendment must be a first- or second-degree amendment. It is not in order to reoffer an identical amendment to an amendment that has already been acted upon.

An amendment may not amend text that has already been amended. In some circumstances, however, a bigger bite can be taken from the measure or amendment. A *bigger-bite amendment* substantively changes the unamended parts of the provision in which the previously amended language appears and is in order.

An amendment must be offered in a timely fashion—only at the time the Committee of the Whole is considering the section or title the amendment seeks to change. An amendment may not affect different parts of a bill unless unanimous consent is granted to offer the amendment *en bloc*.

Germaneness. In addition to the restrictions previously described, an amendment must be germane, or relevant, to the text it would amend. House Rule XVI, clause 7, is one of the most discussed rules of the House and thousands of precedents have resulted from its interpretation or application. Three tests of germaneness are noted in the rule. First, the amendment must relate to the subject matter under consideration. Second, the fundamental purpose of the amendment must be germane to the fundamental purpose of the bill or amendment. Third, the amendment should be within the jurisdiction of the committee reporting the bill. Hence, subject matter, fundamental purpose, and committee jurisdiction represent key tests of germaneness.

Beyond these tests, several principles also relate to germaneness. First, an individual proposition cannot be amended by another individual proposition. Second, a specific subject may not be amended by a general subject. Third, a general subject may be amended by a specific subject. These principles are difficult to interpret, and the Speaker or chair of the Committee of the Whole seeks the advice of the House parliamentarian if a ruling is required. If a point of order is raised that an amendment is not germane, and the point of order is sustained, the amendment cannot be considered. On the other hand, if the question of germaneness is not raised, or if a special rule waives the point of order, it is possible for a nongermane but popular amendment to be agreed upon.

Over 2,000 pages of precedents in *Hinds and Cannon*, *Deschler's Precedents*, and the parliamentarian's annotations in the House *Rules Manual* address germaneness. Links to these documents are online at <*CDDocs.com*>.

Ending the Amendment Process

In the Committee of the Whole, a member can move to *close debate* (end debate) on a pending amendment or to *limit debate* at a specified time. (After the last section of the bill has been read in the House sitting as the House, a member can move the previous question. This motion is not in order in the Committee of the Whole.) Unlike the previous question, closing or limiting debate does not preclude offering additional amendments. It means that all subsequent amendments are decided without debate.

At the conclusion of the amendment process, a member moves that the *committee rise and report*. The motion to rise and report in effect takes a measure from the Committee of the Whole back to the House for final disposition. A *motion to rise*, on the other hand, reports a measure back to the House temporarily. The adoption of a motion to rise indicates that the Committee of the Whole may reconvene at a later time to continue work on a measure.

Separate Vote on Amendments

Once the Committee of the Whole has risen and the House is again sitting as the House, any member may demand a separate vote on any amendment to the text of the measure under consideration agreed to in the Committee of the Whole.

§ 6.130 House Floor: Voting

Voting in the House

There are four types of votes: voice, division, yea and nay, and record votes. *Voice vote* means that members call out "yea" or "nay" when a question is put in the House. The Speaker determines the outcome of the vote by the volume of each response. On occasion, the Speaker can say "without objection," a variation on a voice vote meaning the question is adopted.

A *division vote* can be demanded by any member after a voice vote is taken. First, the members in favor stand and are counted; then, those opposed stand and are counted. A division vote shows only vote totals and does not provide a record of how individual members voted. In recent times, there have been only a few division votes on the floor each year.

Under an automatic *yea and nay vote*, a member may "object on the ground that a quorum is not present and make a point of order that a quorum is not present." The actual vote then determines both the presence of a quorum and the outcome of the pending question.

A *record vote* is taken if one-fifth of a quorum, forty-four members, stand and support the request. Like a yea and nay vote, a record vote is taken by the electronic voting system. (*See § 6.131, House Voting Glossary.*)

Voting in the Committee of the Whole

Both voice votes and division votes are taken in the Committee of the Whole. To obtain a record vote, twenty-five members must support a member's request for a record vote. If fewer than one hundred members are present, which is the minimum number required for a quorum in the Committee of the Whole, a member may demand a record vote, and, pending that, make a point of order that a quorum is not present. The record vote would then be automatic.

Time for Voting

The minimum time for a record vote or quorum call is fifteen minutes in both the House and the Committee of the Whole. The Speaker has the authority to postpone and cluster certain votes and to reduce to five minutes votes after an initial fifteen-minute vote. The chair of the Committee of the Whole may reduce the time for subsequent votes to not less than two minutes.

§ 6.131

House Voting Glossary

Agreed To: Usual parliamentary term for approval of motions, amendments, and simple and concurrent resolutions.

Cluster Voting: Allowance for sequential recorded votes on a series of measures or amendments that the House finished debating at an earlier time or on a previous date. The Speaker can reduce the minimum time for the second and subsequent votes in the series to five minutes each. The chair of the Committee of the Whole may reduce the time to not less than two minutes.

Division Vote: A vote in which a committee chair or the House presiding officer counts those in favor and those in opposition, with no record made of how each member votes. The chair or presiding officer can either ask for a show of hands or ask members to stand.

Electronic Vote: A vote in the House using the electronic voting machine. Members insert voting cards into one of the boxes located throughout the House chamber.

Proxy Vote: The committee practice of permitting a member to cast the vote of an absent colleague. Proxy voting is not permitted in House committees.

Quorum Call: A procedure for determining whether a quorum is present—218 in the House and 100 in the Committee of the Whole House on the State of the Union.

Roll-call (Record) Vote: A vote in which members are recorded by name for or against a measure.

Second: The number of members required to indicate support for an action, such as calling for a vote.

Teller Vote: A House procedure in which members cast votes by passing through the center aisle of the chamber to be counted; now used only when the electronic voting system breaks down.

Voice Vote: A method of voting where members who support a question call out "aye" in unison, after which those opposed answer "no" in unison. The chair decides which position prevails.

Yea and Nay: A vote in which members respond "aye" or "no" on a question when their names are called in alphabetical order.

A larger glossary is located at the back of the book and online at <*TCNLG.com*>.

§ 6.140 House Floor: Motion to Recommit and Final Passage

After the third reading of a bill, but before the vote on final passage, a *motion to recommit* is in order. (The third reading is the required reading to a chamber of a measure by title only before the vote on passage.) The motion is traditionally the prerogative of a minority member to offer, providing the minority with one last opportunity to kill or amend a measure.

A member stands and says, "Mr. Speaker, I have a motion to recommit at the desk." The Speaker then asks if the member is opposed to the measure. That member signifies that he is opposed to the measure "in its current form."

There are two types of motions to recommit. Adoption of a motion to recommit *without instructions* kills a measure. If such a motion is offered, it is not debatable.

§ 6.141

Approval Terminology

Term	Used For
Adopted	Conference Reports
Agreed To	Amendments Simple Resolutions Concurrent Resolutions
Concur	Amendment of Other Chamber
Ordered	Engrossment Previous Question Third Reading Yeas and Nays
Passed	Bills Joint Resolutions
Sustained	Points of Order Rulings of Chair

A motion to recommit *with instructions* attempts to amend a measure. The motion normally instructs that the measure be referred to the reporting committee and that the committee "report the bill back to the House forthwith with the following amendment. . . ." A motion to recommit with instructions is debatable for ten minutes, equally divided between the proponent and an opponent. The time is not controlled, meaning members may not yield or reserve time. At the request of the majority floor manager, the ten minutes can be extended to one hour, equally divided and controlled. If a motion to recommit with instructions is agreed to, the measure is immediately reported back to the House with the amendment, the amendment is voted on, and the House then votes on final passage of the bill.

The vote on final passage is then taken. (*See § 9.60, Versions of Legislation.*) When the results of the vote on final passage are announced, a pro forma *motion to reconsider* is made and *laid on the table*, that is, postponed indefinitely. There is rarely a vote on these motions. To table the motion to reconsider prevents a measure from being reconsidered at a later date. (*See § 6.141, Approval Terminology.*)

§ 6.150 House and Senate Compared

The Senate has an extensive framework of parliamentary procedure to guide its actions. Nevertheless, in practice, its procedures are more flexible than those of the House. While the House emphasizes its procedures, the Senate functions in a more ad hoc manner, adapting its procedures to accommodate individual senators. For example, scheduling and consideration of legislation can be accomplished in almost any manner the party leaders and individual senators can devise. (*See § 6.151, Comparison of Selected House and Senate Procedures.*)

§ 6.160 Senate Scheduling

The Senate sets its floor agenda to accommodate individual senators and to prepare for almost any contingency. Because of the privileges accorded individual senators, the Senate can rarely rely on its rules or customs to set the order of business. Because the rules have different influences at certain times, no Senate session day is truly typical. Scheduling the consideration of a measure can be accomplished in almost any manner the party leaders can arrange. Because the majority leader has priority recognition on the floor, it is that person's job to arrange the schedule.

Some measures can be raised for consideration, or even passage without debate, by *unanimous consent*. However, a single objection can derail a unanimous consent request. Accordingly, the majority leader checks with all interested senators before bringing legislation to the floor by unanimous consent. Other measures are scheduled for consideration pursuant to a *unanimous consent time*

§ 6.151

Comparison of Selected House and Senate Procedures

House	Senate
Four calendars (Union, House, Private, and Discharge)	Two calendars (Legislative and Executive)
Scheduling by Speaker and majority-party leadership, with limited consultation among members	Scheduling by majority-party leadership, with broad consultation among all senators
Role of Rules Committee and special rules to govern floor consideration	Unanimous consent and complex unanimous consent time agreements to govern floor consideration
Presiding officer has considerable discretion in recognition; rulings rarely challenged	Presiding officer has little discretion in recognition; rulings frequently challenged
Debate always restricted	Debate rarely restricted
Debate-ending motions by majority vote (218 representatives)	Cloture invoked by three-fifths vote (60 senators)
Germaneness of amendments generally required	Germaneness of amendments rarely required
Quorum calls permitted in connection with record votes	Quorum calls permitted almost any time and used for constructive delay
Adjourns at end of day	Recesses at end of many days

agreement. A time agreement is negotiated among interested parties to avoid an objection to the unanimous consent request. Still other measures are brought up by a *motion to proceed to consider.* However, a motion to proceed in most instances is debatable.

§ 6.170 Legislative and Calendar Days; Morning Hour and Morning Business

How the Senate begins its session depends on how it ended its business the previous day.

Legislative and Calendar Days

A calendar day is recognized as each twenty-four-hour period. A *legislative day* begins when the Senate next meets after adjourning, rather than recessing, the previous daily session. Indeed, a legislative day can stretch over several calendar days or even weeks.

This practice enables the Senate to maintain flexibility. Because procedures are so strictly determined when a new legislative day is created, the Senate may recess rather than adjourn at the end of the previous day's session. Recessing does not create a new legislative day. A legislative day continues until the Senate adjourns at the end of a daily session. Today, the Senate normally agrees by unanimous consent how to structure its next meeting day.

At the beginning of each day, whether a calendar day or legislative day, a period of *leader time* is set aside. During this time, the majority and minority leaders can be recognized by the presiding officer for ten minutes each to speak on whatever subjects they choose. They often discuss the legislative schedule for the day and the next several days.

Morning Hour and Morning Business

If it is a new legislative day, the Senate proceeds to *morning hour*, which constitutes the first two hours of a legislative day. Based on traditional Senate schedules, morning hour usually extends from 12:00 noon to 2:00 p.m. Within the morning hour, the Senate entertains *morning business*. The first hour is reserved for individual senators to deliver *morning hour speeches* on any subject. Each speech is usually limited to five minutes. By unanimous consent, morning business can be conducted throughout the day, and usually is.

After the completion of morning business, or at the end of the first hour, the other morning hour business occurs. It consists of messages from the president, messages from the House of Representatives, the presentation of petitions and memorials, reports of committees, and the introduction of bills and resolutions.

Because the Senate may remain in the same legislative day for several days, a morning business period is held almost every calendar day.

§ 6.180 Senate Calendars and Legislative and Executive Business before the Senate

The Senate has two calendars. The *Calendar of Business* contains all legislation, both bills and resolutions. The *Executive Calendar* is reserved for executive business, that is, business requiring the Senate to advise and consent on treaties and nominations. Both calendars are published every day the Senate is in session.

Calendar of Business

The *Calendar of Business* contains a list called "General Orders, under Rule VIII," which details all measures that committees have reported and any bills or joint resolutions that have been placed directly on the calendar without first being referred to committee. The order number reflects the chronological order in which a measure was placed on the calendar. Noted on the general order list are the following items:

- the measure's number
- the measure's sponsor
- the measure's title
- date the measure was placed on the calendar
- whether the measure was placed directly on the calendar without being referred to committee
- whether the measure is an original bill
- whether the measure was reported with or without amendment
- whether there is an accompanying report
- whether the report contains minority or additional views

Also included in the Calendar of Business are the following:

- a calendar that shows the days on which the Senate was in session and the anticipated recesses and nonlegislative periods
- a list of senators and the year in which each senator's term expires
- membership lists of Senate committees and Senate membership on joint committees
- a list of bills sent to conference, the names of House and Senate conferees on each bill, and the date either chamber acted on a conference report

The Calendar of Business also contains the text of unanimous consent time agreements and a list of "resolutions and motions over, under the rule." This is a list of simple and concurrent resolutions that have been placed directly on the calendar without first being referred to committee.

The back cover of the calendar shows the history of legislative action on appropriations bills during the current session of Congress.

Executive Calendar

The Executive Calendar has five sections:

- texts of any unanimous consent agreements, which have not been fully implemented, concerning executive business
- Senate executive resolutions that concern executive business (it is rare for there to be any resolutions listed)
- treaties that have been reported from committee, including each treaty's calendar number, document number, and subject, as well as information on how it was reported from the Foreign Relations Committee
- nominations that have been reported from committee, including each nomination's calendar number, the number of the presidential message transmitting the nomination, the name of the nominee and the office for which she has been nominated, and information on how the nomination was reported (a nomination listed for the first time appears under a heading of "new reports")
- routine nominations, such as those in the armed services and the Public Health Service

(For additional information on the calendars, see § 10.20, Floor Documents.)

§ 6.190 Holds, Clearance, and Unanimous Consent

By custom, the majority leader of the Senate, or that person's designee, has the right to set the agenda on the floor. The majority leader decides the order in which bills on the calendar should come to the floor for action, and negotiates with other senators to agree to take up measures the majority leader wishes to consider.

Custom, however, also allows a senator to place a *hold* on the consideration of any legislative or executive business. A hold is a notice that a senator intends to object to any unanimous consent request made on the floor to bring up a matter for consideration by the Senate. *(See § 6.191, Senator's Notice of Hold or Desire to be Consulted.)* Recent policy regarding holds, which has not been consistently followed, dictates that a senator placing a hold should notify the sponsor of the legislation (if legislation is the object of the hold) and the committee of jurisdiction that he is concerned

§ 6.191

Senator's Notice of Hold or Desire to be Consulted

COMMITTEE ON INTELLIGENCE
COMMITTEE ON INDIAN AFFAIRS
COMMITTEE ON HOMELAND SECURITY AND GOVERNMENT AFFAIRS
RANKING MEMBER
PERMANENT SUBCOMMITTEE ON INVESTIGATIONS

United States Senate
Senator Tom Coburn, MD

COMMITTEE ON HEALTH, EDUCATION, LABOR, AND PENSIONS
COMMITTEE ON THE JUDICIARY
RANKING MEMBER
SUBCOMMITTEE ON THE CONSTITUTION

March 23, 2010

The Honorable Mitch McConnell
Senate Minority Leader
United States Senate
Washington, D.C. 20510

Dear Senator McConnell,

I am writing to notify you that I would like to be consulted on any unanimous consent agreements regarding the consideration of H.R. 4851, the Continuing Extension Act of 2010, which would extend a number of federal programs for one month.

No one is arguing that Americans who are currently unemployed should not have their unemployment insurance payments extended. But once again, Congress is refusing to find a way to offset the **$9.15 billion** cost of bill with cuts to less important federal spending.

Time and time again, Congress intentionally waits until the last minute to consider important legislation and then declares the billions of dollars in foreseeable costs as "emergency" spending in order to avoid having to find a way to pay for the bills' price tags.

In the last 6 months, Congress has passed four major extension bills. H.R. 4851 would be the fifth such bill. The total cost of these bills is almost **$30 billion.** Additionally, over the last year Congress has increased funding totaling **$64.9 billion** for the Highway and Unemployment Insurance Trust Funds without offsets.

This short sightedness sticks taxpayers with billions of dollars in additional debt and treats the unemployed, doctors and Medicare patients, hard working men and women who help make our roads and bridges safe, and others relying on federal funds as pawns in Congress' borrowing and spending game.

When the previous last-minute one month extension (H.R. 4691) was brought up days before the funding authority for numerous federal programs, including Unemployment Insurance and the Highway Trust Fund, expired at the end of February, 2010, a United States Senator was attacked for objecting to passing the bill without any debate or amendments because the bill was unpaid for and added **$10 billion** to our nation's debt.

As always, those who prefer to borrow to avoid making tough budget decisions won out, and the taxpayers were stuck with another **$10 billion** of debt.

Congress has continually resisted the need to act like every family in the United States of America and to budget and live within their means. Our debt is now over **$12.6 trillion**. The 2010 deficit is projected to amount to **$1.3 trillion** and we are borrowing 43 cents on every dollar; yet, Congress continues to increase spending without any correlating spending cuts.

Congress' inability to prioritize and manage national needs results in real consequences for Americans, whether it be furloughs, market uncertainty that leads to lower investment and job losses, or Americans being saddled with higher debt and taxes.

If Congress keeps approving temporary extension bills throughout the calendar year without finding offsets, Congress will have added almost **$120 billion** to our national debt. Additionally, the Senate has already

1800 SOUTH BALTIMORE
SUITE 800
TULSA, OK 74119
PHONE: 918-581-7651

RUSSELL SENATE OFFICE BUILDING, ROOM 172
WASHINGTON, DC 20510-3604
PHONE: 202-224-5754
FAX: 202-224-6008

100 NORTH BROADWAY
SUITE 1820
OKLAHOMA CITY, OK 73102
PHONE: 405-231-4941

www.coburn.senate.gov

legislation just

needs to be
ed stimulus
artment
$103 million
nsumer
the cost of a
ill and create

Fiscal Year
obligated
ble for more
tap into **$228**

crease it
sing its
ent.

deral
spending,
al concerns.

but do we
e cost to
cluded to

Thank you for protecting my rights regarding this legislation.

Sincerely,

Tom A. Coburn, M.D.
U.S. Senator

cc: Majority Leader Harry Reid

about the measure. A written notice should also be provided to the senator's party leader and placed in the *Congressional Record*. For the 112th (2011–2013) and 113th (2013–2015) Congresses, in addition, secret holds and rolling holds are not permitted.

In addition, to learn whether there may be objection to bringing up a measure or executive matter if no hold has been placed, or to identify controversy associated with a measure, the party leadership attempts to obtain *clearance* to have a measure considered. To obtain clearance, the party leaders ask individual senators to file *requests to be consulted* with the party leaders. A request signifies that a senator wants to participate in any negotiations regarding when and how a measure or executive matter might be considered on the Senate floor. Further, quorum calls conducted throughout the day—a form of constructive delay—allow the leadership time to conduct negotiations. A hotline telephone, provided to all Senate offices, is often used to obtain clearance. Once all requests have been considered and addressed, the majority leader may choose to call up a measure or executive matter on the floor.

Through these negotiations, the majority leader can determine how best to bring a measure or executive matter to the floor. For most noncontroversial items, the majority leader, or that person's designee, asks "unanimous consent to proceed to the consideration" of a measure or executive matter. By bringing a measure or executive matter to the floor by *unanimous consent*, debate and amendment options are usually unlimited, although a further unanimous consent request could be made to set debate and amendment limitations. A *complex unanimous consent agreement*, also called a *time agreement*, generally limits debate and amendments.

Finally, there is also a class of routine unanimous consent requests that allows senators to obtain floor privileges for selected staff and to "proceed as if in morning business" throughout the day. (*See § 6.192, Who Is Allowed on the Senate Floor?*) Unanimous consent is also obtained to allow the Senate to go into *executive session* to consider business on the Executive Calendar.

§ 6.192

Who Is Allowed on the Senate Floor?

In addition to senators, a variety of staff have permanent or temporary privileges to be on the floor of the Senate.

At the desk immediately in front of the presiding officer are seated the parliamentarian, legislative clerk, journal clerk, and, often, the executive clerk and bill clerk. Reporters of debates sit at a table below the rostrum. Seats near the rostrum are reserved for the secretary and assistant secretary of the Senate and the sergeant at arms. Majority- and minority-party secretaries and other staff members who have floor privileges may be seen on the floor. Pages sit on either side of the presiding officer's desk. Staff members of individual senators are allowed on the floor by unanimous consent.

(*See § 11.21, Senate Floor Plan.*)

§ 6.200 Time Agreements and Motions to Proceed on the Senate Floor

There are three typical ways to bring a measure to the Senate floor for consideration. *Unanimous consent*, often referred to as a *simple unanimous consent agreement*, implies agreement among all senators, as a single objection can stop its implementation. A *complex unanimous consent agreement*, referred to as a time agreement, and a *motion to proceed to consideration*, called a motion to proceed, are the other options available to the majority leader to bring up a measure for consideration.

§ 6.201

Example of a Senate Unanimous Consent Time Agreement

2

UNANIMOUS CONSENT AGREEMENTS

S. 493 (ORDER NO. 17)

1.—*Ordered,* That upon the conclusion of Morning Business on Tuesday, March 29, 2011, the Senate resume consideration of S. 493, a bill to reauthorize and improve the SBIR and STTR programs, and for other purposes. *(Mar. 28, 2011.)*

S. 223

2.—*Ordered,* That when the Senate receives the House companion, as determined by the two Leaders, to S. 223, an act to modernize the air traffic control system, improve the safety, reliability, and availability of transportation by air in the United States, provide for modernization of the air traffic control system, reauthorize the Federal Aviation Administration, and for other purposes, it be in order for the Majority Leader to proceed to its immediate consideration, strike all after the enacting clause and insert the text of S. 223, as passed by the Senate, in lieu thereof; provided, that the companion bill, as amended, be read a third time, the statutory PAYGO statement be read and the bill be passed; provided further, that the motions to reconsider be considered made and laid upon the table; further, that upon passage, the Senate insist on its amendment, request a conference with the House on the disagreeing votes of the two Houses, and the Chair be authorized to appoint conferees on the part of the Senate with a ratio of 5–4; further, that with respect to this order, there be no intervening action or debate. *(Feb. 17, 2011.)*

Time Agreements

The Senate conducts much of its work by agreeing to unanimous consent requests. *Simple unanimous consent requests* cover noncontroversial and routine matters. Complex unanimous consent requests, often called *time agreements*, establish another procedure under which measures are considered on the floor. Without a time agreement, a measure could be debated for as long as senators spoke on the floor, and amendments, whether germane or not, could be offered without restriction. Time agreements are intended to expedite consideration and establish predictability by imposing restrictions on the time available and limiting the amendments that could be offered. (*See § 6.201, Example of a Senate Unanimous Consent Time Agreement.*)

After consultation and negotiation with other senators, which can take days or weeks or months on highly contentious matters, the majority leader obtains a time agreement that satisfies all concerned senators and that meets the policy objectives of the majority party. The majority leader then asks on the Senate floor that a measure be considered "under the following time agreement."

A time agreement can cover consideration of an entire measure or consideration for just one day. It can cover time allocation for all amendments or debate on a particular amendment. It can limit debate on the measure itself or on part of the measure. A time agreement can limit senators to offering only germane amendments, or it can contain a negotiated list of nongermane amendments. It can also restrict the offering of amendments to pending amendments. (*See § 6.202, Comparing a House Special Rule and a Senate Time Agreement.*)

§ 6.202

Comparing a House Special Rule and a Senate Time Agreement

House Special Rule	Senate Time Agreement
Called up as a simple resolution	Called up by unanimous consent
Requires majority vote for passage	Agreed to by unanimous consent
Specifies time for general debate	Specifies time for debating amendments
Permits or prohibits amendments	Generally restricts only the offering of nongermane amendments
Does not specify date for vote on passage of measure	Generally sets date for vote on final passage
Effect is often to waive House rules	Effect is often to waive Senate rules

The Senate often begins consideration of a measure by unanimous consent without a time agreement but then adopts piecemeal agreements. A time agreement can be changed by agreeing to a subsequent unanimous consent agreement.

Time agreements are printed in the *Congressional Record* and the daily Calendar of Business.

Motions to Proceed

Because of the difficulty of negotiating a time agreement, which can be stopped by a single objection, any senator as an alternative can attempt to call up a measure by making a "motion to proceed to consideration," usually referred to as a *motion to proceed.* Although any senator may offer a motion to proceed, by custom the Senate reserves the right to the majority leader or that person's designee. A motion to proceed is generally debatable, and there is no limit on the duration of the debate under Senate rules. (For the 112th Congress (2011–2013), an agreement was reached to reduce the use of filibusters on motions to proceed. It was an agreement announced by party leaders and not a rules change.) Debate on the motion to proceed can be ended by unanimous consent or by invoking cloture. (*See § 6.230, Cloture in Senate Floor Proceedings.*) A motion to proceed, however, needs only a majority vote for passage. (The motion to proceed is not debatable under certain circumstances, such as during a new legislative day.)

§ 6.210 Consideration and Debate on the Senate Floor

Presiding Officer and Recognition to Speak

The presiding officer of the Senate is the vice president of the United States. However, the vice president rarely presides over daily sessions of the Senate. He presides only when a close vote is anticipated and when his vote may be needed to break a tie vote, the only occasion under the Constitution when he is allowed to cast a vote in the Senate.

§ 6.211

Longest Senate Filibusters

- Strom Thurmond, 1957
  24 hours, 18 minutes on civil rights bill
- Wayne Morse, 1953
  22 hours, 26 minutes on Tidelands oil bill
- William Proxmire, 1961
  19 hours, 6 minutes (held floor for 25 hours, 36 minutes, but yielded for 6 hours and 30 minutes to other senators to debate foreign aid bills) on confirmation of Lawrence O'Connor for post at Federal Power Commission
- Robert LaFollette, Sr., 1908
  18 hours, 23 minutes on Aldrich-Vreeland currency bill
- William Proxmire, 1981
  16 hours, 12 minutes on bill raising public debt limit
- Huey Long, 1935
  15 hours, 30 minutes on extension of National Industrial Recovery Act
- Alfonse D'Amato, 1992
  15 hours, 14 minutes on tax bill
- Robert C. Byrd, 1964
  14 hours, 13 minutes on civil rights bill

The president pro tempore, the most senior majority-party senator, generally opens a day's session. Yet the president pro tempore does not preside throughout the day. The president pro tempore designates other majority-party senators to preside, usually in one-hour or two-hour blocks of time. Junior majority-party senators preside often early in their careers, providing them opportunities to learn Senate procedures. In fact, a *golden gavel award* is granted to the first senator in each Congress to preside for one hundred hours.

The main authority of the presiding officer is to recognize members to speak. Priority recognition is almost always granted to the majority and minority leaders if they are seeking recognition, and then to the floor managers of pending legislation. In the absence of any of these senators, the presiding officer must recognize the first senator on his feet seeking recognition. The presiding officer is addressed as "Mr. (Madam) President."

Filibusters

When a senator is recognized to speak on a pending measure, few limitations are placed on her. Debate is generally unlimited on all pending measures. A senator may yield to another senator for a question, but the senator still controls the floor. One of the most visible of Senate characteristics is the right of an individual senator to maintain the floor, that is, to speak for an extended period of time. Continuing, extended debate is referred to as a *filibuster*. The image of James Stewart in the film, *Mr. Smith Goes to Washington*, presents an exaggerated picture of one senator tying up the work of the Senate. (*See § 6.211, Longest Senate Filibusters.*)

A contemporary approach to filibusters is the so-called "tag-team filibuster." A senator speaks for a period and then yields to another senator. When several senators participate in extended debate, it takes some time for the Senate to realize a filibuster is being conducted. Therefore, even the threat of a filibuster carries weight as the Senate attempts to schedule and consider legislation.

Debate is limited only when the Senate:

1. invokes cloture (*see § 6.230, Cloture in Senate Floor Proceedings*),
2. limits debate by unanimous consent or operates under a unanimous consent time agreement,
3. considers a motion to table, or
4. considers a measure governed by a rule-making statute. (Examples of rule-making statutes with built-in debate limitations include the Congressional Budget Act of 1974, and the 1974 Trade Act, which allows so-called *fast-track* procedures.)

Senate rules prohibit a senator from speaking more than twice on the same subject on the same legislative day. Because each amendment is considered a different subject, the so-called two-speech rule is not a practical limit on debate.

§ 6.220 Senate Amendment Procedure

Amendments to a measure in the Senate can be offered at practically any time during consideration of the measure, can be debated for an unlimited amount of time, and, in most situations, can deal with any subject, even if it is unrelated to the measure being amended.

When a measure is being considered on the floor of the Senate, committee amendments are considered first. The Senate often agrees by unanimous consent to committee amendments as a package, called *en bloc amendments*. By unanimous consent, the Senate might then provide that the measure, as amended by the committee amendments, be "considered as an original bill for the purpose of further amendment." This facilitates further amending on the floor by not taking up a branch on the *amendment tree*. (*See one amendment tree in § 6.122, Basic House Amendment Tree.*)

Amendments can be either printed or unprinted. *Printed amendments* are provided in advance of floor consideration of a measure and are printed in the *Congressional Record*. Although a sponsor usually calls up his own amendment, any senator can call up a printed amendment. *Unprinted amendments* are not available in advance and may be drafted on the floor while a measure is being considered.

Senate amendments do not usually need to be *germane*, that is, relevant to the measure. Nongermane amendments are often referred to as *riders*. Measures that contain numerous nongermane amendments have been called *Christmas-tree bills*. Germaneness, however, is necessary for general appropriations bills, bills on which cloture has been invoked, concurrent budget resolutions, and measures regulated by unanimous consent time agreements.

An amendment can also be classified as either *first degree* or *second degree*. A first-degree amendment would change the text of the measure under consideration; a second-degree amendment proposes to change the text of the first-degree amendment.

Both *perfecting amendments* and *substitute amendments* can be offered. Perfecting amendments change or modify language. Substitute amendments add new language as an alternative to the existing text. Perfecting amendments are considered second-degree amendments, and are always voted on before substitute amendments.

Separate *amendment trees* are possible based on the effect of the initial amendment offered. One tree is designed for *motions to strike and insert*, another for *insert*, and a third to *strike*. This complexity is rare in the Senate. Unanimous consent is more likely to be reached so that one amendment can be temporarily set aside to consider a different amendment.

Filling the amendment tree refers to the majority leader's use of his priority for recognition to offer amendments on each branch of an amendment tree. For the 112th Congress (2011–2013), an agreement was reached by party leaders to reduce the frequency of this practice.

A *motion to table* is frequently offered to avoid voting directly on an amendment. To "table" means to kill a provision. Any senator can make a nondebatable motion to table. Often, a senator announces that she intends to offer a motion to table an amendment but does not do so until debate

6

has occurred on the amendment. By agreeing to a motion to table, the Senate does not vote directly on an amendment, and thereby avoids having to vote against it.

§ 6.230 Cloture in Senate Floor Proceedings

A filibuster can be ended by negotiation among senators or by *invoking cloture*. Cloture is the only procedure by which the Senate can vote to set an end to debate without also rejecting the measure under consideration.

Invoking Cloture

Senate Rule XXII describes several stages to invoke cloture. To begin the process, at least sixteen senators sign a *cloture motion*, often referred to as a *cloture petition*. The motion is presented on the Senate floor, where the clerk reads it. The motion needs to "mature" or "ripen" before it can be considered. To do this, it lies over until the second calendar day on which the Senate is in session. For example, if a petition is filed on Monday, it ripens on Wednesday.

On the day the motion is ready for consideration, Senate rules require a vote on cloture one hour after the Senate convenes and after a quorum call establishes the presence of a quorum. However, the Senate can waive the quorum call or change the time by unanimous consent, and often does so. When the vote occurs, it generally requires three-fifths of the senators chosen and sworn; that is, sixty votes if there are no vacancies. (However, to invoke cloture on a motion to amend Senate rules, a two-thirds vote, or sixty-seven senators, is required.)

There are no limits to the number of cloture petitions that can be filed on any measure or amendment. Often, senators file petitions every day so that a vote occurs almost daily with the expectation that cloture will eventually be invoked. (*See § 6.231, Steps to Invoke Cloture.*)

Limitations Following Cloture

If cloture is invoked, certain limitations on how the Senate considers a measure are put into place. Generally, this period, often referred to as *post-cloture consideration*, operates under procedures different from normal Senate process. (*See § 6.232, Senate Procedures under Cloture.*)

Time Cap. The most important effect of invoking cloture is the cap of thirty hours of time for the Senate to continue consideration of a measure. The filibuster—one senator's or a group of senators' unfettered control of the floor—is over. Time for recorded votes, quorum calls, and points of order count in the cap, as does all debate time. Within the cap, each senator is guaranteed at least ten minutes to speak. No senator can speak for more than one hour, although time can be yielded to other senators.

Amendments. Once cloture is invoked, all amendments to be considered must have been submitted in writing during the time the Senate was in session before invoking cloture. First-degree amendments must be filed by 1:00 p.m. on the day the cloture motion is filed, and second-degree amendments must be filed at least one hour before a cloture vote begins. In addition, unlike normal amendment procedures, no amendment is in order unless it is germane to the matter on which cloture was invoked.

§ 6.231

Steps to Invoke Cloture

- Must be filed on a pending question
- At least sixteen senators must sign a cloture motion (also called "cloture petition")
- Amendments must be filed before the vote
- Vote on a motion occurs two days of session later
- Live quorum call precedes the vote and occurs one hour after the Senate convenes
- Vote immediately follows the quorum call
- Roll-call vote is automatic
- Affirmative vote by three-fifths of the senators chosen and sworn is required, except on a rules change, which requires two-thirds of the senators present

§ 6.232

Senate Procedures under Cloture

- Thirty-hour cap on post-cloture consideration
- One hour maximum for debate for each senator
- Amendments must have been submitted before the vote on the cloture motion
- Presiding officer may count for a quorum rather than conduct a quorum call
- No nongermane amendments
- No dilatory motions
- Points of order and appeals not debatable

Presiding Officer. The presiding officer has the authority to count to determine the presence of a quorum. The presiding officer may also make rulings without a point of order being raised. Finally, the presiding officer may rule out of order certain motions or quorum calls if she deems them dilatory. In contrast to regular procedures, no senator can suggest the absence of a quorum once cloture is invoked.

§ 6.240 Senate Floor: Motion to Reconsider and Final Passage

After passage of an amendment, measure, or motion, a senator *moves to reconsider the vote*. Approving this motion to reconsider allows the Senate an opportunity to review its decision and, essentially, revote. Therefore, once a proposition has been agreed to, a senator immediately moves to reconsider the vote, and another senator immediately moves to table the motion to reconsider. The motion to table effectively kills the motion to reconsider and makes the original vote final. Approval of the motion to table also blocks any future attempts to reverse the vote.

Only a senator who voted on the prevailing side or who did not vote at all on a proposition can offer a motion to reconsider. The motion is usually offered by the majority floor manager. The motion to table is made immediately after the motion to reconsider and is generally made by the minority floor manager. Usually, the motion to table is then routinely disposed of: "Without objection, the motion to table is agreed to."

The motion to reconsider can be made on the same day or within the next two days in which the Senate is in session.

When action is completed, a measure is ready for *engrossment and third reading*. Third reading is usually by title only. The measure is then ready for a vote on final passage.

§ 6.250 Voting in the Senate

Voting in the Senate is by *voice, division,* or *roll call.* On a voice vote, the presiding officer normally announces which side seems to have won based on how loudly they voted. More typically, the presiding officer states that "without objection the item is agreed to." This is a variation of a voice vote.

Division votes, often called standing votes, are rarely employed. If used, any senator may demand a division vote. Those senators in favor stand and the chair counts. Those opposed then stand and are counted. A division vote does not provide a record of how each senator voted.

Roll-call votes are known as *yea and nay votes* in the Senate. There is not an electronic voting device as there is in the House. Any senator can seek the yeas and nays. The presiding officer asks if there is a sufficient second. A sufficient second is one-fifth of a quorum—a minimum of eleven senators—which is an easy threshold to reach. Often, a senator receives support for the yeas and nays well in advance of the time the vote actually occurs. Thus, it is possible for debate on a proposition to be held and a request made for a vote. Yet, the vote does not occur until after debate has concluded, which may be minutes or hours after the request for the vote was made. A fifteen-minute period is the time allocated for yea and nay votes, although votes are often kept open beyond this time to accommodate senators trying to reach the floor. (*See § 9.60, Versions of Legislation.*)

§ 6.260 Reconciling Differences between House-Passed and Senate-Passed Legislation

Legislation must pass both chambers in identical form before it can be sent to the president for signature or veto. Differences between the two versions can be worked out either by *amendments between the houses* or by convening a *conference committee.* (*See § 6.261, Reconciling Differences Glossary.*)

After a measure has been passed by one house, an *engrossed version* is transmitted to the other chamber. When a measure is received in the second chamber, it is either ordered "held at the desk" or referred to the appropriate committee.

When the second chamber considers and passes the measure in identical form to that passed by the first chamber, the measure can be sent to the president without further consideration in either chamber.

If the second chamber, the recipient chamber, considers and passes the measure with changes, it returns it to the chamber of origin. The originating chamber has several options. It can accept the second chamber's amendment, it can accept the second chamber's amendment with a further amendment, or it can disagree with the other chamber's amendment and request a conference.

The second chamber can also request a conference immediately rather than returning the measure to the first chamber with an amendment. A chamber must possess the *papers* to request a conference. The papers are the *engrossed measure* (measure as passed by the first chamber), *engrossed amendments* (measure as passed by the second chamber), and *messages of transmittal* between the chambers.

§ 6.261

Reconciling Differences Glossary

Amendments between the Houses: Basic method for reconciling differences between two chambers' versions of a measure by passing the measure back and forth between them until both have agreed to identical language.

Amendments in Disagreement: Provisions in dispute between the two chambers.

Amendments in Technical Disagreement: Amendments agreed to in a conference but not included in the conference report because they may violate the rules of one of the houses and would open the conference report to a point of order.

Concur: Agree to amendment of the other house, either as is or with an amendment.

Conference Committee: Temporary joint committee of representatives and senators created to resolve differences between the chambers on a measure.

Conference Report: Document containing the conference committee's agreements and signed by a majority of conferees from each chamber.

Conferees: The representatives and senators from each chamber who serve on a conference committee; also referred to as managers.

Custody of the Papers: Custody of the engrossed measure and other documents that the two houses produce as they try to reconcile differences in their versions of a measure. (*See Papers*.)

Disagree: To reject an amendment of the other chamber.

Insist: Motion by one house to reiterate its previous position during amendments between the houses.

Instruct Conferees: Formal action by one chamber urging its conferees to uphold a particular position in conference.

Joint Explanatory Statement of Managers: Portion of the conference report providing the history, explanation, and intent of the conferees.

Managers: Representatives and senators serving on a conference committee; also called conferees.

Papers: Documents—including the engrossed measure, the amendments, the messages transmitting them, and the conference report—that are passed back and forth between the chambers.

Recede: Motion by one chamber to withdraw from its previous position during amendments between the houses.

Recede and Concur: Motion to withdraw from a position and agree with the other chamber's position.

Recede and Concur with an Amendment: Motion to withdraw from a position and agree, but with a further amendment.

Scope of Differences: Limits within which a conference committee is permitted to resolve the chambers' disagreement.

Stage of Disagreement: Stage when one house formally disagrees with an amendment proposed by the other house, and insists on its amendment. A measure generally cannot go to conference until this stage is reached.

A larger glossary is located at the back of the book and online at <*TCNLG.com*>.

6

§ 6.270 Amendments between the Houses

The House and Senate must approve identical versions of a measure before it can be sent to the president. This process begins with one house notifying the second house that it has passed a measure and transmitting to the second chamber the measure as passed (the *engrossed measure*). If the second house passes the measure with changes, the two houses can opt to either offer *amendments between the houses* or convene a conference committee to resolve differences.

When one chamber sends a measure, it is *messaged* to the other chamber. At this stage, several actions are possible. The second chamber can ultimately approve, or *concur*, in the first chamber's version. If that happens, the measure is cleared and sent to the president.

Or, the second chamber can ultimately pass the measure with one or more amendments, that is, *to concur with a further amendment*. If that happens, the measure is returned to the originating chamber with "an amendment to the measure."

The first chamber may accept the amendment. If that occurs, the amended measure is cleared and sent to the president. Alternatively, the first chamber may propose a further amendment.

This first option of resolving differences between the two houses—the process of amendments between the houses—allows two degrees of amendments. The amendment of the second chamber is considered text that is subject to amendment. Each chamber has one opportunity to propose an amendment to the amendment of the other chamber. The process is often conducted by informal negotiations between the members and staff of the committees of jurisdiction in the two houses. An extended exchange of amendments is rare.

At any point in the process, either house may choose not to act on the version sent by the other house. It may insist on its own position, and formally disagree with the version sent by the other house. If a chamber insists on its own position, it reaches a *stage of disagreement*. This allows the houses to proceed to the second option of resolving differences by convening a conference committee. (*See § 6.280, Conference Committees.*)

Amendments between the houses is an attempt to reconcile differences in lieu of a conference committee, or even after a conference if items are reported in *true disagreement* or *technical disagreement*. The process of amendments between the houses is most often used when a measure is not controversial, there are few differences between the two chambers' versions of a measure, or it is late in a session and there is insufficient time or will to convene a conference.

House Consideration of Senate Amendments

Assume a fictitious bill, H.R. 1111, is messaged to the Senate and then returned from the Senate with an amendment. Several scenarios are then possible. The House floor manager could ask unanimous consent to "concur" in the Senate amendment. If that option is selected, the House bill as amended by the Senate amendment is the version sent to the president. Alternatively, the House floor manager could ask unanimous consent to concur in the Senate amendment with a further amendment. If unanimous consent is granted, the House bill with the "House amendment to the Senate amendment to the House bill" is returned to the Senate. If objection is heard to either scenario, or is even anticipated, the House manager could seek to bring up the Senate amendment under suspension of the rules or under the terms of a special rule.

Senate Consideration of House Amendments

Assume a fictitious bill, S. 2222, is messaged to the House, which returns it to the Senate with a "House amendment to the Senate bill." The Senate can accept the House amendment by unanimous consent, that is, concur in the House amendment. The measure is then sent to the president. Alternatively, the Senate can concur in the House amendment with a further amendment.

Senate rules provide that a motion to proceed to consider a House amendment to a Senate measure is not debatable. However, if the Senate agrees to concur in the House amendment or to concur with a further Senate amendment to the House amendment, then the amendment itself is debatable. Therefore, the Senate normally disposes of House amendments by unanimous consent or agrees to proceed to conference.

§ 6.280 Conference Committees

Either chamber can request a conference once both houses have passed versions of a measure treating the same subject and using the same bill or resolution number but containing substantive differences. Generally, the chamber that first approved the legislation disagrees with the amendments made by the other chamber and requests that a conference be convened. Sometimes, however, the second chamber requests a conference immediately after it passes legislation, making the assumption that the other chamber will not accept its version.

A conference cannot be held until both chambers formally agree to convene one. The House generally requests a conference by unanimous consent, by motion, or by adoption of a special rule. The Senate usually agrees to a conference by unanimous consent or by motion.

Selection of Conferees

Although House rules grant the Speaker the right to appoint conferees, the Speaker usually does so after consultation with the chair(s) of the committee(s) of jurisdiction. The Senate presiding officer appoints Senate conferees, although the presiding officer, too, draws selections from recommendations of the chair of the committee of jurisdiction and party leaders. Conferees are also referred to as *managers*.

Although seniority on a committee of jurisdiction plays a role in selecting conferees, junior committee members are also appointed to conference committees. A member not on the committee of jurisdiction may be appointed if he had an important amendment included in the chamber's version of the measure or in the other chamber's version. In some instances, especially when a measure was considered by multiple committees, representatives or senators can be appointed as *limited-purpose conferees*. Precedents in both chambers indicate that conferees are supposed to support their chamber's legislation in conference.

The number of conferees can range from three to every member of a chamber. Generally, the size of a chamber delegation reflects the complexity of a measure. Moreover, the size of one chamber's delegation does not necessarily affect the size of the other chamber's delegation. Decisions are made by majority vote of *each delegation*, never by a majority vote of all the conferees. Each chamber appoints a majority of conferees to its delegation from the majority party. (*See § 6.281, Size of Conference Committees.*)

§ 6.281

Size of Conference Committees

The conference committee delegation on the 1981 Budget Reconciliation Act had 280 conferees—208 representatives and 72 senators. This is believed to be the largest conference committee ever assembled.

The smallest conference committee would have six members, three from the House and three from the Senate. That was the practice in early Congresses.

Instructing Conferees

Because a conference committee is a negotiating forum, there are few rules imposed on conferees. However, there are two circumstances under which House conferees may be given direction: first, before conferees are named, and second, when conferees have been appointed for twenty calendar days and ten legislative days and have not yet filed a report.

By custom, recognition to offer a *motion to instruct conferees*—a motion before the conferees are named—is a prerogative of the minority party. The motion is debatable for one hour. Only one motion to instruct conferees before their being named is in order.

For a motion to instruct conferees who have been appointed but have not yet reported, any member, regardless of party, can be recognized to make a motion to instruct, and numerous motions to instruct can be offered.

Motions to instruct House conferees are not binding but express the sentiment of the House on a particular issue in either the House or Senate version of a measure sent to conference.

Motions to instruct in the Senate are rarely made. If made, a motion to instruct is both debatable and amendable, and, as in the House, must be offered before conferees are named. Unlike the House, however, a motion to instruct is not available after conferees have been appointed but the conference committee has not yet reported.

Authority of Conferees

Conferees are expected to meet to reconcile differences between the competing versions of a bill. As such, they are generally limited to matters in disagreement between the versions. They cannot delete provisions that exist in both measures or add provisions not in either measure. However, when the second chamber has adopted a full-text substitute, the latitude in such matters has proven to be quite wide. In appropriations measures, it is often easier to determine the *scope* of differences between House and Senate versions because specific dollar amounts can often be used to determine scope. (*See § 6.282, Authority of Conferees.*)

Conference Committee Deliberations

Conference committees are bargaining sessions. As such, they are characterized by interchamber negotiations and trade-offs as each chamber's conferees try to fashion a compromise that will pass their chamber while upholding the basic position their chamber brought into conference.

There are no formal rules in conference. Staff negotiations are customary, often leaving only the most contentious issues to the members themselves. Decisions on how managers work through these issues are determined by the conferees themselves. All conferees may meet together to consider the two chambers' full alternatives. Conferees might agree to consider a measure in conference title by title and to close a title after it has been considered and reconciled. Conferees sometimes create subgroups or subconferences to consider specific issues in the measure in conference.

§ 6.282

Authority of Conferees

Provision in First Chamber's Measure	Provision in Second Chamber's Measure	Contents Permitted in Conference Report
No provision	No provision	No provision
Provision A	Provision A	Provision A
Provision A	No provision	Provision A or current law or a compromise position between Provision A and current law
Provision A	Provision B	Between Provision A and Provision B

§ 6.283

Authority of Conference Signature Sheet

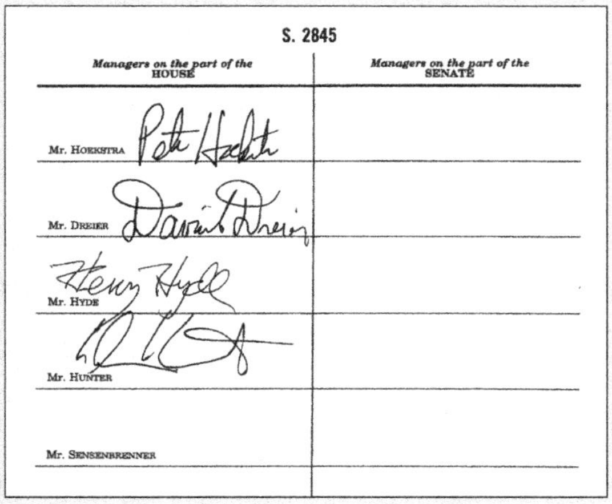
S. 2845

Managers on the part of the HOUSE	Managers on the part of the SENATE
Mr. Hoekstra	
Mr. Dreier	
Mr. Hyde	
Mr. Hunter	
Mr. Sensenbrenner	

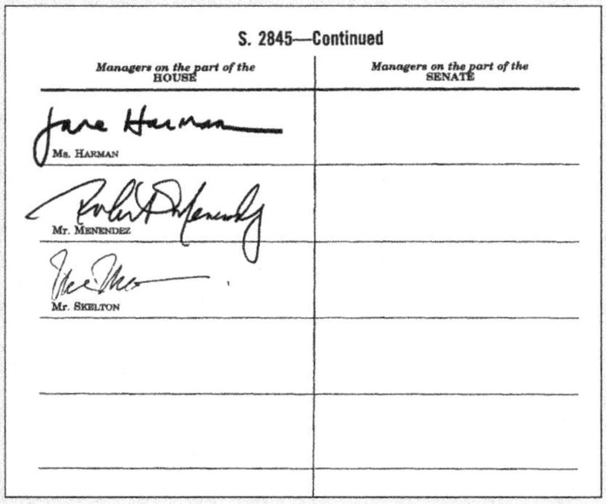
S. 2845—Continued

Managers on the part of the HOUSE	Managers on the part of the SENATE
Ms. Harman	
Mr. Menendez	
Mr. Skelton	

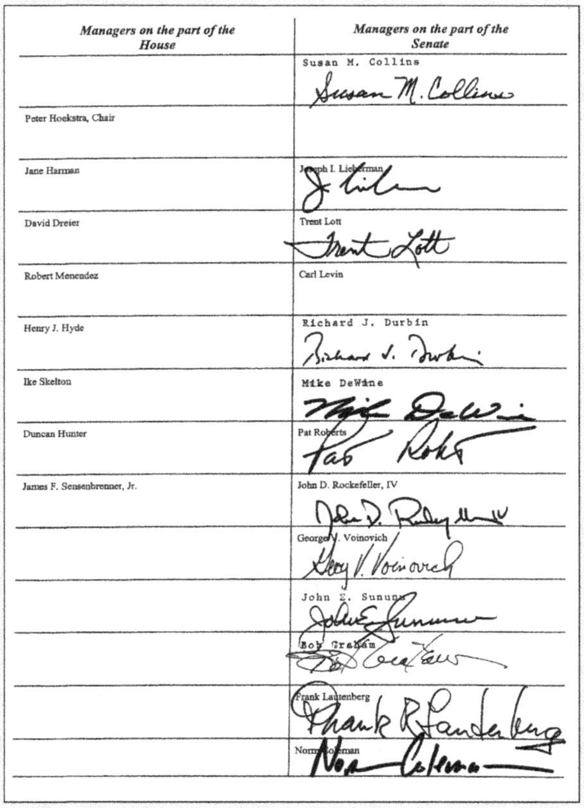

Managers on the part of the House	Managers on the part of the Senate
	Susan M. Collins
Peter Hoekstra, Chair	
Jane Harman	Joseph I. Lieberman
David Dreier	Trent Lott
Robert Menendez	Carl Levin
Henry J. Hyde	Richard J. Durbin
Ike Skelton	Mike DeWine
Duncan Hunter	Pat Roberts
James F. Sensenbrenner, Jr.	John D. Rockefeller, IV
	George V. Voinovich
	John E. Sununu
	Bob Graham
	Frank Lautenberg
	Norm Coleman

There is one restriction placed on House managers. The House in the 110th Congress agreed to new chamber rules that House conferees should "endeavor to ensure" that conference meetings occur only if notice is provided and House managers are given the opportunity to attend.

Conference chairs are determined informally; however, when committees conference regularly, the chair normally rotates between the chambers.

When agreement is reached, a majority of each chamber's conference delegation must agree to the *conference report*. No vote is taken seeking a majority of all conferees. The agreement is formally indicated by signing the report. (*See § 6.283, Authority of Conference Signature Sheet.*)

Conference Report and Joint Explanatory Statement

The conference report and joint explanatory statement are two distinct documents. The conference report contains a formal statement of the procedural actions the conferees took and the formal legislative language the conferees propose. The joint explanatory statement is a more readable document. It identifies the major matters in disagreement, and then summarizes each chamber's position and the conferees' recommendations. The joint explanatory statement also often contains an explanation of the conferees' intent. Two copies of each document must be signed by a majority of the House conferees and a majority of the Senate conferees.

The documents are printed in the House portion of the *Congressional Record*, and are also printed together as a single House committee report. Although Senate rules require printing as a Senate document as well, the Senate usually waives this requirement.

Consideration of Conference Report

The chamber that agrees to a request for a conference is normally the chamber that considers the conference report first. That chamber can agree to, or disagree with, a conference report, or it can agree to a motion to recommit a conference report to conference. However, after one chamber has acted on a conference report, its conferees are discharged, and the second chamber may only accept or reject the conference report.

Consideration on House Floor. House rules provide that a conference report cannot be called up for consideration until the third calendar day (excluding Saturday, Sunday, or holidays, unless the House is in session) after the conference documents have been filed. Furthermore, copies of the conference report and joint explanatory statement must be available at least two hours before the chamber begins consideration. Both requirements can be waived by unanimous consent or by adoption of a special rule from the Rules Committee containing a waiver of the requirements.

Conference reports are privileged and can be brought up when available. They are considered under the one-hour rule. Occasionally, conference reports are brought to the floor by a special rule or under suspension of the rules.

Consideration on Senate Floor. When available, a conference report can be called up. A conference report is debatable under normal Senate rules and procedures. A motion to proceed to consider a conference report, however, is not debatable. A conference report can also be considered under the provisions of a time agreement.

§ 6.290 Presidential Action on Enacted Measures

When a measure has been approved by both chambers, the original papers are provided to the *enrolling clerk* of the chamber that originated the legislation. The enrolling clerk prepares an *enrolled version* of the measure—essentially, the measure printed on parchment. (In infrequent circumstances, Congress may submit to the president a *hand-enrolled measure*, one in draft form and not printed on parchment.) This enrolled measure is then certified by the clerk of the House or the secretary of the Senate, depending on the house in which the measure originated, and signed—first by the Speaker of the House and then by the president pro tempore of the Senate.

The enrolled measure is subsequently sent to the White House, although transmittal can occur any time from a few hours to several weeks after an enrolling clerk has been provided with the original papers. At the White House, the Office of the Executive Clerk logs the receipt of the enrolled measure. (*Information on the status of presidential receipt and action on measures is available from the Executive Clerk's Office, 202-456-2226.*)

Within ten days, not counting Sundays, the president must act on the legislation. Counting begins at midnight of the day he receives the enrolled measure. If the president wishes to approve the measure, he signs it, dates it, and writes "Approved" on it, although the Constitution requires only his signature.

6

Signing ceremonies for major pieces of legislation are often held on the White House lawn, in the Rose Garden, or in a place related to or signified by the legislation. Presidential pens are given to selected people at the ceremony, with the president using several pens to sign and date the document—essentially one pen for each letter or number, to accommodate all those wanting a pen used to sign the measure.

Contemporary presidents have often issued *signing statements* when they signed a measure into law. These statements are often congratulatory toward Congress and the president for having enacted a new law that the president believes will benefit the American people. However, they have in the last three decades become an additional source of information on the president's attitude toward a new law, perhaps expanding on views expressed in statements of administration policy issued during floor and conference consideration of legislation. (*See § 8.20, Congress and the Executive: Legislation.*) Although a president will not have vetoed a measure passed by Congress, he might nonetheless have reservations about provisions in the measure. He may then use a signing statement to explain his reservations and indicate how he will deal with them. A president might indicate that he will seek new legislation from Congress to overcome perceived problems, that implementation of certain provisions will occur pursuant to a certain interpretation of those provisions, or that certain provisions will be carried out consistent with the president's perceived constitutional prerogatives. (*See § 6.291, Signing Statement.*)

A signing statement does not amend or nullify a provision of a law—only Congress and the president together may do that. It may show how the president will use his constitutional duty to execute a law. If the president's interpretation offends Congress, Congress through oversight, appropriations, or new legislation may seek to redirect the president. If the president's interpretation is challenged

§ 6.291

Signing Statement

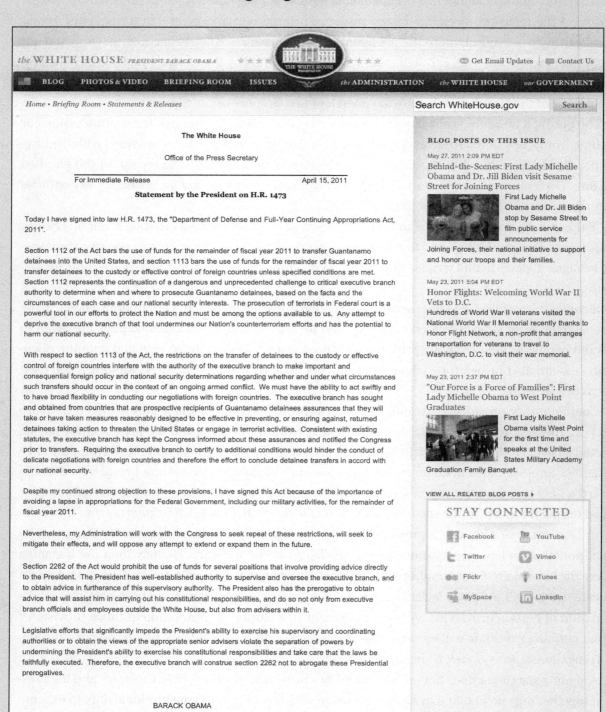

The White House

Office of the Press Secretary

For Immediate Release April 15, 2011

Statement by the President on H.R. 1473

Today I have signed into law H.R. 1473, the "Department of Defense and Full-Year Continuing Appropriations Act, 2011".

Section 1112 of the Act bars the use of funds for the remainder of fiscal year 2011 to transfer Guantanamo detainees into the United States, and section 1113 bars the use of funds for the remainder of fiscal year 2011 to transfer detainees to the custody or effective control of foreign countries unless specified conditions are met. Section 1112 represents the continuation of a dangerous and unprecedented challenge to critical executive branch authority to determine when and where to prosecute Guantanamo detainees, based on the facts and the circumstances of each case and our national security interests. The prosecution of terrorists in Federal court is a powerful tool in our efforts to protect the Nation and must be among the options available to us. Any attempt to deprive the executive branch of that tool undermines our Nation's counterterrorism efforts and has the potential to harm our national security.

With respect to section 1113 of the Act, the restrictions on the transfer of detainees to the custody or effective control of foreign countries interfere with the authority of the executive branch to make important and consequential foreign policy and national security determinations regarding whether and under what circumstances such transfers should occur in the context of an ongoing armed conflict. We must have the ability to act swiftly and to have broad flexibility in conducting our negotiations with foreign countries. The executive branch has sought and obtained from countries that are prospective recipients of Guantanamo detainees assurances that they will take or have taken measures reasonably designed to be effective in preventing, or ensuring against, returned detainees taking action to threaten the United States or engage in terrorist activities. Consistent with existing statutes, the executive branch has kept the Congress informed about these assurances and notified the Congress prior to transfers. Requiring the executive branch to certify to additional conditions would hinder the conduct of delicate negotiations with foreign countries and therefore the effort to conclude detainee transfers in accord with our national security.

Despite my continued strong objection to these provisions, I have signed this Act because of the importance of avoiding a lapse in appropriations for the Federal Government, including our military activities, for the remainder of fiscal year 2011.

Nevertheless, my Administration will work with the Congress to seek repeal of these restrictions, will seek to mitigate their effects, and will oppose any attempt to extend or expand them in the future.

Section 2262 of the Act would prohibit the use of funds for several positions that involve providing advice directly to the President. The President has well-established authority to supervise and oversee the executive branch, and to obtain advice in furtherance of this supervisory authority. The President also has the prerogative to obtain advice that will assist him in carrying out his constitutional responsibilities, and do so not only from executive branch officials and employees outside the White House, but also from advisers within it.

Legislative efforts that significantly impede the President's ability to exercise his supervisory and coordinating authorities or to obtain the views of the appropriate senior advisers violate the separation of powers by undermining the President's ability to exercise his constitutional responsibilities and take care that the laws be faithfully executed. Therefore, the executive branch will construe section 2262 not to abrogate these Presidential prerogatives.

BARACK OBAMA

THE WHITE HOUSE
April 15, 2011

§ 6.292

Vetoes and Veto Overrides: Presidential Clout

(as of May 2, 2011)

Of the 1,460 vetoes exercised by President Washington through President George W. Bush, only 108 were overridden by Congress. In addition, presidents pocket-vetoed another 1,066 measures enacted by Congress, for which Congress had no recourse.

The record for contemporary presidents follows:

President	Regular Vetoes	Regular Vetoes Overridden	Pocket Vetoes
Carter (1977–1981)	13	2	18
Reagan (1981–1989)	39	9	39
Bush, G.H.W. (1989–1993)	29	1	15
Clinton (1993–2001)	36	2	1
Bush, G.W. (2001–2009)	11	4	0
Obama (2009–)	2	0	0

Through the end of his term, President Clinton vetoed thirty-six measures and returned the vetoed measures to Congress. No override attempt was made on twenty-three of his vetoes. On seven occasions, the House voted first and sustained his veto. On three occasions, the House overrode a veto only to have the Senate sustain the veto twice and not attempt an override the third time. On one occasion, the Senate voted first and sustained President Clinton's veto. On the two remaining occasions, the House voted to override the president's veto, and the Senate followed suit.

Through the end of his term in 2009, President George W. Bush vetoed eleven bills. No override attempt was made of two vetoes, one of which President Bush argued was a pocket veto but the House treated as a regular veto. The House failed in its attempt to override five vetoes, but the House and Senate successfully overrode four vetoes.

Through his first term, President Barack Obama vetoed two bills, and seemed to argue that they were pocket vetoes. The House failed to override both vetoes.

For the number of recent presidential vetoes and other summary numbers, see <*CongressByTheNumbers.com*>.

in court, courts have generally looked to the law and its textual development in Congress in their decision-making. *(See § 8.73, Legislative History.)*

If the president does not want to approve the legislation, he may *veto* it. He does this by returning the measure without his signature, but including his objections in writing, called a *veto message.* If Congress, or one chamber of Congress, takes no action on a veto, the measure dies. Neither chamber must take action.

Alternately, Congress can attempt to override a veto and enact the bill "the objections of the president to the contrary notwithstanding." A two-thirds vote of those present and voting is required in each chamber to override a veto. The vote must be by roll call. Once the first chamber successfully overrides a veto, the measure is sent to the second house. The second house does not have to attempt a veto override. However, if a veto override in the second house is attempted and is successful, the measure becomes law. Procedures in each chamber allow debate and motions to table, postpone action, or refer a veto message to committee.

Under the Constitution, a measure may become law without the president's signature if the president does not sign it within ten days, not counting Sundays, provided Congress is in session. Why might a president choose this course of action? President George H. W. Bush allowed two measures to become law without his signature. In both cases he cited his agreement with the legislation's goals, but he also in both cases expressed his belief that the laws would be found to be unconstitutional violations of First Amendment rights in any court challenges. The two measures that became law were the Children's Television Act of 1990 (*P.L. 101-385*) and the Flag Protection Act of 1989 (*P.L. 101-131*).

If Congress is not in session, a measure not signed does not become law. Such measures are considered to be *pocket-vetoed*. Current understanding of the pocket veto allows the practice after Congress has adjourned *sine die*. Pocket vetoes at other times have been challenged in both Congress and the courts. (*See § 6.292, Vetoes and Veto Overrides: Presidential Clout.*)

§ 6.300 Publication of Public Laws

Once the president has signed a measure into law, the president has not signed it within the constitutional ten days, or Congress has passed it over his veto, the measure is transmitted to the National Archives and Records Administration (NARA) and within NARA to the Office of the Federal Register (OFR). At OFR, the measure is assigned a sequential public-law number, such as P.L. 112-2, which would indicate that the law was enacted in the 112th Congress and that it was the second public law of that Congress. (*Public-law numbers are announced in the Congressional Record, Federal Register, and other print and electronic resources, including the NARA web site at <www.archives.gov/federal-register/laws/current.html>; they are also available by phone at 202-741-6043.*)

The law is first published in *slip form*, essentially a pamphlet form similar to that of other congressional documents, and is referred to as a *slip law*. (*Slip laws are available from the House Legislative Resource Center, the Senate Document Room, the Government Printing Office, and other print and electronic resources.*)

OFR also assigns each new public law a *Statutes at Large* page citation. Each new public law is added sequentially to the Statutes at Large. Once a slip law is out-of-print, it is easy to find provisions of a specific public law by using its statutory cite.

Finally, the House's Office of Law Revision Counsel organizes the parts of a new public law in the *U.S. Code*. Unlike the organization scheme of the Statutes at Large—sequential—the U.S. Code organizes all laws by subject matter, and the user can readily understand what is current law. Other print and electronic resources also provide U.S. Code reporting. (*Additional information and samples of the Statutes at Large and U.S. Code are found in § 9.70, Laws and Their Codification.*)

§ 6.310 Chapter Summary and Discussion Questions

Summary

- An understanding of the rules and procedures of the House and Senate can have a significant impact on legislative success, whether a member is employing the rules to advance or impede legislation or a policy advocate is attempting to influence the outcome of legislative activity.
- Members may introduce one of four types of legislation: bills, joint resolutions, concurrent resolutions, or simple resolutions. Only bills and joint resolutions may be used to make law. Many considerations go into the introduction of legislation: drafting to receive a favorable referral, types and numbers of cosponsors, timing of introduction, legislative and media actions preceding introduction, and so on.
- The committee system is at the heart of the consideration of legislation. Each committee has jurisdiction over subject matter identified in House or Senate rules. Legislation is referred to committees based on their jurisdiction and the subject-matter coverage of the bill or resolution.
- Hearings by a committee or one of its subcommittees might precede or follow the introduction of legislation. While a variety of views might be provided at a hearing, a chair usually selects witnesses who support the policy the chair supports.
- Committee chairs tend to select a very limited number of subjects on which to move to the next step—the markup of a piece of legislation, that is, debate and consideration of amendments. Once markup is completed, a committee votes whether to report the marked-up measure to its parent chamber. House committees nearly always file a written report with the House. Senate committees may file a written report, but it is not required by Senate rules.
- Whereas committees are at the heart of the legislative process, action on the House or Senate floor is often the most visible aspect of the legislative process. The majority leadership in each chamber is responsible for scheduling floor activities, including the consideration of legislation. The crux of floor action on legislation is determined by the methods of consideration most commonly used in each chamber: unanimous consent in the Senate, and suspension of the rules and special rules in the House.
- Because Senate rules do not generally limit debate or the amendment process, including the germaneness or relevancy of amendments, the Senate most often accomplishes its consideration of legislation by unanimous consent to one or more ad hoc agreements governing procedures for amending and voting on a measure. If it cannot reach unanimous consent, the majority leader might file a cloture petition, which begins a multiday process that is successful if sixty senators vote to invoke cloture. Since Senate rules protect individual senators' rights and minority points of view, it is difficult for the Senate to move ahead without some degree of consensus on the legislation to be considered and the manner of doing so.
- The House is a majoritarian institution with the opposite problem: stopping the majority from running roughshod over the minority since a cohesive majority can accomplish nearly anything at any time in the House. The House uses its suspension of the rules procedure, limiting debate and disallowing amendments, to consider largely noncontroversial legislation, which is indicated by the requirement of a two-thirds vote for passage of a measure so considered. Controversial

6

or complex legislation is normally considered pursuant to a special rule. First, the House votes on a special rule reported by its Rules Committee that establishes the parameters of floor consideration for a measure: time for debate, amendments allowed, motions disallowed, and so on. If the House adopts the special rule, it then considers the legislation named in the special rule pursuant to the special rule's terms, ultimately voting on final passage. During the consideration of amendments, the majority floor manager leads the effort to defeat amendments his party perceives to be hostile.

- Once the two chambers have acted, any differences in the measures passed by the two houses must be reconciled. One chamber sometimes passes a measure as passed by the first chamber. That measure can then be sent to the president for his signature or veto. If there are differences, the houses might choose to try to reach agreement on the legislative text by passing amendments between the houses. Once both chambers have voted for the same text, the measure may be sent to the president. The two houses might also conclude that a conference committee—members appointed from each chamber—might best be able to reconcile differences. Once they have reached agreement and each chamber has voted to approve the agreement, the measure may be sent to the president.
- Under the Constitution, the president has ten days to act (Sundays excluded). The president may sign or veto a measure. If he signs it, it becomes public law. (A president may also let a measure become law without his signature, but presidents rarely opt for this choice.) If he vetoes it, he returns it to the house that originated the measure. Both houses must vote by two-thirds to override a presidential veto for a vetoed measure to become law. If Congress is not in session when the president vetoes a measure, he is said to have pocket-vetoed it since Congress is not available to receive his veto.

Discussion Questions

- If you were a staff assistant to a member of Congress who wanted to introduce legislation on a subject—you pick the subject the member is interested in—what are all of the considerations inside and outside of Congress on which you would offer advice to the member? How would your advice differ if the member served in the House or in the Senate? In this instance, you want to push legislation forward through the legislative process to enactment.
- House Rule X and Senate Rule XXV are integral to the referral of legislation. Why are they so important?
- If you were a staff assistant to a committee chair who wanted to hold hearings on a controversial subject, what options could you present to the chair on the hearings: for example, whether to hold them before or after legislation is introduced, or both, and when to hold them? What other options would you address? Does it matter that the hearing is held by a House or Senate committee? In this instance, you want to help the chair generate momentum behind legislative action on the subject matter.
- Re-read the section of this chapter dealing with committee rules affecting hearings, and then go to the House or Senate web site and read a specific committee's rules on the calling and conduct of hearings. What did you learn about hearings procedures for that committee,

such as the role of the ranking minority member or the ability of committee staff to ask questions of the witnesses?

- When a committee marks up a bill or resolution, members offer amendments, which are debated and voted on. Think about an amendment that a member of Congress wishes to offer that could lose on a vote in committee. What advantages and disadvantages could you present to the member on whether to offer the amendment in committee, on the floor, or both? Are the advantages and disadvantages different in the House and the Senate? Does it matter whether the member is part of the chamber's majority or minority party?
- What information can be found in committee reports?
- What is the importance of the House Rules Committee? How does its jurisdiction and role affect consideration of a measure on the House floor? How does a special rule in the House compare to a unanimous consent time agreement in the Senate?
- What is the Committee of the Whole and why does the House employ it?
- What options can you identify in each chamber for bringing measures to the floor and considering the measures? Under what circumstances might the majority leadership choose from among these options?
- Lay out a time line for the filing and consideration of a cloture petition and for the conduct of post-cloture consideration of a measure, assuming cloture had been invoked. What deadlines and limitations exist within this time line, such as the deadlines pertaining to the filing of amendments?
- What are the two methods of reconciling differences between the House and Senate versions of a measure? When might either be used or both be used? What legislative documents result from these processes?

Chapter Seven

Legislating in Congress: Federal Budget Process

Contributing Author

Bill Heniff Jr.

with update by

Robert Keith

Analysis

§ 7.00 Introduction: Congress' "Power of the Purse"

Congress is distinguished from nearly every other legislature in the world by the control it exercises over fashioning the government's budgetary policies. This power, referred to as "the power of the purse," ensures Congress' primary role in setting revenue and borrowing policies for the federal government and in determining how these resources are spent.

The congressional power of the purse derives from several key provisions in the Constitution. (*See § 7.01, Congress' Constitutional "Power of the Purse."*) Article I, Section 8, Clause 1 declares in part that Congress shall have the power to raise (that is, "to lay and collect") revenues of various types, including taxes and duties, among other things. Section 8, Clause 2 declares that the power to borrow funds "on the credit of the United States" belongs to Congress. In addition to its powers regarding revenues and borrowing, Congress exerts control over the expenditure of funds. Article I, Section 9, Clause 7 declares in part that funds can be withdrawn from the Treasury only pursuant to laws that make appropriations.

> **§ 7.01**
>
> **Congress' Constitutional "Power of the Purse"**
>
> **Revenues and Borrowing**
>
> The Congress shall have the Power
>
> 1 To lay and collect Taxes, Duties, Imposts, and Excises . . .
>
> 2 To borrow Money on the credit of the United States . . .
>
> (*Art. I, sec. 8.*)
>
> **Spending**
>
> No Money shall be drawn from the Treasury, but in Consequence of Appropriations made by Law . . .
>
> (*Art. I, sec. 9, cl. 7.*)

Under the Constitution, revenue measures must originate in the House of Representatives. Beyond this requirement, however, the Constitution does not prescribe how the House and Senate should organize themselves, or the procedures they should use, to conduct budgeting. Over the years, however, both chambers have developed an extensive set of rules (some set forth in statute) and precedents that lay out complicated, multiple processes for making budgetary decisions. The House and Senate have also created an intricate committee system to support these processes. (*See § 7.02, Federal Budgeting Concepts and Terminology.*)

As American society has grown and become ever more complex, and as the role of the federal government in the national economy has steadily expanded, Congress also has increasingly shared power over budgetary matters with the president and the executive branch. It has refashioned the president's role in budgeting by requiring him to submit to Congress each year a budget for the entire federal government and giving him responsibilities for monitoring agencies' implementation of spending and revenue laws. Accordingly, the president also exercises considerable influence over key budget decisions.

§ 7.02

Federal Budgeting Concepts and Terminology

Federal budgeting involves a complex web of legislative and executive procedures, categories of budgetary legislation, and types of financial transactions. Some concepts and terms fundamental to understanding federal budgeting include those that follow.

Revenues

Income received by the federal government is referred to as *revenues* or *receipts.* (Congress tends to use the former term and the executive branch tends to use the latter.) Revenues are raised from several different sources. In recent decades, revenues have stemmed mainly from individual income taxes, social insurance taxes, corporate income taxes, and excise taxes. Revenues also are raised by tariffs, fees, fines, gifts and bequests, and other means.

A *tax expenditure* is revenue forgone due to an exemption, deduction, or other exception to an underlying tax law. A tax expenditure represents a means of pursuing federal policy that is an alternative to a spending program. For example, home ownership is encouraged by allowing deductions from individual income taxes for mortgage interest paid during the year; the same goal could be promoted on the spending side of the budget by issuing grants or loans for home ownership to individuals.

Spending

When Congress enacts legislation providing legal authority for an agency to spend money, it provides *budget authority*. The most well-known type of legislation that provides budget authority is an annual appropriations act. Budget authority authorizes agencies to enter into *obligations*. An obligation is any type of action that creates a financial liability on the part of the federal government, such as entering into a contract, submitting a purchase order for goods, or employing personnel. When the obligation is liquidated, an outlay ensues. *Outlays* represent the actual payment of obligations, and usually take the form of electronic fund transfers, the issuance of checks, or the disbursement of cash. The stages of spending involving the enactment of budget authority and the incurring of obligations and outlays are referred to informally as the "spending pipeline."

The rate at which funds are spent (that is, converted from budget authority into outlays) is known as the *spendout rate*. Spendout rates vary from account to account, and from program to program within accounts. An account that involves personnel-intensive activities may have a high spendout rate, obligating and expending 90 percent or more of its budget authority during the fiscal year. Conversely, an account that involves the procurement of major weapons systems may have a low spendout rate, with only 5 or 10 percent of its budget authority being disbursed, or converted to outlays, in the first year.

Congress exercises direct control over the enactment of budget authority, but its influence over obligations—and, to a greater degree, outlays—is indirect. Ultimately, federal agencies determine the outlay levels for a particular year through thousands of discrete actions.

Some income to the federal government is not treated as revenue. Rather, it is offset against spending. *Offsetting collections and receipts* arise from fees collected by the federal government for its business-type operations, from the sale of assets, and from other sources. Most such receipts are offsets against the outlays of the agencies that collect the money, but in the case of offshore oil leases and certain other activities, the revenues are deducted from the total outlays of the federal government.

Surplus and Deficit

The relationship between spending and revenues is reflected in the surplus or deficit figure. A *surplus* is an excess of revenues over outlays, while a *deficit* is an excess of outlays over revenues. Congress

Continued on page 305

§ 7.02 (continued)

controls the enactment of legislation providing budget authority and raising revenues, but not the occurrence of outlays. Because of this, Congress' efforts to control the level of the surplus or the deficit are less effective over the short run compared to the long run.

Baseline Budgeting

Congress and the president employ baseline budgeting as a tool to analyze the context in which budget policy choices are made and to assess the impact of particular proposals. In the simplest terms, a *baseline* is a set of projections of future spending and revenues, and the resulting surplus or deficit, based on assumptions about the state of the economy and the continuation of current policies without change. Overall revenue and spending levels usually increase from year to year under the baseline because of demographic trends, workload changes, and other factors. Following the late-2000s recession, however, baseline projections showed declining revenues due to the economic recession.

The Office of Management and Budget develops a budget baseline, referred to as the *current services estimates*, to support the president's budget, while the Congressional Budget Office develops its own baseline, referred to as *baseline budget projections,* to aid the congressional budget process. Although, for the most part, the two agencies share a common approach to constructing budget baselines, differences in aggregate projections and estimates for particular accounts and programs are inevitable. Sometimes the differences may be significant enough to complicate the process of resolving policy differences.

The national economy can exert a significant influence on the federal budget. If projections about economic growth, unemployment levels, inflation, and other economic factors prove to be significantly inaccurate, projected budgetary levels may change by billions of dollars during the course of a year. For this reason, the economic assumptions that underlie the budget baseline are crucially important. Congress and the president usually require that economic assumptions be revised only once or twice a year, to avoid complicating the decisionmaking process.

Statutory Limit on the Debt

When the federal government needs to borrow funds, it issues debt to the public. In addition, the federal government is compelled to incur debt because of requirements that trust fund surpluses be invested in federal securities. As a consequence, the federal government owes debt to the public and to itself. As a general matter, the amount of money that the federal government is able to borrow is constrained by a limit in statute. As long as the federal government incurs annual deficits and trust funds incur annual surpluses, Congress and the president from time to time must enact legislation to raise the statutory limit on the debt.

Federal Funds and Trust Funds

The budget consists of two main groups of funds: *federal funds* and *trust funds*. Federal funds—which comprise mainly the general fund—largely derive from the general exercise of the taxing power and general borrowing. For the most part, they are not earmarked by law to any specific program or agency. One component of federal funds, called *special funds*, is earmarked according to source and purpose. The use of federal funds is determined largely by annual appropriations acts.

Trust funds are established, under the terms of statutes that designate them as trust funds, to account for funds earmarked by specific sources and purposes. The Social Security trust funds (the Old-Age and Survivors Insurance Fund and the Disability Insurance Fund) are the largest of the trust funds; revenues are collected under a Social Security payroll tax and are used to pay for Social Security benefits and related purposes. The use of trust funds is controlled primarily by entitlement laws and other substantive legislation.

Continued on page 306

7

§ 7.02 (continued)

The total budget includes both the federal funds and the trust funds. The merging together of federal funds and trust funds into a single budget sometimes is referred to as the "unified budget approach."

On-Budget and Off-Budget Entities

On-budget entities are federal agencies and programs that are fully reflected in the totals of the president's budget and the congressional budget resolution. *Off-budget entities*, on the other hand, specifically are excluded by law from these totals. The revenues and spending of the Social Security trust funds, as well as the financial transactions of the Postal Service Fund, are at present the only off-budget entities. These transactions are shown separately in the budget. Thus, the budget reports two deficit or surplus amounts—one excluding the Social Security trust funds and the Postal Service Fund and the other including these entities.

Further, off-budget entities are excluded from the budget enforcement procedures applicable to federal programs generally. Congress has established special procedures for the consideration of measures affecting Social Security revenues and spending.

§ 7.10 Key Budget Process Laws

Many different statutes lay the foundation for the modern budget process used by the federal government, but five laws are key: the Budget and Accounting Act of 1921, the Congressional Budget and Impoundment Control Act of 1974, the Balanced Budget and Emergency Deficit Control Act of 1985, the Statutory PAYGO Act of 2010, and the Budget Control Act of 2011. Each of the first four laws has been amended, some on numerous occasions.

Except for the 1921 act, these laws also contain provisions that set forth significant congressional budget procedures. The provisions dealing with congressional procedure were enacted as an exercise of Congress' *rule-making authority*, and effectively serve as rules of the House and Senate. As such, either chamber may modify the provisions that affect its operations without the concurrence of the other chamber and without the enactment of a law.

Budget and Accounting Act of 1921

The Budget and Accounting Act of 1921 (*P.L. 13, 67th Congress; 42 Stat. 20–27*) required for the first time that the president submit to Congress each year a *budget* for the entire federal government. The president is free to submit the budget in the form and detail he deems appropriate, but certain information is required. In addition, the estimates of the legislative and judicial branches must be incorporated in his budget, as submitted by those branches, without change. (*See § 7.40, Presidential Budget Process.*)

The 1921 Budget and Accounting Act also established the Bureau of the Budget, now called the Office of Management and Budget (OMB) and headed by a director subject to Senate confirmation, to assist the president in formulating the budget, in presenting it to Congress, and in monitoring the execution of the enacted budget by agencies. In addition, the 1921 act established the General Accounting Office, later renamed the Government Accountability Office, a congressional agency,

§7.11

Budget Enforcement Act Procedures: 1990–2002

Between 1990 and 2002, Congress and the president were constrained by *statutory* limits on discretionary spending and a pay-as-you-go (PAYGO) requirement on new direct spending and revenue legislation established by the Budget Enforcement Act of 1990 and extended by other laws. These mechanisms supplemented the enforcement procedures associated with the annual budget resolution under the 1974 Congressional Budget Act. However, while the budget resolution is enforced by points of order when legislation is considered on the floor of each chamber, the discretionary-spending limits and PAYGO requirement were enforced by a sequestration process after legislative action for a session of Congress ended. Under the sequestration process, if legislative action was determined to violate the budget constraints, the president was required to issue a sequestration order canceling budgetary resources, on a largely across-the-board basis, in non-exempt programs in the category in which the violation occurred.

Initially, these budget enforcement controls applied to FY1991–1995. In 1993, they were modified and extended through FY1998. Finally, the controls were extended again in 1997 to apply to legislation enacted through FY2002 (and, in the case of PAYGO, to the effects of such legislation through FY2006). In each case, the controls were designed to enforce multiyear budget agreements between Congress and the president. Without any legislative action by Congress and the president to extend them, the discretionary spending limits expired on September 30, 2002 (the end of FY2002), and PAYGO effectively was terminated in December of that year by the enactment of P.L. 107-312. (*See § 7.50, Congressional Budget Process, Points of Order.*)

Beginning in 2002, some members of Congress, as well as President George W. Bush, proposed restoring and modifying these budget enforcement procedures. In 2010, a statutory PAYGO process was reinstituted based largely on a proposal submitted by President Obama in the previous year (*see § 7.12, Statutory PAYGO Act of 2010*). Statutory limits on discretionary spending for FY2012–2021 were imposed by the Budget Control Act of 2012.

7

headed by the *comptroller general*, to audit and evaluate federal programs and perform other budgetary duties. (*See § 4.130, Legislative-Branch Support Agencies.*)

Congressional Budget and Impoundment Control Act of 1974

The 1974 Congressional Budget and Impoundment Control Act (*P.L. 93-344; 88 Stat. 297–339*) requires the House and Senate each year to adopt a *concurrent resolution on the budget*, which serves as a guide for the subsequent consideration of spending, revenue, and debt-limit legislation. (*See § 7.50, Congressional Budget Process.*) The 1974 act created the House and Senate Budget Committees to develop the budget resolution and monitor compliance with its policies, and the Congressional Budget Office to serve as an independent, nonpartisan agency to provide budgetary information and analysis for Congress. (*See § 4.130, Legislative-Branch Support Agencies.*) New procedures were established for congressional review of *impoundments* by the president; the comptroller general was given an oversight role in this process. (*See § 7.150, Impoundment: Deferrals and Rescissions.*)

Balanced Budget and Emergency Deficit Control Act of 1985

To strengthen control over spending and *deficit* levels, and to promote more efficient legislative action on budgetary issues, Congress and the president enacted the Balanced Budget and Emergency Deficit Control Act of 1985 (*P.L. 99-177, title II; 99 Stat. 1038–1101*). At the time, the measure was commonly known as the Gramm-Rudman-Hollings Act, after its three primary sponsors in the Senate (then-Senators Phil Gramm, R-TX, Warren Rudman, R-NH, and Ernest Hollings, D-SC).

The 1985 Balanced Budget Act sought to drive the deficit downward, from nearly $200 billion in fiscal year (FY) 1986 to zero in FY1991. *Sequestration*, a process involving largely automatic across-the-board spending cuts made toward the beginning of a fiscal year, was established as the means of enforcing deficit targets. The sequestration process was designed to trigger automatically if the deficit exceeded prescribed levels, as determined by a report issued by the comptroller general.

The 1985 act was revised in 1987 to meet a constitutional challenge and to modify the timetable for achieving a balanced budget (*P.L. 100-119, 101 Stat. 754*). The Supreme Court, in *Bowsher v. Synar*, 478 U.S. 714 (1986), ruled that the comptroller general, as a legislative-branch official, could not be involved in the execution of laws. Accordingly, the authority to trigger a sequester (based upon conditions carefully set forth in law) was placed in the hands of the OMB director. Also, the target for bringing the budget into balance was shifted to FY1993.

The Budget Enforcement Act of 1990 (*P.L. 101-508, title XIII; 104 Stat. 1388–628*) amended the 1985 Act, fundamentally revising the process. The deficit targets effectively were replaced by two new mechanisms: statutory limits on *discretionary spending* and a *pay-as-you-go* (PAYGO) requirement aimed at keeping the projected effect of *revenue* and *direct-spending* legislation enacted during a session deficit-neutral. Sequestration was retained as the means of enforcing the new mechanisms. Congress and the president enacted several measures after 1990 that extended the discretionary-spending limits and the PAYGO requirement. (*See § 7.30, Budget Enforcement Framework.*) The most recent of these extensions, the Budget Enforcement Act of 1997 (*P.L. 105-33, title X; 111 Stat. 677–712*), extended these budget control mechanisms through 2002. At that time, they were allowed to expire or effectively were terminated.

Statutory PAYGO Act of 2010

In 2009, President Barack Obama proposed that a statutory pay-as-you-go (PAYGO) process be reinstituted, but in significantly modified form compared to the statutory PAYGO process that had existed earlier and was terminated in 2002. The president's proposal, as modified by the House and Senate, was enacted into law on February 12, 2010, as the Statutory Pay-As-You-Go Act of 2010 (*P.L. 111-139, title I, 124 Stat. 8-29*). The goal of the act is to encourage the enactment of revenue and direct spending legislation in a deficit-neutral manner.

Under the new process, the budgetary effects of revenue and direct spending provisions enacted into law, including both costs and savings, are recorded by the Office of Management and Budget (OMB) on two PAYGO scorecards covering rolling five-year and ten-year periods. These effects are determined by statements inserted into the *Congressional Record* by the chairmen of the House and Senate Budget Committees and referenced in the measures. As a general matter, the statements are expected to reflect cost estimates prepared by the Congressional Budget Office. If this procedure is not followed for a PAYGO measure, then the budgetary effects of the measure are determined by OMB.

Shortly after a congressional session ends, OMB finalizes the two PAYGO scorecards and determines whether a violation of the PAYGO requirement has occurred (if a debit has been recorded for the budget year on either scorecard). If so, the president issues a sequestration order that implements largely across-the-board cuts in nonexempt direct spending programs sufficient to remedy the violation by eliminating the debit. Many direct spending programs and activities are exempt from sequestration. If no PAYGO violation is found, no further action occurs and the process is repeated during the next session.

The new statutory PAYGO process was created on a permanent basis; there are no expiration dates in the act. At the conclusion of the first year of operation of the new process (2010), the OMB director determined that there was no debit on either scorecard for that year and that no sequester was required. The same outcome is likely for 2011.

Budget Control Act of 2011

A key issue confronting President Barack Obama and Congress toward the beginning of 2011 was the need to raise the statutory limit on the public debt by a significant amount to accommodate the persistent, high deficits projected by the Office of Management and Budget (OMB) and the Congressional Budget Office (CBO). The president wanted Congress to raise the debt limit by more than $2 trillion, which was the amount judged necessary to last beyond the November 2012 elections.

Members of both parties in the House and Senate were concerned that the public would not accept such an increase, given that the debt limit already stood at the record level of $14.3 trillion, without a strengthened commitment also being made to control spending and curb the deficit.

The Simpson-Bowles Commission (officially known as the National Commission on Fiscal Responsibility and Reform) and various other groups, such as the "Gang of Six" in the Senate, made recommendations to reduce the deficit over the coming decade by as much as $4 trillion. In an effort to reach a "grand bargain" on the federal budget, in which the deficit would be reduced by amounts comparable to what others had proposed, President Obama and Speaker of the House John Boehner carried out negotiations but could not conclude such a deal.

With Treasury Secretary Timothy Geithner issuing dire warnings about economic catastrophe if the debt limit was not raised in a timely way, Standard and Poor's downgrading the federal government's credit rating, turbulence in the stock market, and other factors adding to the urgency of the situation, the president and Congress finally reached a scaled-back agreement. The president signed the compromise measure, the Budget Control Act of 2011, into law on August 2, 2011, as P.L. 112-25 (*125 Stat. 240-267*).

The Budget Control Act (BCA) of 2011 contains many elements, including a phased increase in the statutory debt limit amounting to $2.1 trillion in total, a requirement that the House and Senate vote on a balanced-budget constitutional amendment by the end of 2011, and various changes in House and Senate budget procedures. The core elements, however, involve the reinstitution of statutory limits on discretionary spending and a process under which a Joint Select Committee on Deficit Reduction (the "Joint Committee") is required to develop significant deficit-reduction legislation.

Under the terms of the BCA, the Joint Committee's recommendations would be considered under an expedited timetable and a process that precluded the offering of amendments. If the Joint Committee's recommendations were not enacted into law, spending reductions would occur under a fallback sequestration procedure that was scheduled to take effect in January 2013. The discretionary spending limits and the Joint Committee's recommendations (or, alternatively, the fallback sequestration procedure) together were expected to produce at least $2.1 trillion in deficit reduction over the ten-year period covering FY2012–2021, thus equaling the total amount of the debt-limit increases.

Implementation of the BCA began immediately upon its enactment, with an increase of $400 billion in the debt limit. In late September 2011, the limit was increased by another $500 billion (to $15.2 trillion). A third and final increase in the limit, amounting to $1.2 trillion (bringing the limit to $16.4 trillion), is expected to occur during the first part of 2012. The BCA established procedures under which Congress could block the last two debt-limit increases by means of joint resolutions of disapproval, but it was not anticipated that these procedures would be successful. (The House approved a joint resolution of disapproval, H.J.Res. 77, on September 14, 2011, but it was not acted on by the Senate.)

With respect to the required vote on a balanced-budget constitutional amendment, the House failed to pass such a measure (H.J.Res. 2) under the suspension procedure on November 18, 2011, by a vote of 261 to 165 (twenty-three votes short of the necessary two-thirds threshold). The Senate considered two versions of the constitutional amendment, S.J.Res. 10 and S.J.Res. 24, on December 13 and 14, 2011, rejecting them by votes of 47 to 53 and 21 to 79, respectively.

The BCA reestablished discretionary spending limits for FY2012–2021 by amending the pertinent portion of the underlying law, Section 251 of the 1985 Balanced Budget Act (the Budget Enforcement Act of 1990, which established the original discretionary spending limits, did so by amending the 1985 act). Because the limits are set below the baseline levels of discretionary spending projected at the time by CBO, the enactment of annual appropriations acts in compliance with the limits is expected to reduce such spending (and the deficit) by $917 billion over the ten-year period, according to CBO estimates. Total budget authority available under the limits begins at $1.043 trillion for FY2012 and climbs to $1.234 trillion by FY2021.

Under the revised Section 251 of the 1985 act, discretionary spending is divided into two categories, "security" and "nonsecurity," for FY2012 and FY2013; afterward, there is a single "discretionary" category. The security category is defined as including all discretionary spending for the Defense, Homeland Security, and Veterans Affairs Departments; all budget accounts in the international affairs (150) function, and a few other items. As with the earlier limits, the new ones are adjusted for several factors during the year as the budget process unfolds, such as designated emergencies or changes in budget concepts.

The BCA provided that the Joint Committee, a bipartisan panel consisting of six House and six Senate members evenly divided by party, report its legislative recommendations by a November 23, 2011, deadline. In the event the Joint Committee's legislation was not reported by that date, and enacted into law by January 15, 2012, the BCA provided a fallback procedure intended to produce the $1.2 trillion in savings that the Joint Committee had been tasked to produce. After extensive deliberations, the co-chairs of the Joint Committee (Representative Jeb Hensarling and Senator Patty Murray) announced on November 21 that the group had failed to reach a consensus: "After months

§7.12

Calculation of Automatic Reductions

Section 251A of the 1985 Balanced Budget Act, as amended by the BCA, sets forth the methodology for calculating the dollar amounts of automatic spending reductions that will have to be made in order to achieve the required $1.2 trillion in savings. The reductions are divided evenly between defense and nondefense spending categories, after taking into account debt-service savings (estimated at 18 percent of the total). Under this illustration based on preliminary CBO estimates, after an estimated $216 billion in debt-service savings are subtracted from the goal, $984 billion in automatic reductions would be required, divided evenly ($492 billion) between the defense and nondefense categories. About $55 billion in reductions would be required annually in each category.

Goal	The full $1.200 trillion (because no recommendations from the Joint Committee were enacted)
Determine debt-service savings (18%)	$1.200 trillion * 0.18 = $216 billion
Subtract debt-service savings from goal	$1.200 trillion – $216 billion = $984 billion
Divide remainder by 9 to determine reductions for each year (FY2013–2021)	$984 billion / 9 = $109 billion
Divide annual amount by 2 to determine defense and nondefense allocations	$109 billion / 2 = $55 billion

of hard work and intense deliberations, we have come to the conclusion today that it will not be possible to make any bipartisan agreement available to the public before the committee's deadline" (<*www.deficitreduction.gov*>).

Under the BCA, the failure of the Joint Committee to report recommendations by the November 23, 2011, deadline means that the fallback procedure will be triggered on January 2, 2013. The delay in triggering the procedure gives Congress and the president a little more than a year to intervene by enacting legislation under regular legislative procedures that would prevent the fallback procedure from taking effect, should they choose to do so.

Shortly after the 2011 congressional session ends, the OMB director will issue a final sequestration report for FY2012 determining whether or not the limits for the security or nonsecurity categories of discretionary spending have been breached. If a violation has occurred in one or both categories, then the president must promptly issue a sequestration order implementing largely across-the-board spending cuts in the affected categories sufficient to eliminate the breach. The limits set in the BCA, before any adjustments, were $684 billion for the security category and $359 billion for the nonsecurity category.

If the fallback procedure is activated on January 2, 2013, as provided for under the BCA, the sequestration process for FY2013–2021 is changed in several ways: (1) the process is expanded to encompass reductions in both discretionary spending programs and nonexempt mandatory spending programs, divided evenly (in dollar terms) between defense and nondefense categories; (2) the discretionary spending categories are revised to reflect only spending in the defense (050) function

§ 7.13

Estimated Savings from Automatic Reductions

CBO prepared preliminary estimates in September 2011 of the automatic reductions that would be required in the defense and nondefense categories to achieve $1.2 trillion in savings over the nine-year period covering FY2013–2021, the goal set by the BCA. (Under the act, the OMB director will make the official determinations under the timetable established by the act.) The table shows that in each of the nine years, spending reductions of $55 billion would be required in both the defense category and the nondefense category. Virtually all of the defense reductions come from discretionary spending, while the nondefense reductions include sizeable amounts of mandatory spending reductions ($170 billion) and discretionary spending reductions ($322 billion) over the full period. The estimated debt-service savings of $216 billion are excluded.

By fiscal year, budget authority in billions of dollars

	2013	**2014**	**2015**	**2016**	**2017**	**2018**	**2019**	**2020**	**2021**	**Total 2013–2021**
Defense										
Mandatory sequestration	*	*	*	*	*	*	*	*	*	*
Reduction in the cap on discretionary budget authority	–55	–55	–55	–55	–55	–55	–55	–55	–55	–492
Total	**–55**	**–55**	**–55**	**–55**	**–55**	**–55**	**–55**	**–55**	**–55**	**–492**
Nondefense										
Mandatory sequestration										
Medicare spending subject to 2 percent limit	–11	–11	–12	–13	–13	–14	–15	–16	–17	–123
Other nonexempt programs	–3	–3	–4	–4	–3	–3	–3	–3	–3	–30
Additional sequestration applied to other programs because of the 2 percent limit for Medicare	–2	–2	–2	–2	–2	–2	–2	–2	–2	–17
Subtotal	–16	–17	–18	–19	–19	–19	–20	–21	–22	–170
Reduction in the cap on discretionary budget authority										
Preliminary reductions	–25	–24	–24	–23	–23	–23	–22	–21	–21	–206
Further reductions because of the 2 percent limit for Medicare	–14	–14	–13	–13	–13	–13	–12	–12	–12	–116
Total	**–55**	**–55**	**–55**	**–55**	**–55**	**–55**	**–55**	**–55**	**–55**	**–492**
Memorandum:										
Percentage Cut to Nonexempt Budget Accounts										
Defense	10.0	9.8	9.7	9.5	9.3	9.1	8.9	8.7	8.5	n.a
Nondefense										
Discretionary	7.8	7.4	7.1	6.8	6.6	6.4	6.1	5.8	5.5	n.a.
Mandatory										
Medicare spending subject to 2 percent limit	2.0	2.0	2.0	2.0	2.0	2.0	2.0	2.0	2.0	n.a.
Other	7.8	7.4	7.1	6.8	6.6	6.4	6.1	5.8	5.5	n.a.

Source: Congressional Budget Office

in one category, and all other spending in the other category; and (3) the revised discretionary spending categories are used throughout the FY2013–2021 time frame. For the most part, spending reductions under the sequestration process are applied uniformly (in terms of a percentage cut) to all accounts and programs in a spending category. The fallback procedure is set forth in Section 251A of the 1985 act, as added by the BCA.

For discretionary spending, a sequester for FY2013 would be implemented on January 2, 2013, under the revised categories. For each fiscal year thereafter, when the preliminary sequestration report is issued for that year (in conjunction with the submission of the president's budget in January or February), the limits on discretionary spending for the revised categories are adjusted downward by the appropriate amounts and any required sequester is implemented. The president may exempt military personnel accounts from a sequester, but the reductions in spending for the remaining defense discretionary programs must be increased so that the total required reductions are achieved.

For mandatory spending, a sequester would occur automatically for each fiscal year over the nine-year period, from FY2013–2021. Many mandatory spending programs, such as Social Security, Medicaid, and unemployment compensation, are exempt from the sequestration process. Any required reduction in the Medicare program is limited to 2 percent; if the limitation comes into play, then the reductions in the other discretionary and direct spending programs in the nondefense category must be increased so that the total required reductions are achieved.

The BCA prescribes the method by which the automatic reductions under the fallback procedure are calculated (*§ 7.12 Calculation of Automatic Reductions illustrates how the basic calculations are made*). Although the final determinations will be made by the OMB director as scheduled under the BCA, CBO has made preliminary estimates that provide a general idea of the reductions that will be required (*§ 7.13 Estimated Savings from Automatic Reductions*). According to the estimates, the $1.2 trillion in required savings would be achieved over the nine-year period by reducing defense and nondefense spending categories each by about $55 billion annually, requiring annual uniform reductions ranging from 8.5 percent to 10.0 percent for defense and from 5.5 percent to 7.8 percent for nondefense (except for a 2 percent limit on Medicare reductions).

7

§ 7.20 The Budget Cycle

Federal budgeting is a cyclical activity that begins with the formulation of the president's annual budget and concludes with the audit and review of expenditures. The process spreads over a multiyear period. The first stage is the formulation of the president's budget and its presentation to Congress. The next stage is congressional action on the budget resolution and subsequent spending, revenue, and debt-limit legislation. The third stage is implementation of the budget by executive agencies. The final stage is *audit* and *review*. While the basic steps continue from year to year, particular procedures often vary in accord with the style of the president, the economic and political considerations under which the budget is prepared and implemented, and other factors.

Budget decisions are made on the basis of the *fiscal year*. Originally, the fiscal year used by the federal government coincided with the calendar year. In the 1840s, the fiscal year was changed to a July 1 through June 30 cycle. Finally, the 1974 Congressional Budget Act pushed back the start of the fiscal year by three months, to October 1, to give Congress more time to finish legislative action during a session. Under current procedures, for example, fiscal year 2012 began on October 1, 2011, and will end on September 30, 2012; during the 2011 session, Congress considered regular appropriations and other budgetary legislation for fiscal year 2012, as well as supplemental appropriations for fiscal year 2011.

The activities related to a single fiscal year usually stretch over a period of at least two-and-a-half calendar years. As the budget is being considered, federal agencies must deal with three different fiscal years at the same time: implementing the budget for the current fiscal year; seeking funds from Congress for the next fiscal year; and planning for the fiscal year after that.

§ 7.30 Budget Enforcement Framework

Congress considers budgetary legislation within the framework of budget enforcement procedures established under the 1974 Congressional Budget Act, which are intended generally to uphold the policies underlying the annual budget resolution. Enforcement relies principally on the reconciliation process and, while legislation is under consideration, on points of order to prevent the passage of legislation that would violate established policies (both are discussed in more detail later in this chapter). The House and Senate Budget Committees have primary responsibility for enforcement.

In addition to provisions in the 1974 act, the House and Senate also incorporate enforcement provisions into annual budget resolutions and their standing rules. Internal PAYGO procedures affecting the consideration of direct spending and revenue legislation, for example, were established by the Senate in 1993 as a provision in an annual budget resolution (and modified by subsequent budget resolutions), and by the House in 2007 as an amendment to House Rule XXI (which also has been modified subsequently).

The availability of information is crucial to the effective operation of enforcement procedures. The Budget Committees rely on *cost estimates* on legislation prepared by the Congressional Budget Office (and the Joint Committee on Taxation in the case of revenue measures) and integrates them into a *scorekeeping system*, which shows the impact of budgetary legislation compared to budget resolution levels.

As indicated previously, congressional procedures for budget enforcement may be linked to, or reinforced by, statutory procedures that involve the president and the OMB director. The most recent example in this regard is the Budget Control Act of 2011 (*discussed in § 7.10*).

§ 7.40 Presidential Budget Process

The president's budget, officially referred to as the *Budget of the United States Government*, is required by law to be submitted to Congress early in the legislative session, no later than the first Monday in February. The budget consists of estimates of spending, revenues, borrowing, and debt; policy and legislative recommendations; detailed estimates of the financial operations of federal agencies and programs; data on the actual and projected performance of the economy; and other information supporting the president's recommendations.

Before the deadline for submission of the budget was changed in 1990, presidents usually had to submit their budgets in January. In years in which a new president was inaugurated (which occurs on January 20), the outgoing president usually submitted a budget before the inauguration. Later in the session, the new president submitted revisions to this budget that reflected his priorities and initiatives. In the three transition years since 1990, however, the incoming president rather than the outgoing president has submitted the budget (President Bill Clinton in 1993 for FY1994, President George W. Bush in 2001 for FY2002, and President Barack Obama in 2009 for FY2010).

The president's budget is only a request to Congress; Congress is not required to adopt or even consider the president's recommendations. Nevertheless, the power to formulate and submit a budget is a vital tool in the president's direction of the executive branch and of national policy. The president's proposals often influence congressional revenue and spending decisions, though the extent of the influence varies from year to year and depends more on political and fiscal conditions than on the legal status of the budget.

The Constitution does not provide for a budget, nor does it require the president to make recommendations concerning the revenues and spending of the federal government. Until 1921, the federal government operated without a comprehensive presidential budget process. As stated previously, the Budget and Accounting Act of 1921 provided for an executive budget process, requiring the president to prepare and submit a budget to Congress each year (beginning with FY1923). Although it has been amended many times, this statute provides the legal basis for the presidential budget, prescribes much of its content, and defines the roles of the president and the agencies in the process.

Formulation and Content of the President's Budget

Preparation of the president's budget typically begins in the spring each year, about nine months before the budget is submitted to Congress, about seventeen months before the start of the fiscal year to which it pertains, and about twenty-nine months before the close of that fiscal year. (*See § 7.41, Executive Budget Process Timetable.*) The early stages of budget preparation occur in federal agencies. When they begin work on the budget for a fiscal year, agencies already are implementing the budget for the fiscal year in progress and awaiting final appropriations actions and other legislative decisions for the fiscal year after that. The long lead times and the fact that appropriations have not yet been made for the next year mean that the budget is prepared with a great deal of uncertainty about economic conditions, presidential policies, and congressional actions.

As agencies formulate their budgets, they maintain continuing contact with the Office of Management and Budget (OMB) budget examiners assigned to them. These contacts provide agencies with guidance in preparing their budgets and also enable them to alert OMB to any needs or problems that may loom ahead. (*See § 7.42, Office of Management and Budget Publications for Agencies.*) Agency requests are submitted to OMB in September, and are reviewed by OMB staff in consultation with the president and his senior advisors during September–October. OMB informs agencies of approved budget levels in the "passback"; agencies may appeal these results to OMB or the president. The 1921 Budget and Accounting Act bars agencies from submitting their budget requests directly to Congress. Moreover, OMB regulations provide for confidentiality in all budget requests and recommendations before the transmittal of the president's budget to Congress. However, it is not uncommon for budget recommendations for some programs to become public while the budget is still being formulated.

The format and content of the budget are partly determined by law, but the 1921 act authorizes

§ 7.41

Executive Budget Process Timetable

Calendar Year Prior to the Year in Which Fiscal Year Begins

Date	Activities
Spring	Agencies begin the formulation of budget requests, under guidance from OMB, for the budget that will begin October 1 of the following year.
Spring and Summer	OMB and executive branch agencies discuss budget issues and options.
September	Agencies submit budget requests to OMB.
October–November	OMB conducts its fall review, analyzing agency proposals and briefing the president and senior advisors.
November–December	OMB makes decisions on agencies' requests, referred to as the "passback." Agencies may appeal these decisions to the OMB director and to the president.

Calendar Year in Which Fiscal Year Begins

Date	Activities
By first Monday in February	President submits budget to Congress.
February–September	Congressional phase. Agencies interact with Congress, justifying and explaining president's budget.
By July 15	President submits mid-session review to Congress.
October 1	Fiscal year begins.
October–September (the fiscal year)	OMB apportions enacted funds to agencies. Agencies execute the enacted budget, incurring obligations, and the Treasury makes payments to liquidate obligations, resulting in outlays.

the president to set forth the budget "in such form and detail" as he may determine. Over the years, there has been an increase in the types of information and explanatory material presented in the budget documents.

In most years, the budget is submitted as a multivolume set consisting of a main document setting forth the president's message to Congress and an analysis and justification of his major proposals (the *Budget*). Supplementary documents contain account and program-level details, historical information, and special budgetary analyses, among other things. (*See § 7.43, Volumes Containing and Explaining the President's Annual Budget.*)

During the congressional phase of the federal budget process, the *Appendix* volume in particular is a useful source of detailed financial information on individual programs and *appropriations accounts*. For each annually appropriated account, it provides: (1) the text of the current appropriation and proposed changes; (2) a program and financing schedule; (3) a narrative statement of programs and performance; (4) an object classification schedule; and (5) an employment summary. Among other financial information, the program and financing schedule shows obligations by programs (distinguishing between operating expenses and capital investments, where appropriate),

§7.42

Office of Management and Budget Publications for Agencies

The Office of Management and Budget (OMB) coordinates the preparation of the president's budget, and its submission to Congress, and oversees implementation of the spending laws passed by Congress. The following types of publications contain instructions and guidelines to federal agencies regarding budget-related activities:

- **Circulars**, expected to have a continuing effect of generally two years or more. OMB Circular A-11, updated annually, instructs agencies how to prepare their budget submissions.
- **Bulletins**, containing guidance of a more transitory nature that would normally expire after one or two years. Bulletins often address how apportionment is to occur under a continuing resolution.
- **Regulations** and **Paperwork**, daily reports that list regulations and paperwork under OMB review.
- **Financial Management** policies and **Grants Management** circulars and related documents.
- **Federal Register** submissions, including copies of proposed and final rules.

For information on OMB policies and publications, check the OMB web site (<*www.whitehouse.gov/omb*>) and the Federal Register, at GPO's Federal Digital System, at <*http://fdsys.gov*>, then under "Collections" select "Federal Register." Also see <*CDDocs.com*>.

7

budgetary resources available for obligation, and sources of new budget authority for each of the previous, current, and upcoming fiscal years. (*See § 7.44, Program and Financing Schedule in President's Budget Appendix.*) New budget authority available to an agency for obligation may come from several sources, not just discretionary appropriations. Other typical sources include *mandatory appropriations* and *offsetting collections.*

Much of the budget is an estimate of requirements under existing law rather than a request for congressional action. (More than half the budget authority in the budget becomes available without congressional action.)

The president is required to submit a budget update—reflecting changed economic conditions, congressional actions, and other factors—referred to as the *Mid-session Review,* by July 15 each year. The president may revise his recommendations anytime during the year.

Executive Interaction with Congress

OMB officials and other presidential advisors appear before congressional committees to discuss overall policy and economic issues, but they generally leave formal discussions of specific programs to the affected agencies. Agencies thus bear the principal responsibility for defending the president's program recommendations at congressional hearings and in other interactions and communications with Congress.

Agencies are supposed to justify the president's recommendations, not their own. OMB maintains an elaborate legislative clearance process to ensure that agency *budget justifications*, testimony, and other submissions are consistent with presidential policy. In recent years, agencies have

§ 7.43

Volumes Containing and Explaining the President's Annual Budget

The principal volumes currently part of the president's annual budget submission include the following:

- **Budget** (officially the *Budget of the United States Government*)—includes the president's budget message, presentations on the president's major budgetary initiatives organized by department and major agencies (or, in some years, by budget function), discussions of management initiatives and performance data, and summary tables.
- **Appendix**—sets forth detailed information for accounts within each department and agency, including funding levels, program descriptions, proposed appropriations language, and object classification and employment data.
- **Analytical Perspectives**—contains analyses and information on specific aspects of the budget or budget-related areas, such as budget and performance integration, economic assumptions, and current services estimates; crosscutting programs, such as research and development, federal investment, and aid to state and local governments; and budget process reform proposals.
- **Historical Tables**—provides data, covering an extended time period, on receipts, budget authority, outlays, deficits and surpluses, federal debt, and other matters.

Within a few days of the submission of the budget, the president also transmits an annual ***Economic Report of the President*** to Congress, which includes the report of the Council of Economic Advisers.

The president is required by law to update his submissions, and he does this in a far briefer, more summary fashion in his ***Mid-session Review***, which is due by July 15.

Online access to the president's budget documents is available in several places, including the Office of Management and Budget web site, <*www.whitehouse.gov/omb*>, and GPO's Federal Digital System, at <*http://fdsys.gov*>, then under "Collections" select "Budget of the United States Government." Also see <*CDDocs.com*>.

been required to post their budget justifications on the agency web site shortly after the president's budget has been submitted. The materials typically run to hundreds or even thousands of pages and provide a wealth of details beyond what is provided in the Appendix to the president's budget.

Increasingly in recent years, the president and his chief budgetary aides have engaged in extensive negotiations with Congress over major budgetary legislation. These negotiations sometimes have occurred as formal budget "summits" and at other times as less visible, behind-the-scenes activities.

One tool used by the president to signal his position on legislation in order to influence congressional action is a *Statement of Administration Policy* (SAP). These statements are issued at several different stages of legislative activity and are maintained on the OMB web site. In a SAP, the president may indicate his concurrence with congressional action on a measure, identify provisions in the measure with which he disagrees, and even signal his intent to veto the measure if it is not adjusted according to his wishes. At the conclusion of the legislative process, presidents sometimes issue *signing statements* on legislation that is being signed into law, often using a statement to register objections to particular provisions in the law. (*See § 8.20, Congress and the Executive: Legislation; and § 6.290, Presidential Action on Enacted Measures.*)

§ 7.44

Program and Financing Schedule in President's Budget Appendix

1 Each account is identified by an 11-digit code. The first two digits indicate the agency; the next four digits are the account numbers; the seventh digit is the type of request (regular or supplemental); the eighth digit is the type of fund; and the last three digits specify the budget function. (*See § 7.54; the category 999 indicates that an account involves more than one function*.)

2 The schedule covers three fiscal years: the past year (2010); the current year (2011); and the upcoming year, also referred to as the budget year (2012). The last column contains the president's most recent request. In this case, "CR" in the column for 2011 indicates that funding was provided by a continuing resolution.

3 Agency obligations are classified by program activity and if applicable, by operating and capital investment.

4 New budget authority may be derived from several sources, including discretionary appropriations and (not shown here) mandatory appropriations and offsetting collections.

5 Outlays may be derived from several sources as well. In this example, outlays for the Salaries and Expenses account of the Federal Bureau of Investigation result from new discretionary authority and balances from previous years.

Federal Bureau of Investigation Salaries and Expenses

Program and Financing

(in millions of dollars)

1 Identification code 15-0200-0-1-999	2 2010 actual	CR	2012 est.
3 Obligations by program activity:			
Intelligence	964	1,268	1,324
Counterterrorism/Counterintelligence	3,016	2,795	2,968
Criminal Enterprises and Federal Crimes	1,954	1,858	2,407
Criminal Justice Services	575	445	108
Total operating expenses	6,509	6,366	6,807
Intelligence	274	258	270
Counterterrorism/Counterintelligence	353	381	335
Criminal Enterprises and Federal Crimes	588	615	200
Criminal Justice Services	44	39	383
Total capital investment	1,259	1,293	1,188
Total	7,768	7,659	7,995
4 Budget authority:			
Appropriations, discretionary:			
Appropriation	7,659	7,659	7,995
Appropriation	24	...	...
Appropriations transferred to other accounts	–12	–9	...
Appropriations transferred from other accounts	13	...	...
Unobligated balance of appropriations permanently reduced	–50	–50	...
Appropriation, discretionary (total)	7,634	7,600	7,995
5 Outlays, gross:			
Outlays from new discretionary authority	6,566	7,558	7,875
Outlays from discretionary balances	2,267	1,391	2,353
Outlays, gross (total)	8,833	8,949	10,228

Source: Office of Management and Budget, *Budget of the United States Government, Fiscal Year 2012, Appendix* (Washington: GPO, 2011), p. 724.

7

§ 7.51

Congressional Budget Process Timetable[1]

Deadline	Action
First Monday in February	President submits budget to Congress[2]
February 15	Congressional Budget Office submits report on economic and budget outlook to Budget Committees
Six weeks after president's budget is submitted	House and Senate committees submit reports on views and estimates to respective Budget Committees
April 1	Senate Budget Committee reports budget resolution
April 15	Congress completes action on budget resolution
May 15	House usually begins action on annual appropriations bills
June 10	House Appropriations Committee reports last regular appropriations bill
June 30	House completes action on regular appropriations bills and any required reconciliation legislation
July 15	President submits mid-session review of his budget to Congress
October 1	Fiscal year begins[3]

1. While this timetable is set forth in statute, the deadlines generally are regarded as hortatory and Congress and the president sometimes do not meet them.
2. At any time after the president submits the budget for the upcoming fiscal year, he may submit revisions to the budget, referred to as budget amendments, as well as request supplemental appropriations for the current fiscal year.
3. One or more continuing resolutions may be needed until Congress and the president complete action on all pending appropriations bills.

§ 7.50 Congressional Budget Process

The Congressional Budget and Impoundment Control Act of 1974 established the congressional budget process as the means by which Congress coordinates the various budget-related actions taken by it during the course of the year, such as the consideration of appropriations and revenue measures. The process is structured around an *annual concurrent resolution on the budget* (H. Con. Res. ___ or S. Con. Res. ___) that sets aggregate budget policies and functional spending priorities for at least the next five fiscal years. (The budget resolution and appropriations processes described in the following sections take place each year.)

Because a concurrent resolution is not a bill or joint resolution, it is not submitted to the president to be signed or vetoed. The budget resolution cannot have statutory effect; no money can be raised or spent pursuant to it. However, as a concurrent resolution, it requires House and Senate agreement to the same text to have maximum effect or utility to Congress. The main purpose of the budget resolution is to establish the framework within which Congress considers separate revenue, spending, and other budget-related legislation in a year. Revenue and spending amounts set in the budget resolution (and accompanying joint explanatory statement) establish the basis for the enforcement of congressional budget policies through points of order. The budget resolution also initiates the reconciliation process for conforming existing revenue and spending laws to congressional budget policies. (*For other explanations of the congressional budget process and other budget information, see the Senate Budget Committee's web site at <www.budget.senate.gov>, and the House Budget Committee's web site at <www.budget.house.gov>.*)

Formulation and Content of the Budget Resolution

The congressional budget process begins upon the presentation of the president's budget in January or February. (*See § 7.51, Congressional Budget Process Timetable; and § 7.53, Congressional Budget Process Flowchart.*) The timetable set forth in the 1974 Congressional Budget Act calls for the final adoption of the budget resolution by April 15, well before the beginning of the new fiscal year on October 1. Although the House and Senate often pass the budget resolution separately before April 15, they often do not reach final agreement on it until after the deadline—sometimes not at all. (*See § 7.52, Completion Dates of Budget Resolutions.*) The 1974 act bars consideration of revenue, spending, and debt-limit measures for the upcoming fiscal year until the budget resolution for that year has been adopted. However, certain exceptions are provided, such as the exception that allows the House to consider the regular appropriations bills after May 15, even if the budget resolution has not yet been adopted.

The 1974 Congressional Budget Act requires the budget resolution, for each fiscal year covered, to set forth budget aggregates and spending levels for each *functional category* of the budget. (*See § 7.54, Functional Categories in a Congressional Budget Resolution.*) The aggregates included in the budget resolution are as follows:

- total revenues (and the amount by which the total is to be changed by legislative action);
- total new budget authority and outlays;
- the deficit or surplus; and
- the debt limit.

For each of the functional categories, the budget resolution must indicate for each fiscal year the amounts of new budget authority and outlays. All figures in the budget resolution must be arithmetically consistent.

Amounts in the budget resolution do not reflect the revenues or spending of the off-budget Social

§ 7.52

Completion Dates of Budget Resolutions

The timetable in the 1974 Congressional Budget Act provides for the House and Senate to reach agreement on the budget resolution by April 15, but this deadline is not always met. During the more than 35 years that the congressional budget process has been in effect, the House and Senate did not reach final agreement six times (all shown here). Completion dates for the past 15 years are as follows:

Fiscal Year	Date
1998	June 5, 1997
1999	Not Completed
2000	April 15, 1999
2001	April 13, 2000
2002	May 10, 2001
2003	Not Completed
2004	April 11, 2003
2005	Not Completed
2006	April 28, 2005
2007	Not Completed
2008	May 17, 2007
2009	June 5, 2008
2010	April 29, 2009
2011	Not Completed
2012	Not Completed

7

§ 7.53

Congressional Budget Process Flowchart

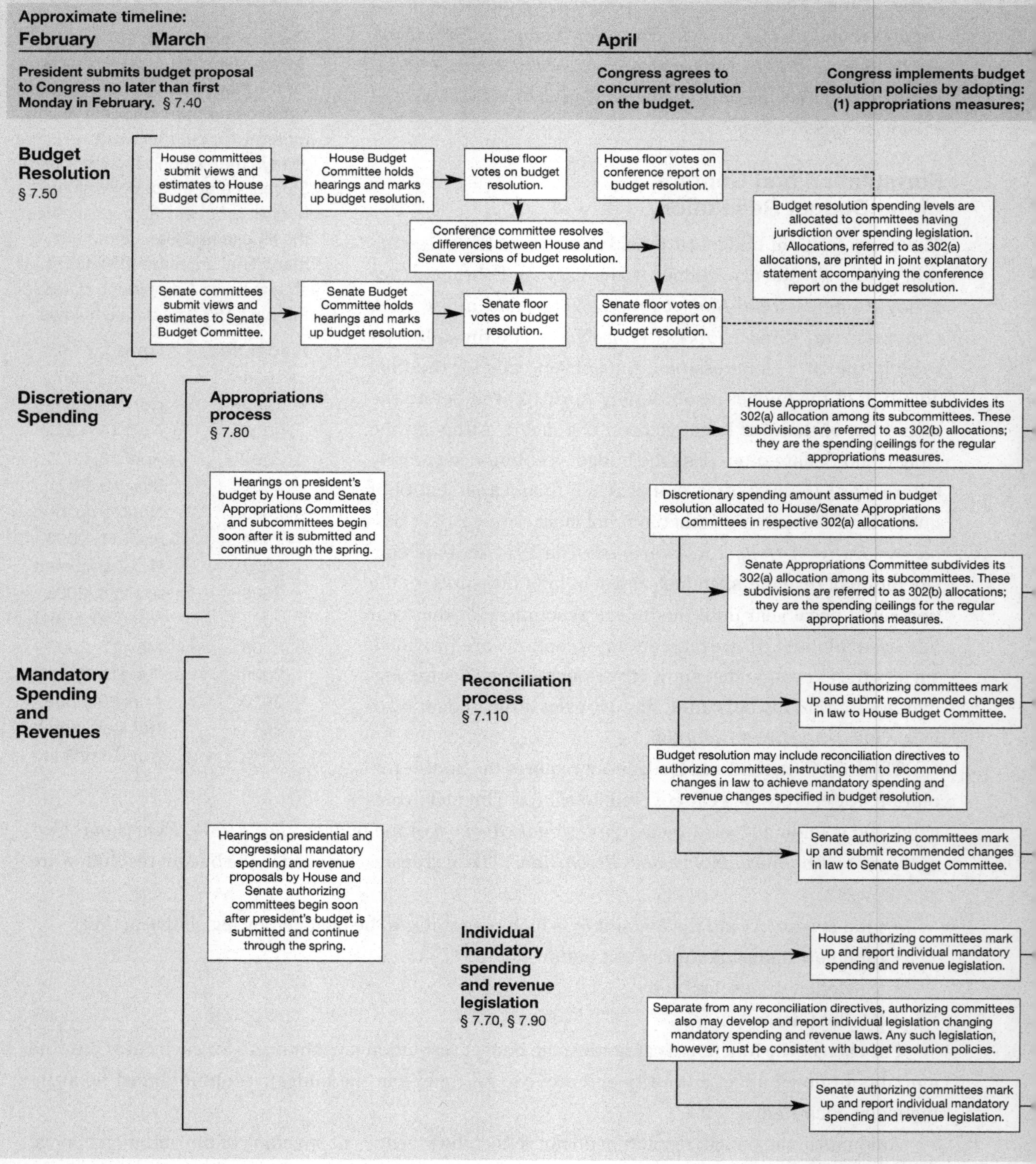
Approximate timeline:
February
March
April
President submits budget proposal to Congress no later than first Monday in February. § 7.40
Congress agrees to concurrent resolution on the budget.
Congress implements budget resolution policies by adopting: (1) appropriations measures;
Budget Resolution
§ 7.50
House committees submit views and estimates to House Budget Committee.
House Budget Committee holds hearings and marks up budget resolution.
House floor votes on budget resolution.
House floor votes on conference report on budget resolution.
Conference committee resolves differences between House and Senate versions of budget resolution.
Budget resolution spending levels are allocated to committees having jurisdiction over spending legislation. Allocations, referred to as 302(a) allocations, are printed in joint explanatory statement accompanying the conference report on the budget resolution.
Senate committees submit views and estimates to Senate Budget Committee.
Senate Budget Committee holds hearings and marks up budget resolution.
Senate floor votes on budget resolution.
Senate floor votes on conference report on budget resolution.
Discretionary Spending
Appropriations process
§ 7.80
Hearings on president's budget by House and Senate Appropriations Committees and subcommittees begin soon after it is submitted and continue through the spring.
House Appropriations Committee subdivides its 302(a) allocation among its subcommittees. These subdivisions are referred to as 302(b) allocations; they are the spending ceilings for the regular appropriations measures.
Discretionary spending amount assumed in budget resolution allocated to House/Senate Appropriations Committees in respective 302(a) allocations.
Senate Appropriations Committee subdivides its 302(a) allocation among its subcommittees. These subdivisions are referred to as 302(b) allocations; they are the spending ceilings for the regular appropriations measures.
Mandatory Spending and Revenues
Reconciliation process
§ 7.110
House authorizing committees mark up and submit recommended changes in law to House Budget Committee.
Budget resolution may include reconciliation directives to authorizing committees, instructing them to recommend changes in law to achieve mandatory spending and revenue changes specified in budget resolution.
Senate authorizing committees mark up and submit recommended changes in law to Senate Budget Committee.
Hearings on presidential and congressional mandatory spending and revenue proposals by House and Senate authorizing committees begin soon after president's budget is submitted and continue through the spring.
Individual mandatory spending and revenue legislation
§ 7.70, § 7.90
House authorizing committees mark up and report individual mandatory spending and revenue legislation.
Separate from any reconciliation directives, authorizing committees also may develop and report individual legislation changing mandatory spending and revenue laws. Any such legislation, however, must be consistent with budget resolution policies.
Senate authorizing committees mark up and report individual mandatory spending and revenue legislation.

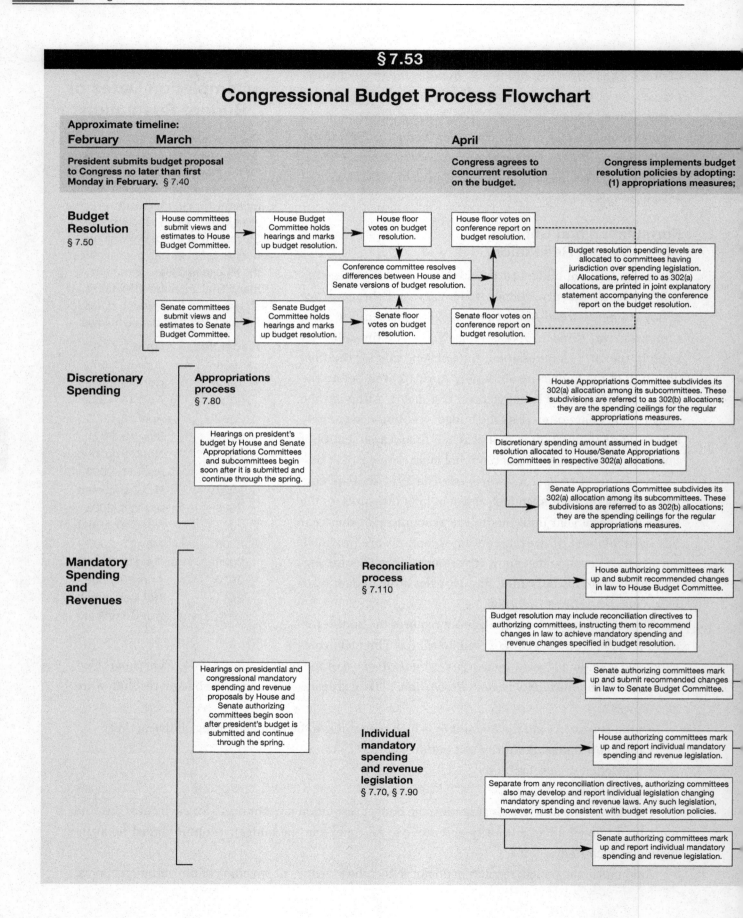

May	June–September	Fiscal Year begins October 1
(2) individual mandatory spending and revenue legislation; and (3) reconciliation legislation (if required).	President signs (or vetoes) budget measures.	

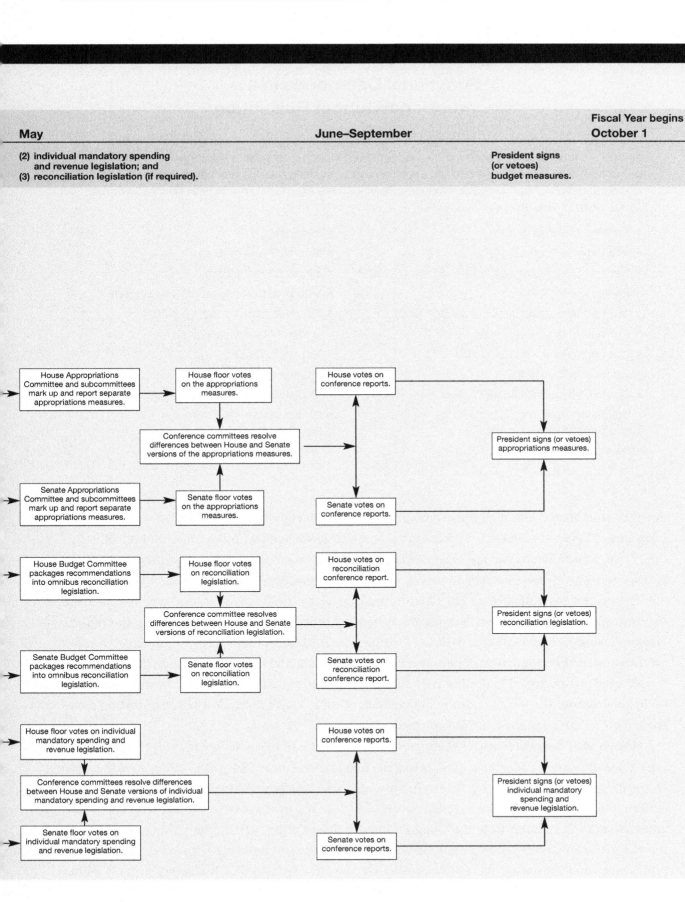

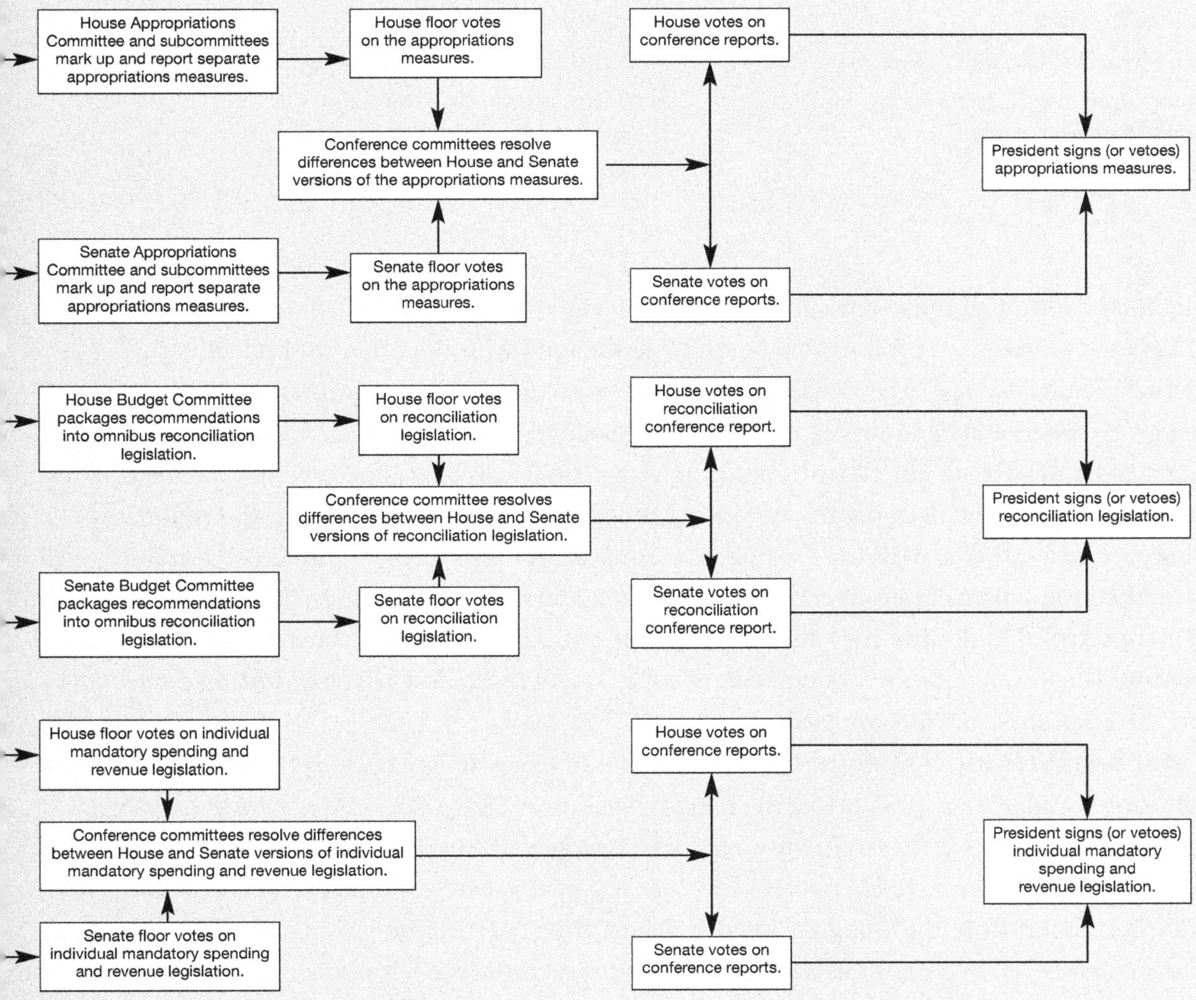
House Appropriations Committee and subcommittees mark up and report separate appropriations measures.
House floor votes on the appropriations measures.
House votes on conference reports.
Conference committees resolve differences between House and Senate versions of the appropriations measures.
President signs (or vetoes) appropriations measures.
Senate Appropriations Committee and subcommittees mark up and report separate appropriations measures.
Senate floor votes on the appropriations measures.
Senate votes on conference reports.
House Budget Committee packages recommendations into omnibus reconciliation legislation.
House floor votes on reconciliation legislation.
House votes on reconciliation conference report.
Conference committee resolves differences between House and Senate versions of reconciliation legislation.
President signs (or vetoes) reconciliation legislation.
Senate Budget Committee packages recommendations into omnibus reconciliation legislation.
Senate floor votes on reconciliation legislation.
Senate votes on reconciliation conference report.
House floor votes on individual mandatory spending and revenue legislation.
House votes on conference reports.
Conference committees resolve differences between House and Senate versions of individual mandatory spending and revenue legislation.
President signs (or vetoes) individual mandatory spending and revenue legislation.
Senate floor votes on individual mandatory spending and revenue legislation.
Senate votes on conference reports.

§ 7.54

Functional Categories in a Congressional Budget Resolution

A budget resolution shows recommended spending both as aggregate levels and as allocations among the functional categories of the budget. The functional categories group programs by broad purposes without regard to the agencies that administer them; a function is further divided into subfunctions. The functional categories have been revised from time to time and their number (21 as of 2012) has changed over time.

- National Defense (050)
- International Affairs (150)
- General Science, Space, and Technology (250)
- Energy (270)
- Natural Resources and Environment (300)
- Agriculture (350)
- Commerce and Housing Credit (370)
- Transportation (400)
- Community and Regional Development (450)
- Education, Training, Employment, and Social Services (500)
- Health (550)
- Medicare (570)
- Income Security (600)
- Social Security (650)
- Veterans' Benefits and Services (700)
- Administration of Justice (750)
- General Government (800)
- Net Interest (900)
- Allowances (920)
- Undistributed Offsetting Receipts (950)
- Global War on Terrorism and Related Activities (970)

Security trust funds, although these amounts are set forth separately in the budget resolution for purposes of Senate enforcement procedures. Amounts associated with the other off-budget entity, the Postal Service Fund, also are excluded from the budget resolutions. Data on off-budget revenue and spending levels are included, however, in the reports that accompany the budget resolution.

The budget resolution does not allocate funds among specific programs or accounts, but the major program assumptions underlying the functional amounts are often discussed in the reports accompanying each resolution and during floor debate. Some recent reports have contained detailed information on the program levels assumed in the resolution. These assumptions are not binding on the affected committees. Finally, the 1974 act allows certain additional matters to be included in the budget resolution. The most important optional feature of a budget resolution is *reconciliation* directives. (*See § 7.110, Reconciliation Legislation.*)

House and Senate Budget Committee Action. The House and Senate Budget Committees are responsible for marking up and reporting the budget resolution. (*See § 7.55, Membership on the House and Senate Budget Committees.*) In the course of developing the budget resolution, the Budget Committees hold hearings, receive *views and estimates* reports from other committees, and obtain analyses and information from the Congressional Budget Office (CBO). The views and estimates reports of House and Senate committees provide the budget committees with information on the preferences and legislative plans of congressional committees regarding budgetary matters within their jurisdiction. (Views and estimates are available from issuing committees and the Budget Committees; they can also often be found on committee web sites.)

CBO assists the budget committees in developing the budget resolution by issuing, early each year, a report on the budget and economic outlook, which includes *baseline budget projections*. The baseline projections presented in the report are supported by more detailed projections for accounts and programs; CBO usually revises the baseline projections once more (in March) before the budget committees mark up the budget resolution. In addition, CBO issues a report analyzing the president's budgetary proposals in light of CBO's own economic and technical assumptions.

The House and Senate Budget Committees include extensive information in their reports on the budget resolution, as required by the 1974 Congressional Budget Act. The Senate Budget Committee is required to report a budget resolution by April 1 each year; there is no reporting deadline for the House Budget Committee. For many years, the Senate Budget Committee has issued a committee print in lieu of a report.

The extent to which the budget committees (and the House and Senate) consider particular programs when they act on the budget resolution varies from year to year. Specific program decisions are supposed to be left to the Appropriations Committees and other committees of jurisdiction, but there is a strong likelihood that major issues are discussed in markup, in the budget committees' reports, and during floor consideration of the budget resolution. Although any programmatic assumptions generated in this process are not binding on the committees of jurisdiction, they often influence the final outcome.

§ 7.55

Membership on the House and Senate Budget Committees

The House Budget Committee, unlike other House standing committees (except the House Committee on Standards of Official Conduct), is composed of a rotating membership. House rules (with certain exceptions) limit a member's service on the committee to four Congresses in a period of six successive Congresses. In addition, House rules require five members from the Appropriations Committee, five members from the Ways and Means Committee, one member from the Rules Committee, one member designated by the elected majority party leadership, and one member designated by the elected minority party leadership to serve on the committee.

In contrast, membership on the Senate Budget Committee is permanent; Senate rules do not limit the duration of a senator's service on the committee.

Floor Consideration. A budget resolution is marked up and reported from a budget committee in the same fashion as most other measures are considered in other committees. Either the House or Senate committee may report first, and either the House or Senate may consider a budget resolution first. Because of the need to adopt a budget resolution to allow orderly and timely consideration of budgetary legislation, action in the two committees and in the two chambers can occur simultaneously and within a short period of time.

Floor consideration of the budget resolution is expedited under procedures set forth in the 1974 Congressional Budget Act and is further guided by House and Senate rules and practices. In the House, the Rules Committee usually reports a *special rule* (a simple House resolution), which, once agreed to by the House, establishes the terms and conditions under which the budget resolution is considered by the House. This special rule typically sets aside a period for general debate, and specifies which amendments may be considered and the sequence in which they are to be offered and voted on. It has been the practice for many years to allow consideration of a limited number of amendments (as substitutes for the entire resolution) that present different major policy choices. In the Senate, the amendment process is less structured, relying on agreements reached by the leadership through a consultative process. The amendments offered in the Senate may entail major policy choices or may be focused on a single issue; unlike most other types of legislation, amendments attached to budget resolutions must be germane. Finally, the number of hours that a budget resolution can be debated in the Senate is subject to a limit of fifty hours. Subsequent consideration of a conference report is also limited.

The House and Senate normally pass budget resolutions with differences that are significant enough to warrant the convening of a conference. Conferees, typically drawn from the two budget committees, reconcile differences and prepare a conference report, which must be adopted in both houses.

Achievement of the policies set forth in the annual budget resolution depends on the legislative actions taken by Congress (and the president's approval or disapproval of those actions), the performance of the economy, and technical considerations. Many of the factors that determine whether budgetary goals will be met are beyond the direct control of Congress. If economic conditions—growth, employment levels, inflation, and so forth—vary significantly from projected levels, so too will actual levels of revenue and spending. Similarly, actual levels may differ substantially if the technical factors upon which estimates are based, such as the rate at which agencies spend their discretionary funds or participants become eligible for entitlement programs, prove faulty.

Budget Resolution Enforcement

Once a budget resolution is agreed to, Congress' regular tools for enforcing it are overall spending ceilings and revenue floors, and committee allocations and subdivisions of spending. (In addition, in some years the House and Senate have enforced discretionary-spending limits in the budget resolution, which paralleled the adjustable discretionary-spending limits established in statute.) For enforcement procedures to work, Congress must have access to complete and up-to-date budgetary information so that it can relate individual measures to overall budget policies and determine whether adoption of a particular measure would be consistent with those policies, as explained below. Substantive and procedural *points of order* are designed to obtain congressional compliance with budget rules. A point of order may bar House or Senate consideration of legislation that violates the spending ceilings or revenue floors in the budget resolution, committee subdivisions of spending, or congressional budget procedures.

In years that Congress is late in agreeing to, or does not agree to, a budget resolution, the House and Senate independently may agree to a "deeming resolution" for the purpose of enforcing certain budget levels. A deeming resolution, sometimes in the form of a simple resolution or a provision in statute, specifies certain budget levels normally contained in the budget resolution, including aggregate spending and revenue levels, spending allocations to House and Senate committees, spending allocations to the Appropriations Committees only, or a combination of these. In some cases, an entire budget resolution, adopted earlier by one chamber, may be deemed to have been passed. Under a deeming resolution, the enforcement procedures related to the Congressional

Budget Act, as discussed below, have the force and effect as if a budget resolution had been adopted by Congress.

Allocations of Spending to Committees. The key to enforcing budget policy is to relate the budgetary impact of individual pieces of legislation to overall budget policy. Because Congress operates through its committee system, an essential step in linking particular measures to the budget is to allocate the spending amounts set forth in the budget resolution among House and Senate committees.

Section 302(a) of the 1974 act provides for allocations to committees to be made in the statement of managers accompanying the conference report on the budget resolution (referred to as the joint explanatory statement). A *section 302(a) allocation* is made to each committee that has jurisdiction over spending. The Appropriations Committees receive allocations for the budget year (and sometimes the current year), while the legislative committees receive allocations both for the budget year and the full period covered by the budget resolution—at least five fiscal years.

The amounts of new budget authority and outlays allocated to committees in the House or Senate may not exceed the aggregate amounts of budget authority and outlays set forth in the budget resolution. Although these allocations are made by the budget committees, they are not the unilateral preferences of these committees. They are based on assumptions and understandings developed in the course of formulating the budget resolution.

After the allocations are made under section 302(a), the House and Senate Appropriations Committees subdivide the amounts they receive among their subcommittees, as required by section 302(b). The subcommittees' *section 302(b) allocations or subdivisions* may not exceed the total amount allocated to the committees. Each Appropriations Committee reports its subdivisions to its respective chamber; the appropriations bills may not be considered until such a report has been filed.

Scorekeeping and Cost Estimates. *Scorekeeping* is the process of measuring the budgetary effects of pending and enacted legislation and assessing its impact on a budget plan—in this case, the budget resolution. In the congressional budget process, scorekeeping serves several broad purposes. First, it informs members of Congress and the public about the budgetary consequences of congressional actions. When a budgetary measure is under consideration, scorekeeping information lets members know whether adopting the amendment or passing the bill at hand would breach the budget. Further, such information enables members to judge what must be done in upcoming legislative action to achieve the year's budgetary goals. Finally, scorekeeping is designed to assist Congress in enforcing its budget plans. In this regard, scorekeeping is used largely to determine whether points of order under the 1974 Congressional Budget Act may be sustained against legislation violating budget resolution levels.

The principal scorekeepers for Congress are the House and Senate Budget Committees, which provide the presiding officers of the respective chambers with the estimates needed to determine if legislation violates the aggregate levels in the budget resolution, the committee subdivisions of spending, or other budgetary levels. The budget committees make summary scorekeeping reports available periodically, usually geared to the pace of legislative activity. CBO assists Congress in these activities by preparing *cost estimates* of legislation, which are included in committee reports, and reflected in the scorekeeping reports of the budget committees.

Cost estimates prepared by CBO show how a measure would affect spending or revenues over at least five fiscal years. While most cost estimates are provided in the committee report to accompany a measure, they may be provided at any stage of the legislative process, subject to available resources of CBO. Estimates for revenue legislation are made by the Joint Committee on Taxation (JCT). (*See § 7.92, Revenue Estimates.*) CBO and JCT cost estimates are available on their respective web sites at <*www.cbo.gov*> and <*www.jct.gov*>.

Points of Order. The 1974 Congressional Budget Act provides points of order (parliamentary objections to the consideration of legislation, including amendments) to block substantive violations of budget resolution policies and violations of congressional budget procedures.

One element of substantive enforcement is based on section 311 of the act. The point of order provided for in this section bars Congress from considering legislation that would cause total revenues to fall below the level set in the budget resolution. It also forbids the consideration of legislation that would cause total new budget authority or total outlays to exceed the budgeted level. In the House (but not the Senate), section 311 does not apply to spending legislation if the committee reporting the measure has stayed within its allocation of new discretionary budget authority. Accordingly, the House may take up any spending measure that is within the appropriate committee allocations, even if it would cause total spending to be exceeded. Legislation that would cause functional allocations in the budget resolution to be exceeded is not prohibited in either chamber.

Another point of order tied to substantive enforcement is found in Section 302(f) of the 1974 act, which bars the House and Senate from considering any spending measure that would cause the relevant committee's spending allocations to be exceeded. In the House, the point of order applies only to violations of allocations of new discretionary budget authority. Further, the point of order also applies (in both chambers) to suballocations of spending made by the Appropriations Committees.

In addition to points of order to enforce compliance with the budget resolution and the allocations and subdivisions made pursuant to it, the 1974 act contains points of order to ensure compliance with its procedures. Perhaps the most important of these is found in section 303, which bars consideration of any revenue, spending, entitlement, or debt-limit measure before adoption of the budget resolution. However, the rules of the House permit it to consider regular appropriations bills after May 15, even if the budget resolution has not yet been adopted.

When the House or Senate considers a revenue or spending measure, the chair of the respective budget committee sometimes makes a statement advising the chamber concerning whether the measure violates these or other budget-related points of order. If no point of order is raised, or if the point of order is waived, the House or Senate may consider a measure despite any potential violations of the 1974 act. When the House waives points of order, it usually does so by adopting a special rule. The Senate usually waives points of order by unanimous consent or by motion under section 904 of the act. The Senate requires a three-fifths vote of the membership (sixty senators, if no seats are vacant) to waive certain provisions of the act.

As mentioned previously, the House and Senate may include additional points of order for budget enforcement purposes as provisions in budget resolutions or as part of their standing rules. The Senate established a "pay-as-you-go" (PAYGO) point of order in 1993 as part of the FY1994 budget resolution and has amended it several times over the years, most recently in 2007 (it currently is in effect though the end of FY2017). (*See § 7.11, Budget Enforcement Act Procedures: 1990–2002.*) The Senate PAYGO rule generally requires direct spending and revenue legislation to be deficit-neutral over six-year and eleven-year periods. These two time periods encompass the current year, the budget year, and the ensuing nine out-years, and in this regard is generally compatible with the time periods used in the House PAYGO rule and the Statutory PAYGO Act of 2010. The Senate PAYGO rule also requires a three-fifths vote to waive.

In 2007, at the beginning of the 110th Congress, the House added a PAYGO requirement to its standing rules (as Clause 10 of Rule XXI) for the first time. The House PAYGO rule provided a point of order against the consideration of any direct spending or revenue measure that would increase the deficit or reduce the surplus during either the six-year period (covering the current year, the budget year, and the four following fiscal years) or the eleven-year period (the previously cited period and the ensuing five fiscal years). In 2009, after the Republicans regained a majority in the House, the House PAYGO rule was replaced by a "cut-as-you-go" (CUTGO) rule. The new rule bars the consideration of legislation that increases mandatory spending over the six-year and eleven-year periods; the revenue effects of legislation no longer are considered for purposes of the rule. (Consequently, the consideration of legislation reducing revenues during these time periods would not be prohibited by this rule.)

§ 7.61

Budgeting for Direct and Guaranteed Loans

The Federal Credit Reform Act of 1990 made fundamental changes in the budgetary treatment of direct loans and guaranteed loans. Among its many provisions, the law required that budget authority and outlays be budgeted for the estimated subsidy cost of direct and guaranteed loans. This cost is defined in the 1990 law as the "estimated long-term cost to the Government of a direct loan or a loan guarantee, calculated on a net present value basis, excluding administrative costs. . . ." Under this law, Congress appropriates budget authority or provides indefinite authority equal to the subsidy cost. This budget authority is placed in a program account, from which funds are disbursed to a financing account.

§ 7.60 Spending, Revenue, and Debt-Limit Legislation

Congress implements the policies of the budget resolution through the enactment of spending (*§§ 7.70, 7.80*), revenue (*§ 7.90*), and debt-limit (*§ 7.100*) legislation. In many of the years since 1980, Congress has employed the reconciliation process (*§ 7.110*) to enact budget changes through legislation considered under expedited procedures. Reconciliation legislation can include revenue changes, changes in direct spending (but not usually changes in discretionary spending), and adjustments to the debt limit. Special procedures also apply to federal credit programs. (*See § 7.61, Budgeting for Direct and Guaranteed Loans.*)

For information on how Congress processes legislation, including budgetary legislation, see Chapter Six, Legislating in Congress: Legislative Process.

§ 7.70 Spending Legislation

The spending policies of the budget resolution generally are implemented through two different types of spending legislation. Policies involving *discretionary spending* are implemented in the context of *annual appropriations acts*, whereas policies affecting *direct* or *mandatory spending* (which, for

§ 7.71

Differences between Discretionary and Direct Spending

Feature	Discretionary Spending	Direct Spending
Budgetary impact of authorizing legislation	No direct impact; authorizes subsequent appropriations	Direct impact; provides budgetary resources
Committees that process budgetary legislation	Appropriations Committees	Authorizing committees; technically, Appropriations Committees for *appropriated entitlements* (like Medicaid)
Frequency of decision-making	Annual	Periodic
Means of enforcing budget resolution	Committee spending allocations and suballocations and points of order under Section 302	Committee spending allocations and points of order under Section 302 and the reconciliation process
Basis of computing budget impact	Current year's spending and president's request	Baseline budget projections
Impact of economic changes	Indirect	Direct, often automatic

the most part, involves *entitlement* programs) are carried out in substantive legislation. (*See § 7.71, Differences between Discretionary and Direct Spending.*)

All discretionary spending is under the jurisdiction of the House and Senate Appropriations Committees. Direct spending is under the jurisdiction of the various legislative committees of the House and Senate; the House Ways and Means Committee and the Senate Finance Committee have the largest shares of direct-spending jurisdiction. (Some entitlement programs, such as Medicaid, do not have their own source of funding and so are funded in annual appropriations acts, but such spending is not considered to be discretionary.) The enforcement procedures under the congressional budget process, mentioned in § 9.50, apply both to discretionary and direct spending.

Congress considers major direct spending legislation in particular policy areas, such as highway spending and farm policy, on a multiyear cycle under regular legislative procedures. In some years, however, significant changes in direct-spending programs, from a budgetary standpoint, are made in the reconciliation process. (*See § 7.110, Reconciliation Legislation.*) The greatest focus usually falls on discretionary spending decisions because annual appropriations acts must be enacted each year.

§ 7.80 Authorizations and Appropriations Processes

To implement the constitutional "power of the purse," Congress has created the annual appropriations process. House Rule XXI and Senate Rule XVI require the prior enactment of authorizing measures before appropriations acts may be considered. Authorizing measures deal with substantive policy issues and appropriations measures deal with funding. In practice, the boundaries between the two types of legislation are not always clear.

Authorizing Measures

An *authorization act* is a law that (1) establishes a program or agency and the terms and conditions under which it operates, and (2) authorizes the enactment of *appropriations* for that program or agency. *Authorizing legislation*, which is used to make authorization law, is one type of legislation that Congress commonly considers. Authorizing legislation may originate in either the House or the Senate, and may be considered at any time during the year. It can prescribe what an agency must do—or proscribe what it may not do—in the performance of its assigned responsibilities. It can give the agency a broad grant of authority and discretion, or define parameters, decision-making, and decisions in great detail.

Unless an authorization measure contains direct spending, which itself enables an agency to enter into obligations, authorizing legislation does not have budgetary impact. It authorizes discretionary spending, for which funding is provided subsequently in annual appropriations acts.

House rules do not expressly require authorizations. Instead, they bar *unauthorized appropriations*. The House may waive the rule against unauthorized appropriations by adopting a special rule before taking up an appropriations bill. The House rule barring unauthorized appropriations applies only against *general appropriations measures*. Under House precedents, a *continuing appropriations measure* is not considered to be a general appropriations bill, and it may thus fund unauthorized programs.

Senate rules also bar unauthorized appropriations, although many exceptions are allowed. Accordingly, the House rule is stricter than the Senate rule.

House rules also prohibit the inclusion of appropriations in authorizing legislation. Senate rules do not contain this prohibition.

House rules bar *legislation in an appropriations bill*, but a special rule from the Rules Committee can waive this requirement. (*See § 6.90, Rules Committee and Special Rules.*) Legislation in appropriations is also prohibited by Senate rules.

Permanent versus Temporary Authorizations. An authorization is presumed to be permanent unless the authorizing law limits its duration. *Permanent authorizations* do not have any time limit and continue in effect until they are changed by Congress. An agency having a permanent authorization need only obtain appropriations to continue in operations. *Annual authorizations* (such as for the Department of Defense) are for a single year and, usually, for a fixed amount of money; specified authorization levels usually serve as a limit on what can be appropriated subsequently. These authorizations need to be renewed each year. *Multiyear authorizations* (such as for Federal Aviation Administration programs) are typically in effect for several years and must be renewed when they expire. New authorizations of programs or activities with annual or multiyear authority are often referred to as *reauthorizations*.

As a general matter, appropriations enacted into law when the authorizing measure has not been enacted may be spent by the agency. The agency also may spend appropriated amounts that exceed authorized levels.

Permanent authorizations rarely specify amounts of money. Temporary authorizations usually do.

An authorization of appropriations in a specific amount is intended to serve as a guideline or limit for the Appropriations Committees in drafting appropriations measures and for Congress in

§ 7.81

Limitations, Earmarks, and General Provisions

In addition to appropriating specific dollar amounts, appropriations and their accompanying reports contain numerous other provisions that affect how federal departments and agencies spend appropriations. The principal categories of these provisions include the following:

- **Limitation**—language in legislation or in legislative documents that restricts the availability of an appropriation by limiting its use or amount.
- **Earmark**—a set-aside within an appropriation for a specific purpose that might be included either in legislation or in legislative documents.
- **Directive**—an instruction, usually in a legislative document, to an agency concerning the manner in which an appropriation is to be administered or requiring a report to Congress on issues of concern.
- **General Provision**—policy guidance on spending included in an appropriations measure; it may affect some or all appropriation accounts in the measure or even have government-wide application; it may also be one-time or permanent.

Appropriations measures might also contain legislative provisions that are included in appropriations measures despite House and Senate rules discouraging the practice.

approving them. However, one regularly finds large differences between enacted authorized and appropriated amounts. A member or group of members advocating "full funding" of a program is often in favor of an appropriation matching an authorization. Moreover, Congress does not need to make an appropriation for an authorization in law if it chooses not to fund an activity.

Annual Appropriations Measures

An appropriations act is a law passed by Congress that provides federal agencies with authority to incur *obligations* for the purposes specified for which payments are made out of the Treasury. As noted in § 7.00, the power to appropriate is a congressional power. Funds in the Treasury may not be withdrawn in the absence of an appropriation. Spending may occur only in accordance with the purposes and conditions Congress established in making an appropriation.

The Constitution does not require annual appropriations, but since the First Congress the practice has been to enact appropriations for a single fiscal year. Appropriations must be used (obligated) in the fiscal year for which they are provided, unless the law provides that they are available for a longer period of time. All provisions in an appropriations act, such as *limitations* on the use of funds, expire at the end of the fiscal year, unless the language of the act extends their period of effectiveness. (*See § 7.81, Limitations, Earmarks, and General Provisions.*)

The president requests annual appropriations in his budget submitted each year. In support of the president's appropriations requests, agencies submit *justification* materials to the House and Senate Appropriations Committees. These materials provide considerably more detail than is contained

§ 7.82

Appropriations Subcommittee Organization

For several decades, Congress considered thirteen regular appropriations acts developed by thirteen parallel subcommittees; each regular appropriations act was developed by the relevant House and Senate Appropriations subcommittee. Realignment of the Appropriations subcommittees in the 109th Congress reduced the number to ten in the House and twelve in the Senate, resulting in subcommittees (and regular appropriations acts) that in some cases were no longer parallel. Further realignment in the 110th Congress resulted in twelve subcommittees in each committee and restored parallelism between them. In some cases, subcommittee jurisdictions were not the same in the 110th Congress as they had been before realignment occurred. The current Appropriations subcommittees are as follows:

- Agriculture, Rural Development, Food and Drug Administration, and Related Agencies
- Commerce, Justice, Science, and Related Agencies
- Defense
- Energy and Water Development
- Financial Services and General Government
- Homeland Security
- Interior, Environment, and Related Agencies
- Labor, Health and Human Services, Education, and Related Agencies
- Legislative Branch
- Military Construction, Veterans' Affairs, and Related Agencies
- State, Foreign Operations, and Related Programs
- Transportation, and Housing and Urban Development, and Related Agencies

in the president's budget and are used in support of agency testimony during appropriations subcommittee hearings on the president's budget.

Congress passes three main types of appropriations measures. *Regular appropriations acts* provide budget authority to agencies for the upcoming fiscal year. *Supplemental appropriations acts* provide additional budget authority during the current fiscal year when the regular appropriation is insufficient. Supplemental appropriations also finance activities not provided for in regular appropriations. *Continuing appropriations acts*, often referred to as *continuing resolutions* (after the form of legislation in which they are usually considered, the joint resolution [H.J. Res. ___]), provide stopgap funding for agencies that have not received regular appropriations. In some years, a series of continuing resolutions (CRs) provide funding for the entire fiscal year. For purposes of House and Senate rules, all regular and supplemental appropriations measures covering two or more agencies or purposes are considered *general appropriations measures*.

The number of regular appropriations acts was fixed for several decades at thirteen, but realignment of the Appropriations subcommittees in the 109th and 110th Congresses reduced that number; at present, there are twelve regular appropriations acts. (*See § 7.82, Appropriations Subcommittee Organization.*) In some years, Congress merges two or more of the regular appropriations bills into an *omnibus measure*. In a typical session, Congress also acts on at least one supplemental appropriations measure. Because of recurring delays in the appropriations process, Congress also typically passes one or more continuing appropriations each year. The scope and duration of these measures depend on the status of the regular appropriations bills and the degree of budgetary conflict between Congress and the president. Funding levels for activities under a continuing appropriations act usually are restrictive and keyed to formulas, such as the lower of the current rate or the president's budget request, or the lower of the House-passed or Senate-passed amount.

In the House. By precedent, appropriations originate in the House of Representatives. In the House, appropriations measures are originated by the Appropriations Committee (when it marks up or reports the measures) rather than being introduced by an individual member.

Before the full Appropriations Committee acts on a measure, the measure is considered in the relevant subcommittee. The House subcommittees typically hold extensive hearings on appropriations requests shortly after the president's budget is submitted. In marking up their appropriations bills, the various subcommittees are guided by the spending suballocations made to them under the budget resolution, as required by section 302(b) of the 1974 Congressional Budget Act.

The subcommittees' recommendations generally are quite influential. It is common for the full Appropriations Committee to mark up and report an appropriations measure prepared for it by a subcommittee without making any substantive changes. The subcommittees also draft the committee reports that accompany appropriations measures to the floor. The Appropriations Committee usually begins reporting bills in early May.

Because general appropriations measures are privileged and thus have direct access to the House floor for consideration, they can be brought to the floor without first obtaining a special rule from the Rules Committee. Nonetheless, most appropriations bills come to the floor under a rule waiving one or more standing rules, such as the rule against unauthorized appropriations. (*See § 7.83, Sequence of Appropriations Measures through Congress.*) Between May and the start of the fiscal year on October 1 (and sometimes until the end of the session), the House often spends many of its days in session processing appropriations measures reported from the House Appropriations Committee or from the conference committees that are normally convened on each of the regular appropriations measures, supplemental appropriations measures, and continuing resolutions. (*See Chapter Six, Legislating in Congress: Legislative Process.*)

In the Senate. Subcommittees of the Senate Appropriations Committee also begin their hearings on appropriations requests shortly after the president's budget is submitted. They are also guided by the section 302(b) spending suballocations. Hearings in Senate appropriations subcommittees may not be as extensive as those held by the counterpart subcommittees of the House Appropriations Committee. Subcommittee markup and reporting to the full Appropriations Committee is followed by full committee markup and reporting.

Up until the latter part of the 1990s, the Senate usually would consider appropriations measures after they had been passed by the House. When the Senate changed a House-passed appropriations measure, it did so by inserting amendments numbered consecutively through the measure.

Under current practice, the Senate sometimes first considers a Senate-numbered measure up to the stage of final passage, routinely using complex unanimous consent agreements to frame floor consideration. When the House-passed measure eventually is received in the Senate, it is amended

§ 7.83

Sequence of Appropriations Measures through Congress

House	Senate
Subcommittee hearings	Subcommittee hearings
Subcommittee markup (no measure number is assigned yet)	Subcommittee markup (either a House-passed measure or an unnumbered Senate measure)
Full committee markup and report (measure is introduced and number is assigned)	Full committee markup and report (either a House-passed measure or a Senate measure is introduced and number is assigned)
House floor action	Senate floor action (if a Senate measure is considered, it is held at the stage of final passage so that the Senate can amend and pass the House measure, fulfilling the tradition that the House originates appropriations measures)

House-Senate Conference
(on a House-numbered measure)

House agrees to conference report (and any amendments in disagreement)	Senate agrees to conference report (and any amendments in disagreement)

Enrolled Measure Sent to President

with the text that the Senate has already agreed to (as a single amendment) and then passed by the Senate. This practice allows the Senate to consider appropriations measures without having to wait for the House to adopt its version, facilitating the timely consideration and completion of the regular appropriations measures.

Like the House, the Senate often spends many of its days in session between June and the start of the fiscal year (or sometimes until the end of the session), engaged in processing appropriations measures reported from the Senate Appropriations Committee or from the conference committees that are normally convened on each of the regular appropriations measures, supplemental appropriations measures, and continuing resolutions.

Conference. As appropriations measures pass both the House and Senate, conference committees are appointed to resolve differences. As is the case on most major pieces of legislation, conference is a critical stage in the legislative process for key policy decisions and many details. Conference reports must pass the House and Senate before an enrolled measure is transmitted to the president for signature or veto. (*See Chapter Six, Legislating in Congress: Legislative Process.*) Recently, the House and Senate sometimes have avoided using a conference to resolve differences over a bill, instead choosing to exchange amendments between the two chambers until differences are resolved. This approach may be used to expedite the process and minimize contentious votes.

Additional Congressional Controls in Appropriations Acts

The basic element of an appropriations act is an *account.* A single unnumbered paragraph in an appropriations act comprises one account. All provisions of that paragraph pertain to that account and to no other, unless the text expressly gives them broader scope. Any provision limiting the use of funds enacted in that paragraph is a restriction on that account alone.

Over the years, appropriations have been consolidated into a relatively small number of accounts with large "lump-sum" appropriations. It is typical for a federal agency to have a single account for all its expenses of operation and several additional accounts for other purposes, such as construction. Accordingly, most appropriations accounts encompass a number of activities or projects.

An appropriation sometimes *earmarks* specific amounts to particular activities within the account, but the more common practice is to provide detailed information on the amounts intended for each activity in other sources, principally the committee reports accompanying the measures. The House and Senate expanded the use of earmarks through 2010, but abuses led both chambers to adopt strict rules governing their use and to significantly curtail earmarks. Extensive information on earmarks, including identification of the requesting member of Congress, is provided in House and Senate Appropriations Committee reports accompanying the appropriations acts. (*See § 7.84, Examples of Appropriations Subcommittees' Requirements for Member Requests.*)

In addition to the substantive limitations and other provisions associated with each account, each appropriations act has *general provisions* that apply to all the accounts in a title or in the whole act. These general provisions appear as numbered sections, usually at the end of the title or act.

In a typical appropriations act, most funding is provided as *one-year appropriations* (the funds are available for obligation during the single fiscal year and lapse after the year has expired). The account language usually does not indicate the period that funds are available; instead, a general provision indicates that all funding provided in the act is available for one year unless otherwise indicated. Congress also makes *no-year appropriations* by specifying that the funds shall remain available until expended. No-year funds are carried over to future years, even if they have not been obligated. Congress sometimes makes *multiyear appropriations,* which provide for funds to be available for two or more fiscal years. *Permanent appropriations,* such as those to pay interest on the national debt or to pay the salaries of members of Congress, remain available without additional action by Congress. (Most, but not all, permanent appropriations are provided in substantive law, not annual appropriations acts.)

Appropriations measures also contain other types of provisions that serve specialized purposes, such as provisions that liquidate (pay off) obligations made pursuant to certain *contract authority* and that *reappropriate* funds provided in previous years. These provisions also *transfer* funds from one account to another; *rescind* funds (or release *deferred* funds); and set ceilings on the amount of obligations that can be made under permanent appropriations, on the amount of direct or guaranteed loans that can be made, or on the amount of administrative expenses that can be incurred during the fiscal year. In addition to providing funds, appropriations acts often contain substantive limitations on government agencies.

Detailed information on how funds are to be spent, along with other directives or guidance, is pro-

§ 7.84

Examples of Appropriations Subcommittees' Requirements for Member Requests

JERRY LEWIS, CALIFORNIA, CHAIRMAN
C. W. BILL YOUNG, FLORIDA
RALPH REGULA, OHIO
HAROLD ROGERS, KENTUCKY
FRANK R. WOLF, VIRGINIA
JIM KOLBE, ARIZONA
JAMES T. WALSH, NEW YORK
CHARLES H. TAYLOR, NORTH CAROLINA
DAVID L. HOBSON, OHIO
ERNEST J. ISTOOK, JR., OKLAHOMA
HENRY BONILLA, TEXAS
JOE KNOLLENBERG, MICHIGAN
JACK KINGSTON, GEORGIA
RODNEY P. FRELINGHUYSEN, NEW JERSEY
ROGER F. WICKER, MISSISSIPPI
RANDY "DUKE" CUNNINGHAM, CALIFORNIA
TODD TIAHRT, KANSAS
ZACH WAMP, TENNESSEE
TOM LATHAM, IOWA
ANNE M. NORTHUP, KENTUCKY
ROBERT B. ADERHOLT, ALABAMA
JO ANN EMERSON, MISSOURI
KAY GRANGER, TEXAS
JOHN E. PETERSON, PENNSYLVANIA
VIRGIL H. GOODE, JR., VIRGINIA
JOHN T. DOOLITTLE, CALIFORNIA
RAY LaHOOD, ILLINOIS
JOHN E. SWEENEY, NEW YORK
DON SHERWOOD, PENNSYLVANIA
DAVE WELDON, FLORIDA
MICHAEL K. SIMPSON, IDAHO
JOHN ABNEY CULBERSON, TEXAS
MARK STEVEN KIRK, ILLINOIS
ANDER CRENSHAW, FLORIDA
DENNIS R. REHBERG, MONTANA
JOHN R. CARTER, TEXAS
RODNEY ALEXANDER, LOUISIANA

Congress of the United States
House of Representatives
Committee on Appropriations
Washington, DC 20515–6015

February 22, 2005

DAVID R. OBEY, WISCONSIN
JOHN P. MURTHA, PENNSYLVANIA
NORMAN D. DICKS, WASHINGTON
MARTIN OLAV SABO, MINNESOTA
STENY H. HOYER, MARYLAND
ALAN B. MOLLOHAN, WEST VIRGINIA
MARCY KAPTUR, OHIO
PETER J. VISCLOSKY, INDIANA
NITA M. LOWEY, NEW YORK
JOSÉ E. SERRANO, NEW YORK
ROSA L. DeLAURO, CONNECTICUT
JAMES P. MORAN, VIRGINIA
JOHN W. OLVER, MASSACHUSETTS
ED PASTOR, ARIZONA
DAVID E. PRICE, NORTH CAROLINA
CHET EDWARDS, TEXAS
ROBERT E. "BUD" CRAMER, JR., ALABAMA
PATRICK J. KENNEDY, RHODE ISLAND
JAMES E. CLYBURN, SOUTH CAROLINA
MAURICE D. HINCHEY, NEW YORK
LUCILLE ROYBAL-ALLARD, CALIFORNIA
SAM FARR, CALIFORNIA
JESSE L. JACKSON, JR., ILLINOIS
CAROLYN C. KILPATRICK, MICHIGAN
ALLEN BOYD, FLORIDA
CHAKA FATTAH, PENNSYLVANIA
STEVEN R. ROTHMAN, NEW JERSEY
SANFORD D. BISHOP, JR., GEORGIA
MARION BERRY, ARKANSAS

CLERK AND STAFF DIRECTOR
FRANK M. CUSHING

TELEPHONE:
(202) 225–2771

Dear Colleague:

It is an honor and a privilege for us to serve as the Chairman and Ranking Minority Member of the Subcommittee on Agriculture, Rural Development, Food and Drug Administration and Related Agencies in the 1st session of the 109th Congress.

As we begin to develop the fiscal year 2006 Agriculture Appropriations bill, we would seek input from both member offices and outside parties interested in expressing their views on matters under the Subcommittee's purview. The Subcommittee will collect member requests via an electronic form posted on the House Intranet. We will collect this information in order to evaluate the need and/or merits of particular projects and programs. The due date is **April 8, 2005.**

As all of you are well aware, the Appropriations Committee faces a tight discretionary allocation in fiscal year 2006. As a result, we cannot guarantee that a particular project or program will be funded, either in part or in full. If your office is requesting funding for specific projects, it is especially important that your office assign a priority number to each project for which you are requesting funding. Each member office should prioritize their projects amongst the total number of requests (i.e., a member's office cannot have a number one priority for projects under the Agricultural Research Service and then another number one priority under the Natural Resources Conservation Service.) The Subcommittee **will only accept requests for project funding or bill / report language from a Member's office**. A signed letter MUST accompany the electronic submission from the Member of Congress to the Subcommittee Chairman that briefly mentions EACH of the items submitted electronically. No electronic file submissions will be considered without delivery of a signed letter that references each submission. Your office may access the electronic request form at the following link: http://onlinecao.house.gov/appropriations/AGApprops.asp .

If you or an outside party are interested in providing written testimony for the record in connection with our fiscal year 2006 budget hearings, please provide three copies to the Subcommittee at 2362A Rayburn House Office Building no later than **April 8, 2005.** Testimony is limited to not more than five single-spaced, letter-size pages, typed on only one side of each page. Although maps, pictures, graphs, letters, petitions and the like may be submitted for the information of the Subcommittee, it is not feasible to include them in the printed hearing record.

Of course, all testimony will be thoroughly reviewed by the Subcommittee. The Subcommittee will also review and consider all information received by Members at any time, whether or not submitted for publication in the formal hearing record.

We hope that this process will help expedite our hearing schedule and result in fewer disruptions and inconveniences for Members. If you have any questions or require further information, please contact the Subcommittee staff at (202) 225-2638.

Sincerely,

Henry Bonilla
Chairman
Subcommittee on Agriculture, Rural Development, Food and Drug Administration and Related Agencies

Rosa DeLauro
Ranking Minority Member
Subcommittee on Agriculture, Rural Development, Food and Drug Administration and Related Agencies

Continued on page 338

§ 7.84 (continued)

Examples of Appropriations Subcommittees' Requirements for Member Requests

LABOR, HHS, EDUCATION AND RELATED AGENCIES SUBCOMMITTEE
FY06 PROJECT QUESTIONNAIRE SHEET

Due to the large number of requests received by the Subcommittee, please assemble your request letter as follows:

- **If the answers to a project questionnaire exceed one page please staple the pages together.**
- **Please provide (3) copies of each completed project questionnaire.**
- **Please clip this set of three copies together.**
- **If you are requesting funding for multiple projects, please collate questionnaires – e.g. three copies of the questionnaire for your project #1 clipped together, followed by three copies of the questionnaire for project #2 clipped together, etc.**

1. Name of Member of Congress.

2. Congressional Staff contact, phone number, and email address.

3. Priority ranking: Due to the funding constraints, please assign a priority number to each project for which you are requesting funding.

4. Name and address of the project grant recipient, and name, telephone number (and e-mail address, if available) of a contact person at the recipient organization. If the potential recipient is a school, please provide the name and location of the school district in which the school is located. Also, if the project is to be carried out in a location that is different from the grantee address, please provide that city and State.

5. Provide a brief description of the activity or project for which funding is requested. **The only construction funding available is for health-related activities.** If the request is for health-related construction, please identify the activity(s) that will be carried out in the health facility.

6. Funding details:
   a. Total project cost (i.e., including all funding sources and all years):
   b. Amount you are requesting for this project in fiscal year 2006 (your FY 2006 request should not exceed the amount that will be used in one year):
   c. **Break down/budget** of the amount you are requesting for this project in fiscal year 2006. (For example, salary $40,000; computer $3,000 etc.)
   d. What other funding sources are contributing to this project? What amount does each of these funding sources contribute?
   e. Has the potential recipient received funding for this project from any Federal agency currently or in the past five years? If yes, include information on the amount of funds, the years received, and the name of the Federal agency and program providing the funding.

7. Describe the organization's main activities, and whether it is a public, private non-profit, or private for-profit entity.

8. What is the national significance of the project, and what specific federal responsibility does the funding of this project or activity further? For example, what measurable improvements in health status, educational achievement, or similar outcomes will result from this project?

§ 7.91

Tax Expenditures

In enacting revenue legislation, Congress often establishes or alters tax expenditures. As defined in the 1974 Congressional Budget Act, "tax expenditures" include revenue losses due to deductions, exemptions, credits, and other exceptions to the basic tax structure. Tax expenditures are a means by which Congress pursues public policy objectives and, frequently, can be regarded as alternatives to other policy instruments such as grants and loans. The Joint Committee on Taxation estimates the revenue effects of legislation changing tax expenditures, and also publishes five-year projections of these provisions as an annual committee print. Every two years, the Senate Budget Committee issues a compendium of tax expenditures (prepared by the Congressional Research Service); the 2010 volume is titled, *Tax Expenditures: Compendium of Background Material on Individual Provisions* (S. Prt. 111-58, December 2010). An example of a well-known tax expenditure is the mortgage-interest deduction available to homeowners.

The current volume can be found on GPO's Federal Digital System, at *<http://fdsys.gov>*, and then searching for "Tax Expenditures: Compendium of Background Material on Individual Provisions." Also see *<CDDocs.com>*.

vided in the committee and conference reports accompanying the various appropriations measures. Although report language typically is not binding legally, agencies ordinarily abide by it in spending the funds appropriated by Congress.

The appropriations reports do not comment on every item of expenditure. Report language is most likely when the Appropriations Committee prefers to spend more or less on a particular item than the president has requested or when the committee wants to earmark funds for a particular project or activity. When a particular item is mentioned by the committee, there is a strong expectation that the agency will adhere to the instructions. (*See § 8.73, Legislative History.*)

§ 7.90 Revenue Legislation

The Constitution requires that all revenue measures originate in the House of Representatives. The Senate, however, may amend a House-originated revenue measure. If the Senate adopts an original Senate measure carrying a revenue provision, the House usually enforces its constitutional prerogative over originating revenue measures by adopting a simple resolution stating that the Senate measure infringes upon the privileges of the House and returning the measure to the Senate, a process referred to as "blue-slipping." The term "blue-slipping" refers to the blue paper on which the resolution is printed.

In the House, revenue legislation is under the jurisdiction of the Ways and Means Committee; in the Senate, jurisdiction is held by the Finance Committee. House rules bar other committees from reporting revenue legislation. Sometimes, however, another committee will report legislation levying user fees on a class that benefits from a particular service or program or that is being regulated by a federal agency. In many of these cases, the user-fee legislation in the House is referred subsequently to the Ways and Means Committee.

§ 7.92

Revenue Estimates

The Joint Committee on Taxation (JCT) <*http://jct.gov*> prepares estimates of proposed revenue legislation for Congress. Generally, the estimates measure the effects of revenue proposals on the revenue projections under existing law. In recent years, some members of Congress have questioned whether or not the estimates of revenue proposals currently provided by the JCT (referred to as "static" by some) adequately take into account macroeconomic effects and incorporate such effects into revenue estimates (referred to as "dynamic estimates").

House standing rules require a "macroeconomic impact analysis" of most revenue measures reported by the Committee on Ways and Means, unless the JCT determines that such an analysis is "not calculable."

The House rule defines a "macroeconomic impact analysis" as:

(i) an estimate prepared by the Joint Committee on Internal Revenue [sic] Taxation of the changes in economic output, employment, capital stock, and tax revenues expected to result from enactment of the proposal; and

(ii) a statement from the Joint Committee on Internal Revenue [sic] Taxation identifying the critical assumptions and the source data underlying that estimate.

Neither the House rule nor the 1974 Congressional Budget Act requires that such estimates be used for budget enforcement purposes. However, neither the rule nor the 1974 Act precludes the use of such estimates for that purpose.

Most revenues derive from existing provisions of the tax code or Social Security law, which generally continues in effect from year to year unless changed by Congress. This tax structure can be expected to produce increasing amounts of revenue in future years as the economy expands and incomes rise, but revenues have dropped in some recent years due to economic decline. Congress usually makes some changes in the tax laws each year, either to raise or lower revenues or to redistribute the tax burden. (*See § 7.91, Tax Expenditures.*)

Congress typically acts on revenue legislation pursuant to proposals in the president's budget. An early step in congressional work on revenue legislation is publication by the Congressional Budget Office (CBO) of its own estimates of the revenue impact of the president's budget proposals, developed with assistance from the Joint Committee on Taxation. The congressional estimates often differ significantly from those presented in the president's budget.

The revenue totals in the budget resolution establish the framework for subsequent action on revenue measures. The budget resolution contains only revenue totals and the amounts by which total revenues should be changed by legislative action. It does not allocate these totals among revenue sources or specify which provisions of the tax code are to be changed.

The House and Senate periodically consider major revenue measures under their regular legislative procedures. (*See § 7.92, Revenue Estimates.*) However, as has been the case with direct-spending programs, many of the most significant changes in revenue policy in recent years have been made in the context of the reconciliation process. (*See § 7.110, Reconciliation Legislation.*)

Although revenue changes sometimes are incorporated along with spending changes (and sometimes debt-limit increases) into a single, omnibus budget reconciliation measure, at other times revenue reconciliation legislation is considered on a separate track (for example, the Tax Increase Prevention and Reconciliation Act of 2005 (*P.L. 109-222; 120 Stat. 345*)).

§ 7.100 Debt-Limit Legislation

When the revenues collected by the federal government are not sufficient to cover its expenditures, it must finance the shortfall through borrowing. In addition, the federal government is compelled to incur debt because of requirements that trust fund surpluses be invested in federal securities. Federal borrowing is subject to a public-debt limit established by statute. As long as the federal government incurs annual deficits and trust funds incur annual surpluses, the public-debt limit must be increased periodically. The frequency of congressional action to raise the debt limit has ranged in the past from several times in one year to once in several years.

Legislation to raise the public-debt limit falls under the jurisdiction of the House Ways and Means Committee and the Senate Finance Committee. Congress has developed debt-limit legislation over the years in three ways: (1) under regular legislative procedures; (2) as part of reconciliation legislation; or (3) in the House, under Rule XXVII (referred to as the "Gephardt rule" after its author, former Representative Richard Gephardt, D-MO). House Rule XXVII required that the House Clerk automatically engross and transmit to the Senate, upon the adoption of the budget resolution, a joint resolution changing the public debt limit to the level specified in the budget resolution. This automatic engrossing process was added to the House rules in 1979, remained in the House rules until it was removed at the beginning of the 107th Congress, was restored at the beginning of the 108th Congress, and was removed again at the beginning of the 112th Congress in 2011. The Senate has no procedure comparable to the Gephardt rule. The Senate may add nongermane provisions to debt-limit legislation considered under regular legislative procedures. For example, the 1985 Balanced Budget Act (Gramm-Rudman-Hollings) was an amendment to a debt-limit bill.

Finally, see the discussion of the Budget Control Act of 2011 (*§ 7.10*) for a discussion of how the Act raised the debt limit in phases.

§ 7.110 Reconciliation Legislation

Beginning in 1980, Congress has used *reconciliation legislation* to implement many of its most significant budget policies. Section 310 of the 1974 Congressional Budget Act sets forth procedures for the development and consideration of reconciliation legislation. Reconciliation legislation is used by Congress to bring existing revenue, spending, and debt-limit law into conformity with the policies in a budget resolution. Reconciliation is an optional process, but Congress has used it more years than not since 1980.

The reconciliation process has two stages—the adoption of *reconciliation directives* in the budget resolution and the enactment of reconciliation legislation that implements changes in revenue or spending laws. Although reconciliation has been used for some time, specific procedures tend to vary from year to year.

Reconciliation is used to change the amount of revenues, budget authority, or outlays generated

7

by existing law. In a few instances, reconciliation has been used to adjust the public-debt limit. On the spending side, the process focuses on entitlement laws; it may not be used, however, to impel changes in Social Security law. Reconciliation sometimes has been applied to discretionary authorizations, which are funded in annual appropriations acts, but this is not the usual practice.

In 2007, the House and Senate adopted rules requiring that the reconciliation process be used only for deficit reduction. In 2009, the House changed its rule to prohibit reconciliation measures that cause increases in net direct spending; reductions in revenues are permitted.

Reconciliation Directives

Reconciliation begins with a directive in a budget resolution instructing one or more designated committees to recommend legislation changing existing law. These directives have three components: (1) they name the committee or committees directed to recommend legislation; (2) they specify the amounts of changes in revenues or outlays that are to be achieved by changes in existing law, but do not usually indicate how these changes are to be made, which laws are to be altered, or the programs to be affected; and (3) they usually set a deadline by which the designated committee or committees must recommend the changes in law. The directives cover the same fiscal years covered by the budget resolution. The dollar amounts are computed with reference to the Congressional Budget Office *baseline* that underlies the budget resolution. Thus, a change represents the amount by which revenues or spending would decrease or increase from baseline levels as a result of changes made in existing law.

Although the instructions generally do not mention the programs to be changed, they are based on assumptions concerning the savings or deficit reduction (or, in some cases, increases) that would result from particular changes in revenue provisions or spending programs. These program assumptions are sometimes printed in the reports on the budget resolution. Even when the assumptions are not published, committees and members usually have a good idea of the specific program changes contemplated by the reconciliation directives.

A committee has discretion to decide the legislative changes to be recommended. It is not bound by the program changes recommended or assumed by the budget committees in the reports accompanying the budget resolution. However, a committee is expected to recommend legislation estimated to produce the dollar changes delineated in its reconciliation directives.

When a budget resolution containing a reconciliation directive has been approved by Congress, the instruction has the status of an order by the House and Senate to designated committees to recommend legislation, usually by a date certain.

Development and Consideration of Reconciliation Measures

When more than one committee in the House and Senate is subject to reconciliation directives, the proposed legislative changes are consolidated by the budget committees into an omnibus bill. The 1974 Congressional Budget Act does not permit the budget committees to revise substantively the legislation recommended by the committees of jurisdiction. This restriction pertains even when the budget committees estimate that the proposed legislation will fall short of the dollar changes called for in the instructions. Sometimes, the budget committees—working with the leadership—develop alternatives to the committee recommendations. These alternatives may be offered as floor amendments to achieve greater compliance with the reconciliation directives.

The 1974 act requires that amendments offered to reconciliation legislation in either the House or the Senate be deficit-neutral. To meet this requirement, an amendment reducing revenues or increasing spending must offset these deficit increases by equivalent revenue increases or spending cuts. In addition, nongermane amendments may not be offered in either chamber.

During the first several years of experience with reconciliation, the legislation contained many provisions that were extraneous to the purpose of the reconciliation measures, such as reducing the deficit. The reconciliation submissions of committees included such things as provisions that had no budgetary effect, that had a budgetary effect merely incidental to a significant policy change, or that violated another committee's jurisdiction. In 1985, the Senate adopted a rule (commonly referred to as the *Byrd rule*, after Senator Robert C. Byrd, D-WV) on a temporary basis as a means of curbing these practices. The Byrd rule has been extended and modified several times over the years. In 1990, the Byrd rule was incorporated into the 1974 Congressional Budget Act as section 313 and made permanent. The Senate, nonetheless, may waive the Byrd rule by unanimous consent or by a waiver motion requiring a three-fifths vote of the membership. Although the House has no rule comparable to the Senate's Byrd rule, it may use other devices to control the inclusion of extraneous matter in reconciliation legislation. In particular, the House has used *special rules* to make in order amendments to strike extraneous matter. (*See § 6.90, Rules Committee and Special Rules.*)

7

Senate debate on reconciliation legislation is limited to twenty hours. The Senate may continue to consider amendments, motions, and appeals after that time, but no additional debate is allowed. The House is not restricted by the 1974 act in debate on reconciliation legislation, but it typically adopts a special rule limiting general debate, amendments, and other floor procedures.

§ 7.120 Implementation of the Budget by Executive Agencies

Federal agencies implement the various spending and revenue measures enacted into law through thousands of discrete actions. While the submission of the president's budget proposals and the subsequent consideration of them by Congress in the legislative process usually garner considerable attention in the media, less scrutiny often is paid to what actually happens to funds after congressional action is finished. Three categories of executive agency actions are of particular interest to Congress: apportionment (*§ 7.130*), transfer and reprogramming (*§ 7.140*), and impoundment (*§ 7.150*).

§ 7.130 Apportionment

After legislation providing budget authority is enacted into law, one of the first steps in making the funds available for spending by agencies is *apportionment.* Apportionment procedures are set forth in the Antideficiency Act (*31 U.S.C. §§ 1341–1342, 1512–1519*), which evolved from legislation first enacted in the 1870s. Under these procedures, the Office of Management and Budget (OMB) determines how increments of budget authority will be advanced to each agency on an account-by-account basis. For a typical account, OMB apportions one-fourth of the available budget authority at the beginning of each fiscal quarter. A violation of the Antideficiency Act may occur when an agency obligates more funds than were apportioned to it; the comptroller general is tasked by Congress with monitoring such violations.

In the absence of an appropriations act, such as when a continuing resolution (CR) is not enacted in a timely manner, the Antideficiency Act requires the affected agencies to shut down.

§ 7.140 Transfer and Reprogramming

After spending measures have been enacted into law, agencies sometimes shift funds from one purpose to another. A *transfer* involves the shifting of funds from one account to another, while a *reprogramming* involves shifting funds from one program to another within the same account. In either case, Congress is involved in these adjustments, although in varying degrees.

Permanent law, in Title 31 (Money and Finance) of the U.S. Code, requires that agencies spend funds only according to the purposes specified in law. For this reason, the transfer of funds from one account to another requires the enactment of a law. In some cases, Congress anticipates the need to transfer funds and may grant a department or agency head transfer authority in advance, subject to limitations. In other instances, Congress might enact legislation providing for specified transfers after the need has been identified.

Unlike transfers, reprogrammings do not shift funds from one account to another and therefore do not require the enactment of a law. The Appropriations Committees exert control over reprogrammings by establishing specific rules that agencies must follow when pursuing such actions. In recent years, these rules have been included as provisions in annual appropriations acts. The rules set forth restrictions such as requiring prior committee notification and approval for reprogrammings beyond a certain dollar threshold and barring reprogrammings from terminating any existing program or creating a new one.

§ 7.150 Impoundment: Deferrals and Rescissions

Although an appropriation limits the amounts that can be spent, it also establishes the expectation that the available funds will be used in full. Hence, when an agency fails to use all or part of an appropriation, it deviates from the intentions of Congress. The Impoundment Control Act of 1974 (*P.L. 93-344, title X; 88 Stat. 332–339*), enacted as part of the Congressional Budget and Impoundment Control Act of 1974, prescribes rules and procedures for instances in which available funds are *impounded.* (*See § 7.10, Key Budget Process Laws.*)

An impoundment is an action or inaction by the president or a federal agency that delays or withholds the obligation or expenditure of budget authority provided in law. The 1974 Impoundment Control Act divides impoundments into two categories and establishes distinct procedures for each. A *deferral* delays the use of funds; a *rescission* is a presidential request that Congress rescind (cancel) an appropriation or other form of budget authority. Deferral and rescission are exclusive and comprehensive categories. An impoundment is either a rescission or a deferral—it cannot be both or something else.

To propose a rescission, the president must submit a message to Congress specifying the amount to be rescinded, the accounts and programs involved, the estimated fiscal and program effects, and the reasons for the rescission. Multiple rescissions can be grouped in a single message. After the message has been submitted to it, Congress has forty-five days of "continuous session" (usually a larger number of calendar days) during which it can pass a rescission bill. Congress may rescind all, part, or none of the amount proposed by the president.

If Congress does not approve a rescission in legislation by the expiration of this period, the president must make the funds available for obligation and expenditure. If the president fails to release funds at the expiration of the forty-five-day period for proposed rescissions, the comptroller general may bring suit to compel their release. This has been a rare occurrence, however.

To defer funds, the president submits a message to Congress setting forth the amount, the affected account and program, the reasons for the deferral, the estimated fiscal and program effects, and the period of time during which the funds are to be deferred. The president may not propose a deferral for a period of time beyond the end of the fiscal year, and he may not propose a deferral that would cause the funds to lapse or otherwise prevent an agency from spending appropriated funds prudently. In accounts where unobligated funds remain available beyond the fiscal year, the president may defer the funds again in the next fiscal year.

At present, the president may defer only for the reasons set forth in the Antideficiency Act, including to provide for contingencies, to achieve savings made possible by or through changes in requirements or greater efficiency of operations, and as specifically provided by law. He may not defer funds for policy reasons (for example, to curtail overall federal spending or because he is opposed to a particular program).

The comptroller general, head of the Government Accountability Office (GAO), reviews all proposed rescissions and deferrals and advises Congress of their legality and possible budgetary and program effects. The comptroller general also notifies Congress of any rescission or deferral not reported by the president. The comptroller general may also reclassify an improperly classified impoundment. In all cases, a notification to Congress by the comptroller general has the same legal effect as an impoundment message of the president. The president's impoundment messages, as well as the comptroller general's reports, are printed as House documents (H. Doc. ___). The GAO also issues its reports separately.

The 1974 Impoundment Control Act provided for special types of legislation—rescission bills and deferral resolutions—for Congress to use in exercising its impoundment control powers. However, pursuant to court decisions that held the *legislative veto* to be unconstitutional, Congress may not use deferral resolutions to disapprove a deferral. Further, Congress has been reluctant to use rescission bills regularly. Congress, instead, usually acts on impoundment matters within the framework of the annual appropriations measures.

President George W. Bush did not propose any rescissions under the Impoundment Control Act. Instead he proposed the "cancellation" of funds; under this approach, he did not have to submit a report on his proposed cancellations to Congress, but neither could he withhold spending the funds while the proposals were pending. Congress responded to the proposed cancellations by enacting many of them—amounting to billions of dollars—into law. President Barack Obama continued the practice of proposing cancellations to avoid complications under the 1974 act.

§ 7.160

Budget Process Glossary

Account: Control and reporting unit for budgeting and accounting.

Appropriated Entitlement: An entitlement for which budget authority is provided in annual appropriations acts.

Appropriation: Provision of law providing budget authority that permits federal agencies to incur obligations and make payments out of the Treasury.

Authorization: Provision in law that establishes or continues a program or agency and authorizes appropriations for it.

Baseline: Projection of future revenues, budget authority, outlays, and other budget amounts under assumed economic conditions and participation rates without a change in current policy.

Borrowing Authority: Spending authority that permits a federal agency to incur obligations and to make payments for specified purposes out of funds borrowed from the Treasury or the public.

Budget Authority: Authority in law to enter into obligations that normally result in outlays.

Budget Resolution: Concurrent resolution incorporating an agreement by the House and Senate on an overall budget plan; may contain reconciliation instructions.

Byrd Rule: A Congressional Budget Act rule (Section 313), named after its author, Senator Robert C. Byrd (D-WV), that prohibits extraneous matter in a reconciliation measure considered in the Senate. Under the rule, extraneous matter includes, among other things specified in the act, any provision that has no direct budgetary effect or that increases the deficit (or reduces the surplus) in a fiscal year beyond those covered in the reconciliation measure.

Continuing Appropriations Act: An appropriations act that provides stop-gap funding for agencies that have not received regular appropriations. (Also referred to as a continuing resolution.)

Cost Estimate: An estimate of the impact of legislation on revenues, spending, or both, generally as reported by a House or Senate committee or a conference committee; the 1974 Congressional Budget Act requires the Congressional Budget Office to prepare cost estimates on all public bills.

Credit Authority: Authority to incur direct loan obligations or make loan guarantee commitments.

Deferral: Action or inaction that temporarily withholds, delays, or effectively precludes the obligation or expenditure of budget authority.

Direct Spending: Spending controlled outside of annual appropriations acts, and specifically including the Food Stamp program (now the Supplemental Nutrition Assistance Program (SNAP)); also referred to as mandatory spending.

Discretionary Spending: Spending provided in, and controlled by, annual appropriations acts.

Earmark: For expenditures, an amount set aside within an appropriation account for a specified purpose.

Entitlement Authority: Law that obligates the federal government to make payments to eligible persons, businesses, or governments.

Fiscal Year: The period from October 1 through September 30; fiscal year 2008 began October 1, 2007, and ended September 30, 2008.

Continued on page 347

§ 7.160 (continued)

Impoundment: Action or inaction by an executive official that delays or precludes the obligation or expenditure of budget authority.

Mandatory Spending: *See Direct Spending.*

Obligation: A binding agreement that requires payment.

Outlays: Payments to liquidate obligations.

PAYGO (Pay-As-You-Go): Process by which direct spending increases or revenue decreases must be offset so that the deficit is not increased or the surplus reduced. A statutory PAYGO requirement was in effect from 1991 through 2002 and was reinstituted in modified form in 2010; the House and Senate each have their own PAYGO rules but the House Rule does not include revenue legislation.

Reconciliation: Process by which Congress changes existing laws to conform revenue and spending levels to the levels set in a budget resolution.

Regular Appropriations Act: An appropriations act that provides budget authority for the next fiscal year.

Reprogramming: Shifting funds from one program to another in the same appropriations account.

Rescission: Cancellation of budget authority previously provided by Congress.

Revenues: Income from individual and corporate income taxes, social insurance taxes, excise taxes, fees, tariffs, and other sources collected under the sovereign powers of the federal government.

Scorekeeping: Process for tracking and reporting on the status of congressional budgetary actions affecting budget authority, outlays, revenues, and the surplus or deficit.

Supplemental Appropriations Act: An appropriations act that provides additional budget authority during the current year when the regular appropriation is insufficient.

Tax Expenditure: Loss of revenue attributable to an exemption, deduction, preference, or other exclusion under federal tax law.

Transfer: Shift of budgetary resources from one appropriation account to another, as authorized by law.

Views and Estimates: Annual report of each House and Senate committee on budgetary matters within its jurisdiction.

A large legislative glossary is located at the back the book and online: <*TCNLG.com*>.

Line-Item Veto

During the 104th Congress, the Line Item Veto Act (*P.L. 104-130*; *110 Stat. 1200*) was enacted as an amendment to the 1974 Impoundment Control Act. President Clinton applied the line-item veto to several measures in 1997, but the Supreme Court ruled the Line Item Veto Act unconstitutional in June 1998 and the earlier line-item vetoes were nullified. (*Clinton v. City of New York*, 524 U.S. 417 (1998).) The authority granted to the president under the Line Item Veto Act, which differed markedly from the veto authority available to most chief executives at the state level, was intended to reverse the presumption underlying the process for the consideration of rescissions under the 1974 Impoundment Control Act. Under the Line Item Veto Act, presidential proposals would take effect unless overturned by legislative action. The act authorized the president to identify at enactment individual items in legislation that he proposed should not go into effect. The identification was based not just upon the statutory language, but on the entire legislative history and documentation. The president had to notify Congress promptly of his proposals and provide supporting information. Congress had to respond within a limited period of time by enacting a law if it wanted to disapprove the president's proposals. Otherwise, the president's proposals would take effect.

In the wake of the Line Item Veto Act's nullification, there have been proposals that the president be given enhanced rescission authority, under which he could propose rescissions that Congress would be forced to act on (but not required to pass) under expedited procedures.

§ 7.170 Chapter Summary and Discussion Questions

Summary

- The Constitution vests governmental power to tax and spend in Congress, which it exercises by passing legislation that the president may then sign or veto.
- Through lawmaking, Congress has given the president many responsibilities for the federal budget, in addition to his constitutional duty to carry out tax and spending laws. For example, the president is required to propose a budget annually to Congress.
- Congress has also exercised its constitutional authority under the Necessary and Proper Clause (*see Chapter Eight, Legislating in Congress: Special Procedures and Considerations*) to direct how the president implements tax and spending laws. For example, the Antideficiency Act prevents an agency from spending more money than Congress has made available to it.
- Congress also in 1974 passed a law, the Congressional Budget Act, to give structure to its own consideration of budgetary legislation. By passing a concurrent resolution on the budget after reviewing the president's annual budget, Congress makes a comprehensive decision on total revenues, total spending, and the deficit for a fiscal year. This comprehensive decision is then enforced against individual pieces of budgetary legislation as they are considered by the House and Senate.
- The Congressional Budget Act added a new process to existing authorizations and appropriations processes, whereby Congress sought to consider two kinds of legislation: policymaking authorization bills, on the one hand, and spending bills, called appropriations bills, that make budget authority available for programs and agencies, on the other. Spending in appropriations bills is called discretionary spending since Congress must pass an appropriation annually for budget authority to be available to a program or agency.
- Another kind of spending is called direct or mandatory spending, where a law requires money to be spent for a program. Only a change in the law can affect coverage or cost of the program; the appropriations process cannot be used to increase or decrease spending. Major social programs such as Social Security, Medicare, and Medicaid are examples of direct spending programs.
- Tax laws generally are permanent, in that they continue to operate as enacted until a new law is passed to change them. An important exception are the tax cuts enacted in 2001 and 2003 under President George W. Bush. They were scheduled to sunset at the end of 2010 but were extended for two more years.

- In the Congressional Budget Act, Congress also established the reconciliation process, which provides a mechanism for Congress to enforce a decision made in a budget resolution by directing committees to report certain budgetary legislation and by expediting the consideration of such legislation on the floor, particularly in the Senate.

Discussion Questions

- Think about the nature of the legislative and executive branches, for example, 535 representatives and senators compared to one president, or decision-making in a bicameral legislature compared to executive authority constitutionally residing in president. Why might Congress have shared its budgetary powers with the president and executive branch, and what might it have hoped to achieve?
- Under the Constitution, what taxing and spending power would Congress be unable to share with the president?
- What political purposes might the budget development process in the executive branch serve? Think about presidential priorities related to taxes, spending programs, and the deficit and debt, and gathering support in Congress and among the public for those priorities.
- Notice that in two of the five years that Congress has not completed action on a congressional budget resolution, the House, Senate, and presidency were all under the same party's control. Single-party control does not mean ready agreement. It suggests that budget decision-making is not just a policy decision but a political decision, as is the case with nearly all decision-making in Congress. Think about the budget debate occurring this year. What does this debate tell you about trying to find a budget policy that a majority in each house of Congress could support?
- What national or international occurrences in recent years have affected levels of revenue and spending? How have these occurrences limited Congress and the president's ability to control spending and the deficit?
- Considering budget enforcement mechanisms Congress uses now or has used in the past, how efficacious might they be in addressing today's federal deficit and debt concerns? What process changes, if any, might assist Congress in controlling the deficit and debt? Are these changes politically feasible—how could a majority in each house be obtained to support the changes?

Chapter Eight

Legislating in Congress: Special Procedures and Considerations

Analysis

§ 8.00 Introduction: Separation of Powers, Checks and Balances, and Federalism

The three branches of the federal government are intertwined by the Constitution and by experience and practice. The executive and the judiciary have explicit and inherent powers under the Constitution. Congress has the authority to legislate not only in areas enumerated in Article I of the Constitution but also, pursuant to the *Spending Clause*, to tax and spend "for the common Defence and general welfare of the United States." (*Art. I, sec. 8, cl. 1.*) It may also "make all Laws which shall be necessary and proper for carrying into Execution the foregoing Powers, and all other Powers vested by this Constitution in the Government of the United States, or in any Department or Officer thereof." (*Art. I, sec. 8, cl. 18.*) The *Necessary and Proper Clause* of the Constitution, also called the *Elastic Clause*, provides Congress with powers beyond those enumerated in Article I. It gives Congress authority to legislate on many of the grants of power to the executive and to the judiciary, and to enact laws to ensure the success of its enactments.

When the Constitution was drafted and ratified, the thirteen original states and the people in them gave certain powers to the national government. After considerable debate, they decided that foreign policy, a common defense, interstate commerce, and other governmental powers were more effectively handled through a constitutionally empowered national government. The states continued as a separate level of government, exercising a separate set of sovereign powers within their physical territories. The federal system, however, is not static. The challenges and advances of the last century and this one—world wars, foreign totalitarian states, religious and ethnic fanaticism, the Great Depression, economic globalization, rights of citizens, and advances in transportation and communications—seem to have favored an expansive and dominant national government.

Separation of Powers and Checks and Balances

The framers of the Constitution differentiated among the three branches of the national or federal government, but they also provided a system of *checks and balances* intended to make the three branches work together and remain in an equilibrium.

The declarative statements introducing the first three articles of the Constitution are the foundation for separation of powers:

- "All legislative Powers herein granted shall be vested in a Congress of the United States. . . ." (*Art. I, sec. 1.*)
- "The executive Power shall be vested in a President of the United States of America." (*Art. II, sec. 1, cl. 1.*)
- "The judicial Power of the United States, shall be vested in one supreme Court, and in such inferior Courts as the Congress may from time to time ordain and establish." (*Art. III, sec. 1.*)

The Constitution then spells out the authority of each of the branches in the three respective articles.

However, the framers interlocked the exercise of the three great governmental powers by assigning roles in each branch that affect or limit power in the other two branches. Perhaps the most important of these to Congress and government affairs professionals alike is the president's role in the legislative process. Article I, Section 7 provides for the presentation of every measure passed by

Congress to the president. If the president signs a measure, it becomes law. Article I also provides for his veto, but, lest the president be arbitrary or autocratic, it also limits his time to weigh approval or veto to ten days (Sundays excepted) and allows Congress, by a two-thirds vote in each chamber, to override a veto.

The president is specifically given the power to make treaties and appoint judges, ambassadors, and designated officers of the federal government. The president's power is limited by the need to obtain a two-thirds vote in the Senate consenting to the ratification of a treaty, and the need to obtain a majority vote in the Senate consenting to those of his appointments designated in law as subject to Senate confirmation.

Other provisions of the Constitution—such as Article II, Section 1, and Article III, Section 1—explicitly constrain another branch. These two sections, respectively, provide for compensation to the president and judges, but the president's salary cannot be increased or decreased during his tenure and judges' salaries cannot be decreased during their service.

The framers also provided checks and balances within the legislative branch. To make law, a measure must pass both houses in identical form before presentation to the president. Revenue measures must originate in the House, but the Senate may amend them. The House has sole power to impeach, and the Senate has sole power to try an impeachment. And, neither house may adjourn for more than three days without the consent of the other house.

Still other constitutional checks and balances have arisen from experience under the Constitution. For example, the power of the judiciary to declare acts of Congress unconstitutional is nowhere explicitly stated in the Constitution. However, in *Marbury v. Madison*, 5 U.S. (1 Cranch.) 137 (1803), the Supreme Court established its authority as an interpreter of the Constitution.

Federalism

In the American system of government, sovereignty is shared between the national and state governments. Through the exercise of its powers, the national government can affect all people in all states, the District of Columbia, and U.S. territories and possessions. Each state government—through the exercise of its inherent police powers—can affect all people within the state's physical territory, except as constrained by the federal and state constitutions, judicial decisions, and other specific limitations.

The national government is a government of enumerated powers. It is important to note that the grant of power to the legislative branch quoted above says, "All legislative Powers *herein granted.* . . ." (*Art. I, sec. 1; emphasis added.*) The phrase reemphasizes the concept of enumerated powers, although the admonition by Chief Justice John Marshall in *McCulloch v. Maryland*, 17 U.S. (4 Wheat.) 316 (1819), is for a generous reading of national powers: "Let the end be legitimate, let it be within the scope of the Constitution, and all means which are appropriate, which are plainly adapted to that end, which are not prohibited, but consist with the letter and sprit of the Constitution, are constitutional." The Bill of Rights nonetheless includes the Tenth Amendment, which provides as follows: "The powers not delegated to the United States by the Constitution, nor prohibited by it to the States, are reserved to the States respectively, or to the people."

The Constitution contains both grants of authority to, and restrictions on, the national government concerning its power over the states. For example, Article IV, Section 4 empowers the national government: "The United States shall guarantee to every State in this Union a Republican Form of Government. . . ." On the other hand, Article IV, Section 3 strictly circumscribes its authority: ". . . but no new State shall be formed or erected within the Jurisdiction of any other State. . . ." States, in turn, are directed to treat each other and each other's citizens without discrimination. For example, the Fourteenth Amendment provides as follows:

> Section 1. All persons born or naturalized in the United States, and subject to the jurisdiction thereof, are citizens of the United States and of the State wherein they reside. No State shall make or enforce any law which shall abridge the privileges or immunities of citizens of the United States; nor shall any State deprive any person of life, liberty, or property, without due process of law; nor deny to any person within its jurisdiction the equal protection of the laws.

Congress, in addition, is authorized by Section 5 of the Fourteenth Amendment to enforce the provisions of the amendment.

States are also prohibited from taking certain governmental action, either unequivocally or in the absence of congressional consent. For example, in the former case, Article I, Section 10, Clause 1 states in part: "No State shall enter into any Treaty, Alliance, or Confederation. . . ." In the latter instance, Article I, Section 10, Clause 3 provides in part: "No state shall, without the consent of Congress . . . enter into any Agreement or Compact with another State. . . ."

Finally, the sovereignty of the states is recognized and protected in the manner by which the Constitution can be amended. Either the legislatures of three-fourths of the states or conventions in three-fourths of the states must ratify a constitutional amendment for it to become effective.

This chapter describes or illustrates some of the ways in which Congress exercises its powers vis-à-vis the executive and judicial branches and the states.

§ 8.10 Congress and the Executive

Within the constitutional framework, Congress and the executive continuously devise and revise formal and informal means of making their relationship work. Over time, Congress has given the executive branch authority and responsibilities that are executive (administering the law), legislative (for example, rulemaking), and judicial (through adjudication). Congress uses its constitutional authority, including the Necessary and Proper, or Elastic, Clause (*art. I, sec. 8, cl. 18: "To make all Laws which shall be necessary and proper . . ."*), to pass laws establishing federal government agencies and programs. In addition to program-specific laws, Congress passes laws dictating government-wide procedures. One way that Congress attempts to ensure that the vast array of federal programs is carried out with due consideration for democratic, constitutional values and a minimum of waste, fraud, and abuse is by passing general management laws, such as the Administrative Procedure Act (*5 U.S.C. § 551 et seq. and § 701 et seq.*), that specify the processes that each agency must follow when carrying out its responsibilities. In addition to its legislative powers, Congress has the power to influence the executive through appropriations, appointments advice and consent, and oversight and investigation. It requires reports from the executive, conducts hearings, monitors the *Federal*

Register, and pursues its checks on executive power in dozens of other ways. Congressional use of these powers and methods for checking the executive varies; some Congresses assert their constitutional prerogatives more than other Congresses.

§ 8.20 Congress and the Executive: Legislation

The president and his administration are key sources of legislative proposals. The president might have an economic program that he wants enacted soon after his election, as Presidents Clinton, George W. Bush, and Obama did. Or, he might request *fast-track* authority to facilitate his negotiation of trade agreements. The president might request legislation on any subject. Department and agency officials, too, regularly seek changes in law in accordance with administration policy, and participate fully in congressional deliberations over new authorization measures and reauthorization measures. (*See § 7.80, Authorizations and Appropriations Processes.*)

The president is likely to make key portions of his legislative program known in his annual State of the Union address (*see § 8.21, State of the Union Address*) and in his annual budget request (*see § 7.40, Presidential Budget Process*). He sends other messages on legislation to Congress, and submits draft legislation or outlines of legislation that he would like to see enacted. The president might also endorse legislation that has been introduced in Congress, and work for its adoption. And his liaison office and affected departments and agencies work together to ensure that legislation moving in Congress is acceptable to the president. (*See § 8.22, White House Legislative Affairs Office; and § 8.23, Letter Expressing Concerns with Legislation (from the General Counsel of the U.S. Department of Commerce).*) The administration also tries to develop common legislative interests with the president's party's leadership in each chamber and, if possible, with the leadership of the other party, especially if the other party is in the majority in a chamber.

Congress also delegates to the president authority to recommend specific actions to Congress. For example, under the Arms Export Control Act (*22 U.S.C. § 2751 et seq.*), the president must notify Congress of major weapons sales, which Congress might then disapprove by a joint resolution subject to presidential signature or veto. Congress has set a high hurdle for itself—a two-thirds vote in each house if it and the president disagree. However, the president usually consults or negotiates with Congress so that Congress does not respond broadly to curtail his discretion in managing foreign relations generally or arms sales specifically.

Congressional committees and chamber leadership may seek the input of the administration on legislation. During the course of congressional deliberations, administration officials testify at hearings, attend markups, and remain active throughout floor and conference proceedings to provide information to members. Committees solicit written agency comments on introduced legislation, usually at the time of hearings or markup. Both chambers' rules require these comments to be included in committee reports on legislation. (*See § 4.170, Congressional Liaison Offices.*) The Office of Management and Budget (OMB) coordinates the administration position, and might also coordinate one or more Statements of Administration Policy (SAPs) on active legislation, which represent the coordinated views of the president and agencies affected by—or interested in—a piece of legislation covered by the SAP. (*See OMB Circular No. A-19, Legislative Coordination and Clearance, <www.whitehouse.gov/omb/circulars_a019>, which continues to express policy guidance, and the*

§ 8.21

State of the Union Address

In contemporary practice, the president appears before a joint session of Congress in late January to deliver a speech popularly referred to as the State of the Union address or message, laying out his legislative program, explaining his policies on the major issues of the time, and exhorting Congress to take specific actions in support of his vision and program. The address emanates from a constitutional provision (*art. II, sec. 3, cl. 1*): "He [the president] shall from time to time give to the Congress Information on the State of the Union, and recommend to their Consideration such measures as he shall judge necessary and expedient[.]"

After consultation with the White House, the House and Senate pass a concurrent resolution setting a day and time for a joint session "for receiving such communication as the President of the United States shall be pleased to make to them." When the day arrives, a special security sweep is made of the Capitol, and other security measures are triggered. The senators are escorted to the House chamber by the Senate sergeant at arms. Other dignitaries are also seated in the chamber—former members, justices of the Supreme Court, the joint chiefs of staff, Cabinet secretaries and Cabinet-rank officials, and ambassadors to the United States. Traditionally, one Cabinet secretary and several members of Congress, representing both parties, do not attend the joint session, to ensure succession should a catastrophe happen at the Capitol while the president is there. The first lady and guests of the president are allocated seats in the gallery. Other gallery guests must obtain tickets.

The Speaker presides over the joint session, but shares the dais with the vice president in his role as president of the Senate. A group of senators and representatives that was previously selected escorts the president into the chamber. The president is announced first at the House door by the House sergeant at arms and then again by the Speaker after the president takes his place on the dais. The group of members also escorts the president out of the chamber after he completes his address.

President Truman's 1947 address was the first to be televised. President Johnson was the first to make his address during prime-time television viewing hours, recognizing the opportunity to speak to the nation that the event presented. A formal opposing-party response was first made in 1966. The State of the Union address has now become an important media event, and both parties use it to publicize their positions on issues covered or not covered in the address, in events both before and after the address.

Immediately following a State of the Union address, members of Congress meet the press in National Statuary Hall to put their "spin" on it. The day after the State of the Union address, the president might travel to several states to publicize his program and to build public support for his proposals.

In years in which a new president takes office, the outgoing president might choose not to deliver an address in person, or might choose to make a televised address at a place other than the Capitol, and the incoming president might choose to make a more focused address several months into office to seek action by Congress on a specific presidential initiative.

OMB director's memorandum on legislative coordination and clearance on the OMB web site at <www.whitehouse.gov/omb/memoranda/_2009> at m-09-09.)

In its guidance to executive branch departments and agencies, OMB has identified the purposes of its legislative coordination and clearance function to be to assist the president in developing a position on legislation, to make the administration's position known to the agencies and to Congress, to ensure that all agencies affected by or interested in specific legislation have had the opportunity to consider and provide their views on the legislation, and to assist the president in decision-making

§ 8.22

White House Legislative Affairs Office

Every president since Dwight Eisenhower has maintained a full-time legislative liaison officer. Organized as an Office of Legislative Affairs, this staff is an important component of the executive office of the president.

As the eyes and ears of the White House, the legislative affairs staff read how members may respond to key presidential initiatives and report back to the White House. As the time for floor votes approaches, this intelligence might guide the White House in determining if a Cabinet official, the vice president, or the president himself needs to be involved in helping to sway any individual members to the president's position. Legislative liaison staff can often be seen outside the party cloakrooms during debates and votes that are particularly important to the president.

By dispensing personal gestures and presidential invitations, the White House lobbying team can have a strong influence with members of Congress. An invitation to a state dinner for a visiting head of state or a seat on Air Force One on an official trip is perceived as very important by most members and as quite persuasive by the White House.

Because knowing the legislative players—both members and staff—is so important, the White House office is often staffed by people who have had experience working on Capitol Hill.

related to bill signature or veto. Therefore, an agency wishing to submit draft legislation to Congress, or to comment or testify on legislation, first submits its legislation or testimony to OMB. OMB in turn circulates the document to affected and interested agencies and to appropriate staff within the Executive Office of the President. OMB also coordinates the reconciliation of differing views, and discussion or negotiation can occur during the clearance process. OMB subsequently advises an agency that the administration has "no objection" to the legislation or testimony, or that the legislation or testimony is "in accord with the president's program." The meaning of the latter designation is that the legislation or testimony implements a presidential proposal, or advances the president's program or policies, and deserves the president's support. (*See § 8.24, Presidential Letter.*) Agencies convey this advice to Congress with their legislation or testimony. Legislation or testimony that conflicts with the administration's program, however, may not be submitted to Congress. (*See also § 4.180, Office of Management and Budget.*)

OMB prepares SAPs, again in consultation with agencies affected by or interested in the specific legislation and with appropriate officials in the Executive Office of the President. SAPs tend to be prepared in anticipation of or during floor debate. OMB's Legislative Affairs Office transmits SAPs to Congress. (*See examples of SAPs at § 12.08 and § 12.13.*)

OMB also coordinates the preparation of a memorandum to the president on measures that have been enrolled and will be sent to the president for his signature or veto. OMB circulates the enrolled measure to affected or interested agencies, and they are expected to submit their analysis and recommendation of the legislation within forty-eight hours. An agency that recommends a signing statement or a veto is also responsible for drafting an appropriate statement for the president's consideration. (*See § 6.292, Vetoes and Veto Overrides: Presidential Clout.*)

§ 8.23

Letter Expressing Concerns with Legislation (from the General Counsel of the U.S. Department of Commerce)

GENERAL COUNSEL OF THE
UNITED STATES DEPARTMENT OF COMMERCE
Washington, D.C. 20230

March 17, 2011

The Honorable Robert A. Brady
Ranking Member
Committee on House Administration
U.S. House of Representatives
Washington, D.C. 20515

Dear Representative Brady:

Thank you for your recent letter to the Under Secretary of Commerce for Standards and Technology and Director of the National Institute of Standards and Technology (NIST), Dr. Patrick Gallagher, regarding H.R. 672, a bill to terminate the Election Assistance Commission (EAC) and to transfer EAC's duties to NIST and other agencies. I appreciate the opportunity to provide the views of the Department of Commerce.

The Department strongly supports the current relationship between the EAC and NIST. However, should the legislation be enacted into law, as currently drafted, the Department would have some serious concerns about the ramifications of the legislation for NIST.

NIST, through its National Voluntary Laboratory Accreditation Program, accredits laboratories in a number of fields of critical national importance, including voting systems. The bill proposes to transfer the EAC's testing and certification program to NIST. This would result in a conflict of interest for NIST because it would put NIST in the position of both accrediting private sector laboratories that test voting equipment and systems, and of certifying the equipment and systems tested by these same labs.

Were NIST to be in a position both to accredit labs and to certify their products, this conflict of interest would be in direct violation of the International Laboratory Accreditation Cooperation, and the Asia-Pacific Laboratory Accreditation Cooperation to which NIST is a signatory.

The legislation also does not provide the resources necessary to absorb the proposed transfer of personnel or the continued work for which NIST is currently funded by the EAC. The Department is concerned that if the EAC is terminated and additional resources are not provided for NIST to carry out EAC activities, NIST's ongoing critical work in voting standards could be compromised.

The Department remains committed to working with you and the members of the Committee as the legislation moves forward. The Office of Management and Budget has advised that there is no objection to the transmittal of these views from the standpoint of the Administration's program. If you have any questions, please contact me or April Boyd, Assistant Secretary for Legislative and Intergovernmental Affairs, at 482-3663.

Sincerely,

Cameron F. Kerry

8

§ 8.24

Presidential Letter

THE WHITE HOUSE
WASHINGTON

June 12, 2010

The Honorable Nancy Pelosi
Speaker of the
House of Representatives
Washington, D.C. 20515

The Honorable Harry Reid
Majority Leader
United States Senate
Washington, D.C. 20510

The Honorable John Boehner
Republican Leader
House of Representatives
Washington, D.C. 20515

The Honorable Mitch McConnell
Republican Leader
United States Senate
Washington, D.C. 20510

Dear Speaker Pelosi, Senator Reid, Senator McConnell, and Representative Boehner:

We are at a critical juncture on our nation's path to economic recovery. I know that each of you is committed to continuing our efforts to help America's families and businesses turn the corner on the deepest and most painful recession America has experienced since the Great Depression. While our efforts over the past 18 months have helped break the freefall and restore growth, it is essential that we continue to explore additional measures to spur job creation and build momentum toward recovery, even as we establish a path to long-term fiscal discipline.

Given the urgency of the continued economic challenges we face, I am writing to urge swift action on several critical priorities that will give our Nation's small businesses added impetus to hire and grow and address the devastating economic impact of budget cuts at the state and local levels that are leading to massive layoffs of teachers, police and firefighters.

As you know, America's small businesses are key drivers of job creation. They have been at the forefront of the dramatic change in the trajectory of private sector job growth we have experienced over the past eighteen months. At the beginning of 2009, our economy was losing over 700,000 jobs per month. Through the first five months of 2010, nearly 500,000 private sector jobs have been created. While this is good news for those who have found work and for businesses large and small that are once again beginning to expand and add more workers, it is cold comfort for the millions of others who want to get back to work.

This is why the extenders legislation being considered in the Senate is so important. It includes provisions like tax cuts to keep research and development jobs in the United States and extends lending programs through the Small Business Administration so that our Nation's small business owners have access to the capital they need to grow their businesses and create jobs.

rewarding states for poor past policy choices.

Because the urgency is high – many school districts, cities and states are already being forced to make these layoffs – these provisions must be passed as quickly as possible. In addition, we should take steps to continue the Recovery Act program that has already helped millions of unemployed workers pay for continuing their health care coverage.

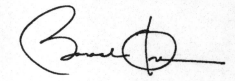

The Lobbying with Appropriated Moneys Act (*18 U.S.C. § 1913*) and other statutes related to agencies and programs generally prohibit the use of appropriated funds for lobbying campaigns directed at Congress. However, the prohibitions, at the very least, do not restrict the responsiveness of executive departments and agencies to congressional requests for information on legislation, including appropriations.

The president also uses his authority to approve or veto measures as part of his leverage with Congress. The president can effectively use the threat of a veto to influence the outcome of legislation. Should a measure with which he disagrees pass, he can veto the legislation to drive home his strong position. As demonstrated by the table in § 6.292 (*Vetoes and Veto Overrides: Presidential Clout*), presidents normally prevail on vetoes. A president might issue a signing statement when he approves a measure that indicates his concerns with the specific provisions and that explains how he will implement those provisions. (*See § 6.290, Presidential Action on Enacted Measures.*) A president does not have any form of so-called item-veto authority, but must sign or veto an entire bill or joint resolution, whatever his reservations over one or more sections.

§ 8.30 Congress and the Executive: Ratification of Treaties and Foreign Policy

The president can negotiate treaties with foreign nations and, subject to the advice and consent of the Senate, ratify them. Under the Constitution (*art. II, sec. 2, cl. 2*), ratification of a treaty requires consent of two-thirds of senators present and voting. The Senate has developed special procedures applicable to treaties. The House and Senate together have also developed other special procedures, including so-called fast-track procedures, applicable to some trade agreements, arms sales, and other foreign policy activities. (*See § 8.150, Congress and Foreign Policy: Treaties and International Agreements; § 8.151, Fast-Track Procedures; and § 8.160, Congress and Foreign Policy: Legislation, Appropriations, and Nominations.*)

8

Congress has developed a number of other formal and informal means to control, guide, or influence the president in his conduct of foreign policy. While only Congress can declare war, it has rarely done so. Today, commitments of American troops to armed conflict may be debated in Congress in the context of the War Powers Resolution (*50 U.S.C. § 1541 et seq.*). The roles of Congress and the president in authorizing the use of U.S. troops in international conflict continue to be in flux. (*See § 8.140, Congress and Foreign Policy: Declaring War and Committing Troops.*)

Through legislation, appropriations, and Senate advice and consent on nominations and treaties, Congress can dictate or influence the foreign policy of the United States and its management by the president. Hearings, fact-finding missions overseas, and other activities assist Congress in being informed and having sources of information independent of the president or the executive branch. (*See § 8.170, Congress and Foreign Policy: Nonbinding Actions.*)

Although Congress has these constitutionally based tools for influencing foreign policy, its level of control vis-à-vis the president has varied over time.

§ 8.40 Congress and the Executive: Rulemaking

Together with taxing and spending, regulation is one of the fundamental ways the federal government implements public policy. Rulemaking is the process by which regulations are developed and given effect. Given the complex and constantly changing modern world, among other factors, Congress does not necessarily enact legislation that is sufficiently detailed to cover every eventuality related to a given area of legislative policy. Therefore, Congress often delegates authority to further refine legislative policy through the assignment of rulemaking authority to executive departments and agencies, as well as to independent regulatory agencies. For example, a statute may contain standards for achieving the statute's purposes and assign responsibility for its administration to a specific governmental entity. The statute might authorize and perhaps guide the promulgation of regulations, or rules, implementing the law by, for example, listing considerations to be included in developing the regulations and mandating a time frame within which regulations are to be issued. Rulemaking authority is sometimes referred to as quasi-legislative authority because it can be seen as an extension of Congress' legislative function.

In addition to enacting laws assigning specific rulemaking authority to various governmental entities, Congress has established government-wide rulemaking requirements that guide the rulemaking process more generally. For example, the Federal Register Act (*44 U.S.C. § 1501 et seq.*), enacted in 1935, created a uniform system for notifying the public of agency rulemaking activity that includes publication of documents in the *Federal Register* and codification of rules in the *Code of Federal Regulations*. The Administrative Procedure Act of 1946 (*5 U.S.C. § 551 et seq. and § 701 et seq.*) established general procedures for rulemaking, including, for example, requirements that a notice of proposed rulemaking be published in the *Federal Register* and that interested persons have the opportunity to comment.

In granting rulemaking authority through numerous laws to various federal entities, Congress still maintains vigilance over the rulemaking process and specific rulemaking initiatives. (*See § 8.41, Congressional Review of Agency Rulemaking.*) Occasionally, Congress acts to increase the importance of certain considerations in the development of regulations, as it did with the enactment of the National Environmental Policy Act of 1969 (*83 Stat. 852*), regarding rules' environmental impact; the Regulatory Flexibility Act of 1980 (*5 U.S.C. § 601 et seq.*) and the Small Business Regulatory Enforcement Fairness Act of 1996 (*110 Stat. 857*), regarding rules' impact on "small entities"; the Unfunded Mandates Act of 1995 (*§ 8.201*), regarding rules' unfunded requirements of state, local, or tribal governments, or the private sector; and the Data Quality Act of 2001 (*114 Stat. 2763A-153*), regarding standards for the quality and use of information underlying rules.

In 1980, Congress passed the Paperwork Reduction Act (*44 U.S.C. § 3501 et seq.*). Among other things, this law was intended to decrease the paperwork burden imposed on individuals and entities by federal regulations. It established the Office of Information and Regulatory Affairs (OIRA) within the Office of Management and Budget (OMB), which is part of the Executive Office of the President. In February 1981, newly elected President Reagan issued Executive Order 12291, which, among other things, gave OMB, and, in turn, OIRA, responsibility for acting as a gatekeeper for new federal regulations. Under the order, all federal agencies except independent regulatory agencies were

§ 8.41

Congressional Review of Agency Rulemaking

When the Supreme Court struck down a form of legislative veto in *INS* v. *Chadha* (*§ 8.51*), Congress still had other means at its disposal for responding to regulations, such as including changes in authorization or appropriations bills, or using oversight hearings. However, with the extensive number of laws through which it had granted rulemaking authority to a large number of governmental entities, Congress sought a flexible mechanism to increase its oversight of regulations.

As part of the Small Business Regulatory Enforcement Fairness Act of 1996 (*110 Stat. 857*), Congress enacted the Congressional Review Act, which provided for congressional review of agency rulemaking (*5 U.S.C. § 801 et seq.*). Among the law's provisions, Congress established a process whereby federal agencies must submit all of their rules to both houses of Congress and the Government Accountability Office (GAO) before the rules can become effective. For each rule that OMB considers "major" (for example, the rule will have a $100 million effect on the U.S. economy), GAO must prepare a report describing the issuing agency's compliance with various rulemaking requirements (for example, cost-benefit estimates under Executive Order 12866). (*For copies of these reports and other information, see the GAO web site at <http://gao.gov>, then select "Legal Decisions & Bid Protests," then select "Congressional Review Act."*) Major rules cannot take effect until sixty days after the rule is submitted to GAO and Congress or published in the *Federal Register*, whichever is later.

The Congressional Review Act provides specific procedures under which Congress can, by joint resolution, disapprove an agency rule. It provides, for example, for expedited procedures in the Senate, but not in the House. Using these procedures, Congress has at least sixty legislative days in which to pass a joint resolution of disapproval. Such a resolution, like any joint resolution, would require passage in both houses and presidential approval. While there are conditions under which a rule might be implemented before Congress acts, if a joint resolution of disapproval is subsequently enacted into law, the rule "shall be treated as though such rule had never taken effect." Once a rule has been disapproved in this manner, "it may not be reissued in substantially the same form, and a new rule that is substantially the same as such a rule may not be issued," unless such a rule is subsequently specifically authorized by law.

As a joint resolution, the measure is subject to possible veto by the president,which is subject to a possible veto override by Congress. The Congressional Review Act was successfully used to overturn a rule on only one occasion between 1996 and the end of 2010. In early 2001, the Republican-led Congress passed, and newly inaugurated President George W. Bush signed, a joint resolution of disapproval nullifying an ergonomics standards rule that had been promulgated by the Occupational Safety and Health Administration (OSHA) during the administration of President Clinton. Although overturning a rule requires overcoming a high political threshold, members of Congress may use the procedures put in place by the law in an effort to draw attention to, and influence the outcome of, specific rulemaking processes. More than forty joint resolutions of disapproval have been introduced since the law was enacted.

required to weigh the costs of a potential rule against its benefits; prepare a regulatory impact analysis for each rule that might impose costs of $100 million or more on the U.S. economy; and submit drafts of proposed and final rules to OMB prior to publication in the *Federal Register*. This executive order was controversial because it unilaterally increased the president's ability to shape public policy through increased control at OMB over the rulemaking process. Executive Order 12866, issued by President Clinton in October 1993, replaced Executive Order 12291. It limited OMB review to "significant" rules from non-independent regulatory agencies, and established certain transparency requirements, while retaining OMB's role in the rulemaking process. In January 2007, President Bush issued Executive Order 13422, which appeared to strengthen the president's control over rulemaking. Among its changes, the Bush executive order seemed to increase the importance of identifying a "market failure" in justifying a new regulation, extended coverage of OIRA's review to agencies' guidance documents, and appeared to increase administration control over decisions to undertake and guide rulemaking. President Obama revoked President Bush's executive order, and restored the framework of President Clinton's executive order. Obama's stated purposes included added transparency and public participation through use of new tools like regulations.gov and the promotion of innovation through a review of existing rules for burdensomeness and effectiveness.

Congress and its members cannot intervene with impunity in regulatory proceedings outside of the legislative process or the formal procedures Congress has enacted. While House and Senate ethics rules recognize the right of members to assist their constituents in matters before executive-branch departments and agencies, criminal laws and ethics rules set parameters on that assistance. (*For sources of information on congressional ethics, see § 3.60, Regulated Activities.*)

§ 8.50 Congress and the Executive: Appropriations

One of Congress' most effective means of exercising control over the executive is through the appropriations process. The Constitution provides that "No Money shall be drawn from the Treasury, but in Consequence of Appropriations made by Law. . . ." (*Art. I, sec. 9, cl. 7.*) By setting the level of funding or denying funding for federal programs, and by attaching strings to funding, Congress ensures its role in establishing the priorities and policies of the executive branch. (*See Chapter Seven, Legislating in Congress: Federal Budget Process.*)

Congress can employ *limitations* in appropriations measures. A limitation restricts spending, such as by prohibiting the use of funds for a specific purpose or setting a ceiling on the amount that might be spent on an activity within an account, or by restricting the management and uses of funds in some other way.

Congress also may include *reprogramming* or *transfer* authority in appropriations measures. (*See § 7.140, Transfer and Reprogramming.*) Reprogramming authority allows a department or agency to shift funds within a spending account, while transfer authority allows a department or agency to shift funds from one account to another. In both cases, Congress usually places limitations on such authority, often requiring the department or agency to notify the Appropriations Committees within a certain period of time before any shifting of funds may occur. In some cases, the reprogramming or transfer authority is contingent on the approval of the Appropriations Committees, a form of the legislative veto still used. (*See § 8.51, Legislative Veto.*)

As explained in § 7.150 (*Impoundment: Deferrals and Rescissions*), the president may also recommend deferrals and rescissions of budget authority in accordance with provisions of the Congressional Budget and Impoundment Control Act. (*88 Stat. 297; 2 U.S.C. § 601 et seq.*)

§ 8.51

Legislative Veto

The practice of giving Congress a "veto" over executive actions is long-standing. With broad grants of discretion to the executive, Congress often found it useful to include a *one-house* or *two-house legislative veto* as part of a grant of authority and discretion. In that way, the executive could shape an outcome to its liking. Congress would then have an opportunity to review the policy decision, and, if unhappy with it, adopt a simple resolution of disapproval in one house or a concurrent resolution of disapproval in both houses.

This type of legislative veto, however, was struck down by the Supreme Court in *INS v. Chadha,* 462 U.S. 919 (1983). Congress exercised a one-house veto regarding a specific type of decision of the attorney general under the Immigration and Nationality Act (*8 U.S.C. § 1101 et seq.*). The Court said that the legislative veto violated the Constitution's principle of bicameralism and the Presentment Clause, which states: "Every Bill which shall have passed the House of Representatives and the Senate, shall, before it become a Law, be presented to the President of the United States." (*Art. I, sec. 7, cl. 2.*)

Congress has responded with procedures in various forms that are constitutional, such as joint resolutions of approval or disapproval. A joint resolution requires the president's signature or an override of his veto to take effect. It has also continued to use the legislative veto formally and informally at the committee level to ensure oversight of the executive branch's exercise of discretion. Many of these legislative vetoes involve the House and Senate Appropriations Committees, and are included in appropriations measures or accompanying documents, such as committee or conference committee reports.

§ 8.60 Congress and the Executive: Management

Congress places controls on the executive branch not only through its appropriations authority but also by making laws for managing the executive branch. Personnel systems (including personnel benefits), procurement systems, financial management, information technology, and other areas of management of the executive branch are covered in laws enacted by Congress. Management of the regulatory process, aspects of which are described in § 8.40 (*Congress and the Executive: Rulemaking*), is another example of the legal imposition of standards for the executive branch to follow in its operations.

Congress can apply a management law to all parts of the executive branch. Through another law, Congress may also exempt an agency from specific management laws, or even exempt a category of agencies from specific laws. Congress might also impose different or additional management standards on an agency or a category of agencies.

Recent administrations have developed federal government management initiatives, such as President Clinton's National Performance Review (NPR), President George W. Bush's President's Management Agenda (PMA), and President Obama's Accountable Government Initiative and Open Government Initiative. Administration officials have sought to implement changes under these initiatives through a combination of the president's existing management authority and legislative proposals. The role of the president as day-to-day "manager-in-chief" of the federal bureaucracy provides him with a prominent vantage point from which to promote and implement particular reforms. Although

Congress might not adopt an administration's plan in its entirety, some members and committees might elect to incorporate elements into their own legislative agenda. Statutory changes are usually necessary in order for a president's management initiatives to take hold and have an impact on the federal government that outlasts the administration.

In addition to providing standards of management and accountability, Congress might also wish to ensure the flow of information to itself to aid in the development of legislation or appropriations, as it did when it enacted the Government Performance and Results Act. (*P.L. 103-62; 107 Stat. 285; subsequently updated by P.L. 111-352; 124 Stat. 3866.*)

§ 8.70 Congress and the Executive: Oversight and Investigation

Congressional oversight and investigation are key components of the system of checks and balances between the branches of the federal government, as well as a means of making determinations about the need for additional lawmaking. With oversight, Congress—through its standing and specially authorized committees—reviews the implementation of public policy. Through investigations, these committees use powers granted them by their parent chambers to probe governmental and private activities for potential misconduct or mismanagement, and to compel the appearance and testimony of witnesses and the provision of documents. Although Congress often conducts oversight and investigatory activities itself, other governmental actors, such as the Government Accountability Office (GAO) and inspectors general (IGs) in departments and agencies, are regularly called upon by Congress to assist with these functions. As one of many elements of congressional-executive relations, oversight and investigations are part of a largely seamless web where one element overlaps with another. Congress sometimes conducts oversight hearings as distinct activities, but the review of agencies and programs also pervades routine congressional activities, such as the appropriations and confirmation processes. (*See § 8.71, Examples of Oversight Letters.*)

Congress' authority to conduct oversight and investigation is implied from its enumerated powers in the Constitution and the Necessary and Proper Clause. This authority is viewed as essential to Congress' lawmaking role. The 1946 and 1970 Legislative Reorganization Acts (*60 Stat. 812 and 84 Stat. 1140, respectively*) directed congressional committees to conduct continuous oversight, and other statutes—such as the Whistleblowers Protection Act of 1978 (*103 Stat. 16*), the Inspectors General Act of 1978 (*92 Stat. 1101*), and the Chief Financial Officers Act of 1990 (*104 Stat. 2838*)—added to committees' capacity to do so. (*See § 8.72, Executive Privilege.*)

Congressional oversight and investigation can serve a number of purposes. Oversight might be undertaken to determine whether or not the executive is administering federal programs and policies as Congress intended. With the broad discretion that laws often grant executive departments and agencies, congressional committees' oversight ensures that Congress is informed of the manner in which the executive is interpreting and carrying out laws. Committees might also use oversight to influence the direction of rulemaking that implements a law. In addition, oversight is an important means of establishing and measuring accountability in the administration of federal programs and policies. Oversight also helps both the executive and Congress to establish priorities within and between federal activities. (See *§ 8.73, Legislative History.*)

With its power to investigate, Congress can publicly expose debasement of government and the rule of law. It can investigate private organizations, economic activities, or any other area where it might legislate.

Although oversight and investigation findings might lead Congress to modify existing law or enact new laws, these activities often lead to changes by other means. They might lead to changes in procedures in governmental or private entities, for example, or additional rulemaking by executive departments and agencies with authority and jurisdiction in the area under investigation. (*See § 8.74, Hearings May Affect Public or Private Practices.*) Either or both chambers of Congress may elect to modify their own rules and procedures as a result of the findings of an investigation. Under some circumstances, investigation might lead to prosecution by the executive for violations of criminal laws. In such situations, congressional committees are mindful of the potential impact on prosecutions of providing witness protections during investigative activities. (*See § 8.75, Committee Investigations and Witness Protections.*)

Congress has many oversight and investigation tools and methods at its disposal, some of which are described briefly here. One frequently used oversight tool is a statutorily required report to Congress from an executive agency. Reports might be required for any number of purposes, such as to detail results of a department's or agency's study of a public policy problem or to inform Congress about a government-wide management concern. Another way Congress might use a report requirement is to monitor the administration of a federal program, particularly at its outset or when significant changes have been made. As suggested above, another frequently used tool of oversight is a committee hearing. Such hearings are carefully planned by members and senior committee staff, and often are used to review governmental activity in a particular policy area and to assess the need for administrative or legislative change. (*See § 6.40, Committee Hearings.*)

As previously noted, members of Congress often use appropriations and confirmation hearings as opportunities to pose oversight-oriented questions. In the latter case, Senate committees with jurisdiction over a nomination often use confirmation hearings to conduct an examination of the administration of the department or agency in which the office is located. They sometimes extract commitments from the nominee to look into certain issues, report back to the committee on certain matters, or effect some change. Individual senators might also place a hold on one or more nominations to exert leverage on the administration for production of information or for a commitment to examine a policy.

Tools available to Congress during investigations include subpoenas, contempt power, grants of immunity, and staff interviews and depositions. (*See § 8.76, Example of Subpoena to Executive Branch Official.*) House and Senate rules authorize standing committees and subcommittees to compel individuals to appear and testify in hearings or to require the provision of documents to Congress. Either chamber could also by resolution delegate that power, or additional powers, to special or select committees. If an individual fails to provide testimony or documents as required, provisions in statute allow the full House or Senate to cite a witness for criminal contempt and refer the matter to the U.S. attorney; the Senate also has recourse to a civil contempt proceeding against witnesses other than executive-branch officials. In the past, the threat of a congressional subpoena or contempt citation has often led to negotiated or full compliance on the part of the targeted individual or office.

§ 8.71

Examples of Oversight Letters

FRED UPTON, MICHIGAN
CHAIRMAN

HENRY A. WAXMAN, CALIFORNIA
RANKING MEMBER

ONE HUNDRED TWELFTH CONGRESS

Congress of the United States

House of Representatives

COMMITTEE ON ENERGY AND COMMERCE
2125 RAYBURN HOUSE OFFICE BUILDING
WASHINGTON, DC 20515–6115

Majority (202) 225–2927
Minority (202) 225–3641

June 8, 2011

The Honorable Margaret A. Hamburg, M.D.
Commissioner
The Food and Drug Administration
10903 New Hampshire Avenue
Silver Spring, MD 20903

Thomas Frieden, M.D., MPH
Director
Centers for Disease Control and Prevention
1600 Clifton Road
Atlanta, GA 30333

Dear Dr. Hamburg and Dr. Frieden:

Pursuant to Rules X and XI of the U.S. House of Representatives, the Committee on Energy and Commerce is examining the recent outbreak of a lethal form of Shiga toxin-producing *E. coli* O104:H4 (STEC O104:H4) in Europe. As of June 6, 2011, case counts confirmed by Germany's Robert Koch Institute include 642 patients with hemolytic uremic syndrome – a type of kidney failure that is associated with *E. coli* or STEC infections – and 15 deaths. We are especially concerned by the Centers for Disease Control and Prevention (CDC) report that, in the United States, there are one confirmed and three suspected cases of STEC O104:H4 infections identified in persons who recently traveled to Hamburg, Germany, the likely site of exposure.[1]

We request that you contact Sam Spector with the Republican Committee staff at (202) 225-2927 and Stacia Cardille of the Democratic staff at (202) 225-3641 to schedule a staff briefing on the Food and Drug Administration's efforts to protect the American food supply. We

[1] U.S. Department of Health and Human Services, Centers for Disease Control and Prevention, *Investigation Update: Outbreak of Shiga toxin-producing* E. coli *0104 (STEC 0104:H4) Infections Associated with Travel to Germany* (online at www.cdc.gov/ecoli/2011/ecoliO104/index.html) (accessed on June 8, 2011).

Letter to the Honorable Margaret A. Hamburg, M.D. and Dr. Thomas Frieden
Page 2

also ask the CDC to participate in the briefing as CDC is monitoring the current outbreak of *E. coli* O104 and tracking illnesses in the United States that may be related to the outbreak.

Sincerely,

Fred Upton
Chairman

Henry A. Waxman
Ranking Member

Cliff Stearns
Chairman
Subcommittee on Oversight and Investigations

Diana DeGette
Ranking Member
Subcommittee on Oversight and Investigations

Joseph R. Pitts
Chairman
Subcommittee on Health

Frank Pallone, Jr.
Ranking Member
Subcommittee on Health

Continued on page 369

§ 8.71 (continued)

U.S. House of Representatives
Committee on Transportation and Infrastructure
Washington, DC 20515

John L. Mica, Chairman — Nick J. Rahall, II, Ranking Member

March 2, 2011

James W. Coon II, Chief of Staff — James H. Zoia, Democrat Chief of Staff

The Honorable Robert Peck
Commissioner, Public Buildings Service
U.S. General Services Administration
1800 F Street, NW
Washington, D.C. 20405

Dear Commissioner Peck:

We write to request information regarding the General Services Administration's (GSA) properties. On several occasions, including directly with you, during a Subcommittee hearing, and subsequently with your staff, requests have been made regarding access to property lists and other information.

In particular, we would request that GSA provide access to the property lists and other information contained in the Federal Real Property Profile database of GSA-controlled properties. Access to this database is critical to ensuring that our Subcommittee can properly conduct oversight and evaluate proposals for space submitted for congressional approval.

We would request that the following be provided to the Subcommittee no later than Friday, March 11, 2011:

- Access to the database as it pertains to GSA-controlled properties; and
- A complete list, both a hard copy and electronically, of all GSA-controlled properties included in the database, including the building address, square footage, estimated market value, how much the property costs the federal government to maintain, current building capacity, current building use, and other associated information.

Should you have any questions regarding this request, please contact the Subcommittee Staff Director, Dan Mathews at (202) 225-3014.

Sincerely,

Jeff Denham, M.C.
Chairman
Subcommittee on Economic Development, Public Buildings, and Emergency Management

Eleanor Holmes Norton, Delegate
Ranking Member
Subcommittee on Economic Development, Public Buildings, and Emergency Management

§ 8.72

Executive Privilege

The phrase "executive privilege" is a shorthand reference to the "qualified privilege" of the executive to decline to respond to a request for information—documents or testimony or both—from either of the other two branches of the federal government. A unanimous circuit court opinion in 1997 distinguished between two different kinds of executive privilege—presidential communications privilege and deliberative process privilege—with different legal bases and different thresholds of need required to compel disclosure.

Presidential communications privilege is based in "the constitutional separation of powers principles and the President's unique constitutional role." (*In re Sealed Case*, 121 F.3d 729 at 745 (D.C. Cir. 1997).) This privilege allows the president to protect from disclosure the details of decision-making and deliberations with close advisors. Presidential communications are considered to be "presumptively privileged," but the privilege is not absolute; it may be overcome by an adequate showing of need. The court indicated that "the privilege should apply only to communications authored or solicited and received by those members of an immediate White House adviser's staff who have broad and significant responsibility for investigating and formulating the advice to be given the President on the particular matter to which the communications relate." The privilege protects such communications where they involve government operations that require the president's direct decision-making. The *In re Sealed Case* court limited the claim of such privilege to those advisors in close decisional proximity to the president. The court specified that "the privilege should not extend to staff outside the White House in executive branch agencies." The reasoning of the court in *In re Sealed Case* was subsequently adopted in *Judicial Watch v. Department of Justice*, 365 F.3d 1108 (D.C. Cir. 2004). Presidential claims of executive privilege are unusual, and they are normally made by the president or at his direction. Such claims usually lead to negotiations between the White House and Congress.

Deliberative process privilege is a common-law privilege and applies to executive officials generally. The threshold of need for overcoming this claim of privilege is lower than for overcoming a claim of presidential communications privilege. If a claim is made by a department or agency that does not involve the president and his assertion of the claim, the practice is for a requesting congressional committee to make a case-by-case evaluation of the claim. The department or agency and Congress normally negotiate over the requested material, and a congressional committee might begin drafting a congressional contempt citation to add leverage to its request. If negotiations between Congress and the executive fail, the parent chamber can adopt a contempt citation and even seek relief in the courts. Alternatively, Congress may use other constitutional powers, such as its appropriations authority or the Senate's confirmation power, as leverage in obtaining the needed information.

The House can also adopt a simple resolution—a *resolution of inquiry*—requesting information or documents from the president or directing a department or agency head to supply such information. Such a resolution is used to obtain factual information, not to request opinions or investigations.

Congressional committees often use staff interviews to collect information as part of an investigation. This staff work provides tighter focus to the questioning and witness list for investigative hearings. On some occasions, House and Senate resolutions have provided specific authority to a committee for staff members to take sworn depositions. Special committee procedures have usually been established under these circumstances. Among other things, depositions, which are con-

§ 8.73

Legislative History

It is impossible to quantify the impact of legislative history on the executive and the judiciary; it is difficult even to define legislative history. In its narrowest sense, legislative history means changes in the text of measures on their way to enactment. Presumably, examining changes to words, sentences, paragraphs, or more allows one to refine an understanding of what Congress meant in enacting a statute. Somewhat more broadly, legislative history includes documents, such as committee and conference reports, that explain congressional intentions in making changes. Even more broadly, legislative history encompasses other congressional documents as well as debate on the House and Senate floors. Some might even argue that a "Dear Colleague" letter signed by the chair and ranking minority member of the committee of jurisdiction, statements of administration policy, a presidential signing message, and other materials are also part of a measure's legislative history.

Executive departments and agencies, which interact with Congress repeatedly on appropriations, authorizations, proposed regulations, liaison activities, and other matters, pay consistently closer attention to the range of legislative history materials than do the courts. Executive departments and agencies seek to understand legislative intent through these materials and to resolve conflicting views expressed in the House and Senate or between a committee report and floor statements. Indeed, committee and conference reports, materials annexed to them, and even committee correspondence and other documents can contain essential information for an agency that is attempting to carry out a law. For example, instructive or directive language might be included in the joint explanatory statement to a conference report on the measure.

Agency practices differ in the manner in which they use legislative history materials. Some give them great deference; others de-emphasize their role in administering programs and writing regulations. Administration policy also strongly influences the regard given legislative history. Nonetheless, an agency might find it risky to ignore instructive language in reports of the Appropriations Committees or legislative committees with which the agency interacts regularly on its programs.

The courts begin with a principle called the *plain-meaning rule* in analyzing a statute. A court will generally look to the plain meaning of a statute's words, and seek any needed guidance within the statute as a whole. A court still might decide to look outside a statute and at the deliberations of Congress at any time, and for any number of reasons—such as to clarify ambiguous language, confirm an interpretation, or learn more about legislative purpose. A court might look first to the textual changes that Congress made during its consideration of a measure at the different stages of the legislative process. It might also seek background information on the purposes of the legislation. Courts, in general, proceed warily if they go further and seek enlightenment from congressional documents or proceedings on the meaning of a word, phrase, or provision of a statute.

A court's attention to varying statutory interpretations regularly arises from opposing counsel's arguments. The court, then, might elect to examine the legislative history as it deems appropriate. However, in appellate rulings and other forums, the judiciary continues to debate the appropriate role of legislative history in interpreting statutes.

ducted in private, might lead to more efficient use of hearing time, facilitate more candid responses from witnesses than they would provide in a hearing, and allow further investigation of witness allegations prior to the airing of those allegations at a public hearing. Under certain circumstances, a committee might seek a court order to grant partial or full immunity to a witness as a means of obtaining testimony. (See *§ 8.75, Committee Investigations and Witness Protections.*)

8

§ 8.74

Hearings May Affect Public or Private Practices

A congressional committee might be the focal point of efforts to change practices in the government or in private entities, even in the absence of lawmaking, through its use of oversight, hearings, and other activities. In the 111th Congress, the Senate Commerce, Science, and Transportation Committee attacked deceptive practices in the debt settlement industry through a variety of means, stimulating actions by both the Federal Trade Commission and the states' attorneys general. The documents shown here indicate the variety of methods used by the committee in its efforts.

U.S. Senate – Committee on Commerce, Science, & Transportation

Home / Press Room / Press Releases

Recent Press Releases

Rockefeller Sends Results of Debt Settlement Industry Investigation to 56 Attorneys General

Democratic Press Office - (202) 224-8374

May 13 2010

WASHINGTON, DC — Senator John D. (Jay) Rockefeller IV, Chairman of the U.S. Senate Committee on Commerce, Science, and Transportation, today sent letters to 56 Attorneys General alerting them to the results of a recent Committee investigation which found that debt settlement companies engaged in fraudulent, deceptive and abusive practices that were harmful to consumers.

"It is my hope that this information will assist you in your efforts to protect citizens of your state from the deceptive claims and practices of this industry," Chairman Rockefeller states in his letters. "I look forward to working with you to end abuses in the debt settlement industry and to address other consumer protection issues."

Chairman Rockefeller sent letters to the Attorneys General of all 50 states, and to the Attorneys General of the District of Columbia, Guam, American Samoa, Puerto Rico, the Northern Mariana Islands and the Virgin Islands.

U.S. Senate – Committee on Commerce, Science, & Transportation

Home / Press Room / Press Releases

Recent Press Releases

Chairman Rockefeller Remarks on The Debt Settlement Industry: The Consumer's Experience

Democratic Press Office - (202) 224-8374

Apr 22 2010

WASHINGTON, D.C.—Millions of American families have suffered serious financial setbacks during the economic downturn. Sometimes it's because someone in the family has lost their job. Sometimes it's because a family member has gotten sick and medical bills are piling up. As we all know, even people who think they have good health insurance can end up owing thousands of dollars out of their own pockets.

For thousands of American and West Virginian families, our economic downturn has meant falling farther and farther behind. It means struggling every month to pay bills. And it means thinking seriously about what happens if they can't make even their minimum monthly payments to their creditors.

One person who found himself in this situation was Mark Spaulding, who lives in South Charleston, West Virginia. Between the credit card bills and the hospital bills, he and his wife owed more than $23,000 dollars. He wasn't behind on these bills yet, but he was worried. He had a job and he believed in paying what he owed, but he wasn't sure how he was going to pay it all off.

So he looked for help and he found a California company called "U.S. Debt Settlement" that looked reputable. He called a toll-free number and talked to a sales representative named Holly Slater. She told him U.S. Debt Settlement could act as his "financial representative" and could negotiate with his creditors to cut his debt by as much as 50 percent.

William and Holly Haas of Concord, New Hampshire had a similar experience with a debt settlement company called "Consumer Credit Counseling of America." I am very pleased to welcome them to our hearing today. Thank you Mr. and Mrs. Hass for sharing your story with us.

What Mr. Spaulding, and the Haas family, and thousands of other Americans have learned the hard way is that these debt settlement companies are not what they claim to be. They promise to reduce consumers' debts by 40, 50, or even 60 percent, and then collect thousands of dollars in fees up front.

Press Releases

February 10, 2010

MADIGAN SUES FOUR DEBT SETTLEMENT FIRMS TO STOP ABUSIVE, DECEPTIVE PRACTICES

Chicago — Attorney General Lisa Madigan today filed four lawsuits against debt settlement companies, alleging that the defendants are engaging in deceptive marketing practices, charging excessive fees and doing little or nothing to improve consumers' financial standing. Along with these suits, Madigan has proposed legislation that would crackdown on the industry's abusive practices.

"These companies are unfairly luring financially strapped consumers with misleading claims that they can effectively eliminate consumers' debt," Madigan said. "The reality is that, after enrolling in a debt settlement program, consumers too often find themselves in even worse financial straits. It's time to clean up this industry so that people struggling to pay off their debts aren't being sold a false bill of goods."

United States Government Accountability Office

GAO

Testimony

Before the Committee on Commerce, Science, and Transportation, U.S. Senate

For Release on Delivery
Expected at 2:30 p.m. EDT
Thursday, April 22, 2010

DEBT SETTLEMENT

Fraudulent, Abusive, and Deceptive Practices Pose Risk to Consumers

Statement of Gregory D. Kutz, Managing Director
Forensic Audits and Special Investigations

Federal Trade Commission
Protecting America's Consumers

[illegible]/2011

FTC Settlements Put Debt Relief Operations Out of Business

Defendants Used Robocalls to Sell Bogus Plans to Lower Credit Card Interest Rates

The FTC has settled two actions that charged marketers with deceptively claiming they could reduce consumers' credit card interest rates. Both operations allegedly made deceptive telemarketing calls, called consumers on the Do Not Call Registry, and used illegal robocalls. The settlements will ban all of the defendants from selling debt relief services.

Advanced Management Services

The FTC charged that Advanced Management Services NW LLC, and several co-defendants called consumers and claimed that they could negotiate with credit card issuers to substantially lower the consumers' credit card interest rates. They allegedly delivered prerecorded "robocalls" with messages urging consumers to "press one" to speak with someone. Many consumers believed the calls came from their credit card company. The defendants charged consumers up to $1,590 and promised a refund if they failed to deliver at least $2,500 in interest rate savings. But, instead of arranging reduced interest rates, the defendants sent consumers instructions to pay down their credit card debts early to save money on interest. Consumers who demanded refunds allegedly were denied outright, got the run-around, or had a $199 "nonrefundable fee" deducted from their refund.

Under two settlement orders, all of the Advanced Management Services defendants are banned from selling debt relief services. The defendants, who were based in Washington and Texas, are also prohibited from misrepresenting material facts about any good or service, selling or using customers' personal information, failing to properly dispose of customer information, and collecting payments from their debt relief customers.

The order against PDM International Inc., also doing business as Priority Direct Marketing International Inc., and William D. Fithian, also bans them from telemarketing and from violating the FTC's Telemarketing Sales Rule, and imposes a $13.8 million judgment. The order against Advanced Management Services NW LLC, also doing business as AMS Financial, Rapid Reduction Systems, and Client Services Group; Rapid Reduction System's LLC; Ryan David Bishop; and Michael L. Rohlf; imposes an $8.1 million judgment. Both judgments, which represent the total amount of money consumers lost, will be suspended when the defendants have surrendered virtually all of their assets, including several luxury cars, a boat, jet skis, and ATVs. The full judgments will become due immediately if the defendants are found to have misrepresented their financial condition.

The FTC acknowledges the assistance of the Better Business Bureau of Eastern Washington, North Idaho, and Montana, and the BBB of Fort Worth, Texas; the U.S. Postal Inspection Service; the Bedford, Texas, Police Department; and the attorneys general of Illinois, Minnesota, North Carolina, North Dakota, Washington, and West Virginia.

Dynamic Financial

In a second case, the FTC alleged that Dynamic Financial Group and other defendants told consumers that, for an up-front fee of up to $1,995, they could save consumers thousands of dollars by reducing their credit card interest rates, and help them pay off their debts faster. The FTC further charged that the defendants promised, falsely, a full refund if consumers did not save a "guaranteed" amount – typically $2,500 or more. However, the defendants allegedly did not negotiate lower interest rates for consumers or failed to provide refunds.

Under five settlement orders in this case, all of the defendants are banned from selling debt relief services. These defendants, who are based in Canada, Florida, and New Jersey, also are prohibited from misrepresenting material facts about any good or service, violating the Telemarketing Sales Rule, collecting payments from their debt relief customers, using or selling customers' personal information, and failing to properly dispose of customer information.

The order against 2145183 Ontario, Inc., also doing business as Dynamic Financial Resolutions Inc.; The Dynamic Financial Group (U.S.A.) Inc.; R&H Marketing Concepts Inc.; America Freedom Advisors Inc.; Joseph G. Rogister; and Christopher M. Hayden also bans them from robocalling and imposes an $8.3 million judgment that will be suspended due to the defendants' inability to pay.

The order against Thriller Marketing LLC, Dwayne J. Martins, and John L. Franks Jr. imposes a $4.9 million judgment that will be suspended when Martins has surrendered the proceeds from selling a 2005 BMW 645 and Franks has surrendered the proceeds from selling two business condominiums in Tampa. The order against Frank Porporino Jr. also bans him from robocalling and imposes an $8.3 million judgment that will be suspended when he has surrendered certain assets. In each instance, the full judgment will become due immediately if the defendants are found to have misrepresented their financial condition.

The orders against Michael Falcone and Sean Rogister also ban them from robocalling and impose judgments of $93,137 and $90,473, respectively, which must be paid immediately.

On April 27, 2011, a default judgment was entered against Alpha Financial Debt Group Inc. That order imposed a $8.68 million judgment and banned the company from robocalling. Litigation will continue against the remaining defendant, Philip N. Constantinidis.

The Commission vote approving the Advanced Management Services proposed consent judgments was 3-1-1, with Commissioner Rosch dissenting and Commissioner Brill recused. The FTC filed the proposed consent judgments in the U.S. District Court for the Eastern District of Washington.

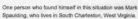

§ 8.75

Committee Investigations and Witness Protections

When a congressional committee (or subcommittee) conducts an investigation, there is no doubt about Congress' power to investigate. But a number of questions or issues often appear as the committee attempts to obtain the specific information it believes it needs.

One set of issues surrounds the committee's authority and conduct. What is the authority in chamber rules or specially adopted resolutions enabling the committee to conduct the investigation? What do the committee's rules of procedure, published in the *Congressional Record*, provide? What are quorum requirements for taking testimony? Are those requirements different for sworn testimony? The committee must also follow procedures in chamber and committee rules for issuing subpoenas, or procedures established in an authorizing resolution. Enforcement through one of the forms of contempt proceedings available to the House and Senate is undertaken only after committee and chamber approval.

Other questions that involve committee conduct include decisions on using staff depositions, taking testimony in open or executive session, and allowing broadcast or photographing of a witness testifying. For example, while the rules of both chambers favor open meetings, in some instances a House rule requires a closed meeting if a majority of the committee agrees on the defamatory or incriminating effect of the testimony. Even when a committee has authority in various aspects of conducting an investigation, it still must consider the strategic and tactical implications of exercising that authority.

At hearings, witnesses are allowed to be accompanied by counsel to advise them on their constitutional rights, but it is generally understood that counsel may not "coach" witnesses. Chamber and committee rules and other factors come into play if a chair believes counsel's behavior is interfering with the committee's hearing.

Yet another set of questions involves the protections afforded witnesses by the freedoms of the Bill of Rights, a matter that can involve the judiciary if Congress or a witness resorts to the courts to validate an assertion of congressional powers or witness rights. The Fifth Amendment freedom against self-incrimination is recognized. The Fourth Amendment requirement of probable cause (for congressional subpoenas) and freedom from unreasonable searches and seizures also seems to be recognized. An assertion of rights under the First Amendment, however, has resulted in weighing committee and witness interests both in committees and, subsequently, in the courts. The courts look especially closely at a committee's authority and legislative purpose in such cases. Congressional committees do not, however, pay the deference to common-law privileges (such as attorney-client) that is given in a court.

If a witness invokes a Fifth Amendment privilege against testifying, a committee might still compel testimony with a two-thirds vote of the committee in favor of seeking a court order to grant immunity and direct the witness to testify. The immunity granted protects the witness from use of the testimony in a criminal prosecution. A grant of immunity might then jeopardize criminal prosecution, the prosecutor bearing the burden of showing that the case is not based on or derived from the immunized testimony. The appellate court decisions that reversed the convictions of Oliver North and John Poindexter in the Iran-Contra scandal made that burden in future prosecutions even more difficult to overcome. (*See § 8.77, Seeking to Compel Testimony.*)

8

Within Congress, the rules of both chambers support their committees' active oversight. Some of these rules have already been discussed. In addition to these, House rules give the Oversight and Government Reform Committee wide latitude in conducting oversight. Senate rules do the same for the Homeland Security and Governmental Affairs Committee. Each committee may conduct oversight government-wide and on intergovernmental programs and activities, and each is given a special responsibility to study GAO reports and recommend action to Congress based on those reports. In addition to general provisions encouraging oversight, House and Senate rules give specific committees "special" or "comprehensive" authority to conduct oversight in certain policy areas, although a particular policy area might fall within the legislative jurisdiction of several committees.

In the House, each standing committee is directed to provide the Oversight and Government Reform Committee and House Administration Committee with an oversight plan for the new Congress by February 15 of the first session of a Congress. The Oversight and Government Reform Committee consolidates these reports and issues an oversight agenda by March 31. House committees are to include oversight findings in their reports on legislation. Each House committee must file a quarterly activities report, including oversight activities.

The House and Senate may also establish temporary committees to conduct oversight. The Senate, for example, created the Special Committee on the Year 2000 Technology Problem to monitor the preparedness of computer systems in the executive branch and various economic sectors to recognize the year 2000. The House and Senate have also acted jointly in the past, such as when both chambers established committees to investigate the Iran-Contra affair, and the committees then worked together. The Speaker may also be authorized by resolution to appoint ad hoc oversight committees.

In addition to the oversight and investigation activities Congress undertakes itself, Congress often calls on certain government organizations to provide support in carrying out these functions. Prominent among these organizations is GAO, which Congress created, in part, to address oversight needs. Generally, at the behest of a congressional committee or pursuant to authority granted to it by statute, GAO undertakes audits and evaluations of federal programs and activities, and reports its findings to Congress. GAO's professional staff has the investigatory experience and authority to ensure that Congress is well-informed on the implementation of laws and options for their improvement. (*See § 4.130, Legislative-Branch Support Agencies.*)

IGs, established statutorily in approximately seventy departments and agencies, also provide support to Congress' oversight and investigation functions. These offices are required, among other things, to report the findings of their audits and investigations semiannually to their respective department or agency heads. These administrative leaders must then forward the reports with their comments to Congress within thirty days. Shorter reporting times apply in some situations, and Congress itself can request information directly from an IG.

From time to time, Congress has also established temporary commissions to investigate particular events or issues. Such commissions have varied in their mandates, authorities, and profiles. The 9/11 Commission, for example, was established by law (*P.L. 107-306; 116 Stat. 2408*), and was populated by experienced and knowledgeable individuals who demonstrated a determination to reach consensus and see the commission's recommendations implemented. The commission had the power to hold hearings and collect evidence, and was granted subpoena power.

§ 8.76

Example of Subpoena to Executive Branch Official

SUBPOENA

BY AUTHORITY OF THE HOUSE OF REPRESENTATIVES OF THE CONGRESS OF THE UNITED STATES OF AMERICA

To The Honorable Alberto R. Gonzales, United States Attorney General

You are hereby commanded to be and appear before the Committee on the Judiciary Subcommittee on Commercial and Administrative Law of the House of Representatives of the United States at the place, date and time specified below.

☐ **to testify** touching matters of inquiry committed to said committee or subcommittee; and you are not to depart without leave of said committee or subcommittee.

Place of testimony: ______

Date: ______ Time: ______

☑ **to produce the things identified on the attached schedule** touching matters of inqui[...] committee or subcommittee; and you are not to depart without leave of said committ[...]

Place of production: 2138 Rayburn House Office Building, Washington, D.C. 20[...]

Date: April 16, 2007 Time: 2:00 [...]

To Any authorized staff member of the House Committee on the Judiciary

______ to se[...]

Witness my hand and the seal of the House of Representatives[...] at the city of Washington, this 10th day of April[...]

Attest: [signature]
Clerk

[signature]
Chairman or [...]

SCHEDULE OF DOCUMENT REQUESTS SUBPOENA TO THE ATTORNEY GENERAL APRIL 10, 2007

Documents requested

1. Complete and unredacted versions, including complete paper and electronic versions, of any and all documents created by or sent to anyone at the Department, referring or otherwise relating in any way to the termination of former U.S. Attorneys David Iglesias, H.E. Cummins, John McKay, Carol Lam, Daniel Bogden, Paul Charlton, Kevin Ryan, or Margaret Chiara (hereinafter "the terminated U.S. Attorneys"), or any of them, or to the consideration or selection of their possible replacements, or any of them.

2. Complete and unredacted versions, including complete paper and electronic versions, of any and all documents referring to or otherwise relating in any way to a communication between anyone at the Department and any Member of Congress concerning any of the terminated U.S. Attorneys occurring in advance of the termination involved.

[...]nd unredacted versions, including complete paper and electronic [...] any and all documents that anyone at the Department submitted to, or [...] otherwise relate in any way to a communication that anyone at the [...] had with, any of the terminated U.S. Attorneys during his or her tenure [...]ncerning any failure in performance, including any failure to comply [...]ment priorities and directives.

[...]nd unredacted versions, including complete paper and electronic [...] any and all documents previously requested in writing by the [...]tee that the Department has withheld, in whole or in part, from [...]on any basis or for any reason, including, but not limited to, those [...]'generated within the Executive Branch for the purpose of responding [...]essional (and media) inquiries about the resignations." as described in [...]ent's March 19, 2007 letter.

[...]om paragraphs 1-4 is the paper version of any document previously [...]complete, unredacted paper form by the Department to the [...]ee on March 13, 19, 20, 23, or 28, 2007.

JOHN CONYERS, JR., Michigan
CHAIRMAN

LAMAR S. SMITH, Texas
RANKING MINORITY MEMBER

U.S. House of Representatives
Committee on the Judiciary
Washington, DC 20515–6216
One Hundred Tenth Congress

April 10, 2007

The Honorable Alberto R. Gonzales
Attorney General of the United States
U.S. Department of Justice
950 Pennsylvania Ave., NW
Washington, DC 20530

Dear Mr. Attorney General:

Attached is a subpoena for documents and electronic information that we previously requested from the Department in connection with its investigation into the circumstances surrounding the recent termination of several United States Attorneys and related matters, which the Department has furnished to us thus far only in redacted form, or has told the Subcommittee it was withholding. The subpoena is being issued pursuant to authority granted by the House Judiciary Subcommittee on Commercial and Administrative Law on March 21, 2007.

I appreciate your cooperation in voluntarily supplying a number of documents in response to the Subcommittee's request. As we have written and told you and your staff on a number of occasions, however, and reiterated most recently in our letters of March 22, March 28, and April 2, 2007, the incomplete response we have received thus far falls far short of what is needed for the Subcommittee and Committee to effectively exercise their oversight responsibilities in ascertaining the truth behind the very serious concerns that have been raised regarding this matter.

8

§ 8.77

Seeking to Compel Testimony

For Immediate Release 4/25/2007

House Judiciary Committee Approves Immunity Order, Authorizes Subpoena for Former DoJ Official Monica Goodling

For Immediate Release
April 25, 2007

Contact: Jonathan Godfrey(202) 226-6888
Melanie Roussell(202) 226-5543

Washington, DC)- Today, the House Judiciary Committee authorized a subpoena and voted in support of seeking a judicial order of immunity to compel testimony for former Justice Department-White House Liaison Monica Goodling. The immunity order required a two-thirds vote of the Committee - 32 Members voted in support, six voted against and two were not present. Chairman John Conyers, Jr. (D-MI) made the following opening remarks at the hearing:

We will first turn to the two items remaining on our agenda from last week, involving Monica Goodling and our continuing investigation into the circumstances surrounding the terminations of U.S. Attorneys, the representations that have been made to Congress regarding those circumstances, and related matters.

There are two resolutions – one to direct the House General Counsel to apply for a court order that would permit the Committee to give Ms. Goodling use immunity for testimony and related information she provides under compulsion to us, and the other to authorize the issuance of a subpoena for Ms. Goodling. Pursuant to notice, I call up first the resolution regarding use immunity.

We had a good discussion of this matter last week, when we decided, at the request of our Ranking Minority Member, Mr. Smith, to postpone voting on the resolutions to permit us all to gain a little more familiarity and comfort with the immunity procedure and to speak informally with the Department of Justice. We have done that this week, and based on that meeting, I believe it is prudent that we proceed with the process of considering immunity for Ms. Goodling.

Allow me to briefly recount how we have come to this point.
The matters we have been examining go to the very heart of the public's ability to rely on the integrity of our legal system, and we have been working diligently to get to the truth. We have encountered some obstacles, and we are working to overcome them. We have been working closely with our Minority in all of these efforts, and we appreciate their support.

We have a subpoena pending with the Justice Department for e-mails and related information, which the Department has thus far only partially complied with, but we continue to be in discussions with the Department regarding their compliance. We have requested interviews with a number of current and former high-level Department officials, and those interviews are being scheduled and conducted.

We have asked the White House for information, and for interviews with selected current and former White House officials who appear, based on information we have obtained thus far, to be significantly involved in the decisionmaking. As of yet, the White House has not been forthcoming, but we continue to hope and expect that we will reach an accommodation with them.

It is against this backdrop that we consider Monica Goodling, who recently resigned from her position as senior counsel to the Attorney General. Among her duties in that position was serving as the Justice Department's principal liaison with the White House.

She was apparently involved in crucial discussions over a two-year period with senior White House aides, and with other senior Justice officials, in which the termination list was developed, refined, and finalized. She was also in the small group of senior Justice lawyers who prepared Deputy Attorney General Paul McNulty and his Principal Associate, William Moschella, for congressional testimony that we believe inaccurately portrayed the surrounding circumstances.

So Ms. Goodling appears to be a key witness for us, as to any possible undue or improper interference, and as to any internal discussions as to how forthcoming to be to Congress. But she has notified the Committee that she would invoke her Fifth Amendment privilege against self-incrimination were she called to testify. And I don't think at this point that all of her potential grounds for invoking the privilege can be dismissed out of hand.

Under these circumstances, it would appear that the Committee has exhausted all reasonable efforts to obtain Ms. Goodling's critical information short of providing her with limited use immunity under the applicable statute, 18 U.S.C. 6005.

Taking this step will compel her to testify, under penalty of contempt, but under the protection that information she provides to us under compulsion could not be used against her for any prosecution, as long as the information is truthful.

Continued on page 377

§ 8.77 (continued)

U.S. Department of Justice

Office of the Inspector General

May 7, 2007

The Honorable John Conyers, Jr.
Chairman
Committee on the Judiciary
U.S. House of Representatives
Washington, D.C. 20515-6216

Dear Mr. Chairman:

This is in response to your letter of April 27, 2007, in which you provided notice to the Attorney General that the House of Representatives Committee on the Judiciary (Committee) has authorized an application to a United States District Court for an order that would grant use immunity to former Department of Justice (Department) employee Monica Goodling in exchange for her testimony before the Committee.

As you know, the Attorney General and Deputy Attorney General have recused themselves from this matter. Therefore, because the Office of the Inspector General (OIG) and the Office of Professional Responsibility (OPR) are conducting a joint investigation of the removal of United States Attorneys and related issues, and after consultation with the Solicitor General in his capacity as Acting Attorney General in this matter, we are responding on behalf of the Department pursuant to 18 U.S.C. § 6005.

As we previously discussed with Committee staff in response to their questions, the OIG/OPR joint investigation is in its early stages, and we intend to take the investigation wherever it leads. As in any investigation that potentially could involve evidence of criminal conduct, we would prefer that any potential subject not be granted immunity at this stage of the investigation.

However, we understand the Committee's interest in obtaining Ms. Goodling's testimony. Therefore, after balancing the significant congressional and public interest against the impact of the Committee's actions on our ongoing investigation, we will not raise an objection or seek a deferral pursuant to the provisions of 18 U.S.C. § 6005.

Please contact us if you have additional questions about this matter.

Sincerely,

Glenn A. Fine
Inspector General

H. Marshall Jarrett
Counsel, Office of
Professional Responsibility

cc: The Honorable Lamar Smith
Ranking Member
Committee on the Judiciary
U.S. House of Representatives

The Honorable Linda T. Sanchez
Chairwoman, Subcommittee on Commercial and Administrative Law
Committee on the Judiciary
U.S. House of Representatives

The Honorable Chris Cannon
Ranking Member, Subcommittee on Commercial and Administrative Law
Committee on the Judiciary
U.S. House of Representatives

The Honorable Paul D. Clement
Solicitor General
U.S. Department of Justice

Continued on page 378

8

§ 8.77 (continued)

UNITED STATES DISTRICT COURT
FOR THE DISTRICT OF COLUMBIA

COMMITTEE ON THE JUDICIARY)

United States House of Representatives)
Washington, D.C. 20515)

Applicant.)

Misc. No. 07-198

FILED
MAY 1 1 2007
NANCY MAYER WHITTINGTON, CLERK
U.S. DISTRICT COURT

ORDER

UPON CONSIDERATION of the Application of the Committee on the Judiciary of the U.S. House of Representatives ("the Committee") for an Order Immunizing the Testimony of, and Other Information Provided by, Monica Goodling, and the Memorandum of Points and Authorities in Support thereof, and having determined that the requirements of 18 U.S.C. § 6005 have been satisfied, it is by the Court this 11th day of May, 2007 ORDERED

That Monica Goodling may not refuse to testify, and may not refuse to provide other information, when compelled to do so at proceedings before or ancillary to the Committee (including its subcommittees) on the basis of her constitutional privilege against self-incrimination, and it is FURTHER ORDERED

That no testimony or other information compelled under this Order (or any information directly or indirectly derived from such testimony or other information) may be used against Monica Goodling in any criminal proceeding, except prosecutions for perjury, giving a false statement, or otherwise failing to comply with this Order.

Thomas F. Hogan
Chief U.S. District Judge

§ 8.80 Congress and the Executive: Appointments

The Senate and the president share the power to appoint the leadership of the executive branch of the federal government and all federal judges. The framework for the appointment of the top officers of the United States is established by provisions in the Constitution and in law. The Constitution states:

> [The President] shall nominate, and by and with the Advice and Consent of the Senate, shall appoint Ambassadors, other public Ministers and Consuls, Judges of the supreme Court, and all other Officers of the United States, whose Appointments are not herein otherwise provided for, and which shall be established by Law: but the Congress may by Law vest the Appointment of such inferior Officers, as they think proper, in the President alone, in the Courts of Law, or in the Heads of Departments. (*Art. II, sec. 2, cl. 2.*)

Over time, this clause has been interpreted to provide that certain officers, including those specifically named and all agency heads, must be appointed with the advice and consent of the Senate. In the case of most inferior officers, the Constitution gives Congress discretion to establish whether or not Senate approval of an appointment will be required. If Congress elects not to involve the Senate, it may delegate the appointment authority to the president alone, a court, or an agency official.

Appointments to more than 1,200 civilian executive branch positions require Senate confirmation at present. These include the leaders of departments (such as secretaries, deputy secretaries, under secretaries, and general counsels), independent agencies (such as administrators and deputy administrators), and boards and commissions (such as commissioners). Presidential appointments of federal judges, U.S. attorneys, U.S. marshals, and certain legislative-branch officials are also subject to the advice and consent of the Senate.

The president and agency heads are authorized to make appointments to several thousand other full- and part-time positions throughout the executive branch without the involvement of the Senate. These positions, some of which have significant policymaking authority, include advisors, senior-level managers, confidential assistants, and advisory committee members. At the end of each presidential election year, the Senate Committee on Homeland Security and Governmental Affairs and the House Committee on Oversight and Government Reform alternate in publishing a book-length committee print of politically appointed positions entitled *Policy and Supporting Positions*, more popularly known as the "Plum Book," named for its serendipitous cover color the first time it was published. (*See the Government Printing Office web site at <www.gpoaccess.gov/plumbook>.*) This cadre of political appointees has grown in recent decades, and political layers have been added at departments and agencies that are intended to increase presidential control over policymaking.

Political appointments are less influential in most independent regulatory boards and commissions, which are structured to be more independent of the president than other parts of the executive branch. For example, rather than serving at the pleasure of the president, as do most presidential appointees, members of these bodies generally have fixed terms and often have some form of protection from removal. Statutes creating such entities may also require that seats must be allocated between members of different party affiliation.

§ 8.81

Confirmation Procedure

Appointments subject to Senate confirmation include most senior government officials and federal judges. Most commissions and promotions of officers in the armed forces, Public Health Service, National Oceanic and Atmospheric Administration, and Foreign Service are also subject to the advice and consent of the Senate.

The president transmits nominations for such appointments to the Senate by message, it is read, and the Senate executive clerk assigns a consecutive number to each message as it is received. Nominations are then referred to the committee with jurisdiction over the agency in which the positions exist. In some cases, a nomination may be referred to more than one committee.

Committees adopt procedures for the consideration of nominations, consistent with Senate rules, and may include those procedures in committee rules. Committees often begin their consideration of a nomination by gathering information about a nominee. About half of civilian nominations, including senior-level executive branch officials and most federal judges, are also subject to a committee hearing. The nominee and others may testify. A nominee is often introduced at a hearing by one or both senators from her home state. Committees generally do not hold hearings on routine nominations such as military promotions, and the 112th Congress adopted expedited procedures applicable to nominations to various boards of trustees, or directors, chief financial officers, and assistant secretaries for legislation.

During consideration of executive branch nominations, many committees exact a commitment from the nominee to testify before committees of Congress. This commitment is intended to strengthen congressional oversight capacity.

A committee has several options regarding the disposition of a nomination. It is not required to act on a nomination at all. If a committee elects to report a nomination, it can report it favorably, unfavorably, or without recommendation. In some cases, a reported nomination will be accompanied by a written report. The Senate may discharge a committee from further consideration of a nomination at any time, but this step, if it occurs, is normally taken by unanimous consent.

Nominations are typically reported to the full Senate by the committee chair, who informs the legislative clerk at the desk. The legislative clerk, in turn, notifies the executive clerk, who assigns the nomination, or, in some cases, the list of nominations, a number and places it on the Senate's executive calendar. (*See § 6.180, Senate Calendars and Legislative and Executive Business before the Senate*.)

When the full Senate considers a nomination it does so in executive, rather than legislative, session. Procedures in executive session are similar to those in legislative session. Floor consideration cannot begin, except by unanimous consent, until a nomination has been on the calendar for one day. In most cases, a nomination is subject to the clearance process and then confirmed by unanimous consent. (*See § 6.190, Holds, Clearance, and Unanimous Consent*.) The Senate sometimes resolves nominations conflicts by crafting unanimous consent agreements providing for limited debate or by bundling a group of nominations that are of interest to a wide group of senators. Nominations that come up frequently are called up en bloc and usually approved without objection.

The Senate rarely votes to reject a nomination; unsuccessful nominations usually die from inaction. Occasionally, a nomination may be sent back to a committee for further consideration. Nominations that have not been acted upon by adjournment *sine die* are returned to the president. Senate rules provide that nominations pending when the Senate adjourns or recesses for more than thirty days are also returned to the president, but the Senate may waive this rule by unanimous consent.

If a nominee is confirmed, the secretary of the Senate attests to a "resolution of confirmation," which is sent to the White House. Of course, the president may withdraw a nomination at any time, thereby ending the process.

Vacancies and Recess Appointments

The Constitution provides the president with the power to make limited-term appointments during Senate recesses to positions that otherwise would require the Senate's advice and consent. Article II, Section 2, Clause 3 states that "[t]he President shall have Power to fill up all Vacancies that may happen during the Recess of the Senate, by granting Commissions which shall expire at the End of their next Session." Presidents have sometimes used this power to circumvent the Senate confirmation process, especially in cases of controversial nominations. In response, Congress has attempted to constrain the president's power through a statute that prohibits payment from the Treasury to recess appointees unless certain nomination guidelines are followed (*5 U.S.C. § 5503*). In addition, a general provision included in the Financial Services (formerly Treasury) appropriations bill has prohibited payment from the Treasury to recess appointees whose nominations have been rejected by the Senate. (*See, for example, P.L. 108-447, Division H, Section 609.*) Nonetheless, recess appointments can be a source of congressional-executive tension. The president's authority to make a recess appointment to a judgeship on the Court of Appeals for the Eleventh Circuit, for example, was challenged in court, with an amicus brief filed by a senator. The Eleventh Circuit upheld the president's authority in this case. (*Evans et al. v. Stephens et al.*, 387 F.3d 1220 (11th Cir. 2004), *cert. denied*, 544 U.S. 942 (2005).)

Although Congress has tried to limit the president's recess appointment power, it has also acknowledged the need to maintain leadership in the federal bureaucracy during the appointment process by enacting the Federal Vacancies Reform Act of 1998 (*5 U.S.C. §§ 3345-3349d*), which allows for three kinds of limited-term appointments to most advice and consent positions in executive-branch departments and agencies. In the event of a vacancy, (1) the first assistant to such position may automatically take over; (2) the president may direct another officer from any agency who holds an advice and consent position to take over the tasks of the vacant office; or (3) the president may select any officer or upper-level employee who has been at the agency where the vacancy exists for more than ninety days of the preceding year.

§ 8.90 Congress and the Executive: Presidential Election and Succession

Under Article II and the Twelfth, Twentieth, and Twenty-fifth Amendments to the Constitution, Congress has critical roles to play in the selection of the president and vice president during the quadrennial election process and in the event of a vacancy between elections.

Article II, Section 1, as modified by the Twelfth Amendment, established Congress' role in the electoral college system. Under these constitutional provisions and federal law, Congress, in joint session on January 6 (or another date set by Congress) following a presidential election, receives and counts electoral votes, and the election of the president and vice president is announced. Congress is empowered to resolve objections regarding the electoral votes at that time. (*See § 8.91, Electoral College.*)

In order to be elected president or vice president by the electoral college, a candidate must receive a majority, and not merely a plurality, of the electoral votes (currently 270 of 538). The Twelfth

§ 8.91

Electoral College

The Constitution provided for *electors* in choosing the president and vice president; the states' electors by long practice are collectively called the *electoral college.* The Constitution in Article II, Section 1, Clause 2, states as follows:

> Each State shall appoint, in such Manner as the Legislature thereof may direct, a Number of Electors, equal to the whole Number of Senators and Representatives to which the State may be entitled in the Congress: but no Senator or Representative, or Person holding an Office of Trust or Profit under the United States, shall be appointed an Elector.

When a voter on election day casts a ballot for president and vice president, she is voting *indirectly* for a presidential and vice presidential ticket and *directly* for a slate of electors. Under authority granted in Article II, Section 1, Clause 3 of the Constitution to set the time of choosing electors, Congress set election day as the Tuesday after the first Monday in November.

There are currently 538 electors. In addition to each state's constitutional allocation based on two senators and its number of representatives—ranging for the 2012, 2016, and 2020 elections from a minimum of three electors to California's fifty-five—the District of Columbia also has three electors pursuant to the Twenty-third Amendment to the Constitution. To be elected president and vice president, the Twelfth Amendment requires candidates to obtain a majority in the electoral college, or, currently, 270 votes.

Electors for a presidential and vice presidential ticket in a state are chosen in accordance with law made by a state's legislature. While state laws vary on the selection of electors, slates of nominees for electors are partisan, usually reflecting choices of state party conventions or state party central committees; electors are expected to support their party's candidates for president and vice president. State law also governs contests involving presidential electors, and, pursuant to federal law, a state's resolution of contests is conclusive when it occurs at least six days before the electoral college meets. As soon as practicable after the election, or after the resolution of any contests, each state's governor sends a certificate of ascertainment of the electors appointed to the archivist of the United States and six duplicate-originals to the state's electors.

In locations designated by state law, electors representing each state's winning slate meet in their states on the first Monday after the second Wednesday in December (following the 2012 general election, December 17, 2012), and cast separate ballots for their party's presidential and vice presidential candidates. All but two states (Maine and Nebraska) award electoral votes on a winner-take-all basis for the presidential and vice presidential ticket—technically, the ticket's slate of electors—that receives the greatest number of votes state-wide. Maine and Nebraska award two electoral votes on the basis of statewide results and the balance of their electoral votes (two for Maine and three for Nebraska) on the basis of congressional district results. Although electors can, and occasionally have, cast ballots for individuals other than the winning ticket's candidates, electors are expected to vote for their party's candidates. Some states have laws that attempt to enforce that expectation.

Records of each state's electors' balloting are transmitted to the vice president of the United States in his role as president of the Senate, to the archivist of the United States, to the state's secretary of state, and to the federal district court of the district in which the electors met.

On January 6 following the election, unless Congress has changed the law to designate another day, the House and Senate assemble at 1:00 p.m. in the House chamber for the counting of the electoral votes. The vice president of the United States presides, although the Senate

Continued on page 383

§ 8.91 (continued)

president pro tempore may preside if the vice president declines or the vice president's office is vacant. The certificates and ballots of each state's electors are opened, proceeding in the alphabetical order of the states. The vice president reads a state's certificate and ballot, and calls for objections. He then presents the ballot to the four tellers—two from each chamber—who were previously selected by their respective chambers. When all the certificates and ballots are opened, read, and counted, the tellers present the results to the vice president. If one of the candidates for each of the offices receives a majority of the electoral votes (currently 270 of 538), the vice president announces the election of the president and vice president. (*For subsequent procedure in the absence of this outcome, see the discussion of contingent election in § 8.90, Congress and the Executive: Presidential Election and Succession.*)

An objection to a state's electoral votes must be in writing and signed by one representative and one senator. If there is a valid objection, the joint session is recessed at that point, the Senate withdraws to its chamber, and the two houses consider the objection. In these sessions, members may speak just once and for no more than five minutes. At the end of two hours, the chambers vote and then reconvene their joint session. Unless both chambers vote to uphold the objection, it fails. If both houses agree to the objection, the vote or votes objected to are not counted. This procedure was followed in 2005 after an objection by Rep. Stephanie Tubbs Jones, D-OH, and Sen. Barbara Boxer, D-CA, to the Ohio ballot. Neither chamber upheld the objection. The principal reasons there might be an objection are that a vote was not "regularly given" by an elector, for example, a "faithless" elector voting for someone other than the winners in his state, or that an elector was not lawfully certified, or both. Federal law (*3 U.S.C. § 1 et seq.*) provides guidance on resolving instances when there might be more than one list of electors.

(*For specific information on electoral college procedures and the reasons therefore, see the web site of the National Archives and Records Administration at <www.archives.gov/federal-register/electoral-college>. Electoral college procedures and the role of Congress are codified at 3 U.S.C. § 1 et seq.*)

Allocation of Electoral Votes for the 2012, 2016, and 2020 Presidential and Vice Presidential Elections

Alabama – 9
Alaska – 3
Arizona – 11
Arkansas – 6
California – 55
Colorado – 9
Connecticut – 7
Delaware – 3
District of Columbia – 3
Florida – 29
Georgia – 16
Hawaii – 4
Idaho – 4
Illinois – 20
Indiana – 11
Iowa – 6
Kansas – 6
Kentucky – 8
Louisiana – 8
Maine – 4
Maryland – 10
Massachusetts – 11
Michigan – 16
Minnesota – 10
Mississippi – 6
Missouri – 10
Montana – 3
Nebraska – 5
Nevada – 6
New Hampshire – 4
New Jersey – 14
New Mexico – 5
New York – 29
North Carolina – 15
North Dakota – 3
Ohio – 18
Oklahoma – 7
Oregon – 7
Pennsylvania – 20
Rhode Island – 4
South Carolina – 9
South Dakota – 3
Tennessee – 11
Texas – 38
Utah – 6
Vermont – 3
Virginia – 13
Washington – 12
West Virginia – 5
Wisconsin – 10
Wyoming – 3

§ 8.92

Presidential and Vice Presidential Succession

In three different places, the Constitution (*art. II, sec. 1, cl. 5*) and amendments to it (*the Twentieth and Twenty-fifth Amendments*) provide for presidential and vice presidential succession, and authorize Congress to enact laws to carry out the constitutional provisions. The Twenty-fifth Amendment restated the original constitutional provision that the vice president becomes president if the president died, resigned, or was removed from office. (Nine vice presidents have succeeded to the presidency on the death or resignation of the president.)

The Twenty-fifth Amendment also authorized the president to nominate a vice president if a vacancy occurred in that office. (The vice presidency has been vacant on eighteen occasions.) The nomination must be confirmed by a majority vote in both the House and Senate. This provision of the Twenty-fifth Amendment has been used twice—President Richard M. Nixon nominated Gerald R. Ford to be vice president after the resignation of Vice President Spiro T. Agnew, and, after Ford succeeded Nixon as president, then-President Ford nominated Nelson A. Rockefeller to the vice presidency. The House and Senate Judiciary Committees conducted investigations of the nominees' fitness, held hearings on the nominations, and reported the nominations. The full House and Senate then debated and voted on the nominations.

In 1947, following the 1945 death in office of President Franklin D. Roosevelt, Congress enacted the Presidential Succession Act. (*62 Stat. 677; 3 U.S.C. § 19.*) Under this act, if vacancies exist in both the presidency and vice presidency, the Speaker of the House succeeds to the presidency if he qualifies (for example, being a naturalized citizen would be a disqualification). If the speakership is vacant or the Speaker is disqualified, then the president pro tempore succeeds to the presidency. If the office of president pro tempore is vacant or its occupant is disqualified, succession moves to the Cabinet, with the order based on the dates on which the departments were created. With ratification of the Twenty-fifth Amendment, however, the likelihood of invoking the Presidential Succession Act was substantially reduced.

The Twenty-fifth Amendment also provided for the event of presidential disability. Under certain circumstances, Congress might be called upon to decide whether a president is unable perform the duties of his office. Congress would be required to assemble within forty-eight hours if it is not in session. A determination of presidential disability would need to be made within twenty-one days of assembling and would require a two-thirds vote in each house.

Amendment, as modified by the Twentieth Amendment, established a system for the *contingent election* of the president and vice president in the event that no candidate attains this threshold. In the case of the president, the House of Representatives chooses the president from among the three candidates with the largest numbers of electoral votes; each state delegation casts a single vote. A majority of states is needed for election. Although an amendment to the Constitution provided electors for the District of Columbia, it did not provide the District with a role in a contingent election. In the event that no vice presidential candidate receives a majority of electoral votes, the Senate chooses between the two candidates with the largest numbers of electoral votes; each senator has one vote, and a majority of votes is needed for election.

The Twelfth Amendment was proposed by Congress in 1803 in response to difficulties encoun-

§ 8.93

Members of Congress Who Served as President

Although only one sitting representative, James A. Garfield, has been elected to the presidency, many presidents have served in the House. Although senators are often thought of as potential presidential candidates, only three have been elected to the White House while serving in the Senate: Warren G. Harding, John F. Kennedy, and Barack Obama. John Quincy Adams and Andrew Johnson were the only presidents to serve in Congress after serving as president. Adams served in the House from 1831 to 1848; Johnson served in the Senate in 1875. A number of sitting or former senators and representatives have been candidates or party nominees.

In addition, several early presidents served in the Continental Congress: George Washington (1774–1775); John Adams (1774–1778); Thomas Jefferson (1775, 1776, 1783–1784); James Madison (1780–1783, 1787–1788); and James Monroe (1783–1786).

Name	Years in House	Years in Senate	Years as President
James Madison	1789–1797		1809–1817
James Monroe		1790–1794	1817–1825
John Quincy Adams	1831–1848	1803–1808	1825–1829
Andrew Jackson	1796–1797	1797–1798; 1823–1825	1829–1837
Martin Van Buren		1821–1828	1837–1841
William Henry Harrison	1799–1800,[1] 1816–1819	1825–1828	1841
John Tyler	1817–1821	1827–1836	1841–1845
James K. Polk	1825–1839[2]		1845–1849
Millard Fillmore	1833–1835, 1837–1843		1850–1853
Franklin Pierce	1833–1837	1837–1842	1853–1857
James Buchanan	1821–1831	1834–1845	1857–1861
Abraham Lincoln	1847–1849		1861–1865
Andrew Johnson	1843–1853	1857–1862; 1875	1865–1869
Rutherford B. Hayes	1865–1867		1877–1881
James A. Garfield	1863–1880		1881
Benjamin Harrison		1881–1887	1889–1893
William McKinley	1877–1883; 1885–1891		1897–1901
Warren G. Harding		1915–1921	1921–1923
Harry S. Truman		1935–1945[3]	1945–1953
John F. Kennedy	1947–1953	1953–1960	1961–1963
Lyndon B. Johnson	1937–1949	1949–1961[4]	1963–1969
Richard M. Nixon	1947–1950	1951–1953	1969–1974
Gerald R. Ford	1949–1973[5]		1974–1977
George H. W. Bush	1967–1971		1989–1993
Barack Obama		2005–2008	2009–

1. Delegate to U.S. Congress.
2. Speaker (1835–1839).
3. Elected vice president in 1944.
4. Senate Democratic leader (1953–1961); elected vice president in 1960.
5. House Republican leader (1965–1973); appointed vice president in 1973.

8

tered during the presidential election of 1800-1801. After ratification by the states, the Twelfth Amendment went into effect in 1804. There have been two contingent elections under its provisions. The president was elected by the House of Representatives in 1825, and the vice president was elected by the Senate in 1837. The Twelfth Amendment mandates some of the specific procedures that must be used during a contingent election. Other procedures were developed by the House and Senate during the respective contingent elections, but those procedures could be altered in the event of another contingent election.

The Twentieth Amendment provided that the vice president serve as acting president until the House is able to choose a president, should the House be unable to reach a decision by inauguration day, January 20. (The Twentieth Amendment provided that a president's and vice president's terms of office end at 12:00 noon on January 20 following a presidential election.) This amendment also allows Congress to establish by law who serves as acting president in the event that neither a president nor a vice president is qualified by January 20. In the Presidential Succession Act of 1947 (*61 Stat. 380; 3 U.S.C. § 19*), Congress addressed this matter, naming first the Speaker of the House, alternatively the president pro tempore of the Senate, and then the Cabinet secretaries in the order in which their departments were created (beginning with the secretary of state). To serve, an individual would need to meet the constitutional qualifications required for any president—a natural-born citizen, a resident of the United States for at least fourteen years, at least thirty-five years old, and not disqualified by previous service as president.

Article II, Section 1, Clause 6 of the Constitution originally provided for presidential succession in the event of "the Removal of the President from Office, or of his Death, Resignation, or Inability to discharge the Powers and Duties of the said Office." The Twenty-fifth Amendment, ratified in 1967, superseded this provision. It established a role for Congress in confirming a president's nomination to fill a vice presidential vacancy. The amendment also provided a role in determining, under certain circumstances, whether a president was "unable to discharge the powers and duties of his office." (*See § 8.92, Presidential and Vice Presidential Succession; and § 8.93, Members of Congress Who Served as President.*)

§ 8.100 Congress and the Executive: Impeachment

One or the most profound powers bestowed on Congress is the power to remove from office the president, federal judges, and other "civil Officers of the United States." Removal requires action by both houses of Congress. The Constitution empowers the House to impeach, or bring charges against, an official in Article I, Section 2, Clause 5, which states, "The House of Representatives . . . shall have the sole Power of Impeachment." After an official has been impeached, the trial is conducted in the Senate, as provided by Article I, Section 3, Clause 6:

> The Senate shall have the sole Power to try all Impeachments. When sitting for that Purpose, they shall be on Oath or Affirmation. When the President of the United States is tried, the Chief Justice shall preside: And no Person shall be convicted without the Concurrence of two thirds of the Members present.

The scope of the judgments resulting from such trials is defined in the next clause:

> Judgment in Cases of Impeachment shall not extend further than to removal from Office, and disqualification to hold and enjoy any Office of honor, Trust or Profit under the United States: but the Party convicted shall nevertheless be liable and subject to Indictment, Trial, Judgment and Punishment, according to the Law.

Although the House has initiated impeachment proceedings more than sixty times since the Constitution was adopted, it has voted to impeach only nineteen times. Eight of these impeachments, all federal judges, led to Senate convictions. Four of these convictions have occurred since 1985. Seven of the nineteen impeachments led to Senate acquittals, and the remaining four resulted in resignations.

Impeachment proceedings have been initiated against nine presidents. In two cases, those of Presidents Andrew Johnson and Bill Clinton, the House voted to impeach, and the president was acquitted in the Senate. In 1974, President Nixon resigned the presidency after the House Judiciary Committee voted for articles of impeachment, but before the full House acted. Since World War II, four other presidents—Truman, Reagan, George H.W. Bush, and George W. Bush—have been the subject of proposed articles of impeachment.

The Constitution sets a high standard for removal in Article II, Section 4, which provides that "The President, Vice President, and all civil Officers of the United States, shall be removed from Office on Impeachment for, and Conviction of, Treason, Bribery, or other high Crimes and Misdemeanors."

Three other standards and restrictions related to impeachment also exist in the Constitution. Article III, Section 1 states as follows: "The Judges, both of the supreme and inferior Courts, shall hold their Offices during good Behaviour. . . ." Article III, Section 2, Clause 3 exempts cases of impeachment from jury trial. And, in Article II, Section 2, Clause 1, the president is disallowed from granting pardons in cases of impeachment.

Impeachment Process

A summary of the principal steps in the impeachment process follows. The impeachment process might begin with a resolution introduced by one or more members of the House or through a referral from an outside entity, such as the Judicial Conference of the United States or an independent counsel. After authorization by the House, an examination or investigation into charges is undertaken, normally by the Judiciary Committee. The committee, by majority vote, may report a resolution and articles of impeachment. It then writes a committee report, which might contain minority, additional, and supplemental views of committee members.

The House considers impeachment resolutions under the one-hour rule or pursuant to a special rule reported from the Rules Committee and agreed to by the House. A majority vote, usually on each article of impeachment, is necessary. The House has voted to impeach on only nineteen occasions; it has voted articles of impeachment on just two presidents, Andrew Johnson and Bill Clinton.

If it adopts one or more articles of impeachment, the House appoints managers (generally members of the Judiciary Committee) to argue the case for impeachment in the Senate, and notifies the Senate of its action. The Senate informs the House when it is ready to receive the managers, who then appear before the bar of the Senate and exhibit the articles of impeachment. The Senate then summons the impeached official, and any pleadings are resolved before the trial begins.

The Senate proceeds under its *Rules of Procedure and Practice in the Senate When Sitting on Impeachment Trials*, a part of the *Senate Manual* (S. Doc. 110-1), as modified by subsequent action of the Senate. The Senate can subpoena witnesses and documents, and may delegate the receipt of testimony and evidence to a committee created for this purpose.

In a presidential impeachment trial, the chief justice of the Supreme Court presides. In all other trials in the Senate, an individual senator serves as the presiding officer, who rules on objections and questions and who may present such matters to the Senate for its decision. The House managers make their opening statements, followed by the impeached official's counsel. Evidence is presented, and witnesses may be called, examined, and cross-examined. Senators may submit questions in writing. Final arguments are presented by each side, but the House managers open and close these last presentations.

The Senate may deliberate in open or closed session. It then may choose to vote on any or all of the articles of impeachment; the Senate might also choose to adjourn an impeachment trial *sine die*. Concurrence of two-thirds of those present is necessary for conviction and removal from office. After adoption of one or more articles of impeachment, the Senate might also, by majority vote, disqualify the convicted official from again holding a federal office.

Under Article II, Section 2, Clause 1, the president may "grant Reprieves and Pardons for Offences against the United States," but this power cannot be used in "Cases of Impeachment." (*A one-page history of impeachment proceedings, from Congressional Directory, 2009-2010* (*Washington: Government Printing Office, 2009*), *p. 561, follows.*)

IMPEACHMENT PROCEEDINGS

The provisions of the United States Constitution which apply specifically to impeachments are as follows: Article I, section 2, clause 5; Article I, section 3, clauses 6 and 7; Article II, section 2, clause 1; Article II, section 4; and Article III, section 2, clause 3.

For the officials listed below, the date of impeachment by the House of Representatives is followed by the dates of the Senate trial, with the result of each listed at the end of the entry.

WILLIAM BLOUNT, a Senator of the United States from Tennessee; impeached July 7, 1797; tried Monday, December 17, 1798, to Monday, January 14, 1799; charges dismissed for want of jurisdiction.

JOHN PICKERING, judge of the United States district court for the district of New Hampshire; impeached March 2, 1803; tried Thursday, March 3, 1803, to Monday, March 12, 1804; removed from office.

SAMUEL CHASE, Associate Justice of the Supreme Court of the United States; impeached March 12, 1804; tried Friday, November 30, 1804, to Friday, March 1, 1805; acquitted.

JAMES H. PECK, judge of the United States district court for the district of Missouri; impeached April 24, 1830; tried Monday, April 26, 1830, to Monday, January 31, 1831; acquitted.

WEST H. HUMPHREYS, judge of the United States district court for the middle, eastern, and western districts of Tennessee; impeached May 6, 1862; tried Wednesday, May 7, 1862, to Thursday, June 26, 1862; removed from office and disqualified from future office.

ANDREW JOHNSON, President of the United States; impeached February 24, 1868; tried Tuesday, February 25, 1868, to Tuesday, May 26, 1868; acquitted.

WILLIAM W. BELKNAP, Secretary of War; impeached March 2, 1876; tried Friday, March 3, 1876, to Tuesday, August 1, 1876; acquitted.

CHARLES SWAYNE, judge of the United States district court for the northern district of Florida; impeached December 13, 1904; tried Wednesday, December 14, 1904, to Monday, February 27, 1905; acquitted.

ROBERT W. ARCHBALD, associate judge, United States Commerce Court; impeached July 11, 1912; tried Saturday, July 13, 1912, to Monday, January 13, 1913; removed from office and disqualified from future office.

GEORGE W. ENGLISH, judge of the United States district court for the eastern district of Illinois; impeached April 1, 1926; tried Friday, April 23, 1926, to Monday, December 13, 1926; resigned office Thursday, November 4, 1926; Court of Impeachment adjourned to December 13, 1926, when, on request of House managers, the proceedings were dismissed.

HAROLD LOUDERBACK, judge of the United States district court for the northern district of California; impeached February 24, 1933; tried Monday, May 15, 1933, to Wednesday, May 24, 1933; acquitted.

HALSTED L. RITTER, judge of the United States district court for the southern district of Florida; impeached March 2, 1936; tried Monday, April 6, 1936, to Friday, April 17, 1936; removed from office.

HARRY E. CLAIBORNE, judge of the United States district court of Nevada; impeached July 22, 1986; tried Tuesday, October 7, 1986, to Thursday, October 9, 1986; removed from office.

ALCEE L. HASTINGS, judge of the United States district court for the southern district of Florida; impeached August 3, 1988; tried Wednesday, October 18, 1989, to Friday, October 20, 1989; removed from office.

WALTER L. NIXON, judge of the United States district court for the southern district of Mississippi; impeached May 10, 1989; tried Wednesday, November 1, 1989, to Friday, November 3, 1989; removed from office.

WILLIAM JEFFERSON CLINTON, President of the United States; impeached December 19, 1998; tried Thursday, January 7, 1999, to Friday, February 12, 1999; acquitted.

Mark H. Delahay, judge for the U.S. district court for Kansas, resigned in 1873 after his impeachment but before his Senate trial began.

In the 111th Congress, the House voted to impeach two federal district judges: G. Thomas Porteous Jr. of the Eastern District of Louisiana on March 11, 2010, and Samuel B. Kent of the Southern

District of Texas, on June 19, 2009. After a trial, the Senate on December 8, 2010, convicted Porteous and disqualified him from office.

The House managers exhibited the articles of impeachment against Kent in the Senate on June 24, 2009, but Kent delivered a letter of resignation to the Senate sergeant at arms on June 25, effective June 30. The House on July 20 voted on another resolution to ask the Senate to dismiss the articles of impeachment, and the Senate agreed to a motion to dismiss the articles on July 22, 2009.

§ 8.110 Congress and the Courts

Congress and the courts do not have the myriad daily interactions that are part and parcel of congressional-executive relations. But, the courts depend on Congress to legislate their organization, and on the Senate to confirm judicial appointees. Congress appropriates money for judicial salaries, personnel, operations, and facilities. The legislative decisions of Congress can have a large impact on the courts' workloads. Congress creates new rights or benefits for citizens and residents, with judicial remedies for disputes; creates or changes regulatory schemes, with rights of appeal to the courts; enacts new criminal laws, which must be prosecuted in the courts; and so on. Congress can also remove judges through impeachment by the House and conviction by the Senate. (*See § 8.100, Congress and the Executive: Impeachment.*)

§ 8.120 Congress and the Courts: Exercising Congressional Powers

There are a number of means by which Congress can exercise checks and balances vis-à-vis the courts. This section does not list exhaustively the extent of Congress' power and influence over the judicial branch, but summarizes some key aspects of that power and influence.

In matters related to the administration of the courts, the Senate confirms presidential nominations to the courts. (*See § 8.121, Nominations to Federal Courts.*) Congress, as a whole, enacts appropriations to operate the courts and, within the constraints of the Constitution, establishes judicial compensation. It creates law courts inferior to the Supreme Court and creates special courts, such as the United States Court of International Trade. Congress long ago created the system of district and circuit courts, but it occasionally legislates additional districts or circuits, as it did in 1980 when it split the former Fifth Judicial Circuit to create a new Fifth Judicial Circuit and a new Eleventh Judicial Circuit. (*94 Stat. 1994.*) Congress decides the number of judgeships that should exist for any court, and appropriates money for new courthouses.

In matters involving judicial power, Congress passes laws under which cases are brought in the federal courts by the executive, other governmental bodies, and private entities and citizens. Among many possible categories of lawmaking, these laws might include initiatives in federal regulation within Congress' enumerated powers, such as changes in immigration and naturalization laws. Congress might federalize what have traditionally been areas of state law, such as new criminal statutes dealing with violent crimes or activities with a potential for violence. Congress might pass laws that respond to court decisions that run counter to majority sentiment in Congress on public-policy issues. (*See § 8.123, Congressional Response to Court Decisions.*)

Congress can also in its lawmaking determine the process by which a matter might be brought

§8.121

Nominations to Federal Courts

Because appointments to federal district and circuit courts, and to the Supreme Court, are essentially lifetime appointments, the Senate often plays a more active (and sometimes contrarian) role in these appointments than when it considers presidential nominations to executive positions. Frequently, senators perceive the stakes in judicial appointments to be very high. That is especially the case with Supreme Court appointments, as indicated by the fact that, over the past 200 years, nearly one in five presidential nominations to the Supreme Court has been rejected or withdrawn.

In making judicial nominations, a president is generally expected to consult the senators from a potential nominee's home state, particularly if a senator is of the same party as the president. Senators of the president's party actually recommend nominees for district judgeships in their home state and for circuit judgeships for seats allocated to their home states, using a variety of methods to identify prospective nominees. The president might also consult more widely, such as with members of the Senate Judiciary Committee or the Senate leadership, or at least with members of those two groups from his own party. And senators, other public officials, and other citizens regularly forward the names of prospective judges to the president and his staff.

Once a judicial nomination is received by the Senate, it is referred to the Judiciary Committee. The committee chair sends a blue-colored form (a "blue slip") to the senators from a state where the president has nominated a circuit or district judge (or a U.S. marshal or U.S. attorney). The senators may use the blue slips to indicate their approval or disapproval of the nominee. The committee reviews any investigation that was conducted by the Federal Bureau of Investigation at the request of the White House. The committee also examines a far-reaching questionnaire that it requires of nominees, the research of its staff, and information supplied by outside groups. (*See § 8.122, Gathering Information on a Judicial Nominee.*) A Supreme Court nominee typically makes a "courtesy call" on members of the committee, and often on other senators as well.

In contemporary practice, the Judiciary Committee will then schedule hearings. A district judge nomination supported by both of a state's senators and with no controversy attached to the nominee might be handled in a hearing covering several judges or several items of committee business. A nomination to the Supreme Court will undoubtedly be subject to at least several days of hearings, with an opportunity to testify afforded to the nominee and an opportunity to ask questions at length afforded to committee members. The nominee may be followed by numerous witnesses providing a range of views on the nominee or on factors for the committee and Senate to weigh in considering the nomination.

The final step is for the committee to vote to report the nomination to the full Senate, which it may do favorably, unfavorably, or without recommendation. The committee reports Supreme Court nominees, unless withdrawn, in one of these ways to give the Senate the opportunity to consider such an important nomination.

Nominations to lesser courts are sometimes tied up in committee or, once reported, in scheduling of floor time. A nomination might be in trouble because of concerns about the nominee's views or character, or because of political factors independent of the nominee. In presidential election years, the Senate may be loathe to oblige a sitting president by confirming a large number of nominees to the federal courts. (*See § 6.190, Holds, Clearance, and Unanimous Consent.*)

Once scheduled for floor time, a judicial nomination proceeds in the same manner as other presidential nominations. The process is described in § 8.81 (*Confirmation Procedure*).

§ 8.122

Gathering Information on a Judicial Nominee

As a nominee to be an associate justice of the U.S. Supreme Court, Samuel A. Alito Jr., a judge on the U.S. Court of Appeals for the Third Circuit, received a twelve-page questionnaire, the first page of which is shown here. In addition to making so-called courtesy calls on many senators, Judge Alito received letters from members of the Senate Judiciary Committee informing him of senators' interests that might be the bases for questions at his confirmation hearing. The first pages of letters from the then-chair and ranking minority member of the committee are shown here.

UNITED STATES SENATE
COMMITTEE ON THE JUDICIARY

NOMINEE FOR THE SUPREME COURT OF THE UNITED STATES

GENERAL (PUBLIC)

1. **Name**: Full name (include any former names used).

2. **Position**: State the position for which you have been nominated.

3. **Address**: List current office address. If state of residence differs from your place of employment, please list the state where you currently reside.

4. **Birthplace**: State date and place of birth.

5. **Marital Status**: (include maiden name of wife, or husband's name). List spouse's occupation, employer's name and business address(es). Please, also indicate the number of dependent children.

6. **Education**: List in reverse chronological order, with most recent first, each college, law school, and any other institutions of higher education attended and indicate for each the dates of attendance, whether a degree was received, and the date each degree was received.

7. **Employment Record**: List in reverse chronological order, listing most recent first, all governmental agencies, business or professional corporations, companies, firms, or other enterprises, partnerships, institutions and organizations, non-profit or otherwise, with which you have been affiliated as an officer, director, partner, proprietor, elected official or employee since graduation from college, whether or not you received payment for your services. Include the name and address of the employer and job title or job description, or the name and address of the institution or organization and your title and responsibilities, where appropriate.

8. **Military Service and Draft Status**: Identify any service in the U.S. Military, including dates of service, branch of service, rank or rate, serial number and type of discharge received. Please list, by approximate date, Selective Service classifications you have held, and state briefly the reasons for any classification other than I-A.

9. **Honors and Awards**: List any scholarships, fellowships, honorary degrees, academic or professional honors or awards, honorary society memberships, military awards, and any other special recognition for outstanding service or achievement you have received.

10. **Bar Associations**: List all bar associations or legal or judicial-related committees, selection panels or conferences of which you are or have been a member, and give the titles and dates of any offices which you have held in such groups. Also, if any such

Continued on page 393

§ 8.122 (continued)

ARLEN SPECTER, PENNSYLVANIA, CHAIRMAN

ORRIN G. HATCH, UTAH
CHARLES E. GRASSLEY, IOWA
JON KYL, ARIZONA
MIKE DeWINE, OHIO
JEFF SESSIONS, ALABAMA
LINDSEY O. GRAHAM, SOUTH CAROLINA
JOHN CORNYN, TEXAS
SAM BROWNBACK, KANSAS
TOM COBURN, OKLAHOMA

PATRICK J. LEAHY, VERMONT
EDWARD M. KENNEDY, MASSACHUSETTS
JOSEPH R. BIDEN, Jr., DELAWARE
HERBERT KOHL, WISCONSIN
DIANNE FEINSTEIN, CALIFORNIA
RUSSELL D. FEINGOLD, WISCONSIN
CHARLES E. SCHUMER, NEW YORK
RICHARD J. DURBIN, ILLINOIS

MICHAEL O'NEILL, *Chief Counsel and Staff Director*
BRUCE A. COHEN, *Democratic Chief Counsel and Staff Director*

United States Senate
COMMITTEE ON THE JUDICIARY
WASHINGTON, DC 20510–6275

November 30, 2005

Honorable Samuel A. Alito, Jr.
c/o The Department of Justice
Washington, DC

Dear Judge Alito:

I write to give you advance notice of some of the issues I intend to ask at your confirmation hearing. In addition to identifying topics, I think it is helpful to outline the background for the questions to save time at the hearing.

Affirmative action is an area of law that has undergone many major changes in the last 25 years. During the late 1970s and early 1980s, when the Supreme Court first began grappling with affirmative action programs, it appeared to have considerable difficulty elucidating clear standards as to determining the constitutionality of such programs. The decisions in Regents of University of California v. Bakke in 1978, Fullilove v. Klutznick in 1980, and Wygant v. Jackson Board of Education in 1986, failed to develop a clear test.

In 1989, in City of Richmond v. Croson, a majority of the Court held that state and local government affirmative action programs are subject to strict scrutiny and thus struck down a Richmond, Virginia affirmative action program that set aside construction contracts for minority-owned businesses. Only a year later, however, the court upheld a federal affirmative action program, applying a lower standard of review in Metro Broadcasting v. FCC.

In 1995, the Court again considered a federal affirmative action program in Adarand v. Pena. In that case, the Court reviewed the Department of Transportation's policy of awarding extra compensation to contractors who hired minority-owned subcontractors. Overruling Metro Broadcasting, decided just five years earlier, the Court concluded that federal affirmative action programs, like state and local affirmative action programs, must be subject to strict scrutiny.

Most recently, the Court considered two higher education affirmative action programs. In Grutter v. Bollinger and Gratz v. Bollinger, the Court rendered a split verdict on the University of Michigan's undergraduate and law school admissions policies. It held that the law school's admission policy was constitutional because it was narrowly tailored and considered race only "a 'plus' factor in the context of individualized consideration of each and every applicant." It did not award "mechanical, predetermined diversity 'bonuses' based on race or ethnicity." In contrast, Michigan's undergraduate admission policy was struck down because it "automatically distribute[d] 20 points, one one-fifth of the points needed to guarantee admission, to every single 'underrepresented minority' applicant solely because of race." The Court held that such rigid policy was "not narrowly tailored to achieve the interest in educational diversity."

Continued on page 394

8

§ 8.122 (continued)

United States Senate

COMMITTEE ON THE JUDICIARY

WASHINGTON, DC 20510-6275

December 19, 2005

The Honorable Samuel A. Alito
United States Circuit Judge for the Third Circuit
357 U.S. Post Office and Courthouse
Federal Square and Walnut Street
Newark, NJ 07101

Dear Judge Alito:

I was glad that we had a chance to meet last month, if only briefly, and look forward to hearing from you at the upcoming hearings. I expect to ask you a number of questions about the role of the courts and judges in our democratic government. I write to you now, in advance of the hearing, so that you will have an opportunity to reflect on these issues and provide fully responsive answers at the hearings.

Last week, we celebrated the 214th anniversary of the adoption of the Bill of Rights to the Constitution. The Framers also embedded protections into the structure of our democracy. The checks and balances among our three branches of government provide fundamental safeguards for the rights of all Americans by ensuring that when one branch overreaches, it can be constrained by the others. Americans rely on this governmental structure to maintain the critical stability and balance necessary to preserve our freedoms and liberty.

At your nomination hearing next month I plan to ask you about your views on the President's power as Commander in Chief under our Constitution and the scope of congressional power in the time of war. There have been times throughout our history when the separation of powers has been tested by Presidents claiming unfettered power. Recent revelations that the President authorized domestic eavesdropping without following the statute that requires approval of the Foreign Intelligence Surveillance Court is but one of several areas where the Court's role as a check on overreaching by the Executive may soon prove crucial. The Supreme Court's role in resolving disputes between the two political branches of federal government involving the withdrawal of troops, and the methods of interrogation, are two other examples of issues that I will want to discuss with you.

Just as with any Federal judge, I view a Supreme Court Justice's willingness to serve as a check on executive power as among the most important issues to consider in a nomination process. It is ironic that after years of issuing decisions that were strongly supportive of executive claims of authority, especially in cases involving so-called "enemy combatants," the Fourth Circuit is now questioning the Bush Administration's switch in its position on whether Jose Padilla can be tried as a civilian in federal criminal court. These issues were also raised in the case of Hamdi v. Rumsfeld, in which Justice O'Connor wrote that our Constitution does not afford the President a blank check, even

§ 8.123

Congressional Response to Court Decisions

Congress, the president, and the courts regularly find themselves at odds over court decisions. But, if Congress has strong feelings about a matter decided by the courts, it might respond with legislation. In 1991, for instance, it enacted a civil rights bill in response to Supreme Court rulings between 1986 and 1991 that had restricted the application of civil rights laws and the remedies available under them in employment discrimination cases. In this example, the three branches spoke to each other through the formal procedures of their constitutional roles, and the two political branches—Congress and the executive—ultimately made a policy decision answering questions raised by the Supreme Court's rulings.

Beginning in 1986, the Supreme Court made a series of rulings on employment discrimination, principally under Title VII of the Civil Rights Act of 1964, which prohibits employment discrimination, and under a post-Civil War law (*42 U.S.C. § 1981*), which prohibits racial discrimination in the making and enforcing of contracts. In the nine rulings subsequently addressed through legislation by Congress, the thrust of the Court's decisions was to make it harder for employees to allege, prove, and obtain relief for employment discrimination.

For example, pursuant to an earlier Supreme Court decision on Title VII (*Griggs v. Duke Power Co.,* 401 U.S. 424 (1971)), employees were able to offer statistical evidence to show the discriminatory effect of an employer's personnel practices. They did not have to prove an intention to discriminate. The courts, in handling cases after that decision, required employers to carry the burden of proof in defending their personnel practices. In 1989, the Court returned to the matter of burden of proof in employment discrimination cases under Title VII. It ruled in *Wards Cove Packing Co. Inc. v. Atonio*, 490 U.S. 642 (1989), that proving discrimination caused by a specific employment practice was a burden carried by plaintiffs and that statistical evidence of the impact of employment practices was insufficient to establish discrimination.

Decisions such as *Wards Cove* alarmed civil rights organizations and a number of members of Congress. In 1990, companion measures were introduced in the House and Senate to deal with the effects of six of the rulings, among the measures' other provisions. An administration bill that dealt with just two of the decisions was also introduced in both chambers. Proponents and opponents of the competing legislation attempted to reach a compromise at various stages of the legislative process, but failed. The administration and those members of Congress opposed to the measures backed by the civil rights organizations were successful at painting those measures with the politically charged moniker of "quota" bills, arguing that employers would adopt quotas for hiring and promotion to avoid lawsuits. Proponents of the measures backed by the civil rights organizations questioned the administration's commitment to enactment of any civil rights measure.

Neither the House nor the Senate mustered veto-proof majorities by the time they voted on the conference report, despite some of the concessions made by civil rights organizations and included in the legislation in an attempt to build wider political support. President George H.W. Bush vetoed the bill (*S. 2104; Oct. 22, 1990*), noting in his veto message a number of areas of agreement between himself and the majority in Congress, but arguing that the effect of the measure would be to create "powerful incentives for employers to adopt hiring and promotion quotas." The Senate took up the veto, and the override attempt failed by a single vote to obtain the two-thirds vote needed to override. (*66 to 34; Oct. 24, 1990.*) The political branches had not yet found a new equilibrium in employment antidiscrimination policy.

When the 102nd Congress convened in 1991, the House Democratic leadership reserved H.R. 1 for a new civil rights bill, giving it prominence and visibility. An administration bill was also introduced

Continued on page 396

§ 8.123 (continued)

in both houses. In the fall of 1991, against the backdrop of the confirmation fight over Clarence Thomas' appointment to the Supreme Court and other political factors, senators and the administration reached compromise on a new bill. The Senate adopted the new measure by a vote of 93 to 5. (*S. 1745; Oct. 30, 1991.*) During Senate consideration of the new bill, senators were very cognizant of how the courts would interpret the measure once it was enacted into law. Because of the number of points on which the bill was not specific, the discretion in interpretation became part of the compromise. Interestingly, the Senate agreed to an amendment attempting to limit the courts' consideration of legislative history surrounding the measure's provisions to a short memo inserted in the *Congressional Record*.

The House followed the Senate in adopting the new measure (*381 to 38; Nov. 7, 1991*), and President Bush signed it (*P.L. 102-166*). The bill that became law addressed policy issues in nine different Supreme Court rulings on employment discrimination, and provided new but limited monetary damages under Title VII. Its language, however, left questions to be resolved by the courts in cases brought before them. The language also allowed the Bush and subsequent administrations leeway in choosing whether and how to participate in those cases.

The political process of making a law does not necessarily result in a law that answers explicitly the variety of cases that might arise under it. As in the situation described above, Congress and the president felt compelled to respond to policy issues raised by the Supreme Court's decisions on discrimination in employment, but the answer eluded them and was ultimately found only in enacting a law with new provisions open to differing interpretations. It might be expected that a future Congress and a future president will find it desirable to address court decisions made under these changes to the employment antidiscrimination laws, again offering new policy direction to the courts.

in the federal courts. For example, appeals from agency adjudicatory decisions are normally taken to a U.S. appeals court. Congress can also say in law which court might hear a matter first, whether administrative remedies must be exhausted before a lawsuit may be filed, what the threshold considerations are for determining that the federal courts are the appropriate judicial forum, and what remedies are available to prevailing litigants. In language included in committee and conference reports and in colloquies on the floor, members are conscious of the potential impact of legislative history on some court decisions. (*See § 8.73, Legislative History.*)

Congress is empowered by the Constitution to impeach and try judges, which it has done as recently as 2010. The Constitution also empowers Congress to make exceptions to the Supreme Court's appellate jurisdiction and to regulate that jurisdiction. (A related, more common exercise of congressional power involving congressional concern about actual or potential judicial decisions is to amend the underlying law on which a decision might be based, for example, amending an environmental law to eliminate a basis for litigation.) Congress might also propose constitutional amendments to the states. (*See § 8.210, Congress and Federalism: Amending the Constitution.*)

Members of Congress themselves might be litigants or *amici* (filing an *amicus*, or friend of the court, brief) in some cases. Finally, the House general counsel and the Senate legal counsel monitor court cases with a view toward the institutional prerogatives and interests of Congress. Members receiving subpoenas for their appearances or for documents notify their chamber by letter. The letter is usually printed in the *Congressional Record*.

§ 8.130 Congress and Foreign Policy

Foreign policy is a power shared by Congress and the executive. The president represents the United States in foreign relations, as head of state and head of government, and as the commander in chief. Beyond that, the framers of the Constitution gave both Congress and the president powers in foreign commerce and foreign policy, and what is now broadly called national security. Congress exerts extensive control over foreign policy and national security, particularly through the appropriations process. The president regularly resorts to his explicit and inherent constitutional powers to take action in foreign and national security policy, including an initial commitment of American troops, but he regularly acts within the framework of policies or grants of authority that exist in law. Either Congress or the executive might initiate a change in foreign policy within its constitutional powers. These actions put the other branch in the position of reacting. Congress and the executive might also work jointly, in either consultative or lawmaking roles.

§ 8.140 Congress and Foreign Policy: Declaring War and Committing Troops

Despite the number of times that American troops have been committed both to large-scale, long-lasting wars and to hostilities or hostile situations of limited duration, Congress has declared war in only five conflicts: the War of 1812, the Mexican-American War, the Spanish-American War, World War I, and World War II. Congress is empowered by Article 1, Section 8, Clause 11 of the Constitution "To declare War . . ." but presidents have rarely asked for declarations of war and Congress has rarely found it necessary to do so. Congress is also empowered in Section 8 "To raise and support Armies . . ." (*cl. 12*) and "To provide and maintain a Navy . . ." (*cl. 13*).

To declare war, Congress passes a joint resolution naming one or more foreign nations. The joint resolution may originate in either house. Normal congressional procedures would apply to the joint resolution. These include normal procedures such as suspension of the rules and a special rule from the Rules Committee in the House, and unanimous consent in the Senate, for waiving procedures that might delay a vote on the joint resolution.

However, for any number of reasons, Congress might instead support a war, limited hostilities, or the potential for hostilities in another way. Congress might choose to "authorize" military action, as it did in 1991 in the instance of the Persian Gulf War (*105 Stat. 3*). It might pass a concurrent resolution, not binding on the president, dealing with some aspect of a foreign crisis, as it did with the Kosovo crisis in March 1999 (*H. Con. Res. 42 and S. Con. Res. 21*). In response to the terrorist attacks of September 11, 2001, Congress passed a joint resolution authorizing the president to use "all necessary and appropriate force" against nations, organizations, or individuals he determined to be responsible (*S.J. Res. 23, P.L. 107-40*). Congress again employed a joint resolution in 2002 to authorize the use of military force in Iraq (*H.J. Res. 114; P.L. 107–243*). Congress did not adopt a bill or resolution concerning Libya after receiving the president's letter on the commencement of military action there. (*See § 8.141, President's Letter on Military Action against Libya.*) Congress also has often supported military action through spending authorization and appropriation measures.

§ 8.141

President's Letter on Military Action against Libya

The White House

Office of the Press Secretary

For Immediate Release March 21, 2011

Letter from the President regarding the commencement of operations in Libya

TEXT OF A LETTER FROM THE PRESIDENT TO THE SPEAKER OF THE HOUSE OF REPRESENTATIVES AND THE PRESIDENT PRO TEMPORE OF THE SENATE

March 21, 2011

Dear Mr. Speaker: (Dear Mr. President:)

At approximately 3:00 p.m. Eastern Daylight Time, on March 19, 2011, at my direction, U.S. military forces commenced operations to assist an international effort authorized by the United Nations (U.N.) Security Council and undertaken with the support of European allies and Arab partners, to prevent a humanitarian catastrophe and address the threat posed to international peace and security by the crisis in Libya. As part of the multilateral response authorized under U.N. Security Council Resolution 1973, U.S. military forces, under the command of Commander, U.S. Africa Command, began a series of strikes against air defense systems and military airfields for the purposes of preparing a no-fly zone. These strikes will be limited in their nature, duration, and scope. Their purpose is to support an international coalition as it takes all necessary measures to enforce the terms of U.N. Security Council Resolution 1973. These limited U.S. actions will set the stage for further action by other coalition partners.

United Nations Security Council Resolution 1973 authorized Member States, under Chapter VII of the U.N. Charter, to take all necessary measures to protect civilians and civilian populated areas under threat of attack in Libya, including the establishment and enforcement of a "no-fly zone" in the airspace of Libya. United States military efforts are discrete and focused on employing unique U.S. military capabilities to set the conditions for our European allies and Arab partners to carry out the measures authorized by the U.N. Security Council Resolution.

Muammar Qadhafi was provided a very clear message that a cease-fire must be implemented immediately. The international community made clear that all attacks against civilians had to stop; Qadhafi had to stop his forces from advancing on Benghazi; pull them back from Ajdabiya, Misrata, and Zawiya; and establish water, electricity, and gas supplies to all areas. Finally, humanitarian assistance had to be allowed to reach the people of Libya.

Although Qadhafi's Foreign Minister announced an immediate cease-fire, Qadhafi and his forces made no attempt to implement such a cease-fire, and instead continued attacks on Misrata and advanced on Benghazi. Qadhafi's continued attacks and threats against civilians and civilian populated areas are of grave concern to neighboring Arab nations and, as expressly stated in U.N. Security Council Resolution 1973, constitute a threat to the region and to international peace and security. His illegitimate use of force not only is causing the deaths of substantial numbers of civilians among his own people, but also is forcing many others to flee to neighboring countries, thereby destabilizing the peace and security of the region. Left unaddressed, the growing instability in Libya could ignite wider instability in the Middle East, with dangerous consequences to the national security interests of the United States. Qadhafi's defiance of the Arab League, as well as the broader international community moreover, represents a lawless challenge to the authority of the Security Council and its efforts to preserve stability in the region. Qadhafi has forfeited his responsibility to protect his own citizens and created a serious need for immediate humanitarian assistance and protection, with any delay only putting more civilians at risk.

The United States has not deployed ground forces into Libya. United States forces are conducting a limited and well-defined mission in support of international efforts to protect civilians and prevent a humanitarian disaster. Accordingly, U.S. forces have targeted the Qadhafi regime's air defense systems, command and control structures, and other capabilities of Qadhafi's armed forces used to attack civilians and civilian populated areas. We will seek a rapid, but responsible, transition of operations to coalition, regional, or international organizations that are postured to continue activities as may be necessary to realize the objectives of U.N. Security Council Resolutions 1970 and 1973.

For these purposes, I have directed these actions, which are in the national security and foreign policy interests of the United States, pursuant to my constitutional authority to conduct U.S. foreign relations and as Commander in Chief and Chief Executive.

I am providing this report as part of my efforts to keep the Congress fully informed, consistent with the War Powers Resolution. I appreciate the support of the Congress in this action.

BARACK OBAMA

War Powers Resolution

To balance the president's responsibility as commander in chief for actions to defend the United States with Congress' powers in foreign policy, Congress, in 1973, enacted over President Nixon's veto the War Powers Resolution (*87 Stat. 555; 50 U.S.C. § 1541 et seq*). The history of the War Powers Resolution has exposed flaws or problems in dealing with situations that arise abroad and with presidential decisions on military actions. Presidents since the enactment of the War Powers Resolution have found it to infringe unconstitutionally on their power as commander in chief, and have interpreted its provisions to favor presidential power and discretion. Yet, whenever troops are committed or may be committed, the War Powers Resolution is now the legal framework invoked and debated by the president and Congress.

The interbranch tensions of the War Powers Resolution begin with its policy statements. These statements assert that, as commander in chief, the president may commit troops to hostilities or imminent hostilities only if there is a declaration of war, a congressional authorization, or an attack on the United States, its territories or possessions, or its armed forces. The War Powers Resolution also requires consultation between Congress and the president before troops are committed. However, presidents have generally chosen to inform Congress rather than consult it, and to do so at varying times in the course of committing troops.

The heart of the War Powers Resolution deals with presidential commitment of troops into "hostilities" or "imminent hostilities." In these circumstances, it requires the president to report to Congress within forty-eight hours after the introduction of troops. A report must explain the reasons for committing troops, the authority under which the president took the action, and an estimate of the scale and duration of the commitment. The president must withdraw the troops within sixty days unless Congress has authorized or extended the commitment by law, or is unable to meet because of an attack on the United States. The president may certify the need for a presence for an additional thirty days to ensure the safe withdrawal of troops.

The War Powers Resolution created expedited, or fast-track, procedures for introducing a joint resolution or bill declaring war or authorizing troop commitments. The procedures apply to committee, floor, and conference proceedings, and operate to bring Congress to a decision by the time the sixty-day period is complete.

The War Powers Resolution also enabled Congress to order the withdrawal of troops by concurrent resolution, a legislative veto presumably invalidated by the Supreme Court's subsequent, unrelated decision in *INS v. Chadha*, 462 U.S. 919 (1983). To rectify this situation, Congress enacted a procedure—independent of the War Powers Resolution—to use a joint resolution, which would then require presidential approval or a congressional veto override to take effect. (*97 Stat. 1062; 50 U.S.C. § 1546a.*)

Among other provisions, the War Powers Resolution also requires reports on troop commitments in situations other than hostilities or imminent hostilities, and includes U.S. troops accompanying foreign military forces in hostilities as an introduction of U.S. armed forces.

The War Powers Resolution was enacted amidst the extraordinary environment of the Vietnam War, Watergate, and congressional actions that led eventually to the House Judiciary Committee's adoption of an impeachment resolution against President Nixon. Nonetheless, it seems to have provided a needed framework for the two branches to debate the commitment of American troops. Except in one instance, presidents have not reported hostilities under the section of the law that would set the sixty-day clock running. However, they have not overtly ignored the War Powers Resolution, and have informed Congress about military engagements consistent with their interpretations of the law. Congress, for its part, has responded differently in different circumstances. For example, it took the initiative in legislation to set the date on which the War Powers Resolution was triggered in 1983 when U.S. Marines were participating in a multinational force in Lebanon.

§ 8.150 Congress and Foreign Policy: Treaties and International Agreements

Article II, Section 2, Clause 2 of the Constitution says of the president: "He shall have Power, by and with the Advice and Consent of the Senate, to make Treaties, provided two thirds of the Senators present concur. . . ." In accordance with Article VI, a ratified treaty, like the Constitution and laws enacted by Congress, is the supreme law of the land.

In foreign affairs, the president often acts under a grant of authority from Congress to negotiate international or executive agreements with foreign nations. For example, Congress might grant negotiating authority to the president pursuant to its constitutional power to regulate foreign commerce. Like a treaty, an agreement is a binding arrangement between the United States and another nation or other nations. Unlike a treaty, it is not submitted to the Senate for its advice and consent. An agreement may, however, be subject to a joint resolution of approval or disapproval by the House and Senate, pursuant to the statute under which the president acted, or, to take effect, it might require implementing legislation.

Some trade agreements serve as examples of the process of congressional delegation of specific negotiating authority to the president, and subsequent congressional action on an agreement negotiated by the president pursuant to that grant of authority. For example, Congress granted the president specific trade negotiating authority (also now being called trade promotion authority) for the "Uruguay Round" of multilateral trade negotiations in 1988 (*102 Stat. 1121; 19 U.S.C. § 2901*). The breadth of the president's authority was spelled out. The president was then to submit implementing legislation to Congress, which would include, among other provisions, changes to existing laws to bring them into conformity with the agreement. To give the president and other nations assurance that Congress would enact what the president negotiated, Congress agreed to consider the agreement under *fast-track procedures*—if the agreement was entered by April 15, 1994. The president submitted the agreement and implementing bill in time, and Congress enacted the bill (*108 Stat. 4809; 19 U.S.C. § 3501*). (*See § 8.151, Fast-Track Procedures.*)

Congress acted in 2002 to give the president trade promotion authority for an agreement to be entered into by June 1, 2005, or, through possible extension, June 1, 2007.

Presidents also claim inherent powers of their own to enter into agreements. Congress, in an attempt to protect its prerogatives and keep the executive in check, has enacted statutes requiring these agreements to be reported to Congress.

While international agreements might be considered in Congress by regular legislative proce-

§ 8.151

Fast-Track Procedures

Fast-track procedures are unique legislative procedures Congress adopts to expedite timely action on a specifically defined type of measure. Fast-track procedures are, therefore, also referred to as *expedited procedures.* The congressional budget resolution and reconciliation bills, resolutions authorizing the use of the armed forces under the War Powers Act, certain foreign military sales, military base closings, and measures to implement international trade agreements are examples of issues considered under fast-track procedures. There is not one form of fast-track procedure; each fast-track procedure is particular to specific legislation or a specific form of legislation.

The *House Rules and Manual* has a section called *Congressional Disapproval Provisions* that contains the complete texts of laws with expedited procedures. These disapproval statutes, applicable in both chambers, are referenced in the rules of each chamber.

Fast-track procedures are in force to limit the opportunity for delay or inaction in either the House or Senate or both. Accordingly, procedures generally require introduction of a measure after Congress receives a presidential message on an expedited procedure issue, and generally require the committee receiving a referral to report on the measure in a specified period of time. If the committee fails to act, an automatic discharge of the committee becomes effective, thereby removing the measure from the committee. Most fast-track procedures provide privilege to the measure for prompt floor action. They also generally impose time limits on debate on the floor and preclude floor amendments.

Examples of laws in which fast-track procedures exist include the Arms Export Control Act *(22 U.S.C. §§ 2776(b), 2776(c), 2776(d), and 2753)* and the 1974 Trade Act *(19 U.S.C. §§ 2191, 2253, 2432, and 2437)*.

dures or by fast-track procedures, treaties—along with nominations—form the *executive business* of the Senate. The Senate has developed special procedures for its handling and consideration of treaties.

Treaty Procedure in the Senate

Consideration of a treaty by the Senate is a type of legislative action that possesses similarities to and differences from regular legislative action.

A treaty may not be ratified for the United States and, pursuant to the treaty's terms, become effective for the nation unless the president obtains the advice and consent of the Senate. That consent is given only by a two-thirds favorable vote of senators present and voting. (The House has no constitutional role in the advice and consent process.)

The Senate might have an informal role before the conclusion of treaty negotiations. Individual senators might serve as observers at the negotiations, or the negotiators might hold periodic briefings for individual senators, leaders, and committees. The Senate's formal role, however, begins with a presidential message—the president's submission of a letter of transmittal and the accompanying treaty documents to the Senate. The treaty documents comprise the text of the treaty, a letter submitted to the president by the secretary of state (usually analyzing the treaty), other documents deemed integral parts of the treaty, and informational documents. The president asks for favorable consideration of the treaty.

Upon receipt, the set of documents is numbered by the executive clerk. Treaty documents are numbered sequentially through a Congress, in a numbering sequence separate from other Senate documents, using the Congress and a sequential number, for example, Treaty Doc. 106-1, where "106" refers to the 106th Congress. Also, upon receipt of the treaty documents, the majority leader may ask unanimous consent on the Senate floor to remove the injunction of secrecy concerning the treaty, which today is usually a pro forma step, treaties having been made public before submission to the Senate by the president.

All treaties are referred to the Foreign Relations Committee. (This referral, however, does not preclude other committees with jurisdiction over the subject matter of the treaty from holding their own hearings or even presenting their views or recommendations to the Foreign Relations Committee.) The committee usually holds hearings, taking testimony from administration officials who participated in treaty negotiations and from others—experts, advocates, and opponents. The committee can choose *not* to act on a treaty. If it takes action and chooses to report the treaty to the full Senate, it may report it favorably, unfavorably, or without recommendation. If the Foreign Relations Committee reports a treaty, it also generally submits a written report, referred to as an executive report. (Executive reports are assigned numbers that run sequentially through a Congress.)

The Foreign Relations Committee also reports a proposed resolution of ratification that may include committee-recommended conditions. Two conditions seem to have become standard in contemporary resolutions. The first is informally called the Byrd-Biden condition, after the late Senator Robert Byrd, D-WV, and former Senator Joseph Biden, D-DE. In essence, the condition says that the Senate may rely on the presentations made by the president and his representatives in developing a shared understanding of a treaty. The second condition, based on concerns most recently raised by the late Senator Jesse Helms, R-NC, notes the supremacy of the U.S. Constitution.

The reported treaty is placed on the Senate's Executive Calendar. To consider a treaty, the Senate must go into executive session. (If the Senate is considering legislative business, it is in legislative session; treaties and nominations are considered in executive session.) The majority leader typically asks unanimous consent that the Senate go into executive session. If unanimous consent is not granted (that is, there is an objection to the unanimous consent request), the majority leader can move that the Senate go into executive session. The motion is not debatable, but it could trigger the first test vote of Senate sentiment on the treaty.

The Senate considers a treaty just as it considers a bill. A treaty is both debatable and amendable (proposed changes to the treaty's text, which the Senate subsequently incorporates into its resolution of ratification). When debate and action on amendments are completed, the Senate considers a resolution of ratification, which is the actual document on which the Senate gives advice and consent. The Senate does not consider further amendments to the treaty. The resolution of ratification is a simple resolution. The Senate can offer, debate, and amend reservations, declarations, understandings, provisos, or statements in connection with the resolution:

- *Reservations* are "specific qualifications or stipulations which change U.S. obligations without necessarily changing treaty language."
- *Understandings* are "interpretive statements that clarify or elaborate the provisions of the treaty but do not alter its language."

- *Declarations* are "statements of the Senate's position, opinion or intentions on matters relating to issues raised by the treaty, but not to its specific provisions."
- *Provisos or statements* do not affect or explain the treaty, but express concern about issues of U.S. law or procedure.

Each of these matters requires a majority vote for adoption. Filibuster and the invoking of cloture are possible, as usual. Approval of a resolution of ratification requires a two-thirds vote of those present and voting, a quorum being present, under the Constitution. Occasionally, several treaties (usually noncontroversial) might be voted on en bloc. Upon approval of a resolution of ratification, it is transmitted by the executive clerk to the White House. A president does not have to ratify a treaty after Senate approval. If the president concludes that any condition attached by the Senate alters obligations under the treaty, he must notify the other treaty parties.

It is important to remember that, unlike bills, a treaty does not die at the end of a Congress. A treaty remains pending before the Senate until it is either agreed to by the Senate or withdrawn by the president. However, floor proceedings on a treaty that remain uncompleted at the *sine die* adjournment of a Congress terminate, and the treaty is returned to the calendar and then to the Foreign Relations Committee. A treaty might also require implementing legislation, which would be in the form of a bill or joint resolution passed in the same form by the House and Senate and submitted to the president for his signature or veto.

The outright rejection of a treaty is rare. Upon rejection, the treaty would be returned to the executive calendar and, at adjournment, to the Foreign Relations Committee. The Senate could adopt a resolution informing the president of its action and return the treaty to him, but the Senate would need to adopt such a resolution.

§ 8.160 Congress and Foreign Policy: Legislation, Appropriations, and Nominations

Legislation

Nearly every year, Congress has at its disposal a number of possible legislative vehicles for reaching its own foreign policy decisions. These bills might include authorization bills for foreign relations and foreign aid, the Department of Defense (DOD), and the intelligence agencies. They also include annual appropriations bills for foreign operations, the State Department, military construction, and DOD. In the course of a year, Congress might also enact other measures that concern or include foreign policy, such as those dealing with trade, international organizations, or supplemental or continuing appropriations resolutions. Despite House and Senate rules generally intended to prevent the addition of legislative provisions to appropriations measures, foreign policy legislative provisions can end up in those measures. (*For a description of the legislative process, see Chapter Six, Legislating in Congress: Legislative Process; and § 8.151, Fast-Track Procedures. See also Chapter Seven, Legislating in Congress: Federal Budget Process.*)

In one of these legislative vehicles or another measure, Congress might enact a program or an extensive set of policies, such as the program to assist Russia in dismantling nuclear weapons (*107 Stat. 1777; 22 U.S.C. § 5951 et seq.*), or the set of policies to guide U.S. diplomacy on other nations' restrictions on religious liberty (*112 Stat. 2787; 22 U.S.C. § 6401 et seq.*), or to prohibit import into or export from the United States of "conflict diamonds" (*117 Stat. 631; 19 U.S.C. § 3901 et seq.*). The president and appropriate executive agencies then carry out these programs.

Congress often conditions U.S. assistance to foreign nations on their observing specified norms of behavior, such as the various aid and arms export laws aimed at curbing nuclear proliferation. It might also prohibit or cut off assistance in one or more forms until behavior changes, as occurs with the various laws that restrict trade and aid to nations that violate U.S. antiterrorism or human rights policies. For example, concerns in recent Congresses over Syria's role in Lebanon were not new. In 2003, Congress passed and the president signed the Syria Accountability and Lebanese Sovereignty Restoration Act (*117 Stat. 2482*), imposing trade restrictions and other penalties.

In the foreign policy area, Congress regularly requires the president to report to it, and to wait to act until Congress has had time to approve or disapprove a proposed policy or action. For example, U.S. trade law requires the president to request permission annually to waive freedom-of-emigration provisions. Until Congress voted for normal trade relations (NTR, formerly called most favored nation) with China, the president's waiver request and congressional action on it made China eligible for NTR status. Once the request was made, Congress had sixty days to adopt a joint resolution disapproving the president's request for waiver authority. Otherwise, the waiver authority was automatically renewed.

Treaties and international agreements can also impose requirements on the United States that require lawmaking. For example, following congressional agreement to legislation implementing agreements reached under the "Uruguay Round" of multilateral trade negotiations (*P.L. 103-465*), the World Trade Organization (WTO) was formed as the new structure for member nations to discuss trade issues, negotiate trade agreements, and settle trade disputes. The United States lost a challenge in the WTO to U.S. tax provisions benefiting U.S. exporters, called the Foreign Sales Corporation (FSC). Congress responded in 2000 by repealing the FSC provisions and creating a new export benefit excluding certain "extraterritorial income" (ETI) from corporate gross income (*P.L. 106-519*). The United States lost a challenge in the WTO to these new tax law provisions, and Congress responded in 2004 with new changes to corporate tax law (*P.L. 108-357; 118 Stat. 1418*) that were intended to comply with WTO rules.

The House or Senate or both often adopt simple or concurrent resolutions (sense of the House, sense of the Senate, or sense of the Congress resolutions) expressing their attitudes on foreign policy issues. Resolutions garnering numerous cosponsors, even if never considered on the floor of the House or Senate, can be important to the administration. In support of an administration policy, a resolution might strengthen the position of the president and his representatives in negotiating with other nations or within a multilateral entity. That appeared to be the case with resolutions introduced early in the 109th Congress to oppose European moves to end the arms embargo against China imposed in 1989 after the Chinese army's assault on demonstrators in Tiananmen Square; the resolutions generally reinforced the Bush administration's position.

A resolution opposing an administration policy might be an early warning, and cause the administration to change course, lest Congress legislate a policy. In the 110th Congress, the House passed a concurrent resolution expressing opposition to the president's so-called troop surge in Iraq (*H. Con. Res. 63, agreed to in the House February 16, 2007*). This resolution was the opening salvo in legislative attempts to force a change in the president's goals and conduct of the war in Iraq. *Sense of* language is regularly included in legislation as a means of bringing a concern to the administration's attention. It may invite compromise with Congress, but without making law.

In legislating on foreign policy, Congress can tie the hands of the president, or, alternately, may allow him to make an independent determination of what course of action is in the best interests of the United States. Congress may require the president merely to report to it, which leaves him considerable discretion, or may direct the president or other executive officials in some way, narrowing his discretion. Congress sometimes acquiesces to a presidential initiative by taking no action. However, the stronger the sentiment in Congress on a foreign policy matter, the more tightly the president's discretion is likely to be circumscribed. So, for example, Congress cut off any funds after September 30, 1994, to maintain U.S. military personnel in Somalia (*P.L. 103–335*).

Appropriations

Congressional influence over foreign policy might be at its strongest in the annual appropriations bills and other appropriations measures. Congress can choose to fund a presidential budget request, not fund it, increase or decrease it, condition or limit funding attached to a request, or fund one or more items that are different from the president's requests. The president is unlikely to win on every budget request and policy matter in a wide-ranging appropriations bill. For example, congressional-presidential disagreement on paying U.S. "arrearages" to the United Nations, and on U.S. policy on international population and family planning assistance, delayed adoption of the foreign operations appropriations legislation in 1999. The president eventually accepted conditions on appropriations (*P.L. 106-113*).

Each year, through the appropriations process, Congress also makes decisions on defense spending. The House, Senate, and president may each have different views, for example, on the effectiveness or need or procurement rate for different weapons systems. Weapons systems are also often positioned by their proponents in policy debates as vital for employment in various states and congressional districts, in addition to being promoted for their contributions to national security. The annual defense appropriations bill can also be a vehicle for foreign policy debates. In the 112th Congress, Congress and the president fought over defense funding regarding the president's goals and conduct of the war in Libya. (*See also Chapter Seven, Legislating in Congress: Federal Budget Process.*)

8

Nominations

The Senate also holds great influence over foreign policy with its constitutional role in confirming presidential nominations to foreign policy posts. The Senate confirms nominations for U.S. ambassadors, U.S. representatives to international organizations, and senior-level staff in the State Department, Defense Department, Central Intelligence Agency, and other government agencies. The confirmation of a nomination cannot be taken for granted, and may occur after the Senate and the president arrive at an understanding concerning a foreign policy issue.

The Senate Foreign Relations Committee, Armed Services Committee, and other Senate committees with jurisdiction over nominations to foreign and national security policy and military posts regularly use nominations to inquire more broadly about foreign policy, in an attempt to influence the nominees or the administration. Nominations to foreign policy posts are handled in the same way as other nominations to executive positions. (*See § 8.80, Congress and the Executive: Appointments.*) However, they regularly become a vehicle that the Senate can use to extract information from the executive branch, cause a reexamination of a policy, or trigger some other course of action. (*See § 6.190, Holds, Clearance, and Unanimous Consent.*)

§ 8.170 Congress and Foreign Policy: Nonbinding Actions

A number of committees have jurisdiction over aspects of foreign policy and national defense policy. The House Foreign Affairs and Senate Foreign Relations Committees are obvious players, and the jurisdiction of the House Ways and Means and Senate Finance Committees over foreign trade is well-known. The House and Senate Armed Services Committees are key committees in national security policy.

Additional committees handle important components of foreign policy. The House Financial Services Committee and the Senate Foreign Relations and Banking, Housing, and Urban Affairs Committees have jurisdiction over international economics and finance. The two Agriculture Committees may assert jurisdiction over international agricultural and food policy. Each chamber has a Select Committee on Intelligence with jurisdiction over the Central Intelligence Agency, the National Security Agency, and other intelligence agencies. Other legislative committees have jurisdictions that are directly or indirectly related to foreign policy; for example, the two Judiciary Committees handle immigration, antiterrorism, and crime legislation; the House Energy and Commerce Committee and Senate Energy and Natural Resources Committee handle energy legislation; and the House Homeland Security Committee and the Senate Homeland Security and Governmental Affairs Committee have jurisdiction over the Department of Homeland Security.

The two Appropriations Committees have several subcommittees that each have jurisdiction over appropriations bills that fund portions of the foreign policy and national defense policy budgets. These subcommittees include those handling foreign operations; the Departments of Commerce, Defense, Justice, and State; agriculture; and military construction. In addition, the House Oversight and Government Reform and the Senate Homeland Security and Governmental Affairs Committees have authority to conduct oversight government-wide.

The import of this list is that numerous committees can claim jurisdiction over aspects of foreign policy, and thereby legislate, conduct oversight, monitor rulemaking, and attempt to influence the administration's conduct of foreign policy. Perhaps one indication of "globalization" is seen in the work of congressional committees, where the distinction between domestic and foreign or international issues is becoming blurred. (*See also § 8.160, Congress and Foreign Policy: Legislation, Appropriations, and Nominations.*)

Legislative and oversight hearings by these committees allow Congress to inform itself about an administration's conduct of foreign policy. Hearings identify possible courses for legislative action, and, in some instances, raise public awareness. Committees also conduct investigations, perhaps drawing on the resources of the Government Accountability Office and other entities, to evaluate the efficacy and efficiency of foreign policy agencies and programs. Committees might also sponsor fact-

§ 8.171

Letter to Foreign Leader

Dave Reichert

Jim Saxton

cc: The Hon
Secretary

The Hon
U.S. Am

Congress of the United States
Washington, DC 20515

February 12, 2008

His Excellency Hu Jintao
President, People's Republic of China
c/o His Excellency Zhou Wen Zhong
Ambassador Extraordinary and Plenipotentiary
Embassy of the People's Republic of China
2300 Connecticut Avenue, N.W.
Washington, DC 20008

Dear Mr. President:

We are writing to once again express our grave concern regarding the continuing atrocities taking place in the Darfur region of Sudan, and to urge you to use your significant influence with the government of Sudan to ensure that it ends its ongoing obstruction of peacekeeping and humanitarian efforts to protect civilians and restore a basic level of stability to the region. Without a much stronger effort from the government of the People's Republic of China (PRC) to convince the government of Sudan to end its obstruction, the real though limited progress made during the past year will be undone, and the possibility of an expanded regional crisis beyond Darfur's borders will continue to grow.

The crisis in Darfur, which for nearly five years has been fueled in large part by the government of Sudan's armed forces and its proxy Janjaweed militias, has already displaced over 2.5 million Darfurians, including over 140,000 in 2007, and has cost hundreds of thousands of lives. As the conflict continues and battles between the Sudanese army, its Janjaweed militias, and the ever-growing number of rebel factions intensify, the field of conflict has expanded to include additional areas of Chad, the Central African Republic, and Sudanese states to the east of Darfur such as Kordofan.

Millions of Sudanese civilians living in villages and in camps for the internally displaced suffer the consequences of the ongoing violence, as do local and international aid workers. This also imperils the basic food, medicine, and assistance on which most of these civilians depend for survival. The absolute need for the civilian protection and a basic level of humanitarian operational security has never been clearer.

We welcomed, therefore, the unanimous passage of UN Security Council Resolution 1769 on July 31, 2007, authorizing the United Nations – African Union Mission in Darfur (UNAMID). We note with gratitude the leading role the PRC played in securing the government of Sudan's commitment to the UNAMID mission, and further note the presence of Chinese military engineers deployed as part of that mission.

8

finding travel to countries or regions to obtain first-hand information on foreign policy issues. (These missions are popularly called CODELS (congressional delegations). The importance of this travel is sometimes dismissed as a "junket," connoting pleasure rather than work and waste rather than results.)

Committees review reports made to Congress on matters within their jurisdiction, consult the president or executive officials on foreign policy matters as required by law or informally, and might organize other means of nonlegislative influence on the administration, such as preparing a letter signed by key members of Congress expressing perspectives on a foreign policy issue. Committee members might also serve as observers at key international meetings or negotiations. In this regard, the views of committee members are important in anticipating and dealing with policy problems that could arise between Congress and the executive. Members of Congress might also serve as intermediaries in international problems, as Senator John Kerry (D-MA) did by meeting on a number of occasions with Afghan President Hamid Karzai. (*See also § 8.171, Letter to Foreign Leader.*)

Congress might also formalize its observation of U.S. participation in international agreements. For example, Congress, in 1976, created the Commission on Security and Cooperation in Europe (*90 Stat. 661; 22 U.S.C. § 3001 et seq.*) to monitor and encourage compliance with the Helsinki Final Act. The Final Act established the Organization for Security and Cooperation in Europe to enhance European security and cooperation in numerous fields, including humanitarian endeavors. (*See the congressional commission's web site, <www.csce.gov>.*) Members of Congress also participate in international organizations and exchanges, such as the Interparliamentary Union, and regularly host foreign officials visiting Washington, DC.

Congress also expresses its approval or support for other nations and specific foreign leaders or dignitaries by inviting them to address a joint meeting of Congress. (*See § 5.34, Joint Meetings and Joint Sessions.*)

§ 8.180 Congress and Federalism

Since the adoption of the U.S. Constitution, creating a federal system of governance, the relationship between the federal government and the states and their political subunits, the localities, has been marked by a history spotted with conflict, cooperation, and indifference. During the more than 225-year history of the republic and the Articles of Confederation, two questions have generated considerable debate among observers of American federalism. What is the nature of the federal union of states? The Civil War challenged the very existence of the United States, but debates over nullification, states' rights, the meaning of the Tenth Amendment, and myriad specific federal or state actions, or a lack of a federal or state action, are regularly part of the national debate on the nature of the federal union. And what powers, privileges, duties, and responsibilities does the Constitution grant to the national government, including Congress, and reserve to the states and the people? The Supreme Court, often the final arbiter of conflicts within the federal system, has sometimes seemed to change its views in its decisions on issues of federalism. It has in recent years identified limits to congressional authority over the states and over the exercise of national powers within the federal structure, after decades of upholding congressional initiatives.

Routinely, federal preemption of state law is a major issue in debates in Congress and cases in federal courts. In debating legislation, members of Congress argue over whether the legislation should be written for federal law to preempt an thereby supplant state law, to co-exist with it, or to forgo legislating on an issue so that states may pursue their own public policy. The Supremacy Clause of the Constitution (*art. VI, cl. 2*) gives rise to this question and answers it in principle:

> This Constitution, and the Laws of the United States which shall be made in Pursuance thereof; and all Treaties made, or which shall be made, under the Authority of the United States, shall be the supreme Law of the Land; and the Judges in every State shall be bound thereby, anything in the Constitution or Laws of any State to the Contrary notwithstanding.

But, Congress might not be clear in its intent or might exceed its constitutional authority in making law. A case in the federal courts will likely ensue. (*See also § 2.90, Laws Protecting and Extending the Franchise.*)

The states and localities have become very dependent on the federal government for fiscal support. In fiscal year 2012, federal outlays for grants in aid to states, localities, and Indian tribes are estimated to be about §584.3 billion, or nearly 16 percent of federal expenditures. Federal grants in aid comprised 24 percent of states' and localities' revenues in 2009, according to the Government Accountability Office (GAO).

Two programs assisting individuals and families in need, Medicaid and Temporary Assistance to Needy Families (TANF), are projected to constitute 49 percent of federal grants in aid outlays in fiscal year 2012. Programs for health, income security, and education together constituted 91 percent of all federal grants in aid to states and localities in 2009, according to GAO. See "State and Local Governments: Fiscal Pressures Could Have Implications for Future Delivery of Intergovernmental Programs," GAO Report GAO-10-899, July 2010.

In addition, in amending the Constitution, Congress and the states are partners. Under the Constitution, three-fourths of the states must ratify a constitutional amendment approved by Congress for the amendment to take effect.

§ 8.190 Congress and Federalism: Exercising Congressional Powers

In the American system of government, national laws on a subject may fully or partially preempt state laws or regulations, or national and state laws on a subject may operate concurrently. The basis for preemption is the Supremacy Clause contained in Article VI, Clause 2 of the Constitution, as noted above.

Congress might make law based in enumerated powers and other powers vested in the national government, or "necessary and proper" to carry out constitutional powers (*art. I, sec. 8, cl. 18*). In doing so, Congress might well act on a subject on which states have also enacted laws. Congress, the executive, the states, and the judiciary all have roles in determining the relationship of federal and state laws on a subject.

In making national law that overlaps with state law, Congress might expressly state a preemption (or non-preemption) in a statute, or preemption might be implied from the construction and provisions of a statute. Within the context of implied preemption three subgroups might be identified:

- Instances where there is conflict between the federal statute and state and local laws. However, under certain circumstances the federal and state law may operate concurrently when the federal statute sets a minimum standard for compliance and the state statute exceeds it.
- Instances where state law impedes or interferes with the federal government's ability to achieve a national objective. Under such a scenario a state legislature might act to amend the state law to be compatible with the federal law or risk partial or complete preemption of the state law.
- Instances where federal law occupies the field, such as foreign policy.

In rulemaking to carry out a federal law, a federal agency might develop regulations that raise the same issues as a statute in terms of preemption or the concurrent exercise of federal and state laws.

Either the courts or Congress might be the final arbiter of the operation of a statute that expressly or implicitly preempts state law. Courts might interpret a statute and find preemption or find an allowance for federal and state statutes to operate concurrently, or courts could find a federal statute to be an unconstitutional exercise of Congress' lawmaking authority. Congress for its part might through amendment clarify its intent or change a statute's operation.

It should be noted that the answer on preemption might not be straightforward, as fifty states and the District of Columbia can have fifty-one different laws. Unless Congress fully preempts state laws, some might continue without change while others might require at least some change to operate concurrently.

Unless Congress expressly preempts state laws, courts weigh federal and state interests and congressional intent. They do not assume federal preemption. Considerations might include the pervasiveness of a federal statute and conflict between federal and state laws. In the words of the late Justice Hugo Black, the courts' function in considering the validity of state laws in light of federal laws and treaties on the same subject is to determine whether state law "stands as an obstacle to the accomplishment and execution of the full purposes and objectives of Congress." (*Hines v. Davidowitz*, 312 U.S. 52, 67 (1941).)

Restraints on Congress

In recent years, the Supreme Court has ruled in several cases on possible restraints on Congress' exercise of its powers within the federal system. In one set of cases, the Court seems to have warned Congress about directing the actions of state legislatures and state executive officials. In another set, the Court seems to have warned Congress about the limits of its powers in the federal system.

The question in the first issue is how Congress may regulate state conduct and activity. In *New York v. United States*, 505 U.S. 144 (1992), the Supreme Court found that the Tenth Amendment constrained Congress in the exercise of an enumerated power. Congress had directed states to dispose of low-level radioactive waste generated in their borders. It then required states that failed to do so to take title to the wastes, take possession of them, and assume liability for them. (*99 Stat. 1842.*) The Supreme Court found that this provision of the law breached state sovereignty in violation of the Tenth Amendment. The federal structure of government under the Constitution, the Court said, disallowed Congress from compelling the states to enact and enforce a federal regulatory program.

Subsequently, in *Printz v. United States*, 521 U.S. 898 (1997), the Court struck down a provision of a federal statute: the part of the Brady Handgun Violence Protection Act (*107 Stat. 1536*) that required state and local law enforcement officers to conduct background checks on individuals wishing to purchase handguns. The Court followed similar reasoning to that in *New York*, finding an unconstitutional violation of state sovereignty in directing state officials to administer a federal regulatory program.

The Spending Clause (*Art. I, sec. 8, cl. 1*), on the other hand, provides Congress with a means of inducing states and localities to enact legislation or to carry out regulatory schemes. In *South Dakota v. Dole*, South Dakota challenged the national minimum drinking-age law (*23 U.S.C. 158*) as exceeding congressional authority under the Spending Clause. The law sought to encourage states to raise their drinking age to twenty-one by directing the secretary of transportation to withhold a portion of federal highway funds from any state that had a lower drinking age. The Court found the law consistent with congressional authority under the Spending Clause as spending for the general welfare, related to a national purpose—safe interstate travel, not prohibited by another constitutional provision, and risking loss of a portion of federal funds that was an inducement but did not make it compulsory that states change their laws.

The Court in *New York* subsequently validated the two other major components of the federal statute requiring that states dispose of low-level radioactive waste, relying in part on the *Dole* decision. The two components of the law challenged in *New York* offered monetary inducements to the states to dispose of wastes and denied access to waste sites for waste generated in states that had not met federal guidelines.

The second issue involving restraints on Congress' exercise of power in the federal system concerns the scope of its powers. Some of these Supreme Court cases have limited congressional authority under the Commerce Clause (*Art. I, sec. 8, cl. 3*). In *United States v. Lopez*, 514 U.S. 549 (1995), the Court struck down a criminal conviction under the Gun-Free School Zones Act (*104 Stat. 4844*). It found that Congress had exceeded its authority under the Commerce Clause, the first such ruling of the Court in nearly sixty years. The Court said that Congress may regulate channels of commerce, instrumentalities of commerce, and activities (presumably largely economic activities) that affect commerce, including only intrastate activities that substantially affect commerce. As enacted, the Gun-Free Zones Act failed to meet these criteria.

The Court reached a conclusion by similar reasoning in *United States v. Morrison*, 529 U.S. 598 (2000), to strike down a provision of the Violence Against Women Act that provided for a federal private cause of action for women who were victims of gender-motivated violence. The Court stated that such crimes were not economic activity, that Congress had not established a jurisdictional relationship between the cause of action and interstate commerce, and that there was not a substantial effect on interstate commerce.

The Court also narrowed the Corps of Engineers' jurisdiction over intrastate waters—in this instance, certain wetlands—under the Clean Water Act. While seeking to avoid constitutional and federalism issues, the Court noted that the grant of authority to Congress under the Commerce Clause is not "unlimited." *Solid Waste Agency of Northern Cook County v. U.S. Army Corps of Engineers*, 531 U.S. 159 (2001).

In *Gonzales v. Raich*, 545 U.S. 1 (2005), in contrast, the Supreme Court held that the Commerce Clause empowered Congress to prohibit local cultivation and use of marijuana permitted under California's Compassionate Use Act. The Court stated that case law had established Congress' power under the Commerce Clause to regulate local activities that have a substantial effect on interstate commerce, and that Congress had a rational basis for regulating local cultivation and use of marijuana to ensure the success of the federal Controlled Substances Act (*84 Stat. 1242*).

The Spending Clause and the Necessary and Proper Clause (*Art. I, sec. 8, cl. 18*) may, however, be a source of authority. The Court found these clauses allowed Congress to enact a law making it a crime to bribe state and local officials of entities that receive at least $10,000 in federal funds. The accused challenged the constitutionality of the statute for its failure to require proof of a connection between federal funds and an alleged bribe. The Court stated that it was sufficient that the statute "condition the offense on a threshold amount of federal dollars defining the federal interest," and that Congress acted within its authority to "ensure that the objects of spending are not menaced by local administrators on the take."

The Supreme Court has also refined its test of Congress' constitutional authority to legislate under the Fourteenth Amendment, striking down the Religious Freedom Restoration Act (RFRA) (*42 U.S.C. 2000bb et seq.*) as an enactment exceeding Congress' power. RFRA prohibited government at any level from "substantially burdening" the exercise of religion unless the government could demonstrate a compelling governmental interest in its law or regulation and that it had chosen the least restrictive means of furthering that interest. In *City of Boerne v. Flores*, 521 U.S. 507 (1997), the Court held that Congress had the power to enforce a right, not decree a right, and that there must be "congruence and proportionality" between the injury to a right to be prevented or remedied and the means adopted to that end. The Court said the application of RFRA to the denial of a church's permit request under a zoning law in Boerne, Texas, was "out of proportion" to the zoning law's "incidental burden" on religion.

The enforcement power of Congress under the Fourteenth Amendment is also key in determining congressional authority to suspend state sovereign immunity from suit under the Eleventh Amendment. In *Kimel v. Florida Board of Regents*, 528 U.S. 62 (2000), the Supreme Court noted that the Age Discrimination in Employment Act of 1967 (*29 U.S.C. § 623 et seq.*) was a valid constitutional exercise of congressional power under the Commerce Clause. State employees had sued under ADEA, alleging age discrimination and seeking monetary damages. The Court stated, however, that congressional power under Article I does not include the power to abrogate the Eleventh Amendment, but that Congress has that power under the Fourteenth Amendment. As it had ruled in *City of Boerne*, the Court stated that Congress could enforce a right, not decree a right, and that there must be congruence and proportionality between the injury to a right to be prevented or remedied and the means adopted to that end. The Court found that Congress failed to identify unconstitutional conduct or to develop a record showing unconstitutional discrimination on the basis of age by state and local governments against their employees. It held that the abrogation of states' immunity under the Eleventh Amendment was disproportionate to any behavior that could be conceived of as unconstitutional under the act and exceeded congressional authority under the Fourteenth Amendment.

The Court followed the same reasoning in *Board of Trustees of the University of Alabama v. Garrett*, 531 U.S. 356 (2002), in finding that Congress had exceeded its authority under the Fourteenth Amendment in abrogating states' sovereign immunity to suit under the Eleventh Amendment in allowing state employees to sue under the Americans with Disabilities Act (*42 U.S.C. 12101 et seq.*).

The Supreme Court, however, followed the same reasoning in *Nevada Department of Human Resources v. Hibbs*, 538 U.S. 721 (2003), to hold that Congress had authority under the Fourteenth Amendment to suspend states' Eleventh Amendment sovereign immunity under the Family and Medical Leave Act, and allowed an employee's suit to proceed. The Court found that Congress sought to protect a right to be free of gender-based discrimination in the workplace, stating that statutory classifications distinguishing between males and females were subject to heightened scrutiny. It noted that Congress had developed a substantial record of evidence of sex discrimination in states' administration of leave benefits, and had tailored a statute specific to that one aspect of the employment relationship.

The Court again permitted a suit to proceed in *Tennessee v. Lane*, 541 U.S. 504 (2004), where it found that a constitutional right—access to the courts by disabled persons—was vindicated by Congress under the Americans with Disabilities Act (*42 U.S.C. 12101 et seq.*). It noted that Congress had developed a substantial record of evidence of exclusion of disabled persons from courthouses and court proceedings due to their disabilities, and that it had authority under the Fourteenth Amendment to abrogate states' immunity under the Eleventh Amendment to enforce disabled persons' right of access to the courts. The Supreme Court also found that Congress had tailored an appropriate statute requiring states to make "reasonable modifications" to remove architectural and other barriers to accessibility.

§ 8.200 Congress and Federalism: Financial Support for State and Local Governments

The financial relationship between the federal government and state and local governments is a critical and far-reaching one. Federal financial assistance to states, local governments, and Indian tribes includes grants, loans, loan guarantees, and tax subsidies and is intended to assist these entities to address national objectives articulated in federal legislation. States maintain offices in Washington, DC, that monitor federal aid legislation and other federal activities. States and localities also belong to associations, such as the National Conference of State Legislatures and the Council of State Governments, and hire lobbyists to advocate their interests.

Federal grants to states and localities cover the range of government-sponsored or -supported services and objectives. Grants include health services, such as the State Children's Health Insurance Program; training of displaced workers; transportation, such as highways, mass-transit, and airports; and empowerment zones and enterprise zones, as part of the federal government's support for community development. Federal grants to state and local governments are estimated to be $584.3 billion in fiscal year 2012, or 16 percent of federal outlays. Of this amount, $385.4 billion is estimated to be in the form of payments to individuals. Federal grants in fiscal year 2012 are estimated to comprise 24 percent of state and local revenues. (*See "State and Local Government Debt: An Analysis," by Steven Maguire, CRS Report R41735, April 14, 2011.*)

§ 8.201

Unfunded Mandates and Congressional Procedures

Congress enacted the *Unfunded Mandates Reform Act* (*109 Stat. 48*) in 1995 to give itself information to identify an unfunded mandate in a bill or joint resolution and a mechanism for explicitly deciding whether to consider a piece of legislation containing an unfunded mandate. An *unfunded mandate* in legislation is a duty that the legislation, if enacted, would impose on state, local, or tribal governments, or the private sector without also providing funds to cover the cost of compliance with the mandate.

A mandate in legislation would be considered *to be funded* in one of two ways. First, the legislation could automatically provide the funding needed to cover the costs of the mandate. Alternately, the legislation could authorize appropriations to cover the costs of compliance. An authorization of appropriations, however, also needs to meet additional criteria for a mandate to be considered funded. It must (1) provide that the mandate would be curtailed or eliminated if insufficient or no appropriations were provided; or, alternately, (2) ensure that Congress would vote to continue the mandate as an unfunded mandate. Only if the legislation made funding automatic or if it authorized appropriations as required would a mandate be considered to be funded.

Under the Unfunded Mandates Reform Act (UMRA), Congress created several exceptions to the law for some types of legislation, including antidiscrimination laws, emergency assistance, treaty obligations, and Social Security. It also exempted appropriations measures, but not legislative provisions in appropriations measures that created unfunded mandates. Finally, the law exempted from its operation any unfunded mandate that failed to meet a threshold (adjusted annually for inflation): for an intergovernmental mandate, $71 million (in 2011) in any year of its first five years in effect, and, for a private-sector mandate, $142 million (in 2011) in any year of its first five years.

Committee Requirements

UMRA set requirements for committees and the Congressional Budget Office (CBO) to study and report on the impact and magnitude of proposed federal mandates. A committee must send CBO a copy of any measure ordered reported that contains a federal mandate, and CBO must prepare a report of estimated mandate costs for the committee. The committee must include this report in its report on the measure or submit it for publication in the *Congressional Record*. (Additional requirements in UMRA govern the CBO report and the committee's response to it.) Early in a year, committees must also identify issues they will address that year, which will have costs for the private sector and state, local, and tribal governments. This information is to be included in the *views and estimates reports* that committees provide to the House and Senate Budget Committees. (*See § 7.50, Congressional Budget Process.*)

Points of Order on the House and Senate Floors

UMRA is implemented in the House and Senate through points of order against legislation containing an unfunded mandate. When an authorization measure is brought up for consideration, a member may make a point of order against its consideration. The point of order would be that the measure contains an unfunded mandate exceeding $71 million (in 2011) for an intergovernmental mandate. A point of order can also be raised if a CBO estimate was not published in either the committee report or the *Congressional Record*.

Normally, a point of order in the House is resolved by a ruling of the presiding officer, but UMRA requires the full House to vote on whether to consider a measure despite a point of order. If a special rule reported from the Rules Committee waives a point of order against consideration of a measure containing an unfunded mandate, the special rule itself is subject to a point of order. Debate on the point of order is limited to twenty minutes, divided between the member raising the point of order and an opponent.

Continued on page 415

§ 8.201 (continued)

In the Senate, if the point of order against consideration is sustained, the measure cannot be considered. The Senate by majority vote can also waive any point of order. In ruling, the Senate presiding officer consults with the Committee on Homeland Security and Governmental Affairs.

Points of order in each chamber can also be raised against the consideration of an amendment, conference report, or motion that contains an unfunded mandate exceeding the threshold amount. There is no requirement that amendments have a CBO estimate. Conferees, however, must request a cost estimate of CBO on a conference report, and CBO must attempt to respond.

Loans (lending federal money) and loan guarantees (indemnification of a lender against default for all or part of a loan made by the lender) include programs such as low-interest loans to localities to assist them in meeting the requirements of the Safe Drinking Water Act. Tax subsidies include such tax expenditures as the exclusion of interest on state and local securities from federal taxation and employment tax credits awarded to qualifying businesses that hire and train disadvantaged individuals in distressed neighborhoods.

Nearly all of these programs are described in detail in the *Catalog of Federal Domestic Assistance*, maintained by the General Services Administration. The catalog exists to assist users—state and local governments, other governmental authorities, nonprofit entities, individuals, and others—in identifying programs that meet their objectives or needs. It provides essential information on each program, such as a précis of application procedures. As described in the catalog's introduction, "assistance" includes "grants, loans, loan guarantees, scholarships, mortgage loans, insurance, and other types of financial assistance, including cooperative agreements; property, technical assistance, counseling, statistical, and other expert information; and service activities of regulatory agencies." The catalog is available online at <*www.cfda.gov*>. Another source is the relatively new federal web site, Grants.gov at <*www.grants.gov*>.

Congress usually attaches conditions to its spending programs, and its authority to do so is well established. Congress creates federal spending programs for purposes stated in law, and it wants to ensure that federal funds are spent for those purposes. In addition, Congress might attach other conditions in law to spending under a program, to ensure the integrity of the program's management, to guide decision-making, to ensure public participation in decision-making, to establish priorities, or for myriad other reasons.

Congress might also attach conditions to a program in order to achieve a national purpose. For example, in order to encourage states to raise the drinking age to twenty-one, Congress conditioned a state's receipt of its full allocation of federal highway funds on its adopting an age twenty-one drinking law. (The Supreme Court case involving this law is described in § 8.190, *Congress and Federalism: Exercising Congressional Powers*.) Congress might also attach financial participation—matching funds—requirements or even "maintenance-of-effort" requirements to a program. The former is in part intended to promote better program administration, since the state or local government also has funds at stake. The latter is to prevent a government from replacing its own funds with federal funds, leaving the activity no better off than it was before federal dollars became available.

While Congress may attach conditions to federal spending, it has established a restraint on itself in doing so. After many years of complaints from states and localities about conditions that imposed costly duties on state and local governments, Congress enacted the Unfunded Mandates Reform Act of 1995. The law, among other provisions, forces committees reporting legislation to obtain from the Congressional Budget Office information on *unfunded mandates* in the legislation. This information may affect procedures in floor consideration of the measure, and ensures that the House and Senate know the cost implications of the proposed legislation to state and local governments. (*See § 8.201, Unfunded Mandates and Congressional Procedures.*)

Grant Programs

Grant programs are a common form of financial support to states and localities. Some of the features of a debate in Congress over providing financial support to state and localities might include a policy decision on what to fund, the level of funding, whether to use a categorical or block grant, and the formula (if any) to be used to allocate the funds between eligible governmental units.

What to Fund? Congress often grapples with the proper federal role in an area of governmental services. For example, in education, states and localities employ teachers, build schools, set promotion and graduation standards for students, and so on. What is the federal role in the education of American schoolchildren? How should the federal government be involved? To what degree should it provide financial support? Among the spending possibilities related to education—schools, teachers, books, special classes, computers, and so on—which should be given financial support? What should be the objectives of the grant—national standards, a lifeline to those most in need, equalization of resources nationally, or other objectives?

The vehicle for policy decisions on a program of aid to state and local governments is normally an *authorization bill*. The measure might be referred to as a reauthorization bill once a program has been created. An authorization bill is often within the jurisdiction of one legislative committee in each chamber. For example, federal aid programs to support education are generally within the jurisdiction of the House Committee on Education and Labor and the Senate Committee on Health, Education, Labor, and Pensions. (*See § 7.80, Authorizations and Appropriations Processes.*)

Categorical or Block Grant? Some federal legislation provides financial assistance to states and localities in the form of *block grants*. In some instances, such as welfare reform in 1996, Congress combined or superseded related, existing *categorical grants* for specific purposes into one or more block grants. A categorical grant provides spending targeted to a specific purpose. In contrast, a block grant provides wider discretion to state and local governments in identifying problems and designing programs that meet the goals of the block grant. In either case, Congress defines some set of eligible activities—in a broad area with wide discretion for a block grant or very specific for a categorical grant. (Congress last used another form of grants, "general revenue sharing," in the 1970s and 1980s.)

According to some estimates, about 95 percent of all federal grants are categorical grants with approximately one-fifth of such grants awarded by formula. There are approximately twenty-seven federal block grants, allocated by formula.

Waivers of federal grant requirements are also an important element of the federal grant matrix, allowing states to experiment with the delivery of assistance. Section 1115 of the Social Security Act is a prime example of the use of waivers. The waiver provision allows a state to restructure its Medicaid program with the aim of fostering innovation and expanding services. Waivers are also an important element in Congress' response to speeding relief to affected areas following natural disasters.

What Formula Factors to Use? When Congress debates legislation for a grant program that uses a formula to distribute federal funds, it can sometimes seem like a rerun of the constitutional convention, but at a programmatic level: large-population states versus small-population states; states with certain population characteristics versus states with different population characteristics; states with certain physical or man-made resources versus states with different resources. What formula factors should Congress use to distribute federal funds associated with a program? Congress as a political institution—"who gets what"—is on display when Congress debates funding formulas. Congress can target grants to certain groups or activities depending on its formula and other considerations.

Because each program has a different purpose—educating children, building highways, providing services to special population groups, and so on—the criteria to be used differ. An education program might use the numbers of school-age children, children within some measure of poverty, or schoolchildren with special learning needs. A highway program might use miles of existing highways, state population, or a needs survey. Members of Congress are on the lookout for combinations of factors that most favor their states, sometimes making it difficult to find a formula that appeals to a majority of members in each chamber.

As an alternative to a formula, Congress might create a project grant program. This kind of program is likely to require an extensive application by potential recipients, create a competitive award process, and place discretion with the agency administering the program. Some programs might also combine a formula and project grant format. For example, a program might allocate federal funds to states based on a formula; money within the states then could be allocated to local governments on a project basis.

Finally, Congress has frequently earmarked spending for particular projects or even entities, designating in law or in a congressional report a beneficiary, purpose, and dollar amount. (*See § 7.81, Limitations, Earmarks, and General Provisions.*)

Level of Funding. Funding for a discretionary grant program is normally a two-step process. An authorization bill is first considered. It typically contains several related programs. An authorization bill normally provides recommended authorizations of appropriations for each of these programs for one, two, or more years. The first decision on spending is a recommendation made in the authorization bill, with the actual funding included in an appropriations measure. It is not without precedent that funding recommendations included in an authorization measure may not match the amount provided in an appropriations measure.

An authorization for a discretionary grant program, once passed by both houses and signed into law by the president, does not make budgetary resources available for spending. Each year, the president submits a budget to Congress with recommended levels of spending for federal programs. The House and Senate Appropriations Committees then develop *appropriations bills*. Once Congress

8

passes and the president signs the relevant appropriations bill, budget authority is available for obligation. The second decision on spending, then, is made in an appropriations bill, and that decision makes funds available. (*See § 7.80, Authorizations and Appropriations Processes.*)

§ 8.210 Congress and Federalism: Amending the Constitution

One of the ways in which federalism is most clearly expressed in the Constitution is in the process for its amendment. Nine of the thirteen original states were required to ratify the Constitution to establish it. Amendments must be ratified by three-fourths of the states (thirty-eight states today) to take effect.

The Constitution provides two methods for proposing amendments and two methods for ratifying amendments. Article V reads as follows:

> The Congress, whenever two thirds of both Houses shall deem it necessary, shall propose Amendments to this Constitution, or, on the Application of the Legislatures of two thirds of the several States, shall call a Convention for proposing Amendments, which, in either Case, shall be valid to all Intents and Purposes, as Part of this Constitution, when ratified by the Legislatures of three fourths of the several States, or by Conventions in three fourths thereof, as the one or the other Mode of Ratification may be proposed by the Congress. . . ."

All amendments to the Constitution that have been adopted have been proposed by Congress. All but the Twenty-First Amendment, which repealed the Eighteenth Amendment (Prohibition), were ratified by state legislatures. The Twenty-First Amendment was ratified by the convention method.

Any member of Congress may propose a constitutional amendment by introducing a joint resolution. A joint resolution may be introduced in the House (H. J. Res.) or Senate (S. J. Res.), or companion joint resolutions might be introduced by like-minded members in each chamber. Joint resolutions proposing to amend the Constitution are within the jurisdiction of the House and Senate Judiciary Committees, to which these resolutions are referred.

If the committees choose to act, they would most likely follow normal legislative procedures—hearings at the subcommittee or full committee level or both, possibly subcommittee markup, full committee markup, and reporting. Floor consideration of a joint resolution proposing to amend the Constitution would also likely happen under a set of procedures that the House or Senate normally crafts to consider important legislation.

The Constitution, however, requires supermajority votes in the full House and Senate—a two-thirds vote in each chamber. This provision has been interpreted as two-thirds present and voting, a quorum being present; it is not two-thirds of the membership. Like other legislation, each chamber must agree to exactly the same proposed amendment before it can be submitted to the states. A conference committee might be needed to reconcile differences in joint resolutions approved in the House and Senate. A two-thirds vote of those voting in each chamber would be needed to adopt the conference report on a joint resolution.

The president does not have a formal role in the amendment process. He might exhort Congress to submit a constitutional amendment to the states on some subject, lending his political support to a movement to amend the Constitution, or he might oppose an amendment. But a proposed amendment does not need the president's review or approval before being submitted to the states.

Once Congress has completed its role in proposing an amendment, the joint resolution is transmitted to the archivist of the United States, who is the head of the National Archives and Records Administration (NARA). The archivist has delegated ministerial functions related to the amendment process to the Office of the Federal Register (OFR) within NARA. OFR adds legislative history notes to the joint resolution, and publishes it in slip-law format. OFR also prepares official and informational documents for the archivist to submit to the states.

The archivist notifies each state governor with a letter and the documents prepared by OFR. Assuming the joint resolution provides for ratification by three-fourths of the states' legislatures, the governors submit the proposed amendment to the legislatures.

State legislatures have adopted different procedures for ratification. For example, some require a supermajority vote. (States also adopted or had in effect differing provisions for the state conventions that ratified the Twenty-First Amendment, repealing the Eighteenth Amendment.) Legislatures must ratify the exact amendment proposed by Congress, and must include a clear statement of ratification in the legislative act they use to express ratification. They may not amend the proposed amendment or attach conditions to ratification. The question of whether ratification by a legislature can subsequently be rescinded is not settled. Because the Constitution requires ratification by state legislatures, governors are not required to approve or sign ratification legislation, although they might lend support or express opposition during legislative debate over the amendment.

States send ratification documents to the archivist, where OFR examines them for legal sufficiency. OFR retains the documents until the amendment is ratified or fails ratification. Once ratification documents are received from the constitutionally required three-fourths of the states, the archivist issues a proclamation certifying ratification. The certification is published in the Federal Register and the Statutes at Large.

Twenty-seven amendments to the Constitution have been ratified. Seven other amendments submitted to the states have failed ratification.

Additional Considerations

In the twentieth century, Congress began the practice of setting a time limit for states to ratify a proposed amendment. Seven years has been the time limit used, although amendments that have been ratified have usually achieved ratification within one or two years.

Like other legislation, members might introduce the same constitutional amendments in one Congress after another, making their opinions known and working to change the Constitution. Even if an amendment is submitted to the states and fails ratification within the prescribed time period, members might introduce a new joint resolution with the same or similar language in another Congress and work for its adoption and submission to the states.

Congress has also extended a time limit once, when it adopted, by majority vote, a joint resolution to extend by just under three years the seven-year limit for considering the Equal Rights Amendment. Congress also acted by passing concurrent resolutions to recognize the archivist's decision to certify ratification of the Twenty-Seventh Amendment (congressional pay) after it had taken over 200 years to obtain ratification by three-fourths of the states.

While two-thirds of the states have not petitioned for an amending convention, applications by a sufficient number of states have prompted congressional action in the past. For example, two-thirds of the states, less one, petitioned Congress in the late nineteenth and early twentieth centuries for a convention to propose an amendment providing for the direct election of senators. Congress responded in 1912 by submitting such an amendment to the states, which was ratified as the Seventeenth Amendment. Not every such movement in the states has been successful, however. For example, Congress failed to adopt a joint resolution on a balanced budget amendment despite applications from nearly two-thirds of the states.

Constitutional scholars have always been concerned about the process of states petitioning for an amending convention. In addition to issues such as the time frame in which applications are made to Congress and the effect of rescinding an application, another procedural issue is the subject for which the application is made, that is, how similar do the applications have to be? Another great concern and subject of debate among other issues involving amending conventions is whether an amending convention could be confined to one or more specified subjects or whether it could recommend additional amendments. Both limited and unlimited conventions have scholarly support.

§ 8.220 Chapter Summary and Discussion Questions

Summary: Congress and the Executive

The relationship of Congress with the other two branches of government—the executive and the judiciary—and with the states and localities is the theme of this chapter. The basis for these relationships is found in the Constitution. The application of the constitutional provisions in practice and experience has resulted in varied, diverse, and changing laws, modes of operating, and means of accomplishing public policy objectives.

The framers of the Constitution vested legislative, executive, and judicial power in three different branches of government. This construction is referred to as the separation of powers, with each branch able to exercise only its respective powers. The framers went further, however, and created a system of checks and balances between the branches to prevent any one branch from becoming too powerful or independent of the other two branches.

While the president and executive branch have all executive authority under the Constitution, Congress has authority to enact laws establishing the structure of the executive branch, creating programs for it to execute, detailing the management of the executive branch, and making money available for the executive branch to perform its responsibilities. The key check and balance in lawmaking is that only Congress may pass legislation, but legislation may become effective as law only with the president's signature or with a congressional override of a presidential veto by a two-thirds vote in each chamber.

Congress also looks to the president for policy and legislative initiatives, and expects the president and other executive officials to be active throughout the legislative process in expressing the executive's views on legislation. The president conveys his legislative desires through an annual State of the Union address, the annual budget, and other means. The president and each department and agency have legislative affairs staffs to handle constant contact with members, committees, and staffs of Congress. The Office of Management and Budget provides a clearance process for legislation and testimony to be delivered to Capitol Hill, and oversees the issuance of Statements of Administration Policy (SAPs) at critical junctures in the legislative process. OMB also coordinates the executive branch process leading to the president's signature or veto of legislation.

Congress regularly delegates rulemaking authority to the executive and to independent agencies. The application of laws may be complex or, as the case in licensing, specific and individual. Congress has therefore established policy in law, but has granted executive departments and agencies authority to implement regulations and adjudicate claims pursuant to law. Congress nonetheless retains the ability to oversee such delegated authority through oversight, appropriations decisions, and laws such as the Congressional Review Act, whereby it has a period of time to consider, and even to vote on, a new regulation before it takes effect.

While there are many ways through the enactment of laws to constrain or direct executive action, Congress' constitutional power of the purse—the appropriation of funds by law—is its most effective authority. The executive may only spend money made available to it by law and may only spend it in accordance with the terms of law. Congress in addition includes instructive and other language in reports and debates that inform the executive of congressional intent; all of these items together are referred to as legislative history.

Second only to appropriations authority in congressional power to constrain or direct executive action is Congress' power to conduct oversight and investigations of both the executive and of private activities. Congress has many means available to it to conduct oversight—hearings, staff investigations, audits by the Government Accountability Office, reports by department and agency inspectors general, resolutions of inquiry, and subpoenas, to name some of the better-known means. The executive may seek to resist some congressional inquiries by asserting executive privilege, but the two forms of this privilege can be overcome, in whole or in part, by Congress. Constitutional rights and other protections are available to witnesses in congressional oversight and investigations.

Another powerful check and balance that exists between Congress and the president is the Senate's constitutional authority to advise and consent to presidential appointments to executive offices, military and other commissions, and the judiciary. Congress may establish by law which positions are subject to advice and consent, or confirmation. The president may be able to make temporary appointments to such offices when they are vacant, but a permanent appointment may be had only with Senate approval.

Congress has an important constitutional role in the selection of the president and vice president. Normally, Congress receives and counts the electoral votes, formally determining which candidate has received a majority. A majority, not a plurality, is necessary to win. The House and Senate may also in the course of counting electoral votes be called on resolve objections to a state's electoral votes. If a presidential and vice presidential team does not obtain a majority of electoral votes, the House chooses the president, with each state voting as a bloc, and the Senate chooses the vice president, with each senator voting individually.

Congress also has the power to impeach and remove from office the president, executive officials, and judges. The House has sole power to impeach, and the Senate has sole power to convict and remove an individual from office, and to disqualify the convicted official from holding a U.S. office again. There have been only nineteen impeachments and eight convictions (all judges) in the history of the United States; an additional four impeached individuals resigned.

Summary: Congress and the Courts

The Constitution gives Congress the authority to structure the federal judiciary and to establish judicial pay. It may not, as a check and balance, reduce the pay of federal judges, and judges, once their nomination is confirmed, are appointed for life. The president nominates federal judges, normally with a degree of input from senators. The Senate Judiciary Committee and the Senate take great care in considering judicial nominations because their appointments are lifetime. Only the Senate advises and consents to a judicial nomination.

Most decisions by courts involve federal statutes rather than constitutional issues. If a court interprets or applies a statute in a manner that many members of Congress find disagreeable, they may seek to amend the law at issue. Members regularly take umbrage at judicial decisions, congressional committees regularly hold hearings on potential changes to statutes following judicial rulings, and Congress on occasion changes law to address concerns with the judicial interpretation or application of a statute.

Summary: Congress and Foreign Policy

The president is commander in chief of U.S. armed forces and appoints ambassadors as part of his administration. The president and his administration closely guard executive prerogatives in national defense and foreign policy. Congress also, nonetheless, has constitutional authority to raise an army and provide for a navy, and to declare and appropriate funds for war. The Senate must advise and consent to nominations to ambassadorships.

Congress has declared war on only five occasions, but it has authorized the conduct of wars in other ways, such as through resolutions and appropriations. Since 1973, Congress and the president have tacitly used the framework of the War Powers Resolution to consider presidential commitments of troops to hostilities. Presidents believe the War Powers Resolution to be an unconstitutional infringement on their constitutionally granted powers, and Congresses have not directly challenged presidents by seeking to closely follow the strictures of the War Powers Resolution.

The Constitution gives a foreign policy power solely to the Senate: to advise and consent to the ratification of treaties. When a president has negotiated a treaty, he submits it to the Senate for its advice and consent, which he must obtain before he ratifies the treaty. A two-thirds vote in the Senate is necessary. Congress also on occasion gives the president authority to negotiate international agreements meeting certain parameters in law. If the president successfully negotiates such an agreement, he then submits it to Congress, which under the law uses expedited procedures to ensure an up-and-down vote on the agreement as negotiated. Treaties and international agreements are laws of the United States.

Congress regularly uses it lawmaking authority to establish foreign policy and national defense policy and to appropriate funds to be spent according to congressional priorities and policies. The president and his administration are active throughout the lawmaking and appropriations process, seeking to bring congressional policy into alignment with the president's views. Congress also uses other means to influence executive actions, such as hearings, sense of the House or Senate resolutions, letters to the president and to other U.S. and foreign officials, participation in international exchanges, and meetings in the United States and abroad with foreign dignitaries.

Summary: Congress and Federalism

The framers divided power between the federal government and the state governments. The federal government is a government of enumerated powers, listed in the Constitution. The states have all power that any sovereign nation has over its territory, except as limited by the Constitution and their own state constitution.

When Congress enacts a law pursuant to its constitutional authority, that law is the supreme law of the land under the Constitution, binding on the states as well as the citizens and residents of the United States. Various congressional enactments, however, might also affect state prerogatives differently. In some instances, states under the Constitution have no authority to make certain laws since Congress' enumerated powers preclude state lawmaking. In other instances, Congress might make law where it shares authority with the states, and might act so that it precludes state lawmaking—called preemption—or might act so that there is room for state as well as federal law.

The courts have frequently been called on to resolve cases involving the federal relationship between the national government and the states. In one set of cases, the courts have prohibited Congress from commandeering state legislatures or state executive officials. They have, however, allowed Congress to offer states inducements to take certain actions, so long as the choice to do so is not compulsory.

In another set of cases, the Court in recent years has constrained congressional use of the Commerce Clause and the Fourteenth Amendment to constitutionally justify enactments. In the instance of the Commerce Clause, the courts have required activities to substantially affect commerce, in addition to other tests, in order for the courts to find constitutional justification for a law under the Commerce Clause. In the instance of the Fourteenth Amendment, the courts have required that there be "congruence and proportionality" between the injury sought to be prevented or remedied and the means adopted to that end.

Federal spending for the states and localities is a substantial component of federal outlays and an even more substantial component of states' and localities' revenues. Nearly 16 percent of federal outlays in fiscal year 2012 are estimated to be for grants to states and localities, and federal grants comprised 24 percent of states' and localities' revenue in 2009. Federal grants address governmental activities across the public-policy spectrum.

Congress might make assistance available as grants, loans, or tax subsidies. It might make grants available as categorical grants or as block grants, the former being for a very specific purpose and the latter for a broader, flexible set of purposes. In its decision-making, Congress determines what to fund, what form of grant to use, what formula factors to use, and what level of funding to use.

Congress has also defined unfunded federal mandates in law, and sought to limit them so that additional fiscal burdens are not placed on states and localities. An unfunded mandate imposes a duty without providing funds to pay for performing that duty. Congressional procedures require such mandates to be identified in legislation, and allow members to make a point of order against the consideration of such legislation.

Congress and the states share responsibility for amending the Constitution. Congress may propose an amendment to the Constitution by a two-thirds vote in each chamber, and three-fourths of the states by action of their legislatures or of state conventions may ratify an amendment. Two-thirds of states may also call a convention for proposing amendments. There have been twenty-seven amendments ratified, and seven amendments submitted to the states have failed ratification.

Discussion Questions

- Read the first three articles of the Constitution, and identify ten examples of checks and balances you find there.
- If the president vetoes legislation, it can become law only if Congress overrides his veto. Look back to the end of Chapter Six where there is a table (*§ 6.292*) showing presidential vetoes and congressional overrides. Why do you think the president is so successful when he vetoes legislation?
- The Office of Management and Budget has been described in a number of places in the *Deskbook*, including in this chapter. Review these descriptions. What conclusions might you draw about the role and importance of this agency in the operation of congressional-executive relations?
- Congress has only once successfully used the Congressional Review Act to overturn a proposed regulation. What makes it so difficult to obtain success? Can you think of other ways in which the Review Act might be successful that is not so evident?
- Re-read the part of Chapter Seven that deals with the appropriations process (*§ 7.80*). Describe some of the ways in which the appropriations process may be used to affect executive actions.
- Executive privilege and constitutional rights might protect witnesses at congressional hearings in certain instances. How effective do you consider these protections from the witness' perspective? How deleterious to an investigation do you consider these protections from a congressional committee's perspective?
- High-visibility nominations often take a great deal of time in the Senate, and senators often find reasons to delay bringing such nominations to a vote. Many scholars have railed against the delay in filling positions and the Senate's slowness. Think of three good reasons that you might oppose any nomination if you were a senator. If you thought the nominee was objectionable for one or more of those reasons, would it be justifiable to use Senate procedures to delay a Senate vote on the nomination? Why or why not?
- Read the debate in the Senate on the trial of Judge Porteous. It appears in the *Congressional Records* of December 7 and 8, 2010. Would you have agreed with the majority in voting to convict him on each article of impeachment, or with the minority in voting against conviction? What were the strongest arguments against convicting him? How persuasive were these arguments? If accepted, what might these arguments mean for behavior in the future by federal judges?

- The Supreme Court made two decisions in recent years that resulted in persistent legislative attempts to rewrite the statutes that the Court had interpreted, wrongly in the eyes of many members. One, the Lilly Ledbetter Fair Pay Act of 2009, became law. The other, the Disclose Act of 2010, did not. One could research these two acts in the *Congressional Record*, newspapers, or other places, but, with even a little research, you should be able to draw some conclusions on why opponents of the Court's decisions were successful in one instance but not in the other.
- The War Powers Resolution has provided a debate framework for Congress but not a decision-making framework for committing or ending the commitment of U.S. armed forces to hostilities. What ideas could you come up with to amend this act that might increase its effectiveness? These ideas need to take into account the reluctance of members of Congress to cast a vote on a controversial issue.
- Expedited procedures can force a vote on an issue. Are they an option for amending the War Powers Resolution? How might you design them? Think carefully about time frames.
- Preemption debates in Congress on a specific piece of legislation often pit business, which usually desires one national standard, against consumer and other groups, such as health groups, who might want federal legislation to establish a floor but to allow states to enact stricter legislation above the floor. Preemption was an issue in the 111th Congress fight over the financial services reform legislation, for example. Can you think of a public policy issue where you would favor a national standard and a public policy issue where you would favor state authority to enact stricter legislation than Congress might enact? Why do you favor the different approaches?
- The Supreme Court approved of Congress' inducing states to change their laws by providing money if they changed their laws and withholding money if they did not. What do you think about this method for getting states to change their laws? Can you identify a law in your state that you would like to see changed, but the legislature has not done so? How might Congress through a new law induce your state and other states to change a law like the one you want changed?
- Go to the *Catalog of Federal Domestic Assistance* online or to Grants.gov online, and use the search engine to identify educational scholarships and loans that might benefit you.
- Draft an amendment to the Constitution. Now what? What arguments would you make to try to persuade members of Congress and then the state legislatures to approve your amendment? How many votes would you need in the House and Senate? How many state legislative bodies (of upper and lower houses in forty-nine states and one legislature in one state) would have to vote their approval?

Chapter Nine

Congressional Documents: Overview, Legislation, and Laws

Analysis

§ 9.00 Introduction

This chapter guides the reader to many types and sources of congressional documents, and to governmental sources of legislative and related research information. These resources are highly useful in monitoring Congress and researching its activities.

There are a few key concepts to keep in mind while reading this chapter and when using the information in it.

First, if a member of Congress wants to introduce legislation that could result in a new law, he must choose the form of a bill or a joint resolution. The other two forms of legislation—concurrent resolutions and simple resolutions—are used only within Congress.

Second, while committees produce many documents, perhaps the most important is a committee's report on a bill or any type of resolution that the committee is recommending to its parent chamber for approval. A committee report is both an advocacy document and an explanatory document, and contains a range of information that cannot be found elsewhere, such as the verbatim changes the proposed legislation makes to existing federal law.

A third key concept is that it is always important to have the most recent version of a piece of legislation. As a bill or resolution makes its way through the legislative process, it is changed by amendment. It is likely that the House and Senate will work on different measures more or less simultaneously, but they will ultimately need to agree to one measure, and decide which one will be the vehicle for agreement between the houses. It is also possible that the legislative vehicle will change when the bill or resolution being considered gets stuck in some parliamentary problem, and House or Senate leaders decide to address an issue with a different measure.

Finally, when the House and Senate have acted and the president has signed a bill or joint resolution into law (or Congress has overridden a presidential veto to make a bill or joint resolution law despite the president's objections), a law is published first as a slip law, then in the Statutes at Large, and, lastly, in the United States Code. Each of these publications uses unique numbers to identify the same law, and each publication is useful for different research purposes.

§ 9.10 Types of Documents

The first critical step is to understand the principal forms of documents that Congress has developed, and the types of information or purposes for which they are used.

Bills and Resolutions. All legislation by which Congress intends to make law is in the form of a *bill (H.R. or S.)* or *joint resolution (H.J. Res. or S.J. Res.)*. An "H" indicates a measure was introduced in the House; an "S" in the Senate. A joint resolution is also the form generally used by Congress to propose amendments to the Constitution. (*See § 9.40, Legislation for Lawmaking: Bills and Joint Resolutions.*)

There are two other types of legislation. *Simple resolutions (H. Res. or S. Res.)* are used in a single chamber to express its opinion on some matter or to administer the chamber. *Concurrent resolutions (H. Con. Res. or S. Con. Res.)* are used by the two chambers together to express congressional opinion on some matter without making law, which by the Constitution must include the president, or to deal with joint administrative matters. (*See § 9.50, Legislation Effective within Congress: Simple and Concurrent Resolutions.*)

Prints. A *print* is a flexible document format used by committees—hence the phrase *committee print.* It might contain almost anything that is of interest to a committee—draft legislation, a committee calendar, a report of a study, the printed transcript of hearings, a compilation of laws in a topical area, and so on. (*See § 10.10, Committee Documents.*)

Reports. *Reports* are also associated with committees, including conference committees. A committee might file a report when it forwards a matter to its parent chamber—such as the results of an investigation, legislation, and, in the Senate, executive business (that is, treaties and nominations). House reports are designated *H. Rept.* and Senate reports, *S. Rept.*; executive reports in the Senate are designated *Exec. Rept.* A two-part number, divided by a hyphen, follows the designation; the first number is the Congress in which the report was issued, the second is a unique number identifying the specific report, for example, S. Rept. 112-12 in the 112th Congress. (*See § 6.60, Committee Reports; and § 10.10, Committee Documents.*)

It is important to remember that the report of a conference committee contains the text of legislation agreed to by the conferees. The House and Senate vote on a conference report. The explanation of a conference agreement appears in a joint explanatory statement, akin to House and Senate committees' reports on legislation. A conference agreeement (the conference report) and its joint explanatory statement are bound together in the conference committee report.

Documents. A print is a document produced by a committee. The House and Senate use *documents*, designated *H. Doc.* in the House and *S. Doc.* in the Senate, for similar purposes. The designation is followed by a number. Documents might be used for matters of interest to the whole House or whole Senate, such as the *Senate Manual* and the *Constitution, Jefferson's Manual, and Rules of the House of Representatives of the United States;* veto messages; administrative documents; and special publications for informing the public, such as *How Our Laws Are Made* or *Our American Government* (available for distribution to constituents by congressional offices). (*The specific documents mentioned here are described in §§ 10.40, 10.50, and 10.60.*)

Congressional Record and Journals. The *Congressional Record* is published each day the House or Senate is in session. It contains a transcript of floor debate and proceedings for that day and a record of other legislative business, such as floor and committee schedules. The official records of floor proceedings are the *Journal of the U.S. House of Representatives* and *Journal of the United States Senate*; the text of debates is not included in the *Journals*. The Senate also maintains the *Journal of Executive Proceedings of the Senate.* (*For detailed descriptions of these documents, see § 10.20, Floor Documents. For information on the Senate's executive business, see § 8.80, Congress and the Executive: Appointments; and § 8.150, Congress and Foreign Policy: Treaties and International Agreements.*)

There are other, special congressional documents not covered by these forms, such as the *Calendars of the United States House of Representatives and History of Legislation*, which are described in Chapter Ten. (*For a complete description of the Congressional Record and the Calendars, see § 10.20, Floor Documents.*)

Congress is also making congressional documents and a vast array of other information available through its World Wide Web sites: THOMAS, the web-based legislative status and information system (<*http://thomas.gov*>) made available through the Library of Congress to the public by the direction of Congress; and the Legislative Information System, a system internal to Congress and legislative-branch agencies and somewhat similar to THOMAS. Few congressional documents before those of the 104th Congress have been available until recently on congressional or other web sites. However, providers, including the Library of Congress, are digitizing historical collections. Over time, information in electronic form, such as hearings transcripts, might eventually replace one or more types of printed congressional documents. Information available in electronic form is also examined below. (*See § 9.20, Finding and Obtaining Congressional Documents.*)

§ 9.20 Finding and Obtaining Congressional Documents

The growth of the World Wide Web has made it easy, convenient, and inexpensive to find and obtain contemporary congressional documents—legislation, committee reports, the *Congressional Record*, and so on. It also matters little whether one is monitoring Congress in Washington, DC, or from any one of the fifty states, the U.S. territories, or foreign countries. The following sources, some more traditional, should answer many needs for contemporary congressional documents.

THOMAS

(*<http://thomas.loc.gov>*)

The place to begin any research on the current Congress—texts of legislation, reports, legislative status, access to committee and member information, and so on—is THOMAS. In conjunction with the House and Senate, the Library of Congress operates this web service to make congressional information and documents easily available to everyone. Some users need more value-added information than THOMAS supplies, but THOMAS' quick, easy access to current status information, texts of documents, schedules, and links to complementary web resources makes it a site to visit daily. At the very least, the potential user should set aside thirty to sixty minutes to explore the site and get to know it before an emergency need for information arises.

GPO's Federal Digital System

(*Accessible through THOMAS, <http://thomas.gov> or directly at <www.fdsys.gov>.*)

For the texts of current congressional documents, including the *Congressional Record*, THOMAS provides links to GPO's Federal Digital System, the web site of the U.S. Government Printing Office (GPO). However, it is worthwhile to explore this site directly to find out what other congressional and governmental documents are available. For example, many government affairs professionals use the *Federal Register* as frequently as they use the *Congressional Record*, and it is available through GPO. GPO's Federal Digital System superseded GPO Access *<www.gpoaccess.gov>*. (*Additional information on GPO appears at § 4.140, Government Printing Office.*)

Federal Depository Libraries

(*Information on the depository library program and on depository libraries in the District of Columbia and each state can be found on the GPO web site, <http://gpo.gov/libraries>.*)

Within the Washington metropolitan area or anywhere in the country, one is likely to be close to a federal depository library—there are more than 1,200 of them around the country. Depository libraries are usually units of public, college, or other libraries, and, as a condition of being a depository library, they are open to all users.

Depository libraries offer an array of congressional and other "core documents of U.S. democracy," as GPO describes the basic collection. The depository libraries provide the public with access to collections of congressional and other federal documents, reference librarians who know the collections, and, often, other useful tools in researching Congress, such as the *CQ Weekly* and Congressional Quarterly annual almanacs.

Congressional Web Sites

(*Accessible through THOMAS, <http://thomas.gov> or directly at the House and Senate web sites, <www.house.gov> and <www.senate.gov>.*)

One of the best developments beginning in the mid-1990s for everyone who monitors Congress has been the growth in the content and currency of committee, leadership, and member web sites. The information available at these sites complements that available from THOMAS and GPO. If THOMAS and GPO's Federal Digital System are the first and second stops on a daily check of congressional information and documents, Congress' own sites are indispensable third and fourth stops.

House and Senate Document Rooms

The House and Senate maintain "document rooms" to distribute—to both members and the public—print copies of current legislation, committee reports, calendars, slip laws, and a limited number of other congressional documents, such as those with an identifier of *H. Doc.* or *S. Doc.* (Printed committee hearings, however, are available from the authoring committees or GPO, and most committee prints are available only from the authoring committee.) While GPO has generally replaced the congressional document rooms and federally designated depository libraries as the source of congressional documents for many individuals, the document rooms continue to be a convenient and free source of printed documents. However, the document rooms quickly run out of sought-after items.

The House document room is a function of the Legislative Resource Center (LRC), a unit within the Office of the Clerk of the House of Representatives. One may visit or write the LRC at B-106 Cannon House Office Building, Washington, DC 20515-6612, and one may fax document orders to the LRC at 202-226-4362. Information on the LRC is available at the clerk's web site (*<http://clerk.house.gov/about/offices_lrc.aspx>* and *<http://clerk.house.gov/legislative/housedoc.aspx>*), and on the House clerk's web site by selecting "Legislative Activities," then selecting "House Documents," or by calling 202-226-5200.

One may visit or write the Senate document room at B-04 Hart Senate Office Building, Washington, DC 20510. One may also fax a document order to the Senate document room at 202-228-2815. Information on the availability of a document can be obtained by calling the Senate document room at 202-224-7701. Additional information on document services is available at *<www.senate.gov/legislative/common/generic/Doc_Room.htm>*, where an order by email may also be placed, and on the Senate web site *<http://senate.gov>* under "Legislation & Records," then selecting "Senate Document Room."

§ 9.30 Sites for Committee, Scheduling, and Member Information

Committee Information. While committees still vary in the content and currency of their sites, the most useful committee sites provide—at no charge—an array of information not likely to be found elsewhere. Many committees, for example, put the following on their web sites: scheduling information, witness testimony, hearings transcripts, lists of measures referred to the committee, lists of committee publications, committee rules, rosters of committee and subcommittee members and staff, and other electronic versions of documents, including noncongressional ones, of interest to members and the public. The sites might also link to THOMAS and GPO and to other web sites with related or supplementary information. Many congressional committees now webcast at least some of their meetings, with links on their web sites.

Committee offices also continue to serve as distributors of certain kinds of information, such as printed committee hearings and committee prints. A committee might have a documents or publications clerk, or someone designated to handle those responsibilities. If one regularly follows the work of a specific committee, it is important to learn how the committee handles its publications.

Scheduling Information. While congressional leaders and party caucuses or conferences also still vary in the content and currency of their web sites, the most useful leadership and party sites are an aid in obtaining long-term and immediate scheduling information, descriptions of the party leadership's legislative priorities, overviews of House-wide or Senate-wide legislative activity, party talking points on important issues, and other information. The whip notices, which are frequently updated, are particularly useful in monitoring floor schedules.

Web access to House and Senate floor schedules (and long-range planning calendars) is available through THOMAS and, among other places, at the following web sites:

- House web site: *<http://house.gov/legislative>*
- Office of the Clerk of the House: *<http://clerk.house.gov>*, then select "Legislative Activities."
- The web site URLs for House leadership positions vary depending on which party is in the majority. The current leadership web sites and schedules can be found on the House web site, *<http://house.gov>*, then selecting "Leadership."
- To see the floor schedules on the web pages of the Majority Leader or the Minority Whip, after clicking on either link select "On the Floor" or "Floor Schedule" or "House Floor."
- Senate web site: *<http://senate.gov>*, select "Legislation & Records," then select "Calendars & Schedules."
- Senate Democrats: *<http://democrats.senate.gov>*
- Senate Republicans: *<http://republican.senate.gov/>*

(*See also § 9.31, Recorded Congressional Information.*)

Member Information. Individual members publish a variety of information on their web sites. A number of members have sites that have been recognized, at least informally, as well-designed and content-rich. Press releases, position statements, home-district or home-state schedules of appearances, staff rosters and photos, constituent services, and continuously running polls are just a por-

§ 9.31

Recorded Congressional Information

Some congressional and related information is regularly updated on telephone recordings.

House of Representatives Floor Schedule Information:
Democratic Recording (advance schedule), 202-225-1600

Democratic Recording (current proceedings), 202-225-7400

Republican Recording (advance schedule), 202-225-2020

Republican Recording (current proceedings), 202-225-7430

Senate Floor Schedule Information:
Democratic Recording, 202-224-8541
Republican Recording, 202-224-8601

Government Printing Office:
New Congressional Publications, 202-512-1809

White House Executive Clerk:
Status of Bills Received, 202-456-2226

Office of the Federal Register:
New Public Law Numbers, 202-741-6043

tion of the information individual members might make available. One is well-advised to take a careful look at a member's web site before paying a call on the member or a staffer in her office. And research on a bill or resolution as it makes its way through the legislative process must include monitoring the web sites of members of the committee of jurisdiction, as well as the sites of the sponsor and cosponsors of the measure.

§ 9.40 Legislation for Lawmaking: Bills and Joint Resolutions

Legislation and amendments are the lifeblood of congressional lawmaking. Several thousand bills and resolutions are introduced in the House and Senate in the two-year duration of a Congress. Thousands of amendments are considered in subcommittees and full committees, on the House and Senate floors, and in conference committees.

At the beginning of a Congress, hundreds of measures are introduced within the first few days of the first session. Members do this because they want to continue to push legislation that did not make it through the legislative process in the last Congress, or they want to fulfill a campaign promise. They might also want to be on record early with a position on certain matters, or they might have spent some time since the election developing new initiatives on which they want to get an early and quick start. At the end of a Congress, when it adjourns *sine die*, all legislation that has made it only to an interim step dies. If a piece of legislation has not been approved in identical form by both the House and Senate, its proponents must introduce it anew in the next Congress and pursue it along the same path of referral to committee, committee consideration, and so on.

The assistance of the House and Senate Offices of Legislative Counsel are integral to members in drafting many of the measures and amendments proposed.

Designation and Numbering

As mentioned in the introduction to this chapter, all legislation by which Congress intends to make law is in the form of a bill or joint resolution—designated *H.R.* and *H. J. Res.*, respectively, in the House, and *S.* and *S. J. Res.*, respectively, in the Senate. A unique number follows the designation. The House and Senate maintain separate series of numbers for their bills and joint resolutions, and assign the numbers in the sequential order in which measures are introduced. For example, H.R. 1 is followed by H.R. 2, and S. J. Res. 1 is followed by S. J. Res. 2. Once both houses of Congress agree to a bill or joint resolution in identical form, the measure is sent to the president for his signature or veto.

The designations *H.R.* and *H. Res.*, and *S.* and *S. Res.*, are often confused. *H.R.* stands for House of Representatives and signifies a bill. *H. Res.* stands for House Resolution and is the form of legislation used within the House for internal matters. *S.* stands for Senate and signifies a bill. *S. Res.* stands for Senate Resolution and is the form of legislation used within the Senate for internal matters. (*See § 9.50, Legislation Effective within Congress: Simple and Concurrent Resolutions.*)

Bills

Most legislation is in the form of a bill (introduced as *H.R.* or *S.*), and nearly all bills on introduction are referred to the committee with legislative jurisdiction over the subject of the bill. For example, a House bill to establish or change a housing program—most likely an authorization bill—would probably be referred on introduction to the House Financial Services Committee, and a comparable Senate bill to the Senate Banking, Housing, and Urban Affairs Committee. Some of the uses of a bill include the following:

- authorization bills
- appropriations bills
- tax bills
- amendments to existing federal laws
- private bills

Some practices involving bills are important to remember. Under the Constitution, all tax bills must originate in the House. That does not mean that the Senate cannot consider tax legislation before passage by the House, but it must wait until a House-passed tax measure is sent to it before it procedurally completes its work. By custom, appropriations bills also originate in the House. Again, the Senate might begin its consideration of an appropriations bill before it has received a House-passed measure, but it may not procedurally complete its work until it receives the House bill. Therefore, tax and appropriations bills agreed to by Congress and sent to the president are designated *H.R.* (or, in the case of most continuing appropriations measures, *H. J. Res.*). (*See § 7.80, Authorizations and Appropriations Processes; and § 7.90, Revenue Legislation.*)

Bills might be introduced in either or both chambers, and might carry an *H.R.* or an *S.* designation, with the exception of tax and appropriations measures, as the two houses attempt to reach agreement on legislation that both houses have passed.

The House Appropriations Committee usually drafts appropriations bills in its subcommittees. Appropriations bills are not introduced as the president transmits a budget to Congress. Rather, each of the subcommittees of the Appropriations Committee holds hearings and drafts a bill as the committee works through the appropriations matters within its jurisdiction. Once subcommittee and committee markups are completed on a draft appropriations bill, the resulting bill is introduced. Like any other bill, it is then assigned the next sequential number; for example, H.R. 2918 was the legislative-branch appropriations bill for fiscal year 2010. The Appropriations Committee develops supplemental and continuing appropriations measures in the same manner.

The Senate Appropriations Committee normally proceeds in a similar fashion. If, however, the House passes an appropriations bill before the Senate Appropriations Committee reports a *companion bill*, the Senate committee has the option of marking up the House-passed bill.

Senate committees are authorized to *originate* measures, and a committee might develop legislation that receives a number after the committee reports it. House committees sometimes work from introduced legislation or legislative drafts and subsequently introduce a *clean bill*. Upon introduction, where a bill number is assigned, the bill is referred to the committee, and the committee automatically reports it. (*See § 6.50, Committee Markup.*)

The numbers of the first bills introduced in a new Congress are often reserved for the legislative priorities of the two parties. For example, S. 1 through S. 10 might be reserved for the Senate majority party's legislative priorities and S. 11 through S. 20 for the minority party's legislative priorities.

As a Congress proceeds, a sponsor might find that he can time the introduction of a measure to obtain a number that relates to the subject matter of the measure, for example, H.R. 1040 or S. 1040 for amendments to the tax code. Or, a member can reserve a specific number for the same reason. A member might also wish to retain a bill number from the former Congress in the new Congress to make it easier for proponents to publicize and build momentum over the course of more than one Congress.

Joint Resolutions

Some of the uses of a joint resolution include the following:

- continuing appropriations resolution
- declaration of war
- approval or disapproval of a presidential action or recommendation (pursuant to procedures under the War Powers Act, for example)
- narrow or very specific purpose, such as establishing a national holiday

As one might conclude from this list, joint resolutions generally serve a narrower or more specific purpose than bills. There are no procedural differences in how they are treated in the legislative process. Indeed, Congress might occasionally opt to use a bill form in instances in which it could use the form of a joint resolution.

The term *continuing resolution* refers to a joint resolution that Congress uses to provide itself with additional time to pass appropriations bills. If Congress has not completed its work on one or more appropriations bills by the time the new fiscal year begins on October 1, it adopts a joint resolution to "continue" the availability of funding at a specific level for a specific time. The president, of course, must sign such a joint resolution for it to become law and take effect. (*See § 7.80, Authorizations and Appropriations Processes.*)

Constitutional Amendments in the Form of Joint Resolution. A joint resolution is also the form generally used by Congress to propose amendments to the Constitution. In this case, however, Congress is not making law and does not send the joint resolution to the president for his signature or veto. Rather, once there is a two-thirds vote on passage in each chamber on an identical joint resolution proposing to amend the Constitution, the measure is transmitted to the archivist of the United States, who is the head of the National Archives and Records Administration (NARA), to begin the ratification process by the states. (*See* § *8.210, Congress and Federalism: Amending the Constitution.*)

§ 9.50 Legislation Effective within Congress: Simple and Concurrent Resolutions

Simple Resolutions

There are two other types of legislation besides bills and joint resolutions. Simple resolutions are used in a single chamber to express its opinion on some matter or to administer the chamber. Simple resolutions are designated *H. Res.* in the House and *S. Res.* in the Senate. A unique number follows the designation, using a separate series and sequential numbering, just as is done for bills and joint resolutions. Some of the uses of a simple resolution include the following:

- additions or changes to chamber rules
- administration of the chamber, such as resolution of election contests
- election of chamber officers
- election of committee members
- sense of the House (or Senate) on some matter (expressing support for an action that could be taken in the executive branch or commending a military unit on an achievement, for example)
- in the House, special rules from the Rules Committee

Special rules from the House Rules Committee, discussed in § 6.90 (*Rules Committee and Special Rules*), are perhaps the most frequent manner in which the House simple resolution is used. Nearly all significant legislation comes to the House floor under a special rule. After the Rules Committee reports a special rule in the form of a simple resolution and the House adopts it, the special rule governs debate and amendment of the underlying legislation.

Concurrent Resolutions

Concurrent resolutions are used by the two chambers together to express congressional opinion on some matter without making law, which by the Constitution must include the president, or to deal with joint administrative matters. Concurrent resolutions are designated *H. Con. Res.* in the House and *S. Con. Res.* in the Senate, with a number following the designation, using a separate series and sequential numbering just as is done for bills and joint resolutions. Some of the uses of a concurrent resolution include the following:

- congressional budget resolution
- adjournment of Congress

- corrections of enrolled measures
- creation of joint committees
- providing for a joint meeting or session of Congress
- sense of Congress on some matter (expressing sympathy over the loss of life in another nation due to a natural disaster, for example)

The important aspect of concurrent resolutions is that they must be passed in identical form by both the House and Senate to have effect between them. The chambers might even convene a conference committee to resolve differences over a very important matter that is contained in a concurrent resolution, such as a congressional budget resolution. (*See § 7.50, Congressional Budget Process.*)

§ 9.60 Versions of Legislation

As a measure makes its way through the legislative process, first in one house and then the other, it changes. To do their work, members of Congress must have the number and text of the latest version of a measure. The House or Senate must have the changes that one of its committees recommended in a measure that was introduced and marked up in committee. Both the House and Senate must have exactly what the full House agreed to and what the full Senate agreed to, and so on. As a measure makes its way through the legislative process, it is reprinted to reflect changes at each major stage of the process; sometimes, additional printings are made because of the complexity of the legislation or the particular procedures being employed.

Progression of Legislation

A case study in Chapter Twelve illustrates the explanation that follows here. Following are common versions of a measure that is first considered in the House:

- as introduced
- as reported from committee
- as passed by the House (the *engrossed* measure; a bill or joint resolution is now labeled *An Act* rather than *A Bill* or *A Resolution*)
- as received by the Senate
- as reported from a Senate committee
- as passed by the Senate (the Senate *engrossed amendment*)
- as reported from a conference committee
- as *enrolled* (the version sent to the president)
- as *public law*

Following are common versions of a measure that is first considered in the Senate:

- as introduced
- as reported from committee
- as passed by the Senate (the *engrossed measure*; a bill or joint resolution is now labeled *An Act* rather than *A Bill* or *A Resolution*)
- as received by the House
- as reported from a House committee

- as passed by the House (the House *engrossed amendment*)
- as reported from a conference committee
- as *enrolled* (the version sent to the president)
- as *public law*

Certain procedural variations occur regularly. For example, House and Senate committees might report bills on the same subject—the House committee reporting a House bill and the Senate committee reporting a Senate bill—and the House might consider the House bill and the Senate, the Senate bill. One must track both bills until both the House and Senate have acted. The second chamber to act would probably take the first step toward agreement between the chambers, possibly by "striking everything after the enacting clause" in the first chamber's bill and inserting the text of the second chamber's bill. This action results in one bill number with a House-passed text and a Senate-passed text. This process is explained in § 6.260 (*Reconciling Differences between House-Passed and Senate-Passed Legislation*).

The versions of a bill might look like this if the House acted first and the Senate second:

- House bill as introduced
- as reported from committee
- as passed by the House (the *engrossed bill*, now *An Act*)
- as received by the Senate
- Senate bill as introduced
- Senate bill as reported from a Senate committee
- as passed by the Senate (the Senate *engrossed amendment*, which uses the House bill number but contains the Senate-passed amendment, or a *public print*, which uses the House bill number but incorporates the Senate-passed text)
- as reported from a conference committee
- as *enrolled*
- as *public law*

Versions of Legislation

It should be relatively apparent from the first one or two pages of a measure what the version is:

- An *introduced version* is labeled *A Bill* or *A Resolution* and shows the measure number, date of introduction, sponsor and cosponsors, and committee or committees to which the measure was referred.
- The *reported version* will still be labeled *A Bill* or *A Resolution*, but it will bear a calendar number, a report number (and part numbers if more than one committee reported the measure), any additional cosponsors, the action of the committee or committees to which the measure was referred (for example, "Reported from the Committee on the Judiciary with an amendment"), and the proposed committee amendment(s) in italicized type. If two or more committees report amendments to a measure, each committee's amendments are printed in a different typeface in the body of the measure.
- The first page of an *engrossed version* is simple in contrast—it contains just the measure number and the designation *An Act* rather than *A Bill* or *A Resolution*.

- The *received version* has the same number and the designation *An Act*, but has the name of the second chamber: "In the Senate of the United States" for House-passed bills and "In the House of Representatives" for Senate-passed bills. It also shows how the second chamber is handling the measure, either by placing it directly on a calendar, in which case there is a calendar number, or by referring it to committee, in which case the referral is noted.
- The second chamber's *engrossed version* appears as an amendment or amendments to the first chamber's measure. (A *public print* might also be printed, incorporating the second chamber's—almost always the Senate's—amendment into the text of the measure.)
- A *conference version* (that is, the conference report) looks on the first page more like a committee report on a measure, but then contains the proposed final text of the measure to be agreed to by the full House and Senate and the joint explanatory statement.
- An *enrolled version* prominently features the Congress and session, uses a formal typeface for the Congress and *An Act*, and shows the measure number in small type in the upper left corner of the first page.
- The *public law* still says *An Act* and shows the public-law number, statutory citation, and date of the president's signing. It also contains margin notes, including the measure number.

One other point to remember about versions of legislation is that more or fewer versions are possible than the examples provided here. In addition, both the House and the Senate leadership may develop different versions of legislation than those reported from committee, and could use those versions for floor consideration.

In the House, the Rules Committee might report a special rule to provide a text reflecting majority leadership desires concerning the floor vehicle. A special rule might also deal with conflicting amendments from several committees acting on a measure. In the Senate, the leadership might negotiate changes to the floor text to deal with individual senators' concerns and to facilitate Senate consideration and passage. These changes or understandings could be reflected in a leadership amendment or a unanimous consent agreement.

If the House adopts the special rule or the Senate majority leader is able to negotiate an amendment or a unanimous consent agreement, the text considered on the floor might be different from that reported from committee. The text considered on the floor might not be separately printed as a bill or resolution before passage by the respective chamber.

§ 9.70 Laws and Their Codification

This section describes the publication of laws and key executive documents produced once the president signs a measure into law, or when Congress passes a measure over the president's veto. These documents are available in federal depository libraries, in addition to the sources included with each document's description.

Presidential Action while Legislation Is Pending

Before and during House and Senate consideration of legislation, or even before and during House and Senate hearings on issues that could result in legislation, the president, White House staff such as the congressional liaison team, and other executive officials are busy informing members of Congress of the president's or the executive branch's views. While the president or other members of the administration might speak directly with individual members of Congress or with groups of members about a pending legislative matter, the Office of Management and Budget (OMB) might also issue on behalf of the executive branch, or on behalf of the president, a Statement of Administration Policy (SAP) on specific pending legislation. SAPs and other legislative information are available on the OMB web site under "Legislative Information," *<www.whitehouse.gov/omb/legislative-affairs>*. (*SAPs are discussed more extensively at § 8.20, Congress and Executive: Legislation.*)

In addition to the White House and OMB web sites, documents on other federal government web sites detail actions and statements by the president related to legislative issues and to legislation and laws. The Daily Compilation of Presidential Documents cumulates all presidential press conferences and statements, speeches, nominations, messages to Congress, and other presidential materials. It is available from GPO's Federal Digital System at *<http://fdsys.gov>*, then select "Browse Collections," then select "Compilation of Presidential Documents." Complementary information in available on the White House web site, *<http://whitehouse.gov>*, under "Briefing Room."

Presidential documents are further cumulated in a collection known as the Public Papers of the President, available on GPO's Federal Digital System at *<http://fdsys.gov>*, then select "Browse Collections," then select "Public Papers of the Presidents of the United States." Some older volumes, dating as far back as the Reagan presidency, are available on the National Archives web site at *<www.archives.gov/federal-register/publications/presidential-papers.html>*.

Presidential executive orders and proclamations are available through the documents and web sites already listed. They are also separately available through the National Archives web site, *<www.archives.gov/federal-register/executive-orders>*.

Public Laws

As explained in § 6.290 (*Presidential Action on Enacted Measures*), a measure must be presented to the president for his consideration and signature to become law. When the president receives an enrolled measure from Congress, he has ten days (Sundays excepted) to sign or veto it if Congress is in session. (If Congress has adjourned *sine die*, he need not take any action if his intent is to prevent a measure from becoming law; he exercises a pocket veto.) The ten days start to run at midnight of the day on which the Office of the Executive Clerk acknowledges receipt of a measure, whether the president is at the White House or traveling inside or outside the United States. The Office of the Executive Clerk manages the official paperwork. The status of legislation at the White House can be obtained from the executive clerk's office by calling 202-456-2226, or by checking the White House web site at *<http://whitehouse.gov>*.

Congress might send the president a measure quickly after final congressional action, such as when a continuing appropriations measure is needed to provide temporary funding to government agencies. Or, at the end of a session, when Congress clears numerous pieces of legislation for the

§ 9.71

Excerpt from a Public Law

Shown in §§ 9.71, 9.72, and 9.73 is how a provision of law appears in a public law (also popularly called a *slip law* after the pamphlet form in which it is published), the Statutes at Large, and the U.S. Code. P.L. 104-4, the Unfunded Mandates Act, was signed into law by President Clinton on March 22, 1995. It had been passed earlier by Congress as S. 1.

This first example shows an excerpt from the public law, section 201.

TITLE II—REGULATORY ACCOUNTABILITY AND REFORM

SEC. 201. REGULATORY PROCESS.

Each agency shall, unless otherwise prohibited by law, assess the effects of Federal regulatory actions on State, local, and tribal governments, and the private sector (other than to the extent that such regulations incorporate requirements specifically set forth in law).

president's consideration, legislation might continue to be transmitted to the president for several weeks after adjournment.

A bill or resolution of a "public character," in the phrasing of House and Senate rules, that the president has signed into law, or that Congress has passed over his veto, is transmitted to the National Archives and Records Administration (NARA) and within it to the Office of the Federal Register (OFR). At OFR, the measure is assigned a sequential public-law number, such as P.L. 112-9, which would indicate that it was enacted in the 112th Congress and that it was the ninth public law of that Congress. (This form for numbering public laws began in the 85th Congress (1957–1958); the Congress designation was then added, for example, P.L. 85-100, rather than P.L. 100.) OFR also assigns a statutory citation (*see Statutes at Large, below*), and its editors add margin notes, citations, and a summary legislative history. (*See § 9.71, Excerpt from a Public Law.*)

Public-law numbers also appear in the *Congressional Record*, *Federal Register*, and other print and electronic resources, including the NARA web site at <*www.archives.gov/federal-register/laws*>. They are also available by phone at 202-741-6043.

Publication occurs first in *slip form*, essentially a pamphlet form similar to that of other congressional documents. *Slip laws* are available from the resources listed in § 9.20 (*Finding and Obtaining Congressional Documents*) and from other print and electronic resources. In addition, convenient resources for retrospective research of public laws include the congressional section of LEXIS-NEXIS and Thomson West's *U.S. Code Congressional and Administrative News*.

The process of presidential signature or veto, possible congressional consideration of a veto, and processing by OFR is the same for bills of a "private character"—a phrase that appears in House and Senate rules—as it is for public bills and resolutions. The same numbering scheme is also used, so that one finds, for example, a Private Law 106-8 as well as a Public Law (P.L.) 106-8.

§ 9.72

Excerpt from the Statutes at Large

An excerpt from P.L. 104-4 is shown in § 9.71. When the National Archives and Records Administration (NARA) received the document signed by the president, it assigned the public-law number and also pages in the U.S. Statutes at Large. The excerpt here shows section 201 in the Statutes at Large; its statutory citation is 109 Stat. 64. The margin notes also show where section 201 appears in the U.S. Code.

109 STAT. 64 PUBLIC LAW 104–4—MAR. 22, 1995

(1) as an exercise of the rulemaking power of the Senate and the House of Representatives, respectively, and as such they shall be considered as part of the rules of such House, respectively, and such rules shall supersede other rules only to the extent that they are inconsistent therewith; and

(2) with full recognition of the constitutional right of either House to change such rules (so far as relating to such House) at any time, in the same manner, and to the same extent as in the case of any other rule of each House.

2 USC 1516. **SEC. 109. AUTHORIZATION OF APPROPRIATIONS.**

There are authorized to be appropriated to the Congressional Budget Office $4,500,000 for each of the fiscal years 1996, 1997, 1998, 1999, 2000, 2001, and 2002 to carry out the provisions of this title.

2 USC 1511 note. **SEC. 110. EFFECTIVE DATE.**

This title shall take effect on January 1, 1996 or on the date 90 days after appropriations are made available as authorized under section 109, whichever is earlier and shall apply to legislation considered on and after such date.

TITLE II—REGULATORY ACCOUNTABILITY AND REFORM

2 USC 1531. **SEC. 201. REGULATORY PROCESS.**

Each agency shall, unless otherwise prohibited by law, assess the effects of Federal regulatory actions on State, local, and tribal governments, and the private sector (other than to the extent that such regulations incorporate requirements specifically set forth in law).

2 USC 1532. **SEC. 202. STATEMENTS TO ACCOMPANY SIGNIFICANT REGULATORY ACTIONS.**

(a) IN GENERAL.—Unless otherwise prohibited by law, before promulgating any general notice of proposed rulemaking that is likely to result in promulgation of any rule that includes any Federal mandate that may result in the expenditure by State, local, and tribal governments, in the aggregate, or by the private sector, of $100,000,000 or more (adjusted annually for inflation) in any 1 year, and before promulgating any final rule for which a general notice of proposed rulemaking was published, the agency shall prepare a written statement containing—

(1) an identification of the provision of Federal law under which the rule is being promulgated;

(2) a qualitative and quantitative assessment of the anticipated costs and benefits of the Federal mandate, including the costs and benefits to State, local, and tribal governments or the private sector, as well as the effect of the Federal mandate on health, safety, and the natural environment and such an assessment shall include—

(A) an analysis of the extent to which such costs to State, local, and tribal governments may be paid with Federal financial assistance (or otherwise paid for by the Federal Government); and

9

§ 9.73

Excerpt from the U.S. Code

An excerpt from the Statutes at Large, in which public laws are placed chronologically, is shown in § 9.72. The Statutes at Large are a convenient place to find all the provisions of a specific public law. However, many times, if not most of the time, one is seeking the current law on a specific subject. The U.S. Code, therefore, places each provision of a public law in the appropriate place in the appropriate subject title. In the example used here, section 201 of P.L. 104-4, which also appeared at 109 Stat. 64, is codified at 2 U.S.C. § 1531. Notes following section 1531 show the public law and statutory origins of the provision, and provide other useful information.

SUBCHAPTER II—REGULATORY ACCOUNTABILITY AND REFORM

§ 1531. Regulatory process

Each agency shall, unless otherwise prohibited by law, assess the effects of Federal regulatory actions on State, local, and tribal governments, and the private sector (other than to the extent that such regulations incorporate requirements specifically set forth in law).

(Pub. L. 104-4, title II, § 201, Mar. 22, 1995, 109 Stat. 64.)

EFFECTIVE DATE

Section 209 of title II of Pub. L. 104-4 provided that: "This title [enacting this subchapter] and the amendments made by this title shall take effect on the date of the enactment of this Act [Mar. 22, 1995]."

REGULATORY PLANNING AND REVIEW

For provisions stating regulatory philosophy and principles and setting forth regulatory organization, procedures, and guidelines for centralized review of new and existing regulations to make the regulatory process more efficient, see Ex. Ord. No. 12866, Sept. 30, 1993, 58 F.R. 51735, set out as a note under section 601 of Title 5, Government Organization and Employees.

Statutes at Large

OFR provides a *statutory citation* for public laws. It also does this for constitutional amendments, private laws, concurrent resolutions adopted in the same form by both houses of Congress, approved executive reorganization plans, and presidential proclamations. The statutory citation refers to the *Statutes at Large*. (*See § 9.72, Excerpt from the Statutes at Large.*)

The Statutes at Large are hardbound books in which each public law appears sequentially in the order it was signed by the president and assigned a public-law number. Constitutional amendments, private laws, concurrent resolutions, and presidential proclamations appear in separate sections after public laws. There are also popular name and subject indices.

One or more volumes are published annually and are available through the Government Printing Office (GPO). The volumes published for each year have a single volume number associated with them. For example, the 105th Congress, first session, coincides with Volume 111, Parts 1, 2, and 3 of the Statutes at Large. Continuing the example, P.L. 105-1 appears in Volume 111 on page 3, Part 1; its statutory citation is 111 Stat. 3.

The Statutes at Large are important for several reasons. Congress by law (*2 U.S.C. § 285b*) has provided that the Statutes at Large are "legal evidence of laws, concurrent resolutions . . . proclamations by the President and proposed or ratified amendments to the Constitution of the United States therein contained, in all the courts of the United States. . . ." This provision of law states that the Statutes at Large are *positive law*; that is, recognized as the determinative text of law by governmental authority. Also, bills and joint resolutions may need to be drafted to amend statutes, as explained below. (*See U.S. Code.*)

The Statutes at Large are found in federal depository libraries, law libraries, and other special libraries. They are also now available for selected years on GPO's Federal Digital System <*http://fdsys.gov*>, under "Collections," select "Statutes at Large," and from private entities such as HeinOnline.

United States Code

Following the assignment of a public-law number and statutory citation, and the publication of a slip law, the House of Representatives' Office of Law Revision Counsel, working largely under the auspices of the Speaker of the House, organizes those public laws that are "general and permanent" into the *United States Code*, popularly referred to as the *U.S. Code* or just the *Code*. (*See § 9.73.*) Unlike the sequential organization scheme of the Statutes at Large, all laws in the U.S. Code are organized by subject matter. The user can readily understand what is current law by checking the Code; all cumulative changes in federal law are reflected in the Code.

The U.S. Code is divided into fifty-one subject *titles*, and each title is divided into *sections*. Sections in a title might be grouped as *subtitles*, *chapters*, *subchapters*, *parts*, *subparts*, or *divisions*. Some titles also have *appendices*. The Office of the Law Revision Counsel has proposed adding four new titles to the U.S. Code: Title 52, Voting and Elections; Title 53, Small Business; Title 54, National Park System; and Title 55, Environment. (See "Codification Legislation of the Office" on the Law Revision Counsel's web site at <*http://uscode.house.gov*>.)

Those titles enacted into positive law by Congress are legal evidence of the law contained in those titles (*1 U.S.C. § 204*). In legislative drafting, amendments to existing law are drafted to positive law, which explains why some legislation amends statutes while other legislation amends the U.S. Code.

The subjects covered by the fifty-one titles of the U.S. Code, with positive law titles so far enacted indicated by an asterisk (*), are as follows:

* 1. General Provisions
2. The Congress
* 3. The President
* 4. Flag and Seal, Seat of Government, and the States
* 5. Government Organization and Employees
6. Surety Bonds (repealed by the enactment of Title 31)
7. Agriculture
8. Aliens and Nationality
* 9. Arbitration
* 10. Armed Forces; and Appendix
* 11. Bankruptcy; and Appendix
12. Banks and Banking
* 13. Census
* 14. Coast Guard
15. Commerce and Trade
16. Conservation
* 17. Copyrights
* 18. Crimes and Criminal Procedure; and Appendix
19. Customs Duties
20. Education
21. Food and Drugs
22. Foreign Relations and Intercourse
* 23. Highways

9

24. Hospitals and Asylums
25. Indians
26. Internal Revenue Code; and Appendix
27. Intoxicating Liquors
* 28. Judiciary and Judicial Procedure; and Appendix
29. Labor
30. Mineral Lands and Mining
* 31. Money and Finance
* 32. National Guard
33. Navigation and Navigable Waters
34. Navy (eliminated by the enactment of Title 10)
* 35. Patents
* 36. Patriotic Societies and Observations
* 37. Pay and Allowances of the Uniformed Services
* 38. Veterans' Benefits; and Appendix
* 39. Postal Service
* 40. Public Buildings, Property, and Works; and Appendix
* 41. Public Contracts
42. The Public Health and Welfare
43. Public Lands
* 44. Public Printing and Documents
45. Railroads
* 46. Shipping; and Appendix
47. Telegraphs, Telephones, and Radiotelegraphs
48. Territories and Insular Possessions
* 49. Transportation
50. War and National Defense; and Appendix
* 51. National and Commercial Space Programs

A citation to the U.S. Code might look like this: 5 U.S.C. § 1101, indicating Title 5 and section 1101.

The full U.S. Code is printed once every six years by GPO. The current edition is the 2006 edition. Annual *supplements* bring the Code up-to-date, but the publishing process is slow and use of supplements is cumbersome. *Classification tables* assist the user in identifying which sections of the Code have been amended and where recently enacted laws appear.

The Code, supplements, and classification tables are available online through the web site of the Office of the Law Revision Counsel, <*http://uscode.house.gov*>, and through GPO's Federal Digital System <*http://fdsys.gov*>, under "Collections" select "United States Code."

Thomson West's *United States Code Annotated*, LEXIS Law Publishing's *United States Code Service*, other print services, and online services such as WESTLAW and LEXIS provide current, cumulative versions of the U.S. Code, and add research aids that enhance the usability and utility of their products.

Federal Register

In the course of its lawmaking, Congress often delegates quasi-legislative authority to executive departments and agencies so that they might effectively implement laws and carry out the broader policy determinations that Congress itself made. Departments and agencies engage in rulemaking in exercising this authority. Congress also often empowers departments and agencies with quasi-judicial authority to make adjudications. To guide the overall use of this authority, Congress enacted the Administrative Procedure Act (APA) (5 U.S.C. § 551 et seq. and 5 U.S.C. § 701 et seq.) and the Federal Register Act (44 U.S.C. § 1501 et seq.), so that there is a prescribed process for rulemaking and adjudications and for public notification.

Rulemaking is the term used in APA to describe the process of drafting, making available for public comment, and issuing rules and regulations. Adjudication under APA might involve a range of activities—a dispute involving a regulation between the federal government and an entity (such as a citizen, an organization, or another governmental unit), the issuance or renewal of a license that an agency has been empowered to grant, or permission to undertake an activity regulated by an agency.

Rulemaking, adjudications, and other activities of the executive branch in carrying out laws enacted by Congress, and actions of the president pursuant to statute or on the basis of his constitutional authority, must appear in the *Federal Register* and can be monitored or tracked there. The *Federal Register* contains federal agency regulations, proposed rules and notices, and executive orders and other presidential documents.

A citation to the *Federal Register* might look like this: 64 Fed. Reg. 34109, indicating volume 64 and page 34109. For convenience, the date of the *Federal Register* in which a cited page appears is often also provided. The *Federal Register* is indexed monthly.

The *Federal Register* is published every business day. It is available in print from GPO, and online through GPO's Federal Digital System *<http://fdsys.gov>*, under "Collections" select "Federal Register." The *Federal Register* is also available in electronic formats from a number of sources.

The publisher of the *Federal Register*, the Office of the Federal Register (OFR) within the National Archives and Records Administration (NARA), provides other services as well in carrying out its mission under the Federal Register Act. Because OFR must make documents available one day before publication in the *Federal Register*, it publishes a *List of Federal Register Documents on Public Inspection* on its web site at *<www.archives.gov/federal-register/public-inspection>*. The documents themselves are available for public inspection at OFR's office, 800 North Capitol St., Suite 700, Washington, DC; 202-741-6000. (*See also the web site <http://regulations.gov>.*)

Twice a year, usually in April and October, OFR also publishes the *Unified Agenda*, also called the semiannual regulatory agenda, which lists rules and proposed rules that federal agencies expect to issue in the following six months. This document is also available in print from GPO and online through GPO's Federal Digital System *<http://fdsys.gov>*, under "Collections," then select "Unified Agenda."

9

Code of Federal Regulations

Just as the U.S. Code provides a subject arrangement of general and permanent federal laws, the *Code of Federal Regulations* (CFR) contains a subject arrangement of general and permanent rules and regulations published in the *Federal Register* and promulgated by federal executive departments and agencies. (Title 3 of the CFR cumulates executive orders, proclamations, and other presidential administrative orders.) Its fifty titles each cover a subject area; the CFR and U.S. Code titles, however, do not correspond to each other. Most CFR titles are further subdivided into *chapters* (usually coinciding with an agency), *parts*, and *sections*, and there also exist *subchapters* and *subparts*.

A citation to the CFR might look like this: 20 C.F.R. 404.1520, indicating Title 20, part 404, and section 1520.

Unlike the U.S. Code, revision of each CFR title occurs annually on a schedule approximately as follows:

- Titles 1–16, as of January 1
- Titles 17–27, as of April 1
- Titles 28–41, as of July 1
- Titles 42–50, as of October 1

To assist the user between revisions, there is the *List of CFR Sections Affected* (LSA), which shows amendments published in the *Federal Register* and not yet incorporated into the appropriate, revised CFR title. The LSA is published quarterly and cumulates amendments to a title until that title is next revised. Available online at GPO's Federal Digital System *<http://fdsys.gov>*, under "Collections," select "Code of Federal Regulations," then select "List of Sections Affected."

The CFR is available online at GPO's Federal Digital System *<http://fdsys.gov>*, under "Collections," select "Code of Federal Regulations."

§ 9.80 Chapter Summary and Discussion Questions

There are four types of legislation, parallel in the House and Senate: bills, joint resolutions, concurrent resolutions, and simple resolutions. Bills and joint resolutions are used to make law, and concurrent resolutions are used for joint actions of the House and Senate internal to Congress. Simple resolutions are used within one house of Congress. As a piece of legislation moves through the legislative process, it is often amended to incorporate new, changed, or deleted text.

Committees also publish committee prints for their own use and committee reports to present recommendations to their parent chamber. Chamber publications might take the form of a House Document or a Senate Document, or they might be undesignated. While the *Congressional Record* is the verbatim transcript of House and Senate proceedings, the official record of each chamber is its journal. Government documents, telephone recordings, and web sites can be used to track legislative information and identify congressional and legislative documents.

Laws are published first as slip laws and then codified into the Statutes at Large and the United States Code. Rulemaking reflecting quasi-legislative powers delegated to the executive may be monitored in the Federal Register and is codified in the Code of Federal Regulations.

Discussion Questions

- Name three purposes of legislation for which a member of Congress would choose the form of a bill.
- Name one purpose of legislation for which a member of Congress would choose the form of a joint resolution.
- Name one purpose of legislation for which a member of Congress would choose the form of a concurrent resolution.
- Name one purpose of legislation for which a member of Congress would choose the form of a simple resolution.
- At what point in the legislative process does a bill or joint resolution become designated as "An Act"?

- When in the legislative process would a measure be said to be engrossed? When in the legislative process is a measure enrolled?
- A measure is printed when it is introduced. In the first chamber to consider it, what are two other times in the legislative process that a measure is likely to be reprinted to reflect legislative action?
- Call up GPO's Federal Digital System on the World Wide Web. What is the first year for which congressional bills, congressional reports, the *Congressional Record*, public laws, the Compilation of Presidential Documents, and *Federal Register* are available? How often is each database updated?
- Identify three government documents or government web sites where you could find meetings scheduled by congressional committees.
- If both houses of Congress have cleared a bill for the president's consideration, what place or places would you monitor to track its presentation to the White House and its status there?
- Where could you find a new public law number?
- What might be some reasons a person would one choose to look up a law in the Statutes at Large? What might be some reasons she would choose the U.S. Code?

Chapter Ten

Congressional Documents: Committee, Chamber, Party, and Administrative Publications

Analysis

§ 10.00 Introduction

The House and Senate produce a number of official publications related to the legislative and administrative functions of their chambers. These publications include ones dealing with rules and procedures, anticipated and past legislative activities, committee matters, and chamber proceedings.

This chapter identifies and describes official committee, chamber, party, and administrative publications, and provides information on online sources where applicable.

Links to many of the documents discussed in this chapter can be found online: <*CDDocs.com*>.

§ 10.10 Committee Documents

House and Senate committees prepare a variety of documents in the process of doing their work. In the conduct of their legislative function, committees publish hearings, drafts of legislation, reports accompanying legislation, reports summarizing their legislative activities over a single Congress, and committee calendars. Within their investigative and oversight roles, they prepare committee prints and reports. Committees also prepare administrative documents on their internal affairs.

Committee Calendars

A committee calendar provides a comprehensive record of a committee's actions during one Congress. All committees *except* the following prepare calendars: the House and Senate Appropriations Committees, the House Administration Committee, the House Committee on Standards of Official Conduct, and the Senate Select Ethics Committee. Many committees publish a calendar at the end of each session; all publish a final calendar at the end of a Congress. Final calendars are cumulative, superseding any interim calendars prepared during a Congress. Some committees post their calendars on their web sites.

Each committee calendar presents similar information, although formats vary. Some present information in a summary fashion; others present detailed information on most or all aspects of a committee's work. Some committees present information arranged by subcommittee; some prepare it by topic; some arrange it chronologically. Some committees prepare entries in several ways within a calendar, such as by subcommittee, by topic, and in chronological order. All committee calendars provide committee and subcommittee membership lists. (*See § 10.11, Excerpt from a House Committee Calendar.*)

Committee Histories

Numerous committees have prepared histories of their panels and published them as official committee documents. Some histories are simple overviews listing former members and briefly describing selected legislation considered by a committee. Other histories have several hundred detailed pages. Some committees prepare histories at the time of historic milestones, such as anniversaries of their organization for fifty, one hundred, or two hundred years. Some panels prepared histories at the time of the 1989 bicentennial of Congress. Most committee histories have not been updated since their original publication.

Many of these histories are available from the respective House or Senate committee. Some com-

§ 10.11

Excerpt from a House Committee Calendar

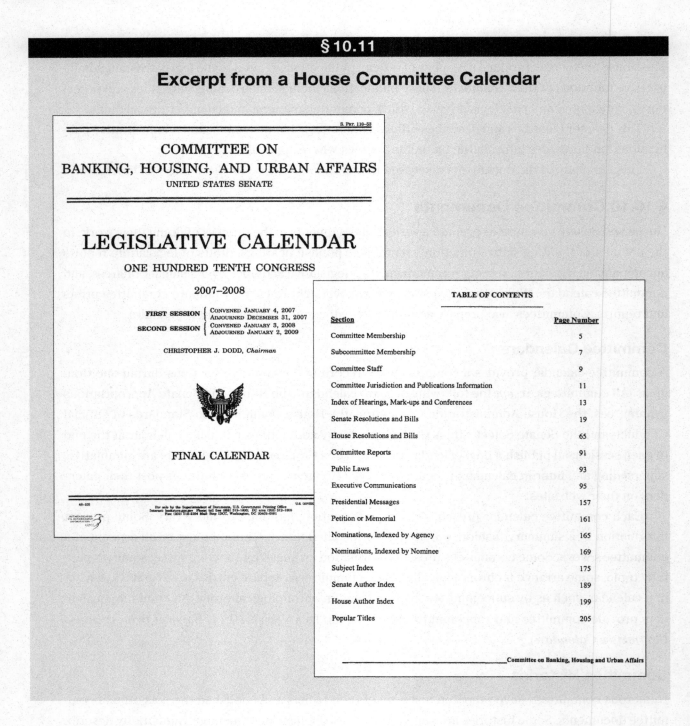

S. Prt. 110–53

COMMITTEE ON
BANKING, HOUSING, AND URBAN AFFAIRS
UNITED STATES SENATE

LEGISLATIVE CALENDAR

ONE HUNDRED TENTH CONGRESS

2007–2008

FIRST SESSION { Convened January 4, 2007 / Adjourned December 31, 2007

SECOND SESSION { Convened January 3, 2008 / Adjourned January 2, 2009

CHRISTOPHER J. DODD, *Chairman*

FINAL CALENDAR

48–105

U.S. GOVER

For sale by the Superintendent of Documents, U.S. Government Printing Office
Internet: bookstore.gpo.gov Phone: toll free (866) 512–1800; DC area (202) 512–1800
Fax: (202) 512–2104 Mail: Stop IDCC, Washington, DC 20402–0001

AUTHENTICATED U.S. GOVERNMENT INFORMATION GPO

TABLE OF CONTENTS

Committee on Banking, Housing and Urban Affairs

mittees provide excerpts on their web sites. Some histories are available from the Government Printing Office (GPO) and depository libraries.

House Committee Histories. The following is a list of published House committee histories:

- *Committee on Agriculture, 150th Anniversary*, printed as H. Doc. 91-350
- *180 Years of Service: A Brief History of the Committee on Interstate and Foreign Commerce*, committee print from the 94th Congress
- *History of the Committee on the Judiciary*, printed as H. Doc. 109-153

- *Historical Information of the Committee on Resources and Its Predecessor Committees, 1807–2002*, printed as Comm. Print No. 107–H
- *A History of the Committee on Rules, 1789–1981*, committee print from the 97th Congress
- *Toward the Endless Frontier: History of the Committee on Science and Technology, 1959–1979*, committee print from the 96th Congress
- *History and Accomplishments of the Permanent Select Committee on Small Business, 77th to 92nd Congress*, printed as H. Doc. 93-197
- *History of House Committees Considering Veterans' Legislation*, committee print from the 101st Congress
- *The Committee on Ways and Means: A Bicentennial History, 1789–1989*, committee print from the 101st Congress

Senate Committee Histories. The following is a list of published Senate committee histories:

- *United States Senate Committee on Agriculture, Nutrition, and Forestry, 1825–1998*, printed as S. Doc. 105-24
- *United States Senate Committee on Appropriations, 1867–2008*, printed as S. Doc. 110-14
- *Committee on Banking and Currency, United States Senate: 50th Anniversary, 1913–1963*, printed as S. Doc. 88-15
- *Committee on the Budget, 1974–2006*, printed as S. Doc. 109-24
- *Brief History of the Senate Committee on Commerce, Science, and Transportation and Its Activities Since 1947*, printed as S. Doc. 95-93
- *History of the Committee on Energy and Natural Resources, 1816–1988, United States Senate*, printed as S. Doc. 100-46
- *History of the Committee on Environment and Public Works, United States Senate*, printed as S. Doc. 100-45
- *History of the Committee on Finance*, printed as S. Doc. 97-5
- *Committee on Foreign Relations, Millennium Edition, 1816–2000*, printed as S. Doc. 105-28
- *Committee on Government Operations, United States Senate, 50th Anniversary, 1921–1971*, printed as S. Doc. 92-31
- *History of the Committee on the Judiciary, 1816–1981*, printed as S. Doc. 97-18
- *History of the Committee on Labor and Human Resources, United States Senate, 1869–1979*, printed as S. Doc. 96-71
- *History of the Committee on Rules and Administration*, printed as S. Doc. 96-27

Committee Prints

Committee prints represent a catchall form of publication and are often used to provide information not directly related to legislative activity. Following are examples of documents usually designated as committee prints: committee and subcommittee membership lists, committee rules, staff studies (including those prepared by the Congressional Research Service), and compilations of laws within a committee's jurisdiction or closely related to its jurisdiction. Draft legislation to be considered in markup is also often prepared as a committee print. (*See § 10.12, Example of a Committee Print.*)

§ 10.12

Example of a Committee Print

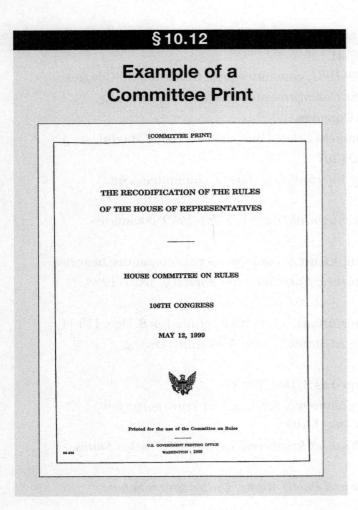

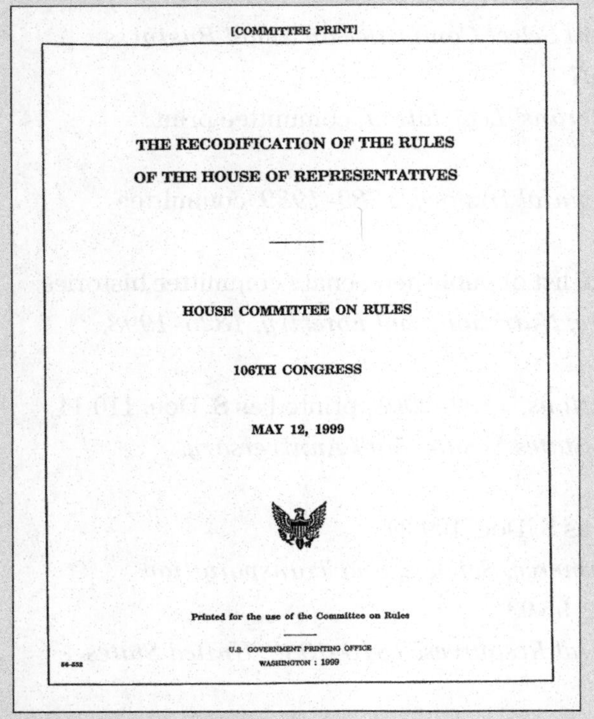

[COMMITTEE PRINT]

THE RECODIFICATION OF THE RULES OF THE HOUSE OF REPRESENTATIVES

HOUSE COMMITTEE ON RULES

106TH CONGRESS

MAY 12, 1999

Printed for the use of the Committee on Rules

U.S. GOVERNMENT PRINTING OFFICE
WASHINGTON : 1999

Some prints are numbered; others are not. The decision to number a print and the numbering system used is left to each committee. Committee prints are available from the respective committee; some are available from the GPO's Federal Digital System, at *<http://fdsys.gov>*, look under "Collections" for "Committee Prints." Also see *<CDDocs.com>*.

Committee Rules

In every Congress, the House Committee on Rules and the Senate Committee on Rules and Administration issue documents that compile the rules of procedure for all committees in their respective chamber. Although committee rules appear in the *Congressional Record*, and are also usually printed by each committee as a committee print and appear on the committee's web site, the House and Senate compilations are useful because all the rules appear in a single publication.

The House compilation for the 111th Congress was published as a committee print by the Committee on Rules. The Senate compilation for the 111th Congress was published as S. Doc. 111-3, prepared by the Committee on Rules and Administration. The documents can be obtained from the issuing committee. Committees' rules are normally also available on their web sites.

Hearings

Witnesses present oral and written testimony at hearings, and are questioned by committee members and, occasionally, by committee staff. Statistical data, correspondence, written answers to questions, and other information can also be submitted by committee members and witnesses for inclusion in the hearing record. Hearings might be broadcast or webcast.

Stenographers are always present at committee and subcommittee hearings. They record transcripts of all the proceedings. The transcripts are then edited by committee staff. Hearing records are generally published by committees, but they are often not available until months after a hearing or series of hearings is held. However, committees maintain transcripts of hearings in the committee offices. The transcripts are usually available for inspection, often the day following a hearing.

Many committees put witness testimony on their web sites soon after a hearing. Many committees are posting transcripts as well, and some make audio or video recordings available online. Although most witnesses provide written testimony to a committee, printed copies may be difficult to obtain before a hearing transcript is printed (unless one attends the hearing). However, for executive-branch witnesses, the respective agency web site, or the Office of Management and Budget web site, often provides the full text of agency witnesses' testimony. If a witness is representing a private organization, testimony may be posted on that organization's web site.

House committees use House stenographers. Transcripts may be purchased when committees grant sale permission. Availability and cost information may be obtained from the Office of Official Reporters, at 202-225-2627.

Senate committees make use of reporting services to transcribe their hearings. Copies may be purchased directly from reporting services, when committees grant sale permission. Individual committees can provide information on the reporting services.

If printed, hearings are available from the respective committee. However, they are generally printed in limited quantities. Printed hearings are also often available online at GPO's Federal Digital System, at *<http://fdsys.gov>*, and look under "Collections" for "Congressional Hearings." Also see *<CDDocs.com>*. (*LexisNexis Congressional is a source for nearly all committee documents. Information can be found at the Lexis-Nexis web site, <http://web.lexis-nexis.com/congcom>.*)

House Committee Oversight Plans

House committees are required to prepare oversight plans and provide them to the Committee on House Administration and the Committee on Oversight and Government Reform. The Committee on Oversight and Government Reform then compiles all the submissions into one publication. The oversight plans provide useful information about issues that a committee intends to study during a Congress. The compilation of 111th Congress oversight plans was published as H. Rept. 111-69. (*House committees' oversight plans are often available on the committees' own web sites.*)

Reports

There are several types of committee reports: those that accompany legislation, those that result from oversight or investigative activity, those from conference committees, and those reflecting the activities of committees over the course of a Congress. (*See § 6.60, Committee Reports, for an extensive discussion of committee reports on legislation and their required contents; and § 6.280, Conference Committees, for a discussion of conference reports and joint explanatory statements.*)

10

An activity report published at the conclusion of a Congress provides a narrative description of a committee's actions over the course of a Congress. These reports usually include summaries of legislation referred to or acted on by the committee, hearings held by the committee and its subcommittees, oversight activities, and the titles of documents issued by the committee. (*See § 10.13, Example of a House Legislative Activity Report.*) Senate committee activity reports include information on nominations and treaties referred and considered.

All reports are designated *H. Rept.* or *S. Rept.* to show whether they are House or Senate committee reports. They are numbered sequentially in the order they are filed with a committee's parent chamber. For example, H. Rept. 112-11 was prepared by a House committee in the 112th Congress and was the 11th report filed by a committee with the House. If two committees filed legislative reports on the same legislation, they would carry the same report number and be designated Part I

§ 10.13

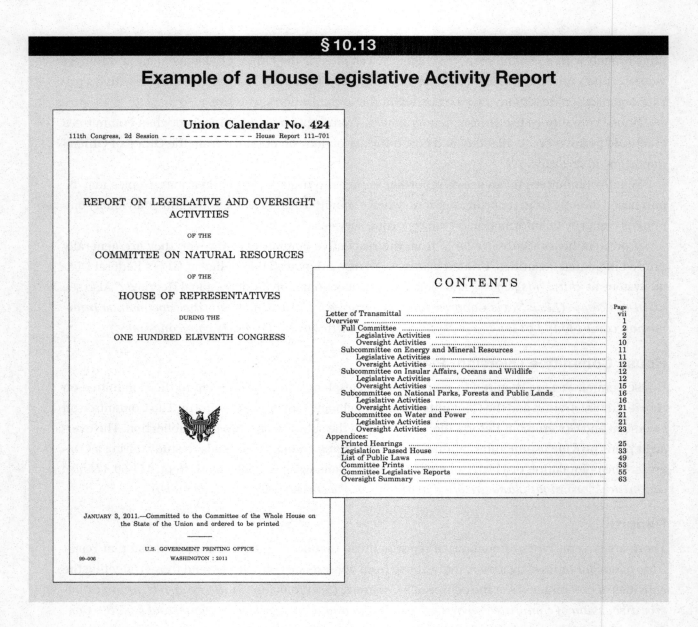

Example of a House Legislative Activity Report

Union Calendar No. 424

111th Congress, 2d Session - - - - - - - - - - - - House Report 111–701

REPORT ON LEGISLATIVE AND OVERSIGHT ACTIVITIES

OF THE

COMMITTEE ON NATURAL RESOURCES

OF THE

HOUSE OF REPRESENTATIVES

DURING THE

ONE HUNDRED ELEVENTH CONGRESS

JANUARY 3, 2011.—Committed to the Committee of the Whole House on the State of the Union and ordered to be printed

U.S. GOVERNMENT PRINTING OFFICE

99–006 WASHINGTON : 2011

CONTENTS

and Part II. Committee reports are available through legislative information databases, including GPO's Federal Digital System, at <*http://fdsys.gov*>, and look under "Collections" for "Congressional Reports." Also see <*CDDocs.com*>.

§ 10.20 Floor Documents

The House and Senate each publish documents related to rules and procedures, anticipated legislation, and chamber proceedings.

Calendars of the United States House of Representatives and History of Legislation ("House Calendar")

The *Calendars of the United States House of Representatives and History of Legislation*, more commonly (if confusingly) referred to as the *House Calendar*, contains a history of each House and

§ 10.21

Calendars of the United States House of Representatives and History of Legislation

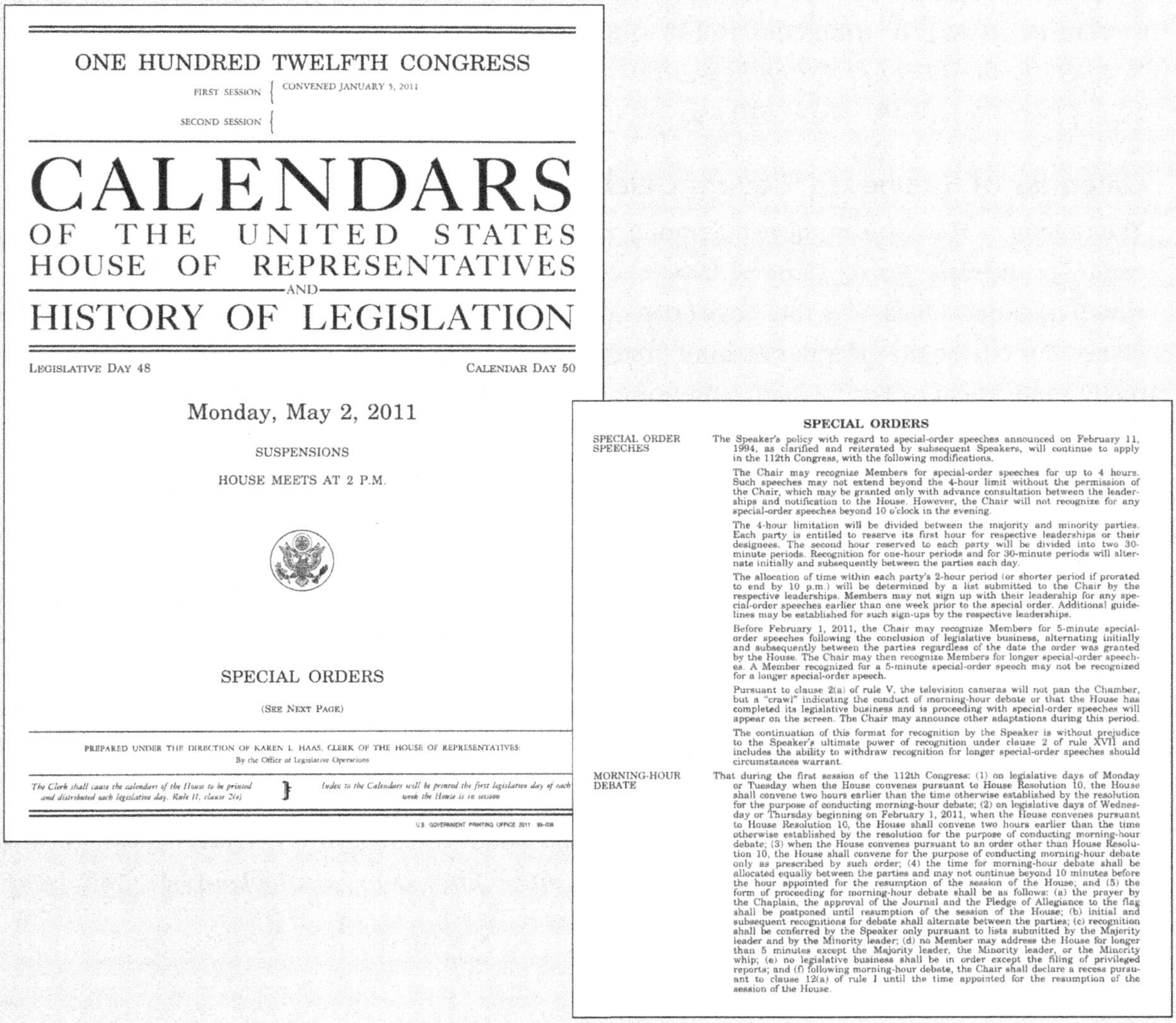

ONE HUNDRED TWELFTH CONGRESS

FIRST SESSION { CONVENED JANUARY 5, 2011

SECOND SESSION {

CALENDARS

OF THE UNITED STATES HOUSE OF REPRESENTATIVES

AND

HISTORY OF LEGISLATION

LEGISLATIVE DAY 48 CALENDAR DAY 50

Monday, May 2, 2011

SUSPENSIONS

HOUSE MEETS AT 2 P.M.

SPECIAL ORDERS

(SEE NEXT PAGE)

PREPARED UNDER THE DIRECTION OF KAREN L. HAAS, CLERK OF THE HOUSE OF REPRESENTATIVES:
By the Office of Legislative Operations

The Clerk shall cause the calendars of the House to be printed and distributed each legislative day. Rule II, clause 2(e) } *Index to the Calendars will be printed the first legislative day of each week the House is in session*

U.S. GOVERNMENT PRINTING OFFICE 2011 99-038

SPECIAL ORDERS

SPECIAL ORDER SPEECHES

The Speaker's policy with regard to special-order speeches announced on February 11, 1994, as clarified and reiterated by subsequent Speakers, will continue to apply in the 112th Congress, with the following modifications.

The Chair may recognize Members for special-order speeches for up to 4 hours. Such speeches may not extend beyond the 4-hour limit without the permission of the Chair, which may be granted only with advance consultation between the leaderships and notification to the House. However, the Chair will not recognize for any special-order speeches beyond 10 o'clock in the evening.

The 4-hour limitation will be divided between the majority and minority parties. Each party is entitled to reserve its first hour for respective leaderships or their designees. The second hour reserved to each party will be divided into two 30-minute periods. Recognition for one-hour periods and for 30-minute periods will alternate initially and subsequently between the parties each day.

The allocation of time within each party's 2-hour period (or shorter period if prorated to end by 10 p.m.) will be determined by a list submitted to the Chair by the respective leaderships. Members may not sign up with their leadership for any special-order speeches earlier than one week prior to the special order. Additional guidelines may be established for such sign-ups by the respective leaderships.

Before February 1, 2011, the Chair may recognize Members for 5-minute special-order speeches following the conclusion of legislative business, alternating initially and subsequently between the parties regardless of the date the order was granted by the House. The Chair may then recognize Members for longer special-order speeches. A Member recognized for a 5-minute special-order speech may not be recognized for a longer special-order speech.

Pursuant to clause 2(a) of rule V, the television cameras will not pan the Chamber, but a "crawl" indicating the conduct of morning-hour debate or that the House has completed its legislative business and is proceeding with special-order speeches will appear on the screen. The Chair may announce other adaptations during this period.

The continuation of this format for recognition by the Speaker is without prejudice to the Speaker's ultimate power of recognition under clause 2 of rule XVII and includes the ability to withdraw recognition for longer special-order speeches should circumstances warrant.

MORNING-HOUR DEBATE

That during the first session of the 112th Congress: (1) on legislative days of Monday or Tuesday when the House convenes pursuant to House Resolution 10, the House shall convene two hours earlier than the time otherwise established by the resolution for the purpose of conducting morning-hour debate; (2) on legislative days of Wednesday or Thursday beginning on February 1, 2011, when the House convenes pursuant to House Resolution 10, the House shall convene two hours earlier than the time otherwise established by the resolution for the purpose of conducting morning-hour debate; (3) when the House convenes pursuant to an order other than House Resolution 10, the House shall convene for the purpose of conducting morning-hour debate only as prescribed by such order; (4) the time for morning-hour debate shall be allocated equally between the parties and may not continue beyond 10 minutes before the hour appointed for the resumption of the session of the House; and (5) the form of proceeding for morning-hour debate shall be as follows: (a) the prayer by the Chaplain, the approval of the Journal and the Pledge of Allegiance to the flag shall be postponed until resumption of the session of the House; (b) initial and subsequent recognitions for debate shall alternate between the parties; (c) recognition shall be conferred by the Speaker only pursuant to lists submitted by the Majority leader and by the Minority leader; (d) no Member may address the House for longer than 5 minutes except the Majority leader, the Minority leader, or the Minority whip; (e) no legislative business shall be in order except the filing of privileged reports; and (f) following morning-hour debate, the Chair shall declare a recess pursuant to clause 12(a) of rule I until the time appointed for the resumption of the session of the House.

10

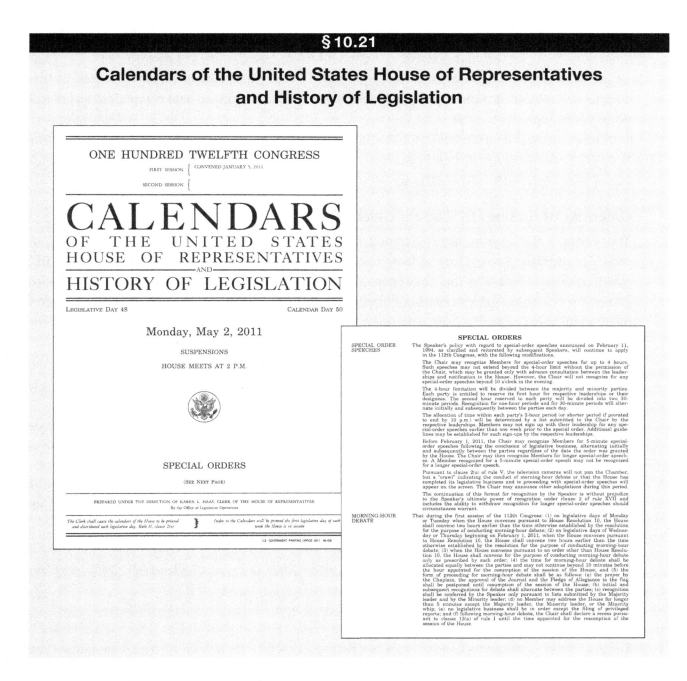

Senate measure once it has been reported from committee, otherwise placed on a House or Senate calendar, or acted on by the House or Senate, and compiles all the calendars published by the House: the House Calendar, Private Calendar, Discharge Calendar, and Union Calendar. A list of motions to discharge committees that have received 218 signatures and are awaiting floor action is included. Also provided is a list of public and private laws, cross-referenced to their corresponding measure numbers. Additional sections contain other useful information. A chart depicting the status of appropriations, tax, and other key budget legislation is displayed on the back page of the House Calendar.

The Monday version of the House Calendar contains information on measures that have completed the conference committee process, an alphabetical index of the short titles of pending measures, and a subject index of House and Senate measures listed in the House Calendar. (*See § 10.21, Calendars of the United States House of Representatives and History of Legislation.*)

A final calendar is published at the end of each Congress; it contains a list of measures that became law, measures vetoed by the president, and statistical workload data comparing the present Congress with prior Congresses.

The calendar is distributed to House offices each day the House is in session. (*Available online at GPO's Federal Digital System, at <http://fdsys.gov>, and look under "Collections" for "Congressional Calendars." Also see <CDDocs.com>.*)

Calendar of Business ("Senate Calendar")

The *Calendar of Business*, more commonly referred to as the *Senate Calendar*, the *Legislative Calendar*, or the *Calendar of General Orders*, contains a list called "General Orders, under Rule VIII," which records all measures that have been reported and any bills or joint resolutions that have been placed directly on the calendar without first being referred to committee. The order number reflects the chronological order in which a measure has been placed on the calendar. (*See § 10.22, Senate Calendar of Business.*)

Included in the Senate Calendar on the general order list are the measure's number, sponsor, and title. Information on when the measure was placed on the calendar and how it was placed there is also included.

One of the most useful parts of the Senate Calendar appears on the inside front cover. The texts of operative or pending unanimous consent agreements are reprinted here. (*See § 6.200, Time Agreements and Motions to Proceed on the Senate Floor.*)

The Senate Calendar shows the days the Senate was in session, and contains a list of senators and the year in which each senator's term expires, membership lists on Senate and joint committees, and a list of bills sent to conference, with the names of the conferees.

The Senate Calendar is distributed to all Senate offices each day the Senate is in session. (*Available online at GPO's Federal Digital System, at <http://fdsys.gov>, and look under "Collections" for "Congressional Calendars." Also see <CDDocs.com>.*)

Executive Calendar

The *Executive Calendar* is used to track the Senate's executive business, such as nominations and treaties. It lists treaties, nominations, and executive resolutions that have been reported by a committee or placed on the calendar. Unanimous consent agreements on treaties or nominations are also carried in the Executive Calendar. (*See § 10.23, Senate Executive Calendar.*)

The Executive Calendar is distributed to all Senate offices each day the Senate is in session. (*Available online on the Senate web site, <http://senate.gov>.*)

Congressional Record

The *Congressional Record* is a substantially verbatim account of daily proceedings of the House and Senate. It consists of five principal parts: House floor proceedings, Senate floor proceedings, Extensions of Remarks, Daily Digest, and time and agenda for the next meeting of the House and Senate.

§ 10.22

Senate Calendar of Business

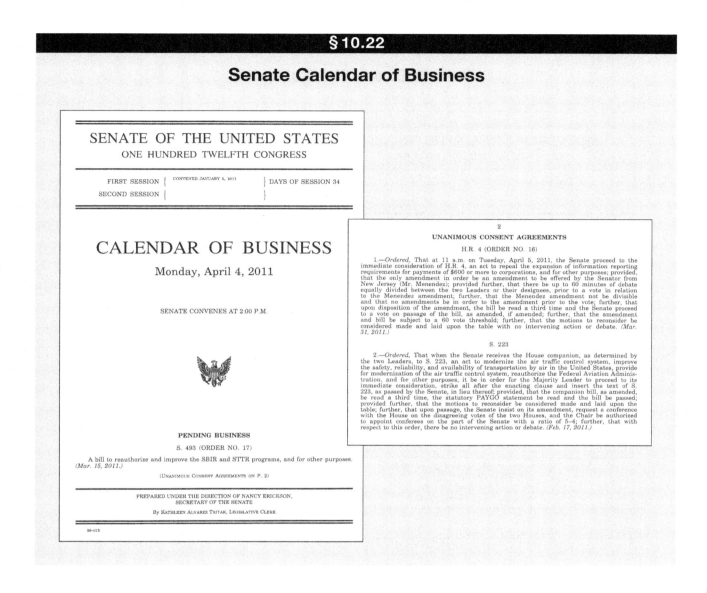

SENATE OF THE UNITED STATES

ONE HUNDRED TWELFTH CONGRESS

FIRST SESSION { CONVENED JANUARY 5, 2011 } DAYS OF SESSION 34

SECOND SESSION { }

CALENDAR OF BUSINESS

Monday, April 4, 2011

SENATE CONVENES AT 2:00 P.M.

PENDING BUSINESS

S. 493 (ORDER NO. 17)

A bill to reauthorize and improve the SBIR and STTR programs, and for other purposes. *(Mar. 15, 2011.)*

(UNANIMOUS CONSENT AGREEMENTS ON P. 2)

PREPARED UNDER THE DIRECTION OF NANCY ERICKSON,
SECRETARY OF THE SENATE

BY KATHLEEN ALVAREZ TRITAK, LEGISLATIVE CLERK

99–015

2

UNANIMOUS CONSENT AGREEMENTS

H.R. 4 (ORDER NO. 16)

1.—*Ordered*, That at 11 a.m. on Tuesday, April 5, 2011, the Senate proceed to the immediate consideration of H.R. 4, an act to repeal the expansion of information reporting requirements for payments of $600 or more to corporations, and for other purposes; provided, that the only amendment in order be an amendment to be offered by the Senator from New Jersey (Mr. Menendez); provided further, that there be up to 60 minutes of debate equally divided between the two Leaders or their designees, prior to a vote in relation to the Menendez amendment; further, that the Menendez amendment not be divisible and that no amendments be in order to the amendment prior to the vote; further, that upon disposition of the amendment, the bill be read a third time and the Senate proceed to a vote on passage of the bill, as amended, if amended; further, that the amendment and bill be subject to a 60 vote threshold; further, that the motions to reconsider be considered made and laid upon the table with no intervening action or debate. *(Mar. 31, 2011.)*

S. 223

2.—*Ordered*, That when the Senate receives the House companion, as determined by the two Leaders, to S. 223, an act to modernize the air traffic control system, improve the safety, reliability, and availability of transportation by air in the United States, provide for modernization of the air traffic control system, reauthorize the Federal Aviation Administration, and for other purposes, it be in order for the Majority Leader to proceed to its immediate consideration, strike all after the enacting clause and insert the text of S. 223, as passed by the Senate, in lieu thereof; provided, that the companion bill, as amended, be read a third time, the statutory PAYGO statement be read and the bill be passed; provided further, that the motions to reconsider be considered made and laid upon the table; further, that upon passage, the Senate insist on its amendment, request a conference with the House on the disagreeing votes of the two Houses, and the Chair be authorized to appoint conferees on the part of the Senate with a ratio of 5–4; further, that with respect to this order, there be no intervening action or debate. *(Feb. 17, 2011.)*

Floor proceedings appear first. On alternate days, the Senate and then the House proceedings appear first. House pages are preceded by an *H* and Senate pages are preceded by an *S*. The pages are numbered consecutively from the previous day's House and Senate pages. Both sections are generally arranged chronologically for the day. Both sections contain floor debate, the text of amendments, and vote tallies. The numbers and official titles of measures introduced are provided in both sections. Amendments submitted for printing and the addition and withdrawal of cosponsors follow the lists of new measures introduced. Floor schedule announcements appear in both sections. Nearly all conference reports are printed in the House section. *(See § 11.10, How to Follow Floor Proceedings in the House; and § 11.20, How to Follow Floor Proceedings in the Senate.)*

The next section of the *Congressional Record*, called Extensions of Remarks, has pages that are preceded by an *E*. Pages are numbered consecutively from the previous day, and contain statements by members (usually House members) on a wide range of topics. Members receive permission on the floor to insert statements into this section.

§ 10.23

Senate Executive Calendar

SENATE OF THE UNITED STATES
ONE HUNDRED TWELFTH CONGRESS

FIRST SESSION { CONVENED JANUARY 5, 2011

SECOND SESSION {

EXECUTIVE CALENDAR

Monday, May 2, 2011

UNANIMOUS CONSENT AGREEMENT
Roy Bale Dalton, Jr. (Cal. No. 74)
Kevin Hunter Sharp (Cal. No. 76)

Ordered, That at 4:30 p.m. on Monday, May 2, 2011, the Senate proceed to executive session to consider the following nominations: Roy Bale Dalton, Jr., of Florida, to be United States District Judge for the Middle District of Florida, and Kevin Hunter Sharp, of Tennessee, to be United States District Judge for the Middle District of Tennessee; provided further, that there be one hour for debate equally divided in the usual form; that upon the use or yielding back of time, the nomination of Roy Bale Dalton, Jr. be confirmed and the Senate proceed to vote without any intervening action or debate on the nomination of Kevin Hunter Sharp; that the motions to reconsider be considered made and laid upon the table with no intervening action or debate; that no further motions be in order to any of the nominations; that the President be immediately notified of the Senate's actions and the Senate resume legislative session.

(April 14, 2011.)

PREPARED UNDER THE DIRECTION OF NANCY ERICKSON,
SECRETARY OF THE SENATE
http://www.senate.gov/ExecutiveCalendar
By Michelle Haynes, Executive Clerk

Issue No. 35

The Daily Digest appears at the end of the *Congressional Record*, and its pages, consecutive from the previous day's Daily Digest, are preceded by a *D*. The Daily Digest is the key to each *Congressional Record* and the place to begin a review. The first section of the Daily Digest is labeled *Senate* and the second, *House*. House and Senate floor proceedings are summarized in the appropriate part of the Daily Digest. Also listed are the sequential numbers of measures introduced that day in each chamber, treaties and nominations received by the Senate, presidential and executive communications received in each chamber, and conferees appointed in each chamber. Individual statements by members are not indexed in the Daily Digest.

In the House and Senate sections of the Daily Digest is a summary of each chamber's committee and subcommittee activities that day. Committees are listed alphabetically, with subcommittees listed under their parent committee. Joint and conference committees and new public-law numbers are also listed. The next day's committee schedules follow the public laws. In the last issue of a week's *Congressional Record*, the next week's floor and committee schedules are printed.

The time and agenda for the next meeting of the House and Senate are listed on the back page of the *Congressional Record*. An index, by House member, of Extensions of Remarks for the day also appears on the back page.

In the course of a week, preceding the Daily Digest, are House and Senate membership lists, each member's office number, and committee rosters. The advance (long-range) Senate committee schedule also appears in these pages. Periodically, the *Congressional Record* prints committees' foreign travel reports and lobby registrations filed with the clerk of the House and the secretary of the Senate. Soon after the end of a month, a *Résumé of Congressional Activity* (summary statistics on the work of the Congress) is printed. (*See § 5.33, Résumé of Congressional Activity, 111th Congress (2009–2011).*)

A noncumulative, biweekly index of the *Congressional Record* is published, about a month after the period covered. The index is organized alphabetically by subject, and under each member's name is a list of measures introduced by that member. A history of bills and resolutions is organized by number at the end of each index.

Permanent bound volumes of the *Congressional Record* are published, but publication lags by several years. In addition, the bound volumes are repaginated sequentially and without the chamber letter designation. A cumulative subject and name index and a history of all measures introduced or acted upon appears in one bound index volume, and a reprint of the Daily Digests of a session and a cumulative index to them appear in a second bound index volume.

Publication of the *Congressional Record* began in 1873. Predecessor publications were the *Annals of Congress* (*The Debate and Proceedings in the Congress of the United States*), which was published from 1789 to 1824; the *Register of Debates*, which was published from 1824 to 1837; and the *Congressional Globe*, which was published from 1833 to 1873. These documents, plus the *Congressional Record* for 1873–1877 are available online from the Library of Congress in "A Century of Lawmaking For a New Nation," *<http://memory.loc.gov/ammem/amlaw>*.

The *Congressional Record* is provided to each congressional office. (*Available online at GPO's Federal Digital System, at <http://fdsys.gov>, and look under "Collections" for "Congressional Records." Also see <CDDocs.com>.*)

House Journal and Senate Journal

The *Journal of the House of Representatives of the United States* is the official record of the House, and the *Journal of the Senate of the United States of America* is the official record of the Senate. A journal for each chamber is required by Article I of the Constitution. The Journals are published on a periodic basis, but at least annually, and they chronicle actions such as bills introduced, amendments offered and agreed to, and votes. The Journals also provide a narrative account of legislative proceedings and contain an alphabetical index. At the beginning of each day, each chamber approves its journal of the preceding day.

The Government Printing Office (GPO) provides copies of the House and Senate Journals to each office, as well as to the Library of Congress and all depository libraries. However, the Journals' contents derive from the *Congressional Record*, so the Journals are of limited practical use. (*The House Journal is available online at GPO's Federal Digital System, at <http://fdsys.gov>, and look under "Collections" for "Journal of the House of Represenatives." Also see <CDDocs.com>.*)

Journal of the Executive Proceedings of the Senate

The *Executive Journal* records the Senate's actions on nominations and treaties—its executive business. Produced by the Senate executive clerk, the Executive Journal is not available for general distribution, although GPO distributes copies to select depository libraries.

§ 10.30 Congressional Rules and Precedents

Rules and procedures can be complicated and cumbersome. Precedents further affect our understanding of the legislative process. The next two sections (*§ 10.40 and § 10.50*) describe the official rules publications that provide definitive information on how the House and Senate operate. The third section (*§ 10.60*) provides a compilation of congressional resources that describe House and Senate procedures in a non-technical format.

§ 10.40 Official Rules Publications of the House

House Rules and Manual

The *Constitution, Jefferson's Manual,* and *Rules of the House of Representatives of the United States,* referred to as the *House Rules and Manual,* governs the House comprehensively. Recodified for the first time in over one hundred years at the beginning of the 106th Congress, the rules themselves describe the selection, powers, and duties of the Speaker and House officials, enumerate the jurisdictions of committees, establish procedures for the House and the Committee of the Whole, prescribe the conduct of representatives, and regulate the House in other ways. Extensive parliamentarian's annotations accompany each rule.

Jefferson's Manual, originally drafted by Thomas Jefferson as president of the Senate while serving as vice president of the United States, supplements House rules to the extent it does not conflict with the rules. The *House Rules and Manual* also contains the Constitution, a list of rules changes from previous Congresses, selections from relevant statutes (such as the Congressional Budget Act), and other provisions governing the House.

The *House Rules and Manual* is generally printed once during each Congress to reflect rules changes adopted at the convening of a Congress and to update the parliamentarian's notes. The edition for each Congress bears a document number from the preceding Congress, because the House typically authorizes the next edition during the preceding Congress. The 111th Congress *House Rules and Manual* was H. Doc. 110-162. (*The 111th Congress House Rules and Manual is available online at GPO's Federal Digital System, at <http://fdsys.gov>, and look under "Collections" for "House Rules Manual." Also see <CDDocs.com>. The House Rules Clerk's Print (see next entry) of House rules for the current Congress is available on the House Rules Committee web site, House Rules Committee web site, <http://rules.house.gov>, and look under "Resources."*)

House Rules Clerk's Print

For each Congress, early in the first session, the clerk of the House issues an unnumbered print containing the rules of the House. This so-called "Clerk's Print" incorporates any rules changes adopted on opening day, and is the first document available containing House rules. No annotations to the rules are included. (*Available online at the House Rules Committee web site, <http://rules.house.gov>, and look under "Resources."*)

House Practice: A Guide to the Rules, Precedents, and Procedures of the House

This volume, commonly referred to as *House Practice*, was compiled by Parliamentarian Emeritus of the House William Holmes Brown, and updated by the House parliamentarian to be current through the 107th Congress. *House Practice* summarizes the most common procedures used by the House and explains their usage in lay language. An update was expected in late 2007.

The book is organized alphabetically by topic and cites other parliamentary reference sources. It is thoroughly indexed. (*Available online at GPO's Federal Digital System, at <http://fdsys.gov>, and look under "Collections" for "House Practice." Also see <CDDocs.com>.*)

Procedure in the House of Representatives (Deschler's)

This single-volume document, referred to as *Deschler's Procedure* (after former House Parliamentarian Lewis Deschler), presents selected precedents from 1959 through 1980. A 1985 supplement covers 1981 through 1984, and a 1987 supplement covers precedents created from 1981 through 1986. *House Practice*, described above, was designed to replace *Deschler's Procedure.*

This document is arranged around topics of procedure, with each chapter divided into broad subtopics. As such, a knowledge of procedure is helpful in navigating the publication.

Deschler's Procedure is out of print. Copies are available for reference at the House Legislative Resource Center, B-106 Cannon House Office Building.

Deschler-Brown Precedents of the U.S. House of Representatives

This multivolume series contains precedents from 1936 to the recent past. Additional volumes are being prepared by the office of the parliamentarian. The first nine volumes are called *Deschler's Precedents of the U.S. House of Representatives*; the volumes thereafter, numbered 10 to 16 as of 2007, are referred to as *Deschler-Brown Precedents*, to acknowledge the work of former Parliamentarian William Holmes Brown. Additional volumes were anticipated in 2011.

The books are organized by topical chapter parallel to those in *Deschler's Procedure.* For many of the topics, the full text of discussion creating or interpreting precedent on the House floor is provided, as well as the page citation from the *Congressional Record.*

Some of these volumes are out of print. Copies are available for reference at the House Legislative Resource Center, B-106 Cannon House Office Building. (*Available online at GPO's Federal Digital System, at <http://fdsys.gov>, and look under "Collections" for "Precedents of the U.S. House of Representatives." The Deschler-Brown Precedents appear under "Deschler's Precedents." Also see <CDDocs.com>.*)

Hinds' and Cannon's Precedents of the U.S. House of Representatives

This multivolume series provides an historical overview of House precedents during the period 1789 to 1936. Volumes 1 through 5 are known as *Hinds' Precedents* and volumes 6 through 11 are known as *Cannon's Precedents.* (Collectively, they are referred to as *Hinds' and Cannon's Precedents.*) Asher C. Hinds was a Republican representative from Maine from 1911 to 1917, and Clarence Cannon was a Democratic representative from Missouri from 1923 to 1964 and a parliamentarian of the House from 1915 to 1920.

These volumes are out of print. Copies are available for reference at the House Legislative Resource Center, B-106 Cannon House Office Building. (*Avaliable online at GPO's Federal Digital System, at <http://fdsys.gov>, and look under "Collections" for "Precedents of the U.S. House of Representatives." Also see <CDDocs.com>.*)

Cannon's Procedure in the House of Representatives

This document is largely of historical interest, as much of it is no longer relevant to contemporary practice.

Cannon's Procedure, published in 1963, is a one-volume summary of the major precedents presented in *Hinds' and Cannon's Precedents*, with a few additional precedents from 1936 to 1963. The document also contains examples of floor dialogue or specific parliamentary actions.

This volume is out of print. Copies are available for reference at the House Legislative Resource Center, B-106 Cannon House Office Building.

§ 10.50 Official Rules Publications of the Senate

Senate Manual

The Senate is the chamber of individual members' rights, and the relative brevity of its rules compared with those of the House of Representatives reflects this fact. The *Senate Manual* contains the Senate's rules, the *standing orders* that function like rules, and additional rules and precedents covering specific activities such as conferences and impeachment trials. Unlike the House, the Senate does not organize itself by adopting rules at the beginning of each new Congress. Since a quorum of the Senate is always serving (only one-third of the Senate is up for election every two years), the Senate views itself as a "continuing body." The Senate adopts standing orders and temporary resolutions to modify the operation of its rules for the duration of a Congress or for a longer period. In addition, Senate precedents guide the Senate and provide an evolving interpretation by the Senate of the operation of its rules.

The *Senate Manual* also contains excerpts from laws affecting the Senate and the texts of four historical documents—the Declaration of Independence, the Articles of Confederation, the Ordinance of 1787 (the Northwest Ordinance), and the Constitution. Extensive historical tables on the Senate, the executive, the Supreme Court, elections, and the states form a unique, convenient reference in themselves. The *Senate Manual* is generally printed once during each Congress. The most recent *Senate Manual* is available online through GPO's Federal Digital System, at *<http://fdsys.gov>*, and look under "Collections" for "Senate Manuals." Also see *<CDDocs.com>*.

Standing Rules of the Senate

The *Standing Rules of the Senate* is a document, issued by the Senate Committee on Rules and Administration, that contains only the standing rules. It was last issued in the 106th Congress as S. Doc. 106-15. Footnotes in this document show changes from 1979, when the most recent extensive revision of the standing rules was made, to 1999. (*Available online at <http://senate.gov>, under "Rules of the Senate."*)

Senate Procedure (Riddick's)

Published in 1992, this single volume presents significant Senate precedents established from 1883 to 1992. Prepared by Floyd Riddick, a former Senate parliamentarian, and updated by Alan Frumin, the current parliamentarian, the document is organized around topics presented in alphabetical order. For each topic there is a review of the general principles governing a procedure, the text of the relevant standing rule, and, where appropriate, citations to the *Congressional Record* or other official publication pages. An extensive index is one of the document's useful features.

All Senate offices were provided with copies of this document. It is otherwise out of print but is available in library collections. (*Available online at GPO's Federal Digital System, at <http://fdsys.gov>, and look under "Collections" for "Riddick's Senate Procedure." Also see <CDDocs.com>.*)

Impeachment

S. Doc. 99-33, *Procedure and Guidelines for Impeachment Trials in the U.S. Senate*, contains basic guidance on Senate impeachment trials. S. Doc. 106-2, *Impeachment of President William Jefferson Clinton, Constitutional Provisions; Rules of Procedure and Practice in the Senate When Sitting on Impeachment Trials; Articles of Impeachment Against President William Jefferson Clinton; President Clinton's Answer; and Replication of the House of Representatives*, a multivolume Senate document; and S. Doc. 106-3 and S. Doc. 106-4 contain relevant items from the impeachment trial of President Clinton. (*Available at GPO's web site at <http://frwebgate.access.gpo.gov/cgi-bin/browse?DB=106_cong_documents&template=cdocuments.tpl&sortoption=alphabetical.html>. For links to the Clinton Impeachment documents in the 106th Congress, and other documents and resources, see <CDDocs.com>.*)

§ 10.60 Other Congressional Sources of Information on Rules and Procedures

Enactment of a Law

This publication, prepared by the Senate parliamentarian, describes a typical day in the Senate, explaining in lay terms Senate procedure, both in committee and on the floor. Descriptions of the functions of Senate officials are also provided. (*Available online at THOMAS, <http://thomas.gov/home/enactment>.*)

How Our Laws Are Made

Prepared by the House parliamentarian, this document is intended for the non-specialist and explains the legislative process, from the drafting of legislation to final approval and presidential action. It

§ 10.61

Byrd and Dole Historical Documents

Historical Almanac of the United States Senate

During the 100th Congress, Senator Bob Dole delivered a series of *Bicentennial Minutes*, short speeches made on the Senate floor. These speeches addressed both substantive and anecdotal aspects of Senate history. Every day the Senate was in session, from January 6, 1987, until the adjournment in 1988, Senator Dole spoke on a discrete topic, delivering speeches on approximately 300 different subjects.

From the first entry in the volume, cited as *June 7, 1787, Method of Senatorial Election Decided*, to the last, cited as *April 6, 1989, Senate Celebrates Its 200th Anniversary*, the volume provides a wealth of information on people and events in the Senate's history.

These bicentennial minutes were compiled under the auspices of the Commission on the Bicentennial of the Senate and published as S. Doc. 100-35, ISBN: 0160064066.

The Senate, 1789–1989

This four-volume history of aspects of the Senate, prepared by Senator Robert Byrd, is commonly referred to as the Byrd books. Volumes I and II are subtitled *Addresses on the History of the United States Senate*. Volume I takes a chronological approach to the Senate's history; Volume II takes a topical approach. Volume III contains *Classic Speeches, 1830–1993*, and Volume IV contains *Historical Statistics, 1789–1992*. Taken together, the Byrd history is rich in historical detail and the flavor and evolution of the life of the nation and the Senate over a 200-year period.

Compiled under the auspices of the Commission on the Bicentennial of the Senate, the volumes were published as S. Doc. 100-20.

200 Notable Days: Senate Stories, 1987 to 2002

A complementary volume to the Dole and Byrd Senate histories is this book by Senate Historian Richard A. Baker. For over a decade, Baker researched and wrote vignettes from the Senate's history; these glimpses of the Senate have been called "historical minutes." This volume collects 200 of these essays. As noted on the Senate's web site: "Read collectively, these stories reveal a larger picture about the uniqueness of the Senate as an institution, providing readers with a more complete image of the modern Senate, and advancing Dr. Baker's belief that to understand today's Senate, one must explore this institution's rich history." *200 Notable Days* was prepared by the Senate historian under the direction of the secretary of the Senate. (*Available online, at GPO's Federal Digital System, at <http://fdsys.gov>, and search for "200 Notable Days." Also see <CDDocs.com>.*)

presents information on both House and Senate procedure, although it focuses primarily on the House. Sample documents that accompany each stage of the process are presented in the back of the publication.

A printed edition exists as H. Doc. 110-49. (*Available online at THOMAS, <http://thomas.gov/home/lawsmade.toc.html>.*)

Our American Government

Prepared by the Congressional Research Service under the auspices of the House Administration Committee, this document uses a question-and-answer format to explain the three branches of the national government and the electoral process. It contains other useful information, such as a table of party control of the two houses of Congress and a glossary of legislative terminology. It is available in print as H. Doc. 108-94. (*Available online at GPO's Federal Digital System, at <http://fdsys.gov>, and search for "H.Doc. 108-94". Also see <CDDocs.com>.*)

Constitution of the United States

Congress has authorized the printing of the Constitution of the United States in several formats. *The Constitution of the United States of America as Amended, Unratified Amendments, Analytical Index* (H. Doc. 111-50) is very useful because the analytical index quickly guides the reader to any phrase in the Constitution. (*Available online at GPO's Federal Digital System, <http://fdsys.gov>, and look under "Collections" for "Constitution of the United States of America." Also see <CDDocs.com>.*) *The Constitution of the United States and the Declaration of Independence* is available in print as S. Doc. 111-4, available online at GPO's Federal Digital System, *<http://fdsys.gov>*, search for "S. Doc. 111-4." These are also available online from the National Archives at *<http://www.archives.gov/exhibits/charters/>*. A print "Pocket Constitution" is available from TheCapitol.Net at *<TCNPocket.com>*. Also see *<CDDocs.com>*.

U.S. Constitution, Analysis and Interpretation, 2002 Edition (S. Doc.108-17), and 2004 Supplement (S. Doc. 108-19), 2006 Supplement (S. Doc. 110-6), and 2008 Supplement (S. Doc. 110-7) is a massive text maintained by the Congressional Research Service, that provides analysis of each clause of the Constitution. The analysis includes examinations of Supreme Court cases and footnotes to case law, scholarly commentary, historical documents, and other sources. All of these documents are available online at GPO's Federal Digital System, *<http://fdsys.gov>* and look under "Collections" for "Constitution of the United States of America." Also see *<CDDocs.com>*.

TheCapitol.Net also has a "Pocket Constitution" containing the Declaration of Independence, the U.S. Constitution and its Amendments; see *<TCNPocket.com>*.

Floor Procedures in the U.S. House of Representatives

Commonly referred to as the *Floor Manual* or the *Republican Floor Manual* (because it was originally prepared by Republican members in the early 1980s), this short document describes the daily order of business in the House and provides references to applicable House rules. Sample language is also provided for selected actions. It is written in "user-friendly" English. An abridged dictionary of parliamentary terms is provided. (*Available in print from the House Committee on Rules.*)

Legislative Manual

Several committees have issued their own legislative manuals. The manuals provide, from the perspective of each committee, an explanation of the legislative process with a sample of the legislative documents generated at each stage of the process. Each document can be obtained from the issuing committee.

Treaties and Other International Agreements: The Role of the United States Senate

Treaties and Other International Agreements: The Role of the United States Senate (S. Prt. 106-71) provides information about the steps involved in making treaties and executive agreements. It covers in detail the procedures that govern Senate consideration of treaties and other international agreements. It is available from the Senate Committee on Foreign Relations. (*Available online at GPO's Federal Digital System, <http://fdsys.gov>, and search for "S. Prt. 106-71." Also see <CDDocs.com>.*)

§ 10.70 Party Publications

Each party in each chamber generates a series of documents generally issued only to each party's members, although several are made available to the public. Some of these publications address party perspectives on legislative issues; others address upcoming floor schedules. Some documents are provided in paper form only, some are sent by email to subscribers, and some are placed on party web sites.

Rules of Party Caucus/Conference

Each party in each chamber adopts rules governing the work of its caucus or conference. These rules are usually adopted by the party members at the early organization meetings held after the election but before the swearing in of the new Congress. (*See § 5.40, Early Organization Meetings.*) The rules cover such topics as the selection of party leaders and the organization of the party leadership, the committee assignment process, and the work of the party organization. Majority-party rules also often affect selected floor procedures. Copies of party rules are generally available only to a caucus' or conference's members, but the House Republican Conference's rules are available online at *<http://gop.gov/about/rules>*.

Whip Advisories and Whip Notices

Each party in each chamber provides to its members *whip notices*, *whip alerts*, *legislative alerts*, or *whip advisories*. Prepared by the party whip, each notice provides information on the anticipated schedule for the day, week, or longer period.

A daily whip notice is distributed before the daily convening of a chamber and usually states the time the chamber convenes, the legislation that is scheduled, how the legislation is expected to be considered on the floor, and, if available, the time the chamber will finish its business that day.

A weekly whip notice is traditionally provided at the conclusion of a week's work and addresses the agenda for the following week. (The paper copies of weekly whip notices distributed to member offices are accompanied by copies of the measures scheduled for floor action and committee reports on those measures.) Oftentimes, a monthly calendar is prepared so members may anticipate the days on which votes are scheduled and periods when the chamber will not be in session.

The House Democratic whip's notices are available online at *<http://democraticwhip.house.gov/>* under "Floor Resources." The House Republican whip's notices are available online at *<http://republicanwhip.house.gov/floor>*. Depending on which party is in the majority, that party's floor notices are available online at *<http://majorityleader.gov/Floor>* or under "Floor Notices." Also see *<CDDocs.com>*.

The Senate Floor schedule is available at *<http://senate.gov>*, and on the Senate Democratic Conference at *<http://democrats.senate.gov>* and on the Senate Republican Conference at *<http://republicans.senate.gov>*. Also see *<CDDocs.com>*.

Legislative Issue Documents

Each party in each chamber prepares a variety of documents—with varying degrees of depth—that address the substantive issues associated with upcoming legislation. These documents can be found at chamber leaders' and party organizations' web sites:

House

For current House leadership see *<http://house.gov>*, then select "Leadership."
Also see *<CongressLeaders.com>*.

- Speaker, *<http://speaker.gov>*
- Majority Leader, *<http://majorityleader.gov>*

Democrats:

- Democratic Leader, *<http://democraticleader.house.gov>*
- Democratic Whip, *<http://democraticwhip.house.gov>*
- Democratic Caucus, *<http://dems.gov>*

Republicans:

- Republican Leader, *<http://republicanleader.house.gov>*
- Republican Whip, *<http://republicanwhip.house.gov>*
- Republican Caucus, *<http://gop.gov>*

Senate

For current Senate leadership see *<http://senate.gov>*, then select "Reference," then "Senate Organization." Also see *<CongressLeaders.com>*.

112th Congress

Democrats:

- Majority Leader, *<http://reid.senate.gov>*
- Assistant Majority Leader, *<http://durbin.senate.gov>*
- Democratic Conference, *<http://democrats.senate.gov>*
- Democratic Policy Committee, *<http://dpc.senate.gov>*

Republicans:

- Minority Leader, *<http://republicanleader.senate.gov>*
- Assistant Minority Leader, *<http://kyl.senate.gov>*
- Republican Conference, *<http://republican.senate.gov>*
- Republican Policy Committee, *<http://rpc.senate.gov>*

For current leaders of Congress and links, see *<CongressLeaders.com>*.

Cloakroom Recordings

Each party in each chamber operates cloakroom recordings for members. Each cloakroom has one telephone line that provides recorded information about the upcoming schedule. A second taped message details the results of votes, ongoing proceedings, summaries of recent actions, and the times of adjournment and convening of the next session. Each of the four cloakrooms operates a *hot line* that automatically notifies members through pagers whenever a major floor action is imminent or, when the bells ring for a vote, the subject of that vote. Members can also call cloakroom staff to ask about pending and anticipated action in the chamber.

The public can obtain the same taped information that is provided to members by calling the following numbers:

- House Democratic Cloakroom: *202-225-1600 for advance schedule and 202-225-7400 for current proceedings*
- House Republican Cloakroom: *202-225-2020 for advance schedule and 202-225-7430 for current proceedings*
- Senate Democratic Cloakroom: *202-224-8541*
- Senate Republican Cloakroom: *202-224-8601*

§ 10.80 Administrative Documents

In addition to the manuals of rules and precedents and the procedural documents prepared by Congress, numerous other publications are integral to understanding Congress. Prepared by the historian's office or the administrative personnel in each chamber, these documents address not the rules but the management of Congress and information about members who have served. (*See § 10.81, Selected Congressional Documents about Members of Congress.*)

Audit of the Financial Statements

Prepared by the House inspector general, these volumes provide the results of audits of the House, mandated by the House Administration Committee. (*Available online along with other inspector general reports at the House inspector general's web site, <www.house.gov/IG>.*)

Statement of Disbursements of the House and Report of the Secretary of the Senate

The quarterly *Statement of Disbursements of the House* and the semiannual *Report of the Secretary of the Senate* provide data on staff salaries and committee expenses during the reporting period. In addition, *Expenditure Authorizations for Senate Committees*, a committee print prepared by the Senate Committee on Rules and Administration, describes existing staffing and budgeting regulations, and provides historical data on committee staffs and budgets. (The Statement of Disbursements of the House, published by the chief administrative officer, was formerly prepared by the clerk of the House, called the *Report of the Clerk of the House*, and commonly referred to as the *Clerk's Report*.)

The most recent *Statement of Disbursements of the House*, H. Doc. 112-6, covered the period October to December 2010; it is available online at *<http://disbursements.house.gov>*. The most recent *Report of the Secretary of the Senate*, S. Doc. 111-17, covered the period April 1, 2010, to September 30, 2010.

Election, Expulsion and Censure Cases, 1793–1990, United States Senate

Prepared by the Senate Historical Office under the direction of the secretary of the Senate, this compilation summarizes all ethics cases considered by the Senate from 1793 to 1990. Printed as S. Doc. 103-33, it is for sale by the Government Printing Office (GPO).

Ethics Manuals of the House and Senate

The House Committee on Standards of Official Conduct and the Senate Ethics Committee publish ethics manuals for their members. The House *Ethics Manual for Members, Officers, and Employees of the U.S. House of Representatives* details the Code of Official Conduct and addresses general ethics standards for members and staff. The Senate *Ethics Manual* addresses the Senate Code of Conduct and provides a compilation of interpretive rulings issued by the Senate Ethics Committee. (*The House Ethics Manual is available online at <http://ethics.house.gov> under "Publications & Forms." The Senate Ethics Manual is available online at <http://ethics.senate.gov> under "Ethics Manual." Also see <CDDocs.com>.*)

Financial Disclosure Forms

Members of Congress and senior government officials are required to file financial disclosure forms. The statements members submit are compiled by their respective chambers. The House disclosure forms are available for inspection at the Legislative Resource Center, B-106 Cannon House Office Building and online at through the House clerk's office at *<http://clerk.house.gov/public_disc/>*. Senate financial disclosure forms are available in the Senate Public Records Office, SH-232 Hart Senate Office Building.

Guide to the Records of the United States House of Representatives at the National Archives, 1789–1989, Bicentennial Edition

This reference work identifies the records of the House and its committees from 1789 to 1989, which are now located at the National Archives. Prepared by the House historian and updated by the clerk of the House, it was originally printed as H. Doc. 100-245. (*An online version is available at <http://archives.gov/legislative/guide/house/>.*)

Guide to the Records of the United States Senate at the National Archives, 1789–1989, Bicentennial Edition

This reference work, located at the National Archives, identifies the records of the Senate and its committees from 1789 to 1989. It was printed as S. Doc. 100-42 (*<http://archives.gov/legislative/guide/senate/>.*).

§ 10.81

Selected Congressional Documents about Members of Congress

Biographical Directory of the United States Congress

This directory provides individual biographies of everyone who ever served in Congress. A print edition of the *Biographical Directory of the United States Congress, 1774–2005* (H. Doc. 108-222) is available from the GPO and available online at <*www.gpoaccess.gov/serialset/cdocuments/hd108-222/*>. Also see <*CDDocs.com*>. The database is available at <*http://bioguide.congress.gov/*>.

Black Americans in Congress, 1870–2007

Prepared under the auspices of the clerk of the House, this volume provides biographical essays on the lives of African-American representatives who served in the House and Senate from 1870 to 2007. The document was printed as H. Doc. 108-224, and is available from GPO. An updated online database is available at <*http://baic.house.gov*>.

The Cannon Centenary Conference: The Changing Nature of the Speakership

This volume contains the 2003 presentations made and papers written to commemorate the centenary of the speakership of Joseph Gurney Cannon, R-IL, perhaps the most powerful Speaker the House has ever known. The presentations examined the modern speakerships of Thomas P. O'Neill Jr., D-MA; James C. Wright Jr., D-TX; Thomas S. Foley, D-WA; and Newt Gingrich, R-GA. Speaker O'Neill is deceased, but Speakers Wright, Foley, Gingrich, and then-sitting Speaker J. Dennis Hastert, R-IL, participated in the proceedings. The proceedings were printed as H. Doc. 108-204.

Guide to the Research Collections of Former Members of the U.S. House of Representatives, 1789–1987

This guide presents a listing of archival repositories housing the papers of former members, related collections, and oral history interviews. It was printed as H. Doc. 100-171. Entries in this volume are appended to the appropriate representatives' biographies contained in the *Biographical Directory of the United States Congress*, listed above. Additional information on members' research collections is available from the National Archives at <*www.archives.gov/legislative/repository-collections/*>.

Guide to the Research Collections of Former Senators, 1789–1995

This guide presents a listing of archival repositories housing the papers of former senators, related collections, and oral history interviews. The collections of 1,658 of the 1,726 senators who served before January 3, 1995, are included, although the document does contain an entry for all 1,726 senators. Printed as S. Doc. 103-35 and prepared under the direction of the secretary of the Senate by the Senate Historical Office, the guide is available for sale by the Government Printing Office. Entries in this volume are appended to the appropriate senators' biographies contained in the *Biographical Directory of the United States Congress*, listed above. Additional information on senators' research collections is available from the National Archives at <*www.archives.gov/legislative/repository-collections/*>.

Hispanic Americans in Congress, 1822–1995

Prepared under the direction of the Joint Committee on Printing and the Hispanic Division of the Library of Congress, this volume provides biographical essays on the lives of Hispanic members who served in the House and Senate from 1822 to 1995. The document was printed as H. Doc. 103-299. (*Available online at* <*www.loc.gov/rr/hispanic/congress*>.)

Continued on page 475

§ 10.81 (continued)

History of the United States Senate Republican Policy Committee, 1947–1997

Prepared by the Senate Historical Office, this compilation provides a narrative history of the Republican Policy Committee. Appendices identify senators who served as Policy Committee chairs and those who served as Republican leaders. Also identified are staff directors of the Policy Committee. It was printed as S. Doc. 105-5 and is available online at GPO's Federal Digital System at *<http://fdsys.gov>*, then search for "S.Doc. 105-5." Also see *<CDDocs.com>*.

Senators of the United States, A Historical Bibliography, 1789–1995

This volume is a compilation of works by and about senators from 1789 to 1995. It presents information on approximately 1,164 senators. Prepared by the Senate Historical Office under the direction of the secretary of the Senate, the volume was printed as S. Doc. 103-34. Entries in this volume are appended to the appropriate senators' biographies contained in the *Biographical Directory of the United States Congress*, listed above.

Vice Presidents of the United States, 1789–1993

This volume presents short biographical essays on vice presidents who served from 1789 to 1993. It was printed as S. Doc. 104-26. (*Available online in an adaptation at <www.senate.gov/artandhistory/history/common/briefing/Vice_President.htm>.*)

Women in Congress, 1917–2006

Prepared by the Office of History and Preservation under the direction of the clerk of the House, this volume provides biographical essays on the lives of the 230 women representatives and senators who served during the period covered in the study. The document was printed as H. Doc. 108-233. (*A version of this publication is updated online at <http://womenincongress.house.gov>.*)

Members' Congressional Handbook

This publication, prepared by the Committee on House Administration, provides nuts-and-bolts information about the official expenses that may be incurred to support a member's legislative and representational duties. It details the regulations promulgated by the House Administration Committee in the administration of members' accounts. *New Member Fact Sheets*, adapted from the handbook, provide one-page overviews of some of the information; these are given to incoming freshmen representatives at early organization meetings. (*An extensive publication is provided to member offices; a summary version is available from the Committee on House Administration web site, <http://cha.house.gov>, then select "Member Services," then "Handbooks." Also see <CDDocs.com>.*)

Committees' Congressional Handbook

A counterpart publication to the *Members' Congressional Handbook*, prepared by the Committee on House Administration, guides committees in the administration of their accounts. (*Online version available from the Committee on House Administration web site, <http://cha.house.gov>, then select "Member Services," then "Handbooks," then "Committee Handbook." Also see <CDDocs.com>.*)

Regulations on the Use of the Congressional Frank by Members of the House of Representatives

This document, prepared by the House Commission on Congressional Mailing Standards, identifies rules pertaining to the use of the *congressional frank*. A June 1998 version is available from the Committee on House Administration. (*Available online from the Committee on House Administration web site, <http://cha.house.gov>, then selecting "Franking & Communications," then "Franking Information," then "Franking Manual" (72-page PDF). Also see <CDDocs.com>.*)

U.S. Senate Handbook, 2006

Prepared by the Senate Committee on Rules and Administration, the *U.S. Senate Handbook* summarizes federal law, Senate rules, and Senate practices regarding the administration, financial management, information management, constituent services, and legislative activity of Senate offices. Written by Senate staff with responsibilities for these activities, the handbook is a good resource for an overview of the work in a Senate office. (*Available from the Committee on Rules and Administration, <http://rules.senate.gov>. The Senate Handbook is available online, but only to Senate offices.*)

§ 10.90 Chapter Summary and Discussion Questions

Each chamber publishes official documents explaining the legislative and administrative work of that chamber. In addition, each committee and each party in both chambers prepare documents detailing aspects of their organization, procedure, and activities. Some documents report and explain actions taken, others announce anticipated actions.

Discussion Questions

- What documents contain the rules of the House and Senate? Obtain a copy of these documents, or browse them online. What other information do they contain? For what purposes might you need this other information?
- What are required contents of House and Senate committee reports? Looking back to Chapter Six, how does the content differ between House and Senate requirements?
- What are the four House and two Senate calendars? What is their purpose? What information is available in the documents in which these calendars are published?
- What part of the *Congressional Record* serves as the table of contents to each daily issue? What information is contained in this section of the *Record?*
- At the beginning and end of each Congress, committees prepare numerous documents. What are they and what information is provided in them?
- Where can one find information about expenditures in each chamber? Where can one find each chamber's ethics rules? What might one need to do to find the rules of each party in each chamber?

Chapter Eleven

Legislative Research: Viewing and Visiting Congress

Analysis

§ 11.00 Introduction

This chapter provides advice on how to follow floor proceedings on the House and Senate floors, by describing what to look for when watching on C-SPAN. Separately for each chamber, there is a description of the normal flow of a legislative day from convening through the consideration of legislation to adjournment. Floor plans and sketches of the chambers appear with each chamber's description of proceedings.

For persons visiting the Capitol or the congressional office buildings, the locations and functions of the Capitol complex buildings are described. Generalized floor plans of the buildings also appear in this section, and the meaning of the signals of the Senate buzzer and light system and the House bell and light system are listed.

The chapter concludes with a basic checklist for tracking legislative action. This section also includes tips for contacting congressional offices by mail, phone, email, or in person.

§ 11.10 How to Follow Floor Proceedings in the House

Proceedings in the House are carried on C-SPAN I, the Cable Satellite Public Affairs Network. For those who need more than a professional interest as a motivating factor for tuning in, watching the House has often been compared to the best soap opera that television has to offer. (*See also Chapter Six, Legislating in Congress: Legislative Process, especially sections on House floor proceedings, beginning at § 6.70, House Floor: Scheduling and Privilege.*)

For those watching outside the Capitol complex, classical music or an excerpt from an earlier program is played while a vote is in progress; for those inside the Capitol complex, there might be no sound during a vote. (Inside the Capitol complex, House proceedings are carried on House channels as well as on C-SPAN I.)

In the course of a day, the Senate or the president might transmit a message to the House of Representatives. In that case, a House clerk walks down the center aisle and bows to the Speaker. The House clerk announces a *message from the Senate/president* and bows again. An accompanying Senate or executive branch clerk bows and reads the message. The message is handed to the House clerk and taken to the desk (also referred to as the rostrum or dais). Business on the message does not necessarily occur then or even soon thereafter.

Steps in the Proceedings

11

Who Is on the Floor? When the president delivers his annual State of the Union message, he is in the House chamber. With some added chairs, there are enough seats to accommodate the entire House membership, all one hundred senators, the president's Cabinet, the justices of the Supreme Court, the joint chiefs of staff, and the diplomatic corps. There are, in fact, more than 700 seats on the floor of the House.

House members do not have assigned seats. Facing the presiding officer's dais, by tradition, Democrats sit to the left of the center aisle, and Republicans to the right. Two lecterns are stationed in the *well*, the open area between the dais and the seats. Four tables, called *party tables* or *committee tables*, are situated among the seats near the front of the chamber. Members may speak only

§ 11.11

House Floor Plan

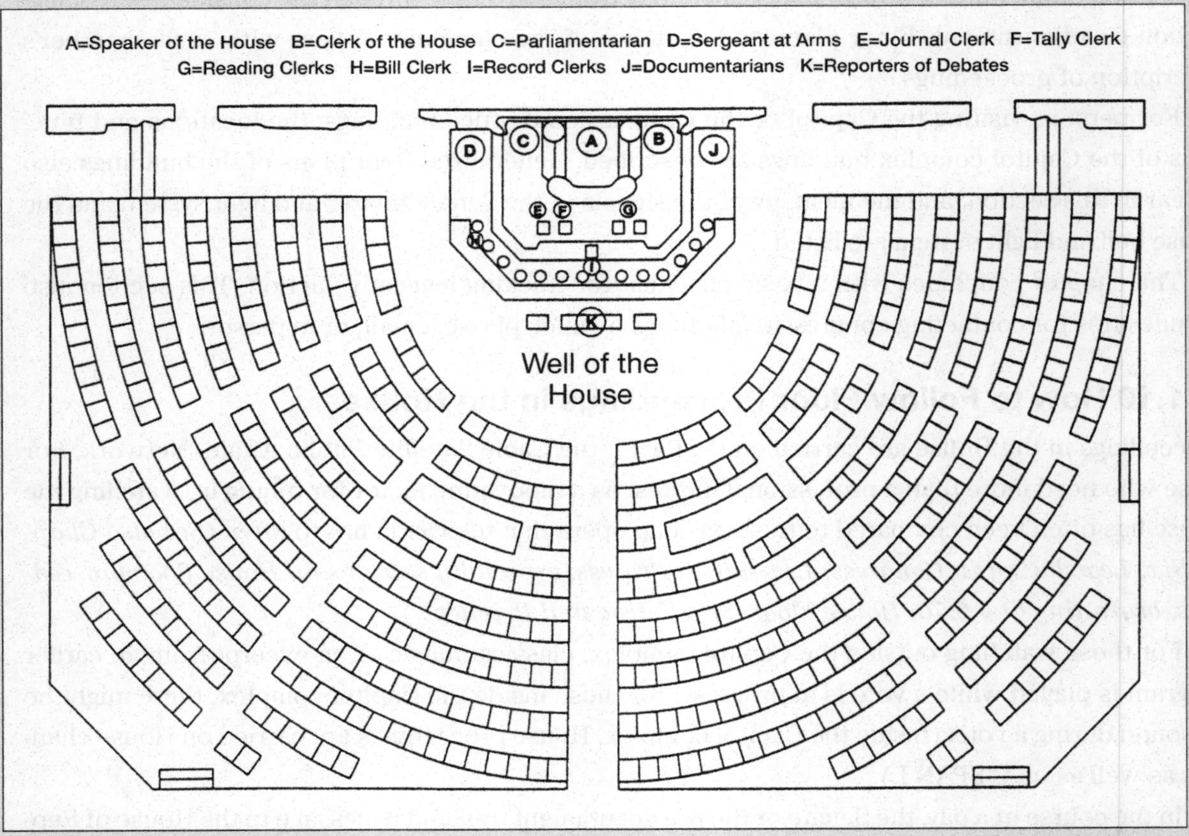

House members do not have assigned seats. The House and Senate Floor Plans are online at <*CongressSeating.com*>.

from the well or from one of the party or committee tables. (*See § 6.113, Who Is Allowed on the House Floor?; and § 11.11, House Floor Plan.*)

At the opening of a session, a staffer in white gloves places the *mace*—the parliamentary symbol of authority of the House—on a pedestal to the Speaker's right. (*See § 6.111, The Mace.*)

Call to Order. The Speaker of the House—the presiding officer—calls the House to order and taps the gavel. The time to convene is set at the end of the previous House session, although there is some regularity of meeting times throughout the year. (*See § 6.72, Daily Starting Times in the House.*) If the Speaker is not presiding that day, another majority member calls the House to order, and a clerk reads a letter from the Speaker designating that member to preside over the House and serve as *Speaker pro tempore* for the day. One may call the Democratic or Republican cloakroom tape to learn the time the House is scheduled to convene and the day's program. (*Democratic cloakroom tape: 202-225-1600; Republican cloakroom tape: 202-225-2020.*) The *Congressional Record* for the previous session also identifies the time and program.

Opening Prayer. The House chaplain or a guest chaplain delivers a brief opening prayer.

Approval of the Journal. The chair announces that he has approved the Journal of the previous day's session. (The *Journal of the House of Representatives of the United States* is the official record of the House and is different from the *Congressional Record (see § 10.20, Floor Documents).*) A member can *demand a vote on the Speaker's approval of the Journal.* This could require a record vote. It can be taken at that time or postponed to a time later in the day. Voting on the Journal provides a count of members who are present for proceedings that day, but it is rarely an indication of a member's support for the Journal itself.

Pledge of Allegiance. A member is called upon to lead the House and those in the gallery in the Pledge of Allegiance.

One-Minute Speeches. At the beginning of most days, some members are seated in the front row of the chamber. This alignment indicates these members' desire to make *one-minute speeches.* These speeches are made in the well of the House. One-minute speeches are allowed when the Speaker recognizes members to *address the House for one minute [and revise and extend his remarks].* The Speaker is authorized to announce a limitation on the number of members recognized on a day for one-minute speeches, and can even announce that no "one minutes" will be allowed or that they will be postponed to later in the day. One-minute speeches can be on any subject, and often are not on legislative issues. A one-minute speech might concern a congressional district issue, such as congratulations for an individual constituent or a winning sports team.

Morning Hour Speeches. On Mondays and Tuesdays the House convenes early to allow members to make five-minute speeches on any subject. No legislative business is conducted during this time, called morning hour. (*See § 6.72, Daily Starting Times in the House.*)

Legislative Business. What happens next is often determined by what day of the week it is. For example, bills under *suspension of the rules* are in order on Mondays, Tuesdays, and Wednesdays. (*See § 6.80, House Floor: Methods of Consideration.*) Other legislation may come to the floor under the provisions of a *special rule* reported from the Rules Committee. Each of these two procedures have time limitations associated with them. For suspension of the rules, forty minutes of debate time is allotted, with twenty minutes to the majority party and twenty minutes to the minority party. When debating a special rule, one hour of debate is provided, again equally divided between the parties. Proceedings in the House sitting as the House are often referred to as proceedings under the *one-hour rule.* (*See § 6.90, Rules Committee and Special Rules.*) At the end of an hour of debate on a special rule, a majority-party member will *move the previous question.* This motion enables the House to end debate on the special rule and proceed to a vote on it. Once the rule is agreed to, the House can consider the underlying legislation. (*See § 6.100, Consideration of a Special Rule on the House Floor.*)

Committee of the Whole. When a special rule is agreed to, the House *resolves into the Committee of the Whole House on the State of the Union,* referred to as the *Committee of the Whole,* to consider the measure referred to in the special rule. The mace is lowered from its pedestal, and the Speaker appoints a member to preside in his stead as chairman of the Committee of the Whole.

All members serve on this fictitious but procedurally significant committee, and nothing physically changes except that the mace is lowered and the Speaker does not preside. However, measures

§ 11.12

View of the Speaker's Dais and Well of the House

The Speaker or Speaker pro tempore sits on the uppermost level of the dais, and the mace is on the pedestal to the Speaker's right if the House is meeting as the House. If the House is meeting as the Committee of the Whole House on the State of the Union, the chairman of the Committee of the Whole occupies this level, and the mace is placed on a lower pedestal. If Congress is conducting a joint session or meeting, the vice president is seated on this level with the Speaker, a second chair having been added. (*See § 6.110, Committee of the Whole: Debate; and § 6.111, The Mace.*)

One might also see one of the parliamentarians to the Speaker's or chairman's right, advising on parliamentary statements or rulings. A time clerk stands on the presiding officer's left.

The reading clerk as well as several other clerks occupy the middle level. The reading clerk is regularly directed by the Speaker or the chairman of the Committee of the Whole to read measures or amendments or provide other information to the membership, which he does from the lectern on this level.

Members may speak from the well of the House, using the Democratic lectern on the Speaker's right or the Republican lectern on the Speaker's left. The official reporters of debate use the table and chairs.

§ 11.13

View of the Speaker's Dais, Floor of the House, and Galleries

While the view of the Speaker's dais in § 11.12 identifies some of the occupants of the dais, this illustration gives a better indication of the size of the dais. On the lowest level of the dais nearest to the viewer are seats occupied by the bill clerk, who is responsible for the "hopper" in which House members place bills and resolutions for introduction.

This illustration also shows in the lower right one of the four committee or party tables from which members may address the House, in addition to the lecterns they may use in the well of the House. Each party has two tables on its side of the center aisle of the House.

The door to the Speaker's left and another out of view to the Speaker's right provide access to the Speaker's Lobby. (The party cloakrooms are in the back of the chamber, out of view in this illustration.)

Immediately above the Speaker's dais is the press gallery. In the walls above the press gallery are the display panels where members' names and votes appear when a vote is taken by electronic device. One of the voting stations is shown at the bottom center-left of the illustration.

Also on the gallery level, to the Speaker's left, one can also see some of the seats that are used for specific guests such as family members and for other visitors and tourists. Visitor seating surrounds the House chamber on the gallery level.

in the Committee of the Whole are not considered under a one-hour rule but under what is called the *five-minute rule*, allowing a proponent, an opponent, and other members on each side five minutes each to speak on an amendment.

The provisions of the special rule dictate what happens in the Committee of the Whole. There is usually a set period for *general debate* to discuss the legislation. Members then offer amendments pursuant to the special rule, either substantive or so-called *pro forma* amendments. These latter amendments can be identified when a member moves to *strike the last word* or *strike the requisite number of words*. Each pro forma amendment enables the member to speak for five minutes. Pro forma amendments are not voted on. (*See § 6.110, Committee of the Whole: Debate; and § 6.120, Committee of the Whole: Amendment Process.*)

Votes on amendments can occur throughout the proceedings. Votes are taken almost always by voice or by *electronic device*, that is, by electronic voting device. To cast their votes electronically, members insert cards into readers located on the backs of the seats throughout the chamber. Television viewers cannot see large panels behind the rostrum that contain the names of all members and a record of how each voted—yea, nay, or present. Viewers see a running tally of vote totals, broken down by party. *Record votes* are left open for a minimum period of fifteen minutes, although votes are also often clustered, with only the first vote running for fifteen minutes or more and subsequent votes taking just two minutes. (*See § 6.130, House Floor: Voting.*)

Committee of the Whole Rises. After consideration of amendments in the Committee of the Whole, the committee *rises and reports* the measure back to the House. The mace is replaced on its pedestal, and the Speaker or Speaker pro tempore assumes the chair. Final action is taken on the measure. A *separate vote* may be requested on any amendment agreed to in the Committee of the Whole. A *motion to recommit* can be offered by the minority party. Upon disposition of this motion to recommit, a vote occurs on *final passage*, and a motion to reconsider is normally laid on the table. (*See § 6.140, House Floor: Motion to Recommit and Final Passage.*)

Special Orders. At the end of legislative business on most days, the House allows members to address the House for as little as five minutes or as long as sixty minutes on any subject they wish. The chamber is usually nearly empty during these *special order speeches*.

End of the Day. When the last special order is concluded, a member *moves that the House adjourn*. The gavel comes down, and the House adjourns for the day.

§ 11.20 How to Follow Floor Proceedings in the Senate

Proceedings in the Senate are carried on C-SPAN II, the Cable Satellite Public Affairs Network. While cable television affords one the opportunity to see important debates, listen to votes as they occur, and monitor the Senate efficiently without leaving the office, it can nonetheless be frustrating to try to view the Senate in session. (*See also Chapter Six, Legislating in Congress: Legislative Process, especially sections on Senate floor proceedings beginning at § 6.160, Senate Scheduling.*)

Oftentimes, for much of the day there is nothing to watch but a sign across the screen saying *quorum call*, a constructive delay of the proceedings. For those watching outside the Capitol complex, classical music or an excerpt from an earlier program is played while a quorum call is in progress; for those inside the Capitol complex, there might be no sound. (Inside the Capitol complex, Senate proceedings are carried on a Senate channel as well as on C-SPAN II.) Quorum calls can last a few seconds, or they can last several hours. And, they can happen repeatedly throughout the day. No senator answers when her name is called. Therefore, any attempt to describe a typical day must start by saying the day will likely be interrupted by repeated quorum calls.

In the course of a day, the House of Representatives or the president might transmit a message to the Senate. In that case, a Senate clerk walks down the center aisle and bows to the presiding officer. The Senate clerk announces a *message from the House* or *president* and bows again. An accompanying House or executive branch clerk bows and reads the message. The message is handed to the Senate clerk and taken to the desk (also referred to as the rostrum or dais). Business on the message does not necessarily occur then or even soon thereafter. Again, this is another kind of interruption that can occur throughout the day.

Steps in the Proceedings

Who Is on the Floor? Senators have assigned desks on the floor of the Senate. Facing the presiding officer's dais, Democrats are seated to the left and Republicans to the right. Seniority (that is, length of service) generally determines desk location, with more senior members often having desks closer to the rostrum. However, senators can choose not to move to a closer desk; for example, Senator Edward Kennedy's desk was in the back row—a desk used by both his brothers.

Certain desks are designated for specific senators. For example, since 1974, the senior senator from New Hampshire has always occupied the desk previously used by Daniel Webster, who represented Massachusetts in the Senate but was born in New Hampshire. Since 1995, the senior senator from Mississippi is assigned the desk formerly occupied by Jefferson Davis.

A so-called "candy desk," filled with sweets, exists on an aisle in the last row on the Republican side of the chamber. The desk is usually assigned to a junior senator. In the 112th Congress, the candy desk was occupied by Senator Mark Kirk.

Floor managers (senators controlling a discussion) might stand or sit at the desks closest to the front of the chamber. (*See § 11.21, Senate Floor Plan.*)

Several people other than senators can be seen on the floor. A committee or personal staffer might be seated on a low chair or stool directly behind a senator who is speaking. Desks in the well are for the party secretaries. For senators with desks in the back row, staff sit on couches against the wall. *Pages*, dressed in navy blue sportcoats and wearing name tags, also are seen either around the presiding officer's dais or walking throughout the chamber. (*See § 6.192, Who Is Allowed on the Senate Floor?*)

Call to Order. The first order of business is the call to order of the Senate. The time to reconvene is set at the end of the previous Senate session. One may call the Democratic or Republican cloakroom tape to learn the time the Senate is scheduled to convene and the day's program, to the extent it is known. (*Democratic cloakroom tape: 202-224-8541; Republican cloakroom tape: 202-224-8601.*) The *Congressional Record* for the previous session also identifies the time, and the majority leader's concluding remarks normally indicate what is known about the next day's program.

The presiding officer taps the gavel, and calls the Senate to order. The constitutional presiding officer, the vice president, rarely presides. The president pro tempore—the majority senator with

§ 11.21

Senate Floor Plan

The current Senate Floor Plan is available online on the Senate's web site *<http://senate.gov>* and at *<CongressSeating.com>*.

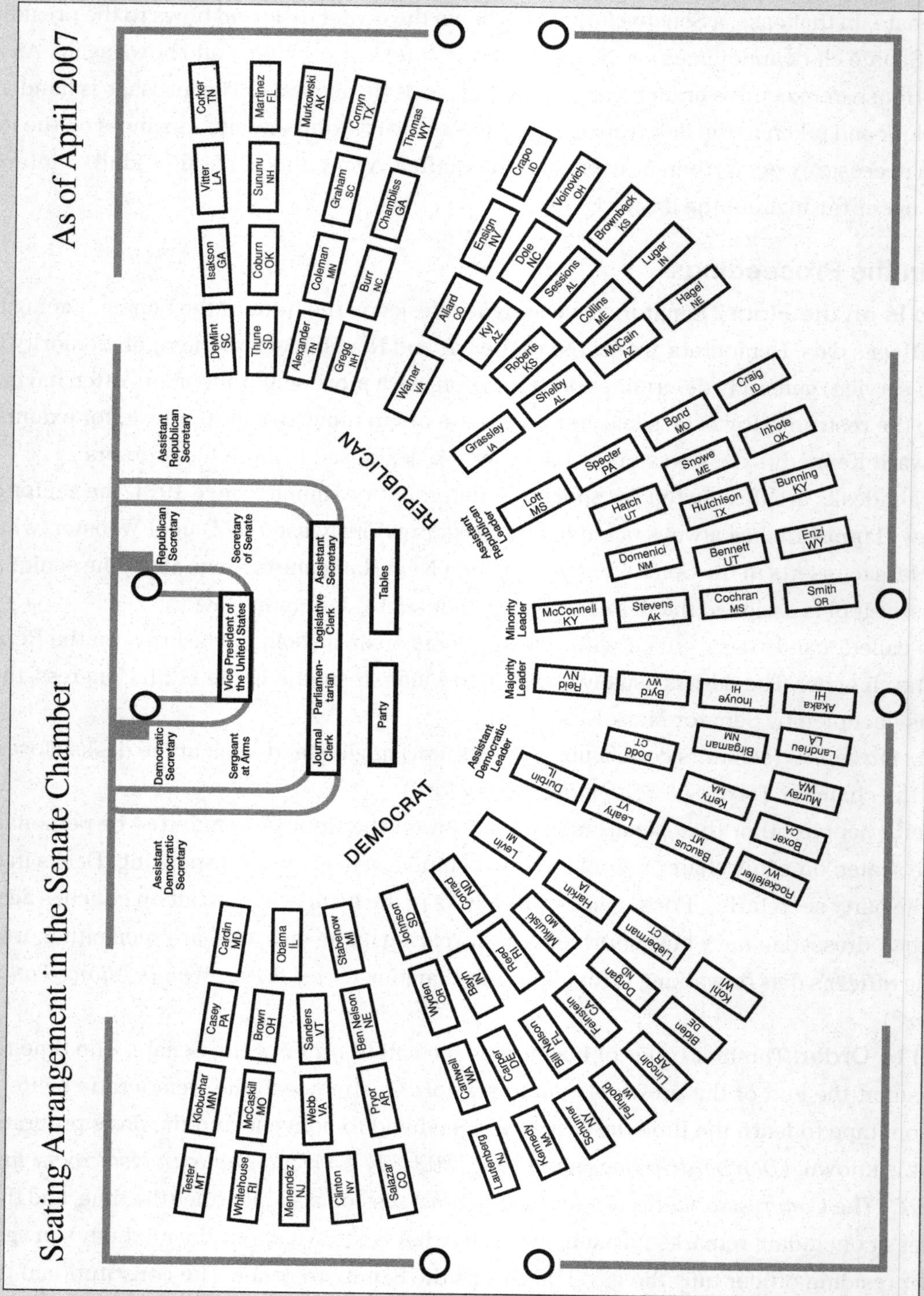

§ 11.22

View of the Senate Rostrum, or Presiding Officer's Dais

The presiding officer of the Senate—the vice president, the president pro tempore, or a designee of the president pro tempore—alone occupies the upper of the two levels of the Senate rostrum.

On the lower level of the rostrum, the journal clerk sits. That person reads bills and amendments and other information as directed by the presiding officer. The journal clerk also calls the roll on votes and quorum calls. The parliamentarian also sits on this level and advises the presiding officer on parliamentary statements and rulings.

The two tables in front of the rostrum are controlled by the parties, the one to the presiding officer's right by the Democrats and the one to the presiding officer's left by the Republicans.

In the foreground, the aisle desk on the presiding officer's right is occupied by the Democratic leader of the Senate and may be used by the Democratic floor manager of legislative or executive business being considered by the Senate. The aisle desk on the presiding officer's left is occupied by the Republican leader of the Senate and may be used by the Republican floor manager of legislative or executive business.

Doors to the presiding officer's left and right lead to the Senate Lobby. Immediately above the presiding officer and outside of this view is the press gallery. Visitor galleries surround the Senate chamber on the same level as the press gallery.

Illustration by Marilyn Gates-Davis. Copyright ©2005 by TheCapitol.Net

the longest service—might open proceedings in the Senate but more often designates a junior senator as acting president pro tem. For one- or two-hour blocks of time throughout the day, more junior senators in the majority party assume the chair.

Opening Prayer. The Senate chaplain or a guest chaplain delivers a brief morning prayer.

Pledge of Allegiance. A senator (although often the presiding officer) is called upon to lead the Senate and those in the gallery in the Pledge of Allegiance.

Leader Time. The majority and minority leaders can make brief remarks at the beginning of the session. They each often use this time to address the business of the day, or to develop their parties' view of issues of the day.

Morning Business. The period of time when bills are introduced and routine matters are handled is called "morning business," often just a period of one hour although the rule calls for two hours of Morning Hour. Morning business, however, usually is conducted throughout the day by gaining unanimous consent to *speak as if in morning business*. As such, morning business can be conducted at any time of day or night. (*See § 6.170, Legislative and Calendar Days; Morning Hour and Morning Business.*)

Legislative or Executive Business. Whether considering legislation (legislative business) or a nomination or treaty (executive business), this activity represents the heart of the Senate's work. How that business is conducted is often difficult to determine in advance. If a measure or executive matter is brought up under a *unanimous consent time agreement*, some order can be foreseen simply by obtaining the text of the agreement.

If no agreement is reached, the legislative measure or executive matter can be brought up under a *motion to proceed to consideration*. Under most circumstances, the motion to proceed is debatable. Most often, a measure or executive matter is brought up by unanimous consent, forgoing debate on a motion to proceed. In either instance, the measure or executive matter itself is debatable. Thus, absent an agreement, the Senate might quickly dispose of the pending business, engage in a longer debate or amendment process, or be caught in a *filibuster*. (*See § 6.200, Time Agreements and Motions to Proceed on the Senate Floor.*)

Watching a filibuster can be interesting (if a senator addresses at great length a policy issue) or frustrating (if a senator reads a phone book or sings). Filibusters may be conducted by a single senator, or by several senators yielding to each other, a so-called *tag-team filibuster*. If a filibuster is being conducted, a *cloture petition* can be filed by sixteen senators, asking in effect to stop the filibuster. A vote on the petition occurs two days after it is filed. It takes sixty votes to *invoke cloture*, that is, to stop debate. And even invoking cloture may not stop the debate immediately. A period of thirty hours is set aside for *post-cloture consideration*. (*See § 6.230, Cloture in Senate Floor Proceedings.*)

Watching a measure being considered on the Senate floor also entails watching *amendments* being offered. This too can be frustrating, as the Senate in many circumstances does not require amendments to be *germane* or *relevant* to the measure being considered. So, an education bill can be amended by an amendment addressing abortion, or a trade bill can have an amendment dealing with student loans. A senator might offer an amendment to a pending amendment, or might ask unanimous consent to set aside a pending amendment in order to offer another amendment. The majority leader might exercise his customary right of priority recognition to offer one or more amendments before other senators or to block other amendments. The Senate also often enters into unanimous consent agreements governing the amendment process on a piece of legislation. (*See § 6.220, Senate Amendment Procedure.*)

Voting. Throughout consideration of a legislative measure or executive matter, the Senate can take votes. Any member may request a *roll-call* vote on an amendment or the measure itself. The vote, however, will not occur until all debate has finished on a proposition. Often a senator will move to *table* an amendment. In essence, if approved, a motion to table kills the amendment. A senator will usually announce in advance that she intends to offer a motion to table the proposition, allowing debate to continue. When a vote occurs either on a motion to table (or on another motion or a point of order) or on an amendment or the measure, the clerk calls the roll. A clock is exhibited on the television screen showing fifteen minutes allotted for the vote. Many votes are held open beyond the fifteen minutes, to enable senators to get to the floor at their convenience. As each member arrives, a clerk announces the senator's name and, after the senator responds, the clerk states how the senator wishes to be recorded. Often, a member will merely put a thumb up or down to indicate voting preference. At tables in front of the dais, senators can read the text of what is being voted on and see the tally of how each senator has voted. (*See § 6.250, Voting in the Senate.*)

End of the Day. When all business for a day has been completed, the majority leader (or a designee) comes to the floor to announce that no further voting or business is expected for that day. The majority leader also normally announces the anticipated schedule for the next session. The Senate at that point either recesses or adjourns, or allows other senators to speak *as if in morning business*. When all senators who wish to speak are finished, a senator will yield the floor. The presiding officer will announce that the Senate is *in recess* or has *adjourned* until the next scheduled session. (*See § 6.170, Legislative and Calendar Days; Morning Hour and Morning Business.*)

§ 11.30 Guide to Public Buildings on Capitol Hill

The Capitol and surrounding congressional buildings are accessible by Metro (subway), bus, taxi, and car. The Metro station closest to the Capitol and the House office buildings is Capitol South; the station closest to the Senate office buildings is Union Station. Public parking is very limited, with Union Station north of the Senate office buildings being the closest place where parking is nearly always available. Visitors with disabilities who have appointments at the Capitol may request parking; the congressional office with whom the visitor has an appointment should contact the Congressional Special Services Office to reserve a parking space. Street spaces are restricted to permit holders or to short-term parking (neighborhood zone and meters).

Public and barrier-free entrances to the Capitol and other public Capitol Hill buildings are shown on the Capitol Hill map. (*See § 11.31, Capitol Hill Map.*) The Congressional Special Services Office assists congressional staff and visitors with disabilities. It provides guided tours, wheelchairs, TDD-TTY support, interpreting, FM systems, and special assistance at events. (*Call 202-224-4048 or, TDD-TTY, 202-224-4049.*)

The principal visitor entrance to the Capitol faces the East Front. Access is through the Capitol

§ 11.31

Capitol Hill Map

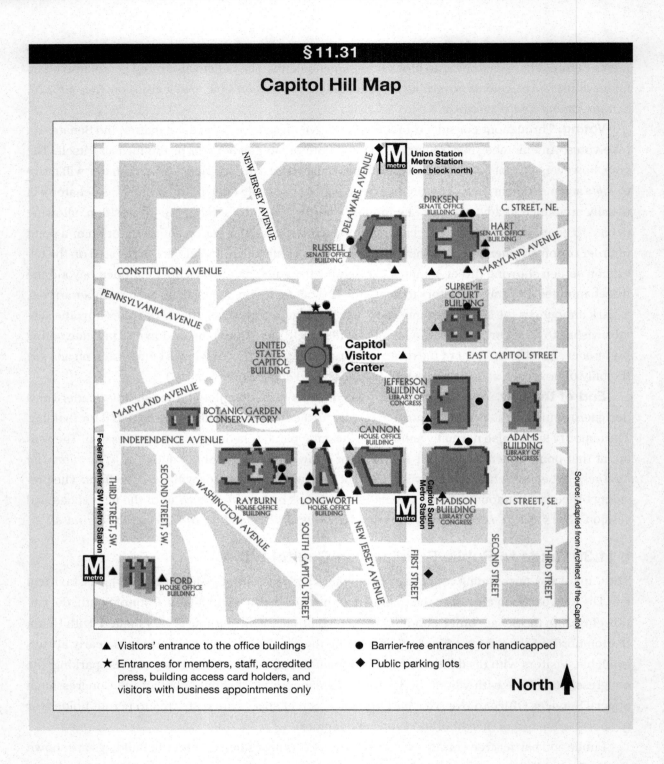

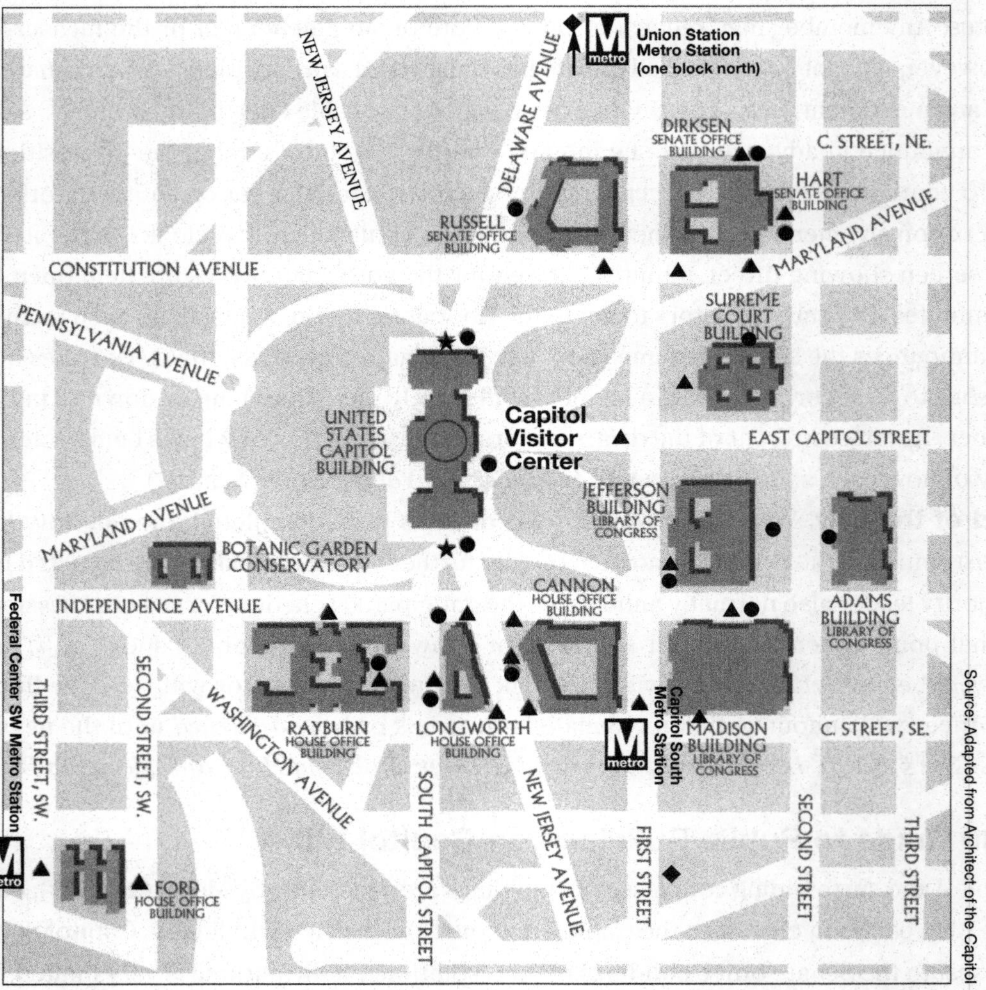

▲ Visitors' entrance to the office buildings
★ Entrances for members, staff, accredited press, building access card holders, and visitors with business appointments only
● Barrier-free entrances for handicapped
◆ Public parking lots

North

Visitor Center, which has entrances from First Street, NE, near the intersection with East Capitol Street (across the street from the Supreme Court building). For tours, visitors must obtain timed-entry admission, reservations for which may be made in advance. (*Visit the U.S. Capitol Visitor Center at <www.visitthecapitol.gov>, or call the Office of Visitor Services at 202-226-8000.*) Guided tours may also be arranged with individual representative's or senator's offices. For visitors with business in the Capitol, House and Senate appointment desks are located in the Capitol Visitor Center, at the north and south entrances to the Capitol, and near tunnels or subways to the Capitol in the House and Senate office buildings. Visitors to the House and Senate galleries, which are open when the respective chamber is in session and during business hours Monday through Friday, must obtain gallery passes from a member of Congress; admission is through the Capitol Visitor Center.

The West Front of the Capitol faces The Mall, with its terraces providing sweeping views of Pennsylvania Avenue, the Smithsonian buildings, and other museums, monuments, and federal office buildings. (*See also § 11.32, The Lantern and Flags.*)

In elevator lobbies in the Capitol and House and Senate office buildings, a visitor finds wall directories for the offices of representatives, senators, committees, and other officials, including both office and telephone numbers. Often there are floor plans in the elevator lobbies, as well, to orient visitors.

Many rooms in the Capitol and congressional office buildings are available for meals, receptions, meetings, and other activities. A person or organization wishing to arrange a Capitol Hill event must work through the office of a member of Congress, a congressional committee or a congressional leader. Dining rooms, cafeterias, cafes, and vending machines are located throughout the Capitol complex.

§ 11.32

The Lantern and Flags

The Capitol Dome is topped by twelve columns encircling a lantern. The lantern is lit when one or both houses of Congress meet in night session. Although there is not a legal requirement for the night lighting or a record of when the lighting began, it is believed that the practice started in about 1864, when members lived in boardinghouses and hotels near the Capitol.

Moreover, when either the House or Senate is in session, a flag flies over the respective chamber. If a chamber recesses rather than adjourns, the flag remains flying until the next adjournment.

Flags also fly over the East and West Fronts twenty-four hours a day, a tradition that started during World War I. They are lowered and removed only when they are worn. (*For information on flags flown over the Capitol that may be obtained through the office of a member of Congress, see § 2.26, Assistance to Constituents.*)

Capitol

The chambers of the House and Senate, National Statuary Hall, and the Rotunda are located on the second ("principal") floor of the Capitol. (*See § 11.33, The Capitol's Second (Principal) Floor.*)

Entrances to the visitor galleries for each chamber are located on the third floor. A visitor must have separate House and Senate gallery passes (both available from a representative's or senator's office), or be accompanied by a guide, or a person with a congressional ID to be admitted to the galleries. Members, congressional staff, the credentialed media, and other staff have IDs that provide them with access to various parts of the Capitol. Special events, such as the president's State of the Union address, generally are not open to guests without event tickets. (*For floor plans and illustrations of the House and Senate chambers, see § 11.10, How to Follow Proceedings in the House; and § 11.20, How to Follow Proceedings in the Senate.*)

Rooms in the Capitol are numbered with an *H* or an *S*, such as S-228, the Old Senate Chamber. *H* rooms are located on the House side of the Capitol, and *S* rooms on the Senate side. One room on the first (ground) floor in the middle of the East Front is numbered EF-100. On the basement level,

§ 11.33

The Capitol's Second (Principal) Floor

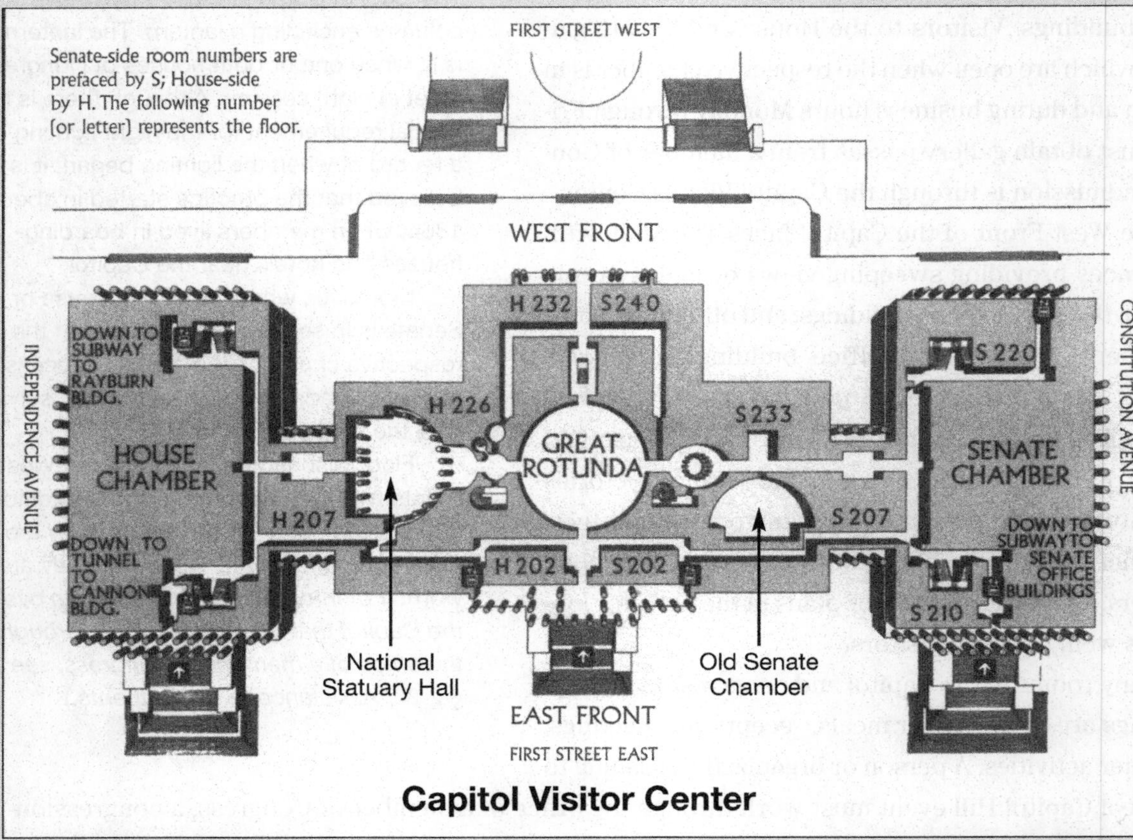

Source: Adapted from Architect of the Capitol

there are rooms designated *HB*, *HC*, and *HT* on the House side of the Capitol, and *SB*, *SC*, and *ST* on the Senate side.

From the Capitol, there is underground access to the House and Senate office buildings. From the southwest elevators on the House side of the Capitol, a visitor can reach the subway and walkway to the Rayburn House Office Building. From the southeast elevators on the House side, a visitor can reach the underground walkway to the Cannon House Office Building, which connects to underground walkways to the Longworth and Rayburn Buildings and, via the Cannon Building, to the Library of Congress' Madison Building. Current security measures restrict self-guided tours from use of these connections to the Capitol.

From the northeast elevators on the Senate side of the Capitol, a visitor can reach the subways and walkways to the Senate's Russell, Dirksen, and Hart Office Buildings. Underground walkways also connect the Russell to the Dirksen and Hart Buildings. Again, current security measures restrict self-guided tours from use of these connections to the Capitol.

Some elevators in the Capitol and the congressional office buildings are reserved for members. When bells ring to summon members to the House or Senate floor, the respective subways and additional elevators are reserved for members.

At street level, when the bells ring summoning members, the police operate the traffic lights at corners next to the congressional office buildings to provide priority to members crossing Independence Avenue on the House side and Constitution Avenue on the Senate side. At evening rush hour, this activity can lead to traffic backups.

While access to the Capitol is strictly controlled and limited, access to the congressional office buildings may be obtained by passing through a security checkpoint at many building doors.

House Office Buildings

There are four House office buildings. The three principal buildings—Rayburn, Longworth, and Cannon—accommodate member, most committee, and most subcommittee offices; they line Independence Avenue from First Street, SW, to First Street, SE. The fourth building, Ford, is located at Third and D Streets, SW. (*See § 11.34, House Office Buildings.*)

Beginning at the foot of Capitol Hill, the westernmost building is the Rayburn Building, named for Representative Sam Rayburn, D-TX (1913–1961; Speaker, 1940–1947, 1949–1953, 1955–1961). Rooms in this building are indicated by four digits, beginning with a *2*, such as 2120 Rayburn HOB, the main office of the Armed Services Committee. The second digit indicates the floor—2120 is on the first floor. (A *B* or *SB* preceding a number indicates a location on the basement or subbasement floor.)

Across South Capitol Street from the Rayburn Building is the Longworth Building, named for Representative Nicholas Longworth, R-OH (1903–1913, 1915–1931; Speaker, 1925–1931). Rooms in this building are indicated by four digits, beginning with a *1*, such as 1301 Longworth HOB, the main office of the Agriculture Committee. The second digit indicates the floor—1301 is on the third floor. (A *B* or *SB* preceding a number indicates a location on the basement or subbasement floor.)

Across New Jersey Avenue from the Longworth Building is the Cannon Building, named for Representative Joseph G. Cannon, R-IL (1873–1891, 1893–1913, 1915–1923; Speaker, 1903–1911). Rooms in this building are indicated by three digits, such as 207 Cannon HOB, the main office of the Budget Committee, located on the second floor. (A *B* preceding a number indicates a location on the basement floor.)

The Ford Building, west of the Rayburn Building and past an entrance to I-395, is named for former Republican representative from Michigan, vice president, and president, Gerald R. Ford (House, 1949–1973; minority leader, 1965–1973; vice president, 1973–1974; president, 1974–1977). Rooms in this building are indicated by an *H2*, followed by a three-digit number, such as H2-405, the Congressional Budget Office, located on the fourth floor.

Senate Office Buildings

There are three Senate office buildings, which line Constitution Avenue, NE. (*See § 11.35, Senate Office Buildings.*) Closest to the Capitol is the Russell Building, named for Senator Richard B. Russell, D-GA (1933–1971). Rooms in this building are indicated by an *SR*, such as SR-328A Russell Build-

§ 11.34

House Office Buildings

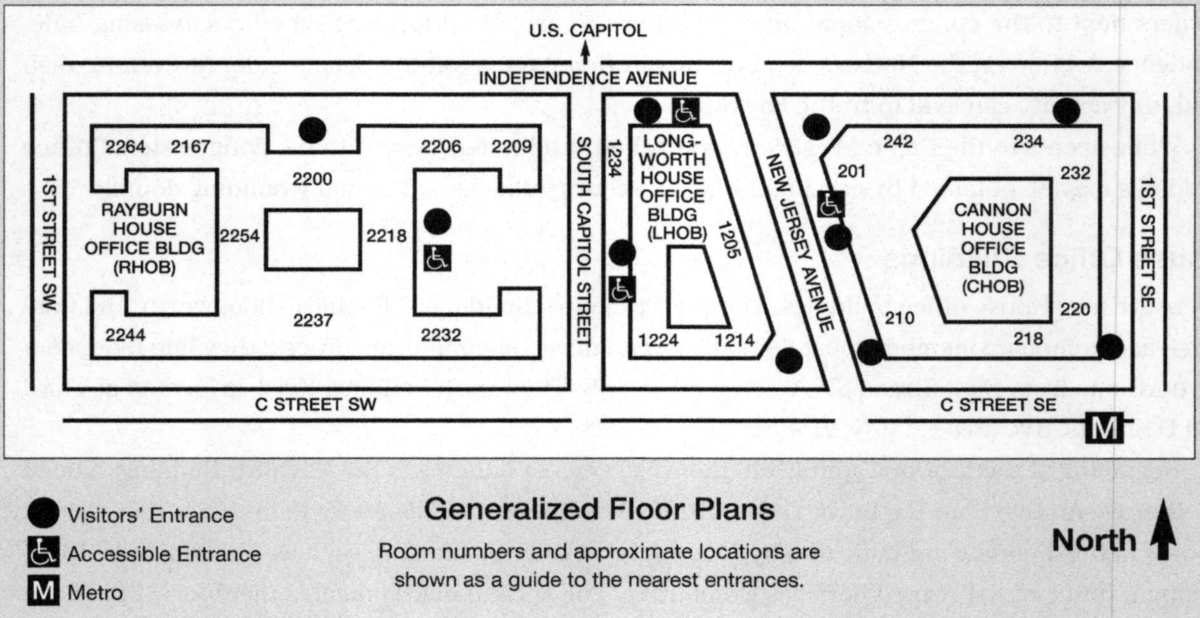

Generalized Floor Plans

Room numbers and approximate locations are shown as a guide to the nearest entrances.

ing, the main office of the Agriculture, Nutrition, and Forestry Committee. (A *B* preceding a number indicates a location on the basement floor.)

Across First Street, NE, is the Dirksen Building, named for Senator Everett McKinley Dirksen, R-IL (House: 1933–1949; Senate: 1951–1969; Republican leader, 1959–1969). Rooms in this building are indicated by an *SD*, such as SD-624 Dirksen Building, the main office of the Budget Committee. (A *B* preceding a number indicates a location on the basement floor.)

Connected to the Dirksen Building is the third Senate office building, the Hart Building, named for Senator Philip Hart, D-MI (1959–1976). Rooms in this building are indicated by an *SH*, such as SH-838 Hart Building, the main office of the Indian Affairs Committee. (A *B* preceding a number indicates a location on the basement floor.)

Members' and Committees' Office Locations

Representatives' and senators' offices are located in the House and Senate office buildings. Members' office locations currently remain the same until the end of a Congress. A new representative elected or new senator appointed to replace a member who resigns from Congress or dies in office before the end of a Congress occupies her predecessor's office.

Shortly after a general election, through the period of the early organization meetings, members bid on vacant offices, based on seniority. Any reelected members who wish to bid on vacant offices, all members filling vacancies and now elected to a new term, and all newly elected members bid on vacant offices. A chain reaction ensues as more senior members decide to move due to a myriad of

§11.35

Senate Office Buildings

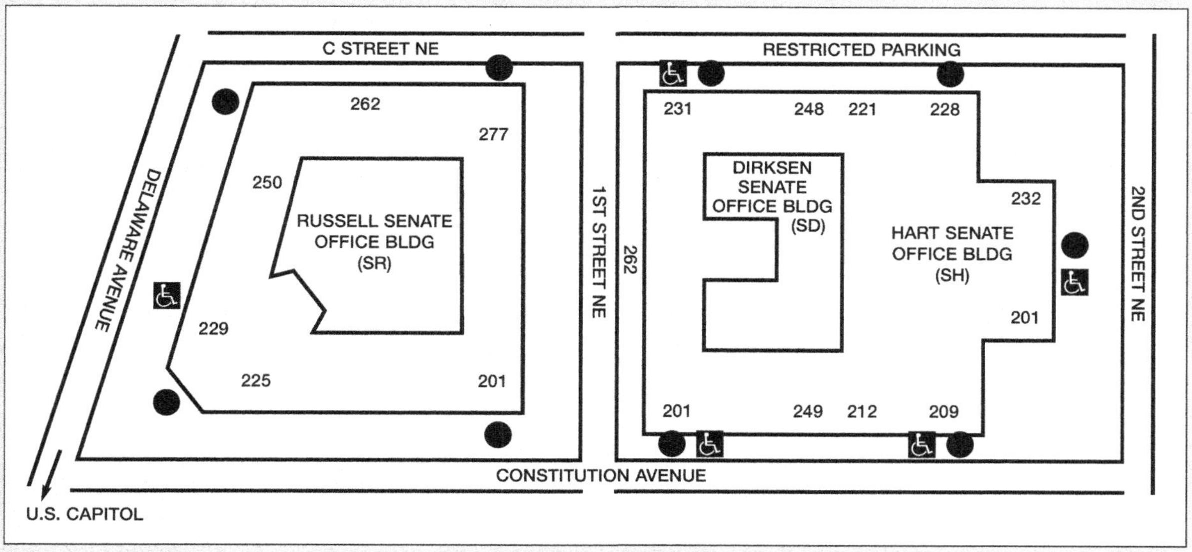

● Visitors' Entrance
♿ Accessible Entrance

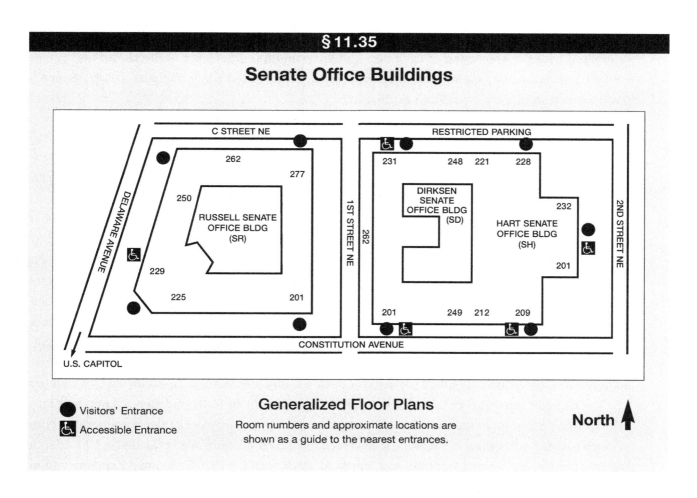

Generalized Floor Plans

Room numbers and approximate locations are shown as a guide to the nearest entrances.

North ↑

reasons—such as the availability of offices closer to Capitol subways and walkways, or closer to their principal committees. A reelected member might also decide *not* to move because a better office is unavailable or because the disruption of moving is undesirable.

By the end of November or early December, new office assignments are completed. Retiring members and those defeated for reelection are given a deadline by which they must vacate their offices. Members-elect work in shared or temporary quarters with temporary mail drops. Space must also be found for retiring or defeated representatives if a lame-duck session lasts past the vacate date. The architect of the Capitol, other congressional support offices, and telephone company and other services then go into action and execute moves in December, right through the holidays, to try to get every representative into his new, repainted, cleaned, furnished, functioning office before the next Congress convenes. New senators might reside in temporary offices for as long as several months after the convening of a Congress. Freshman members in both chambers generally take the phone numbers of the members they are replacing.

In addition, about seventy senators have offices in the Capitol. These small rooms are colloquially referred to as "hideaways."

Committee offices change less frequently. The principal majority and minority offices and main meeting rooms tend to stay the same from Congress to Congress, although the allocation of staff and other resources in both chambers may have an impact on committee room assignments. However, subcommittee rooms often change because subcommittees are regularly abolished, reorganized, or created with the convening of each new Congress and the organizing of the House and Senate committees. Temporary committees also must be accommodated when they are created. Space is freed when a temporary committee expires.

Other Government Buildings

The Supreme Court Building is located on First Street, NE, between East Capitol Street and Maryland Avenue, NE. Visitors are not free to tour this building on their own, but public lecture tours are available.

The Library of Congress has three buildings on Capitol Hill, each named for a president and all connected by underground walkways. The Jefferson Building (named for Thomas Jefferson, the third president), where rooms are designated with an *LJ* followed by a number, is located at the corner of Independence Avenue and First Street, SE. (A new tunnel connects the Jefferson Building to the Capitol Visitor Center.) Directly across First Street is the Madison Building (named for James Madison, the fourth president), where rooms are designated with an *LM* followed by a number. (The Madison Building is also connected to the Cannon House Office Building by an underground walkway, not open to visitors.) At Independence Avenue and Second Street, SE, is the Adams Building (named for John Adams, the second president), where rooms are designated with an *LA* followed by a number.

The Botanic Garden conservatory is located at the corner of Independence Avenue and First Street, SW. The outdoor National Garden, completed in 2006 to the west of the conservatory, comprises a rose garden, a butterfly garden, a lawn terrace, the First Ladies Water Garden, a Mid-Atlantic regional garden, and a small amphitheater. Bartholdi Park, with the 1876 Centennial Exposition fountain created by Frédéric Auguste Bartholdi, designer of the Statue of Liberty, lies across Independence Avenue from the conservatory.

§ 11.40 Bells and Lights: Senate and House Signals

The House and Senate use a system of "bells" and "buzzers," respectively, to announce a vote or quorum call on the chamber floor; the convening, recess, or adjournment of the chamber; and, in the Senate, the conclusion of Morning Business. House bells and lights operate only on the House side of the Capitol and in House office buildings, and Senate buzzers and lights operate only on the Senate side of the Capitol and in Senate office buildings. There are also lights circling many wall clocks throughout the House and Senate, which complement the bells or buzzers. For example, two rings and two illuminated lights on the Senate side of the Capitol and in the Senate office buildings would indicate a quorum call on the Senate floor.

As soon as the bells or buzzers sound, personal and committee staffers check the floor proceedings on television, or BlackBerries®, or by a call to the members' party floor recordings or cloakrooms to find out what is happening in the chamber, and alert members as necessary. The parties in each chamber also use telecommunications systems to notify members of floor action.

The House bells and Senate buzzers are tested early in the day on days in which a chamber will be in session.

In addition, the chandeliers outside the facing entrances of the House and Senate—the north entrance to the House chamber and the south entrance to the Senate chamber—are equipped with bulbs to indicate that a chamber is in session. Beneath the House chandelier hang two red bulbs that are illuminated when the House is in session. Beneath the Senate chandelier hang a white bulb and a red bulb. The white bulb is illuminated when the Senate is in regular session; the red one is lit when the Senate is in executive session.

Senate Buzzer and Light Signals

1. One long ring at hour of convening	• One red light remains lighted at all times while the Senate is in session.
2. One ring	• Yeas and nays.
3. Two rings	• Quorum call.
4. Three rings	• Call of absentees.
5. Four rings	• Adjournment or recess (end of daily session).
6. Five rings	• Seven and one-half minutes remaining on yea-or-nay vote.
7. Six rings	• Morning Business concluded, with lights shut off immediately; or recess during daily session, with lights staying on during period of recess.
8. Twelve rings rung at two-second intervals	• Civil Defense Warning.

House Bell and Light Signals

1. One long ring	• Occurs fifteen minutes before the House convenes, with one ring at the time of convening. One red light remains lighted at all times while the House is in session.
2. One long ring, pause, followed by three rings	• Signals the start or continuation of a notice quorum call. It is terminated if and when one hundred members appear.
3. One long ring	• Termination of a notice quorum call.
4. Two rings	• Fifteen-minute electronically recorded vote.
5. Two rings, pause, followed by two rings	• Manual roll-call vote. The bells are sounded again when the clerk reaches the letter *R* in the roster of representatives. Manual roll-call votes are rare.
6. Two rings, pause, followed by five rings	• First vote under suspension of the rules or on clustered votes. Two rings occur five minutes later. The first vote of a set of clustered votes takes fifteen minutes. Successive votes are taken at intervals of not less than five minutes, and each successive vote is signaled by five rings.

House Bell and Light Signals

7. Three rings	• Quorum call, either initially or after a notice quorum has been converted to a regular quorum call. The bells are repeated five minutes after the first ring. Members have fifteen minutes to be recorded.
8. Three rings, pause, followed by three rings	• Manual quorum call. The bells are sounded again when the clerk reaches the letter *R* in the roster of representatives. Manual quorum calls are rare.
9. Three rings, pause, followed by five rings	• Quorum call in Committee of the Whole, which may be immediately followed by a five-minute recorded vote.
10. Four rings	• Adjournment of the House.
11. Five rings	• Five-minute electronically recorded vote.
12. Six rings	• Recess of the House.
13. Twelve rings rung at two-second intervals	• Civil Defense Warning.

§ 11.50 Checklist of Jobs to Undertake in the Office: Tracking Legislative Action

This section provides a selective list of information needed to track legislative activity. Many congressional offices and outside organizations prepare a "table" on each issue or measure they are tracking to identify key players and actions. Spreadsheet or flowchart software can assist with this task. A checklist such as the following guides the government affairs professional in planning strategy and identifying legislative actions that may require an activity or response at a specific time.

Tracking Legislative Action Checklist

Tracking a Measure: Introduction and Referral

- **Key Documents**

  Measure as introduced

  Sponsor statements and press releases

- **Key Actions and Events**

  Timing of introduction

  Sponsor

  Cosponsors

  Committee(s) and subcommittee(s) of referral

Tracking a Measure: Committee Action, Hearings, and Markup

- **Key Players**

  Members of committee and subcommittee

  Key committee staff

  Key subcommittee staff

  Key committee and subcommittee members and their positions on measure

  Party leadership position on measure

  Outside groups, both proponents and opponents

  Administration position on measure

- **Key Documents**

  Committee rules

  Committee hearing schedule

  Witness testimony

  Hearing transcript

  Agency views

  Congressional Budget Office estimate

  Vehicle for markup consideration

  Amendments offered in markup

  Vehicle reported (for example, clean bill or original bill)

  Committee report

  Additional, supplemental, and minority views, if filed

- **Key Actions and Events**

  Witnesses scheduled

  Hearings held

  Markup schedule

  Markup

  Disposition of amendments

  Votes in markup on each amendment

  Vote to report measure

Tracking a Measure: Floor Action

- **Key Players**

  Leadership, which schedules measure

  House Rules Committee

  Floor managers

  Amendment sponsors

- **Key Documents**

  House and Senate calendars

  Floor schedule/whip notices

  Special rule or unanimous consent time agreement, if appropriate

§ 11.51

Tips for Contacting Members of Congress

Common sense probably tells us that hateful, insulting, or threatening communications do not work. Vague, unfocused, or nebulous requests for action or assistance are also ineffective.

Types of Communication

1. Letters, Faxes, and Email
   - Be brief and to the point
   - Write at the proper time in the legislative process
   - Use your own language
   - Stick to one issue for each communication
   - Personalize the issue
   - Write to your own representative or senator
   - Clearly identify the legislation, using bill numbers if possible
   - Know your facts
   - Be polite and positive
   - Speak for yourself
   - Ask for a reply and include your phone number and postal address, even on email
   - Write on personal stationery, if a letter

2. Telephone Calls
   - Be brief, to the point, and considerate of the member's time constraints
   - Identify yourself as a concerned constituent
   - Indicate the issue
   - Be specific about the action you want
   - Be courteous and polite
   - Compose your thoughts before the call
   - Follow up with a thank-you note

3. Personal Visits
   - Be brief, to the point, and considerate of the member's time constraints
   - Thank the staffer or member by name
   - Put a human face on your issue
   - Begin the meeting by thanking the office for any prior help
   - Respect member's or staffer's opinion
   - "Connect the dots" for the member or staff: explain why the member's help is needed and what specifically the member can do to help

Amendments prefiled
Measure made in order
Measure as passed (engrossed)

- **Key Actions and Events**

Rules Committee meeting (House)
Unanimous consent agreement announced (Senate)
Whip notices
Debate and amendment
Final passage

Tracking a Measure: Reconciling Differences

- **Key Players**

House and Senate conferees
Staff members working with conferees

§ 11.52

Addressing Correspondence to Members of Congress

Addressing Letters to an Individual Member

Honorable [name of representative]
[room number, building]
e.g., 1111 Longworth House Office Building
U.S. House of Representatives
Washington, DC 20515

Dear Representative [last name]:

Honorable [name of senator]
[room number, building]
e.g., 123 Russell Senate Office Building
U.S. Senate
Washington, DC 20510

Dear Senator [last name]:

Addressing Letters to a Committee Chair

Committee on [name]
[room number, building]
e.g., 2222 Rayburn House Office Building
U.S. House of Representatives
Washington, DC 20515

Dear Chairman [last name]:

Committee on [name]
[room number, building]
e.g., 123 Dirksen Senate Office Building
U.S. Senate
Washington, DC 20510

Dear Chairman [last name]:

- **Key Documents**

  Amendments between the chambers
  House-passed and Senate-passed versions of measure
  Side-by-side comparison of measures
  Conference report
  Joint explanatory statement

- **Key Actions and Events**

  Conference meetings
  Amendments offered in conference
  Votes in conference
  Procedures to be followed in conference

Outside the Formal Legislative Process

Proponents and opponents of measure
Lobbying activity on measure
Campaign contributions to sponsors and key opponents of measure
Press coverage of issue, local and national
Polls taken on issue, local and national
Administration activity

§ 11.60 Chapter Summary and Discussion Questions

Watching the House and Senate proceedings on C-SPAN, it is useful first to understand the layout of each chamber, who occupies the dais, who presides, and the locations from which members address their chambers. Representatives do not have assigned seats, but senators do. The House and Senate chambers are located in the Capitol.

A legislative day tends to start in the same way each day, and then develops according to the majority leadership's plan (in the House) or according to the majority leader's iterative pronouncements (in the Senate). Debate and the amendment process in the House is tightly controlled by standing House rules or by special rules reported by the Rules Committee and adopted by the House. Debate and the amendment process in the Senate might be controlled by a unanimous consent agreement, but Senate rules allow senators to debate extensively or to filibuster. Bell (or buzzer) and light systems notify members of quorum calls, votes, and other proceedings in their chambers. Some amount of time each day in each chamber is consumed by non-legislative debate—morning hour, one-minute speeches, and special orders in the House, and morning business in the Senate.

The work of individual representatives and senators and of committees and subcommittees largely occurs in the House and Senate office buildings. There are three Senate office buildings on the Senate side of the Capitol and four House office buildings on the House side of the Capitol. The Supreme Court and the Library of Congress are also located on Capitol Hill.

Government relations professionals develop organized methods of tracking legislative activity and their contacts with members and staff. Experienced government relations professionals also know the value of polite, focused, timely communications.

Discussion Questions

- Who presides in the Senate? Who presides in the House when it is meeting as the House? When it is meeting in Committee of the Whole?
- From what locations do representatives address the House? From what location does a senator address her chamber?
- What three events occur at the convening of each chamber each day?
- What occurs in the Committee of the Whole in the House?
- What is the Senate considering when it is conducting legislative business? What is it considering when it is conducting executive business?
- What area of the national capital does one view from the West Front of the Capitol? What is the name of the access to the Capitol located on the East Front? If you had a meeting in the Capitol, where would you check in to obtain access?
- If you were given the room number for a markup of 1324 in a House office building, in what building would you find that room? If you were given the room number of SR-253 in a Senate office building to attend a hearing, in what building would you find that room?

Chapter Twelve

Putting It All Together: A Working Example

1
2
3
4
5
6
7
8
9
10
11
12

Analysis

§ 12.00 Key Legislative Documents Depicting the History of Financial Services Modernization Legislation in the 106th Congress

Throughout this book, we have presented the legislative process by describing its often esoteric procedures and the documents that are generated at each stage. In this section, our goal is to bring life to the process by describing the progression of a representative piece of legislation—financial services modernization—as it moved through various procedural stages in 1999, the first session of the 106th Congress. It is representative in that more or fewer steps or documents might occur as Congress considers another piece of legislation.

On each following page, the reader will find cover pages and selections from the principal, formal documents generated during the consideration of the financial services legislation. The reader will also find on each of these pages an explanation of the purpose of the representative document in the legislative process and the information that can be gleaned from it. As mentioned throughout this book, many of the documents generated in the legislative process are available from THOMAS, GPO's Federal Digital System, and the House and Senate web sites.

Recall that comprehensive legislation is rarely introduced, considered, and enacted within one session of Congress. It is the product of years of hearings, negotiation, and political timing. For example, the hearings that were held by the House Banking and Financial Services Committee in February 1999, and by the House Commerce Committee's Subcommittee on Finance and Hazardous Materials in April 1999, were the last in a series of hearings on the financial services industry and its regulation by the federal and state governments that had begun years before.

Therefore, to get a full appreciation of the history of this particular legislation, it would be useful to go back at least several Congresses, read the hearings, examine the earlier legislation introduced and perhaps considered, and review statements and any debate that appeared in the *Congressional Record.* There is always a history to a legislative issue, and many members of Congress have participated in at least part of that history before one Congress is able to align policy, politics, and procedure to enact legislation that the president signs into law.

In the 107th Congress, the Banking and Financial Services Committee was renamed the Financial Services Committee, and the Commerce Committee was renamed the Energy and Commerce Committee. In addition, the Financial Services Committee was given jurisdiction over the "business of insurance" and "securities and exchanges," jurisdictional authority that had generally resided in the Commerce Committee. An important cause of the name change and jurisdictional realignment was the enactment of the financial services modernization legislation.

A January 30, 2001, memorandum of understanding that was printed in the *Congressional Record* supplemented the jurisdictional changes to explain certain aspects of insurance and securities issues that would remain in the Energy and Commerce Committee. In the 109th Congress, the Speaker announced that the memorandum of understanding would be modified by deleting a paragraph. The announcement was printed in the *Congressional Record* on January 4, 2005. The paragraph deleted read:

> While it is agreed that the jurisdiction of the Committee on Financial Services over securities and exchanges includes anti-fraud authorities under the securities laws, the Committee on Energy and Commerce will retain jurisdiction only over the issue of setting accounting standards by the Financial Accounting Standards Board.

It is important to know as well that financial services reform as an issue has been considered, in various forms, almost from the time that the Glass-Steagall Act of 1933, the New Deal foundation of twentieth-century financial services regulation, was originally enacted. Major financial services legislation—covering banking, insurance, securities, and related financial services—was subsequently enacted on perhaps a dozen occasions between 1933 and 1999. Other major laws preceded Glass-Steagall, and numerous changes were reflected in amendments and minor legislation after 1933. Likewise, oversight continued and changes to the financial services industry and the economic calamity of 2008 led to massive rewriting of financial services laws, the Dodd-Frank Wall Street Reform and Consumer Protection Act in 2010 (*P.L. 111-203, 124 Stat. 1376*). The government affairs professional, scholar, or anyone working in a subject area needs to develop a good knowledge of the legislative and regulatory history of that subject area.

§ 12.01 Bill as Introduced in the House

H.R. 10 was introduced by Mr. Leach, chair of the House Committee on Banking and Financial Services, on January 6, 1999, the first day of the 106th Congress. Upon introduction there were eleven original cosponsors. The measure was referred to the Committee on Banking and Financial Services (*primary committee*), and in addition to the Committee on Commerce for consideration of provisions within its jurisdiction. Those provisions were not spelled out in the referral language. The Speaker was granted authority to impose time limitations on the referral.

H.R. 10 is designated as *A Bill* at this stage of the process. The *official title* is the language immediately following the bill designation. The *enacting clause*, *"Be it enacted by the Senate and House of Representatives of the United States of America in Congress assembled,"* provides force of law to the measure, if enacted. Section 1(a) identifies the *short (popular) title*; a short title is how most people refer to a measure as it makes its way through the legislative process. (*See § 12.01a.*)

§ 12.01a

Bill as Introduced in the House

(1) Measure number

106TH CONGRESS
1ST SESSION

(1) H. R. 10

To enhance competition in the financial services industry by providing a prudential framework for the affiliation of banks, securities firms, and other financial service providers, and for other purposes.

IN THE HOUSE OF REPRESENTATIVES

JANUARY 6, 1999

(2) Sponsor and original cosponsors

(3) Primary committee referral and sequential referral

(2) Mr. LEACH (for himself, Mr. MCCOLLUM, Mrs. ROUKEMA, Mr. BAKER, Mr. LAZIO, Mr. BACHUS, Mr. CASTLE, Mr. KING, Mr. NEY, Mr. COOK, Mr. LATOURETTE, and Mrs. KELLY) introduced the following bill; which was (3) referred to the Committee on Banking and Financial Services, and in addition to the Committee on Commerce, for a period to be subsequently determined by the Speaker, in each case for consideration of such provisions as fall within the jurisdiction of the committee concerned

---

A BILL

(4) Official title

(4) To enhance competition in the financial services industry by providing a prudential framework for the affiliation of banks, securities firms, and other financial service providers, and for other purposes.

(5) Enacting clause

(5) *Be it enacted by the Senate and House of Representatives of the United States of America in Congress assembled,*

2

SECTION 1. SHORT TITLE; PURPOSES; TABLE OF CONTENTS.

(6) Short (popular) title

(6) (a) SHORT TITLE.—This Act may be cited as the "Financial Services Act of 1999".

§ 12.02 Bill as Reported

The Committee on Banking and Financial Services reported H.R. 10 from committee to the House on March 23, 1999, by a vote of 51 to 8. The vote to report followed two markup sessions held on March 10 and 11. The language on the cover of the reported measure following the phrase "March 23, 1999" indicates that the committee reported a full-text substitute to H.R. 10, *an amendment in the nature of a substitute*. (*See § 12.02a, notes 3, 4.*)

The accompanying committee report was H. Rept. 106-74, the 74th House report filed in the 106th Congress. It was filed in three parts. When more than one committee reports a measure, the report number remains the same for all committees. Each committee version is identified as Part I, Part II, and so forth. (Arabic numbers are gaining popularity for numbering parts, but Roman numerals are traditional.) For H.R. 10, the Banking Committee filed both Parts I and II (*see explanation at § 12.04*). The measure was placed on the *Union Calendar* and was the 105th measure placed on the calendar. (*See § 12.02a, note 1.*)

H.R. 10 was *sequentially* referred to the Committee on Commerce until May 14, 1999. On May 13, the Commerce Committee received an extension until June 11, and, on June 11, it received another extension until June 15. On June 15, the Committee on Commerce reported H.R. 10 from committee to the House with *an amendment in the nature of a substitute*. Within the document (the bill as reported by the two committees), the Commerce Committee amendment followed the Banking Committee amendment. The Banking Committee amendment was printed in italicized type, and the Commerce Committee amendment, in boldface Roman type. (*Compare excerpts at notes 9 and 10 in § 12.02a.*)

On June 15, Mr. Maloney, a member of the Banking and Financial Services Committee, was also added as a cosponsor on the legislation. Members can be added as cosponsors until the measure is reported by all committees that received a referral. (*See § 12.02a, note 6.*)

§ 12.02a

Bill as Reported

❶ Calendar number

❷ Committee report in three parts

❸ Reported from primary committee

❹ Form in which amendment was reported (amendment in the nature of a substitute)

❺ Sequential referral

❻ Additional cosponsor

IB

❶ **Union Calendar No. 105**

106TH CONGRESS
1ST SESSION

H. R. 10

❷ **[Report No. 106–74, Parts I, II, and III]**

To enhance competition in the financial services industry by providing a prudential framework for the affiliation of banks, securities firms, and other financial service providers, and for other purposes.

IN THE HOUSE OF REPRESENTATIVES

JANUARY 6, 1999

Mr. LEACH (for himself, Mr. MCCOLLUM, Mrs. ROUKEMA, Mr. BAKER, Mr. LAZIO, Mr. BACHUS, Mr. CASTLE, Mr. KING, Mr. NEY, Mr. COOK, Mr. LATOURETTE, and Mrs. KELLY) introduced the following bill; which was referred to the Committee on Banking and Financial Services, and in addition to the Committee on Commerce, for a period to be subsequently determined by the Speaker, in each case for consideration of such provisions as fall within the jurisdiction of the committee concerned

MARCH 23, 1999

❸ Reported from the Committee on Banking and Financial Services with an amendment

❹ [Strike out all after the enacting clause and insert the part printed in italic]

MARCH 23, 1999

❺ Referral to the Committee on Commerce extended for a period ending not later than May 14, 1999

MAY 13, 1999

Referral to the Committee on Commerce extended for a period ending not later than June 11, 1999

JUNE 11, 1999

Referral to the Committee on Commerce extended for a period ending not later than June 15, 1999

JUNE 15, 1999

❻ Additional sponsor: Mr. MALONEY of Connecticut

Continued on page 510

§ 12.02a (continued)

Bill as Reported

7 Reported from Commerce Committee

8 Form in which amendment was reported (amendment in the nature of a substitute)

9 Banking Committee amendment

2

JUNE 15, 1999

7 Reported from the Committee on Commerce with an amendment, committed to the Committee of the Whole House on the State of the Union, and ordered to be printed

8 [Strike out all after the enacting clause and insert the part printed in boldface roman]

[For text of introduced bill, see copy of bill as introduced on January 6, 1999]

A BILL

To enhance competition in the financial services industry by providing a prudential framework for the affiliation of banks, securities firms, and other financial service providers, and for other purposes.

Be it enacted by the Senate and House of Representatives of the United States of America in Congress assembled,

9 ***SECTION 1. SHORT TITLE; PURPOSES; TABLE OF CONTENTS.***

(a) SHORT TITLE.—This Act may be cited as the "Financial Services Act of 1999".

(b) PURPOSES.—The purposes of this Act are as follows:

(1) To enhance competition in the financial services industry, in order to foster innovation and efficiency.

(2) To ensure the continued safety and soundness of depository institutions.

Continued on page 511

§ 12.02a (continued)

Bill as Reported

375

of a Federal savings association to a national bank or a State bank after the date of the enactment of the Financial Services Act of 1999 may retain the term 'Federal' in the name of such institution if such depository institution remains an insured depository institution.

"(2) DEFINITIONS.—For purposes of this subsection, the terms 'depository institution', 'insured depository institution', 'national bank', and 'State bank' have the same meanings as in section 3 of the Federal Deposit Insurance Act.".

(10) Commerce Committee amendment

(10) **SECTION 1. SHORT TITLE; PURPOSES; TABLE OF CONTENTS.**

(a) SHORT TITLE.—This Act may be cited as the "Financial Services Act of 1999".

(b) PURPOSES.—The purposes of this Act are as follows:

(1) To enhance competition in the financial services industry, in order to foster innovation and efficiency.

(2) To ensure the continued safety and soundness of depository institutions.

(3) To provide necessary and appropriate protections for investors and en-

12

§ 12.03 Banking and Financial Services Committee Report

Both the Banking Committee and the Commerce Committee reported H.R. 10. Part 1 of H. Rept. 106-74 was filed in the House by the primary committee, the Committee on Banking and Financial Services. When that panel reported H.R. 10 on March 23, 1999, the committee chose to retain H.R. 10 as the legislative vehicle and to report an *amendment in the nature of a substitute.* The committee could have chosen to introduce the amended language as a new, or *clean bill.*

Supplemental, additional, and dissenting views were also filed. They are included in the body of the report. Minority committee members usually request the inclusion of supplemental, additional, and dissenting views in a committee report. Although the request is traditionally made by minority-party members, all committee members are entitled to file such views. To be included, supplemental, additional, and dissenting views must be filed within two days of a committee vote to report. The cover page of the report must indicate when such views are included.

§ 12.03a

Banking and Financial Services Committee Report

❶ Committee report and part number

❷ Reporting committee

❸ Other views

❹ Banking Committee amendment

106TH CONGRESS 1st Session } HOUSE OF REPRESENTATIVES { ❶ REPT. 106–74 Part 1

FINANCIAL SERVICES ACT OF 1999

MARCH 23, 1999.—Ordered to be printed

❷ Mr. LEACH, from the Committee on Banking and Financial Services, submitted the following

REPORT

together with

❸ SUPPLEMENTAL, ADDITIONAL AND DISSENTING VIEWS

[To accompany H.R. 10]

The Committee on Banking and Financial Services, to whom was referred the bill (H.R. 10) to enhance competition in the financial services industry by providing a prudential framework for the affiliation of banks, securities firms, and other financial service providers, and for other purposes, having considered the same, report favorably thereon with an amendment and recommend that the bill as amended do pass.

The amendment is as follows:

❹ Strike out all after the enacting clause and insert in lieu thereof the following:

SECTION 1. SHORT TITLE; PURPOSES; TABLE OF CONTENTS.

(a) SHORT TITLE.—This Act may be cited as the "Financial Services Act of 1999".

(b) PURPOSES.—The purposes of this Act are as follows:

★69–006

12

§ 12.04 Banking and Financial Services Committee Supplementary Report

The Committee on Banking and Financial Services filed in the House a supplementary report containing a cost estimate from the Congressional Budget Office. According to House rules, such an estimate must be included in a committee report. The committee filed a supplementary report to comply with this requirement. The supplementary report also contains an errata correction to Part 1 of the report. The report retains the same number, but is designated Part 2.

§ 12.04a

Banking and Financial Services Committee Supplementary Report

❶ Committee report and part number

❷ Reporting committee

❸ Supplementary report

❹ Purpose of supplementary report

106TH CONGRESS
1st Session
HOUSE OF REPRESENTATIVES
❶ REPT. 106–74
Part 2

FINANCIAL SERVICES ACT OF 1999

JUNE 10, 1999.—Ordered to be printed

❷ Mr. LEACH, from the Committee on Banking and Financial Services, submitted the following

❸ SUPPLEMENTARY REPORT

[To accompany H.R. 10]

❹ This supplemental report shows the cost estimate of the Congressional Budget Office with respect to the bill (H.R. 10), as reported, which was not included in part 1 of the report submitted by the Committee on Banking and Financial Services on March 23, 1999 (H. Rept. 106–74, pt. 1).

This supplemental report is submitted in accordance with clause 3(a)(2) of rule XIII of the Rules of the House of Representatives.

This supplemental report also contains an errata correction to page 2 of part 1 of the report.

U.S CONGRESS,
CONGRESSIONAL BUDGET OFFICE,
Washington, DC, June 10, 1999.

Hon. JAMES A. LEACH,
Chairman, Committee on Banking and Financial Services, House of Representatives, Washington, DC.

DEAR MR. CHAIRMAN: The Congressional Budget Office has prepared the enclosed costs estimate and mandate statements for H.R. 10, the Financial Services Act of 1999. One enclosure includes the estimate of federal costs and the estimate of the impact of the legislation on state, local, and tribal governments. The estimated impact of mandates on the private sector is discussed in a separate enclosure.

If you wish further details on these estimates, we will be pleased to provide them. The CBO staff contacts are Robert S. Seiler (for costs to the Federal Home Loan Banks); Mary Maginniss (for other federal costs); Carolyn Lynch (for federal revenues); Susan Seig (for

57–234

§ 12.05 Commerce Committee Report

Here is the report filed in the House by the House Committee on Commerce, which received a sequential referral of H.R. 10. The report was filed by Mr. Bliley, the chair of the Committee on Commerce, on June 15, 1999, the day the measure was reported with an *amendment in the nature of a substitute*. The report is designated Part 3 of H. Rept. 106-74. Additional views were also filed and included in the body of the report.

§ 12.05a

Commerce Committee Report

❶ Committee report and part number

❷ Reporting committee

❸ Additional views

106TH CONGRESS 1st Session } HOUSE OF REPRESENTATIVES ❶ { REPT. 106–74 Part 3

FINANCIAL SERVICES ACT OF 1999

JUNE 15, 1999.—Committed to the Committee of the Whole House on the State of the Union and ordered to be printed

❷ Mr. BLILEY, from the Committee on Commerce, submitted the following

R E P O R T

together with

❸ ADDITIONAL VIEWS

[To accompany H.R. 10]

The Committee on Commerce, to whom was referred the bill (H.R. 10) to enhance competition in the financial services industry by providing a prudential framework for the affiliation of banks, securities firms, and other financial service providers, and for other purposes, having considered the same, report favorably thereon with an amendment and recommend that the bill as amended do pass.

CONTENTS

57–325

Continued on page 518

12

§ 12.05a (continued)

Commerce Committee Report

❹ Commerce Committee amendment

2

AMENDMENT

The amendment is as follows:

❹ Strike out all after the enacting clause and insert in lieu thereof the following:

SECTION 1. SHORT TITLE; PURPOSES; TABLE OF CONTENTS.

(a) SHORT TITLE.—This Act may be cited as the "Financial Services Act of 1999".

(b) PURPOSES.—The purposes of this Act are as follows:

(1) To enhance competition in the financial services industry, in order to foster innovation and efficiency.

(2) To ensure the continued safety and soundness of depository institutions.

(3) To provide necessary and appropriate protections for investors and ensure fair and honest markets in the delivery of financial services.

(4) To avoid duplicative, potentially conflicting, and overly burdensome regulatory requirements through the creation of a regulatory framework for financial holding companies that respects the divergent requirements of each of the component businesses of the holding company, and that is based upon principles of strong functional regulation and enhanced regulatory coordination.

(5) To reduce and, to the maximum extent practicable, to eliminate the legal barriers preventing affiliation among depository institutions, securities firms, insurance companies, and other financial service providers and to provide a prudential framework for achieving that result.

(6) To enhance the availability of financial services to citizens of all economic circumstances and in all geographic areas.

(7) To enhance the competitiveness of United States financial service providers internationally.

(8) To ensure compliance by depository institutions with the provisions of the Community Reinvestment Act of 1977 and enhance the ability of depository institutions to meet the capital and credit needs of all citizens and communities, including underserved communities and populations.

(c) TABLE OF CONTENTS.—The table of contents for this Act is as follows:

12

§ 12.06 Special Rule from the Rules Committee

On June 30, 1999, the House Rules Committee reported from committee to the House H. Res. 235, a *special rule* providing for consideration of H.R. 10. The special rule was placed on the *House Calendar* as the 81st item. The special rule was reported by Mr. Sessions, a Rules Committee majority member, who was selected to manage the special rule on the floor. The special rule was accompanied by H. Rept. 106-214.

A special rule itself is considered in the House under the *one-hour rule*. Mr. Sessions yielded half of his one hour to a minority member of the Rules Committee *for purposes of debate only*. The two floor managers then parceled out short blocks of time to their colleagues to speak on the rule.

The special rule on H.R. 10 provided ninety minutes of general debate time on the bill, equally divided and controlled by the chairs and ranking minority members of the two committees that reported the legislation, Banking and Financial Services, and Commerce. The special rule also provided for consideration of a new version of H.R. 10, included in the Rules Committee report (H. Rept. 106-214) and cited as "Rules Committee Print dated June 24, 1999." The special rule referred to the Rules Committee report for a list of amendments made in order and the time allocated for each amendment.

§ 12.06a

Special Rule from the Rules Committee

❶ Calendar number

❷ Resolution number

❸ Committee report number

❹ Majority manager of special rule

❺ Special rule for the consideration of H.R. 10

IV

❶ **House Calendar No. 81**

106TH CONGRESS
1ST SESSION

❷ **H. RES. 235**

❸ **[Report No. 106–214]**

Providing for consideration of the bill (H.R. 10) to enhance competition in the financial services industry by providing a prudential framework for the affiliation of banks, securities firms, and other financial service providers, and for other purposes.

IN THE HOUSE OF REPRESENTATIVES

JUNE 30, 1999

❹ Mr. SESSIONS, from the Committee on Rules, reported the following resolution; which was referred to the House Calendar and ordered to be printed

---

RESOLUTION

❺ Providing for consideration of the bill (H.R. 10) to enhance competition in the financial services industry by providing a prudential framework for the affiliation of banks, securities firms, and other financial service providers, and for other purposes.

Resolved, That at any time after the adoption of this resolution the Speaker may, pursuant to clause 2(b) of rule XVIII, declare the House resolved into the Committee of the Whole House on the state of the Union for consideration of the bill (H.R. 10) to enhance competition in the

Continued on page 522

12

§ 12.06a (continued)

Special Rule from the Rules Committee

2

financial services industry by providing a prudential framework for the affiliation of banks, securities firms, and other financial service providers, and for other purposes. The first reading of the bill shall be dispensed with. All points of order against consideration of the bill are

❻ General debate

❻ waived. General debate shall be confined to the bill and shall not exceed 90 minutes, with 45 minutes equally divided and controlled by the chairman and ranking minority member of the Committee on Banking and Financial Services and 45 minutes equally divided and controlled by the chairman and ranking minority member of the Committee on Commerce. After general debate the bill shall be considered for amendment under the five-minute rule.

❼ Alternate version of H.R. 10

❼ In lieu of the amendments now printed in the bill, it shall be in order to consider as an original bill for the purpose of amendment under the five-minute rule an amendment in the nature of a substitute consisting of the text of the

❽ Amendment process

❽ Rules Committee Print dated June 24, 1999. That amendment in the nature of a substitute shall be considered as read. All points of order against that amendment in the nature of a substitute are waived. No amendment to that amendment in the nature of a substitute shall be in order except those printed in the report of the Committee on Rules accompanying this resolution. Each amendment may be offered only in the order printed in

Continued on page 523

§ 12.06a (continued)

Special Rule from the Rules Committee

3

the report, may be offered only by a Member designated in the report, shall be considered as read, shall be debatable for the time specified in the report equally divided and controlled by the proponent and an opponent, shall not be subject to amendment, and shall not be subject to a demand for division of the question in the House or in the Committee of the Whole. All points of order against the amendments printed in the report are waived. The

❾ Cluster voting

❾ Chairman of the Committee of the Whole may: (1) postpone until a time during further consideration in the Committee of the Whole a request for a recorded vote on any amendment; and (2) reduce to five minutes the minimum time for electronic voting on any postponed question that follows another electronic vote without intervening business, provided that the minimum time for electronic voting on the first in any series of questions shall be 15 minutes.

❿ House action

❿ At the conclusion of consideration of the bill for amendment the Committee shall rise and report the bill to the House with such amendments as may have been adopted. Any Member may demand a separate vote in the House on any amendment adopted in the Committee of the Whole to the bill or to the amendment in the nature of a substitute made in order as original text. The previous question shall be considered as ordered on the bill and amendments thereto to final passage without intervening motion except one motion to recommit with or without instructions.

§ 12.07 Rules Committee Report

Accompanying H. Res. 235 was H. Rept. 106-214, a report from the Committee on Rules. The special rule was reported from the Rules Committee by a recorded vote of 9 to 3, and the report filed in the House June 30, 1999, by Mr. Sessions. The report summarized the provisions of the special rule, provided information on all votes taken in the Rules Committee, and, most importantly, designated which amendments would be allowed to be offered on the floor and how much time would be allocated for each amendment. Eleven amendments were made in order under the special rule. Each amendment's sponsor was identified, the amendment was summarized, and the amount of time allocated for each amendment was noted. The full text of each amendment was also included in the Rules Committee report.

§ 12.07a

Rules Committee Report

❶ Committee report number

❷ Purpose of special rule

❸ Provisions of special rule

106TH CONGRESS 1st Session } HOUSE OF REPRESENTATIVES { ❶ REPORT 106–214

❷ PROVIDING FOR THE CONSIDERATION OF H.R. 10, FINANCIAL SERVICES ACT OF 1999

JUNE 30, 1999.—Referred to the House Calendar and ordered to be printed

Mr. SESSIONS, from the Committee on Rules, submitted the following

REPORT

[To accompany H. Res. 235]

The Committee on Rules, having had under consideration House Resolution 235, by a record vote of 9 to 3, report the same to the House with the recommendation that the resolution be adopted.

❸ SUMMARY OF PROVISIONS OF RESOLUTION

The resolution provides for the consideration of H.R. 10, the "Financial Services Act of 1999," under a structured rule. The rule provides 90 minutes of general debate: 45 minutes divided equally between the chairman and ranking minority member of the Committee on Commerce.

The rule waives all points of order against consideration of the bill. The rule makes in order the amendment in the nature of a substitute consisting of the text of the Rules Committee Print dated June 24, 1999, as original text for the purpose of amendment. The rule waives all points of order against the amendment in the nature a substitute.

The rule provides that no amendment to the amendment in the nature of a substitute shall be in order except those printed in this report, which may be offered in the order printed in this report, may be offered only by a Member designated in this report, shall be considered as read, shall be debatable for the time specified in this report equally divided and controlled by the proponent and an opponent, shall not be subject to amendment, and shall not be subject to a demand for a division of the question. The rule waives all points of order against the amendments printed in this report.

The rule allows the chairman of the Committee of the Whole to postpone recorded votes and reduce voting time to five minutes on any postponed question, provided voting time on the first in any se-

69–008

§ 12.08 Statement of Administration Policy (House)

On July 1, 1999, the Office of Management and Budget issued a Statement of Administration Policy on H.R. 10, the House bill. The statement announced the president's support for the legislation and opposition to selected amendments to be offered to it.

§ 12.08a

Statement of Administration Policy (House)

EXECUTIVE OFFICE OF THE PRESIDENT
OFFICE OF MANAGEMENT AND BUDGET
WASHINGTON, D.C. 20503

STATEMENT OF ADMINISTRATION POLICY
(THIS STATEMENT HAS BEEN COORDINATED BY OMB WITH THE CONCERNED AGENCIES.)

July 1, 1999
(House)

H.R. 10 - Financial Services Act of 1999
(Leach (R) IA and 12 co-sponsors)

The Administration supports H.R. 10, the Financial Services Act of 1999. The Administration has been a strong proponent of financial modernization legislation that would best serve the interests of consumers, business, and communities, while protecting the safety and soundness of the financial system. H.R. 10 would:

- allow affiliations among banks, securities firms, and insurance companies, thereby increasing the competitiveness of the U.S. financial services sector and giving consumers greater choice and lower prices;
- preserve the relevance of the Community Reinvestment Act by requiring that banks have and maintain a satisfactory CRA record as a condition for their affiliates or subsidiaries engaging in new financial activities;
- uphold a bipartisan compromise allowing financial services firms to conduct financial activities in the structure -- subsidiaries or affiliates of banks -- that best serves their customers, in a way that is best for safety and soundness;
- generally provide for the continued separation of banking and commerce.

The President has stated the importance of adopting protections to ensure the privacy of consumers' financial records. The amendment to be considered by the House would improve the bill by including new privacy protections, although it does not address all of the issues involved. The Administration will continue to pursue additional protections.

The Administration strongly opposes the medical privacy provisions of the bill. Unfortunately, those provisions would preempt important existing protections and do not reflect the extensive legislative work that has already been done on this complex issue. The Administration thus urges striking the medical privacy provisions and will pursue medical privacy in other fora.

The Administration strongly opposes the Barr-Paul-Campbell Amendment, which would seriously erode our ability to fight financial criminals and the drug cartels. The amendment would effectively eliminate suspicious activity reporting by financial institutions -- one of our

Continued on page 527

§ 12.08a (continued)

Statement of Administration Policy (House)

most important tools in fighting money laundering and fraud. The amendment would mark a significant retreat in our fight against narcotraffickers. The Administration strongly opposes the bill's Federal Home Loan Bank System provisions, particularly a provision that would allow each Home Loan Bank to cut its capital requirement in half and thereby effectively increase the System's taxpayer subsidy without any commensurate return in public benefits. In addition, the Administration believes that the System must focus more on lending to community banks and less on arbitrage activities and short-term lending that do not advance its public purpose. The Administration opposes granting the Federal Housing Finance Board independent litigating authority, which would be inconsistent with the Attorney General's authority to coordinate and conduct litigation on behalf of the United States.

The Administration strongly objects to the refusal to allow House consideration of Representative Lee's anti-redlining amendment, which would help deter violations of the Fair Housing Act. The Administration strongly supports the amendment.

The Administration is concerned that the bill would unduly restrict banks' authority to sell insurance, thereby diminishing competition and reducing choice for consumers.

Because of its commitment to maintaining a separation of banking and commerce, the Administration continues to favor a clear prohibition on existing unitary thrift holding companies selling their subsidiary thrifts to non-financial firms. Allowing such sales could lead to substantial non-financial ownership of insured depository institutions.

The Administration opposes section 154 because it could be seen as undermining principles of normal trade relations and national treatment, which could weaken efforts to negotiate further market access liberalization and expose U.S. firms to additional restrictions abroad.

§ 12.09 Legislation as Passed the House

Pursuant to the provisions of the special rule that had been adopted, the legislation was considered in the Committee of the Whole. Of the eleven amendments made in order under H. Res. 235 (the special rule), five were agreed to by voice vote, four were agreed to by recorded vote, and two failed by recorded vote. The measure passed the House on a 343-to-86 vote.

The measure was now designated as *An Act*, which is how the reader knows that the legislation has passed one chamber. This document is also now referred to as the *House engrossed bill*.

§ 12.09a

Legislation as Passed the House

❶ No longer *A Bill* but *An Act* (engrossed measure)

106TH CONGRESS
1ST SESSION

H. R. 10

❶ **AN ACT**

To enhance competition in the financial services industry by providing a prudential framework for the affiliation of banks, securities firms, and other financial service providers, and for other purposes.

Be it enacted by the Senate and House of Representatives of the United States of America in Congress assembled,

Continued on page 529

§ 12.09a (continued)

Legislation as Passed the House

SECTION 1. SHORT TITLE; PURPOSES; TABLE OF CONTENTS.

(a) SHORT TITLE.—This Act may be cited as the "Financial Services Act of 1999".

(b) PURPOSES.—The purposes of this Act are as follows:

(1) To enhance competition in the financial services industry, in order to foster innovation and efficiency.

(2) To ensure the continued safety and soundness of depository institutions.

(3) To provide necessary and appropriate protections for investors and ensure fair and honest markets in the delivery of financial services.

(4) To avoid duplicative, potentially conflicting, and overly burdensome regulatory requirements through the creation of a regulatory framework for financial holding companies that respects the divergent requirements of each of the component businesses of the holding company, and that is based upon principles of strong functional regulation and enhanced regulatory coordination.

(5) To reduce and, to the maximum extent practicable, to eliminate the legal barriers preventing affiliation among depository institutions, securities firms, insurance companies, and other financial serv-

§ 12.10 Legislation as Received in the Senate

H.R. 10 was received by the Senate on July 12, 1999. It was not referred to a Senate committee, although that could have happened. It was *placed directly on the calendar*, in part because a companion Senate measure had already been considered by a Senate committee.

§ 12.10a

Legislation as Received in the Senate

❶ Calendar number

❷ House-passed measure received by Senate

II

❶ **Calendar No. 204**

106TH CONGRESS
1ST SESSION

H. R. 10

❷ IN THE SENATE OF THE UNITED STATES

JULY 12, 1999

Received; read twice and placed on the Calendar

AN ACT

To enhance competition in the financial services industry by providing a prudential framework for the affiliation of banks, securities firms, and other financial service providers, and for other purposes.

Be it enacted by the Senate and House of Representatives of the United States of America in Congress assembled,

Continued on page 531

§ 12.10a (continued)

Legislation as Received in the Senate

SECTION 1. SHORT TITLE; PURPOSES; TABLE OF CONTENTS.

(a) SHORT TITLE.—This Act may be cited as the "Financial Services Act of 1999".

(b) PURPOSES.—The purposes of this Act are as follows:

(1) To enhance competition in the financial services industry, in order to foster innovation and efficiency.

(2) To ensure the continued safety and soundness of depository institutions.

(3) To provide necessary and appropriate protections for investors and ensure fair and honest markets in the delivery of financial services.

(4) To avoid duplicative, potentially conflicting, and overly burdensome regulatory requirements through the creation of a regulatory framework for financial holding companies that respects the divergent requirements of each of the component businesses of the holding company, and that is based upon principles of strong functional regulation and enhanced regulatory coordination.

(5) To reduce and, to the maximum extent practicable, to eliminate the legal barriers preventing affiliation among depository institutions, securities firms, insurance companies, and other financial serv-

§ 12.11 Legislation as Introduced in the Senate

S. 900 is an *original bill*, which means that it was not introduced and referred to the Senate Committee on Banking, Housing, and Urban Affairs, but rather was drafted in the committee and then reported to the Senate. The chair of the committee, Mr. Gramm, reported the measure on April 28, 1999. A committee report, S. Rept. 106-44, was also filed in the Senate. The measure was placed on the Senate calendar as the 94th item.

§ 12.11a

Legislation as Introduced in the Senate

II

❶ Calendar number

❶ **Calendar No. 94**

106TH CONGRESS
1ST SESSION

S. 900

❷ Committee report number

❷ **[Report No. 106–44]**

To enhance competition in the financial services industry by providing a prudential framework for the affiliation of banks, securities firms, insurance companies, and other financial service providers, and for other purposes.

IN THE SENATE OF THE UNITED STATES

APRIL 28, 1999

❸ Original bill reported from committee

❸ Mr. GRAMM, from the Committee on Banking, Housing, and Urban Affairs, reported the following original bill, which was read twice and placed on the calendar

---

A BILL

❹ Official title

❹ To enhance competition in the financial services industry by providing a prudential framework for the affiliation of banks, securities firms, insurance companies, and other financial service providers, and for other purposes.

❺ Enacting clause

❺ *Be it enacted by the Senate and House of Representatives of the United States of America in Congress assembled,*

SECTION 1. SHORT TITLE; TABLE OF CONTENTS.

❻ Short (popular) title

❻ (a) SHORT TITLE.—This Act may be cited as the "Financial Services Modernization Act of 1999".

12

§ 12.12 Senate Committee Report

The Committee on Banking, Housing, and Urban Affairs reported S. 900 to the Senate, by an 11-to-9 vote. A committee report was filed in the Senate on April 28, 1999, and numbered S. Rept. 106-44, the 44th Senate committee report filed in the 106th Congress. *Additional views* were also filed and included in the body of the report. The calendar number is repeated on the cover page of the Senate report. A section entitled *introduction* and another entitled *history of legislation* summarized the Senate Banking Committee's actions on the legislation.

§ 12.12a

Senate Committee Report

1 Calendar number

2 Committee report number

3 Reporting committee

4 Measure reported

5 Additional views

---

1 **Calendar No. 94**

106TH CONGRESS *1st Session*	SENATE	2 REPORT 106–44

FINANCIAL SERVICES MODERNIZATION
ACT OF 1999

REPORT

OF THE

3 COMMITTEE ON BANKING, HOUSING,
AND URBAN AFFAIRS
UNITED STATES SENATE

TO ACCOMPANY

4 S. 900

together with

5 ADDITIONAL VIEWS

APRIL 28, 1999.—Ordered to be printed

U.S. GOVERNMENT PRINTING OFFICE
69–010 WASHINGTON : 1999

§ 12.13 Statement of Administration Policy (Senate)

On May 3, 1999, the Office of Management and Budget issued a Statement of Administration Policy on S. 900, the Senate bill, announcing the administration's opposition to S. 900. The statement indicated that the president would veto the Senate measure in its current form.

§ 12.13a

Statement of Administration Policy (Senate)

EXECUTIVE OFFICE OF THE PRESIDENT
OFFICE OF MANAGEMENT AND BUDGET
WASHINGTON, D.C. 20503

STATEMENT OF ADMINISTRATION POLICY
(THIS STATEMENT HAS BEEN COORDINATED BY OMB WITH THE CONCERNED AGENCIES.)

May 3, 1999
(Senate)

S. 900 - Financial Services Modernization Act of 1999
(Gramm (R) TX)

The Administration strongly opposes S. 900, which would revise laws governing the financial services industry. This Administration has been a strong proponent of financial modernization legislation that would best serve the interests of consumers, businesses, and communities, while protecting the safety and soundness of our financial system. Consequently, it supports the bill's repeal of the Glass-Steagall Act's prohibition on banks affiliating with securities firms and of the Bank Holding Company Act's prohibitions on insurance underwriting. Nevertheless, because of crucial flaws in the bill, the President has stated that, if the bill were presented to him in its current form, he would veto it.

In its current form, the bill would undermine the effectiveness of the Community Reinvestment Act (CRA), a law that has helped to build homes and create jobs by encouraging banks to serve creditworthy borrowers throughout the communities they serve. The bill fails to require that banks seeking to conduct new financial activities achieve and maintain a satisfactory CRA record. In addition, the bill's "safe harbor" provision would amend current law to effectively shield financial institutions from public comment on banking applications that they file with Federal regulators. The CRA exemption for banks with less than $100 million in assets would repeal CRA for approximately 4,000 banks and thrifts that banking agency rules already exempt from CRA paperwork reporting burdens. In all, these limitations constitute an assault upon CRA and are unacceptable.

The bill would unjustifiably deny financial services firms holding 99 percent of national bank assets the choice of conducting new financial activities through subsidiaries, forcing them to conduct those activities exclusively through bank holding company affiliates. Thus the bill largely prohibits a structure with proven advantages for safety and soundness, effectively denying many financial services firms the freedom to organize themselves in the way that best serves their customers.

The bill would also inadequately inform and protect consumers under the new system of financial products it authorizes. If Congress is to authorize large, complex organizations to offer a wide range of financial products, then consumers should be guaranteed appropriate disclosures and other protections.

The bill would dramatically expand the ability of depository institutions and nonfinancial firms to affiliate. The Administration has serious concerns about mixing banking and

Continued on page 537

§ 12.13a (continued)

Statement of Administration Policy (Senate)

commercial activity under any circumstances, and these concerns are heightened by the financial crises affecting other countries over the past few years.

The Administration also opposes the bill's piecemeal modification of the Federal Home Loan Bank System. The Administration believes that the System must focus more on lending to community banks and less on arbitrage activities and short-term lending that do not advance its public purpose. The Administration opposes any changes to the System that do not include these crucial reforms.

In addition, the Administration opposes granting the Federal Housing Finance Board independent litigation authority. Such authority would be inconsistent with the Attorney General's authority to coordinate and conduct litigation on behalf of the United States.

Pay-As-You-Go Scoring

S. 900 would affect direct spending and receipts. Therefore, it is subject to the pay-as-you-go requirement of the Omnibus Budget Reconciliation Act of 1990. OMB's pay-as-you-go scoring of this bill is under development.

§ 12.14 Legislation as Passed the Senate

The legislation was considered in the Senate by agreeing to a *motion to proceed to consideration.* Numerous amendments were offered and disposed of, either by being agreed to, rejected, withdrawn, or tabled. The measure passed the Senate by a vote of 54 to 44, on May 6, 1999.

The legislation is now designated as *An Act,* which is how the reader knows that the legislation has passed one chamber. This document is referred to as the *Senate engrossed bill.*

§ 12.14a

Legislation as Passed the Senate

106TH CONGRESS
1ST SESSION

S. 900

❶ No longer *A Bill* but *An Act* (engrossed measure)

❶ AN ACT

To enhance competition in the financial services industry by providing a prudential framework for the affiliation of banks, securities firms, insurance companies, and other financial service providers, and for other purposes.

Be it enacted by the Senate and House of Representatives of the United States of America in Congress assembled,

SECTION 1. SHORT TITLE; TABLE OF CONTENTS.

(a) SHORT TITLE.—This Act may be cited as the "Financial Services Modernization Act of 1999".

§ 12.15 Legislation Received in the House from the Senate

On July 20, 1999, the Senate bill, S. 900, was transmitted to the House, which considered it and amended it with its own version. This is evident from the language "strike out all after the enacting clause and insert."

The House and Senate took their first step toward reconciling differences—selecting one bill number, S. 900, to use as the legislative vehicle for further action.

§ 12.15a

Legislation Received in the House from the Senate

❶ House amendment to Senate bill (text of H.R. 10)

In the House of Representatives, U. S.,

July 20, 1999.

Resolved, That the bill from the Senate (S. 900) entitled "An Act to enhance competition in the financial services industry by providing a prudential framework for the affiliation of banks, securities firms, insurance companies, and other financial service providers, and for other purposes", do pass with the following

AMENDMENTS:

❶ Strike out all after the enacting clause and insert:

SECTION 1. SHORT TITLE; PURPOSES; TABLE OF CONTENTS.

(a) SHORT TITLE.—This Act may be cited as the "Financial Services Act of 1999".

(b) PURPOSES.—The purposes of this Act are as follows:

(1) To enhance competition in the financial services industry, in order to foster innovation and efficiency.

(2) To ensure the continued safety and soundness of depository institutions.

12

§ 12.16 Side-by-Side Comparative Print

Before convening a conference committee, it is customary for respective committee staff to prepare a side-by-side comparative print of the two versions of the measure to be reconciled in conference. This document enables conferees to see the differences between the two versions of a measure. A side-by-side often includes a fourth column—current law.

§12.16a

Side-by-Side Comparative Print

COMPARISON OF

S. 900, FINANCIAL SERVICES MODERNIZATION ACT OF 1999

AND

H.R. 10, FINANCIAL SERVICES ACT OF 1999

September 1, 1999

COMPARISON OF H.R. 10 AND S. 900

September 1, 1999

	H.R. 10	S. 900
1. Title	"Financial Services Act of 1999" (p.1)	"Financial Services Modernization Act of 1999" (p.1)
2. Statement of purpose	Purposes of this Act are: (1) to enhance competition in the financial services industry, in order to foster innovation and efficiency; (2) to ensure the continued safety and soundness of depository institutions; (3) to provide necessary and appropriate protections for investors and ensure fair and honest markets in the delivery of financial services; (4) to avoid duplicative, potentially conflicting, and overly burdensome regulatory requirements through creation of a regulatory framework for financial holding companies that respects the divergent requirements of each of the component businesses of the holding company, and that is based upon principles of strong functional regulation and enhanced regulatory coordination; (5) to reduce and, to the maximum extent practicable, to eliminate the legal barriers preventing affiliation among depository institutions, securities firms, insurance companies, and other financial service providers and to provide a prudential framework for achieving that result; (6) to enhance the availability of financial services to citizens of all economic circumstances and in all geographic areas; (7) to enhance the competitiveness of US financial services providers internationally; and, (8) to ensure compliance by depository institutions with the provisions of the CRA of	No provision.

-1-

§ 12.17 Conference Chair's Letter to Conferees

Informal documents relevant to a measure's consideration in conference are often produced, such as letters to conference committee members and leadership memoranda. In this case, Representative Leach, the House Banking and Financial Services Committee chair and the chair of the conference, provided to all conferees a set of ground rules related to consideration of the measure in the conference. Senate conferees were appointed on July 23, 1999. House conferees were named on July 30, 1999. The appointment of conferees is reported in the *Congressional Record*.

§ 12.17a

Conference Chair's Letter to Conferees

JAMES A. LEACH, IOWA, CHAIRMAN

BILL McCOLLUM, FLORIDA
MARGE ROUKEMA, NEW JERSEY
DOUG BEREUTER, NEBRASKA
RICHARD H. BAKER, LOUISIANA
RICK LAZIO, NEW YORK
SPENCER BACHUS, III, ALABAMA
MICHAEL CASTLE, DELAWARE
PETER KING, NEW YORK
TOM CAMPBELL, CALIFORNIA
EDWARD ROYCE, CALIFORNIA
FRANK D. LUCAS, OKLAHOMA
JACK METCALF, WASHINGTON
ROBERT NEY, OHIO
BOB BARR, GEORGIA
SUE W. KELLY, NEW YORK
RON PAUL, TEXAS
DAVE WELDON, FLORIDA
JIM RYUN, KANSAS
MERRILL COOK, UTAH
BOB RILEY, ALABAMA
RICK HILL, MONTANA
STEVEN LaTOURETTE, OHIO
DONALD A. MANZULLO, ILLINOIS
WALTER B. JONES, Jr., NORTH CAROLINA
PAUL RYAN, WISCONSIN
DOUG OSE, CALIFORNIA
JOHN E. SWEENEY, NEW YORK
JUDY BIGGERT, ILLINOIS
LEE TERRY, NEBRASKA
MARK GREEN, WISCONSIN
PAT TOOMEY, PENNSYLVANIA

U.S. HOUSE OF REPRESENTATIVES
COMMITTEE ON BANKING AND FINANCIAL SERVICES
ONE HUNDRED SIXTH CONGRESS
2129 RAYBURN HOUSE OFFICE BUILDING
WASHINGTON, DC 20515–6050

JOHN J. LaFALCE, NEW YORK
BRUCE F. VENTO, MINNESOTA
BARNEY FRANK, MASSACHUSETTS
PAUL E. KANJORSKI, PENNSYLVANIA
MAXINE WATERS, CALIFORNIA
CAROLYN B. MALONEY, NEW YORK
LUIS V. GUTIERREZ, ILLINOIS
NYDIA M. VELAZQUEZ, NEW YORK
MELVIN WATT, NORTH CAROLINA
GARY ACKERMAN, NEW YORK
KEN BENTSEN, TEXAS
JAMES H. MALONEY, CONNECTICUT
DARLENE HOOLEY, OREGON
JULIA CARSON, INDIANA
ROBERT A. WEYGAND, RHODE ISLAND
BRAD SHERMAN, CALIFORNIA
MAX SANDLIN, TEXAS
GREGORY MEEKS, NEW YORK
BARBARA LEE, CALIFORNIA
VIRGIL H. GOODE, Jr., VIRGINIA
FRANK MASCARA, PENNSYLVANIA
JAY R. INSLEE, WASHINGTON
JAN SCHAKOWSKY, ILLINOIS
DENNIS MOORE, KANSAS
CHARLES A. GONZALEZ, TEXAS
STEPHANIE TUBBS JONES, OHIO
MICHAEL E. CAPUANO, MASSACHUSETTS

BERNARD SANDERS, VERMONT

(202) 225–7502

October 13, 1999

** CONFERENCE COMMITTEE **

To: House/Senate Conferees on S. 900
From: James A. Leach, Chairman

All conferences are unique, with rules less stringently observed than in other legislative contexts. The principal rule of conferences is that a majority of conferees in each body must sign the conference report before it can be considered by the full House and Senate.

In this conference, it is my intention to proceed title-by-title through the mark, alternating recognition to the extent practicable between House and Senate Members and Republicans and Democrats for purposes of offering amendments. As Members understand, in conference committees, each body has a single vote, but it will be my intention to assume that any amendment offered by a Member of the conference represents his or her body's position unless another Member of that body requests a vote of that body to determine whether that is in fact the case.

On the House side we have a particularly complex conference arrangement. Conferees will only be able to vote on and offer amendments to those provisions on which they are designated as conferees.

While precedents are mixed, it will be my intention to proceed on the basis that if an amendment is offered by a Member, it may only be amended by Members within the body of the offeror until it is formally presented to the other side, at which point it may be amended by that side. The original offeror, however, may accept suggestions from any member of the Conference and at his or her discretion modify an amendment before it is passed to the opposite side.

I have consulted with the parliamentarian, and while no firm rules apply in this area, the precedent is that each body determines how to proceed in the voting process. This means that on the House side, proxy voting will not be permitted, while in the Senate, it will be.

The first amendment to be offered at the mark-up may be a manager's amendment making certain technical and other revisions to the Chairmen's mark. Any Member who has a proposed technical amendment or other issue that fits a manager's amendment should contact the staffs of one of the relevant chairmen or ranking members.

§ 12.18 Conference Committee Amendment Proposed

Each conference committee conducts its work differently. Some conferences proceed through the engrossed measure *section-by-section;* others consider *full-text substitutes.* The document excerpted in § 12.18a, and the text of the substitute, provided a summary of a *chairmen's mark,* a full-text substitute considered by the conferees.

§ 12.18a

Conference Committee Amendment Proposed

Financial Services Modernization Act

Summary of Provisions of Chairmen's Mark

TITLE I - FACILITATING AFFILIATION AMONG BANKS, SECURITIES FIRMS, AND INSURANCE COMPANIES

- Repeals the restrictions on banks affiliating with securities firms contained in sections 20 and 32 of the Glass-Steagall Act.
- Creates a new "financial holding company" under section 4 of the Bank Holding Company Act. Such holding company can engage in a statutorily provided list of financial activities, including insurance and securities underwriting and merchant banking activities. The financial holding company may also engage in developing activities and activities which the Federal Reserve Board, subject to a Treasury coordinating process, determines are financial in nature or incidental to such financial activities. Complementary activities are also authorized. The nonfinancial activities of firms predominantly engaged in financial activities are grandfathered (subject to a 15% limitation) for at least 10 years, but no more than 15 years. Such financial holding companies must be well capitalized, well managed, and have at least a satisfactory CRA rating.
- Provides for state regulation of insurance, subject to certain specified state preemption standards.
- Provides that a bank holding company organized as a mutual holding company will be regulated on terms and subject to limitations, comparable to any other bank holding company.
- Liberalizes the restrictions governing nonbank banks.
- Provides for a study of the use of subordinated debt to protect financial system and deposit funds from "too big to fail" institutions and a study on the effect of financial modernization on the accessibility of small business and farm loans.
- Streamlines bank holding company supervisions by clarifying the regulatory roles of the Federal Reserve as the umbrella holding company supervisor and the state and Federal nonbank financial functional regulators.

§ 12.19 Conference Report

The conference report, H. Rept. 106-434, was filed in the House on November 2, 1999, by Mr. Leach, the chair of the conference committee. The measure was now officially called the Gramm-Leach-Bliley Act, after the three chairs of the committees that considered the legislation. Negotiations in conference resulted in the naming.

§ 12.19a

Conference Report

106TH CONGRESS 1st Session	HOUSE OF REPRESENTATIVES	REPORT 106–434

GRAMM-LEACH-BLILEY ACT

NOVEMBER 2, 1999.—Ordered to be printed

Mr. LEACH, from the committee of conference, submitted the following

CONFERENCE REPORT

[To accompany S. 900]

The committee of conference on the disagreeing votes of the two Houses on the amendments of the House to the bill (S. 900), to enhance competition in the financial services industry by providing a prudential framework for the affiliation of banks, securities firms, insurance companies, and other financial service providers, and for other purposes, having met, after full and free conference, have agreed to recommend and do recommend to their respective Houses as follows:

That the Senate recede from its disagreement to the amendment of the House to the text of the bill and agree to the same with an amendment as follows:

In lieu of the matter proposed to be inserted by the House amendment, insert the following:

SECTION 1. SHORT TITLE; TABLE OF CONTENTS.

(a) SHORT TITLE.—This Act may be cited as the "Gramm-Leach-Bliley Act".

(b) TABLE OF CONTENTS.—The table of contents for this Act is as follows:

60–398

12

§ 12.20 Joint Explanatory Statement

A second conference document is appended to the conference report and is called the *joint explanatory statement.* This document explains in lay terms what was in the House text and the Senate text of the measure in conference and what is the agreement recommended by the committee on conference. A majority of conferees from each chamber must sign not only the conference report but also the joint explanatory statement.

§ 12.20a

Joint Explanatory Statement

JOINT EXPLANATORY STATEMENT OF THE COMMITTEE OF CONFERENCE

The Managers on the part of the House and the Senate at the conference on the disagreeing votes of the two Houses on the amendments of the House to the bill (S. 900), to enhance competition in the financial services industry by providing a prudential framework for the affiliation of banks, securities firms, insurance companies, and other financial service providers, and for other purposes, submit the following joint statement to the House and the Senate in explanation of the effect of the action agreed upon by the managers and recommended in the accompanying conference report:

The House amendment to the text of the bill struck all of the Senate bill after the enacting clause and inserted a substitute text.

The Senate recedes from its disagreement to the amendment of the House with an amendment that is a substitute for the Senate bill and the House amendment. The differences between the Senate bill, the House amendment, and the substitute agreed to in conference are noted below, except for clerical corrections, conforming changes made necessary by agreements reached by the conferees, and minor drafting and clerical changes.

TITLE I—FACILITATING AFFILIATIONS AMONG BANKS, SECURITIES FIRMS, AND INSURANCE COMPANIES

The legislation approved by the Conference Managers eliminates many Federal and State law barriers to affiliations among banks and securities firms, insurance companies, and other financial service providers. The House and Senate bills established an identical statutory framework (except for minor drafting differences) pursuant to which full affiliations can occur between banks and securities firms, insurance companies, and other financial companies. The Conferees adopted this framework. Furthermore, the legislation provides financial organizations with flexibility in structuring these new financial affiliations through a holding company structure, or a financial subsidiary (with certain prudential limitations on activities and appropriate safeguards). Reflected in the legislation is the determination made by both Houses to preserve the role of the Board of Governors of the Federal Reserve System (the “Federal Reserve Board” or the “Board”) as the umbrella supervisor for holding companies, but to incorporate a system of functional regulation designed to utilize the strengths of the various Federal and State financial supervisors. Incorporating provisions found in both the House and Senate bills, the legislation establishes a mechanism for coordination between the Federal Reserve Board and the Secretary of the Treasury (“the Secretary”) regarding the approval of new financial activities for both holding companies and national bank financial subsidiaries. The legislation

(151)

12

§ 12.21 Special Rule from the Rules Committee for Consideration of the Conference Report

Conference reports are *privileged* in the House and as such do not require a special rule for consideration. However, special rules are often sought for conference reports if *waivers* of existing rules are needed. H. Res. 355 was a special rule providing for the consideration of the conference report on S. 900. The special rule provided that the conference report be considered as read, and waived all points of order against the report and its consideration by the House. The special rule was reported on November 2, 1999.

§ 12.21a

Special Rule from the Rules Committee for Consideration of the Conference Report

❶ Calendar number

❷ Resolution number

❸ Committee report number

❹ Majority manager of special rule

❺ Special rule waiving points of order against the conference report (S. 900)

❶ **House Calendar No. 147**

106TH CONGRESS
1ST SESSION
❷ **H. RES. 355**

❸ **[Report No. 106–440]**

Waiving points of order against the conference report to accompany the bill (S. 900) to enhance competition in the financial services industry by providing a prudential framework for the affiliation of banks, securities firms, insurance companies, and other financial service providers, and for other purposes.

IN THE HOUSE OF REPRESENTATIVES

NOVEMBER 2, 1999

❹ Mr. SESSIONS, from the Committee on Rules, reported the following resolution; which was referred to the House Calendar and ordered to be printed

---

RESOLUTION

❺ Waiving points of order against the conference report to accompany the bill (S. 900) to enhance competition in the financial services industry by providing a prudential framework for the affiliation of banks, securities firms, insurance companies, and other financial service providers, and for other purposes.

Resolved, That upon adoption of this resolution it shall be in order to consider the conference report to accompany the bill (S. 900) to enhance competition in the

Continued on page 548

12

§ 12.21a (continued)

Special Rule from the Rules Committee for Consideration of the Conference Report

2

financial services industry by providing a prudential framework for the affiliation of banks, securities firms, insurance companies, and other financial service providers, and for other purposes. All points of order against the conference report and against its consideration are waived. The conference report shall be considered as read.

§ 12.22 Enrolled Measure

The conference report was agreed to by the Senate by a 90-to-8 vote on November 4, 1999. The House also agreed to the conference report on November 4, 1999, by a vote of 362 to 57. The measure was then cleared for the White House. It was printed on parchment paper and presented to the president on November 9, 1999.

§ 12.22a

Enrolled Measure

One Hundred Sixth Congress
of the
United States of America

AT THE FIRST SESSION

Begun and held at the City of Washington on Wednesday,
the sixth day of January, one thousand nine hundred and ninety-nine

An Act

To enhance competition in the financial services industry by providing a prudential framework for the affiliation of banks, securities firms, insurance companies, and other financial service providers, and for other purposes.

Be it enacted by the Senate and House of Representatives of the United States of America in Congress assembled,

SECTION 1. SHORT TITLE; TABLE OF CONTENTS.

(a) SHORT TITLE.—This Act may be cited as the "Gramm-Leach-Bliley Act".

(b) TABLE OF CONTENTS.—The table of contents for this Act is as follows:

§ 12.23 Public Law

The president signed the Gramm-Leach-Bliley Act on November 12, 1999. The adoption of the *short title* was part of the conference committee agreement. It now was P.L. 106-102, 113 Stat. 1338.

§ 12.23a

Public Law

113 STAT. 1338 PUBLIC LAW 106–102—NOV. 12, 1999

Public Law 106–102
106th Congress

An Act

Nov. 12, 1999
[S. 900]

To enhance competition in the financial services industry by providing a prudential framework for the affiliation of banks, securities firms, insurance companies, and other financial service providers, and for other purposes.

Be it enacted by the Senate and House of Representatives of the United States of America in Congress assembled,

Gramm-Leach-Bliley Act. Inter-governmental relations. 12 USC 1811 note.

SECTION 1. SHORT TITLE; TABLE OF CONTENTS.

(a) SHORT TITLE.—This Act may be cited as the "Gramm-Leach-Bliley Act".

(b) TABLE OF CONTENTS.—The table of contents for this Act is as follows:

Back of the Book

Analysis

Glossary

Account: Control and reporting unit for budgeting and accounting.

Act: Legislation that has been passed by both houses of Congress and signed by the president or passed over his veto, thus becoming law. Also, parliamentary term for a measure that has been passed by one chamber and engrossed.

Adjourn: Formal motion to end a day's session of a chamber of Congress.

Adjourn *Sine Die*: Final adjournment of a session of Congress.

Adjourn to a Day or Time Certain: Adjournment that fixes the next day and time of meeting for one or both chambers.

Adoption (Adopted): Usual parliamentary term for approval of conference report.

Agreed To: Usual parliamentary term for approval of motions, amendments, and simple and concurrent resolutions.

Amendment: Proposal of a member of Congress to alter the text of a measure.

Amendment in the Nature of a Substitute: Amendment that seeks to replace the entire text of the underlying measure. The adoption of such an amendment usually precludes any further amendment to that measure.

Amendment Tree: Diagram showing the number and types of amendments to a measure permitted by the chamber. It also shows the relationship among the amendments, their degree or type, and the order in which they may be offered and the order in which they are voted on.

Amendments between the Houses: Method for reconciling differences between the two chambers' versions of a measure by passing the measure back and forth between them until both have agreed to identical language; sometimes referred to in the media as the "ping pong" approach to reconciling differences in legislation. *Contrast to Conference Committee.*

Amendments in Disagreement: Provisions in dispute between the two chambers.

Amendments in Technical Disagreement: Amendments agreed to in a conference but not included in the conference report because they may violate the rules of one of the chambers and would open the conference report to a point of order.

Appeal: Member's challenge to a ruling made by the presiding officer or a committee chair.

Appropriated Entitlement: An entitlement for which budget authority is provided in annual appropriations acts.

Appropriation: Provision of law providing budget authority that permits federal agencies to incur obligations and make payments out of the Treasury. *See Budget Authority.*

Appropriations Bill: Bill that, if enacted as law, gives legal authority to spend or obligate money from the Treasury. *See Budget Authority.*

Authorization: Provision in law that establishes or continues a program or agency and authorizes appropriations for it.

Baseline: Projection of future revenues, budget authority, outlays, and other budget amounts under assumed economic conditions and participation rates without a change in current policy.

"Bigger Bite" Amendment: Although an amendment cannot amend previously amended language under House rules, a "bigger bite" amendment can be offered because it changes more of the measure or amendment than the original amendment.

Bill: Measure that becomes law when passed in identical form by both chambers and signed by the president or passed over his veto. Designated as *H.R.* or *S. See also Joint Resolution.*

Blue-Slip Resolution: House resolution ordering the return to the Senate of a Senate bill or amendment that the House believes violates the constitutional prerogative of the House to originate revenue measures.

An expanded legislative and budget glossary is available online at <TCNLG.com>.

Borrowing Authority: Spending authority that permits a federal agency to incur obligations and to make payments for specified purposes out of funds borrowed from the Treasury or the public.

Budget Authority: Authority in law to enter into obligations that normally result in outlays.

Budget Resolution: Concurrent resolution incorporating an agreement by the House and Senate on an overall budget plan; may contain reconciliation instructions.

By Request: A designation on a measure that appears next to the sponsor's name and indicates that a member has introduced the measure on behalf of the president, an executive agency, or a private individual or organization.

Byrd Rule: Bars the inclusion of extraneous matter in a reconciliation measure considered in the Senate.

Chairman's Mark/Staff Draft/ Committee Print: Recommendation by committee (or subcommittee) chair of the measure to be considered in a markup, usually drafted as a bill.

Christmas-Tree Bill: Jargon for a bill containing many amendments *(see Rider)* unrelated to the bill's subjects; usually refers to Senate measures.

Clean Bill: New measure reported by a House committee incorporating all changes made in markup. Measure, with new number, is introduced by the chair and referred to the committee, which then reports that measure.

Closed Rule: Permits general debate for a specified period of time but generally permits no amendments.

Cloture: Process by which a filibuster can be ended in the Senate.

Cluster Voting: Allowance for sequential recorded votes on a series of measures or amendments that the House finished debating at an earlier time or on a previous date. The Speaker may reduce the minimum time for the second and subsequent votes in a series of five minutes each. The chair of the Committee of the Whole may reduce the minimum time for the second and subsequent votes in a series to two minutes each.

Colloquy: Discussion between members during floor proceedings, generally to put on the record a mutual understanding about the intent of a provision or amendment. The discussion is usually scripted in advance.

Committee of the Whole: The House in a different parliamentary form. Committee consisting of all members of the House, where measures are considered for amendment. The quorum is one hundred. Members are generally permitted to speak for five minutes. A chair presides in lieu of the Speaker.

Committee Report: Document accompanying a measure reported from a committee. It contains an explanation of the provisions of the measure, arguments for its approval, and other information.

Companion Bills: Identical or similar bills introduced in both chambers.

Concur: Agree to an amendment of the other chamber, either as is or with an amendment.

Concurrent Resolution: Used to express the sentiment of both chambers on some matter without making law, or to carry out the administrative business of both chambers. A concurrent resolution does not require presidential approval or become law, but requires passage in identical form by both houses to take effect between them. Designated as *H. Con. Res.* or *S. Con. Res.*

Conferees: Representatives from each chamber who serve on a conference committee; also referred to as managers.

Conference Committee: Temporary joint committee created to resolve differences between the chambers on a measure. *Contrast to Amendment between the Houses.*

Conference Report: Document containing a conference committee's agreements and signed by a majority of conferees from each chamber. *See also Joint Explanatory Statement of Managers.*

Continuing Appropriations Act: An appropriations act that provides stop-gap funding for agencies that have not received regular appropriations. (Also referred to as a continuing resolution (CR).)

An expanded legislative and budget glossary is available online at <TCNLG.com>.

Cordon Rule: Senate rule that requires a committee report to show changes the reported measure would make in current law.

Cost Estimate: An estimate of the impact of legislation on revenues, spending, or both, generally as reported by a House or Senate committee or a conference committee; the 1974 Congressional Budget Act requires the Congressional Budget Office to prepare cost estimates on all public bills.

Credit Authority: Authority to incur direct loan obligations or make loan guarantee commitments.

Custody of the Papers: Custody of the engrossed measure and other documents that the two chambers produce as they try to reconcile differences in their versions of a measure. *See Papers.*

Deferral: Action or inaction that temporarily withholds, delays, or effectively precludes the obligation or expenditure of budget authority.

Deficit: Excess of outlays over revenues.

Degrees of Amendment: Designations that indicate the relationship of an amendment to the text of a measure and of one amendment to another. Amendments are permitted only in two degrees. *See Amendment Tree.*

Direct Spending: Spending controlled outside of annual appropriations acts, and specifically including the Food Stamp (now SNAP) program; also referred to as mandatory spending. *See also Entitlement Program; contrast to Discretionary Spending.*

Disagree: To reject an amendment of the other chamber.

Discharge a Committee: Procedure to remove a measure from a House committee to which it was referred, to make it available for floor consideration.

Discretionary Spending: Spending provided in, and controlled by, annual appropriations acts. *Contrast to Direct Spending.*

Division Vote: A vote in which the committee chair or House presiding officer counts those members in favor and those in opposition to a proposition with no record made of how each voted. The chair can either ask for a show of hands or ask members to stand.

Earmark: For expenditures, an amount set aside within an appropriations account for a specified purpose.

Electronic Vote: A vote in the House using electronic voting machines. Members insert voting cards into one of the devices located throughout the House chamber.

En Bloc Amendment: Several amendments, affecting more than one place in a measure, offered as a group after obtaining unanimous consent.

Enacting Clause: Phrase at the beginning of a bill that gives it legal force when enacted: "Be it enacted by the Senate and House of Representatives of the United States of America in Congress assembled. . . ."

Engrossed Measure: Official copy of a measure as passed by one chamber, including the text as amended by floor action. Measure is certified by the clerk of the House or the secretary of the Senate.

Enrolled Measure: Final official copy of a measure as passed in identical form by both chambers and then printed on parchment. Measure is certified by the house of origin and signed by the Speaker of the House and the president pro tempore of the Senate before it is sent to the president.

Entitlement Program: Federal program that guarantees specific benefits to individuals, businesses, or units of government that meet eligibility requirements.

Executive Document: A document, usually a treaty, sent by the president to the Senate for its consideration and approval.

Executive Session: Meeting of the Senate devoted to the consideration of treaties or nominations. Also a term used to describe a chamber or committee session closed to the public.

Expenditures: Often a synonym for outlays; a general term to mean spending.

An expanded legislative and budget glossary is available online at <TCNLG.com>.

Fast-Track Procedures: Procedures that circumvent or speed up all or part of the legislative process. Some rule-making statutes prescribe expedited procedures for certain measures, such as trade agreements.

Federal Funds: All monies collected and spent by the federal government other than those designated as trust funds.

Filibuster: Tactic in the Senate to delay or defeat a measure by unlimited debate and other means.

First-Degree Amendment: Amendment offered to the text of a measure or a substitute offered to a first-degree amendment.

First Reading: Required reading of a bill or joint resolution to a chamber by title after its introduction.

Fiscal Year: The period from October 1 through September 30; fiscal year 2011 began October 1, 2010, and ended September 30, 2011.

Five-Minute Rule: House limit of debate on an amendment offered in the Committee of the Whole to five minutes for its sponsor and five minutes for an opponent. In practice, the Committee of the Whole permits the offering of pro forma amendments, each pro forma amendment allowing five more minutes of debate on an amendment. *See Pro Forma Amendment.*

Floor Manager: Member steering legislation through floor debate and the amendment process, usually a committee or subcommittee chair or ranking minority member.

General Debate: Term for period of time at the beginning of proceedings in the Committee of the Whole to debate a measure. The time is generally divided equally between majority and minority floor managers.

Germaneness: Rule in the House requiring that debate and amendments pertain to the same subject as the bill or amendment under consideration. In the Senate, germaneness is not generally required.

Hereby Rule: *See Self-Executing Rule.*

Hold: Senator's request to party leadership to delay or withhold floor action on a measure or executive business.

Hopper: Box on the Speaker's dais near the House clerk's desk where members place bills and resolutions to introduce them.

Impoundment: Action or inaction by an executive official that delays or precludes the obligation or expenditure of budget authority. *See Deferral and Rescission.*

Insert: Amendment to add new language to a measure or another amendment.

Insist: Motion by one chamber to reiterate its previous position during amendments between the chambers.

Instruct Conferees: Formal, although not binding, action by one chamber urging its conferees to uphold a particular position in conference.

Joint Explanatory Statement of Managers: Statement appended to a conference report explaining the conference agreement and the intent of the conferees. *See also Conference Report.*

Joint Resolution: Similar to a bill, though limited in scope (for example, to change a minor item in existing law). Becomes law when passed in identical form by both chambers and signed by the president. It also is the form of legislation used to consider a constitutional amendment. A constitutional amendment requires a two-thirds vote in each house but does not require the president's signature. Designated as *H. J. Res.* or *S. J. Res. See also Bill.*

Lame-Duck Session: Session of Congress held after the election for the succeeding Congress.

Law/Public Law/Private Law: Act of Congress signed by the president or passed over his veto.

Legislative Day: Time a chamber meets after an adjournment until the time it next adjourns.

Managers: Representatives from a chamber to a conference committee; also called conferees.

Mandatory Spending: *See Direct Spending.*

Mark: *See Vehicle.*

Markup: Meeting by a committee or subcommittee during which members offer, debate, and vote on amendments to a measure.

An expanded legislative and budget glossary is available online at <TCNLG.com>.

Minority, Supplemental, and Additional Views: Statements in a committee report presenting individuals' or groups' opinions on the measure.

Modified Closed Rule: Permits general debate for a specified period of time, but limits amendments to those designated in the special rule or the House Rules Committee report accompanying the special rule. May preclude amendments to particular portions of a bill. Also called a structured rule.

Modified Open Rule: Permits general debate for a specified period of time, and allows any member to offer amendments consistent with House rules subject only to an overall time limit on the amendment process and a requirement that amendments be pre-printed in the *Congressional Record.*

Morning Business: In the Senate, routine business transacted at the beginning of the Morning Hour, or by unanimous consent throughout the day.

Morning Hour: In the Senate, the first two hours of a session following an adjournment, rather than a recess.

Obligation: Binding agreement by a government agency to pay for goods, products, or services.

Official Objectors: House members who screen measures on the Private Calendar.

Official Title: Statement of a measure's subject and purpose, which appears before the enacting clause. *See also Popular Title.*

Omnibus Bill: A measure that combines the provisions related to several disparate subjects into a single measure. Examples include continuing appropriations resolutions that might contain two or more of the thirteen annual appropriations bills.

Open Rule: Permits general debate for a specified period of time and allows any member to offer an amendment that complies with the standing rules of the House.

Ordered Reported: Committee's formal action of agreeing to report a measure to its chamber.

Original Bill: A measure drafted by a committee and introduced by its chair when the committee reports the measure back to its chamber. It is not referred back to the committee after introduction.

Outlays: Payments to liquidate obligations.

Papers: Documents passed back and forth between the chambers, including the engrossed measure, the amendments, the messages transmitting them, and the conference report. *See also Custody of the Papers.*

Parliamentary Inquiry: Member's question posed on the floor to the presiding officer, or in committee or subcommittee to the chair, about a pending procedural situation.

Pass Over without Prejudice: A request in the House to defer action on a measure called up from the Private Calendar without affecting the measure's position on the calendar.

Passed: Term for approval of bills and joint resolutions.

PAYGO (Pay-As-You-Go): Process by which direct spending increases or revenue decreases must be offset so that the deficit is not increased or the surplus reduced. A statutory PAYGO requirement was in effect from 1991 through 2002; the House and Senate each have their own PAYGO rules.

Perfecting Amendment: Amendment that alters, but does not completely substitute or replace, language in another amendment. *See Amendment Tree.*

Pocket Veto: Act of the president in withholding approval of a measure after Congress has adjourned *sine die.*

Point of Order: Objection to a current proceeding, measure, or amendment because the proposed action violates a rule of the chamber, written precedent, or rule-making statute.

Popular Title: The name by which a measure is known. *See also Official Title.*

Postpone: There are two types of motions to postpone: to postpone (indefinitely) kills a proposal, but to postpone to a day certain merely changes the day or time of consideration.

An expanded legislative and budget glossary is available online at <TCNLG.com>.

Preamble: Introductory language in a bill preceding the enacting clause. It describes the reasons for and intent of a measure. In a joint resolution, the language appears before the resolving clause. In a concurrent or simple resolution, it appears before the text.

Precedence: Order in which amendments or motions may be offered and acted upon.

Precedent: Previous ruling by a presiding officer that becomes part of the procedures of a chamber.

President Pro Tempore: Presiding officer of the Senate in the absence of the vice president; usually the majority-party senator with the longest period of continuous service.

Previous Question: Nondebatable House (or House committee) motion, which, when agreed to, cuts off further debate, prevents the offering of additional amendments, and brings the pending matter to an immediate vote.

Private Bill: A measure that generally deals with an individual matter, such as a claim against the government, an individual's immigration, or a land title. Private bills are considered in the House via the Private Calendar on the first and third Tuesdays of each month.

Privilege: Attribute of a motion, measure, report, question, or proposition that gives it priority status for consideration.

Pro Forma Amendment: Motion whereby a House member secures five minutes to speak on an amendment under debate, without offering a substantive amendment. The member moves to "strike the last word" or "strike the requisite number of words." The motion requires no vote and is deemed automatically withdrawn at the expiration of the five minutes. *See also Five-Minute Rule.*

Proxy Vote: The practice of permitting a member to cast the vote of an absent colleague. Proxy voting is permitted only in Senate committees if committee rules allow them.

Public Debt: Amounts borrowed by the Treasury Department from the public or from another fund or account.

Public Law: Act of Congress that has been signed by the president or passed over his veto. It is designated by the letters *P.L.* and numbers noting the Congress and the numerical sequence in which the measure was signed; for example, P.L. 112-7 was an act of Congress in the 112th Congress and was the 7th measure signed by the president (or passed over his veto) during the 112th Congress.

Queen-of-the-Hill Rule: A special rule that permits votes on a series of amendments, usually complete substitutes for a measure, but directs that the amendment receiving the greatest number of votes is the winning amendment.

Quorum: Minimum number of members required for the transaction of business.

Quorum Call: A procedure for determining whether a quorum is present—218 in the House and 100 in the Committee of the Whole House on the State of the Union; a quorum in the Senate is 51.

Ramseyer Rule: House rule that requires a committee report to show changes the reported measure would make in current law.

Recede: Motion by one chamber to withdraw from its previous position during amendments between the chambers.

Recede and Concur: Motion to withdraw from a position and agree with the other chamber's position.

Recede and Concur with an Amendment: Motion to withdraw from a position and agree, but with a further amendment.

Recess: Temporary interruption or suspension of a committee or chamber meeting. In the House, the Speaker is authorized to declare recesses. In the Senate, the chamber may recess rather than adjourn at the end of the day so as not to trigger a new legislative day.

Recommit: To send a measure back to the committee that reported it. A motion to recommit without instructions kills a measure; a motion to recommit with instructions proposes to amend a measure. In the House, the motion may be offered just before vote on final passage. In the Senate, the motion may be offered at any time before a measure's passage.

An expanded legislative and budget glossary is available online at <TCNLG.com>.

Reconciliation: Process by which Congress changes existing laws to conform revenue and spending levels to the limits set in a budget resolution.

Reconsider: Parliamentary practice that gives a chamber one opportunity to review its action on a motion, amendment, measure, or any other proposition.

Refer: Assignment of a measure to committee.

Report/Reported: Formal submission of a measure by a committee to its parent chamber.

Reprogram: Shifting funds from one program to another in the same appropriation account. *Contrast to Transfer.*

Rescission: Cancellation of budget authority previously provided by Congress.

Resolution/Simple Resolution: Sentiment of one chamber on an issue, or a measure to carry out the administrative or procedural business of the chamber. Does not become law. Designated as *H. Res.* or *S. Res.*

Resolution of Inquiry: A simple resolution calling on the president or the head of an executive agency to provide specific information or papers to one or both chambers.

Resolution of Ratification: Senate vehicle for consideration of a treaty.

Resolving Clause: First section of a joint resolution that gives legal force to the measure when enacted: "Resolved by the Senate and House of Representatives of the United States of America in Congress assembled. . . ."

Revenues: Income from individual and corporate income taxes, social insurance taxes, excise taxes, fees, tariffs, and other sources collected under the sovereign powers of the federal government.

Rider: Colloquialism for an amendment unrelated to the subject matter of the measure to which it was attached.

Rise: In order only in the Committee of the Whole during the amendment stage, it has the effect of terminating or suspending debate on the pending matter.

Rise and Report: Term to refer to the culmination of proceedings in the Committee of the Whole. The Committee of the Whole sends the measure it has been considering back to the House for final disposition.

Roll-Call (Record) Vote: A vote in which members are recorded by name for or against a measure.

Scope of Differences: Limits within which a conference committee is permitted to resolve its disagreement.

Scorekeeping: Process for tracking and reporting on the status of congressional budgetary actions affecting budget authority, revenues, outlays, and the surplus or deficit.

Second: The number of members required to indicate support for an action, such as calling for a vote.

Second-Degree Amendment: An amendment to an amendment. Also called a perfecting amendment. *See Amendment Tree.*

Second Reading: Required reading of a bill or joint resolution to a chamber: in the House, in full before floor consideration in the House or Committee of the Whole (usually dispensed with by unanimous consent or special rule); in the Senate, by title only, before referral to a committee.

Self-Executing Rule: If specified, the House's adoption of a special rule may also have the effect of amending or passing the underlying measure. Also called a "hereby" rule.

Slip Law: First official publication of a law, published in unbound single sheets or pamphlet form.

Stage of Disagreement: Stage at which one chamber formally disagrees with an amendment proposed by the other chamber and insists on its own amendment. A measure generally cannot go to conference until this stage is reached.

Star Print: A reprint of a measure, amendment, or committee report to correct errors in a previous printing. The first page carries a small black star.

Strike: Amendment to delete a portion of a measure or an amendment.

An expanded legislative and budget glossary is available online at <TCNLG.com>.

Strike and Insert: Amendment that replaces text in a measure or an amendment.

Strike the Last Word/Strike the Requisite Number of Words: Also called a pro forma amendment. Means of obtaining time to speak on an amendment without actually offering a substantive change. *See Pro Forma Amendment.*

Structured Rule: Another term for a modified closed rule.

Substitute Amendment: Amendment that replaces the entire text of a pending amendment. *See Amendment Tree.*

Supplemental Appropriations Act: An appropriations act that provides additional budget authority during the current year when the regular appropriation is insufficient.

Surplus: Excess of revenues over outlays.

Suspension of the Rules: Expeditious procedure for passing noncontroversial measures in the House. Requires a two-thirds vote of those present and voting, after forty minutes of debate, and does not allow floor amendments.

Table/Lay on the Table: Prevents further consideration of a measure, amendment, or motion, thus killing it.

Tax Expenditure: Loss of revenue attributable to an exemption, deduction, preference, or other exclusion under federal tax law.

Teller Vote: A House procedure in which members cast votes by passing through the center aisle of the chamber to be counted. Now used only when the electronic voting system breaks down and for ballot votes.

Third Reading: Required reading of bill or joint resolution to chamber before vote on final passage; usually a pro forma procedural step.

Transfer: Shifting funds from one appropriation account to another, as authorized by law. *Contrast to Reprogram.*

Trust Funds: Accounts designated by law as trust funds for receipts and expenditures earmarked for specific purposes.

Unanimous Consent Agreement/Time Limitation Agreement: Device in the Senate to expedite legislation by spelling out the process for considering a proposal.

Unprinted Amendment: Senate amendment not printed in the *Congressional Record* before its offering. Unprinted amendments are numbered sequentially through a Congress in the order of their submission.

Vehicle/Legislative Vehicle: Term for legislative measure that is being considered.

Veto: Disapproval by the president of a bill or joint resolution (other than a joint resolution proposing a constitutional amendment).

Views and Estimates: Annual report of each House and Senate committee on budgetary matters within its jurisdiction to respective chamber's Budget Committee; submitted in advance of Budget Committees' drafting of a concurrent resolution on the budget.

Voice Vote: A method of voting where members who support a question call out "aye" in unison, after which those opposed answer "no" in unison. The chair decides which position prevails.

Waiver Rule: A special rule in the House that waives points of order against a measure or an amendment.

Well: Open space in the front of the House chamber between members' seats and the podium. Members may speak from lecterns in the well.

Yea and Nay: A vote in which members respond "aye" or "no" on a question.Their names are called in alphabetical order.

An expanded legislative and budget glossary is available online at <TCNLG.com>.

Table of Web Sites

Name	URL	Section
American Association for the Advancement of Science	http://fellowships.aaas.org	§ 4.100
American Political Science Association	www.apsanet.org	§ 4.100
American University	www.american.edu	§ 4.100
Architect of the Capitol	www.aoc.gov	§ 4.112; 4.121
Asian Pacific American Institute for Congressional Studies	http://apaics.org	§ 4.100
Biographical Directory of the U.S. Congress	http://bioguide.congress.gov	§ 4.190; 10.81
Bipartisan Policy Center	http://bipartisanpolicy.org	§ 4.200
Black Americans in Congress	http://baic.house.gov	§ 10.81
Brookings Institution	www.brookings.edu	§ 4.100
Capitol Police	www.uscapitolpolice.gov	§ 4.123
Catalog of Federal Domestic Assistance	www.cfda.gov	§ 2.20; 4.160; 8.200
Census Bureau	www.census.gov	§ 2.40
Census Bureau (apportionment)	www.census.gov/population/apportionment/index.html	§ 2.35
Census Bureau (district maps)	www.census.gov/geo/www/maps/cd112/cd112_mainPage.htm	§ 2.35
Center for Responsive Politics	www.opensecrets.org	§ 2.10; 2.70
Chaplain (House)	http://chaplain.house.gov	§ 4.110
Chaplain (Senate)	www.senate.gov/reference/office/chaplain.htm	§ 4.120
Chief Administrative Officer	http://cao.house.gov	§ 4.110; 4.112
Clerk of the House	http://clerk.house.gov	§ 3.40; 4.110; 9.20; 9.30
Commission on Security and Cooperation in Europe	www.csce.gov	§ 8.170
Committee on House Administration	http://cha.house.gov	§ 3.50; 4.62; 5.120; 5.121; 10.80
Committee on Rules and Administration	http://rules.senate.gov	§ 10.80
Committees' Congressional Handbook	http://cha.house.gov	§ 10.80
Congressional Accountability Act	http://compliance.gov	§ 4.114
Congressional Black Caucus	www.cbcfinc.org	§ 4.100
Congressional Budget Office	http://cbo.gov	§ 4.130; 7.50
Congressional-Executive Committee on China	www.cece.gov	§ 5.130
Congressional Hispanic Caucus Fellowship Program	www.chci.org	§ 4.100
Congressional Institute	http://conginst.org	§ 4.200

Name	URL	Section
Congressional Management Foundation	http://cmfweb.org	§ 4.200
Congressional pages	http://pageprogram.house.gov	§ 4.113
Congressional pay	CongressPay.com	§ 4.20
Congressional Record (online version)	http://fdsys.gov	§ 4.140
Congressional Research Service	www.loc.gov/crsinfo/	§ 4.130
Congressional staff salaries	LegiStorm.com	§ 4.61
Constitution of the United States	http://fdsys.gov	§ 10.60
Department of Commerce	http://commerce.gov	§ 4.173
Department of Health and Human Services	www.hhs.gov	§ 4.172
Department of Transportation	www.dot.gov/ost/ogc/org/legislation/index.html	§ 4.173
Executive orders and proclamations	www.archives.gov/federal-register/ executive-orders	§ 9.70
Foreign Agents Registration Act	http://fara.gov	§ 3.30
Federal Business Opportunities	www.fbo.gov	§ 4.112
Federal Citizen Information Center	http://pueblo.gsa.gov	§ 4.160
Federal Depository Libraries	http://gpo.gov/libraries	§ 4.140; 9.20
Federal Digital System	http://fdsys.gov	§ 3.50; 4.140; 5.10; 7.42; 7.43; 7.91; 9.20; 9.70; 10.10; 10.20; 10.40; 10.50; 10.60; 10.61; 10.81
Federal Election Commission	www.fec.gov	§ 2.10; 2.70
Federal Register (online version)	http://fdsys.gov	§ 4.140
Financial disclosure forms	http://clerk.house.gov/public_disc	§ 10.80
General Services Administration	http://gsa.gov	§ 4.160; 4.172
Global Legal Information Network	http://glin.gov	§ 4.130
Government Accountability Office	http://gao.gov	§ 4.130; 8.41
Government fellowships	http://students.gov	§ 4.100
Government Printing Office	www.fdsys.gov	§ 4.140
GPO Bookstore	http://bookstore.gpo.gov	§ 4.140
Grants.gov	www.grants.gov	§ 4.160; 8.200
Guide to the records of the House	http://archives.gov/legislative/guide/house	§ 10.80
Guide to the records of the Senate	http://archives.gov/legislative/guide/senate	§ 10.80
Guide to the Research Collections of Former Members of the U.S. House of Representatives, 1789–1987	www.archives.gov/legislative/ repository-collections	§ 10.81
Guide to the Research Collections of Former Senators, 1789–1995	www.archives.gov/legislative/ repository-collections	§ 10.81
Heritage Foundation	http://heritage.org	§ 4.100

Name	URL	Section
Hispanic Americans in Congress, 1822–1995	www.loc.gov/rr/hispanic/congress	§ 10.81
History of the U.S. Senate Republican Policy Committee, 1947–1997	http://fdsys.gov	§ 10.81
House Budget Committee	www.budget.house.gov	§ 7.50
House Committee on Ethics	http://ethics.house.gov	§ 3.50; 3.60; 3.61
House Democracy Partnership	http://hdac.house.gov	§ 5.130
House Democratic leader	http://democraticleader.house.gov	§ 10.70
House Democratic caucus	http://dems.gov	§ 10.70
House Democratic whip	http://democraticwhip.house.gov	§ 10.70
House Ethics manual	http://ethics.house.gov	§ 3.50; 10.80
House floor schedule	http://house.gov/legislative	§ 9.30
House inspector general	www.house.gov/IG	§ 4.110; 10.80
House majority leader	http://majorityleader.gov	§ 10.70
House page program	http://pageprogram.house.gov	§ 4.113
House Republican caucus	http://gop.gov	§ 10.70
House Republican Conference	http://gop.gov/about/rules	§ 10.70
House Republican leader	http://republicanleader.house.gov	§ 10.70
House Republican whip	http://republicanwhip.house.gov	§ 10.70
House Rules Committee	http://rules.house.gov	§ 3.50; 10.40
How Laws Are Made	http://thomas.gov/home/lawsmade.toc.html	§ 10.60
Institute for Humane Studies	http://theihs.org	§ 4.100
Internship and fellowship opportunities	http://students.gov	§ 4.100
Joint Committee on Taxation	www.jct.gov	§ 7.10; 7.50; 7.92
Law Library of Congress	http://loc.gov/law	§ 4.130
Law Revision Counsel	http://uscode.house.gov	§ 9.70
Legislative Counsel (House)	http://house.gov/legcoun	§ 4.110
Legislative Counsel (Senate)	http://slc.senate.gov	§ 4.120
Legislative Resource Center	http://clerk.house.gov/about/offices_lrc.aspx	§ 9.20
Lexis-Nexis	http://web.lexis-nexis.com	§ 10.10
Library of Congress	http://loc.gov	§ 4.130; 4.210; 10.20
List of Federal Register Documents on Public Inspection	www.archives.gov/federal-register/publicinspection	§ 9.70
Lobbying Disclosure Act	http://lobbyingdisclosure.house.gov	§ 3.30
Lobbying Registration Form	http://lobbyingdisclosure.house.gov	§ 3.41
Mace	http://artandhistory.house.gov	§ 6.111
Membership changes	www.CongressProfile.com	§ 5.12

Name	URL	Section
Morris K. Udall Foundation	www.udall.gov	§ 4.100
National Academy of Public Administration	http://napawash.org	§ 4.200
National Academy of Sciences	www.nationalacademies.org	§ 4.200
National Academy of Sciences	www.healthpolicyfellows.org	§ 4.100
National Archives and Record Administration	http://archives.gov/legislative	§ 4.190; 6.300; 8.91; 9.70; 10.60
National Association of State Election Directors	www.nased.org	§ 2.11
National Association of Secretaries of State	www.nass.org	§ 2.11
National Conference of State Legislatures	www.ncsl.org	§ 2.11
Office of Compliance	www.compliance.gov	§ 4.150
Office of Congressional Ethics	http://oce.house.gov	§ 3.50
Office of the Law Revision Counsel	http://uscode.house.gov	§ 4.110
Office of Management and Budget	www.whitehouse.gov/omb	§ 4.180; 7.42; 7.43; 8.20; 9.70
Open CRS	http://opencrs.com	§ 4.130
Our American Government	http://fdsys.gov	§ 10.60
Party alignment	www.PartyNumbers.com	§ 5.14
Plum Book	www.gpoaccess.gov/plumbook	§ 8.80
Public Leadership Education Network	www.plen.org	§ 4.100
Regulations.gov	www.regulations.gov	§ 9.70
Secretary for the Majority	http://senate.gov	§ 4.120
Secretary for the Minority	http://senate.gov	§ 4.120
Secretary of the Senate	www.senate.gov/reference/office/secretary_of_senate.htm	§ 4.120
Sergeant at Arms (House)	http://house.gov	§ 4.110
Sergeant at Arms (Senate)	www.senate.gov/reference/office/sergeant_at_arms.htm	§ 4.120
Senate assistant majority leader	http://durbin.senate.gov	§ 10.70
Senate assistant minority leader	http://kyl.senate.gov	§ 10.70
Senate Budget Committee	www.budget.senate.gov	§ 7.50
Senate Document Room	www.senate.gov/legislative/common/generic/Doc_Room.htm	§ 9.20
Senate classes	www.TCNSC.com	§ 5.11
Senate Democratic conference	http://democrats.senate.gov	§ 9.30;10.70
Senate Democratic Policy Committee	http://dpc.senate.gov	§ 10.70
Senate Ethics Committee	http://ethics.senate.gov	§ 3.60
Senate ethics manual	http://ethics.senate.gov	§ 10.80
Senate floor plan	http://CongressSeating.com	§ 11.21

Name	URL	Section
Senate majority leader	http://reid.senate.gov	§ 10.70
Senate minority leader	http://republicanleader.senate.gov	§ 10.70
Senate page program	http://senate.gov	§ 4.113
Senate Republican Conference	http://republican.senate.gov	§ 9.30; 10.70
Senate Republican Policy Committee	http://rpc.senate.gov	§ 10.70
Senate Select Committee on Ethics	http://ethics.senate.gov	§ 3.50
Sergeant at Arms	www.senate.gov/reference/office/sergeant_at_arms.htm	§ 4.120
Speaker of the House	http://speaker.gov	§ 10.70
Statement of Disbursements	http://disbursements.house.gov	§ 4.110; 10.80
Stennis Center for Public Service	www.stennis.gov	§ 4.200
TheCapitol.Net	TCNCE.com	§ 2.11
Biographical Directory of U.S. Congress	CDDocs.com	§ 10.81
Budget process glossary	TCNLG.com	§ 7.160
Calendar of business (Senate calendar)	CDDocs.com	§ 10.20
Capitol Hill Day	CapitolHillDay.com	§ 3.21
Clinton impeachment documents	CDDocs.com	§ 10.50
Committee prints	CDDocs.com	§ 10.10
Committee reports	CDDocs.com	§ 10.10
Committees' congressional handbook	CDDocs.com	§ 10.80
Congressional documents	CDDocs.com	§ 10.00
Congressional election information	TCNCE.com	§ 2.11
Congressional fellowships	TCNCF.com	§ 4.100
Congressional hearing documents	CDDocs.com	§ 10.10
Congressional pay	CongressPay.com	§ 4.20
Congressional Record	CDDocs.com	§ 10.20
Congressional staff salaries	LegiStorm.com	§ 4.61
Daily starting times in House	CongressSchedules.com	§ 6.72
Deschler-Brown Precedents	CDDocs.com	§ 10.40
Ethics manuals of House and Senate	CDDocs.com	§ 10.80
Floor plans, House and Senate	CongressSeating.com	§ 11.11; 11.21
Former governors in 112th Congress	CongressProfile.com	§ 5.16
Former judges in 112th Congress	CongressProfile.com	§ 5.19
Hinds' and Cannon's Precedents	CDDocs.com	§ 10.40
History of U.S. Senate Republican Policy Committee, 1947–1997	CDDocs.com	§ 10.81

Name	URL	Section
House and joint committee ratios in 112th Congress	CongressByTheNumbers.com	§ 5.81
House calendar	CDDocs.com	§ 10.20
House Journal and Senate Journal	CDDocs.com	§ 10.20
House leadership	CongressLeaders.com	§ 10.70
House Practice	CDDocs.com	§ 10.40
House Rules and Manual	CDDocs.com	§ 10.40
Leaders of 112th Congress	CongressLeaders.com	§ 10.70
Legislation glossary	TCNLG.com	§ 6.11; 6.51; 6.91; 6.121; 6.131; 6.261
Legislative process flowchart	LegislativeProcessFlowchart.com	§ 6.01
Members of 112th Congress who served as congressional staff	CongressProfile.com	§ 5.22
Members of 112th Congress who were congressional pages	CongressProfile.com	§ 5.20
Members' congressional handbook	CDDocs.com	§ 10.80
Membership changes	CongressProfile.com	§ 5.12
Numbers of former state and local elected officials in 112th Congress	CongressProfile.com	§ 5.17
Office of Management and Budget publications for agencies	CDDocs.com	§ 7.42
Our American Government	CDDocs.com	§ 10.60
Party alignment	PartyNumbers.com	§ 5.14
Party control of Congress 80th through 112th Congresses	PartyNumbers.com	§ 5.51
Party switchers	CongressProfile.com	§ 5.13
Pocket Constitution	TCNConst.com	§ 5.01
Pocket Constitution	TCNPocket.com	§ 10.60
Pocket Constitution	CDDocs.com	§ 10.60
Pocket Guide to Advocacy on Capitol Hill	PocketGuideToAdvocacy.com	§ 3.21
Precedents for germaneness of amendments	CDDocs.com	§ 6.120
Regulations on use of congressional frank by House members	CDDocs.com	§ 10.80
Resume of congressional activity, 111th Congress	CongressByTheNumbers.com	§ 5.33
Riddick's Senate Procedure	CDDocs.com	§ 10.50
Selected characteristics of 112th Congress	CongressProfile.com	§ 5.14
Senate classes	TCNSC.com	§ 5.11
Senate committee ratios in 112th Congress	CongressByTheNumbers.com	§ 5.82
Senate floor schedule	CDDocs.com	§ 10.70

Name	URL	Section
Senate leadership	CongressLeaders.com	§ 10.70
Senate Manual	CDDocs.com	§ 10.50
Senators in 112th Congress who previously served in House of Representatives	CongressProfile.com	§ 5.15
Tax expenditures	CDDocs.com	§ 7.91
Terms of Congress	TermsofCongress.com	§ 5.31
Treaties and other international agreements	CDDocs.com	§ 10.60
200 Notable Days	CDDocs.com	§ 10.61
U.S. Constitution	CDDocs.com	§ 10.60
Vetoes and veto overrides: Presidential clout	CongressByTheNumbers.com	§ 6.292
Volumes containing and explaining President's annual budget	CDDocs.com	§ 7.43
Whip advisories and notices	CDDocs.com	§ 10.70
THOMAS	http://thomas.gov	§ 4.130; 9.10; 9.20; 10.60
Treaties and Other International Agreements: The Role of the United States Senate	http://fdsys.gov	§ 10.60
Truman Scholars	www.truman.gov	§ 4.100
200 Notable Days: Senate Stories, 1987 to 2002	http://fdsys.gov	§ 10.61
U.S. Association of Former Members of Congress	http://usafmc.org	§ 4.200
U.S. Capitol Historical Society	http://uschs.org	§ 4.200
U.S. Capitol Police	www.uscapitolpolice.gov	§ 4.123
U.S. Capitol Visitor Center	www.visitthecapitol.gov	§ 11.30
U.S. Code	www.gpoaccess.gov/uscode/index.html	§ 4.110
U.S. Geological Survey (district maps)	www.nationalatlas.gov/printable/congress.html	§ 2.40
U.S. Helsinki Commission	www.csce.gov	§ 5.130
U.S. House of Representatives	http://house.gov	§ 4.60; 9.20; 9.30; 10.70; 10.80
U.S. Office of Government Ethics	www.usoge.gov	§ 3.50
U.S. Office of Personnel Management	http://opm.gov	§ 3.60
U.S. Senate	http://senate.gov	§ 3.30; 4.60; 4.113; 9.20; 9.30; 10.20; 10.50; 10.60; 10.70; 11.21
Vice Presidents of the United States, 1789–1993	www.senate.gov/artandhistory/history/common/briefing/Vice_President.htm	§ 10.81
White House	http://whitehouse.gov	§ 9.70
Women in Congress, 1917–2006	http://womenincongress.house.gov	§ 10.81
Women's Research and Education Institute	www.wrei.org	§ 4.100
Woodrow Wilson International Center for Scholars	http://wilsoncenter.org	§ 4.200

Principal Index Terms

Index

A

References are to chapter and section numbers.

References are to chapter and section numbers.

References are to chapter and section numbers.

References are to chapter and section numbers.

References are to chapter and section numbers.

References are to chapter and section numbers.

References are to chapter and section numbers.

References are to chapter and section numbers.

References are to chapter and section numbers.

References are to chapter and section numbers.

References are to chapter and section numbers.

References are to chapter and section numbers.

mation can be obtained
esting.com
USA
240317
V00010B/270/P

9 781587 332081